A HISTORY OF
TECHNOLOGY

A HISTORY OF
TECHNOLOGY

EDITED BY

TREVOR I. WILLIAMS

VOLUME VII

THE TWENTIETH CENTURY

c. 1900 TO *c.* 1950

PART II

CLARENDON PRESS · OXFORD
1978

Oxford University Press, Walton Street, Oxford OX2 6DP

OXFORD LONDON GLASGOW
NEW YORK TORONTO MELBOURNE WELLINGTON
IBADAN NAIROBI DAR ES SALAAM LUSAKA CAPE TOWN
KUALA LUMPUR SINGAPORE JAKARTA HONG KONG TOKYO
DELHI BOMBAY CALCUTTA MADRAS KARACHI

© OXFORD UNIVERSITY PRESS 1978

British Library Cataloguing in Publication Data

A history of technology.
  Vol. VII
  Williams, Trevor Illtyd
  609   T15   78–40068

  ISBN 0–19–858155–6

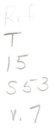
Typeset by Gloucester Typesetting Co. Ltd.
Printed in Great Britain
by Fletcher & Son Ltd., Norwich

CONTENTS

VOLUME VI
Chapters 1-28

VOLUME VII

ILLUSTRATIONS

THE DEVELOPMENT OF THE WORLD TRANSPORT MARKET

K. M. GWILLIAM

THE first half of the twentieth century was an age of radical technical substitution in transport. For inland transport road replaced rail in the dominant role, while for international movement air largely replaced sea transport. In both domestic and international sectors the substitution began, and has been most pronounced, in the passenger market. For freight the substitution has been less complete; the traditional modes have retained, and look like continuing to retain, a dominant share of the long-distance movement of bulk traffic (Fig. 29.1).

The reasons for these changes are not hard to find. For a large proportion of short- and medium-distance passenger journeys the private car became more comfortable, more convenient, quicker and, if multiple occupancy could be achieved, cheaper than rail transport. For the longer international journeys the advantage of air transport in speed became sufficiently overwhelming to overcome disadvantages of cost, and possibly of comfort.

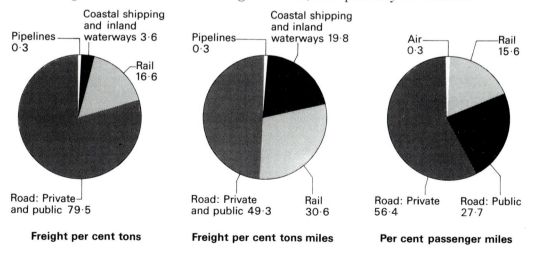

FIG. 29.1. The domestic transport market in Britain, 1960.

One final point should be noted about these main trends. Both air and road transport are viewed as 'superior' goods in the markets in which they are sold, having more highly preferred qualitative characteristics than their main competitors. For air transport this is reflected in the higher price per passenger mile than for other modes. For private road transport this is reflected, not in the cost of the marginal journey, which has always been competitive, but in the costs of car ownership. Hence, the shift between modes depended not only on the relative shifts in technological advantage but also on the increase in income levels during the period, allowing the purchase of the 'superior' goods.

Despite these changes, both in technology and in income levels, neither railways nor shipping have lost all their traditional markets. A major problem facing governments has been to manage the process of adaptation to technical change in such a way that all modes are able to find their proper economic roles. Moreover, as the demands for transport changed over time governments have been faced with the perennial problem of attempting to ensure that the prevailing controls continued to adjust properly for the 'externalities' involved in the provision of transport and did not simply constrain efficient adaptation.

This chapter is divided into two parts. In the first, we consider the way in which changes in world trade and movement-patterns have interacted with technological developments to revolutionize international transport by sea and air. In the second, we are concerned with national and international land transport systems, with special reference to the experience of the developed Western economies.

I. INTERNATIONAL TRANSPORT BY SEA AND AIR

The bulk of international trade of the late nineteenth century was the sea-borne British Imperial trade, which towards the end of the century began to be revolutionized by a number of technological innovations. Although these innovations—the conversion from wooden construction of ships to iron and then steel, the change of propulsion from sail to steam, and the introduction of the triple-expansion engine—all began in the nineteenth century, the main phase of technical change took place in the two decades before the First World War (Ch. 31). Of the U.K. registered tonnage in 1913 two-thirds had been built since 1900 and 85 per cent since 1895. Despite the fact that the subsequent change to diesel engines was to produce great economies in ship operation, the performance of the best ships built in the first decade of this century was not of an entirely different order from those which still sail. For instance, the *Mauretania*, built in 1907, was a vessel of over 30000 tons capable of 25 knots.

The organization of the shipping industry. The dry cargo trades have been divided between two different kinds of shipping operation, 'liners' and 'tramps'. A liner is a ship plying a fixed route according to predetermined schedules, offering space (for cargoes or passengers) at fixed rates. These services were developed in the third quarter of the nineteenth century as combined cargo and passenger carriers. From 1875 onwards, competing liner owners began to associate in 'conferences' to limit competition in particular trades or on a particular route. By the use of tying systems, such as deferred rebates or discriminatory rates for customers contracting to send all their freight by member vessels, the conferences attempted to secure stability in a basically unstable industry. Although some stability does appear to have been achieved, and the conferences also helped to protect unsubsidized U.K. shipping in the inter-war years, it also appears to have had some unfavourable effects. The system dampened profit-earning capacity in times of boom, removed much of the competitive incentive to efficiency, and, ultimately to the detriment of conference members, protected existing technology against developments. By 1900 most of the liner companies had amalgamated into large shipping groups and were members of conferences. With the exception of the North Atlantic trade, where tramps retained their hold, by 1913 most of the cargo exported from the U.K. was handled by the shipping conferences [1].

In contrast to the regular service of the liner, the 'tramp' is usually engaged to load a full cargo between any two ports. The charter is normally by the trip, and the ship searches peripatetically for continued employment. Both freight rates and freight capacity have tended to be more volatile for tramp than for liner shipping.

In the nineteenth century tramps were general cargo vessels, inferior either in construction or age to the liner. This picture has changed as a result of specialization. The employment of the tramp has been stabilized by progressive specialisation in the oil trade in the inter-war period and in dry cargo carriers after 1950, and by time charters. By 1960 the world tramp fleet had an average vessel size of nearly 11000 tons and an average speed of 12 knots; some 25 per cent of this fleet was specialized in its use.

The development of seaborne trade. The value of world trade grew by about 66 per cent between 1900 and 1914, and although this was a period of rising prices, there is little doubt that the volume of trade also grew substantially. The volume of world shipping increased by about 25 per cent during the same period.

This development was interrupted by the First World War, which cut world seaborne trade by nearly 20 per cent. Although it increased by 65 per cent during the 1920s seaborne trade fell back to the 1913 level during the Depression. The 1929 peak was not reached again until 1937. Shipping tonnage was less volatile during the period, rising steadily until 1931, when it stood at 150 per cent of its 1913 level. Thus, in 1932 the world seaborne trade was at about the 1913 level while shipping tonnage was nearly 50 per cent greater. This disparity had two significant consequences. First, 20 per cent of the world fleet was laid up. Secondly, and despite this, freight rates were pushed to very low levels, 25 per cent below pre-war rates. The inter-war period was thus a very difficult time for the world shipping industry.

Ownership of the world shipping fleet. British-owned shipping dominated world sea trade before the First World War. Despite growing competition from Japan in the Pacific and Germany in the Atlantic, in 1914 the British fleet represented 39 per cent of the world fleet of ships over 100 tons and over 40 per cent of sea-going steam and motor ships. This was nearly four times the size of the next largest fleet, that of Germany.

British dominance sprang from a number of sources. An extensive colonial trading policy ensured steady employment for the fleet. Britain had well-established shore facilities and was greatly aided by the technological lead which she had obtained in the late nineteenth century in building iron steam-ships. Above all, Britain's dominance was founded on the export of coal, which accounted for a quarter of all tonnage moved by sea before 1914.

The First World War changed this picture substantially. The U.K. and Germany between them lost 4·5m. tons of capacity between 1914 and 1919 (about 10 per cent of the world total), while the U.S.A. increased her own fleet by over 10m. tons between 1914 and 1920. Japan nearly doubled its fleet during the war, while France and Italy benefited considerably in reparations from the German and Austro-Hungarian fleets. Although the size of the U.S. fleet declined and that of the British fleet was stagnant in the inter-war period, a number of nations (Norway, Greece, Japan, Italy, and the Netherlands) increased their fleet size substantially. By 1939, although Britain still had the largest fleet, her share of world shipping had fallen to about a quarter.

The composition of the world shipping fleet in this period was also very significantly affected by changes in the pattern of trade. British coal exports fell from a high point of 84·5m. tons in 1923 to 38·2m. tons in 1938, and the total volume of all British exports was almost exactly halved during the same period. The basic traffic on which the British tramp shipping fleet depended thus diminished just at the time when the world shipping market as a whole was most depressed. If the British shipping fleet was to maintain its overall share of world seaborne trade it had to find new, non-British, traffics.

The one obvious growth area was the world oil trade. International movements of oil by sea rose from about 14m. tons per annum before 1914 to 84m. tons in 1937, from 5 per cent to 25 per cent of world seaborne trade. The world tanker fleet grew in size from 1·5m. tons in 1914 to 10·4m. tons in 1938, of which over half was owned by the oil companies, more than one-third by Norway, and less than one-fifth by British nationals. Thus, the chief trends in world trade led to radical changes both in the composition of the world fleet and its ownership. Britain's failure to retain her share by developing in the tanker business was due partly to the higher wage costs incurred by the British fleet, but mainly due to the failure of British shipping interests to recognize quickly enough that by the inter-war period the motor ship had superseded the steamship as an economic vessel.

The growth of the fleets of the U.S.A., Japan, and Italy was to some extent aided by government subsidy. But changes in the composition of the world fleet cannot be attributed solely to this cause. In the case of Japan, low labour costs also contributed significantly to the growth; and there are examples both of heavily subsidized fleets which did not grow (France and Germany) and unsubsidized fleets which did grow (Norway). Responsiveness to technical change was almost certainly of at least equal significance in explaining the changing patterns [2].

Shipping after 1939. Despite wartime losses of about 32m. tons, the total world fleet had increased from 61·4m. tons in 1939 to 72·9m. tons in 1946. With the one exception of the U.S.A., the leading shipping nations of the pre-war period suffered both relative and absolute decline. The U.S.A. increased its share of the world fleet from 14·2 per cent in 1939 to a staggering 56·1 per cent in 1946, although its share fell by 20 per cent in the next two years and continued to decline thereafter. In the first full decade after the

Second World War this expanded fleet experienced a period of great prosperity: seaborne dry cargo trade increased by 65 per cent and tanker trade more than doubled.

Two developments conditioned the determination of the national shares of world shipping in the post-war period. The first was flag discrimination. Among the devices used by nations to protect their home shipping industries were bilateral trade treaties containing restrictive shipping clauses; legislation reserving a portion of all inward or outward cargoes to home shipping; preference to national ships through exchange control; and other fiscal means. Although a relatively small proportion of total world trade may have been removed from free competition in this way, the impact was obviously greatest on those fleets that were attempting to gain a living from third-party trade, namely the traditional non-discriminating shipping nations such as Norway and the U.K.

The second important feature of the post-war shipping market was the development of 'flags of convenience'. Some countries, most notably Panama, Liberia, and Honduras, attracted the registration of foreign-owned shipping by offering favourable tax treatment and less restrictive conditions of crew employment and operation. A number of consequences may stem from this. High untaxed profits may lead to high ploughback rates and a more rapid expansion of capacity than would otherwise be the case. Potentially, in the presence of flag discrimination the existence of large fleets with little 'home' trade might concentrate competition further for the non-discriminating nations. In the event of such concentrated competition, arising for this or any other reason, debasement of standards of manning and shifting might be easier to achieve by fleets operated under flags of convenience.

The dominating feature in world shipping after 1939 was the growth of oil movements, which increased fourfold between 1939 and 1960 [3]. This increase was accommodated by an equivalent expansion of the tanker fleet (Table 29.1). Even more striking than the increase in total tonnage was the change in the size of vessel used. In 1939 the typical tanker was 12000 d.w.t.; by 1949 this had increased to about 16000 tons. In the following decade, sizes rose rapidly, so that by 1960 45000 tons d.w.t. was a common size and tankers of 100000 tons had been put into service. Such ships showed a net cost of transportation only a little over a third that of the 16000-ton vessel.

Thus, for the shipping industry the first half of the twentieth century had seen the replacement of steam power by motor power with associated increases

TABLE 29.1
Growth of world tanker fleets 1900–60

	World tonnage (million tons d.w.t.)
1900	0·5
1919	3·7
1939	16·6
1960	64·0

Source: Institute of Petroleum

in speed and reduction in cost; a general increase in the size of vessel associated with changed organizational and contracting arrangements; and, above all, the development of a seaborne movement of oil which overwhelmed the shipping market and resulted in dramatic changes in the sizes of freight ships and in the national ownership of fleets [4].

II. AIR TRANSPORT

The counterpart to the growth in seaborne freight trade was an even more startling growth in the transport of passengers by air. The role of air transport has been to carry passengers over long distances or where land transport is not possible. It has never been competitive with surface transport for distances of less than about 200 miles in Europe, though in the U.S.A. in 1960 about 25 per cent of domestic passengers were carried on stages of less than 200 miles. But it rapidly achieved dominance on the longer distance international routes; by 1960, 50 per cent of passengers moving into or out of Britain from other countries did so by air, and 75 per cent of transatlantic passenger movement was by air.

In contrast, because air transport is a high-cost mode, the movement of freight by air can be justified only for commodities with a high value-to-weight ratio, for which speed of movement is essential. Thus, although air freight movement increased by about 300 per cent in the 1950s, by 1960 it still accounted for only a small proportion of the total movement of freight. For instance, freight and mail together accounted for 20 per cent of the revenue of British European Airways (B.E.A.) in 1951/2 but grew so much more slowly than passenger traffic that by the early 1960s it produced only a little over 10 per cent of revenue. Moreover, though some specialized freight operations had begun in the 1950s, by 1960 over two-thirds of air freight in Europe was still carried as a 'fill-up' cargo on passenger services.

The development of aircraft (Ch. 33) can be expressed in four dimensions: capacity, speed, range, and utilization. To some extent the first three are independent of each other; for instance, the Zeppelin LZ 129 airship of 1935 had a capacity of 50 passengers and 10 tons of freight and a range of 8000 miles, but a speed of only 80 miles/h, whereas the Douglas DC3 could carry only 21 passengers for 800 miles but could go twice as fast. The potential utilization is, for any type of aircraft, a function of its range, its overhaul time, and its reliability. The actual utilization would also depend on the conditions in which it could operate and the level of demand. The annual utilization rate of the first generation of aircraft was therefore commonly 1000 flying hours per annum or less. By 1960 an average figure would be about 3000 hours [5].

The statistic which encapsulates all of these elements is the working capacity of the plane: the number of passenger miles or ton miles that it could achieve in the year. As Table 29.2 shows, from the earliest aircraft types used for regular scheduled services after the First World War—such as the De Havilland 34—to the most technically advanced in 1960—such as the Boeing 707–320—the productivity of the individual aircraft increased by a factor of over 400.

Despite the fact that the Boeing 707 cost 2000 times as much as the DH34 at current prices, the high performance of the modern aircraft and its relatively smaller labour and operating resource requirements per unit of output resulted in a falling real cost per passenger mile between 1922 and 1960 to accompany the very significant increases in speed, comfort, reliability, and safety that were achieved.

TABLE 29.2
Development of aircraft 1922–59

Aircraft	Year	Seating capacity	Cruising speed (mile/h)	Range (miles)	Utiliza-tion (h/year)	Working capacity (passenger miles/year)
De Havilland 34	1922	8	105	250	1000	0·89
Douglas DC3	1935	21	160	800	2000	6·72
Douglas DC4	1946	44 (+freight)	239	1760	2500	26·29
Boeing 707–320	1959	189	544	4625	3500	359·8
Factor 1959/1922	—	23·6	5·1	17·5	3·5	428·4

Source: K. R. Sealy [5]

The development of this potential was a chancy business. Although the Wright brothers had established the practicability of engine-powered flight in 1903, civil aviation had made little progress as a mode of transport by 1914. Blériot's first Channel crossing by air in 1909 stimulated some interest but essentially the aeroplane remained a fascinating novelty.

Recognition of the potential military significance of aviation during the First World War completely changed the situation. For example, Britain created an Air Ministry in 1917 (two years before the creation of a separate Ministry of Transport) and by the end of the war was producing planes in great numbers. But although the technology improved consistently throughout the inter-war period, commercial flying could be achieved only with the aid of substantial government support. In Britain it was decided that the only way in which development would take place was by the formation of a single airline as the 'chosen instrument' of government support. Eventually this led to the creation of a domestic nationalized flag carrier, British Overseas Airways Corporation (B.O.A.C.), in the international sector and the rigorous control, through a licensing procedure, of the smaller private companies operating in the domestic market. This was a pattern common to several of the major western European powers.

The Second World War caused an acceleration in technical progress in air transport, including the invention of the jet engine, which enhanced the prospects of profitable commercial operation. It also produced a supply of trained aviation manpower which ensured that there would be no shortage of entrepreneurs willing to enter the industry. International air transport was about to 'take off'. But before it could do this some intractable problems of international relations had to be resolved.

The concept of sovereign rights in national airspace was enshrined in the Paris Convention in 1919 and was the basis on which international civil aviation was developed in the inter-war period. With the prospect of a much more rapid and extensive development of civil aviation after the Second World War, the representatives of 52 nations met at Chicago in 1944 to discuss policy for post-war regulation of international air transport. The Chicago Convention set up the International Civil Aviation Organisation (I.C.A.O.) to further collaboration in international aviation and achieved much agreement on standardization of practices.

On the crucial question of the freedom to develop international commercial services no agreement could be reached at Chicago. The American desire for the minimum of control was frustrated by the British determination that the world air transport market should not be dominated by the U.S.A. Britain therefore advocated detailed government regulation of all aspects of air transport, including nomination of routes, selection of carriers, control of capacity, and determination of fares and rates. As a common international agreement could not be reached, the British insistence on continued close government control through bilateral agreements prevailed.

The terms of the first bilateral agreement between Britain and the U.S.A. thus became of crucial importance as a pattern for post-war developments. The representatives of the two governments met in 1946 in Bermuda, where they negotiated an agreement which formed the basis for a satisfactory reconciliation of conflicting national interests.

The principles of the 1946 Bermuda agreement were clear. The routes to be operated by the airlines of both countries were to be agreed in the negotiations but there were to be no capacity or frequency limits on routes directly connecting the two countries. If this resulted in excess capacity there would be an *ex post facto* review of the problem. It was also recognized that economic operation of long-haul services required rights to carry traffic on intermediate sectors; this was permitted so long as the amount of capacity provided was sensibly related to the end-to-end potential of the route and not to the exploitation of the intermediate traffic. Finally, it was agreed that fares and rates should be decided in the first place by the airlines themselves through the International Air Transport Association (I.A.T.A.) but should also be subject to government approval.

In the following year, I.C.A.O. organized a conference at Geneva in the hope that the Bermuda compromise might form a basis for a multilateral agreement on air transport rights. But several nations were worried by the absence of any capacity or frequency control in the Bermuda pattern and wished to reserve the right to predetermine the share of their own national airlines.

Two aspects of this outcome have had particularly important consequences on the structure of the air transport industry. First, the reservation of rights to predetermine capacity has formed the basis on which a number of emergent nations (and others) have been able to foster and protect their national airlines. In strictly economic terms this has probably meant that there have been too many small airlines in the market. Secondly, the control of rates has complemented predetermination and prevented the more efficient airlines from expanding their market share at the expense of the less efficient. In the absence of price competition other forms of promotion have been sought.

Greater seating space, better meals, free drinks, and cinema shows have emerged and each have in their turn been strictly controlled in I.A.T.A. agreements. But it has not been possible to constrain the quality of the air-craft itself. Consequently there has always appeared to be a premium attach-ing to the possession of the fastest and most modern aircraft which has led to competitive improvement of service quality even when, in global terms, it has not been in the interests of the airlines to do so. Thus the combination of rates control, predetermination of capacity, and the willingness of some coun-tries to subsidize their national airlines for prestige reasons has resulted in a steady pressure for rapid technological innovation in air transport which, in its turn, further stimulated the growth in demand.

The greatest single stimulus to this growth came from the development of the jet aircraft as a transport vehicle. In Britain it was decided that in the post-war period civil aircraft should be designed to use the turbine engines which had shown so much promise in the military sphere. In 1953 B.E.A. introduced the Viscount, in which turbine engines were used to drive a propeller. Even earlier, in May 1952, B.O.A.C. had introduced its first pure jet aircraft, the Comet I, into long-haul service. The jet revolution had begun, and by 1960 the international air transport industry had increased its 1948 output more than fourfold (Table 29.3).

The advantages offered by the pure jet aircraft—speed, comfort, and, on long haul, economy—stimulated the traditional business market. The release of much of the pre-jet capacity, and ultimately the extension of jet service itself, also stimulated the development of an entirely new leisure market. Between 1950 and 1960 expenditure on foreign travel rose twice as quickly as consumer expenditure as a whole in Britain and the U.S.A. as a conse-quence of the development of 'package holidays'. By 1960, half a million people were being carried annually from Britain in such services, pioneered

TABLE 29.3
World civil aviation statistics (excluding China, the U.S.S.R., and other non-I.C.A.O. countries)

	1948	1960
Distance flown (million km)	1270	3000
Passenger traffic (million km)	21 000	109 000
Cargo traffic (tons × million km)	420	2180
Mail traffic (tons × million km)	170	610

Source: *U.N. Statistical Yearbooks.*

largely by the tour operators and the independent (non-nationalized) airlines. The stage was set for a further burst of rapid growth in the air transport market.

III. LAND TRANSPORT

World inland transport markets. At the turn of the century the inland transport markets of the world could be divided into two groups. Those of most of the developed western economies were dominated by the railways. A certain amount of bulk traffic was carried on canals, on inland waterways (notably the Rhine and Danube systems in Europe and the Great Lakes in North America), and by coastal shipping (notably coal in Britain). This apart, long-distance carriage of freight was by rail. Similarly, for the movement of passengers the undeveloped state of the road network and the constraints imposed on mechanical vehicles on roads in many countries gave the railways an effective monopoly. In contrast to this, in the developing world of Africa, South America, the Middle East, and the Far East railways were still in the period of expansion and development and operated generally as a local, occasionally as a national, but only very rarely as an international mode of transport.

National rail networks. The nineteenth century had been the age of the railways (Vol. V, Ch. 15). In the more developed countries, the rail networks were effectively complete by the turn of the century, and certainly so by the First World War. In the inter-war period the railway mileage of Western Europe increased by only about 5 per cent. Although in many countries the railways were privately owned, in most they were very strictly and comprehensively controlled by the state. For instance, in Britain the railways were largely subjected to traders' interests and were unable to vary their rates at all without the permission of the Railway and Canal Commission.

In North America the railway system developed in an atmosphere of private enterprise and intense competition which also produced ample track systems and equipment by the early twentieth century. In South America, in contrast, the railway system was less well developed, and such development as existed was heavily dependent on foreign capital. For instance, as late as 1937 British companies owned and operated 25 000 km of the 40 000 km of railway in Argentina.

For the rest of the world railways were disconnected and mainly local in character, and the first two or three decades of the twentieth century were decades of great activity in the construction of major national and international rail trunk routes. For instance, in China about £45m. of loans for railway construction were issued in the period 1899–1923. Similarly in the inter-war period from 1921–38 the railway system of Soviet Russia increased its route mileage by over 60 per cent from 36000 to 55000. By 1945 this had reached 66000 miles.

International coordination of rail transport. Europe not only entered the twentieth century with well-developed national rail networks but also had the makings of an essentially international rail transport system. The Unité Technique, an international conference for promoting technical unity on railways, had been founded in 1882, and in 1890 an agreement on the common conditions for rail carriage was reached in the famous Berne Convention. Although the First World War seriously disrupted this sytem, the creation of the International Railway Union (U.I.C.) in 1922 re-established channels for the development of an international system of railways in Europe.

Not all matters could be brought within the scope of international agreement. Although the European system was largely developed to common track and loading gauges, standardization was not easily achieved. For instance, in many countries railway electrification policy was determined by the national electricity policy. Thus, at the end of 1938 three different, incompatible, systems of electrification were in operation in Europe (Ch. 45).

Similar problems of technical coordination had to be faced in North America, where fierce competition between companies could have produced incompatible systems. In the event, a number of inter-administrative organizations dating from the late nineteenth century ensured a good deal of technical conformity. In 1934 the various specialist technical organizations merged to form the American Association of Railroads. Thus, the standard 4 ft 8½ inch gauge is common to virtually all Canadian and U.S. railways, wagons are standardized, and there is general conformity, though not total uniformity, in overall loading gauge; for instance, engines operating on lines west of Chicago tended to be built to a more liberal clearance limit than those on lines east of that city.

For the rest of the world technical standardization had appeared less important and was less easily achieved. For instance, in 1927 only 10 per cent of African railways were standard gauge, 57 per cent was of 3 ft 6 inch gauge, 22 per cent was metre gauge, and a further 11 per cent was of even narrower gauge. In South America there was no accepted standard gauge, even in individual countries, and even by 1946 the railways did not form part of an internationally linked system.

The development of mechanized road transport. By the end of the nineteenth century the major technological developments necessary in both road and vehicle construction for the growth of a competitive road transport industry had been achieved (Vol. V, Ch. 18). But in 1900 this potential lay almost totally unexploited. There were only 11 000 motor-cars in the world, 5000 of which were in France.

The twentieth century motor-car (Ch. 30) is a combination of several nineteenth-century inventions: the petrol engine, the clutch, the universal joint, the electric generator, the pneumatic tyre, etc. Regular production of petrol cars was commenced by Panhard in France only in 1891. Early production in the U.K. by such manufacturers as Daimler, Lanchester, Riley, Rover, and Triumph was on a very small scale. It was the American Ford Company which developed mass-production of cars, which it introduced to Western Europe with the opening of a plant to assemble the successful Model T at Manchester in 1911. For the most part, however, the industry consisted of many small firms producing in short runs at relatively high prices until the inter-war period.

The development of the car market was most rapid in the U.S.A. Lower prices due to production on a larger scale, the development of facilities for the motorist, and keen marketing (including the development of the 'hire-purchase' system) quickly took the motor-car from being a luxury owned only by the rich to become the reasonable expectation of the professional and the skilled artisan classes. By 1922 there was one car for every nine people in the U.S.A. This development was also aided by the absence of the dense public transport networks generally to be found in developed Western Europe.

The scale of vehicle production increased in the inter-war period with progressively greater use of line production bringing down real costs and prices. For instance, between 1920 and 1929 the price of the Morris Cowley fell from £525 to £199. A substantial concentration of production also took place, so that by 1939 90 per cent of car output in Britain came from the 'Big Six': Morris, Ford, Austin, Vauxhall, Rootes, and Standard. But labour productivity in the British and European car industry was only one-third that in the U.S.A. and in real terms the cost of the average British car was about 30 per cent above that of its American counterpart.

TABLE 29.4
Vehicles in use in the U.K. 1904–60

	Cars	Motor cycles	Hackneys			Goods and other vehicles	Total
			Buses and coaches	All	Taxis		
1904	8465	—		5345		4000	17810
1910	53196	36242		24466		30000	143877
1920	186801	287739		74608		101000	650148
1930	1056214	724319	52648		48483	391997	2273661
1939	2034400	418000		90000		606200	3148600
1945	1486600	309100		98700		658100	2552500
1950	2257873	751738	77636		58845	1263151	4409223
1960	5525828	1861247	78722		14543	1958800	9439140

Source: British Road Federation, *Basic road statistics: public passenger transport in towns.*

During the Second World War car production was almost totally discontinued. In contrast, commercial vehicle output was increased to record levels and the major car manufacturers also turned their hands—and acquired space and capacity—to produce a wide range of war goods. In the post-war period this capacity was used to expand car production. By 1954, virtually all the small companies had been forced out of the industry in Britain and the 'Big Five' (Austin and Morris having merged in 1952), together with Rover and Jaguar, accounted for over 99 per cent of British production.

By 1960, one household in four owned a car in Britain, and the car had already become the dominant mode of personal movement in Western Europe as in the U.S.A. (Table 29.4).

By the turn of the century the public transport of passengers in urban areas was already predominantly by road. For the most part this had been by horse bus, the development of mechanically propelled road vehicles having been constrained very severely. In Britain, for instance, the 4 mile/h speed limit and the crippling licencing restrictions, which had first been introduced to limit the activities of steam coaches, were relaxed for vehicles of less than 3 tons only by the Locomotives on Highways Act of 1896. Even then the speed limit was raised only to 14 mile/h. However, once the relaxation had begun it proceeded rapidly. In 1905 both the speed limit and the maximum weight to which the freedom applied were raised. This encouraged the rapid replacement of horse-drawn by mechanically propelled vehicles. For instance, by October 1911 the London General Omnibus

Company had completed the replacement of its 17 800 horses by a fleet of motor buses.

In urban areas the other mode of transport to offer significant competition to the railways was the tram. In Britain the tramways were largely in municipal operation as a result of the constraints put on private operation by the Tramways Act of 1870. Although many municipalities had hardly constructed their tramways before they came under technological threat from the trolley-bus and motor bus, they dominated urban public transport in many towns for the first thirty years of the twentieth century.

Road–rail competition. The First World War did not produce any revolutionary technological developments in transport but it did accelerate and accentuate some emerging trends and problems. It cause a large expansion of the fleet of road vehicles and experienced operators, both of which were to be released into the civilian sector after the war. In constrast to the expansion of the vehicle fleet, the war caused a reduction in the already modest programmes of road development. Road capacity was not keeping up with the rate of growth of the demands made upon it. But the threat to the rail domination of inland transport markets had emerged.

In Western Europe the railways were in a relatively weak state to meet this competition. Not only had they borne the brunt of the war effort—and in some cases, as in the U.K., received quite inadequate compensation for their contribution—but also they were severely constrained in their ability to offer commercial competition. As a consequence of their former monopoly position they were expected—and in many cases legally obliged—to accept some unprofitable social service obligations and also were constrained in their freedom to set commercial rates.

In the post-war period there was no effective control of entry into, and operation of, the road haulage and road passenger transport industries. As a result, road transport made serious inroads into traditional rail traffics during the 1920s. The financial viability of the railways, which had suffered very badly as a consequence of the war, deteriorated further.

A second major consequence of the freedom in road transport was internal to that sector. Low levels of employment, low rates of return on capital, and the release of large amounts of ex-military capacity and manpower combined to produce a state of fierce competition within the road transport industry itself. Consequently the industry was suspected of becoming unacceptably unsafe through inadequate vehicle maintenance and dangerous driving practices.

The combination of excessive competition in road transport and inadequate coordination between road and rail led to government intervention to control road transport, and particularly road haulage, in the mid-1930s in most of the developed countries. This normally took the form of control of conditions of operation in the road haulage industry and restrictions on the areas within which, commodities for which, or rates at which, road transport services could be offered. Such constraints were introduced in Britain in 1933, in France in 1934, and in Germany in 1936. Even in the U.S.A. the Motor Carriers Act of 1935 required the licensing and publication of rates by 'common carriers' in road transport and gave to the Interstate Commerce Commission the power to regulate minimum tariffs in such a way as to prevent excessive competition between road and rail. This pattern of state intervention thus seemed to hold irrespective of whether the railways were state-owned (as in France) or not, of whether the railway sector was itself essentially competitive (as in the U.S.A.) or not, or of the extent to which railways were being used as a conscious instrument of national economic and military strategy (as in Germany). The problem of protecting the railways in the face of intensified road competition dominated all these differences in situation.

The tide could not easily be turned. In Britain the railways continued to lose general merchandise traffic, which fell from 68·4m. tons in 1919 to 44·3m. tons in 1938. The four major privately owned railways were rapidly approaching bankruptcy. In France the newly unified Societé National des Chemins de Fer (S.N.C.F.) showed an overall deficit of 6m. francs in 1938. In the U.S.A. over 30 per cent of total railway mileage was in trusteeship or receivership by the end of 1937. But in each of these countries there was a strong body of opinion which considered that the railways had a proper role in the national transport system, which was somehow being subverted by the nature of the existing institutional structures. Thus by the end of the decade each of these countries was preparing a new set of policy measures to obtain better 'coordination' between the modes.

In Britain this took the form of the 'Square Deal' campaign aimed at releasing the railways from many of their traditional, restrictive obligations. In France it took the form of developing a national and regional administrative structure (Conseil Supérieur des Transports) through which a conscious policy of transport co-ordination could be pursued. In the U.S.A. it took the form of a call by the Interstate Commerce Commission in its 1939 report for the Federal Government to set up a Transportation Board and to take a more positive role in determining the structure of the transport industry.

Inland transport after 1945. The Second World War truncated these efforts and produced conditions in which rail transport regained dominance in handling the strategically important flows of men and materials in the war effort. But it did not eliminate the fundamental underlying trends, which were certain to reassert themselves in the course of post-war reconstruction. For, among other things, the development for strategic reasons of a system of custom-built, limited-access primary roads in Germany during the late 1930s, together with developments in vehicle size and power, had demonstrated the potential of road transport to compete even in the longer-distance freight markets.

The post-war problem of the developed economies was that of permitting this developing technology of road transport to find its proper role without losing the advantages which could still be obtained in many markets from rail transport. One serious difficulty which had to be faced in seeking this reconciliation lay in the physically depreciated state of much transport infrastructure, particularly that of the railways. For example, it has been estimated that between 1937 and 1953 British railways disinvested to the extent of £440m. at 1948 prices. In the early post-war period, despite the initial good intentions of the government, the combination of physical shortages and the use of public sector investment cuts as an instrument of macroeconomic management made it impossible to make up the accumulated arrears of maintenance and investment. Introduction of new technology, as well as maintenance of capacity, was thus retarded.

Some major technological changes had already achieved widespread introduction. After the First World War the price of coal had risen to such an extent that new forms of traction were sought, particularly for main line working. In the U.S.A., where oil was relatively cheap, the answer was to use diesel traction. By 1946 a quarter of passenger car mileage in the U.S.A. was diesel-hauled and the production of steam locomotives had virtually ceased. In Europe electric traction proved more attractive, and by 1937 there were over 16000 km of electrified track in continental Europe (including 3000 km in Sweden). In Britain, though over 30 per cent of the Southern Railway had been electrified by 1939 little further progress in the direction of innovation in motive power was made until the end of the 1950s.

A number of other significant improvements in rail technology were available, or had been introduced, by this time. By the early 1960s 60 per cent of all German Federal rail mileage had long welded rail, which substantially improved ride comfort. Power signalling and control techniques produced notable improvements both in economy and safety.

Despite these improvements in rail technology, and the introduction of further legislation aimed at securing a 'proper co-ordination' of the transport sector (such as the nationalization of all long-distance public transport in Britain in 1948), the development of road transport could not be halted. For instance, in the U.K. road transport accounted for 50 per cent of the domestic ton mileage of freight and $62\frac{1}{2}$ per cent of the inland transport (excluding coastal shipping and air transport) by 1960. For passenger movement it was even more dominant, with nearly 85 per cent of passenger mileage, of which over 55 per cent was by private car. Moreover, in the post-war period the rapid development of vehicles had become a world-wide phenomenon, with rates of growth in the Third World (albeit from very low base figures) greater than those of the U.S.A. Nevertheless, by 1960 the great majority of motor vehicles in the non-Communist world were still be to found in the U.S.A. and Western Europe (Table 29.5).

This expansion was far from exhausted by the end of the 1950s. Car ownership was still rising rapidly and was indeed being encouraged in many countries by a growing programme of road investment which continued and accelerated in the following decade.

This development of road transport has had very important economic and social effects in the developed industrial countries. The advent of motor transport has permitted a much wider dispersion of industry. Light industries in particular have been able to relocate or develop away from the old industrial concentrations served only by rail.

TABLE 29.5
World vehicle fleets (excluding Iron Curtain countries, North Korea, North Vietnam)

	Cars (000)		Commercial vehicles (000)	
	1948	1960	1948	1960
Africa	640	1850	290	740
North America	35 160	66 560	8450	13 100
South America	650	1650	530	1170
Asia	380	1710	500	2240
Europe	5130	22 690	2750	5760
Oceania	910	2470	510	950
Total	42 870	96 930	13 030	23 940

Source: *U.N. Statistical Yearbooks.*

Social habits have been equally affected. The motor-car has opened up a wide range of possibilities for entertainment and relaxation. For instance, Londoners made three times as many trips in 1936 as in 1906. Above all, the patterns of residential location have been transformed. Initially, improved suburban rail services allowed new developments outside the traditional confines of the major conurbations. In smaller urban settlements the motor-car made it possible for those with the time and money to work in the town and live in the country. The inner centres of cities thus lost population while the suburbs expanded both in area and in population. Entirely new life-styles have been created, at least partly, by the transport developments of the twentieth century.

Technological change in transport, both national and international, has thus been at the very heart of the process of economic and social development in the most rapidly changing half-century of man's history.

REFERENCES

[1] STURMEY, S. G. *British shipping and world competition*. Athlone Press, London (1962).
[2] Report of the Committee of Inquiry into shipping. (*The Rochdale Report*.) Command 4337, H.M.S.O., London (1970).
[3] COUPAR, A. D. *The geography of sea transport*. Hutchinson, London (1972).
[4] BEAVER, S. H. Ships and shipping: the geographical consequences of technological progress. *Geography*, **52**, 133–56 (1967).
[5] SEALY, K. R. *The geography of air transport*. Hutchinson, London (1966).

BIBLIOGRAPHY

ALDCROFT, D. H. *British transport since 1914*. David and Charles, London (1975).
BARKER, T. C., and SAVAGE, C. I. *An economic history of transport in Britain* (3rd edn.). Hutchinson, London (1974).
COUPAR, A. D. *The geography of sea transport*. Hutchinson, London (1972).
SEALY, K. R. *The geography of air transport*. Hutchinson, London (1966).
STURMEY, S. G. *British shipping and world competition*. Athlone Press, London (1962).

30

ROAD VEHICLES

LORD MONTAGU OF BEAULIEU

I N 1900 the motor vehicle was still in a fairly rudimentary state of development, and was of negligible importance in social and economic life (Vol. V, Ch. 18). Owners of private cars were few in number and generally objects of suspicion, ridicule, or both, while goods traffic was the province of the railways, except for local deliveries which were horse-drawn. Three factors in particular hampered the acceptance of the motor-car: anti-motoring laws, especially with relation to speed, the atrocious state of most country roads, and the unreliability of the car itself. Of these the last was the earliest to be improved, and in the first decade of the century a journey of over 30 miles became, from an adventure with almost certain breakdown, a reasonably reliable and everyday event.

I. PASSENGER CARS

The design of cars varied more in the first five years of the century than at any time since, for manufacturers had no set ideas to work from, and a great variety of solutions seemed equally attractive. Thus engines were mounted horizontally or vertically, in the front, rear, or middle of the frame. The latter might be made of wood, either plain or armoured with metal flitch plates, channel steel, or tubular steel. The sliding pinion gearbox was becoming the norm, but many cars, especially in America, used an epicyclic or planetary system. The final drive might be by chain from a countershaft to the rear axle, single chain on light cars, double on heavier cars or commercial vehicles; or by belts; or by a propeller shaft and bevel gears on the rear axle. The last gradually became the usual system, and by 1910 only a few old-fashioned cars used chain drive, while belts were confined to motorcycles and cyclecars. The drawbacks of chains were that they were noisy and required regular maintenance, including boiling in Russian tallow. Belts slipped and broke, and were unsuitable for transmitting more than limited power. A major problem of the early motorist, and one which caused more involuntary halts than any mechanical defect, was the pneumatic tyre. This had been introduced on bicycles in 1888 and on cars in 1895, and despite the frequency of punctures motorists preferred them to solid rubber tyres because of the jolting that the latter gave at any speeds over 10 mile/h. Solid tyres were customary on heavy lorries and buses up to the mid-1920s, while steam traction engines, slower still, had iron-shod wheels. The detachable wheel did not become common until about 1910, so a tyre change involved removing the tyre from a fixed wheel. An alternative was the Stepney wheel, which was a spare wheel and tyre which could be fitted next to the punctured one, and enabled the car to be driven at least as far as the nearest garage.

Bodies on the earliest cars were mostly open two-seaters, because the shortness of the wheelbase made it difficult to accommodate more passengers. By 1900 a popular solution was the rear-entrance tonneau, in which the rear passengers sat in tub seats on either side of the door, which was in the back of the body. Very occasionally, such a body might have an enclosed top, but the great majority were open. By 1904 the more expensive and powerful cars like the Daimler, Panhard, and Mercedes, had wheelbases sufficiently long to allow for a side entrance to the rear seats. These had doors, although doors for the driver and front passenger did not become widespread for another six years. Closed bodies were still very rare, and in fact did not exceed open cars in numbers until the late 1920s. The two closed styles which did achieve some currency were the two-seater coupé—often called the doctors' coupé because of its popularity with medical men who had to be out in all weathers—and the limousine with glass partition between the chauffeur and his passengers. Some cars could be had with two bodies, an open tourer for summer and a limousine for winter, and the body not in use would be suspended from the roof of the garage.

The impact of the motor-car on society was very small at first, and the attention it attracted was quite out of proportion to its influence. By 1900 practically everyone in the industrialized world had heard of the horseless carriage through the popular press, but few in country districts had ever seen one, and still fewer owned a car or earned their living from it. The motor industry, such as it was, consisted of a few companies with a maximum output of perhaps 1000 vehicles a year, some of which had come to prominence through the bicycle industry, and a host of small tinkerers who assembled a few cars, or sometimes only a single prototype, and on the strength of their hopes rather than actual fact, called themselves 'motor-car makers'. The growth of the industry was greatly helped by those firms who

FIG. 30.1. 1902 Oldsmobile Curved Dash Runabout.

FIG. 30.2. 1914 Ford Model T tourer.

made engines for sale to other manufacturers, for the casting of a cylinder block was beyond the facilities of most of the small enterprises. The most important engine makers were de Dion Bouton and Aster, who between them supplied engines to over 200 firms in Europe and America. Total world production of passenger cars in 1900 was about 9000, of which 4192 came from the U.S.A., where steam and electric cars outsold petrol-engined ones. The first large-scale maker of petrol cars was Ransom E. Olds who launched his Oldsmobile Curved Dash Runabout (Fig. 30.1) in 1901. A rugged simple vehicle with horizontal single-cylinder 7-hp engine and a two-seater body, the Oldsmobile sold 425 units in its first year despite a disastrous factory fire. The figure rose to 2500 in 1902, 4000 in 1903, 5508 in 1904, and 6500 in 1905. It was largely thanks to the Olds that American production figures increased by 100 per cent between 1903 and 1904, and it is significant that the only other year when there was a comparable leap was 1908–9, after the introduction of the Model T Ford (Fig. 30.2). Ford had, in fact, taken the lead in production in 1906; production of the T was 17771 in its first year, and within five years of its appearance Ford factories were turning out ten times this number. This was possible only because of the conveyor-belt system whereby parts for assembly were brought to the workers on a timed schedule.

This was not a Ford invention, for it had been used in the Connecticut clock and watch industry for years; Henry Ford was said to have got the idea from watching the overhead trolleys used by Chicago meat packers. The results of mass production were dramatic, for the greatly increased sales lowered unit costs, and allowed Ford to slash prices almost every year from 1909 to 1916. Despite price reductions from $850 to $360, profits were such that Ford could increase wages, paying $5·00 per day in 1914 when the industry average was $2·50, and reducing a working day from ten hours to eight. Potential workers flocked to Detroit from all over America, lured not only by the money but by Ford's special aid programmes for immigrants and his willingness to engage the handicapped who were considered unemployable by the industry at large.

Although by far the biggest, Ford was not the only American mass producer of motor-cars in the second decade of the century; in 1916, after Ford's 735 000 cars came Willys–Overland with 140 000, Buick with 124 834, and Dodge with 71 400; some 95 other car makers brought the nation's total to over $1\frac{1}{2}$m. There were then nearly 3·3m. cars on American roads, compared with 105 000 ten years earlier. Not only was the car a great liberator, enabling townspeople to visit the countryside and reducing the isolation of rural farms, but it and the ancillary industries of oil, rubber, glass, and so on were becoming significant employers of labour.

By the outbreak of the First World War the design of the passenger car had reached a fairly standardized pattern which was to remain for many years. The engine was almost universally front-mounted, driving through a three- or four-speed sliding pinion gearbox and propeller shaft to a live back axle. Some popular small cars, such as the Humberette, had two-cylinder engines, but four was the usual number, with six in the larger cars. The V-8 engine had been built by de Dion Bouton in small numbers since 1910, but it was Cadillac who really established the V-8 as a popular power unit, making some 15 000 to 20 000 a year from 1914 onwards. Brakes were normally found on the transmission (hand brake) and rear wheels (foot brake), although some four-wheel braking systems had been used from 1910. These were not very satisfactory as they required simultaneous operation of hand and footbrake. In 1919 the French Hispano–Suiza company introduced a coupled system in which brakes on all four wheels were operated by the footbrake; moreover the action was assisted by a mechanical servo driven from the transmission. A more widely used system of assistance was the hydraulic servo in which a master cylinder filled with fluid multiplied the braking effect. This was

introduced on the American Duesenberg in 1921, and became commonplace
on the more expensive cars in the 1920s while mechanical four-wheel brakes
spread throughout the motor industry; by 1928, there were very few cars
made anywhere with brakes on the rear wheels only. For a while there was
much suspicion of four-wheel brakes, which were thought to cause skidding.
Those manufacturers who were slow to adopt the system were loud in con-
demnation, but their real objection was cost, for the chassis had to be modified if four-wheel brakes were to operate satisfactorily. A variation on the
hydraulic system was the vacuum servo used on some luxury cars such as
Packard, Pierce–Arrow, and Stutz.

An important engine development in the 1920s was the straight-eight or
eight-in-line as it was sometimes called in America. This was pioneered on
the Italian Isotta–Fraschini Tipo 8, which with the Hispano–Suiza and the
Rolls-Royce Silver Ghost was one of the great European luxury cars of the
1920s. It was a logical development of the in-line six, but even more than
that layout it needed an exceptionally strong crankshaft, which is why it was
slow to appear. After the Isotta, came straight-eights by Duesenberg and
Packard in America, Leyland in England, and Bugatti in France. All these
were expensive cars, but within a few years makers of proprietary engines
such as Continental and Lycoming launched straight-eight units, which
enabled manufacturers of assembled cars to join the ranks of the eight-in-
lines. By 1931 60 per cent of the models listed on the American market had
straight-eight engines, though not, of course, 60 per cent of the cars sold, for
the mass-producers like Chevrolet, Ford, and Plymouth were still wedded to
four or six cylinders.

The V-8 which had been so popular up to about 1922 fell from favour, so
that in 1929 only five American companies were offering one. In 1932, however, Ford launched their low-priced V-8, and this car with its spectacular
performance and prices starting as low as $460 did much to regain the prestige
which Ford had lost during the last years of the old-fashioned Model T and
its humdrum successor, the Model A. Multi-cylinderism went even further
with the V-12, which had been briefly popular from 1915 to about 1923 when
Packard was the best-known exponent, and was revived in the 1930s when a
dozen manufacturers on both sides of the Atlantic turned to this complex
but turbine-smooth power unit. Even more exotic was the V-16, of which
only Cadillac and Marmon made any numbers.

One of the most interesting cars of the 1920s was the Italian Lancia
Lambda, which went into production in 1923. Its engine was a narrow-angle

FIG. 30.3. 1922 Lancia Lambda chassis.

V-4 with an angle between the cylinders of only 13°, as compared with the 90° of Cadillac's V-8. This allowed for monobloc casting instead of the two separate banks of cylinders in a traditional Vee engine. More important than the engine, though, was the Lambda's construction; in place of the conventional pressed steel chassis, to which was attached a metal and wood body, Lancia used a monocoque hull built up from hollow steel pressings (Fig. 30.3). This combined the chassis with the lower half of the body, in which the seat squabs acted as cross-members of the frame. Above this was mounted a saloon or tourer body top. The weight of the Lambda frame was 2352 lb, less than the bare chassis of other cars of comparable size. It was made from 1923 to 1931, though a separate chassis frame was available from 1927 and standardized from 1929. This was to satisfy specialist coachbuilders who needed a conventional bare chassis on which to build. The Lambda was lower in appearance than its contemporaries, and had excellent road-holding, causing it to be thought of as a sports car in England, though on the Continent it was regarded more as a good, fast tourer.

The next important step towards combining chassis and body came in 1931 when William Muller and Joseph Ledwinka of the Budd Company of Philadelphia built a prototype saloon with an all-steel shell in which door pillars, roof, and underframe were all part of a complex welded structure. They showed the design, which also had a V-8 engine and front-wheel drive, to the major U.S. manufacturers, but they were too conservative to adopt it, and the company which put the idea into production was Citroen of France. André Citroen had already made use of Budd pressed-steel bodies, and in 1934 he launched his *traction avant*, a four-door saloon with unit construction, independent torsion-bar suspension, and front-wheel drive. Other manufacturers then followed the Budd/Citroen example; Opel, General Motors' German subsidiary, introduced unit construction on their 1935 Olympia, as did another General Motors company, Vauxhall, in 1938. Others to use the principle in one form or another were Lincoln (1936), Lancia (1937), Renault (1938), and Nash (1941). Unit construction is particularly suited to mass production, for the material costs are lower than a conventional chassis and body, although tooling costs are higher and can be justified only by a high production volume. Also the possibility of custom coachwork is eliminated, which is why unit construction has generally been found in the cheaper, non-specialist cars. However, in 1966, even Rolls-Royce turned to it for their Silver Shadow saloon.

Suspension was another field in which the time-honoured system gave way to new layouts between the two world wars. The type which had come to be accepted was that of four leaf springs, one for each wheel, of which those at the front were semi-elliptic in pattern and the rear the same, quarter-elliptic, or three-quarter elliptic. Some cars, including the Model T Ford, had a transverse semi-elliptic spring at the front. Although sprung, the wheels were linked by the axles, so that a deflection caused by a road irregularity on one wheel was automatically transmitted to the whole body. To avoid this the principle of independent suspension was developed, and though it had been seen on a steam carriage as early as 1873, it did not become commonplace on cars until the 1930s. Two systems were used at first, sliding pillars acting against a coil spring (Lancia, Morgan) and pivoting wishbones acting against a coil spring (Buick, Cadillac, Oldsmobile). On the Dubonnet system the coil springs were located in oil-filled cylinders. Another system, little used before the war except on the Volkswagen prototypes, was the torsion bar, in which the strain is taken by the twisting of a bar rather than the compression of a spring. Independent suspension was used at first on the front wheels only, but some advanced Continental cars, such as Skoda and Steyr, used independent rear suspension, and this has become widespread since the Second World War.

From about 1905 up to the 1930s almost every car had a front-mounted engine driving the rear wheels. In 1929 the American Erret Lobban Cord launched his dramatically long and low Model L29 which had front-wheel drive; this was followed by another small-production American car, the Ruxton. The first mass-produced front-wheel drive car was the Citroen *traction avant* of 1934—already mentioned in the context of unit construction—of which more than 762000, of a basically unchanged design, were made up to 1957. Other European front-wheel drive cars of the 1930s were the German D.K.W. and Adler; French Rosengart; and Czech Aero and Jawa. Britain lagged behind, and only the B.S.A. was front-driven. The U.S.A. was also conservative: apart from the small-production Cord, which was not made after 1937, no American car used front-wheel drive until after the Second World War. Rear-mounted engines, which were another way of eliminating a drive shaft running the length of the car, began to appear in the 1930s, the best-known exponents being the Czech Tatras. These were streamlined and very fast, but the concentration of weight at the rear of the chassis made them dangerous to handle, and it was not until the advent of the mid-engined car (engine behind the seats but ahead of the rear axle) in the 1960s that anything but a front-engined layout was used for really powerful cars. Mercedes-Benz made a few small rear-engined cars and Ferdinand Porsche's Volkswagen, of which prototypes appeared in 1936, used the layout too. After the Second World War, and probably influenced by the success of the Volkswagen, other manufacturers began to mass-produce rear-engined cars, including Renault (1948), Fiat (1955), Chevrolet (1960), and Hillman (1963).

More important to the everyday motorist than the position of the engine were aids to easy driving. Two which did more than anything else to popularize motoring were the electric starter and the synchromesh gearbox. The first attempts to eliminate cranking the engine by hand involved compressed air, which was fed to each cylinder in firing order. The air was compressed by the engine, and could also be used for inflating the tyres or raising the jack. In 1912 Cadillac introduced the electric starter, using a small motor originally developed for operating cash registers. The key to this development was the recognition by C. F. Kettering that electric motors can, for very short periods, be quite substantially overloaded. Thus a relatively small motor sufficient to turn the automobile engine until it fired. This gradually spread to other makes and smaller cars, so that by 1930 cranking was a thing of the past except in emergencies, although the starting handle continued to be featured on most cars for some time longer. The synchromesh gearbox, which automatically synchronized the speeds of gear wheels before the teeth meshed, was introduced by General Motors on their 1929 Cadillacs, followed by Rolls-Royce and another General Motors car, Vauxhall, in 1932. By doing away with the necessity for double-declutching, the synchromesh box made driving easier than ever, but there were still those who wanted greater simplicity, and for them the automatic transmission was developed. Many systems were proposed, but the first to be adopted on a large scale was again a General Motors development, Hydramatic drive. This used a fluid coupling and epicyclic gear trains which gave four forward and one reverse speed automatically. First available on the 1940 Oldsmobile as an option, automatic transmission became standard on the larger American cars during the 1950s, and on many cars today, including Rolls-Royce, a manual gearbox is unavailable.

The early post-war years saw the appearance of minicars in a number of countries, a response to shortage of petrol and the high price of ordinary cars. They were mostly rather crude machines, and far from reflecting developments in technology, they harked back to an earlier era, with single-cylinder or two-cylinder air-cooled engines, kick starters, and chain drive. With growing European prosperity in the 1950s the minicars disappeared.

Steam cars. At the turn of the century there were many people who claimed that steam had as bright a future as internal combustion for the motorcar (Vol. V, pp. 420–6). Indeed, in 1901 and 1902 the largest-selling American car, the Locomobile, was a steamer and there were over fifty makes of steam car on the American market. They were mostly similar in design and appearance, having two-cylinder engines fed by boilers of about 180 to 200 lb/in² working pressure; single chain drive to the centre of the rear axle; bicycle-type tubular steel frame; full-elliptic springs; and wire wheels. The boiler was paraffin-fired, and top speed was about 25 mile/h. The complete vehicle weighed not much more than 7 cwt, and the normal body style was a simple open two-seater. Once they were running, these light steam buggies had several advantages over the contemporary petrol cars; they were virtually silent except for a hiss when accelerating, and free from the vibration which was a curse of cars powered by 'nasty explosion engines' as they were called. More important, the flexibility of the steam engine made a gearbox unnecessary; so the problem of changing gear with an unsynchronized box, perhaps the most difficult aspect of early driving, was avoided. Against these assets had to be set the starting procedure. This could take anything up to 45 minutes, and involved 21 separate steps, of which the first was 'head the car into the wind'.

The flash generator, which admitted a small quantity of water to coils which had been heated to red heat, thereby converting it instantly to high-pressure steam, was an alternative to the conventional boiler. Invented by Léon Serpollet, whose cars naturally used it until their demise in 1907, it was also employed on the American White.

Steam cars achieved very little popularity outside America, however, and even there the boom was over by 1905. Thereafter, only two makes of importance struggled on, White and Stanley. As they tried to keep up with the growing sophistication of the petrol car they became more expensive, so that whereas a 1902 Stanley cost $750, the price of a 1918 Stanley was $2750, putting it among the higher-priced cars. White went over to petrol engines in 1910, but Stanley struggled on with falling sales until 1927. Meanwhile a new make of steam car had appeared which exceeded anything previously seen in this field, in sophistication, performance, and price. This was the Doble (Fig. 30.4), made initially in Detroit, and later in San Francisco. It had

FIG. 30.4. 1924 Doble E-type steamer, showing the boiler under the bonnet. The engine was just ahead of the rear axle.

a four-cylinder horizontal double-acting compound engine with a flash generator which could produce 750 lb/in² pressure in 30 to 45 seconds, thanks to
electric ignition. A really efficient condenser consumed practically all the
steam generated. With a light body, the Doble could accelerate from 0 to 40
mile/h in 8 seconds, and had a maximum speed of 108 mile/h. However. with
all these attractions went a price of $11 200, which made the Doble the most
expensive American-built passenger car. Buyers who were both wealthy and
sufficiently adventurous to go in for steam at this date were very few (one was
the young Howard Hughes), and only 45 Dobles were sold between 1923 and
1932. After the eclipse of the Doble there were no steam cars made anywhere
in the world, though a few isolated experimenters have toyed with the idea up
to the present day.

II. GOODS VEHICLES

Internal combustion. The first load-carrying commercial vehicles were based
on contemporary passenger cars, and appeared in the late 1890s. With limited
power and short wheelbases their utility was very restricted, and the early
vans operated by such companies as the Paris stores Galeries Lafayette and
Grands Magazins du Louvre were of more value for publicity purposes than
as load carriers. The first step towards a purpose-built commercial vehicle
was the placing of the driver over the engine instead of behind it. This layout
was pioneered by the German Daimler company in 1898 and became widespread in America, where it was normal for larger trucks until 1914. However, a major drawback was the vibration transmitted to the driver, and as the
distances to be covered grew, so the forward-control position fell from favour,
only to be revived in the 1930s when engine vibration had been reduced; the
driver and his mate then sat on each side of the engine rather than on top of it.

During the years up to 1914 the use of goods vehicles increased greatly,
though horses remained more important in this field than with either passenger cars or buses, and there were still many more horse-drawn than motor
goods vehicles in 1914. Motor lorries were seldom used for journeys of more
than 50 miles, for their low speeds made it impossible for them to rival
the railways. Long-distance demonstration runs, however, were made quite
early, and the first trans-American motor-truck run was made by a Packard
in 1912. Its time was 46 days, but by 1931 this had been reduced to five days.
The most important work of the truck before 1914 was to act as feeder to the
railheads. These services were often operated by the railways themselves, on
condition that they would only carry goods destined for onward transit by

rail. By this means, remote valleys and fishing villages were brought into the orbit of railway services. Another important work of the medium-distance lorry was to bring fresh fruit, vegetables, and eggs from farms for distribution in a market town. Apart from this widespread work, motor lorries were being used for wholesale and retail deliveries of coal, oil, beer, ice, groceries, furniture, and mail, to mention only a few commodities. Municipal vehicles included motor fire engines, ambulances, and street-cleaning equipment.

In design, goods vehicles did not deviate greatly from passenger cars. Light vans with one or two-cylinder engines turned from chain or belt-drive to shaft-drive, though the larger lorries retained chains until well into the 1920s. The six-cylinder engine was practically unknown in commercial vehicles before the First World War, the typical power unit being a large four-cylinder T-head or L-head engine of up to 8 litres capacity, delivering about 40 b.h.p. at 1000 rev/min. Few lorries were rated for more than 5 tons load capacity, though the Hewitt Motor Company of New York listed a 10-tonner which used the same engine and frame as the 5-tonner, but with larger springs and wheels. The rated capacity was no guide to the actual load that a lorry might be subjected to, and manufacturers usually allowed for a 100 per cent overload factor when deciding a rating. The enormous Hewitts had a maximum speed of no more than 8 mile/h, while a smaller lorry of, say, 3 tons capacity, might be capable of 20 mile/h.

An articulated lorry had been made as early as 1898, by the British Thornycroft company, but it had no immediate successors, and the first to manufacture tractor/trailer units for sale was Knox of Springfield, Massachusetts. Designed by Charles H. Martin, the Knox system involved a 'fifth wheel' turntable which was carried on semi-elliptic springs attached to the tractor's rear axle. The trailer's weight was taken by the wheels rather than by the tractor's frame, which could therefore be of lighter construction. This turntable was originally used with a three-wheeled tractor with a long steering column which stretched over the bonnet to the single front wheel. The early Knox tractors, made from 1909 to 1915, were often used in conjunction with horse-drawn trailers, including ladder trucks for fire service. A four-wheeler replaced the three-wheeler in 1915, largely because it was found more suitable for rough ground to have two tracks instead of three. More famous in the long run than the Knox was the British Scammell, a four-wheeler tractor with 47 hp four-cylinder engine and double chain drive; this went into production, using a Knox-type turntable, in 1920. The manufacturers went ahead with this on the understanding that it would be regarded for legal

FIG. 30.5. The Scammell frameless articulated tanker, c. 1927.

purposes as a single-unit vehicle rather than a lorry and trailer, and so have a
speed limit of 12 mile/h instead of the 5 mile/h to which vehicles towing full
trailers were still subject. Weight restrictions were calculated according to
the load per axle rather than overall weight; so with three axles the Scammell
had a loading of less than 6 tons per axle. It could carry a 50 per cent greater
load with the same axle as a four-wheeler, being rated as a 7-tonner though it
was sometimes asked to carry as much as 15 tons.

An important development of 1926 was the frameless tanker (Fig. 30.5) in
which a large cylindrical tank provided its own frame, being supported
merely by the 'fifth wheel' turntable at the front and the axle at the rear.
Used for carrying fuel oil, beer, milk, vermouth, molasses, industrial chemicals, and many other liquids and gases, the Scammell frameless tanker has
been made up to the present day. By the late 1920s the articulated semi-
trailer was widespread in most countries, with load capacities from $2\frac{1}{2}$ to
100 tons. During the 1930s two-axle trailers began to appear, and are commonplace today. A specialized form of articulated vehicle, also pioneered by
Scammell, was the 'mechanical horse'. This was a three-wheeled tractor
powered by a small passenger car engine, for towing loads of 2–6 tons. Widely
used by the railway companies as replacements for their vast numbers of
horses, Scammell mechanical horses were made from 1932 to 1965; another
British company, Karrier, made them from 1932 to 1941.

Apart from the semi-trailer, the other method of increasing load area was to use three axles on a rigid chassis. This was first proposed by the British Foden company as early as 1903, but the first rigid six-wheelers to be built came from the American Goodyear Tyre Company, who made several in 1920 to demonstrate their large pneumatic tyres. American companies who made rigid 'sixes' for sale included the Six Wheel Company of Philadelphia (better known for their six-wheeled buses), Douglas, Fageol, and Moreland, later joined by the big producers like Mack, Autocar, G.M.C., and White. For work on level ground where loads were not too heavy, only the leading axle of the rear bogie would be driven, the rear one acting as a support only, but for heavy work in hilly country more traction was necessary, and both axles were powered. This was known as the 6×4 (six wheels driven by four) layout. The usual drive system was by shaft and bevel or worm gear to both axles, but some very heavy American trucks, and some British steam wagons, used chains to couple the two axles. Load capacities of the rigid sixes in the pre-war era were in the 10–15-ton range. To increase this still further, a number of British companies added an extra non-driven axle at the front, making an 8×4, or rigid eight. The first of thes was the Sentinel DG8 steam waggon of 1929, which was followed in the 1930s by most of the well-known heavy lorry-makers such as A.E.C. (Fig. 30.6), Leyland, Albion, and Scammell.

Fig. 30.6. 1934 A.E.C. Mammoth Major 15-ton rigid eight lorry.

The powered front axle, giving four-wheel drive, appeared in the U.S.A. in 1908 when two engineers from Wisconsin, Otto Zachow and his brother-in-law William Besserdich, invented a double-Y universal joint encased in a ball-and-socket joint; this allowed power to be applied to driving wheels which could still be steered. Originally used on a passenger car, the principle was applied in 1912 to a 3-ton lorry which was manufactured by a newly formed company, the Four Wheel Drive Auto Company of Clintonville, Wisconsin. The new 4×4 vehicle had infinitely better traction than a 4×2 in sandy or muddy ground, and over 15000 were supplied to the U.S. Armed forces during the First World War. Production continued in the 1920s, and the FWD company has included 4×4s, as well as other layouts such as 6×4, 6×6, and 8×6, in its range up to the present day. Other American companies who built early four-wheel-drive trucks included Duplex, Jeffery (later Nash) and Oshkosh. The principle of three driven axles (6×6) came into use experimentally in the 1920s, and was widely used in military vehicles in the Second World War.

Probably the most important commercial vehicle development of the inter-war period was the diesel engine. First developed for stationary engines in the 1890s, the compression ignition engine was applied to road vehicles by the German Benz and MAN firms in 1923. The idea was slow to catch on at first, largely because it was untried, more expensive, and because the high compression ratio of anything up to 25:1 (compared to 5 or 6:1 for ordinary petrol engines of the 1920s) made starting very difficult. Various methods were employed including a compression lever to make hand starting of one or two cylinders possible, electric glow plugs to warm the cylinders, or a small petrol engine turning the diesel's flywheel by friction. The conventional electric starter was found to be insufficiently powerful. However the diesel's advantages of fuel economy (more miles to the gallon and cheaper fuel), and greater pulling power than a comparable petrol unit gradually encouraged manufacturers to offer diesels, at first optional, then as standard. By 1931 Mercedes–Benz were making no petrol-engined commercial chassis, and in 1938 45 per cent of all German commercial vehicles in production were diesel powered. Most diesels were conventional in layout with four or six vertical in-line cylinders, but an exception was the Junkers opposed-piston unit which was made in France under the name CLM. Diesels first appeared in America in the early 1930s but, with an abundance of cheap petrol, that country did not turn to the diesel on a large scale until well after the Second World War.

FIG. 30.7. 1916 Foden overtype steam wagon.

Steam. The steam traction engine had been in widespread use since the 1880s, and by the turn of the century the steam lorry, or waggon as it was often called, was beginning to be of commercial significance, especially in Britain. Two basic designs emerged; the overtype and the undertype. The former had a horizontal locomotive-type boiler with the engine mounted above, driving the rear axles by a long chain. They had the appearance of a traction engine with a load-carrying space behind, and although there was less space than in an equivalent-sized undertype the overtype was a proved design and engine accessibility was excellent. The best-known make was Foden (Fig. 30.7), who built overtypes from 1901 to 1927 in much larger numbers than any other firm. The undertype had a vertical boiler, either ahead of the driver or just behind him, and the engine was mounted on the chassis frame. There were also a small number of undertypes with short locomotive boilers, and the Yorkshire undertype with transverse horizontal boiler. Engines were mostly two-cylinder compounds, and boilers fire-tube or water-tube operating at pressures of 200 to 276 lb/in^2.

Because of the abundance of cheap coal the steam lorry was much more widespread in Britain than anywhere else, and for loads of 5 tons or more it was almost universally used up to 1914. As late as 1926 there were over 10000 steam lorries in use in Britain, costing not more than 2d. a mile to run. However, as the petrol engine became able to cope with heavier loads, the steamer's drawbacks became more noticeable. Chief among these was the skill needed to get the best out of it, and the fact that it needed a crew of two. Skilled men were not easy to find, especially as operators were not willing to pay higher wages for steam drivers. The diesel engine was an enemy behind steam's own lines, for it possessed the same advantages of cheap fuel and suitability to heavy work. The final blow came in 1933 with a new British system of taxation based on unladen weight. Steamers were inevitably heavy vehicles, and the new system meant that a 10-ton steamer was taxed at a much higher rate than a diesel of equivalent capacity. The last steam lorries, the Sentinel S4, S6, S8, and the last-mentioned a rigid eight-wheeler for 15-ton loads, were excellent machines with rotating firegrates giving automatic stoking, 4-cylinder single-acting horizontal engines, and widespread use of aluminium alloys. Several internal-combustion vehicle features such as shaft drive, electric lighting, and pneumatic tyres were employed.

III. PUBLIC SERVICE VEHICLES

For the first quarter of the twentieth century the motor bus developed along generally similar lines to the goods vehicle. The first buses were very small open charabancs for no more than nine or ten passengers, on private car chassis, but by 1905 many lorry makers were advertising that their chassis were suitable for bus bodies. They were not, however, purpose-built for passenger work, and had a high loading line necessitating several steps for passengers. Double-deckers were widely used, as this layout had been familiar with horse buses. By 1910 London had 1142 motor buses and an approximately equal number of horse buses, but four years later the last horse bus had been withdrawn, and motor buses numbered more than 2500.

For several years after the First World War the motor bus changed little, though forward control came to London's buses with the K type of 1919. Then, within the space of a few years, several epoch-making designs appeared. In 1921 the brothers Frank and William Fageol of Oakland, California, introduced their Safety Coach, a 22-passenger single-decker coach with fully enclosed body and a chassis whose side members were swept up over the axles, so that between the axles the floor was only 19 inches from the ground.

FIG. 30.8. 1928 Twin Coach side-engined bus.

This feature, together with a wider track than was customary, gave the Fageol Safety Coach a totally new and lower appearance. Hundreds were sold over the next few years, and there were many imitators among American manufacturers. Drop frames, for both single and double deckers, came to Britain in 1924, and pneumatic tyres were widely adopted at the same time. In 1927 the Fageol brothers produced another milestone design. The Twin Coach (Fig. 30.8) looked almost identical at front and rear, and was powered by two four-cylinder engines mounted on each side of the chassis, behind the front axles. Seating capacity was 43, compared with 29 for the largest conventional single-decker. Revolutionary in 1927, it would not look particularly archaic today. The dual engines were replaced in 1934 by a single transverse engine behind the rear axles, but the principle of a flat front with entrance ahead of the axle (and driver-controlled pneumatic doors) was continued by Twin Coach and soon adopted by all American bus builders for vehicles of 30 passengers capacity or larger. In 1935 Twin Coach built the first American diesel bus.

European manufacturers were slower to abandon the traditional front-engined bus, although the British A.E.C. Company made 233 single-deckers and four double-deckers of the Q type between 1932 and 1936. These had a single side-mounted engine, as did the German Bussing–NAG six-wheeled Trambus of 1931. In 1941 the Birmingham and Midland Motor Omnibus Company, an operating company who designed and built their own buses, introduced a single-decker bus with horizontal underfloor engine which they put into production after the war in 1946; in 1948 A.E.C. launched their Regal IV range of underfloor-engined buses. Within a few years nearly all bus manufacturers adopted the underfloor or rear-engined position, leaving only small buses of less than 20 seats and school buses with front engines.

Another important bus development of the 1930s was monocoque, or integral, construction of chassis and body. The Twin Coach Model 23R of 1935 onwards had heavy cross-members, a single longitudinal stiffener between the axles, and a continuous encircling angle rail. In 1935 Gar Wood Industries of Detroit began production of William B. Stout's design for a 24-passenger bus which had welded steel tubes covered by a thin aluminium alloy skin. This had a Ford V-8 engine mounted in the tail and driving forward to the rear axle. It and its successor, the Aerocoach (Fig. 30.9), were made until 1952.

FIG. 30.9. 1941 Aerocoach 'Mastercraft'.

The social impact of the bus was enormous in country districts, for it took the poorer villagers from their immediate neighbourhood to market town and seaside, whereas previously they had relied on, at best, a seat on the carrier's cart, and otherwise their own feet. The country bus also collected milk and mail from remote villages, and like the lorry, acted as a feeder to the railways, many of which operated large fleets of buses. After the First World War many ex-servicemen invested their gratuities in a charabanc or two, and large fleets of these open buses swarmed from industrial towns at public holidays. They offered little in the way of comfort or speed, but they gave the working man an escape from his immediate surroundings for the day, and at a price he could afford.

IV. ELECTRIC VEHICLES

Two distinct types of electric vehicle have flourished in the twentieth century: the self-contained machine powered by batteries and the trolley vehicle drawing its current from overhead wires. Battery vehicles were already popular by 1900, both for private and commercial use, and more than 300 cabs built by the Electric Vehicle Company of Hartford, Connecticut were operating in New York and other American cities. They were not entirely successful because of the high cost of setting up battery-charging depots, a problem also encountered by the operators of London's electric cabs in the 1890s. In 1900 the Electric Vehicle Company, whose products were called Columbia, made more vehicles than any other U.S. manufacturer; they ranged from small two-passenger runabouts to heavy 5-ton trucks. The former had 44-cell batteries and motors geared directly to the rear axle, with a top speed of 20 mile/h. Battery-electric trucks were popular in American cities, where their limited range and low speed, sometimes no more than 6 mile/h, were not seen as serious drawbacks. For the really heavy trucks no single motor was powerful enough. A popular solution was to have four separate motors, one mounted in each wheel, drawing current from a battery of 44 cells which took up most of the space between front and rear axles. An alternative was the petrol-electric system, whereby a conventional petrol engine drove a dynamo to generate current for the motors. These might be mounted in the wheels, as in the American Couple Gear, or a single motor in the centre of the frame, as in the British Tilling-Stevens.

The electric car was more popular in the U.S.A. than elsewhere, and from 1900 to 1920 the electric brougham or coupé was widely used by ladies for social calls and shopping in cities. A typical example of 1914 would have a battery of 40 cells, wheel or lever steering, and four or five speeds controlled by lever or pedal. The latter operated in the opposite way to the accelerator of a petrol car; when it was fully depressed the brakes came on, and as it was progressively released the speed increased.

During the 1920s the building and use of electric cars dwindled to practically nothing. Their limited range between replacement or recharging of batteries, seldom more than 50 miles, was a drawback that few motorists were prepared to suffer, especially as improved roads made out-of-town journeys more practicable. Similarly, the heavy electric truck was superseded by internal combustion vehicles with greater speed and range, but the electric found a new field in house-to-house delivery work, especially of milk and bread. This had been the province of the horse until the early 1930s, when purpose-built small electric vans and milk floats, seldom of more than 25 cwt capacity, began to appear in large numbers. They were especially popular in Britain, which has remained the leading manufacturer of this type up to the present day. The smallest were pedestrian-controlled 'prams' of 5 cwt capacity, used for delivery of milk or mail, and also as small refuse collectors operating in confined spaces.

The trolley vehicle first appeared in Germany in 1882, and in 1901 the first trolleybus service began, at Bielethal in Saxony. Designed by Max Schiemann, this replaced the bow collector familiar on trams by a slide contact running under the wire. Between 1901 and 1914 many trolleybus routes were opened in Germany and Austria. Britain followed somewhat later, with a first system in 1911. All these early vehicles were single-deckers with artillery wheels and solid tyres, and they were unsatisfactory in that they were derived from tramcar practice rather than being conceived as trackless trolleys from the ground up. This came with the Tilling–Stevens buses built for Wolverhampton in 1923, and a further step forward was the introduction of the double-drive six-wheeler and of pneumatic tyres, both by Guy in 1926. Double-deckers were now common, both four- and six-wheelers. In the late 1930s a number of integral construction double-deckers were made for London Transport. An important improvement developed by London Transport was the use of carbon-lined skids in the trolley booms. These greatly increased the life of the overhead line.

The trolleybus seemed to be the natural replacement for the tram, and the peak years for numbers were probably just after the Second World War. At that time there were over 6000 throughout the world, but in the succeeding 25 years numbers were considerably reduced. Several factors account for this, including the increased cost of electricity and overhead equipment, and the inflexibility of the trolleybus in adapting to changing one-way schemes.

V. MOTORCYCLES

Production of motorcycles was very limited until the early 1900s. Early designs were mostly motorized bicycles in which various engine positions were tried, including horizontal mounting ahead of the rear wheel and vertical above the front wheel, which was driven by a leather belt. Many motorcycles were, in fact, ordinary bicycle frames to which specially built proprietary engines, such as Clément or Minerva, were fitted. An important step forward was taken by the Werner brothers in France who, in 1901, built a motorcycle with a 262-cc 2-hp single-cylinder engine mounted vertically behind the front wheel, the aluminium crankcase being an integral part of the frame instead of merely attached to it (Fig. 30.10). This practice was soon adopted by British manufacturers including Phelon and Moore, Humber, and Robinson and Price. Early motorcycles had single-cylinder engines but the search for increased power led, as with the motorcar, to two cylinders. The most logical form of this was the V-twin because, when mounted sideways, it fitted naturally into the triangular-shaped frame between front and

FIG. 30.10. 1902 Werner 2-hp motor bicycle.

rear wheel. Among the V-twin pioneers was the British firm of J. A. Prest-wich, who made a small number of complete cycles but were much more famous for their V-twin engines which they supplied to other manufacturers of motorcycles and light cars.

Two other forms of two-cylinder engine were the vertical twin, little used until the 1930s, and the horizontally opposed, or flat twin. The latter was made famous by Douglas Motors of Bristol, who made flat twin engines in many sizes from 1906 to 1957. Four-cylinder in-line engines were a speciality of the Belgian F.N. Company from 1904 to 1923, and were also made by Laurin and Klement (Austria), Dürkopp (Germany), and Henderson (U.S.A.). Belt transmission was customary, though chains became more popular for the more powerful machines from about 1912 onwards. Clutches and gearboxes were completely lacking on early motorcycles, and starting was effected by running alongside the machine and vaulting into the saddle when the engine fired. The increasing weight of the more powerful machines made a variable-speed system necessary, and the variable pulley and belt, or epicyclic gear in the hub, became popular.

In the early days motor tricycles were popular, in particular the de Dion Bouton whose engine of 1895 turned at a much higher speed than any other (1500 rev/min). The makers favoured the tricycle because of its inherent stability compared with two-wheelers, which were very prone to skidding on wet roads or when attacked by dogs, a frequent occurrence. De Dion Bouton tricycles were made in quite large numbers until 1901, and were followed by more sophisticated designs with wickerwork basket seats for a passenger between the front wheels. These were called tricars, and gradually they took on the characteristics of the car, a steering wheel replacing the handlebars and a seat the rider's saddle, while the air-cooled single-cylinder engine gave way to a water-cooled twin. The heyday of the tricar was from about 1903 to 1908, after which the side-by-side two-seater car took over in popularity.

The most popular means of increasing the two-wheeler's carrying capacity was the sidecar. This first appeared as a simple canework affair in 1903, but soon more comfortable versions appeared, with such refinements as wind-screens, folding hoods, and doors. Completely enclosed coupé-type sidecars did not appear until the 1930s.

Between the wars motorcycles were at the peak of their popularity, bringing independent transport to many who could not afford to run a car. The classic engine design was the big V-twin, with capacity as high as 1000 cc, developing 70 b.h.p. One of the finest of these was the Brough Superior with 998 cc

J.A.P. side-valve or overhead-valve engines, the latter guaranteed to reach 100 mile/h. Flat twins were a speciality of Douglas and B.M.W. The vertical twin was re-introduced by Triumph in 1935. It was more compact than the V-twin and, mounted transversely gave more even cooling of both cylinders. The two-stroke engine was popular in a variety of light machines by such makers as Dunelt, Levis, Velocette, and, especially, Scott.

The scooter had a brief vogue in the early 1920s and was revived by the Italian aircraft firm, Piaggio, just after the Second World War. Their Vespa had a 98 cc single-cylinder two-stroke engine driving through a three-speed gearbox and chain to the rear wheel, and a stressed-skin, spot-welded spine frame. Other Vespas with engines sizes up to 150 cc followed, and the design started a vogue which was taken up by numerous manufacturers in Italy, France, Germany, Great Britain, Spain, Austria, Czechoslovakia, and the Soviet Union. Another post-war development was a return to the cyclemotor, or motorized bicycle. Engines were as small as 49 cc, and in the more primitive designs drove the front wheel by friction roller, though this was replaced by chain drive to the rear wheels on such models as the N.S.U. 'Quickly' and Honda C50.

BIBLIOGRAPHY

Automobile Quarterly. The American car since 1775. Dutton, New York (1971).

BOLSTER, JOHN. *The upper crust.* Weidenfeld and Nicholson, London (1976).

BUCHANAN, C. D. *Mixed blessing, the motor in Britain.* Leonard Hill, London (1958).

CORNWELL. E. L. *Commercial road vehicles.* Batsford, London (1960).,

DAY, JOHN. *The Bosch book of the motorcar.* Collins, London (1975).

GEORGANO, G. N. *A history of sports cars.* Nelson, London (1970).

—— (ed.) *The complete encyclopedia of motorcars 1885 to date.* Ebury Press, London (1973).

MONTAGU OF BEAULIEU, LORD, and BIRD, ANTHONY. *Steam cars 1770 to 1970.* Cassell, London (1971).

NICHOLSON, T. R. *The vintage car, 1919–1930.* Batsford, London (1966).

PLOWDEN, WILLIAM. *The motorcar and politics, 1896–1970.* Bodley Head, London (1971).

SEDGWICK, MICHAEL. *Cars of the 1930's.* Batsford, London (1970).

SETH-SMITH, MICHAEL. *The long haul, a social history of the British commercial vehicle industry.* Hutchinson Benham, London (1975).

31

SHIPS AND SHIPBUILDING

B. BAXTER

I. SHIP DESIGN

FROM time immemorial wood was the only material used in shipbuilding because it was readily available throughout the world and was easily worked with simple hand tools. Wooden ships were transversely framed and covered by planks which were fixed to the wooden frames by bolts or screws of copper, iron, or steel. Although their subdivision was poor and their stability often inadequate some wooden ships were still being built at the end of the nineteenth century (Fig. 31.1). Generally speaking, however, their history belongs to earlier volumes of this work.

During the early part of the nineteenth century the construction of ships from wrought iron began and the invention of steam propulsion, which required more space for machinery and coal bunkers, accelerated the change from wood to iron. The design of iron ships followed that of wooden ships and a system of transverse framing was still used. The hull plates were riveted to the frames and the decks were riveted to beams; the beams and frames were connected by riveted brackets. The use of wrought iron was curtailed because it was subject to excessive corrosion and fouling, but many iron ships were still in service in the early years of the twentieth century.

Steel was introduced to shipbuilding about 1870. After 1877, when Lloyd's Register of Shipping published their *Rules for steel ships*, mild steel hulls quickly superseded wrought iron and by 1890 about 90 per cent of British ships were being built of steel. The introduction of steel had a less spectacular effect on design than the introduction of iron. The transverse framing method of construction continued to be used but advances in the science of naval architecture improved the general design of ships. Sizes increased, weights were reduced, and different methods were used for fabricating the hull structure. The latter changed greatly through the application of scientific principles of structural design and through the replacement of riveting by electric welding. The first all-welded ship, the *Fullagar*, 45 m in length, was launched at Cammell Laird in 1919. She was ultimately lost after 17 years of service as the result of a collision.

Experiments carried out in the 1940s on two similar tankers, the welded *Neverita* and the riveted *Newcombia*, showed that under static and dynamic conditions welded ships, although lighter than similar riveted ships, were subjected to and successfully met the same stresses. Basically, however, the improvements in the design of the hull structure of ships have been less than might be expected in comparison with advances in other aspects of ship-building, mainly because—for the first half of this century—the basic material, mild steel, had remained largely unchanged.

II. SHIP TYPES

The majority of merchant ships can be divided into one of the following broad categories: dry cargo ships, bulk carriers, oil tankers, and passenger ships.

The design and development of dry cargo ships from 1900 to 1950 can be divided into two phases. For the first twenty years standards were maintained, but thereafter there was rapid and substantial progress.

As was natural, the first iron and steel cargo ships of the latter years of the nineteenth century followed in many respects the design of the sailing ships which they superseded, and were mainly of the flush-deck type. These were gradually improved by the extension of the bridge structure amidships to the ship's side; the raising of the quarterdeck to form a poop; and an increased height for the forecastle. These resulted in the 'three-island' type ship which was modified when any two of the islands were joined.

When the weather-deck erections were small, surrounding weather-deck areas were used for stowing cargo protected by light coverings. This led to the awning-deck or spar-deck type of ship. When these areas were plated in, and tonnage openings fitted, the complete superstructure or shelter-deck type of ship was evolved. This type was very popular because the tonnage openings made the upper tween-deck spaces technically open spaces and therefore exempt from tonnage measurement. The strength deck in this type is the shelter-deck, although the freeboard is measured from the deck below the shelter-deck.

When the tonnage openings were made into permanent hatchways and completely closed, and the scantlings of the upper plating and frames were increased, the freeboard deck then became the uppermost continuous deck and the ship became a full scantling ship.

These two types of ships, the complete superstructure and the full scantling, are the true forerunners of the modern dry cargo carriers. The advan-

Nº 131. ADMIRALTY PIER EXTEN: 15.7.02
GENERAL VIEW

—FIG. 31.1. Wooden sailing ships and iron-hulled paddle steamers in Dover Harbour, 1902.

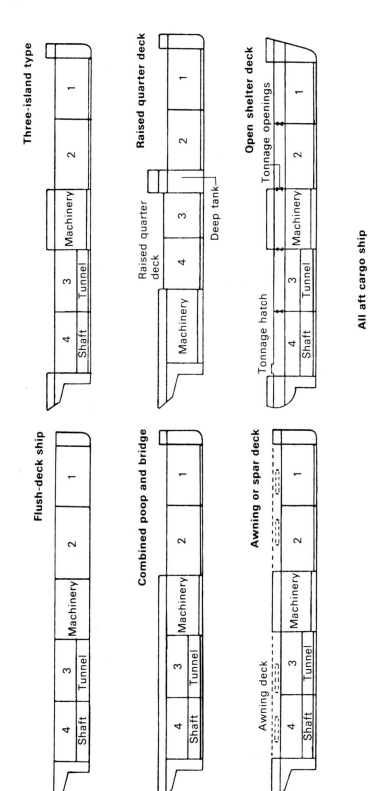

FIG. 31.2. Development of the cargo ship.

tage of the latter, however, is that it is given a greater draught than the former because of its greater strength and lack of openings in the weather-deck; perhaps the most striking feature of a large modern dry cargo ship is that there are fewer decks than in the older ships. Fig. 31.2 shows the development of the cargo ship.

After the standard ships of the First World War were designed and built, there were marked increases in the speed and size of cargo ships. Because of the increased speeds and the need to increase stability the slender narrow ships of the early years have given way to gradual increases in beam relative to length.

The further development of the design of steel ships has resulted in a steady growth in the average size of all types of cargo ships, accompanied by a constant demand for economy in weight and cost and for greater safety. Fig. 31.3 shows the profile of various cargo ships.

The development of the bulk carrier is less well documented than that of the cargo carrier and tanker but recently there have been very large increases in the size of this type of ship. It was first developed in the Great Lakes, where large single-deckers were used for the carriage of ore at the beginning of this century. In 1903 iron ore was first taken from Narvik. Iron ore carriers were then developed with the machinery aft and ballast tanks in the wings.

In the early days the unloading was done by hand, but this was rapidly replaced by mechanical discharging using grabs. In 1910 self-loading apparatus was installed. To overcome the inherent disadvantage of a normal ore carrier which could be used only to carry ore in one direction the combined oil/ore carrier was developed.

Many features of the bulk carrier, such as large hatchways, clear holds and decks, and steel hatch covers are now increasingly used in dry cargo ships.

III. TANKERS AND LINERS

Oil was discovered in Pennsylvania in 1859 and thereafter the export of oil from the U.S.A. gradually increased. In the beginning the trade was conducted mainly by carrying oil in drums, cases, barrels, and similar small containers, in sailing ships, but the expanding demand resulted in the introduction of the oil tanker in the form known today when the *Gluckauf* of about 3200 tonnes deadweight was built on the Tyne in 1886. Since that time there has been continuing progress in the size and sophistication of tankers (Fig. 31.4). Figs. 31.5(a) and (b) show two of the famous U.S. 'T.2' tankers (1945), of which 480 were built.

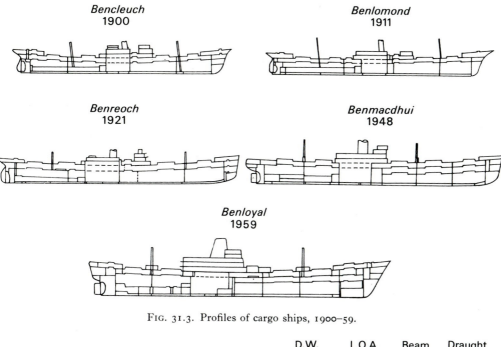

FIG. 31.3. Profiles of cargo ships, 1900–59.

		D.W. (Tonnes)	L.O.A. (m)	Beam (m)	Draught (m)
1886	First tanker S.S *Gluckauf*	3200	92	11	5
1918		8000	120	17	7
1930		10 000	140	18	8.5
1945	American T.2 Tanker	16 600	160	21	9
1960		104 000	289	41	16·3

FIG. 31.4. Growth in the size of tankers.

The design of tankers has been marked by their uniformity of progress and the speed/length ratio has changed only little, possibly because the economic justification for very high speeds has been absent.

The structural design of oil tankers rapidly incorporated the longitudinal system of framing developed by Sir Joseph Isherwood. Their design was also assisted by the ability to designate certain tanks as permanent empty spaces, which allows smaller scantlings than would be required if the tanker carried a homogeneous cargo through its whole length. Another trend now

FIG. 31.5(a). The launching of the first T.2 tanker, the *Gettysburg*.

(b). A T.2 tanker converted for transportation of aircraft during the Second World War.

FIG. 31.6. The *Queen Elizabeth*.

universally adopted in tanker design is to concentrate the bridge and accommodation at the after end of the ship. This arrangement has many advantages from an economic, structural, and safety point of view.

The *Great Eastern* (1858), because of its size, dominated the passenger liner scene until the building of the *Oceanic* just before 1900; this was the first liner to exceed the *Great Eastern* in size (Vol. V, pp. 361–5).

A new era started with the directly driven turbine liners *Lusitania* and *Mauretania* which went into service in 1907 and 1909 respectively. These ships were capable of maintaining, during the voyage across the Atlantic, a minimum average speed of 24–5 knots in moderate weather. The requirement for this speed was dictated by the strong competition from German liners on the same international run. Later, very large but much slower ships, the *Olympic, Titanic, Britannic*, and *Aquitania* were built. The *Titanic* was lost in 1912 and the *Britannic* was torpedoed in 1917.

In the early 1930s the geared steam-turbine liners *Queen Mary* and *Queen Elizabeth* incorporated the best features of the very early liners and were designed to maintain a weekly schedule on the Atlantic crossing. Fig. 31.6 shows the *Queen Elizabeth*, which was for a long time the largest ship in the

FIG. 31.7. The 30000-ton cruise liner *Arcadia*.

world. Other famous liners in service in the 1930s were the *America* (U.S.A.); *Conte Di Savoia* (Italian); *Europa* (German); *Manhattan* (U.S.A.); *Normandie* (French); and *Arcadia* (British) (Fig. 31.7).

A notable difference between the passenger liners of the nineteenth and twentieth century was the absence of built-up superstructures in the earlier types. This was because the 1894 Merchant Shipping Act limited the number of passengers which could be carried on the upper deck. When, in 1906, this restriction was removed two and three tiers of superstructures were immediately fitted in new liners. This had the effect of increasing the beam in relation to the length and the increased space available to passengers also increased the relative depth of the ship. Consequently, the modern liner is relatively less slender than its predecessors. Steel superstructures were used at first but later aluminium alloy replaced these, permitting greater strains to be endured than with steel.

In addition to the types of ships already considered, two new different types of craft have entered the high-speed passenger ferry service on short routes. These are the air-cushioned hovercraft and the hydrofoil.

The first commercial hovercraft was designed by Sir Christopher Cockrell in 1950 and development has been concentrated in Britain. There are two principal types: the amphibious with flexible skirts, and the side-wall type. The side-wall designs are more economical but the increased drag reduces their operating speed.

The first commercial sea-going hydrofoils were introduced in about 1956 in Italy, and their service quite rapidly spread to the Mediterranean, Scandinavia, Hong Kong, Japan, and South America.

IV. SAFETY OF SHIPS

Ships are now very much safer than they were in the nineteenth century. One of the reasons for early casualties was the poor stability of the designs, which were not based on scientific principles. The factors governing adequate stability are now much better understood. There was a dramatic fall in the number of deaths of crews in merchant ships from 0·14 per cent in the first decade of the twentieth century to 0·03 per cent during the period 1953–7. In addition, the tonnage of ships lost as a percentage of the total owned has fallen steadily from 2 per cent in 1900 to 0·23 per cent in 1959.

In a general way the safety of a ship is allied to its freeboard. The greater the amount of freeboard the greater the amount of reserve buoyancy and, therefore, the greater the chance of remaining afloat when damaged. A Load Line Act came into force in Britain in 1890 which made it compulsory for sea-going ships to be marked with a loadline, and the calculation of the amount of freeboard was agreed in 1906.

An International Conference on Load Lines was held in London in 1930 and proposed Rules for the Calculation of Freeboard and for the condition of assignment were agreed unanimously. Thus, for the first time in history, the regulations for controlling the loading of sea-going ships became international, ensuring a uniform degree of safety for all ships and their crews throughout the world.

After the sinking of the *Titanic* in 1912, in which 1502 people were drowned, a committee was appointed to study efficient subdivision in all types of ships and to consider other ways of raising the standard of safety. This was a forerunner of the International Conferences on the Safety of Life at Sea held in London in 1914 and 1929. In 1948 another International Conference was held to add desirable modifications to the 1929 Conference. Separate committees considered, among other items, the safety aspects of construction: that is, watertight subdivision and stability, life-saving appliances, and navigation.

The 1913 Conference laid down the fundamental principle that a ship must have lifeboats and liferafts capable of carrying all on board. The 1930 Conference added the requirement that in addition buoyant apparatus for 25 per cent of the persons on board should be available. It also required that a certain number of motor boats must be carried. The 1948 Convention increased the scope to cover cargo ships. Cargo-carrying ships must never carry more than 12 passengers or they become classed as passenger ships, in which case the number and spacing of bulkheads is determined by the 1948 Convention.

There are no government requirements for the number of transverse watertight bulkheads which need to be fitted in a normal cargo ship, but the Rules of Classification Societies—such as Lloyd's Register of Shipping—state that the minimum number of bulkheads to be fitted in any cargo ship is four if the machinery is amidships, and three if the machinery is aft. The number of bulkheads to be fitted is governed by the length of the ship, ranging from four for ships less than 65 m in length and nine for lengths of 165 m to 290 m.

The protection of ships against fire is concerned with both the prevention of fires and methods of suppressing them. The first line of defence is to detect the fire as early as possible and to restrict its spread by correct and adequate fire-fighting measures. If these fail it is necessary to use the inherent fire resistance of the ship's structure to prevent a major disaster, but it is clearly desirable to avoid this stage.

One of the chief concerns of the 1948 Safety Convention was to obtain standardized methods of fire protection in accommodation and service spaces as well as fire detection and extinction devices in both cargo and passenger ships. There are three types of automatic fire detection systems readily available; namely heat-sensitive, smoke detection, and infra-red.

The ready availability of water make it the most suitable fire-fighting agent in ships. It may be used either from hand appliances or fixed installations, such as pipes or spray nozzles. Flammable liquid fires are best extinguished by the use of carbon dioxide in foam or froth form. The use of water for electrical fires must be avoided, and for these also carbon dioxide is suitable.

V. RESEARCH

Research into the design of ships and machinery has in the main been evolutionary rather than revolutionary, and this tends to obscure the fact that substantial progress has been made in several directions. This can be most easily seen by making comparisons between the specifications and appearance of ships designed at the start of the century and those being designed fifty years later.

In Britain, there has been a long history of successful work on resistance and propulsion at the Ship Division of the National Physical Laboratory and in private tanks in Scotland and England, as well as work on high-speed forms at the Admiralty Experiment Works at Haslar. Systematic research on welding was carried out during the Second World War for the Admiralty Ship Welding Committee, and in 1944 the British Ship Research Association (B.S.R.A.) and PAMETRADA (Parsons and Marine Engineering Turbine Research and Development Association) were established by the ship and marine engineering industries with financial and technical support given by the British Government.

The work of B.S.R.A. was divided into three main groups—naval architecture research, marine engineering research and production research—resulting from the Report of the Patton Committee (Industry Report on Productivity in Shipbuilding). Projects started and developed during the first years included accurate recording of ships' performance at sea; reduction of model resistance and propulsion data to empirical formulae; measurement of interaction between main hull girder and superstructures; development of new welding methods; corrosion of propellers; the adoption of a standard code of practice for measured mile trials; and testing of bulbous bows. On the engineering side they included stresses in steam pipes; fatigue in bolts and main shafting; fabrication of aluminium alloys; ventilation in cargo and crew spaces; and noise insulation.

Advances in the science of naval architecture have enabled the general design of ships to be improved, resulting in increased size, reductions in weight, and, in particular, increased speeds brought about by improved propulsion efficiencies resulting from the increased knowledge of ship resistance. There have been no radical alterations in the standards of strength over the past hundred years but great improvements have been made in the standards of subdivision, minimum freeboard, statical and dynamical stability, and fire prevention, and all of these have contributed to make ships much safer. In general, while there has been a natural increase in the size, speed, and efficiency of hull and machinery under the pressure of economic considerations, the comparable improvements in the amenities for the crew and in the safety of life have resulted from different causes.

VI. SHIPBUILDING

Shipbuilding is an industry that has expanded from a traditional craft, and is now pre-eminently an assembly industry, with much general engineering work. The three main stages in the production of a completed ship are: design, production of specification and drawings, and pre-production planning; building the hull and launching; and fitting out and trials. The organization, staff, and labour required for each of these stages is different.

The process of obtaining a new merchant ship involves five successive stages. First, the shipowner decides on the requirements for the new ship. These will usually specify, as a minimum, the amount and type of cargo to be carried; the service speed under normal conditions on a specified route; and the maximum draught. These requirements will then be sent to a shipbuilder or consultant naval architect, who will prepare one or more alternative designs.

After the approval of the design and the choice of a shipbuilder a contract is signed and the shipbuilder then produces the working drawings for approval by one of the seven major Classification Societies, such as Lloyd's Register of Shipping. The building of the ship is supervised by the surveyors of the Classification Society to obtain the relevant classification certificates for hull, machinery, and electrical installation. Without these certificates insurance would be virtually impossible. Finally, after satisfactory completion of trials at sea, usually lasting two or three days, the ship is accepted by the owners.

The responsibility for conforming to the terms of the contract remains firmly with the shipbuilder, and failure is often covered by severe penalty clauses.

The hull production process starts when the steel bars and plates enter the shipyard, where they are inspected and checked. If these plates and bars have not been shot- or grit-blasted at the steelmakers they will be subjected to this process in the shipyard and then coated with a primer to prevent rust. Thereafter the plates and bars are transferred to a prefabrication shop where they are welded into prefabricated assemblies consisting of flat panels of plating strengthened by stiffening bars. These sub-assemblies are then incorporated into a three-dimensional prefabricated unit (Fig. 31.8), which in turn is positioned on the building berth by travelling cranes. The midship units are normally placed on the berth first and these are followed by the units forming the after end of the ship. The after end has to be completed before the forward end since it is usual for the propeller shafts and propellers to be fitted prior to launching. This requires a considerable amount of structural machining and perhaps the fitting of 'A' brackets for twin-screw ships.

Machines used in the pre-launch stage of construction include magnetic or vacuum-type cranes for lifting plates and bars; conveyors for transporting

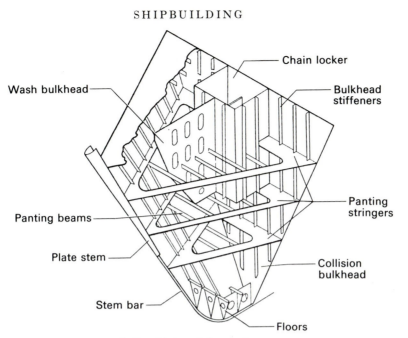

Chain locker

Wash bulkhead

Bulkhead stiffeners

Panting stringers

Panting beams

Plate stem

Collision bulkhead

Stem bar

Floors

FIG. 31.8. Pre-fabricated fore-end structure.

plates throughout the yard: plate-straightening rolls for flattening plates that have been distorted; shot-blasting equipment for removing the mill scale and rust prior to the application of paint; automatic paint-spraying machines for quickly applying rapid-drying special primers to top and bottom surfaces simultaneously; bending rolls, used to roll shell plates and flanged bulkheads; presses of various types to bend, straighten, joggle, and flange plates; guillotines for shearing smaller pieces of plate; plate edgers which mechanically prepare plate edges for welding; frame benders, used to bend ships' frames while cold (the old method of bending frames immediately after furnacing having disappeared); and flame planers and profilers used for preparing rectangular plates or burning shapes from plates.

Most large shipyards now use manual methods of welding fillets but submerged and open-arc machines are used for the welding of seams and butts. Approximately 10 per cent of all metal deposited is carried out by automatic or semi-automatic machines and this figure is continually increasing. Gravity fillet-welding machines are used to deposit weld material simultaneously on both sides of stiffeners to meet the increasing demand for faster speeds of welding. One-side welding is being developed and complete depth penetration is being obtained. The remote side is protected by a copper strip or some coated refractory backing material.

A ship is built on permanent blocks placed underneath the keel. When it is ready for launching the total weight is transferred from these blocks to a launching cradle, which supports about three-quarters of the length of the ship. It consists of a structure forward called the fore poppet, fitting closely to the hull just aft of the stem; a structure just forward of the rudder post, or cut-up, called the aft poppet; and a portion intermediate between these two. In Britain, this cradle usually rests on two 'ways' parallel to the centreline of the ship, the distance between the ways being about one-third of the beam of the ship. Just before the actual launch a lubricant is inserted between the sliding and standing ways, and during the actual launching process the cradle and the ship slide down the ways until the ship is completely waterborne.

In some shipyards, and particularly on the Great Lakes, the launching site is so restricted that side launching has been developed. The ships are built on an even keel and are often dropped off the way ends into the water with a consequent large angle of heel. In many of the large modern yards ships are floated out of a building dock and are not launched in the traditional way (see below).

After launching the process known as fitting out continues. This means that the main engines, diesel-generating sets, compressors, pumps, piping, valves, etc., are installed in the engine room, and the superstructure, deck-houses, masthouse, bridge, etc., are completed. The accommodation spaces and living quarters are fitted with all services including plumbing, wiring, ventilation, etc.

The modern tendency is to instal as much equipment as possible on board the ship before the launch. For merchant ships the fitting out process lasts for about one-third of the building period; for warships the period is two-thirds.

Riveted ships predominated in the first three decades of the twentieth century. Hand riveting gave way to hydraulic riveting, which in turn was superseded by pneumatic riveting.

The shipyards required plenty of building berths where the ships were assembled plate by plate on frames attached to the keel, the whole hull being faired and bolted together before riveting and caulking. Berths were therefore equipped with many light derricks, rarely exceeding five tons in capacity. Punching, shearing, frame-bending, and material preparation were carried out in sheds at the head of the berth.

The task of fairing the various sections of the ship, that is, making certain they were uniform and consistent, was solved by drawing the ship full scale on the mould-loft floor, a procedure that gradually gave way in modern yards to $\frac{1}{10}$-scale lofting. The lines thus drawn full scale could be made readily available; they were either copied on scrieve boards, which were then used to determine the shape of the frames, or templates were prepared giving information for the preparation of plates.

The structure when completed was tested by hammering for soundness and by flooding tanks and compartments for watertightness.

During the First World War, large-scale production of standard designs of ships was, for the first time, made possible and prefabrication was practised in Britain and elsewhere. A Merchant Shipbuilding Advisory Committee, set up in 1916, decided on an extensive shipbuilding programme to build ships of a simple design which would, as far as possible, have hulls, engines, and equipment of a standard type.

The main lessons learned in Britain were that large-scale production of standard designs of ships and engines could be successfully undertaken and was an essential part of the nation's fighting strength. In addition, it was learned that hull prefabrication by shipbuilders with the assistance of the civil engineering industry was essential.

Before, during, and immediately after the First World War productivity in British shipyards was high by the standards of the time and ahead of that in the U.S.A. and other rival shipbuilding countries. This gave Britain a technical lead in ship construction which, in part, accounted for British supremacy as a ship-owning nation.

After the First World War British shipowners had four sources from which to replace their wartime losses; among these was the acquisition of standard ships built by the British Government and ceded German ships. This saddled the British ship-owning industry throughout the 1920s and 1930s with a large number of pre-war ships, and the retention of these by British owners was a great misfortune for the British shipbuilding industry.

In the period up to the Second World War the German, Dutch, Swedish, and Japanese shipyards, backed in many cases by open or hidden state subsidies, increased their building while Britain's remained static. The British share of the world shipbuilding market continued to fall from 60 per cent in 1912 to 50 per cent in 1939; even in 1939 it was only large naval orders that fully utilized British yards, which were working well below capacity with 20 per cent unemployed.

This depression in British shipyards was blamed on difficult and overpaid labour forces. Although a solution was found by contraction of capacity,

FIG. 31.9. H.M.S. *Hood*, a battle cruiser of 41 000 tons displacement, completed in 1923, and sunk by the German battleship *Bismark* in May 1941.

what was really needed were more modern shipyards; more orders for modern ships; and new methods of working. The world economic stagnation in the early 1930s led to pessimism about the future of shipbuilding and in 1933 the level of unemployment in the industry rose to 63 per cent.

Instead of the accepted, and apparently normal, slump and boom there was a continuous slump. To counter this the National Shipbuilders Security Ltd. (N.S.S.) was founded in 1930 to eliminate surplus shipyards, but the role and intervention of N.S.S. in the shipbuilding industry had probably less importance than is now historically attached to it. Nevertheless, the experience of British shipbuilding in the 1930s has left its mark, and fears of over-capacity and over-expansion have never been fully removed.

For shipbuilders the inter-war years saw the culminating era of the great passenger liners. Warship building programmes involving battleships (Fig. 31.9), aircraft carriers, cruisers, destroyers, and submarines were limited by the Washington Treaty of 1922. Tankers formed an important part of building demand, but the ubiquitous tramp cargo ship represented by far the largest proportion of output. Specialized craft, container, and passenger ships as well as colliers, coasters, trawlers, tugs, and other small craft were also in demand.

It was necessary in both world wars to produce a large number of merchant ships very quickly to replace those sunk by the enemy and also to provide the increased sea transport required for world-wide military operations. It was also necessary to build all types of warships to defend merchant fleets and to engage and subdue enemy fleets.

During the Second World War the Allies decided to concentrate on the building of naval ships and special types of ships for war transportation. A high degree of standardization of machinery and equipment was achieved to help and speed production. In 1942 and 1943 27m. tons of freighters and tankers were launched in U.S. shipyards, which also delivered 1238 Liberty ships from fourteen yards.

The technical factors which helped to achieve such remarkable production rates were the widespread introduction of welding—which was also accepted because it was easier to train newly recruited labour to weld than to rivet—and the development of the block sub-assembly on berths, building at first 10-ton blocks and finally 200-ton blocks. Jigs were used to ensure a good fit for the blocks and also to permit the maximum use of down-hand welding. In addition, there was a detailed and complete scheduling and control of the flow of material and equipment through the shops to the berths. Fig. 31.10 shows the numbers of man-hours per ship for ships built in new yards and the advantage gained by building standard ships.

Electric arc welding of mild steel plates in shipbuilding has superseded riveting as the main form of structural attachment. The main advantages are a substantial saving in steel weight; economy of construction; greater fabrication potential; better continuity of strength; greater freedom of design; and

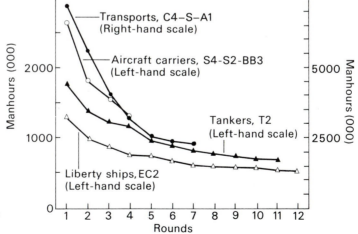

FIG. 31.10. Manhours per ship for ships built in new yards in the U.S.A. This shows the reduction in manhours for building standard ships such as T2 tankers, Liberty ships, etc.

the provision of watertightness without caulking. On the other hand, the efficiency of the joints depends upon the welder and the position in which he is operating; also, the rapid heating and cooling tend to distort the plates, and locked-up stresses occur owing to contraction. These can be minimized if the structure is suitably prepared and the correct sequence of welding is followed. X-ray and gamma-ray techniques are used for checking welds, but at present these are generally restricted to butt welds. Because early welding tended to be brittle, welded structures in the 1930s were suspect and the acceptance of welded ships by shipowners was very slow.

Two separate occurrences hastened the acceptance of welding. The first was the development of the coated electrode, and the second was the London Naval Treaty which gave the incentive to build the lightest possible warship; in order to save weight welding was widely adopted. This required the training of many welders and gradually the skills and techniques spread from warship construction to merchant ship construction.

Undoubtedly, however, it was the widespread welding adopted in the building of Liberty and Victory ships in the U.S.A. during the Second World War, which showed that ships welded under most production methods were generally successful. Welded ships could also be more economically powered because of their lighter and smoother hulls, and this made the technique still more acceptable to shipowners.

There is no doubt that British shipyards before the Second World War were in general better equipped than many continental shipyards. After the war, the position was reversed; many of the well-known modernized continental yards were then much better equipped than the majority of British yards.

The modernization and reconstruction schemes in most shipyards were carried out in three distinct stages. First, the replacement of worn-out conventional equipment. Secondly, the introduction of modern welding equipment and practices. Thirdly, changes in layout to meet the increasing dimensional trends. In particular, the construction of very large tankers gave rise to a close comparison of the advantages of building docks and slipways. The main advantage of the building dock is the elimination of expensive launching arrangements and all their associated activities, and this was the system which gradually took preference.

A number of new shipyards have been established in traditional ship-building countries, and also in some countries having little or no previous knowledge or experience of the industry. In Britain modernization of existing

FIG. 31.11. Gotaverken's new shipyard at Arendal, Norway.

yards so fully engaged those in the industry that there was little time for serious thought on new shipyards. In western Europe, and Scandinavia in particular, entirely new shipyards were built by long-established, well-known, successful companies. Fig. 31.11 shows the layout of Gotaverken's shipyard at Arendal, Norway. This shipyard introduced the conveyor-belt system of shipbuilding in which the fabricated sections, each weighing up to 300 tons, are conveyed gradually from the fabricating hall and along the building dock as each section is completed and added to the hull section immediately preceding it.

Each of these new yards can construct and accommodate tankers up to 100 000 tons deadweight. Their layout is ideal for the rapid production of ships of reasonably standard type. If repetitive production of fewer specialized standard ships is also the objective, then these yards undoubtedly have competitive advantages.

Developments in the structural design of ships have been influenced by three considerations, namely, eliminating internal obstructions to give large clear holds for carrying and working cargo; reducing the weight of the ship by the most efficient distribution of material; and ensuring that the hull structure is strong enough to withstand the forces of the sea.

The elimination of internal obstructions in cargo ships in particular has been accomplished by the substitution of deep transverse and horizontal underdeck girders for widely spaced hold pillars.

The efficiency of the structure has been increased by the increased use of welding and a consequent reduction in the weight of steel. In addition, the advantages of framing the bottom and decks of cargo ships longitudinally instead of transversely is now universal.

Design methods now use the results of the separate calculation of the wave bending moment and the still-water bending moment. The addition of these gives the total bending moment to which the ship will be subjected, and this in turn enables structures to be designed and built with an adequate margin of safety.

During the period under review the shipbuilding and marine engineering industries maintained their loyalty to traditional materials, that is, mild steel, brass, and wood. As larger ships with higher speeds entered service the use of new materials was closely studied. The advantages to be obtained by reducing hull scantlings, made possible by the introduction of steels of higher tensile strength, were being examined in the 1950s, although the effects of increased deflection and vibration, notch ductibility, fatigue, welding, and fabrication all needed to be carefully assessed before economic and technical changes were made.

Light alloys have been used increasingly in both the internal structure and superstructures. Laminated foam or resin-based materials have been developed as strong, sound absorbing, cheap materials for internal bulkheads and partitions. Weight reductions have been made possible by using non-slip anti-corrosive plastic materials for decking and the use of plastic and pre-formed pipes.

The materials engineer is primarily interested in improving strength, life, and reliability, while at the same time reducing weight. Economic savings will, more often than not, also come from reduced costs in maintenance and inspection.

The changes in shipbuilding materials from wood to iron and from iron to steel, as well as changes in the method of propulsion, produced changes in

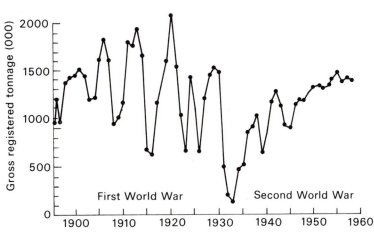

FIG. 31.12. U.K. shipping output reached over 2 000 000 gross tons for the first and last time in 1920.

management structures. As at first most shipyards built and repaired their own steam engines, an engineering department separate in function and control from the shipyard became necessary. With more recent changes from riveting to welding and from plate assembly to the prefabrication of large hull units, the work in the drawing office became more important, as it then became the first process in the overall production cycle.

To procure and fit at the right time the many thousands of parts which go into a ship requires careful planning. The most difficult stages are at the beginning of the contract and at the end, where very close cooperation is required between the shipbuilder, the subcontractors working in the shipyard, and the outside suppliers of equipment. As shipyards increased in size and the ships built in them became larger and more complicated, sales and estimating departments became necessary for selling ships. Works management, maintenance, security, and safety arrangements became necessary for the yards. In order to help boost sales, specialist designers and marketing and research staff were often added.

While the technological function was increasing, the administrative function also grew to include personnel, buying, legal, secretarial, and investment departments.

The history of world shipbuilding in the first half of the twentieth century is largely reflected by the history of British shipbuilding simply because of its dominant position. Figs. 31.12 and 31.13 show the U.K. annual output and the U.K. annual tonnage as a percentage of the world total. It was only after 1950 that the rapid and sustained growth in the output of countries such as

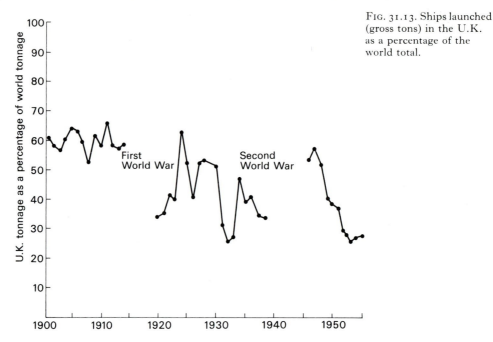

FIG. 31.13. Ships launched (gross tons) in the U.K. as a percentage of the world total.

Japan, Sweden, and Norway made the relatively unchanging annual output from British yards an ever-decreasing percentage of the world total.

VII. PROPULSION

The triple-expansion engine (Vol. V, p. 149) went into service in 1880 and was well established by 1890. The introduction of steel boilers, associated with the triple-expansion engine, allowed working pressures to be raised to about 150 lb/in² and although there was little external change in the appearance of reciprocating engines in the inter-war period the triple-expansion engine reached its ultimate stage of development when the reheating system, which in various ways gave appreciable improvements in performance, was introduced.

The steam turbine (Ch. 41) first came into prominence after its use in the *Turbinia* in 1897 and was in general use in warships by about 1910. Although the steam turbine has a high power-to-weight and power-to-volume ratio and is quieter and causes less vibration than a reciprocating engine, it also has disadvantages: it is not economical at cruising speeds; it cannot be reversed; and a high standard of quality control is required to achieve the same standards of reliability in a turbine as a reciprocating engine. Steam turbines are considerably more expensive than diesel engines of comparable power and their fuel consumption is 20 per cent higher. However, many shipowners would prefer the smooth running, easy handling, and lower maintenance costs of turbine machinery if the running costs could be reduced.

The changeover to steam turbines was, therefore, slow other than in warships and large liners. The first turbine-engined ship for transatlantic service, the *Virgina*, was in service in 1904 and was followed by the liners *Aquitania*, *Lusitania*, and *Mauretania*. Steam turbines with reduction gearing were first fitted in the cargo ship *Vespasian* in 1909, being followed by the liners *Coronia* and *Franconia*.

Before the Second World War little progress was made in the introduction of the steam turbine in cargo ships except in the U.S.A., but since that time its range of application has been extended to smaller ships. More recently, steam turbine machinery has been used in a number of large container ships because of the high power required (over 30000 s.h.p.).

A radical change in marine propulsion was caused by the introduction of oil as a fuel, first in place of coal and then with the oil engine invented by Rudolph Diesel in 1897 (Vol. V, p. 163). The change was accelerated by the rapid adoption and development of this engine in most European countries, with the exception of Britain. The new era of the heavy oil engine really started in Britain in 1912, when the *Selandia* was fitted with two single-acting four-stroke engines. The double-acting four-stroke engine predominated in the 1920s, but the two-stroke engine is now generally used for slow-speed engines, although the four-stroke is still used for medium- and high-speed engines. The slow-speed marine oil engine, with a range from of about 110 to 150 rev/min is the predominant propulsion unit for most types of merchant ships.

The three outstanding developments in marine oil engines, two of which have been introduced since the Second World War, are as follows. First, the use of solid fuel injection, which replaced blast air injection in the 1930s and led to a reduction in specific fuel consumption. Secondly, the use of cheap and readily available heavy boiler oil instead of diesel fuel. Thirdly, the introduction of turbo-charging, which enables an engine to use more oxygen and more fuel in each cylinder; this has increased power output by up to 50 per cent. Outputs of up to 2000 s.h.p. per cylinder may now be obtained.

The increased efficiency of the marine engine from 1900 to 1950 is best described in terms of the reduction in fuel consumption. On this basis the

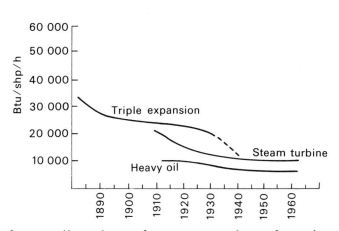

FIG. 31.14. Thermal efficiency of marine engines.

heavy oil engines of 1950 were about four times as efficient as the triple-expansion engines and boilers of 1900 (Fig. 31.14).

The overall propulsive efficiency of cargo ships, expressed in terms of the quasi-propulsive coefficient (QPC), increased from about 0·50 in 1900 to about 0·80 in 1950. In addition, the specific fuel consumption per hour was reduced from about 3 lb of coal per s.h.p. to 0·4 lb oil per b.h.p. in the diesel engine (for all purposes); that is, from about 37 000 b.t.u. to 8000 b.t.u. Taken in conjunction with improvements in resistance and propulsion this means that the efficiency of marine propulsion as a whole improved about eight-fold during those 50 years. In 1950 approximately 30 per cent, by gross tonnage, of world merchant ships were driven by diesel engines.

Steam turbines and diesel engines are now being slowly replaced, almost exclusively in warships, by gas turbines and—in a very few instances—nuclear-powered machinery. The gas turbine system, which eliminates the need for steam as a transfer medium, has been slowly developed for marine use. The first gas-turbine driven warship, MGB 2009, went to sea in 1947, exactly 50 years after the revolutionary steam turbine was fitted in the *Turbinia*. Both ships had a speed of 34 knots. The first ocean-going merchant ship to use a single-unit, mechanically driven gas turbine was the *John Sergeant*, converted from a Liberty ship in 1956. The thermal efficiency of these new engines is not as high as that of the heavy oil engine, but this disadvantage may be outweighed by the advantages of a 'repair by replacement' philosophy which the multiple unit offers.

BIBLIOGRAPHY

BAXTER, B. Comparison of welded and riveted ship construction. *Engineering*, 22 July 1955
——. *Qualifications for shipbuilding*. Royal Institution of Naval Architects, London (1971).
BEER, W. *Analysis of world merchant ship losses*. Royal Institution of Naval Architects, London (1969).
DANIEL, G. *International Conference on Safety of Life at Sea, 1948*. Institution of Naval Architects, London (1949).
EYRES, D. *Ship construction*. Heinemann, London (1972).
HURST, R. *Ship research*. Royal Institution of Naval Architects, London (1964).
——. *Towards a technology of shipbuilding*. North East Coast Institution of Engineers and Shipbuilders, 1966–7.
LENAGHAN, J. *Present trends in the shipbuilding inbustry*. Royal Institution of Naval Architects, London (1962).
MITCHELL, W., and SAWYER, L. *Empire ships of World War II*. Journal of Commerce, Liverpool (1965).
—— ——. *British standard ships of World War I*. Journal of Commerce, Liverpool (1968).
MURRAY, J. M. *Merchant ships 1860–1960*. Royal Institution of Naval Architects, London (1960).
NASH, P., and ASHRON, L. *Research in fire fighting and fire protection in ships*. Royal Institution of Naval Architects, London (1965).
PALMER, S. *The impact of the gas turbine on the design of major surface warships*. Royal Institution of Naval Architects, London (1973).
PARKINSON, J. R. *The economics of shipbuilding*. Cambridge University Press (1960).
SHEPHEARD, R. *The challenge of our marine environment*. North East Coast Institution of Engineers and Shipbuilders, 1968–9.
SMITH, D. *The 1966 International Conference on Load Lines*. Royal Institution of Naval Architects, London (1969).
STURMEY, S. *British shipping and world competition*. Athlone Press, London (1962).
TATTON-BROWN, P. *Main propulsion gas turbines in the R.N.* North East Coast Institution of Engineers and Shipbuilders, 1970.
WALTON, T. and BAXTER, B. *Know your own ship*. Griffin, London (1970).

32

RAILWAYS

O. S. NOCK

I. LOCOMOTIVES AND ROLLING STOCK

Steam locomotives. At the turn of the century the motive power of railways all over the world was almost entirely steam. Although many attempts had been made during the latter part of the nineteenth century to break away from the basic Stephensonian concept, embodied in the *Rocket* of 1829, with the important addition of the brick arch in the firebox to make possible the effective burning of coal, rather than coke, it was this original and simplest form that had prevailed (Vol. V, Ch. 15). Much experiment had taken place with two-stage, or compound expansion of the steam, but except in France, with the work of Alfred de Glehn, and in Austria, with that of Karl Gölsdorf, the results were not generally lasting. The outstanding advance in the early 1900s came from the work of the Prussian engineer Wilhelm Schmidt in developing the practice of superheating the steam above its temperature of formation. This eliminated the disadvantages of condensation, and increased the volume of steam produced. Yet although Schmidt's work was widely taken up on the continent of Europe, its most striking early success was in England, on the London and North Western Railway, where locomotives designed by C. J. Bowen Cooke and incorporating the Schmidt superheater showed an economy in fuel consumption over otherwise identical non-superheated locomotives of 27 per cent (Fig. 32.1) It was one of the greatest advances in the entire history of the steam locomotive.

As the demands of increased traffic required larger, and inevitably heavier, locomotives the effect of heavier axle loads on the track and underline structures became critical. In the early 1900s a classic development took place in Holland, where the spongy nature of much of the ground on which railways had necessarily to be laid made the problem acute. To secure smooth running of the locomotives themselves the art of balancing the revolving and reciprocating parts had been postulated, notably by W. E. Dalby, professor of engineering in London University. However, balance weights added to the wheels to secure smooth running could, in many circumstances produce a dynamic

FIG. 32.1. The high superheat 'George the Fifth' class 4–4–0 of 1910 by C. J. Bowen Cooke exemplified by the London and North Western Railway's *Coronation* engine of 1911.

augmentation of the dead load on the axle—a 'hammer-blow' effect. In certain of the simplest types of locomotive, with two inside cylinders, this could be as much as a 50 per cent addition to the dead load. Hammer-blow could, however, be eliminated entirely by using four cylinders, all driving on to the same axle, and by the introduction of this principle the Dutch civil engineers were able to accept larger locomotives, with a greater axle-load than the previous two-cylinder types. This collaboration in design between the locomotive and the civil engineers was no more than a beginning, and in Britain the full flowering of such cooperation did not begin to take shape until the setting up of the Bridge Stress Committee, in the 1920s.

The introduction of highly superheated steam with its greater fluidity, and the use of piston valves instead of the older traditional slide valves for providing steam distribution to the cylinders, gave a much improved performance and faster running. One of the most significant collateral developments, however, took place in the design of the valve gears themselves. The success of the de Glehn four-cylinder compound locomotives in France had attracted world-wide attention, and G. J. Churchward arranged for three French-built 'Atlantic' engines to be purchased for experimental purposes by the Great Western Railway in Britain. He then set out to produce a single-expansion design that would equal the thermal efficiency of the French compound,

FIG. 32.2. The Great Western Railway's *Queen Philippa* 4-cylinder 4–6–0 of G. J. Churchward's 'Star' class, forerunner of the later 'Castle' and 'King' classes.

FIG. 32.3. One of the Chapelon rebuilt 4–6–2 locomotives of the Paris–Orleans Railway, as used on the Northern Railway.

without the complications in mechanical design and handling that were so necessary on the imported locomotives. The Stephenson link motion still remained one of the simplest forms of valve gear, and Churchward devised an improved layout, whereby better openings for steam entry and exhaust were obtained. This involved a longer travel of the valve, a feature at first not favoured by other engineers because of a fear of undue wear. But the long-travel valves developed by Churchward at Swindon resulted in greater efficiency with a simple engine than was achieved by the much more complicated French compounds.

It was a time also of much development in boiler design. As steam pressures were increased, to provide greater power, many refinements became necessary in the avoidance of sharp bends and angles in the plate construction, to avoid points of high stress concentration; in the study of water circulation, and the shapes desirable to promote free flow and rapid steam-raising; and to overcome the problems of increased weight by the proliferation of the number of driving and carrying wheels. So far as the actual machinery was concerned, while engineers appreciated the advantages in balancing to be derived from four-cylinder locomotives the Dutch development was not generally favoured because of the high stresses and bearing loads imposed on the one axle. Something of a compromise was effected in certain British and overseas designs by having three or four cylinders with the drive divided between two axles. This did not eliminate 'hammer-blow' but made it much less than was common in the simple two-cylinder types. It should be emphasized, however, that this was almost entirely a British trend. In North America the machinery layout was reverting almost universally to the two-cylinder type, with all the running gear outside the frames and readily accessible for maintenance.

At the same time the streamlined era was commencing, and at first it might seem that the fitting of external fairings covering much of the exterior was a negation of the *desideratum* of accessibility. But in this respect designers were torn between the demands of showmanship, when in a time of severe trade depression no means of attracting publicity for railways could be neglected, and the practical aspects of running the trains. Technically, the internal streamlining of steam passages, and the points of entry and exit on the valves, together with the freedom of exhaust in the smokebox, were far more important towards the attainment of higher speeds than any streamlined external shape. The scientific study of steam flow through the motive power circuit of a locomotive was conducted with outstanding success on the

FIG. 32.4. The first engine of Sir Nigel Gresley's streamlined 'A 4' Pacifics, the London and North Eastern Railway's *Silver Link* of 1935.

Paris–Orleans Railway by M. André Chapelon, and the modifications he recommended to the standard four-cylinder de Glehn compound 'Pacific' engines of that railway (Fig. 32.3) increased the maximum output by no less than 50 per cent. In Britain new records for maximum speed were attained, on special test runs, of 108 mile/h (174 km/h) by Sir Nigel Gresley's non-streamlined Pacific engine *Papyrus* in 1935; of 114 mile/h (184 km/h) by Sir William Stanier's *Coronation* in 1937; and finally the ultimate world record with steam of 126 mile/h (203·5 km/h) by the Gresley streamlined 'Pacific' *Mallard* in 1938. The highest speed ever attained by a British train in service carrying ordinary fare-paying passengers was attained by another Gresley streamlined 'Pacific', *Silver Fox* in 1936: 113 mile/h (182·5 km/h).

The development of the articulated steam locomotive, to gigantic proportions, must also be noted: this took two distinct forms. The American 'Mallet', which first appeared in 1904, had two engine units beneath one very long boiler. In this design the rear unit was carried on the main frame, while the forward one was on a swinging frame that adapted itself to the curvature of the track. There were many complications in providing flexible steam pipe connections and in carrying the weight of the front part of the boiler on a movable support. In the U.S.A., however, this form of articulated locomotive was, by 1941, built up to the maximum of the Union Pacific 'Big Boys', with 4–8–8–4 wheel arrangement and a total engine weight of 346 tonnes, not including the very large tender. The British development, built for many different rail gauges and operating conditions, was the Beyer–Garratt, consisting of two complete engine units, fed by a single, very large boiler carried on a central cradle suspended from the two engine units. A highly flexible machine resulted, ideally suited to negotiating severely curved sections of line, and by its physical make-up making possible a boiler of ideal proportions for free steaming—with a short barrel of large diameter, and a firebox unrestricted in proportions by any large wheels beneath.

Diesel traction. The first applications of the diesel engine to railway traction came soon after the end of the First World War, and at once revealed considerable differences of opinion as to how the engine power should be transmitted to the driving wheels. In Poland Professor Lomonossoff designed a 1200-hp locomotive with electrical transmission. In 1926 the German firm of Hohenzollern A.G. of Dusseldorf built a locomotive for Russia with direct geared drive, and in 1929 the German Railways took delivery of a diesel locomotive on which the transmission was by compressed air. In Europe, at any rate, there was at first a general desire to avoid electrical transmission, which was considered costly, heavy, and to give no more than moderate overall efficiency. After early experience direct mechanical drive was also discarded for large power units, because of the difficulty of changing gear without interrupting the continuity of the drive. A notable early project with which British manufacturers were associated was on the Buenos Aires Great Southern Railway, which introduced an electric multiple-unit train that derived its power supply from a travelling power station consisting of a diesel-driven generating plant; it was built by Sir W. G. Armstrong-Whitworth and Co. of Scotswood-on-Tyne (1929).

In the U.S.A. the Electro-Motive Corporation of General Motors was the earliest and most powerful advocate of diesel traction, and in their case there was no doubt about the type of transmission; it was electric from the outset, and nothing else. The advantages of diesel traction over steam were not only those of considerably higher overall thermal efficiency, which in early days were largely offset by the higher initial cost, and the cost of fuel compared to the then-prevailing cost of coal. The diesel had virtually no stand-by losses; it required considerably less skill to operate; and in certain quite extensive running conditions need have no more than a one-man crew. Above all, it had a much higher availability because it spent no long periods 'on shed' for fire-cleaning, ash removal, and general servicing. Although a great deal had been done, particularly in the U.S.A., to reduce the turn-round times on steam locomotive operations, these, however improved, could not approach what was attained with diesels.

As introduced into railway traction during the later 1930s, diesel operation took four forms:

(1) The diesel-electric locomotive of around 1500 engine horsepower.
(2) The high-speed multiple-unit electric train with electrical transmission.
(3) The single-unit railcar, usually with mechanical transmission.
(4) The medium-powered locomotive, with electrical transmission, purely shunting work.

The last-mentioned, with its advantage in avoiding stand-by losses, was the first category extensively adopted in Britain. Attention was directed to the second group listed above by the spectacular schedules worked by the two-car 'Flying Hamburger' on the German State Railways, with a start-to-stop average speed of $77\frac{1}{2}$ mile/h (125 km/h) in each direction between Berlin and Hamburg (1932). Nevertheless, it became evident later that the conditions on this particular route were particularly favourable to making a high average speed, because when the makers of the train were invited to submit proposals for a similar train to run on the London and North Eastern Railway between King's Cross and Newcastle the fastest schedule they could promise gave an average speed of only 63 mile/h (101·5 km/h). So, for a time, British high-speed development continued with steam.

By far the most important step in the introduction of diesel traction came from the U.S.A. in 1935. General Motors having produced, and wellnigh perfected, their '567' engine, determined on complete standardization, with positive refusal to make any other. There were originally four models with 6, 8, 12, and 16 cylinders respectively. The engine was of the V-type, with two banks of cylinders set with their centrelines at $45°$ to each other and driving on to a common crankshaft. It was a two-stroke engine, with solid unit direct injection, and had the vital feature of developing full horsepower at low speeds. Its power characteristics were to prove of immense importance when the time came for the general superseding of steam in the U.S.A. by diesel traction. The largest version of the '567' engine in its original form provided a locomotive of 1800 hp. This was far below the maximum capacity of the largest steam locomotives then operating in the U.S.A., but against this General Motors made a further stand on the grounds of standardization. Rather than produce larger single units to compete with the largest steam locomotives, they incorporated arrangements in their basic design to enable two or more of the 1800-hp locomotives to be coupled and operated as a multiple unit, thus providing, when needed, composite units of 3600, 5400 hp, or even more. In this there was clear recognition that a diesel, unlike a steam locomotive, is at its highest thermal efficiency when working at maximum capacity. Care had thus to be taken in allocating units to the various assignments to ensure that this was so over as wide a field of duties as possible.

The '567' engine, and its counterparts subsequently developed in Europe, was relatively slow running, and of the very robust marine type. Its characteristics at varying speeds show how it came to demonstrate its great superiority over steam when working at maximum power slowly, on a heavy gradient. Table 32.1 relates to a steam 4–8–4 and a diesel locomotive, both with a nominal horsepower of 3000.

When diesel-electric locomotives of General Motors design were introduced on the Canadian Pacific Railway it was on the very severe divisions in British Columbia that they were first allocated, and with good reason.

In Britain, diesel engines with basically similar characteristics to those of the '567' were introduced, with success, in the 1940s and locomotives of similar design were exported to many overseas countries (Fig. 32.5). A notable exception is the high-speed 'Deltic' engine, deriving its name from the cylinder formation, in the form of an equilateral triangle. The basic assembly consists of three separate cylinder blocks bolted together and each carrying a crankshaft at each apex of the triangular form. This is the principle of the Napier aero-engine, and unlike the '567' it is quick-running. It has a high power-weight ratio and has been most successfully applied into the 22 'Deltic' locomotives of 3300 hp (1961) that have achieved a remarkable record of high-utilization, high-speed performance on the East Coast main line between King's Cross and Edinburgh. Although a considerable amount of gearing is necessary to combine the output of the three crankshafts into a single output shaft, this has not proved a disadvantage in the very intensive service in which these locomotives have been employed.

TABLE 32.1

Tractive force for steam and diesel locomotives of 3000 hp (nominal)

Speed (mile/h)	Available tractive force (tons)	
	Steam	Diesel
8	24	45
15	22	28
25	18	18

FIG. 32.5. A typical main line diesel-electric locomotive of the 'first generation'; an example built by the English Electric Company for the Sudan Government Railway.

Electric traction. In their eagerness to apply electrical power to railway traction the pioneers of the nineteenth century, notably those in the U.S.A. and on the continent of Europe, introduced a diversity of traction systems (Vol. V, p. 346), some of which have not withstood the test of time. Among early installations were those using low-voltage direct current at 600–50-V in Britain and the U.S.A.; 3000-V three-phase alternating current in Italy and Hungary; and 11000-V single-phase alternating current in the U.S.A. Almost from the outset there were rival systems in the U.S.A., and in Britain there was a major confrontation when it came to electrifying the Inner Circle underground line in London (1905) between the 600-V d.c. system and the three-phase 3000-V a.c. proposals of Messrs. Ganz, of Budapest. The latter is of historical interest only at the present time, being obsolete, but at one time it was extensively used in Italy. The three-phase traction motor runs at constant speed, and it was successfully used on the Giovi Incline, inland from Genoa, and at a steady speed of 60 mile/h (97 km/h) along the Mediterranean Coast; but in modern conditions it lacked flexibility.

Passing to the systems in use in 1950, the low-voltage direct current, as installed on the Southern Region of British Railways, has the merit of simplicity, though use of the third-rail pick-up brings incidental complications in country districts, where there are level crossings used by the farming community. The return traction current is passed through the running rails, in this way differing from the system used on London Transport, which has a separate fourth rail for the traction return. The Southern Region system was originally designed for the suburban network of the London and South Western Railway (L.S.W.R.), and after grouping of the British railways in 1923, when further electrification in the London area was planned, a choice had to be made between the L.S.W.R. 600-V d.c. system with third-rail pick-up and the 6600-V single-phase a.c. system of the London, Brighton, and South Coast Railway (L.B.S.C.R.), with overhead wire current collection, recommended by Sir Philip Dawson on the earlier understanding that the entire main line network of the Brighton Railway would be converted to electric traction at an early date. After grouping, the low-voltage d.c. system of the L.S.W.R. was chosen as the future standard, and subsequently, except for a few lines on the periphery, it covered the entire network of the Southern Region, with an increased voltage of 750 on the later extensions.

In recalling the Southern decision of 1923 it must equally be remembered that in Britain railways embarking on electrification then had to generate their own power; large plants were installed, supplied by batteries of coal-fired boilers. Before the end of the 1920s, however, work had begun with installing the national electricity supply grid (Ch. 12), from which the railway could purchase supplies. Faced with a short mineral line in County Durham operating on 1500-V d.c. from an overhead wire supply, in addition to the L.S.W.R. and L.B.S.C.R. systems in London, discussions took place as to the future standard system to be adopted for main-line electrification in Britain. By that time the Paris–Orleans Railway had begun electrification with 1500-V d.c. and an overhead wire supply. This was also adopted for the first railway electrification in India, on the Great Indian Peninsula Railway. Finally, a committee under the chairmanship of Lord Weir in 1931 endorsed a recommendation of an earlier committee in favour of this latter system as the future British standard, and it was adopted for the electrification of the heavily used Manchester–Sheffield main line of the London and North Eastern Railway. It was also adopted as standard on the Netherlands State Railways. It had the advantage of simplicity of electrical control, while the higher voltage reduced the transmission losses over lengthy mileages. It was generally agreed that an overhead line was essential for main-line work. Two other European countries, Belgium and Italy, adopted d.c. traction, but with the still higher voltage of 3000. In Italy, the older three-phase a.c. lines were gradually converted.

In the meantime developments in a different direction were taking place on the continent of Europe, following experimental work in the early 1900s in Switzerland. In the U.S.A. the Norfolk and Western Railway in adopting 11 000-V single-phase a.c. on its overhead wire used locomotives with phase converters supplying three-phase traction motors. This was a consequence of early difficulties experienced in getting satisfactory commutation on an a.c. motor using single-phase current. But in 1903 Behn-Eschenburg devised a circuit that would give acceptable results provided a current of low frequency was adopted. For the newly constructed Lötschberg line, opened in 1913, single-phase current of 15 000-V at $16\frac{2}{3}$ cycles per second was adopted, with single-phase a.c. traction motors. These were arranged to adjust their speed to the load, and thus gave a much more flexible performance than the three-phase motors then generally used in Italy. The new Lötschberg locomotives were rated at 2500 hp, to provide a specified performance of 26 mile/h (42 km/h) hauling a load of 315 tonnes on a gradient of 1 in 37. The Lötschberg line was a complete success and the 15 000-V single-phase a.c. system at $16\frac{2}{3}$ cycles became standard on the Swiss Federal Railways, and in Germany, Austria, Norway, and Sweden.

Until just after the Second World War it seemed that world electric railway practice was dividing itself between four established and well-tried systems, thus: 1500 and 3000-V d.c. with overhead wire collection; 15 000-V single-phase a.c. at $16\frac{2}{3}$ cycles; and low-voltage d.c., with third rail collection, on the Southern Region of British Railways. In this period once again the Lötschberg Railway proved a pioneer in the introduction of the all-adhesion type of locomotive, running on two four-wheeled bogies without any leading or trailing non-powered wheels (Fig. 32.6). Until then it had been generally thought that leading or trailing wheels were essential on a high-speed locomotive, but the French Railways adopted the Lötschberg design and in 1955 demonstrated that with skilful design of the suspension this type of locomotive was stable at quite exceptional speed on two test runs when maxima of 206 mile/h (332 km/h) were attained.

Just at the end of the period under review, a new factor in railway electrification supervened. One of the greatest obstacles to the rapid spread of electric traction had been the high cost of the overhead line and its structures, and of

FIG. 32.6. One of the 'Ae 4/4' all-adhesion electric locomotives on a passenger train, on the Bern–Lötschberg–Simplon Railway.

the substations. An experimental installation in France (1951) using 25 000-V single-phase a.c. at a commercial frequency of 50 cycles per second, however, showed that the capital cost of equipping a main line would be no more than two-thirds of that using the 1500-V d.c. system. This fact posed immediate problems both for France and Britain, both ready to go ahead with considerable schemes of electrification. Both countries decided to change to the 25 000-V a.c. system; and although the decision itself, and its implementation, came after 1954, it can be added that the successes of the British and French installations were followed by the adoption of the same system for new electrifications in many other parts of the world, including Japan, India, Czechoslovakia, Hungary, Yugoslavia, Portugal, and Turkey.

Passenger rolling stock. At the beginning of the twentieth century the design of coaches was in a transitional stage. Wood had hitherto been the principal material of construction, even for the underframes; and while many large and luxurious carriages were being introduced in Europe, and to a lesser extent in Britain, a large number of express trains included small non-bogie vehicles. In North America much larger and heavier cars were the rule, and the open saloon type of interior, as distinct from the compartment style favoured in Europe, prompted the more rapid introduction of steel bodies. In Britain steel underframes were coming into use in the early 1900s, and with the general introduction of corridor stock and more lavish accommodation, designers were paying considerable attention to reduction of the dead weight of their coaches to lessen the haulage tasks of locomotives. On the Great Western Railway, in particular, in 1904, G. J. Churchward built third-class corridor coaches 70 ft (21·5 m) long, carried on two four-wheeled bogies, and seating no fewer than 80 passengers in comfort, yet having a tare weight of only $33\frac{1}{2}$ tonnes. Such coaches were designed for relative short journeys of four to five hours, and luxury as such was not required. At the other extreme, in 1908, the London and North Western Railway built for the Anglo-Scottish day services twelve-wheeled coaches weighing $42\frac{1}{2}$ tonnes tare, and yet seating only 48 passengers.

There continued to be a great variety in the sleeping accommodation provided on night trains. In North America the 'open' type of coach interior had no greater privacy than that of drawn curtains across the sleeping 'bunks', while on the otherwise luxurious trains sponsored by the Wagon-Lits company the private berths were all two-tiered. It was only in Britain that first-class passengers enjoyed the privacy of single berths. Third-class sleeping cars were introduced in Britain in 1929 with four berths within a compartment.

On the continent of Europe the aftermath of the First World War left many old wooden-bodied carriages in use on fast express trains. Often, unhappily, they were marshalled between heavier modern vehicles, and suffered severely in the event of accidents. In their replacement steel vehicles became universal. After the First World War much was done also to improve the braking of passenger trains generally. After the grouping in 1923 the four British main-line railways decided to standardize on the automatic vacuum rather than the air brake, which was used almost everywhere on the continent of Europe. With the gradual increase in speeds of running the limitations of both types of brake became more acute in respect of the speed of propagation of the braking effect down the pipe of a long train. With the air brake the reduction in pressure made by application of the driver's brake valve took several seconds to take effect at the rear end, with consequent slight delay in applying the brakes on the rear coaches. A similar time-lag was experienced with the automatic vacuum brake. To overcome difficulty with the first the electro-pneumatic brake was invented, to provide simultaneous application of the brakes throughout the length of a train. With the vacuum brake the Great Western Railway developed a 'direct admission valve', which was fitted on to each vehicle, and made possible a considerably quicker application at the rear end of a long train. Various refinements of the air brake were developed in the U.S.A. to provide for effective control of very long and heavy freight trains.

In design of passenger rolling stock in Britain, the accommodation gradually changed from the traditional compartment type to the open saloon, with tables between the seats, with doors only at the ends, and facilities for light meals or snacks to be served to every passenger at his or her seat. With this type of coach individual control of window openings was rendered unnecessary by the general introduction of air-conditioning. On the continent of Europe, however, the coaches run on many of the Trans-Europ-Express (TEE) services from 1961 included stock of both open and compartment type. The French *grand-confort* coaches represented a degree of luxury in travel that was probably unsurpassed. The suspension was first class, and provided exceptionally smooth riding at speeds in excess of 100 mile/h (160 km/h). By contrast—in type of service, that is—the intensive commuter services around great cities presented a constant problem to coach designers, as much as to traffic operators, as to how to provide mass transportation for the brief periods of the morning and evening peaks. On a number of railways on which the height of the loading gauge is greater than in the United Kingdom, double-deck cars were introduced, notable examples being those of the Canadian Pacific in the Montreal area, and of the New South Wales Railways at Sydney. But while the carrying capacity of individual cars is thus increased there is the time of loading and unloading to be considered. It is for this reason that on the Southern Region of British Railways, probably the most intensive commuter service in the world, the coaching stock remained of the compartment type, non-corridor, with separate doors for every compartment; this was simply to enable passengers to get in and out quickly.

Freight rolling stock. Freight traffic on most railways of the world also underwent a fundamental change during this period. From being common carriers, taking any consignment, large, small, packaged, or in bulk, they tended to become specialists, taking such traffic as it was impracticable, or uneconomic, to convey by road or other means. From the simple, general-purpose goods wagon, vehicles were introduced for exclusive use in special traffics, such as wagons for conveyance of motor-cars from works to port of shipment; cement in bulk; grain; iron ore; and coal. Freight trains are now operated on the block-load principle; they are of fixed formation, shuttling back and forth—in the case of coal—from colliery to power station, with tracks arranged for continuous running at each terminal without the need for shunting, or detaching the main-line locomotive. Wagons have been designed for mechanized operation of the discharging doors.

While it is not possible to organize all railway freight traffic into block loads, or to convey it in nominated trains chartered by large industrial organizations, the application of the container principle has largely eliminated marshalling in the case of many fast overnight freight services. In these cases the 'block load' consists of a fixed set of flat cars, on to which standard-sized containers are loaded. Not all the flat cars may be loaded to capacity on each trip, but with mechanized handling plant at the goods terminals, transferring the containers from lorry to railway truck, or vice versa, the operation of transhipment is rapid and efficient. Modern freight trains are all fitted with continuous automatic brakes, and run at speeds up to 70 mile/h.

II. THE ROAD AND ITS EQUIPMENT

The Track. Until the mid-1940s standard-gauge railways in the British Isles were laid with the bullhead type of rail supported in cast-iron chairs, generally on transverse timber sleepers. This type of track was also used on certain Indian railways, and on the former Western Railway of France. Elsewhere in the world the flat-bottomed, or Vignoles, type of rail was used, spiked down directly to the wooden sleepers. This was relatively cheap and easy to install, and thus ideal for use on railways built for colonizing, and elsewhere in areas where speed was of no great consideration. On the other hand, the British home railways prided themselves on the quality of their track; this was subject to constant and careful maintenance, with little more than simple hand tools, and the skill and experience of dedicated permanent-way inspectors. As speeds rose, in North America, France, and elsewhere, the standards of maintenance with flat-bottomed rails were enhanced to the extent that British engineers came to reconsider their traditional practice on the 'home railways', and made a basic comparison of the technical features of the two kinds of rail.

Development began in the worsening economic conditions of the 1920s, with improvement in the metallurgical composition of the standard rail, by inclusion of a manganese content to provide a harder surface and better wearing qualities. The heavy wear occurring at intensively used junction layouts led to the substitution of specially fabricated cast members, in nickel steel, for the previously hand-forged crossing noses, and similar details, made out of standard rails. Simultaneously, on railways using flat-bottomed rails there was constant development of rail fastenings beyond the traditional 'spike' to provide a more durable maintenance of gauge and line under conditions of heavy and fast traffic. Greater precision was introduced in day-to-day maintenance, relying less on the skill of the individual man, and more upon increasingly sophisticated equipment, though not yet to the extent of partial, let alone complete, mechanization. An interesting development during the great recession of the 1930s in Britain was the use of steel sleepers. These were introduced for the twofold purpose of avoiding the need for importing foreign timber (unquestionably the best for railway track work) and supporting the steel industry, then much distressed. Much experimental and development work took place, with rather inconclusive results. The ultimate answer for the railway track of the future came later.

The decision of the British railways to standardize on the flat-bottomed type of rail for the future was made before the nationalization of 1948, and was based on the fact that for a given weight per unit length the flat-bottomed rail had a greater lateral stiffness, and thus could be expected to keep its line with less maintenance. This was an important consideration at a time when skilled labour was scarce and becoming increasingly expensive. In adopting the flat-bottomed rail British Railways included in its mounting a specially-shaped bedplate between the rail and the sleeper to give the same inward inclination of the vertical axis that had been found beneficial with the old standard bullhead rail. The combined effect of inclining the two rails very slightly inwards towards each other imparted a centring effect on rolling stock, counteracting the tendency to yaw or hunt while running.

At the same time as the flat-bottomed rail was introduced in Britain there was a general movement in all countries having heavy and fast railway traffic to mechanize as much as possible of the maintenance work, and a number of special-purpose machines have been designed for such operations as ballast packing, track aligning, and levelling, while the task of renewing and relaying track was facilitated by specially designed lifting gear that could place lengths of prefabricated track into its final position. The rail joint had always been a point of weakness in track, no matter how carefully the bolted connections were made and the adjoining sleepers packed; and in this post-war period the practice, hitherto experimental, of welding the rails at the joints to make continuous lengths became standard practice. In order to absorb the stresses set up by varying ambient temperatures, previously reflected in expansion and contraction of the rails, and accommodated by the slight gap between rails at the joints, additional care had to be taken to provide adequate ballasting to prevent any risk of the track buckling in hot weather. Throughout the railways of the world ballasting had always been variable in quality, ranging from sleepers laid on the surface of the ground with little surrounding packing to the massive ballasting with broken stone used in the Eastern States of the U.S.A., on the London and North Western Railway, and on other heavily trafficked lines.

The period after the Second World War saw the widespread introduction, and eventual standardization, of the reinforced concrete sleeper. French practice in this respect is to use a concrete block under each rail, connected by a steel tie-bar, whereas in Britain the concrete is continuous. This form of sleeper, being moulded, has the great advantage that the cross-section can be varied, between one rail and the other, according to the varying distribution of stresses. Thus the material can be used to the best advantage, reducing the section at the mid-point where the stresses are least, and consequently reducing the weight. Concrete sleepers, as developed in both Britain and France, have proved most effective in carrying very fast, heavy, and frequent traffic.

III. SIGNALLING AND TRAFFIC MARSHALLING

The ever-growing intensity of train working at large stations, and the need for closer co-ordination to improve traffic flow, led to various systems of power actuation of points and signals. Not only was the physical labour of lever pulling eliminated, but miniaturizing the equipment enabled a greater number of functions to be operated from one signal box. In the earliest installations of this kind, in the U.S.A., in Britain, and to a lesser extent in France and Germany, all the signals themselves were of the existing conventional types, with semaphore arms. In point operation separate equipment was provided for the facing-point locks and locking bars, as in mechanical actuation. Various power systems were introduced, the most generally favoured being the electro-pneumatic, with compressed-air cylinders providing the motive power and valves controlled by electromagnets, and the all-electric, in which point and signal operation was effected through small electric motors driving through gear trains.

The invention of the track circuit in 1872 had made possible an outstanding advance towards the safer operation of trains, though its introduction came rather slowly, except in the U.S.A. One of its most striking first applications came in 1905 at the time of the electrification of the Metropolitan District Railway, in London, when a young Cornish engineer, Bernard H. Peter, installed at Mill Hill Park station (now Acton Town), the first illuminated track diagram in the world. Previously, on the earliest American power interlocking machines, there had been a mechanical indicator on a pictorial diagram of the tracks to show the direction in which each pair of points was lying. Peter introduced a much larger track diagram, on which all the track circuits were illuminated; and because the lamps were extinguished when a train passed over the track circuit the progress of all train movements was constantly in front of the signalman, without his having to look out of the window. It was one of the greatest milestones in the history of railway operation. The use of track circuits also eliminated the need for the old-fashioned locking bars installed on the approach side of facing points to prevent the inadvertent operation of the points while a train was passing over. The actuation of the facing-point lock could henceforth be incorporated in the power-operating mechanism of the points, instead of requiring a separate lever.

The increasing intensity of train working in the advanced countries of the world inevitably led to errors, either through signalmen inadvertently omitting some step in the rules of procedure laid down, or by drivers misinterpreting signals or misjudging their speed and distance. To counteract the effects of such human failures the period from 1905 onwards was a time of much scheming among railway engineers and operating officers, not to mention individual inventors, and signalling contractors. The track circuit was universally acclaimed as the ideal medium for guarding against the risk of stationary trains or locomotives being forgotten, but the problem of alerting a driver to a potentially dangerous situation involved questions of operating psychology. It was generally agreed that only as a last resort should control of the train be taken out of his hands, and the brakes automatically applied. American developments that began in this epoch were many and complex, and are discussed later. In Britain it was the principle embodied in the system of audible cab-signalling developed on the Great Western Railway from 1906 that later became the standard arrangement on the nationalized British

Railways after 1948. The principle was to give dissimilar audible signals in the engine cab when each distant signal was passed: the ring of a bell when the signal was clear, and a siren for caution. The latter had to be acknowledged by the driver; if he failed to do this, the brakes were applied and the train stopped. With proper acknowledgement he retained full control of the train.

From a time roughly marked by the outbreak of the First World War, the whole field of signal indication was in transition. Leaving out of account the distinctive, and often perplexing, arrangements of discs, boards, and semaphores to be seen on the continent of Europe, the first moves away from the traditional lower-quadrant semaphore came with the use of upper-quadrant signals in the U.S.A., from which it was a natural transition to units displaying three, rather than two positions: horizontal for 'stop'; inclined upwards for 'caution'; and vertically upwards for 'clear'. Then, and again first in the U.S.A., came the development of light signals, which had the advantage of showing the same indication by day and by night. While some American railroads adopted daytime signals showing red, yellow, and green indications, to correspond with the night indications of a three-position upper quadrant semaphore, others adopted the so-called 'position light signal'. This used no colours, but displayed on a large circular background a row of white lights: horizontal for stop, inclined for caution, and vertical for clear. One of the largest users of this type of signal was the Pennsylvania Railroad. In Britain, after much study of the problem, the colour-light signal was adopted, and (except on the Great Western Railway) the familiar red, yellow, and green aspects were standardized, with the important addition of the 'double-yellow', providing a preliminary caution, on heavily worked lines.

The earlier power interlocking machines, using miniature levers, had small-size mechanical interlocking between levers, in the same style as the older manually actuated plants. But with the increasing size and complexity of working, these miniaturized locking frames not only became very intricate in design, but difficult to alter if changing traffic requirements entailed a rearrangement of the track layouts. In 1929 a British development provided all-electric lever interlocking, and this was the first step towards the elimination of the lever itself. An important principle now became involved. Lever interlocking, whether effected by a mechanical engagement of locking 'dogs' or by electromagnetic locks, imposed a physical restraint against the chance of a signalman making a wrong movement; if it was unsafe for a certain action to be taken the lever could not be pulled. With the further miniaturization arising from the substitution of push-buttons or thumb-switches for a conventional lever the physical restraint was removed. The safeguard was now that if an attempt was made to set up an unsafe condition the electric interlocking device prevented the apparatus from responding, and the signalman had a visual indication on the control panel that this was so. The use of relay, or more correctly 'circuit interlocking', on large control machines was entirely a British development.

In the U.S.A. the use of small control panels with signalling movements set up by thumb-switch actuation was being developed for a different purpose in the 1930s. On very many single-track main lines running through sparsely populated country, train movements were regulated by telegraphic orders, by which the drivers were given written instructions to proceed, or to wait at a specified passing loop for a train coming in the opposite direction to arrive and cross. It was a simple, cheap system, relying on the good judgement of the train despatchers to arrange the 'meets' so as to cause the minimum of waiting time, and on the responsibility of enginemen to observe the written orders correctly. But as traffic increased it proved cumbersome and slow; and the occasional error arising in a system so dependent upon the human element led to disastrous head-on collisions on the single-line sections. A division, or subdivision over which a despatcher might have jurisdiction could extend to as much as 100 miles (160 km). While centralized electrical control, with an illuminated diagram, would be ideal the cost of cable for direct wire operation of distant functions would have been prohibitive. To meet these conditions, a system of coded remote control was devised. In this there were only two or three line wires throughout, and each function—signal, or point operating machine—had a distinctive code, in precisely the same way that individual subscribers are dialled on an automatic telephone system. Known as Centralized Traffic Control (CTC), it was applied with great success on many lines in the West and Middle West, particularly when such lines became more heavily utilized during the Second World War. Later, the system was extensively applied also in New Zealand and Rhodesia by British manufacturers.

Until the end of the Second World War colour-light signalling had not been installed to any great extent on the continent of Europe. In the period of reconstruction after 1945 all new works embodied light signalling, in preference to semaphores, or in the French case to the elaborate system of chessboards, diamond signs, and discs that had previously characterized those railways. While each country developed its own individual code of aspects, most were similar to that standardized in Britain, though in North

FIG. 32.7. Modern signalling. An illuminated panel diagram at New Canada Junction, near Johannesburg, South African Railways.

America colour-light signalling was based on a different principle. The British code provided geographical indications: the driver was advised as to the route he should take at a junction. The American code embodied the principle of 'speed signalling', in that the driver was advised as to whether he should run at high, medium, or low speed, the respective values of which were laid down in the rules of the road. Instead of a single casing containing three or four lens units, as in Britain, the Americans use the 'searchlight' type of unit, which can display a red, yellow, or green indication from the same lens, through a three-position relay unit inside. Three of these searchlight units are mounted vertically on the same mast, and by combination of the relative positions of the red, yellow, and green indications that each can display, a number of different 'speed' messages can be set up for the driver of an approaching train to read, and act upon.

The great advantages to be derived from concentration of signalling control in a relatively small number of large signal boxes had been amply demonstrated on British railways even before the Second World War; but the extension of such control to extensive geographical areas, as in the American CTC schemes, was not practicable, because the time taken for transmission of the control codes, about four seconds, was too long. The traffic

FIG. 32.8. Modern panel signal box, of the one-control-switch panel type, an example at Bologna, Italian State Railways.

conditions were very much more intense than on the long single-tracked lines in the U.S.A. Then, however, the science of electronics was applied to the problem of railway signalling remote control, and by the use of transistors instead of the former electro-mechanical stepper switches, codes could be sent almost instantaneously. The new techniques were only in their infancy at the end of the period covered by the present survey; but it may be mentioned that now, in the 230 miles (370 km) of the West Coast main line of British Railways, between Weaver Junction, Cheshire and Glasgow, electrified in 1974, there are only five signal boxes.

Legislation imposed because of the frequency of serious accidents at that time, led to the rapid introduction of a variety of Automatic Train Control systems in the U.S.A. in the 1920s. These took a variety of forms—understandable because of the diversity of lineside signalling equipment then installed. The various systems of automatic train control included forms of cab signalling that, unlike the British system derived from the pioneer work on the Great Western Railway, were based on visual indications. On certain railways the cab signalling indications showed no more than illuminated letters H, M, L—high, medium, low speed—as appropriate, while on others there was a miniature repetition of the wayside signal indications. With all

FIG. 32.9. Mechanized marshalling yards: an aerial view of St. Luc yard near Montreal, Canadian-Pacific Railway.

the earlier installations there was included also an automatic control of the brakes. On certain railways the control was intermittent, coming into effect at successive signal locations, whereas on others the speed control, derived from an inductive link between current flowing in track circuits and a receiver on the locomotive, was continuous, and included regulation of the running speed according to the limits laid down for various sections of the line. Then, as a result of much experience, the Pennsylvania Railroad dispensed with the automatic brake feature, and relied entirely on continuously controlled cab signals. During the Second World War, the wayside signals also were dispensed with on an all-freight line in the Pittsburgh area, and reliance was placed solely on the cab signal indications. This was indeed a precedent for what subsequently became the standard signalling system on the high-speed Shinkansen lines in Japan.

Efforts to put the laborious and time-consuming job of shunting goods wagons on to a more rational basis had begun before the nineteenth century had ended. The introduction of the hump principle, by which a train to be remarshalled was propelled over the hump crest in one continuous movement, was accompanied by the centralized control of all the points operation. Wagons already detached from each other, and destined for different reception yards, separated rapidly when passing over the crest of the hump, attaining speeds of around 15 mile/h. This gave no time for hand operation of the points. A notable installation of power points was made in Britain at the Wath concentration yard on the Great Central Railway, near Barnsley, in 1906. Even though the points operation was centralized a great number of men had to be employed in this, and in similar yards on both sides of the Atlantic, to check the speed of the running wagons, and bring them gently into contact with the wagons already in the sidings to which they had been routed.

It was early in the 1920s that the 'car retarder', or 'rail brake', was first introduced in the U.S.A. This consisted essentially of an articulated system of beams running longitudinally for 50 ft (15 m) or more on each side of the rails, and designed to move inwards to grip the wheels of a wagon as it passed through (Fig. 32.10). The actuation was powered either by electro-pneumatic or all-electric means. With centralized control from the main operating cabin the operators there, with a high-level view over the whole yard, could apply such braking effort to each wagon, or group of wagons coupled together, as was necessary to bring them down to a speed just sufficient to carry them to the furthest extent of available space in the siding concerned. The introduc-

FIG. 32.10. A close-up view of one of the wagon retarders at the Carlisle yards, British Railways.

tion of retarders eliminated the need for men on the ground in the yards. A great number of yards of this kind were installed in the U.S.A. between the two world wars. There were also a few in Britain, notably at March (Cambridgeshire) opened in 1929, Hull, and Toton, near Nottingham.

It was found, however, that in practice the control-tower operators could not always judge accurately the degree of braking required, and after the Second World War further steps towards complete automation were made. The operation of the retarders was controlled by a computer, into which were fed statistics of all the varying factors that affect the running of wagons: its weight, initial speed, and 'rollability'—that is, whether it was free running or not—the physical characteristics of the siding into which it was routed, and not least the direction of the prevailing wind. The siding characteristics included not only the distance available up to the last wagon standing, but the amount of curvature of the line, because that can substantially affect the running. Yards embodying this remarkable degree of sophistication were installed in Britain in the early 1950s, and to a larger extent during the modernization plan of British Railways from 1955 onwards.

The gradual elimination of steam traction, and the need to obtain maximum utilization of rolling stock and locomotives has led to new conceptions of station layout and operation. By 1950 it was not unusual for a long distance express train to arrive at a terminus, unload, reload, and depart again on a long journey after a turn-round time of no more than 20 minutes. The diesel or electric locomotive which had brought the train in could thus be quickly released and available for a return working in little more time than that in which the coaching stock was standing in the terminus. At the same time, passenger facilities at modern stations became more like those of a large airport, with all the amenities grouped round a large central concourse. The platforms and their decor then answer much more appropriately to the American term 'train shed' than to the elegant Victorian departure platform, with bookstalls, cafés, kiosks, and other amenities actually abreast of a long-distance express train about to depart.

IV. EXTENSIONS TO THE WORLD'S RAILWAY NETWORK

While the growth of railways during the nineteenth century had been remarkable, Table 32.2 shows how development has continued since, with Japan, South Africa, and the U.S.S.R. more than doubling their mileage since 1900. At the same time some of the old networks, built up in the heat of competition between privately owned railways, have been reduced, and figures for the year 1980 are likely to show still more drastic reductions.

TABLE 32.2

Expansion and contraction of railways in the leading countries of the world

| Country | Total route distance operating (km) | | | |
	1900	1920	1940	1960
Brazil	***	28533	34252	37670
Canada	***	63382	68502	70858
France	36799	41600	40000	38857
Germany*	51958	57698	59139	46899
Great Britain	29039	32712	32552	30209
Indian Empire	39835	59119	66234	—
India—Republic	—	—	—	56669
Italy	14375	16170	17858	16339
Japan	6300	10437	18399	20403
South Africa	7005	16362	21863	21824
Sweden	11304	14869	16610	15219
Switzerland	3599	5737	5222	5118
U.S.A.	311187	406941	376880	350114
U.S.S.R.	44492	71597	106105	120000†

* Figure for 1960 includes both East and West Germany.
† Estimated figure.
*** Statistics not available.

Apart from the general extension of the networks, some notable trunk line projects may be specially mentioned:

Canada: *National Transcontinental*, 1913

    Moncton (New Brunswick) to Winnipeg: 2900 km
    Grand Trunk Pacific, 1914
    Winnipeg to Prince Rupert: 2870 km
    Canadian Northern, 1915
    Winnipeg to Vancouver: 2800 km

Persia: *Trans-Iranian*, 1938

    Persian Gulf via Teheran, to Caspian Sea: 1492 km
    Tehran-Djolfa Line, 1958, 882 km

Angola: *Benguela Railway*, 1928

    Lobito Bay, on the Atlantic, to the Belgian Congo (Zaire) frontier at Dilolo (1349 km), linking up with the established system of the Congo, and with that of Northern Rhodesia (Zambia) and the South African system.

BIBLIOGRAPHY

AHRONS, E. L. *British steam railway locomotive 1825–1925*. Locomotive Publishing Co., London (1927).
——. *British railways track*. Permanent Way Institution. London (1943).
BRUCE, A. W. *Steam locomotive in America*. Norton, New York (1952).
CHAPELON, A. *La Locomotive a vapeur*. J. B. Baillière et Fils, Paris (1938).
COX, E. S. *British Railways standard steam locomotives*. Allan, London (1966).
FERGUSON, T. *Electric railway engineering*. Macdonald and Evans, London (1955).
GAIRNS, J. F. *Locomotive compounding and superheating*. Griffin, London (1907).
HINDE, D. W., and HINDE, M. *Electric and diesel-electric locomotives*. Macmillan, London (1948).
JOHNSON, R. P. *The steam locomotive*. Simmons–Boardman, New York (1942).
MEEKS, C. L. V. *The railway station*. The Architectural Press, London (1957).
NOCK, O. S. *British Railway Signalling*. Allen and Unwin, London (1969).
——. *British steam railway locomotive 1925–1965*. Allan, London (1966).
——. *Locomotion*. Routledge and Kegan Paul, London (1975).
——. *Railways of Australia*. A. and C. Black (1971).
——. *Railways of Canada*. A. and C. Black, London (1973).
——. *Railways of Southern Africa*. A. and C. Black, London (1971).
——. *Railways of Western Europe*. A. and C. Black, London (1977).
PHILLIPSON, E. A. *Steam locomotive design: data and formulae*. Locomotive Publishing Co., London (1936).
WEIL, PIERRE. *Les chemins de fer*. Larousse, Paris (1964).

33

AIRCRAFT AND THEIR OPERATION

PETER W. BROOKS

I. THE FIRST PRACTICAL AEROPLANES

FIXED-WING flight—as distinct from the more popular flapping-wing, rotating-wing, or buoyant systems—interested thinkers and experimenters for more than a thousand years before practical results, in the form of short gliding flights, were achieved during the nineteenth century (Vol. V, Ch. 17). An Englishman, Sir George Cayley, flew a stable man-carrying glider in 1809. Forty years later, he tested at least two others. Before the end of the century, a German, Otto Lilienthal, and several who followed his example were making thousands of controlled flights with various types of glider. At about the same time, another form of fixed-surface flying machine, the kite, which had existed (initially in China) in small sizes for 2500 years and had been employed occasionally in larger sizes for man-lifting for 500 years, was first adapted to practical purposes (meteorology and military reconnaissance) mainly as a result of the invention in 1892 of the improved box-kite by Lawrence Hargrave in Australia.

The turn of the century thus saw the coming together of a developed airframe, deriving from kite and glider, with the internal combustion engine (Ch. 40), developed after 1886 for road transport. With hindsight, this development can be seen as inevitable. The first successful exponents of the combination were the American brothers, Wilbur and Orville Wright, although others at this time contemplated making, or even attempted to take, this crucial step—including the American S. P. Langley, who received a $50000 subsidy from the U.S. Government in 1898. Using only their own very modest financial and technical resources, the Wright brothers achieved the first powered, sustained, and controlled aeroplane flights at Kitty Hawk in North Carolina on 17 December 1903.

The Wrights' 1903 Flyer (Fig. 33.1), with its 12-hp petrol engine, could just make short straight flights over level ground with the help of a stiff breeze to assist take-off from a launching rail. The brothers continued their experiments the following year near Dayton, Ohio and made several flights,

FIG. 33.1. The Wright Flyer achieved the first powered, sustained, and controlled flights on 17 December 1903.

FIG. 33.2. The Henri Farman III, one of the first truly practical aeroplanes produced in Europe (1909), established the finalized form of pusher biplane.

including two of about five minutes, with an improved machine whose take-off was normally assisted by a simple catapult. In 1905, a third Flyer made numerous circular flights, including one of more than 24 miles in 38 minutes. The practical aeroplane had arrived.

The Wrights kept their early work secret and it attracted little publicity. Moreover, they stopped flying for nearly three years after their final success in 1905 so that their triumph was not generally recognized until they demonstrated their aircraft in public in 1908. Meanwhile, other experimenters, influenced to some extent by scanty information about the Wrights, were pursuing alternative lines of development.

The Wright Flyer successfully combined a sufficiently light and powerful propulsion system with an effective airframe. It had a petrol engine driving airscrews, as had been tried by a number of airship and aeroplane experimenters in the latter part of the nineteenth century, but used more efficient slow-turning propellers. However, these suffered from the drawback of being duplicated and of having long chain transmissions. The Wright airframe was a significant advance because it incorporated, for the first time, a responsive three-axis control system, including, in particular, wing-warping for lateral control. Less satisfactory were the tail-less configuration with front elevator, which made the aircraft unstable and difficult to fly, and the skid landing gear, which demanded a launching rail for take-off plus, usually, the catapult device.

Other experimenters in Europe and North America avoided the deficiencies of the Wright design but, initially, had less satisfactory propulsion and control arrangements. The brothers Gabriel and Charles Voisin, Louis Blériot, and a number of less prominent European pioneers—almost all in France—plus the 'Aerial Experiment Association', including particularly G. H. Curtiss, in North America produced designs which, while still inferior to those of the Wrights in 1908, were soon to eclipse them. During its brief period of ascendancy, which ended in 1910, the Wrights' tail-less biplane was widely demonstrated and about 30 were built by the brothers and by subcontractors.

A Brazilian, Alberto Santos-Dumont, made the first tentative powered flight in Europe on 23 October 1906. However, his tail-first biplane was unsatisfactory and contributed little to further progress. More significant in Europe were the Voisins, whose Standard pusher biplane first appeared in 1907, and Blériot, who advocated the tractor monoplane which he personally demonstrated in dramatic fashion with the first flight across the English Channel on 25 July 1909. The Voisin Standard was the first aeroplane put into serious production (more than 100 were built), while variants of the cross-Channel Blériot XI were also sold in large numbers.

The Voisin biplane was progressively developed, particularly by Henri Farman, an Englishman living in France who was perhaps the greatest of the pioneer pilots. In the latter part of 1908, Farman fitted ailerons to his Voisin, which had previously relied on its rudder for lateral as well as directional control. Farman soon achieved notable flights, including the first across country. In 1909, his further refined Henri Farman III (Fig. 33.2) offered new standards of performance and practicability and established the definitive form of pusher biplane, soon to be widely copied.

The Blériot monoplane was similarly imitated and a variety of externally-braced high-wing and parasol monoplanes came into use alongside the more numerous biplanes. Monoplanes at this time, with their external bracing, offered little aerodynamic advantage over biplanes, while their structures tended to be weaker or heavier; after a few years, their popularity declined. The type was to revive in new forms years later. The pusher biplane combined with the tractor engine of the monoplane was to inspire an entirely new configuration, that of the tractor biplane. The first tentative examples were due to F. Ferber (1905), A. de Pischof (1907), and A. Goupy (1909), and the first practical design was developed by Louis Breguet in 1909. The superiority of the tractor biplane became clear from 1910. It was soon dominant and so remained for the next 20 years.

Engine development—mainly in France and, to a lesser extent, Germany—made major contributions to progress during these years. Many of the early aero-engines derived from motor-car practice but perhaps the most significant during this period was the entirely original air-cooled rotary, of which L. Seguin's Gnome of 1907 was the first serviceable example. Rotaries continued in use until the 1920s. Almost as important were water-cooled in-line engines, notably the Mercedes in Germany, and air-cooled and water-cooled vees (particularly as developed by Renault in France and Hispano-Suiza in Spain).

Rapid progress in airframe design—towards greater aerodynamic efficiency, stronger and lighter structures, and the use of improved materials—continued until 1914 when the First World War provided new incentives and much greater resources. By then, defence budgets were already paying for almost all aeronautical research and development, as they have continued to do ever since. These years were also to see, particularly in the few Government research establishments, the belated evolution of aerodynamic theory and its first correlation with practical design. An Englishman, F. W. Lanchester, had defined the basis of aerodynamic theory in 1897, and the Germans Ludwig Prandtl and Albert Betz developed it considerably during the First World War. Nevertheless, the actual practice of aircraft design was to remain largely empirical for many years.

II. AEROPLANES AT WAR

By the outbreak of war in August 1914, the armed forces of all the great powers understood the potential importance of aircraft for military purposes and had formed aeronautical offshoots of their armies and navies. Aircraft had by then also been used on a small scale in the Italo–Turkish War (1911–12) and the Balkan War (1912–13).

The First World War was to have a profound effect on aircraft development: aeronautics became overnight an important part of the nations' war potential. Probably only about 5000 uncertain, under-developed, tentative aeroplanes, with little background of manufacturing or operating experience, had been built in the whole world up to 1914. By the end of the war, aeroplanes were being designed, built, and operated against a substantial background of experience: nearly 200000 had been built and several million hours had been flown.

Nevertheless, progress in the design of the majority of aircraft was, with a few notable exceptions, surprisingly limited during the war. Advances were made in aircraft size and weight and in the power and reliability of aeroengines, but the methods of construction in most general use remained largely unchanged. Aerodynamic improvements were modest, no doubt mainly because the emphasis was on large-scale production of proved equipment.

Almost all aeroplanes pressed into military service in 1914 were unarmed two-seaters weighing 1500–2000 lb (700–900 kg) with speeds of 70–80 mile/h (110–130 km/h), a radius of action of under 100 miles (160 km), and an effective ceiling of perhaps 10000 ft (3000 m). These two-seaters were to be used for reconnaissance. The most important initially were the French Voisin III, the German Albatross C.III, and the British B.E.2c designed at the Government's Royal Aircraft Factory.

A few two-seater aeroplanes, mainly of the pusher type, had been fitted with machine guns before 1914 and these gradually became involved in desultry air combats. Single-seat 'scouts' originally designed for unarmed reconnaissance—of which the Royal Aircraft Factory's B.S.1 (1913) designed by G. de Havilland was one of the first—promised, however, to be more suitable for air fighting, if they could be armed effectively. In April 1915 a famous French pilot, Roland Garros, shot down several enemy aircraft while flying a Morane-Saulnier N monoplane fitted with a machine gun firing forward through the airscrew disc, the revolving blades of which were protected by bullet deflectors. Garros was forced to land in enemy territory later that same month and the Germans promptly followed his example and introduced the Fokker E.1 Eindecker armed with forward-firing machine gun and interrupter gear to protect the revolving airscrew. From August 1915, flown notably by Max Immelmann, the E.1 became the first effective fighter aircraft and enabled the Germans to gain 'command of the air'. Only about 400 Fokker Eindeckers of four types were built but by June 1916 the so-called 'Fokker Scourge' had clearly demonstrated the importance of fighting in the air.

The Allies reacted to the Fokker with the Nieuport 11 and 17, de Havilland D.H.2, and Royal Aircraft Factory F.E.2b, which soon established Allied superiority. This was maintained until late 1916. In September 1916, at the suggestion of the first great fighter leader Oswald Boelcke, the Germans introduced *Jagdstaffeln* fighter squadrons equipped particularly with Albatross D.I/II/III aircraft. These formations swung the advantage once again to the German side, culminating in 'Bloody April' (1917) when Allied losses were particularly severe. By July, however, a new generation of Allied fighters, including L. Béchereau's SPAD S.7, and the Sopwith Pup and Triplane, had regained the advantage despite the introduction by the Germans of the Fokker Dr.I Triplane and the improved Albatross D.V, which continued in service until the end of the war.

Even more potent Allied fighters appeared in 1917, including three famous British types (Frank Barnwell's Bristol F2B, H.P. Folland's Royal Aircraft Factory S.E.5, and Herbert Smith's Sopwith Camel) and three French (Nieuport 24 and 27 and SPAD S.13). Single-seat fighters were now armed with at least two fixed forward-firing machine guns, speed had increased to 110–125 mile/h (180–220 km/h), and effective ceilings to nearly 20000 ft (6000 m). These types maintained Allied superiority right up to the Armistice in November 1918, despite German adoption of strong *Jagdgeschwaden* fighter formations and their large-scale introduction, from May 1918, of the highly successful Fokker D.VII fighter designed by Reinholt Platz. By now, fighters were also intervening in the land battle, being used extensively for 'ground strafing'. The air war was fought mainly over the Western Front and had as its most-publicized practitioners the so-called 'aces': fighter pilots

FIG. 33.3. The de Havilland D.H.4 (1917) was the most successful light bomber of the First World War. It was later adapted into one of most widely used pioneer civil transports in Europe and America.

whose success and fame was measured in numbers of aircraft shot down. The greatest of these were the German Manfred von Richthofen (80 victories), the Frenchman René Fonck (75 victories), and Edward Mannock (73 victories) from Britain.

Bombing had been envisaged before the war but not on any scale. However, bomb-dropping on and directly behind the battlefield soon became commonplace both sides of the largely fixed 'front line' trenches. The Germans used their rigid airships to bomb strategic targets deep in enemy territory and, from the other side, some of the first long-range attacks made by Allied aeroplanes were on German airship sheds. As the war progressed, special bombing aircraft were developed: smaller single-engine bombers mainly for tactical daylight operations and larger multi-engine types mainly for night attacks on more distant strategic targets. The former evolved from reconnaissance aircraft but the latter were an entirely new development, the first of which, the Russian Igor I. Sikorsky's IM series, were developed from a pre-war design.[1]

[1] Most notable in the two categories were:
Light bombers: French Voisin III (1914), VIII, and X (1916), and Breguet XIV (1917), British de Havilland D.H.4 (Fig. 33.3) (1917), and D.H.9 and D.H.9A (1918), and German D.F.W. C.V (1917).
Heavy bombers: Italian Caproni Ca 32 (1915), Ca 33 (1916), and Ca 46 (1918), British Handley Page o/100 (1916) and o/400 (1917), and German Gotha and Friedrichshafen G-types (1917), and Staaken (1916) and Siemens-Shuckert (1917) R-type Giants.

During the war aircraft became important auxiliaries to armies on land and, less so, to navies at sea. Independent air action with long-range bombers on strategic targets was also developed from the spring of 1917 by both sides, notably by the German Bombengeschwader 3, the British Royal Naval Air Service (41st Wing), and the R.A.F's Independent Force. This development was a factor in the recommendations of the distinguished South African soldier-statesman Jan Christian Smuts which led to the formation on 1 April 1918 of the Royal Air Force as the first air service independent of other armed forces. The R.A.F. was later nearly disbanded, under political and economic pressures between the wars, but survived to set the pattern for similar services in other countries.

Aircraft played a modest but increasing role in the war at sea. Floatplanes made coastal patrols from shore bases and, launched from seaplane carriers, struck against land and sea targets. A British Short 184 seaplane first torpedoed a ship on 12 August 1915. Flying boats, particularly those developed by J. C. Porte at Felixstowe in Britain (initially derived from designs of G. H. Curtiss in the U.S.A.), became the most important shore-based maritime aircraft. In the later stages of the war, landplanes began to be operated from ships at sea: initially from rudimentary flying-off platforms, followed by ditching at sea or landing at a shore base if within reach. In 1917–18, experiments were made with deck-landing aeroplanes, and a month before the end of the war the first through-deck aircraft carrier, the British H.M.S. *Argus*, was commissioned with an embarked squadron of landplane Sopwith Cuckoo torpedo bombers. Although the aircraft carrier took no part in the First World War, it was to have an important role in the Second.

III. AIRSHIPS

'Dirigible balloons' or 'airships' are powered lighter-than-air craft which were first flown experimentally during the second half of the nineteenth century (Vol. V, p. 400). However, practical airships like aeroplanes had to wait for the petrol engine. An early Daimler petrol engine was fitted to an airship by the German Karl Wölfert in 1888 but the first truly serviceable airship, the French Lebaudy brothers' *Le Jaune* designed by H. Julliot and D. Simoni, did not fly until 13 November 1902, only thirteen months before the Wrights' first flight in an aeroplane.

The Lebaudy was a pressure airship, that is to say it had a hydrogen-filled envelope like that of a gas balloon but of elongated form. An internal ballonet, kept pumped up with air, provided a small internal pressure which maintained the shape of the envelope. A long spar, suspended on rigging lines beneath the envelope, supported the engine and car slung below. The latter feature meant that the Lebaudy was a semi-rigid, as distinct from a non-rigid airship, whose engines and cars are suspended directly from the envelope or are attached to it. The Lebaudy was practical because it was controllable and because its 40-hp German Daimler engine gave a speed of about 25 mile/h (40 km/h)—just enough for a worthwhile speed across country on calm days. On 12 November 1903, it made a flight of 32 miles in 1 hour 41 minutes from Moisson, where it was built, to Paris where it was placed on public exhibition in the Galerie des Machines. Later, this historic airship was wrecked, rebuilt, enlarged, and modified. Finally handed over to the French Army, it remained in service until 1909.

Because less efficient in large sizes, pressure airships never became serious contenders for transport or offensive military applications despite numerous attempts and a few notable pioneer long-distance flights in the 1920s by the semi-rigids of the Italian Umberto Nobile, who flew in the *Norge* to the North Pole in 1926. Something like 800 pressure airships were built between 1900 and 1960. They were used mainly for military reconnaissance (by the Italians, French, and Germans); anti-submarine patrol (by the British, French, and Americans); and commercial advertising (by the Americans and Germans). Almost all were of less than 450000 ft³ (13000 m³) capacity, giving a gross lift of less than 30000 lb (14000 kg); the majority were much smaller—usually of less than half this capacity.

The mainly Italian semi-rigids built between the two world wars and some of the later American Goodyear naval blimps were larger. The last few of the latter (the ZPG-3W class of 1958, which were used as radar pickets) had capacities of up to 1·5m. ft³ (42000 m³), gross lifts of about 90000 lb (41000 kg) and maximum speeds of nearly 80 mile/h (130 km/h). However, sizes and capabilities of this order—and, indeed, much more—were provided more effectively by rigid airships. These differed fundamentally from the pressure type in being typically much larger and in having long cylindrical or cigar-shaped hulls with a framework of light alloy or wood covered with fabric enclosing up to 21 separate gas-bags.

The basic rigid design originated at the end of the nineteenth century with a retired German general, Count Ferdinand von Zeppelin. He was influenced by the earlier ideas of a Croatian, David Schwarz, who had built unsuccessful airships with rigid hulls in Russia in 1893 and in Germany in 1897. The Schwarz airships did not have gas-bags, their lifting gas being contained

FIG. 33.4. The Zeppelin L30, the most influential design of rigid airship, developed for the German Navy in 1916.

directly within the metal-covered hull. Much later (1929–41) the United States Navy operated the Metalclad ZMC-2 designed by R. H. Upson on similar lines, but the design was not developed further. Important steps in development were:

(1) The first Zeppelin: the LZ1 of 1900, which was a failure.
(2) The first truly successful Zeppelin: the LZ4 of 1908.
(3) The first rigid to be operated commercially for an extended period: DELAG'S Schwaben of 1911.
(4) The first successful four-engine rigid airship: the wooden Schutte-Lanz SL2 of 1914, which also introduced a number of other important design innovations.
(5) The first type of rigid airship built in quantity: the Zeppelin Naval L3 Class of 1914, of which 12 saw service with the German Army and Navy.
(6) The type of rigid airship which proved most effective in military operations: the Zeppelin Naval L10 and L20 classes of 1915, of which 34 were built.
(7) The rigid airship whose design represented the biggest advance and which had the greatest potential for further development: the Zeppelin Naval L30 class of 1916, (Fig. 33.4), from which were later derived: the L59, which made a notable 4200-mile (6760-km) return

flight to central Africa in 1917; the British Beardmore R34, which made the first return flight across the North Atlantic in 1919; *Shenandoah*, the first American rigid airship and the first to use non-inflammable helium gas, which appeared in 1923.

(8) The American 'reparations' Zeppelin: the *Los Angeles* of 1924, which had a longer life than any other rigid, being finally broken up in 1939.

(9) The most successful airship and the first to operate long-distance scheduled services—between Europe and South America in 1932–7: the *Graf Zeppelin* of 1928.

(10) The British rigid airship programme of 1924–30, aimed at linking the Empire by air: the private-enterprise R100 and Government-built R101 of 1929.

(11) The American rigid airship programme of 1928–35, intended to provide long-range naval reconnaissance: the U.S. Navy's Goodyear-Zeppelin *Akron* of 1931 and *Macon* of 1933.

(12) The last rigid airships: the transport Zeppelins *Hindenburg* of 1936 and *Graf Zeppelin II* of 1938, whose operations ended in 1939.

Some 160 rigid airships of basically Zeppelin type were built between 1900 and 1938. These flew a total of about 80000 hours and, for a time, the type was regarded as potentially superior to the aeroplane for long-range bombing, reconnaissance, and transport. Rigid airship development and operation remained chiefly in German hands and particularly with the Zeppelin company and its operating associates. Less important programmes were undertaken by the British before and during the First World War and by the British and Americans after the war, as tabulated above.

In addition to Count Zeppelin, the other most important protagonists of rigid airships were also German. They included: Dr Ludwig Durr, who supervised the design of all the Zeppelins; Johann Schutte, responsible for the wooden Schutte-Lanz rigids, who introduced several important advances in design; Captain Peter Strasser, of the Imperial German Navy and Head of the Naval Airship Service during most of the First World War, who pushed to the ultimate the development of the Zeppelin for military purposes; and Dr Hugo Eckener, prime mover of the Zeppelin organization after its founder's death, who also became the most successful and famous airship captain.

The airship failed for several reasons, the most important being difficulties of handling on the ground, low operating speeds and heights, and vulnerability to adverse weather. Many airships (including nearly 40 per cent of rigids built) were lost in accidents, particularly from burning of the highly inflammable hydrogen lifting gas. Although this particular hazard was later removed by the general adoption of helium (first used in the U.S. Army's C-7 blimp of 1921), other deficiencies proved decisive. The U.S. Navy stopped using airships in the early 1960s and only a very few small blimps have survived since, in peripheral advertising roles.

IV. BEGINNINGS OF AIR TRANSPORT

Before the First World War, aircraft were too unreliable for sustained regular scheduled operations. First attempts at carrying passengers and goods by air included: local passenger sightseeing flights with Zeppelin airships operated by DELAG from a number of German cities (1910–14); the 'Coronation Aerial Post', an experimental aeroplane service operated in Britain by the Grahame-White Aviation Company Limited to carry mail between Hendon and Windsor (9 to 26 September 1911); and the St Petersburg–Tampa Airboat Line, operated with a Benoist flying boat, which carried passengers on a regular basis in Florida, U.S.A. (January–February 1914). Towards the end of the war, however, when the new vehicles had become more dependable, several military mail and passenger services were attempted in Europe and America. Some of these were sustained for periods of up to about a year. However, civilian air transport did not start until after the war.

The first regular scheduled daily air service for passengers was probably that of the German company, Deutsche Luft Reederei, between Berlin, Leipzig, and Weimar (and later to Hamburg) started on 22 February 1919 and continued for more than five months. The French, British, and Americans began similar operations soon afterwards. The first international daily scheduled service was operated for 16 months between London and Paris from 25 August 1919 by a British company, Aircraft Transport and Travel Ltd., founded in 1916 by the Englishman G. Holt Thomas who later formed the International Air Traffic Association—the ancestor of the International Air Transport Association (I.A.T.A.), the powerful Association of the world's airlines.

The first transport aircraft were adaptations of proved military types: bombers crudely modified for passengers. Later, new civil types appeared but these were basically straightforward developments of military designs. The practice of adhering closely, in the design of the great majority of civil aircraft, to lines of development already paid for by the military started at this time and has continued ever since—inevitably, because defence budgets pay for by far the greatest part of all aeronautical research and development.

Airliners in the 1920s were mostly biplanes built of wood, wire, and fabric in the Wright tradition although, towards the end of the decade, steel or duralumin began to be substituted for wood in their framework structures. Also in service were smaller numbers of all-metal German Junkers low-wing monoplanes, Dutch Fokker high-wing monoplanes, with wooden wings and fuselages of welded steel tube covered in fabric; and types inspired by them, notably Ford's metal Tri-Motor in the U.S.A. and the Savoia-Marchetti low-wing monoplanes in Italy.

The first civil aircraft were mostly single-engined. A few were more costly adaptations of multi-engine military types. Engines were unreliable and there was greater risk of forced landing with multi-engine aircraft because they had more engines to fail and could not continue flying after a failure of any one. Only later did multiple power units increase safety and reliability—first with the trimotors of the mid-1920s, starting with the Fokker F.VII-3m (Fig. 33.5).

FIG. 33.5. The Fokker F.VIIA-3m, the first practical multi-engine transport aircraft (1925), widely used in many parts of the world.

Equally important was the development of more reliable and durable aero-engines. Times between overhaul of aero-engines in civil service rose from 150–200 hours or less immediately after the war to 400–500 hours by the early 1930s and thus helped to reduce operating costs. Overhaul times were, and continue to be, much shorter in military service. Air-cooled radials, which first appeared in Britain (Bristol Jupiter and Armstrong Siddeley Jaguar), and then in the U.S.A., were particularly important and were generally adopted for civil and military purposes from the later 1920s.

During the first ten post-war years, Europe led in air transport develop-ment. The larger European countries all had several small airlines from 1919. These pioneer companies soon found, however, that the level of traffic and the fares which could be charged, in competition with surface transport, were too low for profitable operations with available aircraft. In practice, revenue covered only some 10 to 20 per cent of costs and survival depended on Government subsidies.

The first national 'flag carriers' were established at this time, KLM in Holland (1920) and SABENA in Belgium (1923) being among the earliest. Imperial Airways in Britain (1924) and Lufthansa in Germany (1926) grew out of the amalgamation of earlier companies. By 1930, the European airlines had developed a comprehensive network of government-subsidized services covering the whole continent and European interests had started numerous services in or to colonial or other territories overseas. Notable early European airline developments in distant parts of the world included: the French to North Africa (1919) and in South America (1919); the Belgians in the Congo (1920); the Germans in South America (1921) and Persia (1925); and the British from Egypt to the Persian Gulf (1927) and from Europe to India (1929).

Surprisingly, development of air transport in the U.S.A., as of its military aviation during the First World War, lagged behind Europe through the 1920s. From 1918 to 1927, the most important American operations were subsidized air mail services run by the Post Office. After the passage of the Kelly Act in 1925, which provided that the Government should not engage in private business, subsidized private contractors were brought in to take over and extend the mail network. The new airlines were soon carrying passengers as well as mail and, from these uncertain beginnings, rapid expan-sion began. From a position in which they had no significant scheduled passenger air traffic in 1926, the Americans were, by 1929, carrying a third more than the next busiest air transport nation (Germany). By then also,

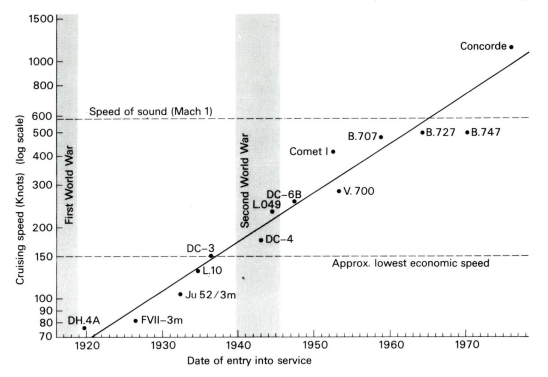

FIG. 33.6. Trends in transport aircraft cruising speeds.

four large groups had emerged as the dominant U.S. domestic airlines, in addition to Pan American Airways, operating international services.

In 1930, the European airlines were still operating old-fashioned biplanes and Junkers and Fokker monoplanes, although these were of considerably improved design compared with those in use immediately after the war. Speeds had increased only slightly (Fig. 33.6) but there had been significant advances in reliability and safety. Fares per mile had, on average, been reduced by perhaps a third, but costs (Fig. 33.7) had also come down so that about 25 per cent of costs was now covered by revenue. American airlines were doing even better, covering an average of perhaps 30 per cent of their costs by 1930. For a few of the most successful carriers, in both Europe and America, revenue represented as much as 50–60 per cent of expenditure.

V. GENERAL AVIATION: PRIVATE FLYING AND GLIDING

The British Moth (Fig. 33.8) designed by G. de Havilland, was the first widely used light aeroplane. A conventional two-seat biplane of wood, wire, and fabric with a 4500 cc Cirrus engine of 60 hp, it flew for the first time on

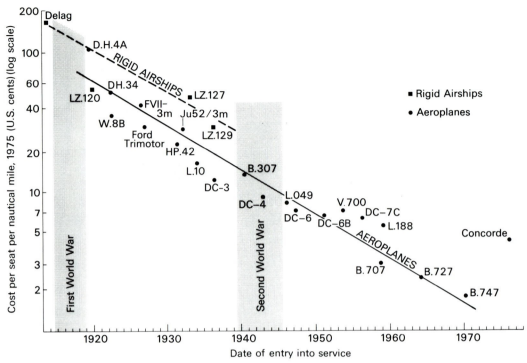

FIG. 33.7. Trends in transport aircraft operating costs.

22 February 1925 and sold initially for £650. The Moth was used to establish a State-subsidized flying-club movement in Britain, which was copied in many countries. About 2000 Moths were built, followed by about 9200 of a developed version, the Tiger Moth, which was later widely used for military as well as civil training. As significant as the Moth were the wooden cantilever low-wing monoplanes of the German Hanns Klemm. His L.25 started as an ultra-light two-seater in 1927 but, fitted later with more powerful engines, was widely sold and inspired many similar types by other manufacturers.

Two pioneer American light aircraft were particularly important: the Aeronca, which appeared as the C-2 single-seater in 1928 and as the C-3 two-seater in 1930 (price $1550), and C. G. Taylor's E-2 Cub of 1930 (price $1325) which later became the Piper Cub and also led to the Taylorcraft and British Auster series. The Cub and improved Super Cub were built in great numbers (37000) and the latter is still in production. Both Aeronca and Cub were high-wing monoplanes—the former with a wire-braced fabric-covered wooden wing on a fabric-covered steel tube fuselage, and the latter with a strut-braced wooden (later metal) fabric-covered wing on a tubular fuselage.

FIG. 33.8. The de Havilland Moth, the first widely used light aeroplane (1925) with which private and club flying started in the U.K.

D. A. Luscombe, in the U.S.A., was the first to go into production with a stressed-skin all-metal light aeroplane in 1934 at about the time this form of construction became established for larger aircraft. All-metal construction was not, however, generally adopted for light aircraft until after the Second World War. It followed large-scale production of all-metal training aircraft in the U.S.A. during the war.

Important to light aircraft development from the early 1930s were air-cooled horizontally opposed piston engines, particularly the numerous American Lycoming and Continental models. These succeeded the vertical and inverted air-cooled in-line engines which were popular, particularly in Europe, during the 1920s and 1930s.

Throughout this period there was a great variety of specialized general aviation types, in addition to light aircraft, including special designs for air survey, rugged convertible land–sea–ski-planes, for remote areas like the 'frozen north' of Canada; seaplanes and amphibians for use over coasts and inland waters; and specialized sporting and racing aircraft. Light transports were developed for charter and executive use and also for the airlines.

Many notable flying competitions took place between the wars, of which must be mentioned those for seaplanes for the Schneider Trophy (1919–31), which significantly encouraged development of high-speed aircraft, and the 'MacRobertson' England–Australia Race (1934), which confirmed the ascendancy of the modern monoplane. Adapted military or transport aircraft were used for many long distance flights which were a feature of aviation development between the wars. Amongst the most important of these flights were: the first direct crossing of the North Atlantic (J. Alcock and A. Whitten Brown in 1919); the first flight from England to Australia (R. and K. Smith in 1919); the first flight round the world (U.S. Army Air Service team in 1924); the first flights over the North and South Poles (R. E. Byrd and Floyd Bennett in 1926; R. E. Byrd and B. Balchen, 1929); the first solo flight across the North Atlantic (C. A. Lindbergh in 1927); and the first flight across the Pacific (C. Kingsford-Smith and C. T. P. Ulm in 1928). There were many others. Later, many long distance 'record flights' across the world were made in light aircraft, fame and fortune (from prizes, sponsorship, or advertising) came to many pilots whose names hit the headlines in every country.[1]

Following the Second World War, light aircraft development gained a new impetus, especially in the U.S.A. where general aviation expanded rapidly during the next 30 years. Its scale is indicated by the fact that, by the mid-1960s, general aviation flying hours in the U.S.A. exceeded those of the airlines and military taken together yet the American airlines themselves were flying more hours than the total for the rest of the Western world. By the 1960s, a great variety of single and multi-engine light aircraft were being produced in large numbers, particularly in the U.S.A. by the Piper, Cessna, and Beech companies. These aircraft were almost entirely of all-metal construction, the great majority with piston engines. However, small but increasing numbers of turboprop and pure-jet aircraft were also coming into service. Light aircraft and smaller numbers of larger types were being used for a wide variety of industrial, commercial, administrative, and recreational purposes as well as for flying training.

Gliding and soaring is a form of private flying which started in Germany in the early 1920s, originally largely at the instigation of Dr Oskar Ursinus, editor of the journal *Flugsport*. Because of restrictions on power flying under

---

[1] Alan Cobham, Amy Johnson, Wiley Post, Kingsford-Smith, Jim Mollison, Charles Scott, Jean Batten, Amelia Earhart, Jean Mermoz, Bert Hinkler, James Melrose, Paul Codos, Dieudonné Costes, Francis Chichester, and many more.

the Treaty of Versailles after the First World War, the Germans adopted gliding as an inexpensive way of encouraging flying.

Initially, the sport was confined to slope-soaring along hills. Later, techniques of thermal, thunderstorm, and wave soaring were discovered, making possible remarkable performances. By the 1960s, world soaring records stood at 46000 ft (14000 m) altitude, nearly 650 miles (1000 km) straight-line distance, and 80 mile/h (130 km/h) average speed around a 100-km ($62\frac{1}{2}$-mile) triangular course. Technical development of sailplanes went hand-in-hand with advances in flying technique. In the early days, emphasis was on staying up at low speeds; early wooden gliders had low rates of sink at low speeds but were unable to fly faster without rapid loss of height. Sailplane development in the 1920s contributed significantly to reductions in aeroplane drag and to improved stressed-skin wood structures.

After the Second World War, sailplanes acquired higher-speed characteristics, albeit with some increase in minimum rate of sink, so that they could fly faster across country between areas of thermal lift and get quickly through areas of sink. Some types had fabric-covered steel tube fuselages; a few had riveted stressed-skin light-alloy sheet structures, like contemporary aeroplanes (Section VI). Sailplanes built of fibreglass, chiefly from Germany, became the most popular in the 1960s. Another development, mainly for training, was the motor-glider—a sailplane with auxiliary engine for take-off and climb which could be shut down in soaring flight.

VI. DEVELOPMENT OF THE METAL MONOPLANE

Aerodynamically clean all-metal monoplanes—built mainly of riveted aluminium alloy sheet—which were to become familiar as the most important long-distance passenger vehicles of the second half of the twentieth century, began to appear in numbers for both military and civil purposes in the early 1930s.

Construction of aeroplanes in metal had been attempted from the earliest days. Metal framework structures covered with fabric were much used in France and Germany during the First World War. After the war, there was a general trend towards this form of construction, mainly because of doubts about the availability of suitable timber in sufficient quantities in the event of another war. Metal can, however, be more effectively used for monocoque or stressed-skin construction, in which the outer skin is part of the load-bearing structure.

Stressed-skin wings in wood had originally been suggested by the Frenchmen A. Penaud and P. Gauchet as early as 1876. The first to try them on an actual aeroplane was another Frenchman, M. Blanc, in 1912. He was followed by two Germans, F. D. Hergt and Oesterlen, in 1916. The Dutchman A. H. G. Fokker was the first to use this form of construction on a large scale. Combined with fuselages of welded steel tube covered with fabric, he employed it for the wings of highly successful military aircraft produced for the Germans during the First World War (Fig. 33.9) and thereafter for many military and civil aircraft until the 1930s. The Germans introduced wooden stressed-skin wings for sailplanes and light aircraft in the 1920s and were soon widely copied elsewhere.

Monocoque wooden fuselages were first built by the Englishman F. Handley Page and by the Frenchmen E. Ruchonnet and L. Béchereau in 1911. Wooden monocoques were much used by the Germans during the First World War and afterwards for sailplanes and light aircraft.

Monoplane cantilever wings (without external bracing) were first employed by L. Blériot in two partly successful designs in 1907. José Weiss in England showed that thick wings were aerodynamicly efficient with his model gliders from 1905. He thus pointed the way to light cantilever structures although his own designs (full-size gliders in 1907 and aeroplanes from 1909) continued to be strut-braced. The German Hugo Junkers proposed an all-wing aeroplane with thick wings in 1910, but the first cantilever monoplane built with thick wings was a more conventional low-wing design, the Antoinette Monobloc of 1911 due to the Frenchman Leon Levavasseur, who was also responsible for the famous Antoinette cable-braced monoplanes. The Monobloc was a failure, the wing lacking stiffness.

The French Morane-Saulnier Company built an aeroplane with a steel monocoque fuselage before the First World War and the German F. Huth did the same in aluminium but it was Junkers who produced the first practical all-metal aeroplanes (Fig. 33.10). His 'Tin Donkey', a cantilever monoplane with a welded tinplate stressed-skin structure, flew successfully in 1915 but proved excessively heavy, as was a similarly constructed low-wing monoplane fighter produced in 1916. However, in 1917 Junkers switched to the much lighter aluminium alloy duralumin, and used it in corrugated sheet form over a load-bearing tubular structure of the same material. The skin was no longer fully stressed and made only a limited contribution to structural strength, but Junkers aircraft built in this way continued in widespread use for the next 25 to 30 years. Duralumin was first used in the British Vickers *Mayfly* rigid airship in 1911 and later in Zeppelins. In improved forms, it was to become the most important material for aircraft construction (p. 439).

FIG. 33.9. The Fokker D.VIII. A highly successful German fighter aircraft (1918) with cantilever wooden wing and welded steel tube fuselage.

FIG. 33.10. The Junkers F13, the first civil all-metal aircraft. The F13 (1919) and a number of developments were widely used between the wars.

The next, more important, step was to stressed-skin construction in light alloy with smooth skins. German designers were the first to try this during the First World War, but they did not apply the technique to production aircraft until the 1920s and then on only a limited scale. C. Dornier and A. Rohrbach pioneered stressed-skin wings in metal, and G. Baatz was responsible for the first duralumin monocoque fuselage. The Short brothers in Britain and M. Wibault in France were also early in the field after the war. Rohrbach was responsible for the Zeppelin-Staaken E.4/20, a prototype four-engined all-metal high-wing transport monoplane flown in Germany in 1920. This remarkably advanced design, based on a projected heavy bomber, pointed the way to large aircraft in duralumin.

Another German, W. Messerschmitt, made important contributions to the design of metal wings, and still another, H. A. Wagner, developed a comprehensive theory for stressed-skin structures. Early corrosion problems with duralumin were reduced by the adoption of Alclad, with a rolled-on coating of pure aluminium (p. 441), first used on the American ZMC-2 airship of 1929.

Americans were the first to exploit these advances fully in production aircraft. Late in the 1920s, several American designers—in particular J. K. Northrop at Lockheed—developed clean cantilever monoplanes (initially in wood) with higher wing loadings than had been attempted previously. These were made possible by new higher-powered, lightweight, air-cooled radial engines (such as the Wright Whirlwind and the Pratt and Whitney Wasp) and by acceptance of increased stalling speeds and take-off and landing distances. The Lockheed Vega of 1927 was a notable example of such a design. Higher wing loadings reduced overall dimensions, saving weight and improving performance, thus starting a spiral of interdependent improvements which transformed the aeroplane and enormously increased its capabilities and economy.

By the mid-1930s, several American manufacturers had produced all-metal monoplanes of riveted duralumin sheet and extrusions which exploited the new concept: the Martin B-10 bomber, the Boeing 247 and Douglas DC-2 and DC-3 transports, which also incorporated such further refinements as retractable landing-gear, improved wing sections, flaps, wing-mounted fully-cowled radial engines, and variable-pitch propellers. Parallel developments in instruments, equipment, and operating techniques, at about the same time (Ch. 34), transformed aircraft operations and led to notable advances in bad-weather flying ability and in reliability and safety.

VII. AIR POWER BECOMES DOMINANT

The primitive aeroplanes of the First World War were only auxiliary to armies and navies. However, they gave promise of much more in the future. During the Second World War, more than three times as many aeroplanes, of immeasurably increased capabilities, were built and employed in almost every conceivable role.

A view widely held between the wars was that bombing towns would be devastating and could break their inhabitants' will to resist. This seemed to be confirmed by exaggerated reports of the effects of bombing during the 'Chinese Incident' (1931–41) and the Spanish Civil War (1936–9). A decisive role for strategic bombing had first been claimed by the Italian Giulio Douhet in a widely publicized book, *Command of the air* (1921). British air doctrine, as propounded by Sir Hugh (later Lord) Trenchard, agreed with this view. As a result, the R.A.F. concentrated on heavy bombers and, as war again drew near, on means of defence against them. William Mitchell and his supporters in the U.S.A. also advocated land-based bombers in a much-publicized 'bombs-versus-battleships' controversy, but carrier-based air power, supported by long-range shore-based aircraft, was adopted as the basis of American strategy and one which Japan shared. The Germans, and less decisively the Russians and a few military thinkers in France and Britain, saw aircraft as of the greatest value in direct support of land forces, themselves now made highly mobile by armoured fighting vehicles and motor transport.

These attitudes affected the way in which the Second World War was fought from its outbreak in September 1939. The German *Blitzkreig*, which depended on mechanized armoured forces on the ground closely supported by tactical air power, was rapidly and decisively victorious in Poland, Norway, and the West during 1939–40. German air power was exercised mainly by the Junkers Ju 87 single-engined dive-bomber and by twin-engined Dornier Do 17, Heinkel He 111, and Junkers Ju 88 bombers, supported by Messerschmitt Me 109 fighters—all modern monoplanes of all-metal stressed-skin construction, mostly powered by inverted-vee liquid-cooled piston engines. The Me 109 was built throughout the Second World War in large numbers (33 000) and in successively improved versions. It was later supplemented by Kurt Tank's Focke-Wulf Fw 190, of which 25 000 were built. Some of these aircraft and operating techniques had been tried out by the German Condor Legion in Spain during the Civil War.

The small Polish air force was overwhelmed in a few days. In Norway,

British air opposition with carrier-based aircraft and from fighters put ashore in the far north was ineffective. When the Germans turned west, the story was repeated: the French air force was weak, partly because the aircraft industry was disorganized after its nationalization. Their fighters (Morane 406, Dewoitine 520, and imported American Curtiss Hawks) and bombers (LeO 45 and Potez 63) were largely inferior to German equipment in quality and numbers. R.A.F. assistance was inadequate in scale and quality. France collapsed in June 1940.

The Battle of Britain, fought that summer between the R.A.F. and the German Luftwaffe, was the first major battle entirely between air forces. At issue was control of the air over the approaches to, and the southern part of, the British Isles which the Germans had to have if they were to invade. They failed to gain it after prolonged bomber and fighter attacks which were repulsed by an R.A.F. Fighter Command inferior in numbers, which succeeded over home territory in inflicting far heavier losses than it suffered. The defensive fighters responsible were Sidney Camm's Hawker Hurricane and R. J. Mitchell's Supermarine Spitfire (Fig. 33.11) with their eight machine-gun armament, reflector sight, and HF or VHF radio telephone which kept them in touch with a highly effective control system depending on the first early warning radar net and an elaborate ground observer organization. Fighter maximum speeds were 300–350 mile/h (480–560 km/h) at this time and effective ceilings were about 30000 ft (9100 m).

After failing in the daytime Battle of Britain, the Luftwaffe turned to night attacks, which were sustained on London and other British cities until May 1941. Their effectiveness was limited by the unsuitability of the German bombers for such operations. Moreover, British radar-directed night fighters (notably the Bristol Beaufighter) inflicted rapidly increasing losses on the attackers.

In June 1941, the Germans and their allies turned on the Soviet Union and launched a massive *Blitzkrieg* which again achieved spectacular successes, carrying the invaders nearly to Moscow and as far as the Caucasus until the advance was slowed and finally stopped early in 1943 at Stalingrad (now Volgograd). Important Russian aircraft during this bitter and protracted campaign were the single-engine Ilyushin Il-2 Sturmovik ground-attack monoplane and the Yakovlav series of fighters. Air fighting on the Eastern Front gave scope for the development of outstanding fighter pilots who, as in the First World War, measured their successes by numbers of aircraft shot down. Leaders amongst these were the German Erich Hartmann (352 vic-

FIG. 33.11. The Supermarine Spitfire (1938), the most famous fighter aircraft in the history of air warfare—a classic example of a stressed-skin metal monoplane with a liquid-cooled piston engine.

tories); the Austrian Walter Nowotry (258 victories); and the Russian Ivan Kozhedub (62 victories). Leading pilots in western Europe and North Africa were the German Hans-Joachim Marseille (158 victories); the South African St John Pattle (41 victories); and James Johnson (38 victories) from Britain. In the Pacific the American Richard Bong (40 victories) and the Japanese Heroyoshi Nishizawa (103 victories) were the most successful.

The Japanese entered the war in December 1941 with a surprise carrier-launched air attack on the American Pearl Harbour naval base in Hawaii which immobilized a major part of the American Pacific fleet. Thereafter, sea–air warfare between the American and Japanese navies spread across the Pacific Ocean, fought largely with specialized naval aircraft which both had developed. Prominent amongst these on the American side were the Grumman F4F and F6F and Vought F4U fighters, and the Douglas SBD and Grumman TBM bombers. The Japanese relied heavily on Mitsubishi A6M (Zero) fighter, and Aichi D3A (Val) and Nakajima B5N (Kate) bombers.

The American Army Air Force deployed its first major war effort in Europe. There the four-engined Boeing B-17 and Consolidated B-24 bombers, later supported by escorting fighters—H. L. Hibbard's Lockheed P-38,

A. Kartveli's Republic P-47, and R. Rice and E. Schmued's North American P-51—started a daylight bombing offensive to complement R.A.F. Bomber Command's night attacks. The latter was also using large four-engine bombers—Short Stirling, Handley Page Halifax, and, particularly, Roy Chadwick's Avro Lancaster—and the high-speed twin-engined de Havilland Mosquito built of wood.

American land-based air power built-up more gradually in the Pacific, being based on islands successively nearer Japan and finally on the Marianas, Iwo-Jima, and Okinawa. A new long-range four-engined bomber, the Boeing B-29 (Fig. 33.12), launched a strategic offensive against the Japanese islands from these bases.

Meanwhile, German submarines, and to a lesser extent surface ships, had been blockading Britain and, from early 1941, inflicting massive Allied shipping losses. Aircraft played as important a role in the struggle against the U-boats as they did in the Pacific, while the latter were aided by shore-based Focke-Wulf Fw 200 patrol aircraft, developed from a pre-war civil transport. The Allies replied to the blockade by re-introducing convoys (as used in 1914–18) and by massively deploying surface escorts and aircraft. Aircraft proved to be the most effective U-boat killers, operating from merchant ships (catapulted from CAMships or from rudimentary flight decks on MACships), from small escort carriers, and, most important of all, from shore bases. The big fleet aircraft carriers, introduced between the wars by the British, Americans, and Japanese, also took part in the anti-submarine war but were mainly used for offensive operations against enemy surface ships and shore bases. A notable British attack of this type, in November 1941, was on the Italian fleet at Taranto. The Americans and Japanese fought a whole series of major air–sea battles in the Pacific, starting with that at Midway, in which aircraft from carriers played the main role.

Air power played major roles in every theatre of war. Particularly significant for the future was the part played by German transport aircraft (Junkers Ju 52/3m) in the invasion of Crete in 1941 and by Allied transport aircraft (Douglas C-47 and C-54 and Curtiss C-46) in carrying supplies in Africa, Burma, and China; in the latter, across 'the Hump' after China's only surface link with the West, the Burma Road, had been cut by the Japanese. Aircraft used in these and other roles were almost entirely stressed-skin all-metal monoplanes with radial air-cooled or vee liquid-cooled piston engines of up to about 2000 hp of American, British, German, Italian, and Japanese design, which had been developed or were under development before the war.

FIG. 33.12. The Boeing B-29 (1943), the decisive bomber of the Second World War in the Pacific, used for the great fire-raids on Japan and to drop the first two atom bombs.

The invasion in 1944 of a German-occupied Europe, weakened and disorganized by the British and American bombing offensives, led to defeat of the German armies and collapse of the German economy—helped particularly towards the end by lack of oil caused by air attack. The Second World War ended in Europe in May 1945 but not before the Germans had, from September 1944, fired about 4300 of the first ballistic missile, the V-2, nearly half of them against Britain. This weapon had been designed by a team under W. von Braun (Ch. 35). It anticipated the dominant strategic position that such weapons were to attain in the second half of the twentieth century when ballistic missiles would supplement and, for all-out war (or the threat of it, as a deterrent), later replace bombers as the decisive strategic weapon.

Before the end of the Second World War bombers, using high explosives and incendiaries, had confirmed pre-war fears of their ability to destroy towns. The fire-storm attack on Hamburg in July–August 1943 killed nearly 42000 people. An incendiary attack on Tokyo in March 1945 killed nearly 84000—more than either of the atomic bombs dropped on 6 and 9 August 1945 on Hiroshima (80000 killed) and Nagasaki (nearly 40000 killed). The two atomic bombs caused immediate Japanese capitulation, thus abruptly ending the war and finally confirming the absolute dominance of air power. Nuclear weapons with aerospace delivery systems, both aircraft and missile, subsequently proved an effective deterrent to total war.

VIII. GROUND FACILITIES AND NAVIGATIONAL AIDS

For take-off, the Wright Flyer required a launching rail and, usually, the assistance of its catapult. It landed on skids. However, except for seaplanes and a few on skis, almost all aeroplanes since have had wheeled landing-gear. The Frenchman Henri Fabre was the first to fly a seaplane, on 28 March 1910. Seaplanes, on floats or as flying boats, have been widely used ever since but mainly in roles where their ability to operate with few ground facilities has justified higher cost, lower performance, and reduced convenience.

Until the early 1930s, landplanes could operate from any reasonably smooth, firm, and level field with a clear run of about 1500 ft (450 m) into the wind. During the biplane era wing loadings were low and they increased only slowly (from about 4 to about 12lb /ft²). When the new all-metal monoplanes appeared, wing loadings started to rise rapidly. The introduction of flaps, other high-lift devices, and improved wing sections enabled wings of a given area to provide more lift but the increases were insufficient to prevent take-off and landing distances from increasing. By the late 1930s, major aerodromes had runs of 4000–5000 ft (1200–1500 m) and these had grown to 6000–7000 ft (1800–2100 m) by the end of the Second World War. At about the same time, heavier aircraft made hard-surface runways necessary. Then came nose-wheel landing gear which helped take-off, reduced cross-wind limitations, and made heavier braking possible after landing—soon aided by reverse pitch and, later, reverse jet thrust.

The runways required by large military and civil aircraft of high performance continued to get longer and stronger. By the 1950s, they were 7000–8000 ft (2100–2400 m) long. By the 1960s, with the general introduction of jet propulsion, 10000 ft (3000 m) or more were required at major aerodromes and wing loadings had reached 100 lb/ft² or more.

Night flying started in a small way soon after practical aeroplanes appeared in 1909–10. During the First World War, it was quite widely practised for bombing and air defence, but was still a somewhat hazardous business on all but moonlit nights and it remained so until the adoption of gyroscopic blind flying instruments in the early 1930s. The first gyro instruments were a German artificial horizon (used on their Giant bombers from 1916) and a turn indicator, demonstrated by the American Lawrence Sperry in 1917. However, few pilots knew how to use such instruments to fly safely in cloud or on dark nights. Some of the early spectacular record flights between the wars provided the first practical demonstrations of prolonged flight on instruments (Section V).

The first complete flight on instruments, including an instrument approach, was made by the American J. H. Doolittle on 24 September 1929 using radio and gyroscopic artificial horizon and a directional gyro. The first completely blind landing was made by M. S. Boggs on 5 September 1931. From the early 1930s, instrument flying gradually became general, enormously increasing the bad-weather capabilities of aircraft when combined with anti-icing equipment and appropriate pilot training—the latter greatly assisted by ground simulators, starting with the Link trainer.

Radio was tried experimentally for communication soon after aeroplanes became practical. During the First World War it was used for air-to-ground communication and (mainly by airships) for navigation. From the early 1920s the Americans were the first to adopt radio extensively for both two-way communication and navigation on their Government-run Post Office air mail routes and, from 1927, on the then rapidly-expanding domestic airline network. They favoured radio telephony (using the spoken word), whereas in Europe wireless telegraphy (using the Morse code) was more popular. The medium-frequency (MF) four-course radio range, which provided guidance from beacon to beacon along defined air routes, was introduced in the U.S.A. from 1927. By 1939, it had spread elsewhere and, after the Second World War, became the basis of a worldwide system of airways. The Europeans had previously used wireless for homing (QTEs and QDMs). Another American navigation aid was the radio compass (later: automatic direction finding, ADF) used with any ground station or non-directional medium-frequency beacon (NDB).

Improved aerodrome lighting and the first approach-light systems, in place of earlier primitive 'flare paths', appeared in the 1930s. These developments in lighting, instrumentation, and radio, and improved aircraft characteristics, gradually made night and bad-weather flying a routine matter, eventually limited only by the need for adequate visibility for take-off and landing. Subsequent developments have been concentrated in two main areas: Approach and landing[1] and navigation *en route*.[2] Automatic pilots to control particularly large aircraft in cruising flight began to be used in the later 1930s. After American experiments during 1936–8, automatic pilots started being coupled to navigation and approach and landing aids in the 1950s. This made possible largely automatic flight, including landing in very low visibilities. The automatic equipment has to be 'fail-safe' and highly reliable, operating in some systems with intervention by the human pilot and in others without.

Control of aircraft traffic from the ground started between the wars, initially by visual signals. Air traffic control services (ATC), using radio, and later radar and computers, were continuously developed from the mid-1930s,

[1] In the early 1930s, the German Lorenz approach aid (later: standard beam approach, SBA) was developed from the radio range, using the principle of the Equisignal beacon first proposed by Scheller before the First World War. During the Second World War, this was overtaken by radar (used initially for aircraft and ship detection and location) which led to a 'talk-down' system, ground-controlled approach (GCA). Radio communication was much improved by the British-led switch to very high frequency (VHF) from the previously used medium-frequency radio telephony. GCA was largely replaced after the war by an instrument landing system (ILS) developed by the American Civil Aeronautics Authority at Indianapolis from work started in 1928–30 on the Equisignal beacon and F. W. Dunmore's ultra-short-wave landing beam. ILS continues in general use in improved forms.

[2] 'Sonne', a long-range navigation system developed by the Germans during the Second World War, was later improved by the British (as 'Consul') and is still used. The British also developed a secondary radar system, 'Rebecca', for homing on a responder beacon, 'Eureka'. A hyperbolic pulse system ('Gee'), employed for bomber navigation by the R.A.F. during the war, was later developed into 'Loran' which, in newer versions, continues in use. 'Decca' is another type of widely-used 'area navigation', as distinct from 'beacon', system. In the late 1950s, the Americans brought in the VHF omnirange beacon (VOR), which has since been adopted as the basis of airway systems over most of the world. With distance-measuring equipment (DME), it also becomes an 'area' system ('Vortac'). Navigational aids introduced in the 1960s, such as Doppler and inertial navigation systems (INS) are also 'area' aids. They are completely self-contained, being independent of ground facilities.

when they were first started by four of the U.S. domestic airlines. There were similar earlier developments in Europe. By the 1950s, almost all airline traffic, as well as a great deal of other civil and military flying, was in controlled airspace where track, height, and separation from other aircraft were continuously monitored by ground controllers. Major airports, where traffic, as at all busy aerodromes, is supervised by a control tower, usually became centres of control zones (CTR), themselves enclosed within larger terminal areas (TMA). TMAs, under the control of ATC centres, are linked by airways, the track, width, and height of which is defined by beacons and reporting points. Aircraft movements are normally planned ahead and defined in a flight plan. They are watched by surveillance radar and identified by transponders (IFF) which reply to radar interrogation.

In addition to these elaborate operational facilities at aerodromes and *en route*, extensive traffic-handling buildings, surface transport systems, and other arrangements for air passengers and cargo have developed all over the world. The intensive operation of military and civil aircraft also requires widespread and elaborate maintenance and overhaul bases equipped with engine test-cells, electronic, and systems maintenance shops, and other specialized facilities.

IX. JET PROPULSION

In the late 1930s a few farsighted people foresaw future limitations to the piston-engine for the propulsion of high-speed aircraft. Interest was thus stimulated in the possibilities of the gas turbine (see Ch. 40) and the rocket (see Ch. 35).

A. A. Griffith and F. Whittle in Britain in the late 1920s independently made the first practical proposals for the use of gas turbines in aircraft. In 1926 Griffith evolved a new aerodynamic theory of turbine-blade design and in 1929 he suggested an axial compressor for a gas turbine driving a propeller, the so-called turboprop engine. An axial compressor was built in 1936 which led to an axial Metrovic pure-jet engine which ran in 1940 and flew in 1943. Jet propulsion by gas turbine with a centrifugal compressor had been suggested by Whittle in 1928, patented in 1930, and published in 1932, probably inspiring similar developments from 1936 by H. von Ohain and M. Mueller in Germany.

Ohain developed a centrifugal jet engine like Whittle's; Mueller initially proposed a turboprop which by 1938 had become an axial pure-jet. The first Ohain jet engine ran in 1937 at about the same time as the first Whittle

FIG. 33.13. The Messerschmitt Me 262, the first jet fighter in operational service (1944). The British Gloster Meteor was also used on operations during the War.

engine. The first jet aeroplane, the German Heinkel He 178 with a developed Ohain engine flew on 27 August 1939 and was followed on 15 May 1941 by the first British design, the Gloster E.28/39 with Whittle engine. The first operational jet aeroplanes were fighters. The German Messerschmitt Me 262 (Fig. 33.13) and the British Gloster Meteor entered service in 1944 and were used on a limited scale towards the end of the Second World War. American and Russian jet development started at this time, deriving mainly from earlier British and German work.

Jets then gradually took over from piston engines for military and civil purposes in all but the smallest aircraft: the first jet light bombers, reconnaissance aircraft, and all-weather fighters were coming into service at the end of the war. They were followed by jet medium bombers (1951), transports (1952), heavy bombers (1955), all-through military training (1955), executive aircraft (1961), and finally maritime patrol aircraft (1969).

Turboprop engines have had a useful, although probably limited, career as aeroplane power units alongside pure jets since their adoption for several roles in the early 1950s. Of from about 400 to about 15000 hp, they were in widespread service in the 1950s, 1960s, and 1970s but there were signs that they might not survive in competition with the jet, at least in large sizes. Up to that time, turboprops had, moreover, failed to supplant the still almost universal piston engines in light aircraft, although in turboshaft form they had become the main helicopter power plant by the 1960s.

The most important developments of the jet engine after the Second World War were towards greater thrusts, lower fuel consumption, and higher thrust-to-weight ratios. Special efforts were also directed at reducing atmospheric pollution (exhaust smoke) and noise—or at least minimizing such increases as would otherwise have accompanied the higher powers of later engines. The main contribution to these improvements came from the adoption of the dual-flow principle, by which only part of the air passing through the engine's compressor is burnt with fuel and drives the power turbines. This change was accompanied by the introduction of twin- or three-spool layouts which enable different parts of the compressor (and propulsive fan) to be driven by separate power turbines and thus to operate more efficiently at different speeds.

After the Second World War, the rocket engine, which must be supplied with both oxygen and either liquid or solid fuel, became of prime importance for the propulsion of missiles and for the launching of space vehicles (Ch. 35). However, this power unit has been little used for aircraft. The first tentative rocket-propelled aircraft was the German RRG Ente glider, which made a short flight powered by two Sander solid fuel rockets on 11 June 1928. A longer flight with another rocket-propelled glider was made by F. von Opel on 30 September 1929. The first aircraft to fly under the power of a liquid-fuel rocket was the Heinkel He 176 which made its first flight on 30 June 1939. Subsequently, the Germans used the Messerschmitt Me 163 rocket-powered interceptor fighter (first flight: April 1941) on a limited scale during the Second World War. Since the war, rocket propulsion of aircraft has been almost exclusively for experimental purposes—mainly for high-speed research. There was no sign that it would replace air-breathing engines in the foreseeable future.

X. HELICOPTERS

Helicopters were a twentieth-century invention: several pioneers during the two previous centuries thought about rotary wings and flew crude models, but man-carrying helicopters did not leave the ground until 1907. The first helicopter—really a tethered test rig—was built in France by the Breguet brothers and C. Richet. Four biplane rotors driven by a 45-hp Antoinette petrol engine first lifted a pilot on 29 September 1907. Six weeks later, on 13 November, Paul Cornu flew a machine with two tandem counter-rotating two-blade rotors powered by a 24-hp Antoinette. Neither aircraft was really controllable, nor had significant stability, but the second was reported to have flown untethered for about 20 seconds. Progress towards stability and control came in the 1920s. G. de Bothezat in America developed a four-rotor helicopter powered by a 220-hp Gnome-Rhone engine which flew for 1 minute 42 seconds on 18 December 1922. L. Brennan at the Royal Aircraft Establishment in Britain achieved similar results in the summer of 1925 with a single-rotor design powered by shaft-driven airscrews mounted on two of the four blades. Both types could be controlled to some extent, were marginally stable while hovering, but became unstable in translational flight.

De Bothezat was sponsored by the U.S. Army; Brennan by the British Air Ministry. In 1920, the latter also offered a £50000 prize for a successful helicopter. This was not awarded, but a prize of 90000 francs, offered by the French Government for the first circular flight of one kilometre by a helicopter, was won by E. Oemichen on 4 May 1924, with a flight of 14 minutes. Oemichen also established the first officially recognized helicopter world records. Starting in 1920, he developed a design like de Bothezat's with four main rotors and no less than eight auxiliary airscrews for control. An Argentinian, the Marquis R. de Pateras Pescara, experimenting in France at about the same time, retained de Bothezat's more practical method of control by rotor pitch variation. Pitches of the two co-axial superimposed rotors of his helicopter could be altered, both collectively and cyclically, by warping their biplane blades. Cyclic pitch control had originated with G. A. Crocco in 1906. Pescara's design was unstable but made flights of up to about 12 minutes in 1924. Propulsion was by tilting the lift vector and the rotors could free-wheel after engine failure, thus permitting a safe descent in autorotation.

Autorotation—windmilling a rotor in the airflow—was first demonstrated in Madrid on 9 January 1923 by the Spaniard, Juan de la Cierva, inventor of the Autogiro. This is an intermediate type of rotary-wing aircraft propelled by a normal airscrew in which the rotor freewheels in flight. Something like 700 Autogiros were operated worldwide over the following 20 years, thus providing valuable practical experience which read across to the helicopter. Cierva also adopted articulated rotor blades (first suggested by C. Renard in 1904 and tried by Breguet in 1908) which reduced vibration and blade stresses; removed undesirable gyroscopic effects; and overcame the unbalanced lift of advancing and retreating blades in translational flight. The first effective articulated blades on a helicopter were on the co-axial design of the Italian C. d'Ascanio, who made flights of up to about nine minutes in 1930.

From 1931 to 1933, the Russian Central Aero-Hydrodynamic Institute

(TsAGI) near Moscow produced a series of three single-rotor helicopters with articulated blades and collective and cyclic pitch control. Two small airscrews offset main rotor torque. Flights of 10 to 15 minutes were claimed.

The first practical helicopters appeared in 1935–6: the co-axial Breguet-Dorand 314 made a satisfactory free flight near Paris on 26 June 1935. Later, it achieved flights of over an hour and speeds of about 65 mile/h (105 km/h), continuing to fly until 1939. On 6 June 1936, the German Fw 61, with two side-by-side rotors, designed by H. K. J. Focke, made its first free flight. Within a year, several world records (1 hour 20 minutes endurance; 50 miles (80 km) closed-circuit distance; 8000 ft (2400 m) height; and 76 mile/h (122 km/h) speed) confirmed its practicality. Both types had articulated rotor blades and collective and cyclic pitch control. The Breguet did not lead to production, but a larger development of the Fw 61 went into small-scale service in Germany during the Second World War.

The first helicopters produced and used in numbers were designed by Igor I. Sikorsky in the U.S.A. As first flown on 14 September 1939, the Sikorsky V.S.300 had a single 28-ft main rotor powered by a 75-hp Lycoming petrol engine, collective and cyclic pitch control of three articulated blades, and a small torque-compensating tail rotor. The original design was, however, unsatisfactory and was modified with two additional auxiliary rotors replacing cyclic pitch control. The definitive V.S.300A (Fig. 33.14), which reverted to the original simple configuration, flew on 8 December 1941. Thereafter, some 400 examples of three developed Sikorsky designs saw service before the end of the war.

After the war, on the strength of their hovering and vertical take-off and landing capabilities, and despite their higher complexity and cost, helicopters gradually established themselves as the most important aircraft after aeroplanes. By the 1960s, many thousands were in world-wide military and civil use: close-support 'gunships' and transports over the battlefield; for anti-submarine warfare; crop-spraying; charter and limited scheduled commercial passenger and freight transport; servicing of oil rigs; and many rescue and emergency roles.

Gas-turbine power units began to be adopted for all but the smallest types from the early 1960s. These helped to reduce two major deficiencies of helicopters: their small disposable loads and low maximum speeds. Most helicopters were small although larger multi-engine machines, some weighing up to about 100000 lb (45000 kg), were becoming more numerous. The most popular types have a single main rotor and a small torque-compensating tail

FIG. 33.14. The Sikorsky V.S. 300A (1941) was the first successful helicopter of 'penny-farthing' configuration with single main rotor and small anti-torque tail rotor, which was later to become the most common type of helicopter.

rotor, as pioneered by Sikorsky. Others have two main rotors: tandem, side-by-side, intermeshing, or co-axial. Control and propulsion are almost always by collective and cyclic pitch variation. Rotor blades are usually articulated, although rigidly interconnected two-blade 'see-saw' rotors (pioneered in 1942 by A. D. Young of the American Bell Company) are also common. New developments point towards rigid or semi-rigid rotors, the latter with torsion-bar blade attachment.

XI. GROWTH OF THE AIRLINE INDUSTRY

Economic transport aeroplanes had emerged by the mid-1930s. For the first time passengers could be carried at costs which, allowing for a competitive load factor, were less than air fares low enough to attract an expanding volume of traffic. Numerous technical and operational advances contributed to this development (Section VI) but the American Douglas DC-3 (Fig. 33.15) was particularly significant. This aeroplane had been developed at a cost of about $2·5m. ($10m. in mid-1970s values) by a team led by A. E. Raymond and E. F. Burton to the order of American Airlines. It derived from the earlier DC-2, itself built for T.W.A. In one step, the DC-3 lifted the airlines out of the pioneer era and, within a few years, brought U.S. operators close to profitability without subsidy. This new equipment, and the improved operating techniques which it made possible, soon gave the American airlines a lead over the rest of the world. Through the 1930s, they carried as many passengers as all other countries together. The 'Big Four' (American, Eastern, T.W.A., and United) became the core of a booming domestic airline system while the 'chosen instrument', Pan American Airways, expanded overseas—first to Latin America and then across the Pacific and the Atlantic.

The DC-3 was widely exported, and introduced new airline standards throughout the world. Later, military variants of the same aircraft would, in their thousands, transport the necessities of war. After the war, the DC-3 returned to civilian service and performed a major task in rehabilitating the airlines and thereafter, for many years, in providing a work-horse for countless secondary air routes. Hundreds of DC-3s were still in service 40 years after the type first appeared.

The DC-3 (20–30 passengers) led to the larger (40–60-passenger) DC-4 four-engined long-haul transport. Its development was originally sponsored by four major U.S. airlines and it first entered service, as the military C-54, in 1942. The DC-4 incorporated several significant innovations, including a rounded-section, tubular fuselage (with underfloor freight holds) which was suitable for pressurization—although the DC-4 itself was not, in fact, pressurized—a nose-wheel landing gear, and a more efficient wing section (NACA 230 series) with improved high-lift devices (slotted flaps). It cruised at about 200 mile/h (320 km/h) and required about 6000 ft (1800 m) of runway.

The DC-4 and its post-war developments, the pressurized DC-6 and DC-7 series, and H. L. Hibbard's rather similar Lockheed Constellation, were to do for long-haul air transport what the DC-3 had done on the shorter hauls. These new aircraft each cost about $30m. to develop (equivalent to about $70m. in mid-1970s values). Right through the 1950s these aeroplanes enabled the airline industry of the western world to extend its route network between and across all the populated continents.

The U.S. domestic airlines carried about 60 per cent of the western world's air traffic in 1945. This share had declined to about 43 per cent by 1950.

Fig. 33.15. The Douglas DC-3 was the most successful transport aircraft in the whole history of airline development. The DC-3 incorporated many features of the modern metal monoplane.

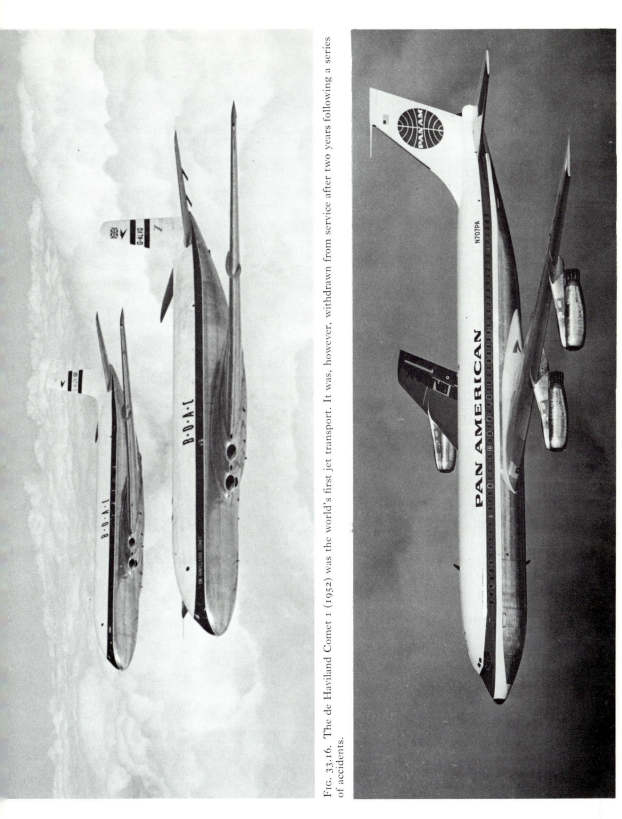

FIG. 33.16. The de Haviland Comet I (1952) was the world's first jet transport. It was, however, withdrawn from service after two years following a series of accidents.

FIG. 33.17. The Boeing 707 was the aeroplane which launched the jet transport era in the west (1958) and set the pattern for many later airliner developments.

Nevertheless, U.S. domestic traffic increased more than sevenfold from 1940 to 1950 and nearly fourfold from 1950 to 1960, so that increases elsewhere were even more spectacular. Specific operating costs of the best piston-engined aircraft during this 20-year period were reduced by something like 75 per cent in constant values. This enabled the industry, and particularly the American airlines carrying more than half the western world's traffic, to achieve profitability without subsidy much of the time from the early 1950s, despite large reductions in real fares—of as much as 37 per cent between 1940 and 1950.

The piston-engined airliners of this era were progressively developed so that, by the later 1950s, cruising speeds had reached 300–30 mile/h (480–530 km/h) at operating heights of 15000–20000ft (4500–6000 m). Passenger capacity of the long-haul types had increased to about 100 and ranges were sufficient for non-stop North Atlantic operations. Stalling speeds increased to about 100 mile/h (160 km/h) and required runway lengths to about 7500 ft (2300 m).

On shorter hauls, I. M. Laddon's twin-engine Convair CV-240/440 series, which appeared in the late 1940s, was outstanding. From 1953, George Edwards' British turboprop Vickers Viscount appeared alongside the Convair as the first non-American airliner seriously to challenge the ever-dominant U.S. types. This aeroplane was joined in the late 1950s by a number of other turboprop aircraft which were to have a limited vogue until succeeded by jet equipment.

The Berlin airlift, which saw 2362000 tonnes of supplies flown into the city by American and British aircraft in 15 months in 1948–9—thus completely sustaining a blockaded population of 2·1m. people—demonstrated another capability of air transport. A different kind of landmark was passed in 1957 when, for the first time, more passengers flew the Atlantic than crossed by sea.

The British were the first to introduce jet transport (in 1952). However, the original de Havilland Comet (Fig. 33.16) designed by a team under R. E. Biship suffered from deficiencies which led to its withdrawal from service after about two years, so that the jet era proper did not start in the west until 1958. Meanwhile, the Russians had put their first jet transport, the Tupolev Tu-104, into service in 1956.

The jet engine had been initially a British and German development (Section IX) but parallel aerodynamic advances sprang largely from German work started in the late 1920s. In 1933, Adolf Busemann at Göttingen had shown that thin aerofoils delay and reduce sharp increases in drag (air resistance) which occur as an aircraft approaches the speed of sound (Mach 1, equivalent to 660/760 mile/h, (1060–1220 km/h) according to the temperature). In 1935, Busemann suggested swept-back wings, and in 1939, also at Göttingen, Albert Betz demonstrated that these delay and reduce the sonic drag rise. Alexander Lippisch similarly deserves credit for his advocacy of delta wings. The new jet transports, following the pattern of previous military developments (Section XII), exploited to the full the higher cruising speeds made possible by these aerodynamic advances.

The airlines' introduction of jets able to cruise at speeds approaching that of sound resulted in spectacular reductions in journey times. Traffic response was, however, initially disappointing. Air traffic was suffering from one of its periodic recessions in the late 1950s, and several years passed before it resumed its rapid growth and thus enabled the new larger aircraft to achieve their full economic potential. Traffic was, in due course, to be markedly stimulated by the jets' higher speed and greater comfort. Jet cruising speeds rose to 500–50 mile/h (800–900 km/h) and cruising heights to 30 000–40 000 ft (9000–12 000 m), while stalling speeds of 120–25 mile/h (190–200 km/h) and runway lengths of up to 10 000 ft (3000 m) became the norm. The specific operating costs of the new larger jets (with 150–200 passenger seats) offered, in due course, reductions of something like 50 per cent as compared with the best piston-engine equipment.[1]

At the end of the 1960s, the scheduled airlines were carrying more than 300m. passengers a year and had become the principal method of long-distance passenger transport on most international and domestic routes. On the world's busiest route, across the North Atlantic, more than 40 times as many people were travelling by air as by sea. Air cargo traffic was also growing rapidly. Air transport had become as important to peacetime civilization as air power had already proved in war.

XII. SUPERSONIC AND VTOL/STOL AIRCRAFT

In the first half of the twentieth century, powered human flight was at last achieved and then exploited for practical purposes, the aeroplane establishing

---

[1] The most important of the new jet types were the four-engined American Boeing 707 (Fig. 33.17), designed by a team led by E. C. Wells and G. Martin, and Douglas DC-8. Various versions of these aircraft were soon catering for the bulk of the western world's long-haul traffic. The development of each type cost something like $300m. ($550m. in mid-1970s values). The three-engined Boeing 727 became the most important medium-haul type. Short-haul equipment included the twin-engined American Douglas DC-9 and Boeing 737; the French Sud Caravelle; and the British B.A.C. One-Eleven. The Russians developed similar equipment: the Ilyushin Il-62 and Tupolev Tu-154 and Tu-134.

itself as the most important type of aircraft as it followed well-defined lines of development almost entirely under the impetus of defence expenditure. The main trends were towards higher speeds, greater lifting capacity, longer range, lower operating costs, and increased all-weather capabilities, safety, and reliability. This applied in every category, from the smallest and most modest recreational or training light aircraft to the largest transports and military types with the highest performance. These improvements involved ever-greater complexity which required enormous increases in development and manufacturing effort (Figs. 33.18–33.21) to take advantage of notable advances in aerodynamics, structures, materials, equipment and power plants and the acceptance of steadily rising minimum flying speeds and more extensive and elaborate ground facilities. Minimum speeds increased from about 40 mile/h (65 km/h) in the early period to 120–130 mile/h (190–210 km/h) for jet aircraft of the 1950s and 1960s, and would have been higher but for great progress in the development of high-lift devices. Take-off and landing distances for the largest and highest-performance types rose at the same time from 1500 ft (450 m) or less to 10 000 ft (3000 m) or more.

Adoption of jet propulsion and parallel advances in aerodynamics (Section XI) had spectacular effects on performance and particularly on operating speeds, which soon increased for many types into the subsonic region (500–600 mile/h, 800–1000 km/h). The research which made this possible was first applied by the Germans during the Second World War to new aircraft and missile developments, but the main practical benefits were not realized until after the war, and then first by the victorious nations—Germany being excluded at that time from aircraft development. The Russian MiG-15 jet fighter (Fig. 33.22), which first flew on 2 July 1947, was the first aeroplane with swept surfaces to enter widespread service. It was followed by the North American F-86 fighter (first flight 1 October 1947) and the Boeing B-47 bomber (first flight 17 December 1947). These aircraft all took advantage of the results of German research.

The introduction of jet aircraft capable of high subsonic speeds led to development of supersonic aircraft. The first flight at a speed exceeding that of sound was achieved by Captain C. E. Yeager, U.S.A.F., in the Bell XS-1, an American rocket-powered research aircraft which was launched in flight from a Boeing B-29 bomber on 14 October 1947.

The first conventional aeroplane to achieve supersonic speed (in a dive on 26 April 1948) was the prototype of the F-86 jet fighter. The first production aircraft capable of over Mach 1 in level flight was the North American F-100

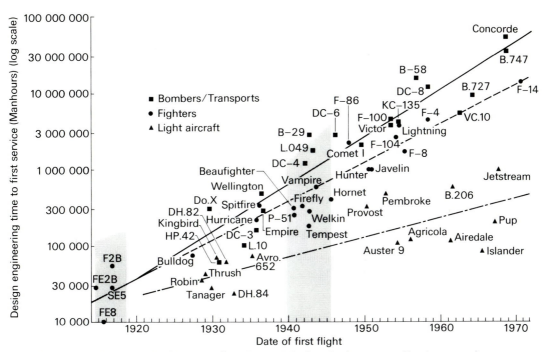

FIG. 33.18. Trends in development effort. Industrial effort (and corresponding investment) required to develop and manufacture all types of aircraft has steadily increased over the years (see also Fig. 33.19).

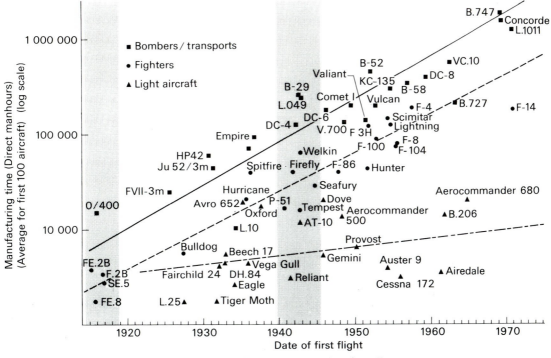

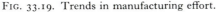

FIG. 33.19. Trends in manufacturing effort.

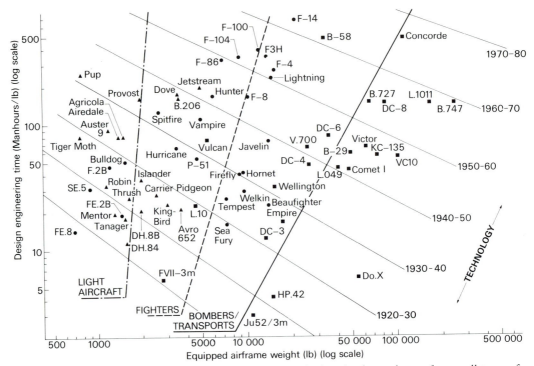

FIG. 33.20. Development complexity. Industrial effort required to develop and manufacture all types of aircraft, when related to their weight, has progressively increased with each advance in technology (see also Fig. 33.21).

fighter, which entered service in September 1954. Mach 2 (twice the speed of sound) had been first attained by the American Douglas Skyrocket research aircraft in 1953. Fighter aircraft with supersonic capabilities became commonplace in the 1950s and maximum speeds of more than Mach 2 were attained by many fighters in the 1960s. A few experimental or military types were by then capable of Mach 3. From 1961, an air-launched rocket-powered research aircraft, the North American X-15, achieved speeds of up to more than Mach 6 and heights exceeding 50 miles (80 km), which bridged the step to space flight. The latter was first achieved by the Russian Y. A. Gagarin in an Earth orbit on 12 April 1961 (Ch. 35).

Supersonic speeds had become commonplace for comparatively small, short-range military aircraft by the later 1950s. By then also, as we have seen, large subsonic jet aircraft were established for long-range military and civil duties. Long-range supersonic aircraft were slower in coming. A small number of American and Russian supersonic bombers entered service in the late 1950s and early 1960s but these aircraft normally operated subsonically, their maximum speeds being mainly to provide a brief 'dash' capability only.

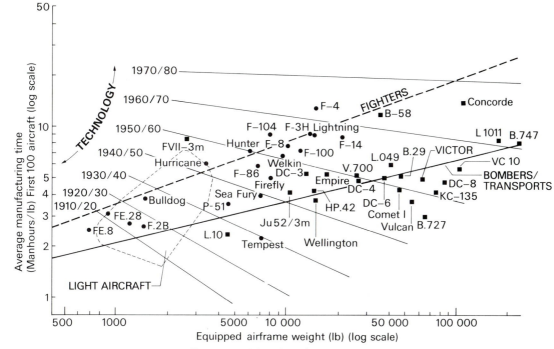

FIG. 33.21. Manufacturing complexity.

FIG. 33.22. The MiG-15, the famous Russian jet fighter (1947) of the Korean War which was the first to exploit the results of German transonic research with the use of swept wing and tail surfaces.

Long-range military aircraft, which cruised at supersonic speeds, were still a rarity in the mid-1970s when the Anglo-French B.A.C./Aerospatiale Concorde (Fig. 33.23) and Russian Tu-144 supersonic transports entered airline service.

Another line of aeronautical development from about the mid-century was one of increased emphasis on short and vertical take-off and landing (STOL, VTOL). Such aircraft were being developed for both military and civil pur-purposes from the 1950s and several STOL types entered service in the 1960s and 1970s. Short take-off and landing was not, however, a new idea: all early aeroplanes could take-off and land in quite small spaces, but the inexorable pressures of development led to aeroplanes weighing up to 400 tons, with engines of up to 80 000 hp, requiring runways 2 miles (3 km) long. These great vehicles, and smaller types with similar characteristics had revolutionized long-distance transport and the strategy and techniques of warfare but they had also created environmental problems—particularly of noise—to which shorter take-off and landing, as well as new, quieter engines, were seen as possible solutions.

By 1950 the helicopter was already the established VTOL vehicle in widespread and ever-expanding service. Helicopters are, however, comple-mentary to, rather than competitive with, fixed-wing aeroplanes. Moreover, the high power-to-weight ratio of jet engines created new opportunities for the integration of lift and propulsion, which for fixed-wing aircraft had been kept separate since Cayley. A. A. Griffith in Britain suggested VTOL by means of special light-weight jet-lift engines and this was first demonstrated by the Rolls-Royce 'Flying Bedstead' in 1953. In 1954, the American Con-vair XFY-1 'Tailsitter' turboprop fighter prototype was the first aeroplane to make a vertical take-off and landing with transition to level flight. In 1946, a Frenchman, M. Wibault, proposed swivel-jet engines for VTOL. Sir Sidney Camm's British Hawker P.1127 first demonstrated this system in 1960. Other VTOL systems were being developed but the swivel-jet Hawker Harrier (Fig. 33.24) was the first to enter service (1969).

Smaller STOL aircraft continued to be required for a great variety of uses, including many military and general aviation applications, and for scheduled transport into airports which are small or surrounded by noise-sensitive areas. Trends of development in the later 1940s already reflected these needs. They were to gain emphasis and momentum after 1950.

FIG. 33.23. The B.A.C./Aerospaciale Concorde, the first supersonic (Mach 2) transport aircraft, developed jointly by France and the U.K., entered service in 1976.

FIG. 33.24. Hawker-Siddeley Harrier, the swivel-jet which was the first V/STOL aircraft to enter service (1969).

BIBLIOGRAPHY

BEAUBOIS, H. *Airships: an illustrated history*. Macdonald and Janes, London (1973).

BROOKS, P. W. *The modern airliner: its origins and development*. Putnam, London (1961).

——. *Historic airships*. Hugh Evelyn, London (1973).

CHAMBE, R. *Histoire de l'aviation*. Flammarion, Paris (1948).

DAVIES, R. E. G. *A history of the world's airlines*. Oxford University Press, London (1964).

DOLLFUS, C., BEAUBOIS, H., and ROUGERON, C. *L'homne, l'air et l'espace*. L'Illustration, Paris (1965).

DOLLFUS, C., and BOUCHE, H. *Histoire de l'aeronautique*. L'Illustration, Paris (1932).

GIBBS-SMITH, C. H. *A history of flying*. Batsford, London (1953).

——. *Aviation: an historical survey*. H.M.S.O., London (1970).

——. *The re-birth of European aviation*. H.M.S.O., London (1974).

——, and BROOKS, P. W. *Flight through the ages*. Hart-Davis MacGibbon, London (1974).

HODGINS, E., and MAGOUN, F. A. *Sky high*. Little, Brown, and Co., Boston (1929).

HOOREBEECK, A. VAN. *La conquete de l'air*, Vols. 1 and 2. Marabout Université, Verviers (1967).

JOINT DOD–NASA–DOT STUDY. *Research and development contributions to aviation progress* (RADCAP). Department of the Air Force, Washington, D.C. (1972).

KARMAN, T. VON. *Aerodynamics*. Cornell University Press, Ithaca, N.Y. (1954).

KELLEY, F. C. *The Wright brothers*. Harrap, London (1944).

KING, H. F. *Aeromarine origins*. Putnam, London (1966).

MILLER, R., and SAWERS, D. *The technical development of modern aviation*. Routledge and Keagan Paul, London (1968).

NESSLER, E. *Histoire du vol à voile de 1506 à nos jours*. Oeuvres Francaises, Paris (1948).

PENROSE, H. *British aviation*, Vols. 1, 2, and 3. Putnam, London (1967, 1969, and 1973).

PETIT, E. *Histoire mondiale de l'aviation*. Hachette, Paris (1967).

RAE, J. B. *Climb to greatness: the American aircraft industry, 1920–60*. M.I.T. Press, Cambridge, Mass. (1968).

ROBINSON, D. H. *Giants in the sky*. Foulis, Henley-on-Thames (1973).

SCHLAIFER, R., and HERON, S. D. *Development of aircraft engines and fuels*. Harvard University Press, Boston, Mass. (1950).

SIMONSON, G. R. *The history of the American aircraft industry*. M.I.T. Press, Cambridge, Mass. (1968).

STEWART, O. *The story of air warfare*. Hamish Hamilton, London (1958).

TAYLOR, J. W. R. *A picture history of flight*. Hulton Press, London (1955).

——. *A history of aerial warfare*. Hamlyn, London (1974).

——, and MUNSON, K. *History of aviation*. Octopus Books, London (1973).

TURNER, C. C. *The old flying days*. Samson Low, Marston, London (1927).

VIVIAN, E. C., and MARSH, W. L. *A history of aeronautics*. Collins, London (1921).

WARD, B. H. (ed.) *Flight—a pictorial history of aviation*. Published by Year—the Annual Picture History, Los Angeles (1953).

WELCH, A., and WELCH, L. *The story of gliding*. John Murray, London (1965).

34

NAVIGATIONAL EQUIPMENT

E. W. ANDERSON

IT must have seemed to the mariner that the techniques of navigating had reached a plateau in 1900. The compass had developed from a piece of iron ore floated in a bowl of water (Vol. III, p. 523) into a sophisticated device mounted on gimbals within a binnacle, with pieces of magnetic material inserted to counteract iron in the ship.

Measurement of speed, originally a matter of throwing overboard a log at the end of a knotted line and counting the knots paid out while a half-minute sand-glass ran dry, now relied on a propeller trailed astern. Steamships were able to estimate the rate of progress from the engine revolutions.

Hydrographic offices had been in existence for a hundred years and charts had reached a high standard. Channels were marked by buoys and, for guidance at night, there were powerful coastal lights (Vol. V, p. 181), the descendants of the first lighthouses built over two thousand years before. In the open sea, astro-navigation had become a well-established art following John Hadley's invention of the sextant's forerunner in 1730 and the successful tests of John Harrison's remarkable timepiece in 1763.

The aids and instruments then used in navigation had one common feature: they relied on the eyes and the hands of the navigator. Instruments could be illuminated, but if the visibility were poor position could not be fixed. The mariner could reckon where he might be only from an extrapolation from past courses and speeds and use leadline soundings close to land to feel his way uncertainly towards harbour.

After 1900 equipment emerged that could support, or even supplant, the senses of man. An automatic system is able to distil into a moment of time the energies of people working many years before the journey and in an environment far more favourable than that of the craft. Technology has, however, its Achilles heel: it can perform only according to the programme laid down when it was conceived. It needs the support of the human navigator to ensure that the circumstances in which it is operating conform to those for which it was designed.

I. TWO GREAT INVENTIONS

In 1901, Guglielmo Marconi set the seal on his earlier work by bridging the Atlantic with a radio signal, and the world saw that a new dimension had been added to communications. In 1903, the Wright brothers made the first flight in a heavier-than-air machine among the sand dunes at Kitty Hawk. A new dimension had been added to transport but it took nearly five years before this great step was appreciated.

Initially, the reaction of the mariner to radio was confined to relief that his chronometer could now be checked at sea. Marconi's work had stemmed partly from the experiments of H. R. Hertz, who in 1880 transmitted a signal a distance of a few feet using parabolic reflectors. The possibilities of directional antennae were therefore already proved and direction-finding came into being in the early days of the First World War. Radio was thus destined to give the navigator eyes that could see the way even in thick fog.

The changes that the aeroplane was to introduce into navigation were longer in making an impact, and were not connected primarily with the three-dimensional nature of flight nor with the high speeds of aircraft compared to ships. The key to the Wright brothers' success was their appreciation that although a model aircraft had to be stable in order to fly itself, a manned machine could not be given this stability if it had to be flown.

It was fortunate that a suitable control sensor was now available. Originally a demonstrator's toy, the gyroscope had become a precision instrument by 1900. Indeed, the future performance of sea, underwater, air, and space control equipment was to develop in parallel with improvements in methods of gyroscope manufacture, until eventually it was feasible to control movement from place to place by self-contained navigation systems.

The non-stable aeroplane introduced a demand for control equipment fundamentally different from that of the ship or the land vehicle. This demand not only reacted on systems in the marine and surface navigation and made space flight possible, but had its influence on the broad stream of manufacture and process control. We shall now examine separately the early developments in the two fields of radio and control instrumentation.

II. DIRECTION-FINDING

As in all fields of technology, acronyms are in common use by navigators, and direction-finding is known as DF. Originally, an antenna in the form of a loop was employed. This reacts to radio waves in the same way that a strip of wood rocks in the sea swell following the slope of the waves and produces signals according to the rate of rise and fall. When at right angles to the direction in which the waves are running, no signal is produced. The null is more distinctive than the comparatively vague maximum signal and is therefore used to measure direction.

To find from which side of the loop the signal is coming, the antenna is turned so that it measures the rise and fall of the waves. To these rate signals is added the output from a conventional antenna which reacts only to the crests and troughs and is placed a quarter of a wavelength ahead of the loop so that its maximum positive signal coincides with the maximum rise of signal in the loop (Fig. 34.1). When the normal antenna is connected to the loop, the total signal will be increased.

If the waves come from the opposite direction, the normal antenna will register a trough for a maximum rate of rising signal in the loop and the total output will therefore decrease when the switch is made. Thus, by turning the loop from the null position and switching in the fixed 'sense' antenna, ambiguity in direction is resolved. The movement of the 'sense' antenna by a quarter of a wavelength is achieved electronically by phase shift.

The first radio receivers had no amplification and the large rotating loops needed for direction-finding on ships would have been too cumbersome. Therefore two fixed loops were erected at right angles and the signals were fed into two small coils correspondingly aligned, which thus reproduced the radio waves in a concentrated model form. The bearing of the transmitter could now be measured by a third small rotating 'gonio' coil. Similar systems were used for direction-finding on land.

For position-finding at sea, transmitters known as radio beacons were sited along coastlines to enable ships to measure bearings in all weathers. Similar beacons were located at airfields when airborne direction-finding became practicable. With the appearance of beacons of other types, these became known to airmen as NDBs (non-directional beacons) since they radiate equally in all directions.

By the early 1930s, improvements in radio techniques made possible the fitting of small loops in aircraft. This equipment was developed into automatic systems, displaying to the pilot the direction of the transmission to which he had tuned so that he could 'home' to his airfield beacon. The equipment was consequently known as a radio compass but, after the Second World War, it gradually acquired the more dignified name of automatic direction finding (ADF).

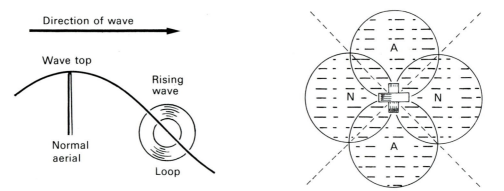

FIG. 34.1. Loop antenna with 'sense'.   FIG. 34.2. The principle of operation of radio range.

DF stations were also set up on land to find the position of a ship or an aircraft in distress by measuring the direction from which the SOS signal had come, using two fixed loops and the goniometer system. In the 1930s, the signals from the loops were amplified and fed into a cathode ray tube to operate the orthogonal deflector plates which steer the 'electronic paintbrush'. By this means, the direction of the transmission could be traced as a line radiating from the centre of a circular cathode ray tube display, direction being measured against a compass ring fitted round the perimeter of the face.

In 1928, a system of radio tramlines, known as radio range, was introduced into the U.S.A. to steer aircraft from point to point along routes clear of high ground. At each station, two fixed loops were erected and into one loop a series of As in morse was injected and into the other a parallel series of Ns. In the four diagonal lines, the signals would interact to produce a continuous steady note (Fig. 34.2).

Any deviation from one of the four chosen directions would begin to introduce more of the A or the N signal according to which side of the diagonal line the aircraft had moved. Thus, armed only with his radio and a list of the radio range stations, call signs, and frequencies, the airman could travel all over the U.S.A. so long as the weather did not cause undue interference. Similar stations were sited in Australia and Canada, but European nations were concerned mainly with overseas operations and were slow to equip their relatively small homelands.

Later in the 1930s, the ability of antennae to concentrate transmissions into narrow beams began to be used to assist aircraft approaching the runways that were now appearing. The early German systems used pairs of beams set at a fine angle, one carrying an A signal and the other an N signal, so that by using his radio the pilot could fly his aircraft down the equisignal line. In the absence of a reflector, the antennae would transmit in the opposite direction as well, forming a 'back beam' which could also be employed.

III. INSTRUMENTS

Although radio applied equally to ships and aircraft, developments in instrumentation were generally orginated by the special needs of aircraft. The first requirement was to measure distance in the third dimension. Mountaineers and balloonists already carried barometers and pilots were soon provided with similar devices known as altimeters, calibrated in feet according to a 'standard atmosphere', which assumed a certain relationship between air pressure and height. The atmosphere is, however, variable and the height recorded could be seriously in error although the actual sea-level pressure, as supplied by the meteorological forecaster, would be fed in as a datum setting and a correction made for local air temperature. Similar instruments were fitted in submarines to record depth below the surface. A barometric device with a carefully designed leak in the capsule was later developed to indicate rate of change of height or depth.

Early pilots estimated speed by the pressure on a hand held out into the slip-stream but, as early as 1911, French and English engineers were working on forward pointing Pitot tubes (after Henri Pitot (1695–1771)) leading to a barometer, the additional pressure due to the speed being calibrated in miles per hour, assuming a standard sea-level air density. Actual air density could be derived from the altimeter, allowing for the sea-level pressure setting and the local air temperature.

Had a true airspeed indicator, automatically corrected by feeding in information from the altimeter and thermometer, been available, the pilots would not have used it. The uncorrected airspeed indicator, by registering the frontal pressure on the Pitot tube also indicates the lifting pressure on the wings. Provided the reading does not fall below a certain value, the negative lift over the wings will not degenerate suddenly and cause a stall. Hence the uncorrected airspeed indicator is an essential instrument for aircraft handling. The same requirement does not apply to Pitot tubes fitted to submarines or ships.

Speed over the ground has to take account of ocean currents and tides in marine navigation, and of winds in the air. The latter, particularly for slow aircraft, may represent a large fraction of the true airspeed. A wind from one side of the craft will cause crabbing and the path over the ground will be deflected by an angle known as drift. Early pilots estimated this drift by painting diverging lines on the wings but eventually, in aircraft carrying a navigator in addition to the pilot, special drift meters were put into service.

The first aeroplane compass was a mariner's instrument set in a box of cotton wool to absorb vibration. Except at the equator, lines of magnetic force dip downwards towards the poles; this introduces major errors when the aircraft banks for a turn and may indicate a change of course in the wrong direction. The dip also holds the magnetic needles slightly to one side causing violent swinging when the craft changes course or speed. Hence the magnetic compass can be used only when flying straight and level.

Gyroscopic devices. The problems inherent in airborne magnetic compasses were solved by the directional gyroscope (DG), which appeared in the cockpits of certain long-range aircraft in the early 1920s, but was not in general service until 1928. It consisted of a gyro-wheel driven by compressed air and linked to a rotatable compass scale. At intervals, when flying straight and level, the pilot would reset this scale so that the reading agreed with the magnetic compass.

The directional gyroscope was not the first use of a gyro-wheel for course-keeping, for torpedoes had been steered by this method since 1895, and as early as 1909 Elmer Sperry was able to control a United States floatplane by use of it. However, the outstanding use of the gyroscope for steering was the gyro-compass, first built by Hermann Anschütz-Kaempfe and fitted to a German warship in 1910. In the next twenty years, instruments similar to that shown in Fig. 34.3 replaced the magnetic compass as the main steering indicator in large ships.

When a force is applied to tilt a spinning gyro-wheel, it reacts by precessing or tilting at right angles. As the Earth rotates, its surface tilts except at the poles. If a gyroscope is lying with its axis pointing east–west and is kept horizontal by a weight suspended below, the tilting of the Earth will introduce a force causing the gyro-wheel to precess until it is aligned north–south. Any drifting from this direction will re-introduce the tilting, which will precess the gyroscope back to the north–south alignment.

It was only a short step to link the gyro-compass to the helm of a ship. The first auto-helmsman was fitted by Anschütz to a Danish ship in 1916. However, the conventional gyro-compass cannot be used in an aeroplane, for the craft will follow paths not fixed to the Earth's surface and travels so fast that the gyroscope will be tilting even when flying north–south. Correc-

Fig. 34.3. The Sperry Mk II marine gyro-compass.

tions are possible but changes of course and speed introduce gross errors in high-speed craft.

The major problem in aviation was not maintenance of course but keeping the craft level, particularly at night and during long flights. The artificial horizon, produced by Sperry in 1916, was the initial solution. A gyroscope, with its axis vertical and a weight below to correct any tendency to tilt, was made to display, through linkages, a model of the real horizon which would rotate in the same direction and move up and down in the same sense as the visible horizon. The first production instruments did not appear for another 12 years, but shortly afterwards the vertical gyro-wheel was being linked to the aircraft controls to produce automatic stabilization. By the late 1930s, the autopilot had appeared, driving the control surfaces of the aeroplane by pneumatic power and steering the craft through a directional gyroscope.

The gyroscope had also been applied to the stabilization of ships by the crude method of using the energy of a large gyro-wheel to discourage rolling. Starting in 1915, about forty ships were gradually fitted with these monsters, typically weighing 600 tons with wheels 13 ft (4 m) in diameter spinning at 15 revolutions a second. By 1925, the Japanese were controlling roll in moving vessels by underwater fins driven by motors responding to a small gyroscope, and thus the modern marine stabilizer was born.

IV. SONAR AND THE BIRTH OF RADAR

In 1916, the scourge of the submarine had led the Allies to fit underwater microphones to their warships to listen to the motors of their enemies. Not unnaturally, the U-boats would shut down their propulsion systems when they heard ships approaching. Consequently, two years later these 'passive' systems were replaced by 'active' Asdic detectors (after Anti-Submarine Detection Investigation Committee) in which a pulse of sound was transmitted and the echo received. The time taken for the 'ping' to travel to and from the target was measured in order to find the range. The peacetime application was the 'echo-sounder' in which the clearance between the ship's hull and the sea bottom was recorded, generally on a continuous strip of paper. By 1930, the lead-line was fast disappearing from ships.

Subsequently, methods of concentrating the transmissions of Asdic systems into beams were developed so that direction could be found as well as distance. Particular effort was directed towards converting electrical power into sound waves and sound waves back into electrical signals. Transducers similar to loudspeakers were replaced by piezoelectric crystals and, more recently, by devices whose dimensions are altered by electrical inputs and which produce electrical outputs when they are distorted. By 1960, such systems were in common use on trawlers to detect shoals of fish (p. 350).

It is sad to reflect that so many technological innovations have been sparked off by the needs of battle. The submarine threat triggered off work on sonar in the First World War and fears of mass air raids were to lead to the development of radar in preparation for the Second. As early as 1930, the effects of a passing aircraft on signals used for direction finding were being studied in the U.S.A. and a ship detection system was being developed in Germany. Britain did not enter the field until 1935, and though the French had started earlier they were not committed to a major programme until 1939.

The basic principle of radar is identical to that of sonar. Pulses are transmitted along radio beams and the echoes are picked up by a receiver. The displays were originally linear traces on the face of a cathode ray tube. The 'electronic paintbrush' travelled across from left to right at a steady speed and was then blacked out and flicked back to the starting point. The process was synchronized with the pulse generator, so that the transmitted pulses appeared as a steady kick or 'blip' upwards and the echoes as blips to the right; the separation from the transmitting blip indicated the range. Information regarding the direction of the radio beam was taken separately from the rotating antenna.

Although Britain had started work on radar nearly five years after the U.S.A. and Germany, by 1938 a crude chain of radar stations was operational in southern England, whereas the Germans did not even start production until a year later. Robert Watson-Watt, who directed the work in Britain, was not concerned with radar as an end in itself but regarded it only as an element in an overall system. He was thus one of the early examples of a new breed of technologist, the systems engineer. He understood, to use his own words, 'the best we shall never achieve, the second best will take too long; we must settle for the third best'.

V. ELECTRONIC NAVIGATION

Early radar antennae were too bulky to be mounted on any craft except big ships. In 1939, the British invention of the cavity magnetron made high-power transmission possible in centimetre- and millimetre-wavebands. Radar antennae could now take the form of small parabolic reflectors known as 'dishes' which, in 1942, were to appear in maritime patrol aircraft and a year later in night fighters and bombers.

The plan position indicator (PPI), was already being used in ground radar stations. The cathode ray trace starts at the centre and travels outwards with blacked out returns so as to draw a series of radial lines following the rotation of the dish. As each echo is received, it brightens up the trace and produces a map in which aircraft are seen as fast-moving dots of light.

PPI displays were used for anti-submarine patrol and for blind bombing. Fig. 34.4 shows a typical radar picture taken from an aircraft. Water does not reflect radio waves unless it is rough, and therefore it appears black. Diffuse echoes from the land produce light areas, while the vertical walls of towns reflect the waves strongly and are seen as bright patches. The airborne dishes could not be made sufficiently large for accurate weapon delivery but high precision was obtainable from ground- and ship-borne antennae, and by 1943 gunlaying radars were in service.

From the outset, it was appreciated that some means to distinguish friend from foe was necessary. Accordingly, small transmitters were fitted in friendly craft which would respond to a radar beam by a signal appearing as a distinctive pattern on the radar picture. These devices belonged to a new family of equipment in which 'transponders' replied to signals from radar transmitters. Such systems were known as 'secondary radar' to distinguish them from the original echo devices known as 'primary radar'.

The highly accurate 'Oboe' bombing system employed secondary radar.

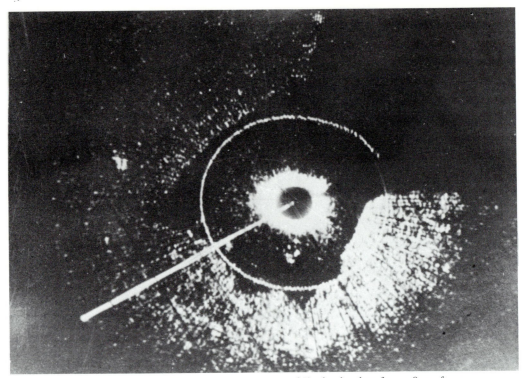

FIG. 34.4. A radar picture of the Wash, on the east coast of England, taken from 18000 ft on 12 December 1943. The photograph shows Skegness, Boston, and Sutton Bridge aerodrome.

The 'cat-and-mouse' ground stations transmitted signals which were sent back by transponders in the bomber. The 'cat' station used the response to calculate guidance information which was transmitted to the pilot as As or Ns and enabled him to follow an arc crossing the target. The 'mouse' station followed the aircraft and sent a signal when the bombs were to be released. A converse system named 'Shoran' (short range navigation) was used by the Americans. In this the aircraft initiated the transmissions and the transponders were sited on the ground.

Other secondary radar systems included the airborne transmitter 'Rebecca' which used a transponder 'Eureka', typically sited by soldiers on the ground. The responses were received by aerials on each side of the fuselage to give a crude left–right indication. Another transponder known as BABS had a beamed antenna and was used with Rebecca as an aid for approaching an airstrip.

During these developments, the Germans were not inactive although, as discussed below, their technical effort was diverted into other fields. By 1941, a most effective radar defence system was in operation but their airborne work lagged behind because they knew nothing of the magnetron until 1943, when they shot down a radar bomber. At once the Germans set to work building airborne devices to home their fighters on to the transmissions of the British bombers.

The immediate reaction of German scientists to the discovery of the magnetron illustrates the new technological war that was in progress. In the First World War, it was found that engineering advances could lead to great military success. The interrupter gear by which Fokker made it possible for German fighters to fire ahead through their propellers (p. 794) nearly succeeded in driving the Allied aircraft out of the Flanders sky.

There was another lesson to be learnt from those days. The British tank, which would probably have broken through the German army had it been properly exploited, was frittered away by the inability of military commanders to grasp its potential. In the Second World War, 'operational research' teams of mathematicians and scientists were included in the higher military staffs and played an important part in decision-making.

Let us consider some relevant examples of the so-called 'war of the wizards'. For night bombing, the Germans relied on very accurate long-range beam systems. The British scientists retaliated by injecting a suitable transmission so that the null line of the pair of beams was shifted to one side and the bombs thus fell wide of their targets. In 1942, the Germans suddenly produced a jamming system that blinded British coastal radars long enough for two German battleships besieged in Brest to escape up the English Channel.

By 1942, the British had the system known as Gee in operational service. Chains of stations transmitting coded pulses were established in Britain and the bombers were fitted with receivers to identify the time-intervals between the arrivals of the pulses. Each pair of pulses would locate the aircraft as being along a hyperbola which was marked on a special chart with the time difference. The angles at which the hyperbolae intersected over Germany were too fine for accurate bombing and the Germans soon started to jam the signals. Nevertheless, the system was invaluable for returning aircraft.

The U.S.A. produced a pulse system shortly afterwards using a lower frequency and siting the stations in pairs around the Pacific. Known as Loran (long range navigation), the equipment enabled ships and aircraft to position themselves, and it was never jammed effectively by the Japanese. A very accurate American medium-frequency hyperbolic system was introduced specially to guide the Normandy armada. The receiver measured phase differences and the system was known as Decca. Like Loran and Gee, it was an example of a new family of navigational aids that provided positional information over an area and not from specific points.

The scientists were not always destructive. For position finding at sea, the Germans developed a long-wave system of Sonne beacons, later to be known as Consol, in which patterns of waves carrying dots and dashes were rotated electronically through small sectors. With a normal loop, the U-boat could identify the sector and, by listening to the dots and dashes, locate itself along a bearing within that sector. A second Sonne station would give a second line and hence a position. The scientists decided that the stations were so useful to Allied ships and aircraft that they should be neither jammed nor faked!

VI. MISSILES AND INSTRUMENTS

As early as 1918, pilotless bomb-carrying aircraft were on the drawing boards in Britain and the U.S.A. Subsequently, the Allies concentrated on electronics but the Germans designed missiles (Ch. 35), having built rocket motors in the early 1930s. The first of these weapons, the V-1 pilotless aeroplane steered by an autopilot, appeared in 1943. An accelerometer recorded deviation from the flight path; a barometer gave height information; and a small propeller in the nose drove a counter which put the machine into a terminal dive when the distance covered was correct. The accuracy was low, for it depended on the winds across the English Channel being as forecast.

The second missile was the far more revolutionary V-2. An integrating gyroscope was carried, in which the wheel gimbals were unbalanced so that acceleration due to motor thrust built up a precession. When this reached a preset value, the motor was cut and the missile would follow a supersonic trajectory to its target. The Germans also steered bombs by signals passed by a parent aircraft along fine wires trailing from bobbins on the fins. Had the war in Europe not ended, *Wasserfall*, an anti-aircraft missile guided by radar, would soon have been in full production.

These three brilliant conceptions formed the pattern for future intercontinental ballistic, anti-tank, and anti-aircraft missiles. Meanwhile the Allies assumed that the war would be over before such novel systems could be put into operation, but they were wise enough to collect German technologists as a top priority immediately hostilities ended. Thus Wernher von Braun, who led the V-2 team, was later to launch the first United States satellite and to develop the Saturn rockets for the *Apollo* space flights.

The great advantage possessed by the V-1 and the V-2 was immunity from jamming or faking. Similar considerations led to continuing interest in astro-navigation. The Germans built gyro-stabilized sextants which were remarkably easy to use. The Allies developed bubble sextants for use in aircraft and fitted ingenious graphical systems for converting observations into positions, using optical projectors directed on to the navigator's chart.

At sea and in the air, automatic plotting devices were introduced, one device tracing a point of light across the chart according to the progress of the craft. Stabilized bombsights were also introduced. These were of two types. The British favoured models of the vector triangle of air speed, wind speed, and speed over the ground. The Americans preferred tachometric sights which followed the progress of the target and released the bomb automatically according to the angular speed and the height.

It is perhaps worth commenting on the way in which the German and the American technological philosophy differed from that of the British. The Germans in particular tended to use simple designs beautifully manufactured to produce the requisite accuracy. British engineering was generally far cruder, the accuracy being achieved by inelegant but most effective complexities.

By these contrasting methods, control systems generally, and autopilots in particular, were gradually improved. Hydraulic actuators replaced the original pneumatic drives, and were superseded after the war by all-electric systems. Gyroscopes were now driven by electric motors, and the rate gyroscope was in use in which the force of precession acted against a spring to record the rotational rate of tilt in pitch and roll.

Airborne magnetic compasses were developing in two different directions. In fighters, detectors were being mounted in wing-tips away from the engines and, in large aircraft, the directional gyroscope and the magnetic element were being combined into bulky 'gyro-magnetic' compasses. The Americans stabilized their detectors by beautifully manufactured gyroscopes but the British used cruder gyro-wheels corrected by continually switching-in the magnetic detectors. In the end, the latter system was preferred, as it became possible to place the bulky gyroscope in the fuselage and a small magnetic element in the wing-tip.

VII. COLLISION AVOIDANCE

In any form of navigation, the first step is to find the way. After a time, other people follow the pioneers; tracks are worn across the fields; and signposts erected. Finding the way becomes progressively easier but a new problem arises: collision with other travellers. Thus, in all fields, the emphasis shifts from finding the way towards avoiding collision.

At sea, collision had become a progressively more serious problem since the later years of the nineteenth century. When visibility was poor, there was no alternative to slowing down and in fog in a crowded seaway it might be a matter of heaving to or dropping anchor. The introduction of radar made it possible for the mariner to see other ships and to avoid them. In the decade following the end of hostilities, radar became the normal fitment in ships of all sizes using a PPI presentation and antennae shaped like a slice of Dutch cheese. It has been said that, in those ten short years, more money and effort was spent on navigational equipment than in all the previous centuries of marine history added together. In addition to radar, Decca had become the standard short-range aid, and Loran the long-range system.

The original radar presentation showed the ship at the centre of the display with the heading upwards though, for air operations, a compass input had been applied to give a north-up picture. The sailor preferred the display that showed him the ships in the directions that he saw them, but since the display showed relative motion it gave a false impression of the speed of other craft. A buoy, for example, appeared as a vessel moving down the face of the cathode ray tube. After a time, a 'true motion' display was designed but not introduced until the 1950s. The focus of the radiating traces on the c.r.t. was made to move according to the speed of the craft, and so the land remained static on the screen. After a time, the focus would disappear over the edge of the face and the picture would have to be shifted electronically back on to the screen. However, the true motions of other craft were now represented correctly and buoys appeared as stationary dots.

We have seen that radar can identify land shapes. In ships, radar pictures have been projected optically on to the coastlines portrayed by the navigator's chart. Transponders were also sited at crucial points to make identification more certain. The inputs from radar were eventually to be fed into computers in the hope that automatic anti-collision advice could be presented to the mariner.

In the air, it was found that an aeroplane coming head-on presents too small a target, and travels too fast, for individual avoiding action to be practicable. Hence, air traffic control (ATC), was developed rapidly after the war to maintain adequate separation between aircraft travelling along airways. Radar was the tool used by the ground controller. It included not only a PPI picture to show the horizontal situation but also height-finding radars to measure the vertical position. Radars working over small sectors were also used to guide aircraft down towards touch-down. Once again, radar became the main collision avoidance aid, to be supported later by computing.

Airborne radar was still carried on commercial airliners but only in order to detect the large water droplets which accompany thunderstorms and serious turbulence. It will also be remembered that the altimeter measures pressure in the guise of an inaccurate representation of height above sea level. With the growth of air traffic control, this reading became a key item in collision avoidance. Provided two aircraft had a separation figure of, say, 1000 ft (300 m) on their respective altimeters, they would not collide. That the altimeter readings gave rather vague measures of absolute height was of less significance.

VIII. AIRBORNE NAVIGATIONAL AIDS

When the U.S.A. became involved in the Second World War, the other aircraft-producing nations had been concentrating on military needs. It was accepted by the Allies that American air transport manufacture would continue, and the International Civil Aviation Organization (I.C.A.O.) was subsequently inaugurated at Chicago in 1944. Thereafter, aircraft equipment was to become increasingly standardized on aids approved by I.C.A.O.

The radio range had tended to concentrate the ever-growing volume of air traffic along specific paths. The medium frequency was vulnerable to interference, and control of aircraft by aural means was found to be tiring over long distances. The U.S.A. therefore proposed a new 'point navigation' system originally known as ORB (omnidirectional range beacon) but later to be developed as VOR (the prefix V standing for V.H.F.).

At each beacon, two continuous waves modulated with a steady oscillation are transmitted, one from a beam rotated electronically and the other from a fixed antenna. The modulations are arranged to be in step when the beam points north, 90° out of phase when the beam is east, 180° out of phase when south, and 270° when west. In the aircraft, the phase difference of the modulations is measured and displayed on a dial as a direction.

A long-drawn-out battle was to be fought at I.C.A.O. between protagonists of the 'point navigation' VOR system and the British Decca, the short-range marine 'area navigation' aid. VOR was selected although, in the event, concentrations of traffic over VOR stations would have been avoided by the adoption of Decca. However, the introduction of computing has made it

Fig. 34.5. Indicator for zero reader flight director.

feasible to achieve area navigation using a reference system based on points. At each VOR station, it was planned to site a transponder to be operated by a simple non-directional radar in the aircraft. The device, known as DME (distance measurement equipment) was not introduced for many years.

Concurrently, the radio approach beams were gradually replaced by ILS (instrument landing system) designed with vertical U.H.F. 'glide path' beams of high precision in addition to the horizontal V.H.F. 'localizer' beams. In place of As and Ns, modulations were superimposed on the transmissions and compared, the results being displayed on a combined up–down and left–right meter. The early type of instrument is shown in Fig. 34.5; it was later combined with the artificial horizon to form the 'attitude director'.

Both VOR and ILS gave signals that could be coupled into an autopilot, and the way was open for 'push-button' air navigation and automatic landing. The latter required a radio altimeter to measure ground clearance. It was a continuous-wave downwards-beamed radar, the modulation transmitted being compared to the modulation of the returning echo. A phase measurement could then determine distance above the runway over a limited range. It is interesting to find measurement of phase difference appearing in so many types of post-war equipment.

Before the Second World War, civil aircraft had generally been operated by one or two pilots, a separate navigator being carried for flights overseas. After the war, this practice continued for a time and astro-navigation was made possible in the new high-altitude aeroplane by a periscopic sextant protruding through the roof of the pressure cabin. However, by 1950 it became apparent that radio could measure speed by the well-known Doppler principle. This had already been applied in 1944 to the detection of moving targets.

It had been believed that Doppler radar could not work over water, but British engineers persisted until it became possible to record speed along the line of the fuselage and at right angles to it except over a flat calm. This ability, combined with the new gyro-magnetic compasses, enabled a continuous plot of ground positions to be presented to the pilot. There was no more need for navigators and their periscopic sextants.

Aircraft instruments were basically unchanged but warning devices were added to show when a malfunction had occurred. In addition, the high-speed jet aircraft was provided with a Mach meter which registered speed through the air as a mach number, a multiple of the local speed of sound (after Ernst Mach (1838–1916)).

IX. INERTIAL NAVIGATION

The V-1 and the V-2 autopilots paved the way for systems that could follow the position of a craft without the need for any external sources of information. Initially, these 'inertial navigators' were developed to steer the new long-range ballistic missiles which the Americans and the Russians were building with the help of German technologists. The object was to ensure that before the end of the two or three minutes' burn of the rocket motors the warhead would be on its correct trajectory towards the aiming point and travelling at the correct speed according to the position at which the thrust was cut off.

It was considered reasonable to produce accelerometers and integrators that were sufficiently accurate for these short periods of time, and this has suggested that the new branch of navigation was based on the double integration of accelerations. However, resulting errors would have depended on the square of the time of operation, and would thus have grown rapidly. Fortunately, it became apparent that the accelerometers were in effect measuring the direction of the local force of gravity and the gyroscopes were 'remembering' the direction of gravity at the point where the journey started, position depending on the difference between these directions. Thus the key component became the gyroscope; for example, in long submarine journeys below the Arctic ice, the requirement for accelerometer accuracy was found to be relatively low. For every minute of angle of gyroscope drift, however, the 'memory' of the starting point would be in error by a nautical mile.

X. THE TECHNOLOGIST

Only in the early days were trains and automobiles regarded by the public as dangerous but aircraft, although a hundred times safer than private motor vehicles in terms of deaths per passenger mile, have never outlived their reputation for being unsafe. For this reason, the makers of air navigation equipment and instruments have always taken great pains to ensure the reliability of their products. Very rigorous inspections have been instituted since the early days to ensure that, should an accident occur, the manufacturer would not be burdened by heavy liabilities. The procedures were in many instances defined by government agencies; they affected design in all fields of navigation and had a wide influence on industry as a whole.

To meet the stringent safety requirements, the 'reliability engineer' appeared, his task being to ensure that the design would meet the necessary safety standards. As soon as manufacture starts, the 'quality engineer' comes into his own, making certain that the materials and components employed will pass the final tests. From the work of such specialists, the new 'clean rooms' were to appear, work on navigation equipment being undertaken in conditions of asepsis previously associated only with surgical operating theatres.

To provide insurance against malfunction, a philosophy of redundancy was adopted, originally taking the form of the human redundancy implicit in the two pilots of commercial airliners with their two sets of instruments. The method proved to be invaluable for another reason. The reliability of the new complex systems could not be proved except over a period of test so long that the device might be obsolete before it was accepted. However, by carefully planned redundancy, the reliability of each part could be tested in the field in perfect safety over relatively short periods of time and the fault rate of the whole redundant system estimated with certainty.

'Systems engineering' (Ch. 43) has already been mentioned in connection with pre-war radar. Although navigation did not originate the term, this new approach to problems was evident in the development of instruments and equipment during and after the Second World War. Radio and instrumentation were integrated, the linking of the autopilot to ILS and to the radio altimeter being a typical example. With the invention of the transistor in 1948 and the subsequent appearance of miniaturized modules, the digital computer

TABLE 34.1
Navigational technology 1900–50

| Date | Radio | | Control instrumentation | |
	Navigation aids	Radar (& sonar)	Instruments	Control equipment
Before 1900			Sextant, chronometer, magnetic, compass, and log	Torpedo steering systems
1900				
1910			Altimeter	
1920	Marine DF	(Asdic) (Echo sounder)	Airspeed indicator	Experimental autohelmsman Marine stabilisers
1930	Radio range, Airborne DF		Directional gyro	Artificial horizon
1940	Gee	Land based radar Naval radar	Bubble sextants	Autopilots, pneumatic & hydraulic
1950	Decca Loran VOR and ILS	Airborne radar Shipborne & ATC radars Radio altimeter	Gyro-magnetic compass Periscopic sextant	Missile autopilots Electric autopilot
After 1950	DME	Doppler (fish sonar)	Pitot log	Inertial navigator

appeared, able to link together an extraordinary diversity of equipment to serve a common purpose.

Thus the systems engineer came into his own, acting as the midwife of technology to ensure the timely and effective delivery of the new, extremely complex systems. His first step would be to identify the objectives, a task that could be extremely difficult since conflicts could arise between aims. A mathematical model might then be set up, leading to optimization studies in which the advantages of various approaches would be compared.

When the best solution had been chosen, a flow diagram would be constructed to demonstrate how the various processes would be dovetailed to meet the target dates. The prototype equipment would generally be tried out on a simulator, using mathematical models of the situations that could be met in actual operations. From then onwards, the systems engineer would continually be reverting to his original questioning role, asking not only 'How?' but also 'Why?'.

Table 34.1 shows the overall technological development during the half-century from 1900 to 1950. The engineers responsible learnt one other lesson during this period. Navigation is a matter of guiding people and their goods over land and sea, through the air and, more recently, through space. None of those concerned can avoid being aware of the significance of social and of environmental factors. Perhaps this is the greatest lesson that navigation has to teach technology as a whole.

BIBLIOGRAPHY

ANDERSON, E. W. *Principles of air navigation*. Methuen, London (1951).
HITCHENS, H. L., and MAY, W. E. *From lodestone to gyro-compass*. Hutchinson, London (1952). (1952).
INTERNATIONAL HYDROGRAPHIC BUREAU. *Radio aids to marine navigation*. Monaco (1952).
PORTER, A. *Introduction to servo-mechanisms*. Wiley, New York (1950).
PUCKETT, A. E., and RAMO, S. (eds.) *Guided missile engineering*. McGraw Hill, New York (1958). (1958).
RICHARDSON, K. I. T. *The gyroscope applied*. Hutchinson, London (1954).
SONNENBURG, G. J. *Radar and electronic navigation*. Newnes, London (1952).
WEEMS, P. H. V., and LEE, C. V. *Marine navigation*. Van Nostrand, New York (1952).

The following books lead on from 1950:

ANDERSON, E. W. *Principles of navigation*. Hollis & Carter, London: Elsevier, New York (1966). (1966).
DRAPER, C. S. W., WRIGLEY, W., and HOVORKA, J. *Inertial guidance*. Pergamon Press, London and New York (1960).
RIDENOUR, L. N. (ed.). *Radar system engineering*. McGraw Hill, New York (1965).
SAVANT, C. J. *Control systems design*. (2nd edn.). McGraw Hill, New York (1964).

35

SPACE TECHNOLOGY

ANTHONY R. MICHAELIS

NEIL A. ARMSTRONG, an American civilian, took 'a small step' on to the surface of the Moon on 20–1 July 1969. This was 43 years after R. H. Goddard achieved the first liquid fuel rocket flight; 12 years after *Sputnik 1*; and only 8 years after Yuri A. Gagarin first circled the Earth in space. The *Apollo* Programme—six men had walked and six men had driven their vehicles on the Moon by 14 December 1972—was indeed a giant technological leap for mankind, the greatest so far.

During the Second World War, research and development of the A-4 (V-2) rocket were forced to a successful conclusion by the German Army at a cost of about $150m. At precisely the same time in history, the American Government, using its Army, industry, and best scientists, paid $2000m. for the Manhattan Project, which produced the first plutonium bomb. The American National Aeronautics and Space Administration (NASA), used a budget of $24000m. for the *Apollo* Programme; although the American Department of Defense made not inconsiderable contributions, *Apollo* was a technological peacetime achievement that came within its original 10-year time limit and within its original budget. Never before had so many technological problems been solved in so short a space of time and at such small cost in human life. Three astronauts, R. Chaffee, V. Grissom, and E. White, lost their lives during a fire in a ground test of an *Apollo* capsule on 27 January 1967.

In contrast, the Russian space effort was entirely controlled by a secret military bureaucracy. At first highly successful, it rapidly fell behind when difficulties arose with their *Soyuz* spacecraft [1]. The Russians made every effort to be the first on the Moon, but when they lost four cosmonauts, V. Komarov (April 1967), G. T. Dobrovolsky, V. N. Volkov, and V. I. Patsayev (June 1971), both tragedies occurring on *Soyuz* flights, their Moon programme came to a halt.

Apollo's spectacular success was, in the last analysis, due to a management revolution which welded government, industry, and the universities into a unique partnership. In practice, it meant inventing new systems and techniques, particularly for quality control, frequently supported by computer programmes, which directed, in time and space, the mental and physical activities of the 500000 people engaged on the *Apollo* programme. Only thus was it possible for each partner to contribute its own excellence. Industry could give its own research and manufacturing facilities as well as technological expertise and flexibility in manpower, which the public service could never match economically. NASA's function was primarily that of integrating and directing. It acted as the focus of transfer for management skills and experience from one industrial company to another. From the wisdom of the universities, accumulated over centuries in all branches of knowledge, came the basic sciences from which space technology grew with such astonishing rapidity.

This management revolution was foreshadowed during the construction and massive production of the A-4 rocket, and it arose again independently in the Manhattan Project. As both these examples of 'big technology' were secret wartime activities, no lesson has been learned from them. Robert Oppenheimer, Director of the Los Alamos Laboratory and the brilliant mind behind the research and development of the first atomic bombs, once expressed his experience in the following manner [2]: 'We know that the only way to avoid error is to detect it and that the only way to detect it, is to inquire. We know that in secrecy error undetected will flourish and subvert.' And this very simple truth may well explain why an American first walked on the Moon and not a Russian.

The management revolution is undoubtedly the most important benefit and lesson from the *Apollo* programme; unfortunately, it has also remained the least well-known, although none of it is secret. James E. Webb, the Administrator of NASA until 1969, wrote a book about it [3a], and further technical details can be elicited from NASA headquarters in Washington (see Bibliography and particularly [3b]).

I. THE DREAM AND THE PRECURSORS

The dream of travelling to the stars and planets is as old as man himself. Once he had learnt that at least the planets might be solid bodies, he peopled them with mythological gods and goddesses; we have Lucian of Samosata's account (about A.D. 150) of the first fictional voyage to the Moon—by sailing ship—and how men from Earth joined in the war between the Sun and the Moon gods. As century followed century, writers learnt to base their fictional tales on soundly established astronomical and physical facts and theories. They knew that Galileo (1610) had described the mountains of the Moon. Newton in his *Principia* (1687) had stated his Third Law: 'Actioni contrariam semper et aequalem esse reactionem', the immutable and universal basis of all rocket propulsion. In 1783 the first Montgolfier balloon had risen in the sky. Jules Verne's *De la Terre à la Lune* (1865) forecast quite accurately many features of the *Apollo* Programme a hundred years later, a remarkable achievement indeed. However, like many other precursors, Verne grossly underestimated the technological difficulties which man was to solve before flying the 800 000 km from the Earth to the Moon and back again.

Before 1900, three outstanding pioneers of space flight were born: the Russian Konstantin Tsiolkovski, the German–Rumanian Hermann Oberth, and the American Robert H. Goddard. Tsiolkovski worked out the basic principles of space flight, such as staging (one rocket firing when its carrier rocket's fuel was exhausted); the importance of high exhaust velocity from liquid-fuel rockets; and the possibility of using plants to produce oxygen for long space voyages. He had conceived these ideas by 1895.

Oberth in his two books of 1923 and 1929 [4] set out the mathematics and design concepts of large spacecraft with clustered liquid fuel rockets for space travel. In August 1930, he even carried out a static firing in Berlin of a rocket engine that developed a thrust of 7 kg, using petrol and liquid oxygen (LOX) as propellents, and it was due to his writings that German rocket enthusiasts were inspired to start their Rocket Society in 1927.

II. THE FIRST ROCKET FLIGHTS

Rockets, using a mixture of saltpetre (potassium nitrate), sulphur, and charcoal, the so-called gunpowder or black powder, were apparently first used by Chinese military engineers in A.D. 1232. (A definitive account awaits publication in Vol. V Part I of Joseph Needham's *Science and Civilization in China*.) Using various mixtures of these solid propellents, war rockets proved decisive in India against the British in 1792; in the burning of Copenhagen in 1807, started by W. Congreve's rockets; and in the battle leading to the capture of Washington by the British in 1814. Solid fuel rockets were also used extensively in the nineteenth century for life-saving (Fig. 35.1) and whaling.

Soon after the formation of the German Rocket Society, solid fuel rockets were attached to racing cars, built by Fritz von Opel in 1928, and speeds up to 290 km/h were reached on roads and rails. Today, solid fuel rockets are chosen for strap-on boosters and for atomic warhead missiles which need to

FIG. 35.1. Firing a Carté rocket (solid fuel) and line across the wreck of the *Mary Grey*, lying off Seaton Carew, Durham (1851).

be stored in a state of instant readiness over long periods. For example, the boosters of the *Titan–Centaur* launch vehicle, which sent the *Viking* life-searching spacecraft on its voyage to Mars in 1975, used in their motors powdered aluminium as fuel with ammonium perchlorate as oxidizer, the two chemicals being incorporated in a synthetic rubber binder. The two solid fuel booster rockets, each 3 m in diameter and 25·9 m long, produced a combined thrust of 10·6m. newtons (1088 tons), accelerating the 640-ton vehicle from rest to 5000 km/h in 111 seconds.

A rocket, in order to move, must generate a propulsive force, namely its thrust. This is expressed in newtons, tons, or kilograms. In present designs this force is generated by the combustion of chemical fuels in a rocket engine, and these fuels can best be compared by their exhaust velocities, measured in metres per second. The overall efficiency of the rocket is defined by its specific impulse, measured in seconds; this is the thrust (in kilograms) per kilogram of propellant burned per second.

This basic theory of rocket propulsion was clear to Tsiolkovski, Oberth,

FIG. 35.2. Professor Robert Goddard with his first gasoline and liquid oxygen rocket (1926), the small apparatus at the very top of the structure; he thought then that greater stability would result during flight if the remainder trailed behind.

FIG. 35.3. Goddard's later rocket experiments (1935) used a quite sophisticated launch platform, shielded from the wind.

and Goddard, and they also knew that no solid rocket fuel could compare in exhaust velocity with that of liquid fuels. For example, the specific impulse of a black-powder rocket motor would be about 60 seconds; that of the A-4 engine, using alcohol and LOX, 218 seconds; and that of the liquid hydrogen and LOX engine of the *Saturn V*, 450 seconds. Alternatively, if theoretical exhaust velocities for chemical fuels are calculated, solid dynamite would produce 3300 m/s; gasoline or kerosene in LOX about 4500 m/s; and liquid hydrogen in LOX about 5600 m/s. In practice, none of these theoretical values can be achieved.

Goddard, a genius of mechanical ingenuity, was the first to translate theory into successful practice; near Worcester, Massachusetts, on 16 March 1926, his gasoline and LOX propelled rocket (Fig. 35.2) rose 12·5 m in 2·5 seconds and fell to Earth at a distance of 56 m. It was the world's first liquid-fuel rocket flight, an event comparable to the Wright Brothers' achievement at Kitty Hawk in 1903.

During the next 15 years, Goddard, while Professor of Physics at Clark

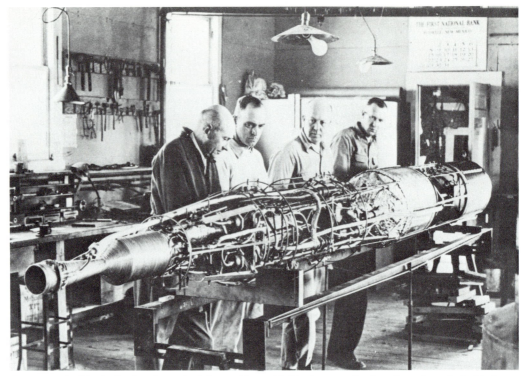

FIG. 35.4. Goddard, the first from the left, working with his three mechanics, the only technical help he had at Roswell, New Mexico, U.S.A. (1939).

University, pursued his lonely progress towards a research rocket to carry meteorological instruments to great heights (Figs. 35.3 and 4). In the course of this work, mostly at Roswell in east-central New Mexico, helped by three instrument makers, a machinist, and a technical assistant (his devoted wife, Esther C. Goddard), he tried out most aspects of current rocket technology in his laboratory, in static engine firings, or in actual flight. His financial support first came from the Smithsonian Institution (1917–29), and later from the Guggenheim family (1929–41)—at about $15000 a year—on a recommendation by Charles Lindbergh.

Goddard's full experimental notes of his Roswell work [5] were published after his death and are an impressive record of his far-sightedness, his outstanding skill as one of the first engineer-physicists, and, above all, his patience. Here is the briefest record of his life's work:

Considered liquid hydrogen and liquid oxygen as rocket fuels (1909); first research paper ridiculed in the *New York Times* (13 January 1920); first rocket flight at Roswell: height 610 m (30 December 1930); automatic launch sequential system invented (29

September 1931); first used gyroscope in gimbals to actuate vanes in exhaust stream to steer rocket (19 April 1932); first tests of centrifugal pumps for gasoline and LOX in laboratory (spring 1934); A-series rockets achieved velocity of 1125 km/h and height of 2·3 km (February–October 1935); K-series rockets achieved specific impulse of 135 seconds (November 1935–February 1936); first gimbal-mounted rocket engine, controlled by gyroscope (28 July 1937).

Goddard constantly refined his complex designs. His last rockets, the P-series— 6·7 m long, 45 cm in diameter, launch weight 210 kg—had centrifugal pumps for gasoline and LOX, and an umbilical compressed nitrogen pipe to start them (September 1938–10 October 1941, last test). Although there were numerous minor explosions, there was never a major accident during the many static firings and 31 rocket flights from Roswell.

Because of the derisive newspaper sarcasm in 1920, Goddard published little except patents. Were the major steps of his work known to the German rocket technologists, the only other serious workers in this field? In spite of much research on this question, some doubt still persists; H. F. Guggenheim [5] was affirmative on this point in 1948, yet F. C. Durant (private communication) in 1975 denied the existence of such a link after he had searched for it for 25 years.

In the first German rocket flight tests by Willy Ley [6] and Klaus Riedel (1931 and 1932) a water–alcohol mixture was used as fuel and LOX as oxidant. A total of 270 static tests and 87 ascents were carried out at the famous *Raketenflugplatz*, in the suburbs of Berlin. The interest of the German Army in liquid-fuel rockets dates from the spring of 1932, and in November of that year, three months before Hitler came to power, Wernher von Braun joined their Weapons Development Branch with the comment that 'the Army's money would be the only hope of putting our work on a sound financial basis' [7]. During the next year he carried out static firing tests of the A-1 (A stands for *Aggregat*) a thrust of 150 kg being achieved. The next model, the A-2, reached a height of 2·4 km in a 16-second flight using alcohol and LOX (December 1934). At that time, von Braun had 80 assistants of various qualifications working for him, and his hope had come true: the German Army offered the huge sum of 11m. marks for rocket research (summer 1935). With such means at their disposal, von Braun and his team could rapidly equal and surpass Goddard's research efforts. A vast new rocket experimental station, at Peenemünde on the Baltic Sea, became operational (April 1937) with von Braun as Technical Director. Eight years later (1945) there were 20000 people working there, and a total of 400m. marks had been spent on research and development.

Using alcohol and LOX, like all subsequent German rockets, the A-3 was designed for 1500 kg thrust with gyro-controlled molybdenum vanes in its exhaust, but it was a failure (1937). The A-5, the next series, proved successful and heights of over 12 km were reached; graphite vanes were employed and parachutes were used to recover some of the 25 rockets launched (1938 and 1939).

At the outbreak of the Second World War a work-force of 3500 German Army officers and men was drafted to Peenemünde, and scientific problems were given out to German universities (for example, the development of integrating accelerometers, pump impellers, Doppler radio-tracking of trajectory, and computers). However, it was not until 3 October 1942 that the first A-4 flew successfully, reaching a height of 96 km, with a range of 190 km and a supersonic speed of 5280 km/h. For propaganda purposes, the A-4 was also called the V-2: the 'V' here stands for *Vergeltungswaffe* or vengeance

FIG. 35.5. A German A-4 or V-2 test-fired by its crew for the British Army at Cuxhaven at the mouth of the Elbe (1945). A fair number of A-4 rockets were captured by the Allies.

weapon. It incorporated many advances in rocket technology initiated by Goddard: for example, centrifugal pumps driven by a steam turbine of 540 hp, and lubricated by LOX. Walter R. Dornberger, then the General in Command of Peenemünde, commented at the celebration following this flight: 'We have proved rocket propulsion practicable for space travel' [8]. (For an account of navigational aids see Ch. 34.)

But over a hundred further test firings, some with warheads, were necessary before large-scale production at a rate of 10 A-4s a day—later increased to 30 a day (spring 1944) with concentration camp labour—could proceed at the underground factory of Mittelwerke in the Harz. A total of 518 A-4 rockets reached London, the first falling on 7 September 1944; in southern England 2511 men, women, and children were killed, and 5870 seriously injured. A further 642 A-4s were launched (Fig. 35.5).

III. MANNED SPACE FLIGHT

Dornberger's prediction was indeed correct, although it took almost exactly two decades before Yuri Gagarin in *Vostok 1* made space travel a reality with his single orbit around our planet (12 April 1961). It is impossible to tell here the detailed history of space technology during these two decades, most of which is in any case beyond the assigned end of this work. Eugene M. Emme [9], and Monte D. Wright [12] have chronicled contemporary American space events. All historical American material is freely available to the interested scholar, but only on rare occasions—for example in the articles by J. E. Oberg, R. F. Gibbons, and A. Kendon [1]—can a critical glimpse be obtained of Russian space technology.

Rocket engines, fuel pumps, turbines, valves, tubing, tanks, gyroscopes, accelerometers, guidance and control systems, computers (for use both inside rockets and spacecraft as well as on Earth) had to be designed, tested, and manufactured to hitherto unimagined specifications of reliability. For the 12m. individual parts of the *Apollo* rockets and spacecraft, 99·9999 per cent reliability was sought and attained. Mechanical and electronic instruments, pressure and strain gauges, transducers, beacons and recorders—often miniaturized, always of minimum weight—had to be created. New material processing techniques, for example explosive forming and chemical milling, were required, both for standard materials and for the newer metals—tungsten, molybdenum, beryllium, and titanium—so extensively used in space technology. New rocket fuels, particularly liquid hydrogen, had to be produced in tonnage quantities, and vast world-wide telecommunication networks had to be erected, many of them in space, if the American astronauts on the Moon were to keep in touch with their home planet.

In addition to the pure engineering aspects of space technology, a second range of completely novel problems, partly physiological and partly psychological, had to be assessed, explored, and solved, if man was to travel safely and in moderate comfort for many days or weeks in space. Temperature protection against the cold of space and against the heat of re-entry, including space-suit design; precautions against meteorite impact, cosmic rays, and ultraviolet radiation from the Sun; the provision of food and drink, and of a breathable atmosphere inside the spacecraft; of reliable telecommunications; of computerized navigational aids; the generation and storage of electric power; and finally the management of human waste—these were all problems which were solved, often brilliantly, before Man could set foot on the Moon.

Between *Vostok 1* (1961) and *Apollo 11* (1969), the first lunar landing by a man, there had been 20 American manned space flights of the *Mercury*, *Gemini*, and *Apollo* series, solving step by step the engineering and physiological problems. The Russians had launched flights during the same period, the *Vostok*, *Voskhod*, and *Soyuz* series, all of which however remained in Earth orbit, with a greatest apogee of 492 km. A joint *Apollo–Soyuz* Earth orbital flight took place in July 1975; a novel piece of docking equipment, called androgenous, was the only technological advance.

One of the many great engineering achievements of the *Apollo* Programme was the Lunar Roving Vehicle (LRV), first used on *Apollo 15* (Fig. 35.7) (31 July 1971). From an operational point of view, the safe recovery of the *Apollo 13* spacecraft, which partially exploded on 13 April 1970, was most remarkable. The record-breaking performance of the 100-ton *Skylab* on its 112m. kilometre journey around the Earth in 2476 orbits, with its third crew who returned on 8 February 1974 staying 84 days in space, remained unbeaten for just four years. The Russian 19-ton *Salyut 6* with two cosmonauts aboard broke this record in March 1978.

IV. UNMANNED SPACE VEHICLES

Of the two thousand unmanned space vehicles launched by the end of 1977, roughly one-third were devoted to pure science, astronomy, planetary exploration, the life sciences and selenographic research; one-third were application satellites for Earth resources, weather data, telecommunications, and navigation; and one-third were for military surveillance—the photographic and television reconnaissance satellites.

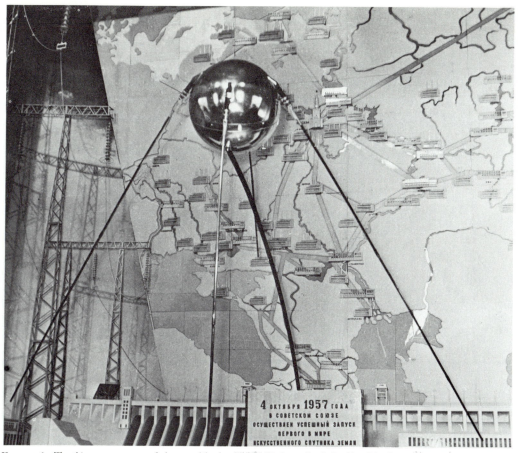

FIG. 35.6. To the amazement of the world, the U.S.S.R. launched the Earth's first artificial satellite on 4 October 1957, thus demonstrating their advanced rocket technology. The satellite's radio emission provoked fear and admiration and led in America to a complete re-evaluation of science, the foundation of NASA, and, four years after its launch, to President Kennedy's demand to land an American astronaut on the Moon. *Sputnik 1* here seen in replica at a Russian exhibition weighed 84 kg had a diameter of 60 cm and an elliptical orbit ranging from 224 km to 896 km, circling the Earth every 90 minutes. It carried two radio transmitters working in phase; it disintegrated on 4 January 1958.

From the simple 'beep-beep' radio signal of *Sputnik 1* (1957) (Fig. 35.6) developed tens of thousands of telecommunication channels spanning the Earth in 1975; they were relayed from satellites in synchronous orbit, 35 900 km above the equator. (*Early Bird* was the first, launched on 16 April 1965.) American and Russian planetary probes have regularly impacted and soft-landed on other heavenly bodies (*Luna 2* was the first on the Moon; 12 September 1959) and photographed them (*Luna 3*, provided the first photographs of the far side of the Moon on 4 October 1959). More sophisticated probes to the planets have landed robot vehicles (*Luna 16*, 12 September 1970); explored the

FIG. 35.7. *Apollo 15* near the base of the Apennine Mountains on the Moon. On the left the Lunar Module, on the right the Lunar Roving Vehicle, both at Hadley Base (1971).

FIG. 35.8. *Apollo 15*'s Command and Service Module in deep space, as seen by an artist (1971). The astronaut on the left, Al Worden, is collecting a film cassette while James Irwin is paying out to him the umbilical-tether line. This event is pictured at about 320000 km from Earth.

FIG. 35.9. The end of an era was reached when *Apollo 17* astronauts walked in the Taurus–Littrow area of the Moon (1972). The scientific instruments which they and previous *Apollo* crews left on the Moon continued to send their results for many years after the last astronaut had returned to Earth.

asteroid belt and Jupiter; left the solar system (*Pioneer 10*, 2 March 1972); and have searched for life on Mars (*Viking*, August 1975).

Apart from Russia and America, France (26 November 1965), Japan (11 February 1970), China (24 April 1970), and Britain (28 October 1971) have launched satellites of their own, mostly for political prestige. Furthermore, Russian and American launch vehicles were placed at the disposal of their respective friends for national satellites and even for single experiments. It was expected that the American *Shuttle*, a re-usable rocket-propelled space vehicle, operational by 1980, would replace at much lower cost almost all previous American launchers and place 30 tons of payload, either manned or unmanned, into low Earth orbits.

V. THE OUTLOOK

The launch of the last, the 32nd, *Saturn* rocket for the joint *Apollo–Soyuz* flight in July 1975, brought to an end the *Apollo* era. No American astronaut is expected in space until the *Shuttle* becomes operational in 1980, although with the now perfected *Soyuz*, Russian cosmonauts are expected to continue Earth-orbital and perhaps to attempt Moon-orbital flights.

The vast amount of technological benefits gained during the *Apollo* era and from other American space programmes is contained in more than 750000 scientific and technical reports, all available from NASA headquarters in Washington. But other, more intangible, effects have become apparent, some favourable and others unfavourable. C. P. Boyle in 1973 wrote a highly readable review of 90 examples [10]; they range from art and poetry inspired by space technology, to the use of reconnaissance satellites for making arms limitation agreements practical.

Still less tangible is the hypothesis that a new renaissance of the spirit of mankind is in the making, just as the new geography of Columbus and Magellan, as well as the new astronomy of Galileo and Copernicus revolutionized the thinking of Europe. Emme [9] and particularly Arthur C. Clarke, have advanced this challenging idea. There can be no doubt that technologists will not fail when their skills are required for more daring space exploration. Chemical fuels for rocket engines reached their limits with the end of *Apollo* and much prototype work has already been carried out in America with electrical (ion) and nuclear propulsion systems; these have been reviewed by Durant [11].

Will space technology ever achieve its ultimate goal and bring Man from this planet into contact with intelligent inhabitants of another solar system?

At present, at least, this seems unlikely since the velocity of light, 300000 km/s, and the short span of human life, set natural limits to space exploration in time, and hence distance, in the vast expanse of the Universe.

REFERENCES

[1] OBERG, JAMES E. The hidden history of the *Soyuz* project.
KENDON, ANTHONY. An analysis of the masses of Russian spacecraft.
GIBBONS, RALPH F. Soviet military space tests. All in *Spaceflight*, **17**, Nos. 8–9 (1975).

[2] DAVIS, NUEL PHARR. *Lawrence and Oppenheimer*. Simon Schuster, New York (1968).

[3] (a) WEBB, JAMES E. *Space Age management—the large-scale approach*. McGraw-Hill, New York (1968).
(b) SEAMANS, ROBERT C., and ORDWAY, FREDERICK I. The *Apollo* tradition—an object lesson for the management of large-scale technological endeavors. *Interdisciplinary Science Reviews*, **2**, 270 (1977).

[4] OBERTH, HERMANN. *Die Rakete zu den Planetenräumen* and *Wege zur Raumschiffahrt*. R. Oldenbourg, Munich (1923 and 1929, respectively).

[5] GODDARD, ROBERT H. *Rocket development. Liquid-fuel rocket research 1924–1941*. (Edited by E. C. Goddard and G. E. Pendray.) Prentice-Hall, New York (1948).
See also: *The Papers of R. H. Goddard*. (Edited by E. C. Goddard). McGraw-Hill (1970). and: 'The Robert H. Goddard Collection' at the National Air and Space Museum, Smithsonian Institution, Washington D.C.; representative of his life's work, correspondence, reports, photographs, and motion picture films.

[6] LEY, WILLY. *Rockets, Missiles and Space Travel*. Chapman and Hall, London (1951).

[7] BRAUN, WERNHER VON. Reminiscences of German Rocketry. *Journal of the British Interplanetary Society*, May 1956.

[8] DORNBERGER, WALTER R. *A Faultless Launching—The First V-2*. Bechtle Verlag, Esslingen am Neckar. (1952).

[9] EMME, EUGENE M. Space and the Historian. *Spaceflight*, **15**, No. 11, 1973.

[10] BOYLE, CHARLES P. *Space among us. Some effects of space research on socity*. Goddard Space Flight Center, Greenbelt, Maryland (1973).

[11] DURANT III, FREDERICK C. Rockets and missile systems and Space exploration. *Encyclopaedia Britannica* (15th edn.) (1974).

[12] WRIGHT, MONTE D. *Documents in the History of NASA*. HHR 43. NASA History Office. (Available on request from NASA, Washington.) (1975).

BIBLIOGRAPHY

CLARKE, ARTHUR C. *The coming of the Space Age*. Meredith Press, New York (1967).
An anthology of 36 reprints of original articles on all aspects of astronautics, including [7] and [8] above.

LEY, WILLY. *Rockets, Missiles and Space Travel*. Chapman and Hall, London (1951).
Undoubtedly the most complete bibliography, listing English, American, German, French, Italian, Russian, Spanish, and Dutch books, periodicals, and Government publications, including historical works of the eighteenth and nineteenth centuries.

NATIONAL AERONAUTICS AND SPACE ADMINISTRATION (NASA). By 1973 the American Space Agency had published about 750000 scientific reports, most of them non-secret. Enquiries about them should be addressed to: The Director, Public Information Division, NASA Headquarters, Washington, D.C. 20546, U.S.A. See also [12] for historical data.

36

CIVIL ENGINEERING

P. S. A. BERRIDGE

PART I: ROADS, BRIDGES, AND TUNNELS

I. ROADS

THE development of highways during the twentieth century is a story of changes brought about through conflicting forms of transport. Where civilization had been established, dusty turnpikes and city cobbled streets suited to the plodding horse sufficed for automobile, bicycle, and tramcar only for as long as it took to provide separate ways for each.

At the turn of the century there were 8000 motor vehicles in the U.S.A. On the French Riviera, 500 automobiles seen in a day on the *Grande Corniche* equalled the number of horse-carriages. In the first long-distance drive, from Peking to Paris sponsored by *Le Matin* in 1907, the first man home, driving an Italian car, took 60 days; his nearest rival, at the wheel of a French car, took 80 days.

In Britain in 1901, the motor-car was a rarity. Roads were for horse-drawn vehicles: rolled macadam, untarred and dusty, in the country and the suburbs; paved with stone setts in industrial towns, and with wood blocks, usually jarrah, in high-class residential districts. Crossing-sweepers kept road junctions clean for pedestrians; drinking-water troughs and bins for manure were common street furniture; water-carts 'laid' the dust; and straw spread across the carriageway deadened the sound of hooves and iron-rimmed wheels outside the mansion when the owner was ill. The horse-tram had not disappeared from London's thoroughfares. Except for the steam-roller with scarifier, and occasionally the tar-boiler, the engineers' plant was innocent of machinery. The stone-breaker, squatting, hammer in hand, was a common sight beside the country lane and the mud scraper for boots was a necessity outside every front door.

Serious consideration was first given to adapting British highways to the motor vehicle in 1909. A Road Board was set up by Parliament with Colonel R. E. Crompton, who had promoted the Government Steam Train that trundled along the Grand Trunk Road in India in 1872, as consulting engineer. The works recommended by the Road Board were paid for out of the revenue: 3d. per gallon from the Motor Spirit Import Duty, and an annual vehicle tax of £1 for motor-cycles and from three to eight guineas (£3·15 to £8·40) for cars according to their horsepower. From 1909 the growth of the number of mechanically propelled vehicles accelerated rapidly. In 1911, of the 772 vehicles passing a given point in 24 hours on a main road in Kent, 41 per cent were motors; in 1912, that percentage had risen to 62; in 1922, only 5 per cent were horse-drawn; and in 1954, all the 15 268 vehicles that passed then were powered mechanically.

In 1919, the Road Board had been replaced by the Ministry of Transport. Two years later, a spate of road-widening and straightening and new bypass works, urged on to relieve unemployment during post-war trade depression, was put in hand. The first full-scale traffic census in England, in 1922, showed that the most heavily used road in Essex carried 14 540 tonnes in 24 hours, and in London during the same period, 115 000 tonnes passed busy Hyde Park Corner. In 1929 the first electric colour-light traffic signals were installed at intersections; a year later a Road Traffic Act restricted waiting in congested streets and started traffic regulation in one-way thoroughfares. In 1931, the first steps were taken to rid the king's highway of that most danger-ous of hazards to cyclists, the tram-rail. Another Road Traffic Act, in 1934, inaugurated tests for drivers of mechanically propelled vehicles and intro-duced the speed limit of 30 mile/h (48 km/h) in built-up areas, Percy Shaw, a Yorkshireman, invented 'cat's-eyes,' the rubber-mounted reflectors that 'line' traffic lanes so effectively in fog and darkness. In 1935, the too-long-delayed Restriction of Ribbon Development Act reflected the importance of controlling the spread of building construction alongside traffic arteries. In 1949, the Special Roads Act allowed the building of roads reserved exclu-sively for the motor vehicle. The motorway in Britain had been given the green light.

Abroad, the motorway had come sooner. The Avus *Autobahn* was an attraction for motorists attending Germany's first post-war Motor Show in Berlin in 1921. Five years later, Professor Robert Otzen was planning to link Frankfurt with Basle by autobahn instead of adapting existing highways to the special needs of the automobile. In 1929, construction of an autobahn was started to relieve the pressure between Dusseldorf and Bonn, where 1800 vehicles an hour were jamming a two-lane highway. In the 1930s, 4000 km of autobahn were opened in Germany. In 1950, all European coun-tries except Ireland, Spain, the U.S.S.R., and Bulgaria signed an agreement for the integration of an international highway network of 42000 km. Four years later, tourist concerns, car-builders, tyre manufacturers, and civil engineering construction firms in Italy joined forces to finance a 725-km *Autostrada* from Milan to Naples.

In 1958, the world's car population was 82m. in the U.S.A.; 16m. in Europe; 2·2m. in Australia; 1·4m. in Asia; and 1·1m. in Africa. India had 258000 km of surfaced roads and 480000 km unsurfaced. In China, where a factory was turning out 40000 commercial motor vehicles a year, Mao Tse-Tung boasted 4000 km of motor roads with more being built at the rate of nearly 100 km every month. In Britain, valuable land was being usurped at the rate of 60 ha for every 10 km of new motorway.

Construction. Modern roads range from the simple earth track cleared of vegetation, the soil compacted by the traffic, to the busy motorway with its structural road-base which distributes the weight of the traffic to the drained and compacted soil of the consolidated subgrade. Sandwiched between the formation (that is, the top of the prepared subgrade) and the surfacing, and perhaps including an insulating sub-base underneath, the road-base will be of either 'flexible' bituminous macadam or 'rigid' concrete. Whatever the construction may be, the fundamental principle is the same as that expressed by John Loudon McAdam: 'It is the native soil which really supports the weight of traffic; while it is preserved in a dry state it will carry any weight without sinking.' The earth road may suffice, climate permitting, where the daily traffic does not exceed 50 lightweight vehicles. An all-weather motorway with dual two-lane carriageways can carry 1800 vehicles per hour each way on a clear day, and the weight on a single wheel may be nearly 7 tonnes.

The pavements of most twentieth-century roadways are laid by mechanical means, and they may vary in thickness from 600 mm down to 200 mm or even less, according to the soil conditions and the method of construction used. The subgrade will have been stabilized by the compaction of the native soil to a depth of about 500 mm, and overlaid with dry stone screenings or sand; and, in the 'flexible' pavement, the layers of the macadam road-base will have been spread and levelled by machine and compacted by rolling. The Barber–Greene Finisher, which originated in the U.S.A. in 1937, became the most commonly used machine on the construction of macadam roads in Britain in 1951. Since the mid-1960s, the road-bases of high-quality roads have consisted of either rolled asphalt or one of the dense-coated macadams—tar macadam or bitumen macadam—which are well-graded

FIG. 36.1(a). The Banihal
Cart Road zigzags down from
the tunnel (2740 m above
sea-level) and into the Vale
of Kashmir. This early motor
road, 308 km long, from
Jammu to Srinagar, over the
Pir Panjal range of the
Himalayas was opened in
1922.

FIG. 36.1(b). Heavy
construction on the Banihal
Cart Road: a tunnel gives
protection from minor
avalanches.

aggregates premixed with tar or bitumen binders before being spread in the pavement. The binders impart a degree of flexibility to the road-base so that slight adjustments can take place in the pavement without the risk of it cracking. The hot-mix rolled asphalt is the most stable and durable of all the bituminous road mixtures laid by machine. For the surfacing, the asphalt wearing coat, a mortar of sand and bitumen added to a coarse aggregate, is rendered more skid-resistant by the rolling-in of coated chippings.

In contrast to rolled asphalt, manufactured mastic asphalt used for surfacing the roadway on large suspension bridges is trowelled or 'floated' by hand. On the carriageways of the middle span of the Forth Road Bridge (1964) the single 38-mm layer was applied directly on the steel which was freshly grit-blasted to ensure adherence; on the Severn Bridge (1966), a thin layer of hot rubber–bitumen topped with a priming coat of rubber solution was interposed between the steel and the mastic asphalt to improve the bond.

The so-called rigid pavement had a road-base of concrete which, because it acts like a large stone slab, distributes the traffic load over a much bigger area of the subgrade than is possible under 'flexible' macadam. Disadvantages of the concrete road-base, whether plain or reinforced with steel, were the long time required for the concrete to mature, and the tiresome need for joints to counter cracking of the slab as the concrete set. As late as 1935, concrete roads in Britain were being constructed by hand, and the road-base had to be left for 28 days before it could be used by traffic. Gradually, the curing time was cut; where Portland cement was used, to 13 days; with rapid-hardening cement, to 7 days.

Motor roads and motorways. Some concession to road users in Britain followed a dust-laying demonstration near Reading in 1907. Macadam pavements were hand-painted with tar; later, the idea of using compressed air to spray on the hot tar was introduced from France.

One of the first motor roads in England was planned during the First World War: it was the 9-km Winchester bypass. Initiated as a single 9-m wide pavement, the design was changed to dual 6-m carriageways in 1935. When opened on 1 February 1940, it had a central reservation; the sharpest bend had a radius of 244 m; and the minimum vertical line of sight at 1·14 m above the surface was 121 m. The rigid road-base was of reinforced concrete laid in slabs 203 mm thick, 3 m wide, and 27 m long which were separated from a 254-mm sub-base of gravel by waterproof paper. Subsequently, the 9-mm construction joints were submerged under an all-over bitumen wearing course. The Winchester bypass boasted the first grade-separated roadway junctions in Britain. In 1954, 7000 vehicles were using it in a day.

The 111-km London–Birmingham motorway was opened on 2 November 1959. The biggest road project in Britain since the Roman occupation, it had been completed in 19 months and, except for the short Preston bypass, it was the country's first motorway. With dual three-lane carriageways, it had a capacity of 60000 vehicles a day each way. Construction on a 152-mm granular sub-base was a 355-mm course of plant-mixed cement-stabilized gravel and, on top, a two-coat surfacing of hot-rolled asphalt 100-mm thick. The work was highly mechanized and a labour force of 5000 was augmented by 72 scrapers and 150 excavators. The project involved planting a million hedge bushes and erecting 306 km of fencing.

The building of more motorways in Britain has continued. By November 1966, there were 700 km in use and 225 km under construction; rural motorways aligned for a top speed of 70 mile/h (112 km/h), and urban ones 50 mile/h (80 km/h).

II. BRIDGES

Principles and practice. Since 1900 many important changes have taken place in bridge engineering. Two world wars and the neglect of ageing structures, plus the significant effect of increasing labour costs outstripping the rise in prices of steel and cement, led to more precise knowledge of bridge capacity, more economical fabrication of steelwork through electric-arc welding instead of riveting, better bolt fasteners, and a greatly improved use of concrete. The bulky riveted truss was to give place to the neat 'tailored' line of welded steelwork, the torsionally superior box girder, and the streamlined decks of stay-assisted and suspension bridges. Spalling reinforced concrete was to be replaced by concrete of improved quality made crack-proof through efficient vibration and the technique of prestressing. Advances in technology were to lengthen the greatest distance practicable between the towers of the longest hypothetical suspension bridge to a span of 3·25 km. Nevertheless, twentieth-century history was to record a surprisingly large number of bridge failures, which without exception had been caused by the vagaries of *Homo sapiens*.

In 1901, the Engineering Standards Committee was formed in Britain to correlate the qualities of alloyed steel produced by different makers and to systematize the hundreds of different shapes and sizes of rolled sections on the market. From that original committee the British Standards Institution was born. In those early days, bridges were being built to a factor of safety of four; in other words, it was believed that the load a bridge had been built to carry repeatedly *ad infinitum* would have to be multiplied by four before the girderwork would suffer permanent injury. Calculations were rudimentary. They were known to be so because thousands of ageing structures were being crossed regularly by loads many times heavier than the weights their designers had allowed for, and there appeared to be no evidence of serious injuries. In 1923, a Bridge Stress Committee was appointed to look into the matter; in particular, they were to make the determination of loading capacity more precise. With the collaboration of engineers in many different countries, they studied the deformation stress caused by the bending of the parts of a framework in which the joints were rigid; the effects of load-sharing caused through the interaction between the main girders and the floor of a bridge; the distribution of loading affected by different thicknesses and kinds of road-metalling; the increments of stress caused by the effects of impact; and so on. Their report was published in 1928. A year later, the so-called factor of safety was reduced by increasing allowable stresses by $12\frac{1}{2}$ per cent; and because this was taken to apply to existing as well as new bridges, the capacities of many thousands of ageing structures, of wrought iron and of mild steel, were suddenly increased at the stroke of the pen. Such was the tolerance shown by the riveted bridge, which never was known to fail through metal fatigue. The rivet hole arrested the progress of the crack that started from brittle fracture; and although prone to attack from rusting, which could lead to deadly corrosion fatigue (quite different from, and not to be confused with, metal fatigue), the end came slowly. The riveted bridge never broke suddenly; always it could be depended upon to give ample warning of imminent catastrophe. Not so the bridge that was welded. With it there was no plastic yield to ease the burden of high stress concentration, as the splitting of the welded hulls of Liberty ships had shown during the Second World War. Steel that was heated to 1500 °C by the electric arc could become embrittled, and in the vicinity of a notch there could be a risk of brittle fracture initiating a crack that would progress with alarming rapidity. It was to guard against such a calamity, and against the possible incidence of failure through metal fatigue, that the British Standards Institution issued some astonishing advice in 1962: like the fortune-teller looking into the crystal ball, the bridge designer was asked to peer into the future and guess how many times various different categories of loading could be expected to cross his bridge during the next

120 years, before he could choose the maximum stress that his particular piece of steelwork might be allowed to carry. Evidence indeed that bridge engineering is an art and the capacity of a bridge is not to be determined with mathematical exactitude!

The coming of the welded steel bridge was the most significant event since the first wrought-iron girders were riveted for a road bridge near Glasgow in 1841. The change-over from riveting started in the 1920s; but it was very gradual; abroad, some new bridges erected in the 1970s were riveted. In Britain, the economic advantages of welded construction could not be ignored, for the savings were enormous. In rolling-mill and stockyard, the demand for hundreds of different shapes and sizes of channels, angles, zed-bars, etc. vanished. On the drawing-board, aeons of time were saved because there were no bothersome rivet-pitches to work out and detail; no rivet-lists to write out in quadruplicate. In the template-loft, no rivets to show. In the workshop, no holes to mark off and centre-pop and drill; no matching of holes in different parts of the steelwork; no reamering of holes; no temporary black-bolting and unbolting; no rivets to sort for size, to heat, to hold-up, and squeeze; the list was endless. Besides, riveting was fast becoming a dying craft; on Clydeside in 1948, the number of apprentice riveters could be counted on the fingers of one hand. But, ranged against the change-over to welding were the reluctance of contractors opposed to scrapping their valuable riveting plant; the trouble of learning how to counter distortion caused through the ill-judged programming of operations during fabrication by welding; and a conservatism among designers slow to appreciate that the shape of a properly designed welded bridge bears no resemblance to the riveted structure with its mass of different rolled sections and parts apportioned to facilitate the operation of closing the rivets.

Complementary to welding is the high-strength friction-grip bolt, first used in British railway bridges in 1948. This fastener was invaluable in the field where conditions often made good-quality welding difficult. The shank is not machined, and the high-strength friction-grip bolt is used in holes which are 3 mm larger in diameter. Tightened by a torque-multiplying wrench to grip with a predetermined tension which is visibly proved through the quashing of 'pimples' on the washer used under the nut, the high-strength friction-grip bolt grips the faying surfaces like a vice. It will not loosen through vibration. Unlike the rivet, the high-strength friction-grip bolt can be correctly used where the shank is loaded in direct tension.

Apart from the benefits from the reduction in the labour-content at the works and on the erection site, there was a remarkable saving in dead weight in the structure of a welded bridge. A road bridge of 30 m span built across the River Rhône in 1930 contained 25 per cent less steelwork than it would have required if riveted.

The third important twentieth-century development was the prestressing of concrete; a Frenchman, Eugene Freyssinet, is said to have initiated the idea. By it the concrete in a beam is compressed by forces of such magnitude that when the beam deflects under load, the surface of the concrete at the bottom (which, of course, would be in tension in a ferro-concrete beam) does not crack. The pre-compressing force in the concrete is carried by high-tensile steel tendons. If these tendons are tensioned against anchorages in the manufactory before the concrete is poured and vibrated around them, the prestressed beam is said to have been pre-tensioned. When released from the anchorages, the tendons transfer the force into a compression of the concrete after it has matured. Thus, in a pre-tensioned beam the transfer of force from tendon to concrete depends solely on the bond between steel and concrete. Alternatively, if the tendons are stretched by jacks reacting against the ends of precast concrete units the process is called post-tensioning. By either method prestressed concrete is the greatest boon since 1808, when Ralph Dodds proposed the reinforcement of concrete with wrought-iron bars 'to give greater strength in tension' (Vol. V, p. 512). By eliminating surface-cracking and the unsightly spalling caused by the rusting of internal reinforcement which marred so many earlier concrete structures, prestressing was to make the concrete bridge almost maintenance-free.

The heyday of the rivet. At the dawn of the twentieth century riveted steelwork for bridges was being fabricated in western Europe and the U.S.A. and shipped abroad in small parts for opening up communications in under-developed countries.

In 1900, the Indus was being bridged at Kotri, just above its delta. Temporary pontoon crossings excepted, it was only the third time this river had been bridged in a distance of 1600 km. Kotri Bridge has six spans and they carried a railway and a road; the 111-m girders for five of the spans were the longest that had then been shipped to India. Made in Britain, their fabrication was typical. Rivet holes were drilled from wooden templates and, because of wear, the spacings were apt to vary. Consequently, it was not practicable to interchange similar members between the different spans; as a result, every span had to be assembled and the parts numbered before shipment. In

FIG. 36.2. The Indus Bridge at Kotri, built in 1900, after it had been strengthened and separate roadways added in 1933. The simply supported girders were the longest in any railway bridge in India.

1931, Kotri Bridge had to be strengthened (Fig. 36.2): the main girders were duplicated; the flooring replaced for heavier railway loads; and brackets added outside the trusses to carry two 3·5-m roadways. In the thirty years since the original construction, there had been many improvements in the methods of fabricating riveted steelwork. Among these, was the use of jigs made of steel case-hardened to ensure perfect accuracy in the spacing of holes for field-driven rivets, so that all similar parts would be readily interchangeable. The ten new trusses for Kotri Bridge were made in India and this time only one girder had to be put together to check the fabrication at the works.

In 1901, Burma became the owner of the world's loftiest bridge. The Gokteik Viaduct, 687 m long, was a typical American trestle bridge with trusses spanning between four-legged and six-legged braced towers. The riveted steelwork was made in Pennsylvania and erected on site with cantilever travellers working outwards from each end. The tallest trestle was 97 m high, and because it was founded on the rock of a natural arch beneath which the Chungzoune River flows, rail level was 252 m above the bottom of the gorge. The Gokteik Viaduct was destroyed by the Japanese in 1945; subsequently, with new steelwork from England, it was restored.

In 1903, the Connel Ferry Bridge, a notable cantilever structure, was built across the Falls of Lora in Scotland with a single span of 153 m. Four years

later, and with the same length of span, the imposing arch of the Victoria Falls
Bridge was completed across the Zambezi River in a spectacular gorge 122 m
deep. The erection of this flat-topped and spandrel-braced arch aroused
great interest. A rocket was first fired across the chasm; it carried a light rope
which was used to draw a steel hawser over. A Blondin cableway followed to
handle the pieces of riveted steelwork which had been made in Darlington,
England. Held back and anchored to the cliffs on each side of the gorge, the
steelwork advanced in two cantilevers to be joined at midspan. The total
length of the Victoria Falls Bridge is 198 m. Truss girder spans join each end
of the arch to the tops of the cliffs. When opened, it carried two railway tracks
of 1·067-m gauge. Twenty-five years later, with the steelwork of the deck
suitably modified, it accommodated a roadway and a single line of railway
side by side. The Connel Ferry Bridge was similarly altered to carry a roadway instead of a single line of standard-gauge railway.

Four bridges completed in 1909 were important landmarks in the develop-
ment of bridge-engineering. They were the Manhattan Bridge and Blackwell's
Island Bridge (later renamed Queensboro) across the East River in New
York City; the Queen Alexandra Bridge over the River Wear in England; and
the Fades Railway Viaduct 133 m above the River Sioule in France. The
Manhattan Bridge was the first suspension bridge in which the design included allowance for the horizontal displacement of the cables under load.
With a centre span of 447 m and side spans of 220 m carried by four suspension cables, each made up of 9472 wires 4·8 mm in diameter, held aloft by
flexible steel towers, this bridge set the pattern which was to be followed in
all the world's great suspension bridges built in the twentieth century.

Blackwell's Island Bridge is of the cantilever type. Double-decked like the
Manhattan Bridge, it carries a centre roadway 11 m wide flanked on each side
by two trolley-car tracks on the lower deck, and, above, four railway tracks
and two footwalks. Its total length is 1137 m and the two cantilever spans are
each 360 m long. The riveted steelwork was delivered in enormously heavy
pieces which had to be pinned together at the joints during erection. Some of
the parts of the trusses weighed 122 tonnes. In some places as many as
twenty eye-bars had to be grouped together while a single pin, 40 cm in
diameter and more than 3 m long, was coaxed through the holes, which were
only half a millimetre larger than the diameter of the pin. Such difficult
assembly operations were not repeated in bridges built after Blackwell's
Island. The Queen Alexandra Bridge was also double-decked, with two railway tracks on the upper deck and a roadway below. The relatively puny

101·5-m span was the heaviest in Britain. On the average, there were 29·9 tonnes of steelwork in every metre in the length of the span. The main girders were Linville trusses, the web system arranged like the strokes of two **N**s with one **N** half a letter forward of the other. The merit of this arrangement is that the cross-girders, which were spaced at every vertical, were close together. Consequently, the longitudinal stringers were short and therefore shallow, thus permitting the thickness of the upper deck to be kept to a minimum so as to give adequate headroom for the road vehicles on the lower deck. Extravagant in steelwork, and vulnerable to rapid corrosion because the paint brush could not reach where the diagonals crossed the verticals, the Linville truss was soon to go out of fashion after the Queen Alexandra Bridge. The Fades Viaduct had three principal spans: the middle one 144 m long, the side ones each 116 m. All the girders had a constant depth of 12·2 m and were typical of French practice at the time. They were lattice trusses with the web system resembling trelliswork, without any intermediate verticals. At Fades, as with the English bridge, erection was by cantilevering from each end, the girders being converted into simply supported beams after the steelwork had been joined at mid-span. The multiplicity of parts in the lattice girders meant that each piece was light to handle, and this was an important convenience during erection. But the fact that the lattice members were riveted together at every intersection led to excessive local deformation, and so this great French railway bridge was to become one of the last to be built with lattice girders.

At the 15-span Hardinge Bridge (1915) which carried the double-track railway across the River Ganges between Calcutta and Siliguri (for Darjeeling), the method of erection was unusual. A single service span was used to support the permanent steelwork while it was being put together in each of the 105-m spans. While in use, this service span rested on the piers and on completion of one permanent span it was carried on barges and floated to the next opening. Afterwards, the service span was modified and used as a permanent structure in a bridge carrying the Grand Trunk Road across the Haro River in the north of the Punjab. But the idea of using a service span on which to put together accurately fabricated truss girders was not repeated. At the Willingdon Bridge (1932) across the tidal Hoogly, the spans—which were 107 m long and similar to those at the Hardinge—were assembled, one by one, on an erection platform built on the river bank. The completed spans, lifted off the camber jacks by barges on the rising tide, were floated out to the bridge and landed on the piers as the tide ebbed. The Willingdon Bridge

carried two railway tracks of 5 ft 6 in (1·67 m) gauge between the main girders
and, cantilevered out on each side, a 5·5-m roadway and a footpath. There
were seven spans, each containing 2025 tonnes of steelwork; they were the
heaviest spans of their kind ever built in India. The service span idea was not
used at this Hoogly bridge because at the Ganges the gradually increasing
deflection of the temporary erection platform had proved to be troublesome
in accurately aligning the parts of the trusses. It is questionable whether such
a high standard of accuracy was justified. In 1931, at the Nerbudda River
Railway Bridge the diagonal members of the trusses had to be made to within
0·39 mm of the designed length of more than 16 m because the 88-m spans
were to be prestressed during erection. This refinement was intended to
eliminate deformation stresses caused by the rigidity of the riveted joints,
which resulted in the secondary bending of members as the trusses deflected
under a train. The designers claimed the prestressing saved 9 per cent weight
of steelwork. The tied arch is less demanding than the truss. At the building
of the Vila Franca Bridge for a road across the River Tagus in 1951, a service
span used to support the steelwork of the five 103-m spans proved to be very
suitable.

After the First World War, a large programme of bridge reconstruction
was undertaken in India. Collectively, the railway bridges dealt with to the
north and west of Delhi would have stretched a distance of 57 km. It was the
proud boast of the engineers that traffic, rail and road, was never interrupted
for a single period longer than three and a half hours. The Alexandra Bridge,
opened in 1876 to carry a metre-gauge railway and the Grand Trunk Road
across the River Chenab, was shortened from 64 spans (each 40 m long) to
17 in 1919 and regirdered in 1927. All the discarded girderwork was re-used
in building road bridges. Similarly, bridges across the Ravi, Sutlej, Jhelum,
and Indus were reconstructed. At the Jhelum Bridge (Fig. 36.3) where the
30-m spans, separate for road and rail, shared the same piers in the 1·6-km
long structure the workmen became so expert that in changing the thirty-
third of the fifty spans, interference with the train service was cut to a mere
70 minutes. At Attock (Fig. 36.4), the historic bridge which had been the
first permanent structure built across the Indus (1883) and which led to the
famous Khyber Pass, the new girders of the two 94-m double-decked spans
over the water were cantilevered out from the piers and the new cross-girders
threaded through the old trusses (1929). The new steelwork had been made
in Germany and the old trusses taken out of Attock Bridge had been India's
first to be made of mild steel instead of wrought iron.

FIG. 36.3. The Jhelum Valley Road Bridge at Kohala, 570 m above sea-level and 102 km from
Rawalpindi on the way to Srinagar, was reconstructed in 1931 to prevent the girderwork being damaged
by landslides; the hillsides on the right bank of the river being highly unstable during the monsoon rains.

The Lower Zambezi Bridge, 3·6 km long, was finished in 1935. At that time
the third longest bridge in the world, it was an example of the high standard
of accuracy attained in the mass production of girders in Britain. There were
thirty-three identical 80-m spans, and all similar parts were interchangeable.

The simply supported truss, a beam that spanned an opening and had no
intermediate supports, had been gradually increased in span-length. In 1917,
Sciotoville Bridge over the Ohio River was the longest, at 236 m. In 1936
that was surpassed by the Admiral Graf Spee Bridge at Duisburg, 20 m
longer. In 1966 Japan had one that topped the 300-m mark, and at the
Astoria Bridge in Oregon the Americans built the longest of all, more than
375 m. But the steel arch, needing no falsework below while the two halves
were built as cantilevers to meet at mid-span, was more economical. The
Sydney Harbour Bridge, opened in 1932, had the biggest and heaviest
arch, 504 m. But it was never the longest; the Bayonne Bridge in New
York City, which had been completed the year before, was just 60 cm
longer. The Sydney 'coat-hanger' contained the heaviest riveted steel fabrication of all time: rivets 34·9 mm in diameter gripping plates and rolled angles
totalling more than 30 cm in thickness. Where the enormous thrust of 2000
tonnes bore on the pins at the skewbacks the accuracy of workmanship in the

FIG. 36.4. The historic Attock Bridge during reconstruction in 1929. Completed in 1883 and some
1500 km from the sea, the Attock Bridge was the first permanent structure to be built across the Indus
and the original girders were among the very first in which mild steel was used in India.

fit between the girderwork and the steel saddle castings was within 0·025 mm.
When the Sydney Harbour Bridge was being tested 81 railway locomotives
were left standing on the arch for eight days.

Cantilever bridges did not increase in span-length in so spectacular a
fashion. The Quebec Bridge (1918) has the longest span in the world: a
single one 27·4 m longer than each of the two 520-m spans at the Forth
Bridge (1890). Howrah Bridge, India's busiest highway bridge, across the
Hoogly in Calcutta, was opened in 1943. It is a cantilever bridge with a single
span of 458 m, and is a unique structure. The huge load-carrying trusses are
elevated aloft so that the anchor arms, which stretch 120 m shorewards behind
the great towers that stand on the river's edge, shall be high enough to clear
the tops of trams, buses, lorries, and other traffic surging on to the bridge
from the roads that run parallel with the waterway and hug the banks. The
roadway, 21 m wide, and the two footpaths are on a platform, which is hung
below the main structure, and they are at such a level that the inclines leading
on to the bridge are gentle enough for the humble bullock-cart to negotiate
without trouble. Busier than London's London Bridge, Howrah Bridge was
in 1946 being crossed by 121 100 pedestrians, 2997 cattle, and 27 400 trams
and motor vehicles every day.

FIG. 36.5. Spanning the Rohri Channel of the River Indus near Sukkur, two unique bridges. On the right, the Lansdowne Bridge which boasted the world's longest cantilever span in 1889. On the left, Pakistan's Ayub Arch is the only railway bridge in which the deck is slung on coiled wire rope suspenders.

The Howrah and Sydney Harbour Bridges were of riveted steelwork. So too were the Ayub Arch (1962); the Verrazano Narrows Suspension Bridge (1964); and the Salazar Bridge (1967). The Ayub Arch (Fig. 36.5) was the pride of Pakistan. Designed in the U.S.A., fabricated in England, and erected by Pakistani engineers, it spanned the Rohri channel of the Indus at Sukkur and replaced the famous Lansdowne Bridge which, in 1889, had been the longest cantilever span in the world. The Ayub Arch has a span of 246 m and it has the distinction of being the only railway bridge where the deck is slung on locked-coil rope suspenders. The Verrazano Narrows Bridge, at the entrance to New York harbour, has the longest span in the world, 1298 m, which is 18 m more than the previous record held by the Golden Gate Bridge (1934) at San Francisco (Fig. 36.6). Verrazano is double-decked and has four carriageways, each 11 m wide; the stiffening trusses are 7·3 m deep; the four suspension cables each contain 26 108 pencil-thick wires; and the two towers soar 206 m above the water. At high tide, the headway for shipping passing under the Verrazano Bridge is just less than 70 m. Portugal's Salazar Bridge, astride the Tagus at Lisbon, has a span of 1013 m; it was the longest in Europe until the Bosphorus was bridged in 1973. But the steelwork of the suspension bridge that joins Europe to Asia was not riveted.

Welded steelwork. Australia had a welded footbridge in 1926; it had a span of 27·5 m and belonged to a gasworks in Melbourne. Two years later, the first welded steel bridges appeared in America and Britain. The English one was a five-span portal-frame road bridge, 66 m long, over railway tracks in Teesside. The first all-welded railway bridge in Britain spanned Ladbroke Grove in London in 1938. It was a half-through-type plate girder bridge used by the Hammersmith and City line trains of the Underground. But the design slavishly followed the form common to riveting practice; it contained none of the advantages afforded by the easy tailoring to shape that is the essence of good design of steelwork fabricated by welding. Ten years later, after eight bridges between Berwick and Edinburgh had been swept away after a cloudburst, all the new girderwork was welded. The first major development was in 1962 when Brunel's famous suspension-bridge spans (1852) at Chepstow were replaced with the world's first welded trussed box girders (Fig. 36.7). Separate for each railway track, they were 94 m long, shop-welded and prefabricated, and all the site-joints were connected with Torshear bolts which were automatically tightened to a predetermined grip by machine. The mild steel in each span, only 296 tonnes, amounted to just over 3 tonnes per lineal metre, which was less than any other span of similar capacity and length.

FIG. 36.6. The Golden Gate Bridge, San Francisco, which when opened in 1936 had the longest span in the world, 1280 m (4200 ft). The riveted trusses of the suspended structure were built of small members put together piece-meal on site.

FIG. 36.7. Reconstructing Brunel's historic bridge across the Wye at Chepstow in 1962. The new welded truss box-girder span, used on a railway bridge for the first time, is being launched across the water on the underside of the 1852 ironwork which carried the Up line.

FIG. 36.8. A 19-m long section of the suspended structure of the Severn Road Bridge complete with roadways, foot-way, and cycle-track being lifted from the water by a crane that ran on the permanent suspension cables.

FIG. 36.9. Slung from the stiffening trusses of the suspension bridge, the transporter 'sails' across the Manchester Ship Canal and the River Mersey on its 304-m ride at Runcorn.

Welding had made possible the development of the box girder, with its advantage of immense torsional strength. Within a few more years, the box girder form of construction was to be found in nearly every new bridge, be it for railway, road, or motorway. It was to make possible that most technically advanced of bridges, the Severn Road Bridge (1966) (Fig. 36.8) with its 988-m span which, though a mere 18 m shorter than the span of the Forth Road Bridge (1964), required only just over half the amount of steel used in the Scottish bridge. Bigger, but fashioned on the Severn design, the Bosphorus Bridge has a span of 1074 m.

Movable bridges. Twentieth-century movable-span bridges across shipping channels include bascules, rolling-lift, swing, vertical-lift, and transporter bridges. With the exception of London's Tower Bridge (1894) with its high-level footbridges fixed above the bascules, only the transporter and the vertical-lift bridges have overhead structures which, of course, have to be high enough to clear the tallest ship.

The transporter bridge carries a travelling platform for road traffic; its function is that of a ferry but without the inconvenience of fluctuations in the level of the water. In Britain, transporters bridged the River Usk at Newport in South Wales (1906), the Tees at Middlesbrough (1911), and, in a single stride of 305 m, the Mersey and the Manchester Ship Canal at Runcorn (1903) (Fig. 36.9). The Middlesbrough bridge has a centre span of 143 m and the capacity of its travelling platform is 600 passengers plus six vehicles. At Runcorn, the 'road' car could carry 300 pedestrians and four loaded boiler-wagons, and make the crossing in $1\frac{3}{4}$ minutes; this bridge was scrapped after the completion of a steel arch bridge alongside in 1962. Transporter bridges were also to be found in France: a 142-m span at Nantes (1902), and, at Marseilles, one with a span of 166 m that bridged Le Vieux Port until the Second World War.

By Act of Parliament, owners of movable bridges in Britain are responsible for manning them. Because the bridges often have to be operational day and night throughout the year, the cost in terms of the number of times a bridge has to be opened to allow a ship to pass seems to be exorbitant. At the dawn of the twentieth century, for example, there were 212 men on the payroll at London's Tower Bridge, which was being opened for shipping more than 6000 times a year and crossed by 8000 vehicles and 60000 pedestrians. Whether a bridge is opened thousands of times in a year or only half a dozen times, the number of men on the payroll remains almost constant. The

FIG. 36.10. The rolling-lift bridge at Inchinnan, Scotland, completed in 1923, carries a road across the River Cart. Rolled back, it gives a clear channel 27·5 m wide for shipping.

rolling-lift span of Scotland's Inchinnan Bridge (Fig. 36.10), which spans the River Cart, is a case in point. Built for road traffic and completed in 1924, it had to be a movable bridge to give passage for dredgers built in a shipyard that was located upstream from the crossing. By 1971, the number of 'openings' was averaging one in twelve months, yet the cost of manning was £18000 a year.

Typical road swing-bridges in Britain are the Booth Ferry Bridge over the River Ouse near Goole, and the Kincardine Bridge across the Forth in Scotland. The former, completed in 1929, uses 1016 tonnes of girderwork 68 m long to bridge a navigable channel which is only 38 m wide. Kincardine Bridge (1936) was the longest swing span in Europe: with girderwork 111 m long and weighing 1625 tonnes, it swings to give two navigation channels, each 45 m wide. In the U.S.A. there are longer swing bridges: across the Willamette River, the moving girderwork (1908) is 158 m long; and on the Mississippi at Fort Madison, there is a swing span (1927) of 160 m. These were eclipsed in 1965 by the twin swing spans at al Firdan in Egypt, where the pivots of the two moving leaves of the bridge across the Suez Canal were built 168 m apart.

Typical of a vertical-lift bridge is the Kingsferry Bridge completed in 1963, it is the third movable bridge to be built on the site. Crossing the Swale, it connects the Isle of Sheppey with the mainland of Kent. There are seven spans, the middle one lifting to give a headroom of 29 m over a navigable channel 27·5 m wide. The superstructure consists of plate girders, shop-welded and site-bolted except for the main joints in the main girders, which were riveted after delivery. But the towers are of reinforced concrete; and the appearance of this utilitarian structure has been enhanced by carefully tapering the pillars upwards. Each pair of columns on either side of the waterway is joined just below the top by a concrete portal, and their function is to carry the 'sash' rollers which accommodate the 159-mm circumference ropes of plough steel attached to the counterweights. The Kingsferry Bridge carries a 7·3-m roadway, a 1·8-m pathway, and a single line of railway. The latest bridge replaced a Scherzer rolling-lift bridge which fifty years before had replaced a hinged bascule built in 1863. The modern Kingsferry lift-span weighs 472 tonnes and is raised or lowered by two electric motors moving it at a rate of 19·5 m in a minute. It is a fine bridge, but as lift-spans go it is a puny affair. The Arthur Kill Bridge between Staten Island, New York City, and New Jersey (1959) has a truss-borne platform with a length of 179 m.

Foundations. The world's deepest bridge foundations are under Australia's Hawksbury River Road Bridge (1942) and the San Francisco–Oakland Bay Bridge (1936) in the U.S.A. Both go down 73 m below low-water level. Both are monolith structures which stood initially with the tops above the water so that they could be sunk by mucking out with grabs and without the need for men to work in compressed air. At the American bridge, work went according to plan, but at Hawksbury the monolith made three sudden plunges as its cutting edge broke through crusty strata and into running sand. The height of the monolith had to be increased by 60 m; compressed-air working had to be introduced; and parcels of gelignite had to be exploded to break up troublesome boulders before that monolith was safely founded on solid rock.

An important development in foundation engineering was the introduction in 1938 of the ICOS (*Impresa Construzioni Opere Spedializzate*) process. Attributed to a research worker, Christian Veder, it depends on the injection of a high-density mud slurry into an excavation so that the ground-water and the material of the ground itself do not fall into the hole. The mud slurry is bentonite, a highly colloidal plastic clay which swells to several times its original volume when mixed with water, and forms a low-viscosity solution. Foundations in an excavation filled with bentonite are made by lowering steel reinforcement and concrete into the slurry-filled hole. The steel and concrete displace the bentonite which is recovered for re-use. Compared with pile-driving, the ICOS process is noiseless. It was first used in England in 1962, when the retaining walls for the Hyde Park Corner underpass were being built close to St. George's Hospital in London.

The ICOS process is also quick. It was used at the building of the Sui Gas Bridge, 1·75 km long, across the River Sutlej in Pakistan in 1964. All the 27 piers, each 1·5 m in diameter and going down 40 m, were completed in 98 days. Never before had a bridge across a river in the alluvial plains of the Punjab been completed in a single dry season. In the past, the founding of a single pier had frequently occupied two working seasons.

Concrete in construction. The development of prestressed concrete so that it would not crack was to remove the prime objection to the use of concrete in bridge construction. It began in 1907, when the two halves of a 30-m arch in France were forced apart by jacks in a gap at the crown; thirty years later, the prestressed concrete bridge, made of beams in which all parts of the concrete remained in compression even when the bridge was fully loaded, was established as a reliable and long-lasting structure. Prestressed concrete led to the use of much higher safe working stresses in the concrete, which resulted in savings in both concrete and steel by as much as 50 and 75 per cent respectively. It led also to the building of bridges more strikingly slender in their appearance. Freyssinet's span of 74 m across the River Marne at Esbly was a good example; one of five similar bridges he made with pre-cast concrete units post-tensioned on site, it was completed in 1949.

The first prestressed concrete railway bridge was built by the London Midland and Scottish Railway in 1945. Constructed near Wigan, the Adam Viaduct has four 9-m spans, each consisting of a platform of pre-tensioned concrete beams precast in the railway company's own factory. The bridge carries a double-track main line. Since 1946, the railways in Britain have used prestressed concrete for all new bridges and structures whenever conditions have permitted, because of the resulting economies in maintenance costs.

The technique of ensuring that parts of concrete structures will not crack has greatly enhanced the appearance of new bridges. One of the most elegant is Gladesville Bridge (1964) which carries a six-lane highway over the

FIG. 36.11. The Royal Tweed Bridge at Berwick. On a gradient rising towards the north and built 1925–8 to carry the A1, the London to Edinburgh road, the bridge has four arch spans which from the south progress in length from 51 m to 110 m, the longest reinforced concrete span in Britain.

FIG. 36.12. The Gladesville Bridge near Sydney has the world's longest concrete arch span. The monolithic rib, 25 400 tonnes, is here shown during erection on falsework. One of the voussoirs awaits hoisting from a barge near mid-span prior to transfer to the rail track and lowering down the falsework; another waits in the foreground. Three of the four separate ribs are shown complete, and the voussoirs for the last one are being assembled.

Parramatta River near Sydney, Australia. Its 304-m arch is the longest in the world and the design was one of Freyssinet's last preoccupations before his death. The arch rib (Fig. 36.12), a monolith weighing 25 400 tonnes, was constructed as four separate ribs consisting of hollow precast reinforced-concrete voussoirs erected on falsework and made into arches by means of jacks that sprung the ribs about 90 mm at each quarter point. There are 108 voussoirs in each rib, and they weigh some 50 tonnes each. So accurate was their construction that after the ribs had been combined into the huge single unit, the centre-line varied from the true linear arch by not more than 9·5 mm, and the expanding of the ribs to levels above their true funicular shapes countered all future movements due to creep and shrinkage of the concrete.

No less impressive are the Medway Bridge (1963) and London Bridge (1973). There is a similarity between the river spans of the Kentish motorway bridge (95 m + 152 m + 95 m) and the City of London's newest bridge (79 m + 103 m + 79 m). In each, the prestressed concrete box form of construction in the shoreward spans is continued in cantilever style over the middle opening, which is completed with a suspended span; at each, the slender piers support the superstructures through narrow-throated hinges of reinforced concrete. But there the similarity ends. The earlier bridge was built by casting the concrete beams *in situ* and post-tensioning them in lengths of about 9 m. The procedure was to prop the growing superstructures on temporary towers and to erect shuttering on steelwork cantilevered out ahead of the completed work. At London Bridge, on the other hand, the concrete units were precast and slung from a steel gantry while they were post-tensioned like beads threaded on a taut string.

Unit construction. The development of unit construction for the rapid building of bridges reached a peak in the Second World War. In Britain, the Royal Engineers had the UCRB (Unit-Construction Railway Bridge) which later was superseded by the ESTB (Everall Sectional Truss Bridge). There was military trestling too, a welded version of the Interchangeable Unit Trestling developed for the N.W.R. in India in 1924. Another was the Callender–Hamilton bridge, designed by A. M. Hamilton while he was building the Rowanduz Road through Kurdistan in 1934; its components were mass-produced in England by firms used to turning out steelwork for electric power lines. And, most important of all, there was the Bailey bridge devised by Sir Donald C. Bailey and the Royal Engineer Board's Experimental Bridging Establishment.

FIG. 36.13. A pontoon bridge of double and treble side-by-side Bailey girders, somewhere in Europe during the Second World War. The pinning together of the basic 3-m long framed units which formed the individual girders is clearly shown in the foreground. Note also the arrangement of beams that supported the transverse timber roadway decking.

A UCRB construction on military trestling thrown across the Seine at Le Manoir in September 1944 was typical. Carrying a single line of railway and founded on 'camel's feet', it survived an abnormal flood stream of 10 knots. Examples of Callender–Hamilton bridging restored rail communication in Assam before the war, and were carrying road traffic over the Severn at Gloucester, England, long after fighting had stopped. But the Bailey bridge became the soldier's favourite; the only purpose-made unit construction, it was universally adopted by the Allies in 1941 (Fig. 36.13).

In the Bailey system there was a complete break from conventional girder design. The basic unit was a rectangular framework of welded steelwork, 3 m long and 1·5 m deep, which consisted of two open-diamond braced squares. A unit was easily managed by six men. A girder could be quickly formed by joining units end to end; and, with a minimum of extra parts, the girders could be doubled or trebled side by side, and mounted one above the other to make double- or triple-storey Bailey bridges. The steel was of special alloy. The rolled channels and joists in the units and the cross-girders all had the highest possible mechanical properties. Instant interchangeability of parts was the keynote of success, and the manufacture of these construction units was a proud achievement. In the months preceding the Allies' invasion of Normandy, more than 600 firms in Britain alone were making Bailey units and the fit of every part had to be checked. Of the total number made (696 544) only 469 units had to be rejected, such was the accuracy in gauging and jigging achieved in this nation-wide project.

Many Bailey bridges helped to restore communications in Europe. Examples demonstrated the versatility of the system. There were 400-m pontoon bridges launched across the Rhine in 40 hours. On piles, the 700-m long Montgomery Bridge at Wesel had triple-triple Bailey construction cantilever spans and triple-double suspended spans; it carried two carriageways, foot-walks, and a cycle track. On Bailey units built into trestles founded on the stumps of piers of a former Italian bridge across the River Po, the Springbok Bridge was built by South African engineers; it had four 83-m spans with triple-double trusses—the longest Bailey construction unit bridge spans ever built—and was completed in just eight days. In south-east Asia, a 120-m suspension bridge which incorporated towers and stiffening girders made of Bailey units, was built by 120 soldiers, aided by 15 skilled erectors; it was finished in 26 hours.

Failures. One of the worst bridge disasters happened at Tangiwai in New Zealand on Christmas Eve 1953. A railway bridge was swept away by an unpredecented flood; an act of God perhaps, or had the engineers misjudged the size of opening needed for the stream? More failures in the twentieth century have been caused through apathy than through lack of knowledge. Siting slender piers in navigable waterways had put at risk the Severn Railway Bridge (1875) and Australia's Tasman road bridge (1964). The former lasted until one foggy night in 1960; the latter survived for nine years. On the Severn, a couple of tanker craft collided with a broken pier and knocked it down; five seamen were killed, but providentially there was no train on the bridge. At the Tasman Bridge, a ship knocked over two piers and brought down three spans; seven people lost their lives.

In 1907, 9100 tonnes of steelwork being erected for the first Quebec Bridge collapsed because the slowly worsening buckle in a principal strut was

FIG. 36.14. Failure in the building of the Shri Yuvraj Karan Singh Bridge across the River Chenab in the State of Jammu and Kashmir. Because the lacing-bars in an important temporary steel strut had been insecurely fastened, the falsework collapsed and the permanent steelwork of one half of the bridge fell into the water. Completed successfully in 1935, this span of this road bridge is the longest simply supported truss in India.

ignored. The progress of the buckle had been observed and reported over several days to the engineer's office in New York, but no orders were given to halt construction, which continued to add to the danger; 75 men were killed.

In 1916, the suspended span of the second Quebec Bridge slid into the St. Lawrence while it was being raised to complete the cantilever span. A supporting casting had broken, and 13 men were killed.

These catastrophes showed an alarming disregard for safety. It was a diagnosis that was to be heard all too often at inquiries into bridge failures, even as recently as the 1970s. In 1935, one half of the Shri Yuvraj Karan Singh Road Bridge fell into the River Chenab and eight lives were lost (Fig. 36.14). It was to become India's longest simply supported span (137 m). The steelwork was being erected as two cantilevers extending out from each bank of the river; to save money, the lacing bars in a temporary strut had been clamped to the main parts of the post instead of being securely bolted. That strut buckled, with disastrous results. During the building of the Second Narrows Bridge in Vancouver in 1958, the steel joists in a grillage folded over because their thin webs had not been stiffened; there were eight fatalities. And twice in 1959, tragedy marred the erection of a large road bridge at Barton in Lancashire and on each occasion four men were killed. Once, a steel trestle collapsed because it was not strong enough; once, four plate girders folded over sidways because there was no bracing fitted to hold them upright.

In 1970, box girder bridges under erection in Wales and Australia fell, each with heavy loss of life. At Milford Haven a 60-m cantilever buckled because it had been underdesigned; at Melbourne, the high-level West Gate Bridge came to grief because, following a labour dispute, the work had been entrusted to men who were inexperienced in cambering steelwork and who tried by overloading one half of a girder to match it with the camber of the other half. With attention focused on box girder design and construction by these two catstrophes, an investigation in Britain in 1971 led to the strengthening of no fewer than sixty motorway bridges which had been underdesigned. Disregard of long-established and safe practice had given the box girder an ill reputation, which its torsionally sturdy properties did not deserve.

However, in spite of unfortunate lapses, twentieth-century bridge construction has been remarkable for the improvements in care of personnel on construction sites. In the building of Britain's three major suspension bridges there were only four fatalities: at Tamar (1962), ignoring an accident to an overloaded boat, there were none; at the Forth (1964) there were three, which compares with 57 killed in the building of the great railway bridge (1890); and, at the Severn Road Bridge, one man was gassed when welding inside a box girder. The history of ageing bridges, on the other hand, does show some complacency. Brunel's Chepstow Bridge buckled dangerously in 1944 because it was being used to carry locomotives which were far too heavy; and, in the 1930s, the central suspenders of his suspension-bridge spans at Saltash broke because they had been weakened through corrosion fatigue. Robert Stephenson's box girders (1850) at the Britannia Tubular Bridge could barely hold themselves up after a fire consumed a timber roof above them in 1970; the wrought iron had not suffered in the blaze, but for many years those spans had been carrying locomotives ten times heavier than those for which the bridge was built. Less spectacular, but nonetheless evidence that the factor of safety is sometimes being allowed to sink dangerously close to unity, is given by the following examples. In 1952, 175 persons were injured when a footbridge gave way because hidden ironwork had been weakened through corrosion. In 1953, the middle girder of a railway bridge over the old Holyhead road suddenly split over a length of 5·5 m and the train service had to be halted. A road bridge at Ardrossan also collapsed in 1953, under an abnormally heavy load; it consisted of cast-iron beams and they had been stressed to four times the limit for safety.

In 1940, the Tacoma Narrows Suspension Bridge succumbed to wind-flutter, a violent up-and-down thrashing of the deck structure caused by powerful eddies set up by a moderate wind gusting across the solid-web stiffening girders. At this American bridge, the last throes of 'Galloping Gertie' were filmed and documented, and the failure caused a furore because the symptoms were well known. Captain Brown's suspension-bridge spans at Brighton Pier had succumbed to wind-flutter in 1833; Telford's famous bridge over the Menai Strait suffered from the same affliction in 1836 and the Irish mail coach had to be refused passage. Fortunately, the only victim at Tacoma was the bridge itself. The disaster led to important research with models in wind-tunnels, which resulted in the design of bridge decks that are aerodynamically stable in all winds.

III. TUNNELS

The Simplon Tunnel was opened in 1906. Construction of the two single-line bores for this railway tunnel, 20·11 km long, had started in 1898. The bores were 17 m apart, centre to centre, and they were connected with transverse tunnels at intervals of 200 m. Half a century later, the Woodhead Tunnel was being driven through the Pennines for British Railways. More than 4·8 km long and with a single bore for the double-track electrified main line between Manchester and Sheffield, it was completed in 1953, England's third longest railway tunnel. Typical of twentieth-century tunnelling, Simplon and Woodhead demonstrated that in spite of new and improved techniques, burrowing through the unknown was still the least dependable branch of civil engineering. The meeting of the twin Alpine bores in 1905, after a total of 2392 working days, had been delayed for more than six months because headings unexpectedly left hard rock—gneiss, mica-schist, and 'sugar marble' limestone—and suddenly ran into treacherous formations of decomposed calcareous mica-schist where the high ground pressure defeated, for a time, all efforts to stabilize the material by shoring with heavy timbers. Ultimately, with closely spaced steelwork and rapid-hardening cement, work had been able to go ahead; but only after the cost of progress per metre had rocketed from £162 to £980. At Woodhead the modern bore replaced two single-line tunnels, the maintenance of which had ceased to be economic under the unpleasant conditions caused by frequent steam-hauled trains. Completion was delayed more than two years because the original construction plans turned out to be quite impracticable. The final bill for the 4·9-km tunnel soared to £1100 per metre. The idea of driving a 3·65 m × 3·65 m pilot tunnel from four working faces (begun at each portal and from a single shaft located about midway) and subsequently enlarging by radial drilling had to be abandoned. Enlargement by radial drilling in blocky gritstones and shaly sandstones proved to be impossible without excessive overbreak. The method then had to be changed from radial drilling to face drilling. This fundamental change entailed driving bypass tunnels to gain access to nine chambers that were needed to start the headings for face drilling. It also resulted in a loss of efficiency because it was impossible to keep inwards and outwards construction traffic separate. Prior knowledge of the geology is essential to the correct choice of method of excavation and the design of lining, both temporary shoring-up and permanent construction, to withstand bursting and crushing forces.

The longest pressure tunnel in Britain is at Lochaber. It was finished in 1930. Divided into twelve lengths for convenience of construction, it is 24 km long and the cross-sectional area varies between 15 and 17·5 m². Driven through hard rock and almost completely in the dry, the best weekly progress from each of 22 working faces was 27·5 m. Another Scottish hydro-electric power project, the Clunie, has a tunnel with a cross-sectional area of 38·5 m². Finished in 1949, it was the first tunnel in Britain to be taken out to its full dimensions without a preceding pilot bore; it was driven through 850 m of hard rock. In the Breadalbane hydro-electric scheme (1957), the raising instead of sinking of a vertical pressure tunnel was remarkable for the improved facilities this construction method gave for the removal of the broken rock. The shaft, 183 m deep and 3·65 m in diameter, excavated through hard igneous rock, leads to the penstock tunnel at St. Fillans generating station. The construction procedure started with the drilling of a 162-mm pilot hole vertically downwards into the penstock tunnel. Then with a hoisting cable passed down the hole and shackled to an armoured-steel stoping cage, the shaft was driven upwards, working from the bottom. The cage accommodated two drill operators and a telephonist who passed orders to the shot-firers and winchmen outside. As the shattered rock fell to the bottom it was removed by plant working in the penstock tunnel. The armouring protected the men in the cage against falling rock, and before the charges were fired the cage was lowered and all personnel evacuated to a safe distance.

The method of tunnelling through soft rock for a motorway near Monmouth in 1965 was unusual. The twin bores were short, only 188 and 183 m, but the excavation, 111 m² in cross-sectional area, was too large for the face to be left standing without support. The strata, sandstones and marls, varied between hard conglomerate, which had to be blasted, and soft, friable clayey material. A vertical face would have been dangerous; besides, the tunnels were to be lined with double reinforced concrete. Steel shields were used. They followed conventional form, spanned the full width, and were propelled forward on skids laid down in small pilot tunnels driven slightly ahead of the excavation. Each shield projected right up to the top and sides of the face, which sloped from the bottom inwards into the hillside at the top. Thus the personnel were protected by a substantial buttress of material lying more or less at its natural angle of repose, and excavation proceeded in absolute safety. Shuttering for the concrete lining followed immediately behind the shield, and after a 'pull' of 1·22 m (the advance achieved after a single blasting) the shield was skidded forward by jacks thrusting against concrete which had been poured and vibrated only 2½ hours before.

The Rotherhithe Tunnel was the largest subaqueous tunnel in the world when it was opened in 1908. It has an inside diameter of 8·25 m and it was designed to allow room for two horse-drawn pantechnicons to pass; the approach gradients, 1 in 36, were suited to horse-drawn buses. This vehicular tunnel runs from Lower Road, Rotherhithe, to Commercial Road, Stepney; it is lined with cast iron and it was driven with a conventional shield through soft and water-bearing ground (Fig. 36.15). The length of bore lined with cast iron is 1010 m and in every ring—which advanced the tunnel through 0·75 m—there are seventeen separate castings which were machine-finished on the faying surfaces of every flange. Where the tunnel is on a curve, every casting was machined so that on bolting the rings together the road would follow the intended line.

The Rotherhithe Tunnel had followed a pedestrian tunnel opened in 1902 between Greenwich and the Isle of Dogs. Both had been driven with the aid of compressed air to keep the water out of the workings. A tunnel of 3·5 m bore for electric cables from Tilbury Power Station to Gravesend, driven in 1967–8, was unlike any previous bore constructed in water-bearing strata under the Thames. It was built without exposing the workmen to the risk of

FIG. 36.15(a). One of the shields used in driving the Rotherhithe Tunnel shown here after it had emerged into a steel-lined vertical shaft. The picture shows clearly the front of the shield and the compartments in which the men worked, shovelling away the 'muck' as the shield advanced through the London clay.

contracting bone necrosis, the dreaded disease suffered by one out of every five men who have been actively employed in tunnelling under compressed air. This Thames Cable Tunnel was successfully driven through ground where the water pressure rose to $6·2 \times 10^5$ N/m². It was driven through chalk with a 298-kW electrically powered tunnelling mole; this had a continuously rotating head that chiselled away the muck and deposited it on conveyors that led to muck wagons and so to the bottom of a shaft, whence the spoil, mixed with water, was pumped to the surface. Combinations of deep drainage wells and ground treatment with injections of clay–cement grout, and continuous pumping, prevented the ingress of water to the workings.

There have also been developments in the lining of shield-driven tunnels. At the Potters Bar railway tunnels (1955–9), and in an entirely new system of tunnelling known as the rotating shield method (1958), precast concrete units

FIG. 36.15(b). The back of a shield used for driving the Rotherhithe Tunnel. This photograph, taken during the final stages of the erection of the shield, shows the hydraulic rams which, when pressing against the cast iron lining of the tunnel, thrust the shield forward into the clay. The two swivelling hydraulic rams were used to lift and place the heavy iron lining units in position.

have been used instead of cast iron (Fig. 36.16). Moreover, the concrete units, which cost only about one-eighth the price of the cast-iron ones, are innocent of bolts. At Potters Bar three straight circular bores were driven in the dry through London clay; in the aggregate they measured 1665 m and were for two lines of railway worked by diesel traction. Except at the portals, where for short lengths bolted cast-iron lining had to be used, plain concrete segments were used in rings which were prestressed against the clay as it was cut through by the shield. Metallurgical supersulphated cement was used to ensure that the concrete would be resistant to the effects of sulphuric acid present in the locomotive exhaust. The moulds in which the concrete units were cast were very accurately machined, to within limits of ± 0.25 mm; each ring was 68 cm thick radially and advanced the tunnel by 45.7 cm. To provide for the pre-stressing, special units near axis level admitted jacks which pressed the top

FIG. 36.16. The novel system of lining introduced by British Rail in their 1959 tunnels near Potters Bar: six interlocking concrete blocks being positioned by an erecting machine.

and bottom halves of the ring apart. Subsequently, the jacking spaces were filled with concrete and the jacks removed; apart from painting abutting surfaces with a bituminous mixture to act as a lubricant and a bedding, no other preparation of the concrete segments was necessary. Cast with nibs and recesses, the units were interchangeable and they fitted perfectly. The expanding of the rings hard against the clay eliminated all need for costly grouting outside the lining.

The rotating shield system was invented by Eric Bridge, and in it he cleverly devised an entirely new method of auger tunnelling. Instead of a shield thrust straight ahead by jacks pushing against the tunnel lining, the rotating shield turns like an auger. The lining, mass-produced precast concrete blocks, is in the form of a double spiral and the shield, shaped to accord with the spiral, is thrust round and forward by two jacks pushing against the last concrete lining units to have been erected. The front of the shield is conical, with the cutters brought to a point. In operation the spoil, automatically cut from the rotation of the shield through a twist equal to the spiral length of one lining unit, falls into the tunnel and is ready for removal while, the jacks retracted and two more lining units positioned, the shield is set for the next push along the spiral. Driven through clay at Tolworth, a Bridge spiral tunnel 1·8 m in diameter advanced through 1·75 m in an hour. The shield was operated by one man and power for the jacks came from a 4-kW motor.

All the vehicular tunnels under rivers in Britain were driven with Greathead-style shields like the one used for the Tower Subway in 1869. Queensway (3·25 km) under the Mersey was opened by H.M. King George V on 18 July 1934; overwhelmed by increasing traffic, it was relieved by Kingsway, opened by H.M. Queen Elizabeth II on 24 June 1971. Kingsway had been dug by the world's largest mechanical mole after it had bored the water tunnels for Pakistan's irrigation project at Mangla. Tunnels were twice driven under the Tyne: the first, for pedestrians and cyclists, was completed in 1951; the second, nearly 2 km long and for vehicles, was opened in 1967. The Clyde Traffic Tunnel was opened in 1964, and Dartford Tunnel under the Thames the year before. All were lined with cast iron.

Submerged tunnelling, in which prefabricated steel and concrete tubes are laid in a trench dredged across a river bed, began in 1910. The first was for railway trains under the Detroit River; twenty years later a vehicular tunnel built in the same fashion linked Detroit and Windsor. Elsewhere submerged tunnels carry road traffic beneath rivers in Argentina, the U.S.A., Holland, and Belgium. In the last, a platform on spuds firmly planted on the river bed ensured that the tunnel units could be accurately set in position at a depth of 32 m.

Similar highway tunnels, but of rectangular cross-section, have been constructed in Europe: under the Nieuwe Maas at Rotterdam (1941); the Coen Tunnel at Amsterdam (1966); the Benelux at Rotterdam (1967); under the IJ at Amsterdam (1968); and under the Scheldt at Antwerp (1969). The last was the largest; its units, 47·85 m wide and 10 m high, accommodate six lanes for road traffic and, separately, a double-track railway.

BIBLIOGRAPHY

BAILEY, DONALD COLEMAN, FOULKES, R. A., and DIGBY-SMITH, R. The Bailey Bridge and its Developments. *Minutes of Proceedings of the Institution of Civil Engineers: Civil engineer in war* (1948).
BAXTER, J. W., GEE, A. F., and JAMES, H. B. Gladesville Bridge. *Minutes of Proceedings of the Institution of Civil Engineers*, **30**, March 1965.

BERRIDGE, P. S. A. *The girder bridge, after Brunel and others*. Robert Maxwell, London (1969).
——, *Couplings to the Khyber*. David and Charles, Newton Abbot (1969).
BROWN, C. D. London Bridge: planning, design and supervision. *Minutes of Proceedings of the Institution of Civil Engineers*, **54**, part I, February (1973).
BUCHANAN, C. D. *Mixed blessing, the motor in Britain*. Leonard Hill, London (1958).
FREEMAN, R., and LONG, A. E. The erection of military road bridges, 1939–1946. *Minutes of the Proceedings of the Institution of Civil Engineers: Civil engineer in war* (1948).
HAMMOND, R. *Tunnel engineering*. Heywood, London (1959).
HINDLEY, G. *A history of roads*. Richard Clay (The Chaucer Press), Bungay (1971).
HOPKINS, H. J. *A span of bridges*. David and Charles, Newton Abbot (1970).
INGLIS, C. E. Theory of transverse oscillations in girders, and its relation to live-load and impact allowances. *Minutes of Proceedings of the Institution of Civil Engineers*, **20**, September (1923).
KERENSKY, O. A., and LITTLE, G. Medway Bridge: Design. *Minutes of Proceedings of the Institution of Civil Engineers*, **29** (1963–4).
KIER, M., HANSEN, F., and DUNSTER, J. A. Medway Bridge: Construction. *Minutes of Proceedings of the Institution of Civil Engineers*, **29** (1963–4).
LEEMING, J. J. *Road accidents, prevent or punish?* Cassell, London (1969).
MEAD, P. F. London Bridge: demolition and construction, 1967–73. *Minutes of Proceedings of the Institution of Civil Engineers*, **54**, part 1, February (1973).
NICHOLS, H. J. Pre-stressing bridge girders. *Journal of the Institution of Civil Engineers*, **5** (1936–7).
O'FLAHERTY, C. A. *Highways*. Edward Arnold, London (1974).
PARRY, R. R., and THORNTON, G. D. Construction of the Monmouth Tunnels in soft rock. *Minutes of Proceedings of the Institution of Civil Engineers*, **47**, September (1970).
PEQUIGNOT, C. A. *Tunnels and tunnelling*. Hutchinson, London (1963).
REMFRY, D. H. The interaction in bridgework of the deck system on the main girders and the consequent modification of stresses therein. *Minutes of the Proceedings of the Institution of Civil Engineers*, **20**, September (1923).
SCHREIBER, H. *The history of roads*. Barrie and Rockliff, London (1961).
SHIRLEY-SMITH, HUBERT. *The world's great bridges*. Phoenix House, London (1953).
STEINMAN, D. B., and WATSON, S. R. *Bridges and their builders*. Dover Publications, New York (1957).
TABOR, E. H. The Rotherhithe Tunnel, in *Engineering wonders of the world*, vol. 1. Nelson, London (1912).
TERRIS, A. K., and MORGAN, H. D. New tunnels near Potters Bar in the Eastern Region of British Railways. *Minutes of Proceedings of the Institution of Civil Engineers*, **18**, April (1961).
TURTON, F. Three prestressed concrete railway bridges. *Minutes of Proceedings of the Institution of Civil Engineers*, **27**, September (1961).

PART II: LAND RECLAMATION, CANALS, PORTS, AND HARBOURS

I. LAND RECLAMATION

In 1930 the world's population was 2000 million. The figure had doubled during the preceding hundred years. By 1975 it was to have been doubled again. Not surprisingly therefore, there have been in the twentieth century some major engineering projects to reclaim more land to provide food and water for the rapidly increasing population. Two outstanding examples are the keeping of the sea out of the former Zuiderzee, and storing fresh water in a former inlet of the sea for crowded Hong Kong.

The IJsselmeer polders (Fig. 36.17). The project for enclosing three-quarters of the Zuiderzee had been planned in 1891 by Cornelis Lely, but it was not until nearly thirty years later, when the Dutch faced an alarming shortage of food, that work was put in hand on the greatest land reclamation scheme the world has ever known. During the First World War (in which the Dutch were neutral) shipping blockades stopped the import of food into Holland, and in 1916 the home-produced crops were lost through the accidental inundation of rich agricultural lands by the sea when the ancient dykes were breached.

The building of embankments joining North Holland to the island of Wieringen and that island to Friesland, 48 km to the north-east, was started on 29 June 1920. Closure was effected on 28 May 1932 (Fig. 36.18).

By then the Wieringermeerpolder (20 000 ha), the first of five polders, had been drained. Next, the Noordoostpolder (48 000 ha) was drained in 1942; Eastern Flevoland (54 000 ha) in 1957; and South Flevoland (44 000 ha) in 1968. The last polder, Markerwaard (60 000 ha) will have been drained by 1980 and the freshwater lake, the IJsselmeer, will have been almost stabilized at its reduced area of 125 000 ha. IJsselmeer water comes from rivers and the lake will partially empty into the Wadden Zee through non-return sluices when the tide is on the ebb. The IJsselmeer will irrigate the rich polders, float ships of up to 2000 tonnes, and maintain the level of the ground-water at Amsterdam so that the timber piles on which the city buildings are founded shall not dry out and suffer decay.

Another benefit from the IJsselmeer is the ridding of the old polder lands

of a terrible plague of malarial mosquitos, a plague so pestilential that motorists, in spite of windscreen wipers, had often been stopped because their
vision had been impaired by layers of insects crushed against the glass.
Scientists found that eels would eat the larvae of the mosquito if they were
admitted to the lake. So, through the utilization of one of the most remarkable
of natural phenomena—namely the migration of elvers from the Sargasso
Sea, swarming in their millions in search of freshwater food—the organized
'locking-in' of these creatures through the sluices and into the IJsselmeer was
to solve a difficult problem and rid the Dutch of a major health hazard.

The embankment which shuts out the sea consists of 13·5m. m³ of boulder
clay and 23m. m³ of sand, dredged up from the bed of the Zuiderzee by
eleven bucket dredgers and seven suction dredgers. In all, the floating plant
numbered 505 vessels. Brush-wood for fascines to consolidate the dam was
brought from woods in Holland. The stone, of which 920000 m³ armour the
sloping sides against wave action, had to be imported from Germany and
Belgium. At its base, the embankment has a width of 183 m, and on the crest,
9 m above high water at spring tides, there is room for a dual two-lane motor
road and a separate cycle-path. The provision of this splendid highway has
given the Dutch improved access to the north-east part of their country.
There are locks for shipping passing in and out of the IJsselmeer along two
navigation lanes: one close to the shore of North Holland, the other nearer to
Friesland. To control the water-level in the lake—20 cm below Dutch Mean
Water-level in summer and 40 cm below it in winter—there are massive
sluices grouped near the locks. In all there are twenty-five sluices; each is
12 m in diameter and can be closed by a pair of giant steel valves which weigh
41 tonnes apiece.

The construction of the embankment was remarkable for the patience and
ingenuity displayed. The concrete works for the locks and sluices were built
in excavations dredged out in the open sea and pumped dry behind temporary cofferdams. Thus, the sluices were ready for use well in advance of
the most difficult operation, namely making the final closure of the dam
against the powerful scouring action of the tides. Under water, the embankment was built up by dumping clay from self-discharging lighters; above
this, dredgers discharged boulder-clay on to the dam to bring the top up to
the level of high spring tides. Above low water, the brush-wood fascines used
to consolidate the bank were weighted down with stones. Finally, the stone
armouring to give protection against wave action was set by hand on a
mattress of straw and rubble.

Construction, programmed to minimize interference with the ebb and flow of the sea, was started in the shallower regions. In between these 'islands' of construction, specially designed underwater banks were formed of clay protected by weighted mattresses, which could be depended upon to remain undisturbed even by swift currents flowing at speeds of 22 km/h. It had been intended to effect the final closure in the spring of 1932; but, because ship-worm threatened early damage to the brush-wood mattresses, the work was speeded up and the shorter length of the embankment, from Wieringen to North Holland, was finished in November 1931. At the closure of the 48-km dam in 1932, scour had reached a depth of 30 m before the flow was finally checked.

Work on the Wieringermeerpolder had gone on ahead of the completion of the Zuiderzee embankment. It was finished and pumped dry on 21 August 1930. A dyke 19 km long had been built to hold back the partially tamed tidal water of the sea and it was completed on 27 July 1929. Five pumps then drained the polder dry in $6\frac{1}{2}$ months. While this was going on, a complete network of minor shipping canals and drainage ditches had been dredged to service the new arable land. Sixty bridges, 250 km of roads, and 500 farm-steads—together with the necessary schools and churches—were being built ready to meet the needs of the settlement. The first of the new villages came into being in 1931 and the first satisfactory harvest after the desalinization of the soil was reaped nine years later. Such was the pressing demand to meet the growing population of a country which was about to surrender an empire that for every new farm leased by the Dutch government there were more than 300 applicants.

The construction of the Noordoostpolder, the second of the Zuiderzee reclamations, was started in 1936; the 55 km of dykes which enclosed it were finished in December 1940; and it had been pumped dry by 9 September 1942. There were, in addition to the navigation canals and drainage ditches, 483 km of roads and 69 bridges to serve a carefully planned layout of 11 small centres of population. To speed up the settlement, many of the buildings for the farmsteads had been prefabricated.

Land reclamation works throughout the Netherlands suffered delay and serious damage during the Second World War. The Wieringermeerpolder was inundated on 17 April 1945 when the Germans blew two gaps in the enclosing dyke. Within 48 hours fresh water from the IJsselmeer covered the whole 20000 ha and wrought havoc in every farmstead. Fortunately, due warning had been given and the inhabitants escaped with their lives. No

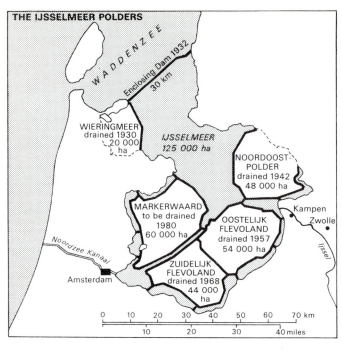

THE IJSSELMEER POLDERS

WADDENZEE

Enclosing Dam 1932
30 km

WIERINGMEER
drained 1930
20 000 ha

IJSSELMEER
125 000 ha

NOORDOOST
POLDER
drained 1942
48 000 ha

MARKERWAARD
to be drained
1980
60 000 ha

OOSTELIJK
FLEVOLAND
drained 1957
54 000 ha

Kampen
Zwolle

Noordzee Kanaal

ZUIDELIJK
FLEVOLAND
drained 1968
44 000 ha

Amsterdam

IJssel

0   10   20   30   40   50   60   70 km

10   20   30   40 miles

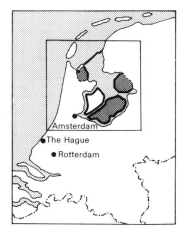

Fig. 36.17. The Zuiderzee area in 1961 showing the reclaimed polders and other areas to be drained in the future.

Amsterdam
The Hague
Rotterdam

Fig. 36.18. Engineers battle to stem the strong tidal race and close the gap between the two arms of the Zuiderzee barrier-dam in 1932.

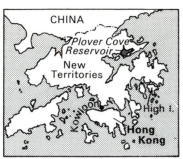

FIG. 36.19. Plover Cove, a sketch map of the coast showing the reservoirs reclaimed from the sea at the inlet and in the strait in relation to crowded Hong Kong and Kowloon.

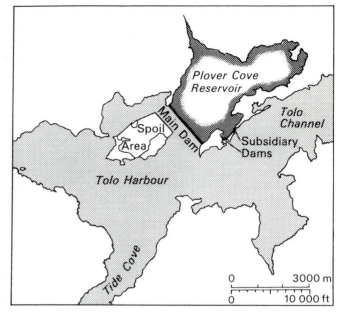

FIG. 36.20. In building the Panama Canal, all the plant used to remove the excavated material from the huge Culebra cutting was rail-borne.

damage was done either to the dam which kept out the sea or to the pumping stations. As soon as Holland had been liberated the dyke was repaired and the pumps were set to work; by 11 December 1945, 7 teralitres[1] of fresh water had been pumped out of the Wieringermeerpolder. Five months later the rich arable land had been restored and in that very year, 1946, a normal crop was harvested.

Plover Cove reservoir (Fig. 36.19). Begun in 1964 and completed in four years, Plover Cove is a lake 5·5 km long of fresh water stored in what was formerly an inlet of the sea. It is the major part of a scheme that was planned to double the quantity of drinking water available to the inhabitants of Hong Kong. The scheme increases storage capacity fourfold and it taps all possible sources within the 1035 km² of the island and the mainland territory. British engineers were responsible for the scheme. French, Swedish, Japanese, and Chinese contractors carried out the reclamation project with a labour force which at one time numbered 4500 and was recruited from America, Australia, Holland, Germany, and Norway.

The Plover Cove reservoir was sealed off from the open sea by a barrage 2070 m long and two subsidiary dams, 198 and 210 m long respectively. In between, there is a spillway 244 m long built across an outcrop of hard rock on an island. At the barrage, the seabed consisted of very soft mud 15 m deep, and the depth of the tidal sea ranged from 9 to 12 m. When this dam was finished, the crest was 11 m above low tide; and when the reservoir was in use, the difference in levels between the sea at high tide and the fresh water at its lowest was equivalent to a head of about 10 m. Built of material from local quarries, it took two years continuous dumping before the stone in the embankment started to show above the sea. Of the 16·25m. tonnes of fill that went into the barrage, 90 per cent had been placed under water.

So successful was the reservoir at Plover Cove that in 1970 work was started on a similar project at High Island. There, dams rising 91·5 m above the bottom of the sea close the two ends of a strait. Together, the inlet and the strait contain 802·5 gigalitres[2] of much-needed fresh water for the people in Hong Kong.

II. CANALS

The development of canals has continued during the twentieth century. With the exception of the inland navigations in Britain, where the extensive

---

[1] tera = a million million.   [2] giga = one thousand million.

use of locks made transport by canal barge uneconomic in competition with the railway train and the road lorry, the world's canals have been extended very considerably. The enlarged Kiel Canal (1914) gave the German dread-noughts a short cut from the Baltic to the North Sea just in time for the First World War; in spite of sea-locks, it was being used by more ships per day than any other canal in 1964. The origin of the Panama Canal, too, was due to naval requirements, but so valuable was it to prove in shortening commer-cial shipping routes that by 1965 plans were being drawn up for constructing another canal between the Atlantic and Pacific oceans. The Welland Canal (1932) and the St. Lawrence Seaway (1959) were built so that large ocean freighters could voyage right into the heart of the North American continent.

The Panama Canal. The Panama Canal was constructed by the U.S.A. between 1907 and 1914. Opened initially on 15 August 1914, it was closed shortly afterwards by a serious landslide and it was not in regular use until 1915. It is 64·8 km long and has another 16·9 km of sea approaches. The canal runs between Colon on the Atlantic Ocean and Panama on the Pacific, and can be used by any ship drawing not more than 12·2 m in salt water and capable of being taken through locks that are 304 m long and 33·5 m wide. Locks at each end lift vessels through about 26 m so that they can proceed along a freshwater channel cut through a mountain range and a lake where the water-level was raised by the construction of a huge earth dam. At the time of construction, that dam was claimed to be the greatest structure of its kind ever undertaken by man; the weight of spoil, 305m. tonnes, excavated to take the canal through the isthmus exceeded by 58 times that of the volume of the Pyramid of Cheops.

The Panama Canal was cut by rail-mounted machines (Fig. 36.20). As recorded on the 1962 memorial unveiled at the opening of the Thatcher Ferry intercontinental highway bridge, John F. Stevens, the main architect of the canal, was a railroad engineer who was renowned for his work in taking a transcontinental railway through the Rocky Mountains. More than any other twentieth-century project, the building of the Panama Canal depended on steel wheels rolling on steel rails. The route paralleled the very first American railroad that joined the Atlantic and Pacific coasts in 1885. With the exception of floating dredgers used in cutting the channels through the lake and the sea approaches, all the construction plant was worked by steam and it moved on railway tracks. After completion of the canal, the electric tugs that pull ships through the locks were mounted on railway tracks and fitted with rack and pinion gear to negotiate the short steep inclines between locks. Still in the railway era, the opening of the canal heralded the building of a second Panama railroad.

The construction of the canal was remarkable for the immensity of the task of moving the spoil from cuttings and dumping it in embankment dams. The plant used was representative of the all-time zenith in the development of portable rail-borne machines powered by steam raised by burning coal. Through the mountain, the spoil was scooped up by steam-driven bucket-ladder dredgers mounted on rails; these worked along temporary tracks laid on terraces dug out of the hillside by rail-mounted steam shovels. The spoil was taken away in trains of low-sided flat trucks hauled by powerful 4–6–0 steam locomotives. There were more than a hundred steam shovels, by Bucyrus and Marion; each weighed between 70 and 95 tonnes, and, at a single bite, the biggest could handle 3·8 m³ of broken rock and earth. Each shovel stood on its own short length of railway track and deposited its loads, up to 10 tonnes at a time, on to trucks being drawn by slowly on an adjacent track. Tracklaying and moving; the unloading of the trains; and the spreading of the unloaded spoil were operations that were fully mechanized. Working along the track which was to be slued sideways, a track-thrower with its gang of nine men could move 1·6 km of standard-gauge railway line laterally through 2·7 m in eight hours. The track-thrower resembled a long-jibbed travelling steam crane; it slued the track without removing the fish-plates from the rails or the rails from the sleepers. Done by hand, this work would have required an army of 600 labourers. The train-loads of spoil were unloaded by means of Lidgerwood discharging ploughs. These were heavy steel blades drawn over the floors of the trucks and along the full length of a train by a hawser wound on to the barrel of a steam winch. The latter was mounted on a special truck placed next to the locomotive, which supplied the steam. The blade of the plough was angled so that spoil was pushed off to one side of the train. The ends of the trucks let down to bridge the gaps over the couplings and the sides were hinged so that they could be released on the off-loading side of the train and held locked upright on the other. A Lidgerwood with its crew of ten men could unload a train of seventeen 40-tonne trucks, each with a burden of 34·4 m³ of spoil, in five minutes. To have done the same work in the same time by hand would have needed 400 men with shovels. And to spread and level the unloaded heaps of earth and rock, a mechanical spreader was used. This, a forerunner of the modern bulldozer, consisted of a steel blade that was slung out on a rigid frame from the side of a special

FIG. 36.21. Vessels negotiating the locks in the Panama Canal are controlled by electric rack-and-pinion railway 'tug' locomotives.

railway truck and angled so that the material was pushed over and spread out evenly as the truck was propelled forward by a locomotive. A spreader with its crew of five did the work of an army of 400 labourers in less than a fifteenth of the time.

The locks in the Panama Canal are arranged in duplicate. Side by side, separate locks deal with northbound (Pacific to Caribbean) and southbound traffic. At the Atlantic end at Gatun (Fig. 36.21) there are three double sets of locks in a single staircase; descending to the Pacific, a lake separates the top stair from the two lower steps. Each lock shares equally the height of lift, and all the pairs of the steel mitre lock gates, 23 m in height, are identical. A feature of the locks is the strong chain stretched across the approach to each flight. These chains are attached to powerful springs and they can arrest the progress of any ship that may threaten to ram the gates.

Locks are especially vulnerable to damage in time of war. It was for this particular reason that the building of the Panama Canal was so long delayed. That story is past history, but there is a sequel. The idea of building a second

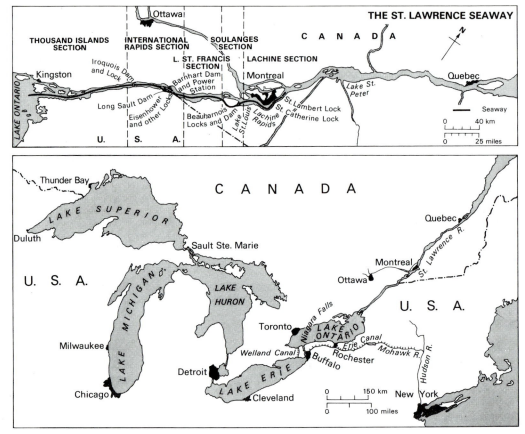

FIG. 36.22. The St. Lawrence Seaway.

Panama Canal as a sea-level waterway, with only one set of locks to cater for the difference in levels between the two oceans, was discussed by the U.S. Congress in 1945–7. Such a canal, planned for the nuclear age, would have duplicate shipping lanes and would give passage to ships with a draught of 18·25 m; the locks would be 61 m wide and 475 m long; and, because the tidal range at the Pacific end is 6 m and at the Atlantic end it is minimal, the lift to be provided for would be very small compared with the ups and downs in the present canal.

The Panama Canal shortened the sea routes from New York to San Francisco by 8047 km and from Liverpool to the west coast of the United States by 4184 km. The benefits in 1915, when steamships had to sacrifice valuable cargo space for coal and had to make time-consuming calls at ports for rebunkering, were even greater than they were later when oil had replaced coal as the most commonly used fuel. Nevertheless, and in spite of the incidence of air travel, the annual number of ships passing through the canal was to rise from 4443 in the 1920s to 10794 in 1960; by 1950, the figure was only 5448, but in 1965 it had risen to more than 12000. Although locking through the canal usually takes no longer than three hours in the journey from ocean to ocean, the 1915 canal suffers from two disadvantages: the Pacific locks are sited too close to the narrow channel through the mountain range, and the locks are too small to accommodate many large ships. The first objection leads to delay through the bunching of ships; the second precludes the passage of the latest aircraft-carriers belonging to the U.S. navy.

The St. Lawrence Seaway (Figs. 36.22 and 23). Planned during the first half of the twentieth century, the St. Lawrence Seaway was constructed between 1954 and 1958. The project, the development of navigation between Montreal and Lake Ontario, was combined with a scheme to harness the river for the generation of electrical energy, known as the St. Lawrence Power Project. The official opening was performed jointly by H.M. Queen Elizabeth II and President Eisenhower on 26 and 27 June 1959. The seaway removed the last remaining hindrance to the through passage of ships drawing not more than 8·26 m. The power undertaking, half in the U.S.A. and half in Canada, has a generating capacity of 1·880 MW and an average annual energy output of 13 000 GWh. It was the demand for energy, together with the need to ship iron ore from Labrador to Lake Erie (because the ore deposits west of Lake Superior were insufficient to meet all the demands of the steel industry in the U.S.A.) that had finally led to an international agreement which was to turn Duluth–Superior, the second port of the U.S.A., into a sea-port.

The St. Lawrence Seaway is ice-free from April until mid-December. The facts that it is closed for part of the year; that navigation by canals with a depth of 4·25 m had circumvented the rapids in the St. Lawrence since 1903; and that alternative ice-free routes existed for the movement of grain from the mid-West to Europe accounted for the delay in the authorization of the gigantic project, which was eventually to cost $1200m.—$650m. for power and the balance for navigation, including improvements in the Upper Great Lakes. Even the opening of the Panama Canal was blamed for adding to the delay; in 1925, because railway rates were reduced, it was cheaper to ship grain destined for Europe via Vancouver and the Panama Canal.

However, the advantages of through passage from the Gulf of St. Lawrence right into the heart of the most industrialized area of the North American continent had long been appreciated and they were gradually provided for

(Vol. IV, p. 551). By 1906, a dredged channel with a depth of 9 m had made Montreal into an ocean port. The Welland Canal which bypasses the Niagara Falls and provides navigation between lakes Erie and Ontario had been deepened for lake steamers drawing 4·25 m in 1887; a new Welland Canal, 169 km long and opened in 1932, had a depth of 7·6 m throughout and, most wisely, 9·1 m of water over the sills in its eight locks. The deepening of the Welland Canal was included in the Great Lakes–St. Lawrence undertaking. In the St. Lawrence River itself, when a hydro-electric power station was built in 1928, the Beauharnois Power Canal, 1000 m wide (to meet pondage requirements for the power-station intakes under the ice in winter) was dug more than 8·26 m deep with the future seaway in mind.

The Seaway involved controlling the outflow from Lake Ontario; damming the St. Lawrence River so as to drown the International Rapids; constructing a canal to bypass the dams; and, at the lower end, building two locks and connecting channels to surmount a rise of 12·8 m from the harbour at Montreal to the natural Lake St. Louis at the head of the Lachine Rapids. To regulate the water-level in Lake Ontario, the Iroquois Dam and lock were sited 11 km below a natural rock weir which formerly controlled the outflow. The dam is a straight buttressed gravity concrete structure with gated sluice-ways; the lock gives a maximum lift of only 1·8 m. Below Iroquois, the artificial stretch of water, 48 km long and from 2·4 to 6·4 km broad, is known as St. Lawrence Lake; it is the head-pond for the American and Canadian power-houses which are combined in the international power station built astride the frontier. Power is generated from a head of 24·7 m. At this point the river flows in two channels separated by the Barnhart Island; this natural feature was of the greatest significance in the planning of the entire project. The northern channel is closed by the power dam and the international power station. The power dam is a straight reinforced concrete structure 1000 m long, rising 49 m above the foundations. The dam across the southern channel is a concrete gravity curved-axis spillway structure, 880 m long and 44 m high above the foundations. The Wiley–Dondero Canal, which bypasses the dams, is 16 km long and includes two locks; it is wholly within American territory.

All the dams were constructed in the dry and behind temporary coffer-dams. The power dam was built in a single stage after the rapids had been dried out and the river diverted to the south of Barnhart Island. The dam across the south channel was built in two stages to avoid disturbing navigation on the existing canal system. In fact, all the construction works had to be most carefully programmed to meet three conditions that had been laid down in the international agreement. There was to be no interruption to canal traffic; there was to be no interference with the flow of water to existing power stations and other concerns; and the level of the water in Lake Ontario was to be retained within close limits in order to meet the needs of farmers and others living and working along its shores. In addition, the rate of flow above the power stations, existing and planned, had to be slow enough for the water to freeze as a solid ice-cover across the power-pools without the risk of ice-jams blocking the intakes.

To contain the water impounded by the dams, large compacted earth-fill embankments were built; on the U.S. side they extend for 27 km, and on the Canadian for 5 km. The land permanently inundated occupied 728 ha in the U.S.A. and 809 ha in Canada. This part of the project affected 6500 persons, 360 farms, 18 cemeteries, 56 km of Ontario Provincial Highway No. 2, and 64 km of the Canadian National Railway double-tracked main line. In moving and resettling the populace, more than 500 houses, and even a 127-year-old church, were transported bodily on special pneumatic-tyred vehicles.

It was not the immensity of the scheme so much as the intricacy of the planning needed to ensure compliance with the terms of the agreement that was to make a significant contribution to the advance of modern technology. Eleven hydraulic models were used to study the effects construction would have on the flow of water over 61 km of the river that were crucial to the whole programme. These models assisted in the overall design of the Seaway and the Power project. They demonstrated what the changes in the rate of flow would be under the ice in winter. The measurement of flow down the models had to be very accurate; for this, an improved miniature propeller-driven current meter was devised. It had to detect velocity changes that ranged between 55 mm/s and 60 cm/s, and the readings had to be recorded some distance away from the meter. Previously, all such instruments had suffered from errors caused by frictional drag in the commutator. But for the St. Lawrence, a new invention avoided such inaccuracies. This ingenious device registered the minute changes in the electrical resistance of the water surrounding the blades of the propeller. Those changes were caused by the tiny differences in conductivity across 1·27 mm of water, which altered as the speed of rotation of the propeller conformed to the changing rate of flow of the water. The rate of change in the electrical resistance indicated the velocity of the water. This meter was used to measure flow below the surface.

To trace direction and speed of movement on the surface, an elegant method was evolved. With a camera mounted in the roof of the laboratory, the passage of illuminated floats was recorded on film. With the shutter left open in the dark, and the field of view interrupted by a holed disc which was rotated at a constant speed, the developed negative revealed a succession of dashes that indicated the path and speed of each float.

Those models, and the ingenuity displayed in the University of Toronto, saved a great deal of expenditure. In the post-war developments at Niagara, Ontario Hydro had saved about $5m. by studying flow down similar models; through the use of the models of the St. Lawrence a far larger sum of money had been saved. Checking the results obtained from the hydraulic models with site recordings taken after the Seaway had been in operation showed the remarkable accuracy attained in the design of the immense scheme. In a 22·5-km stretch of the river, the fall in water-level was within 30 mm of that predicted by the model.

Seldom has scientific study proved more rewarding. The St. Lawrence Seaway and its ancillary works had multiplied by ten the tonnage of cargo that could be carried in a ship voyaging 4000 km from the Atlantic Ocean to Lake Superior. It had cut the number of locks involved in climbing 183 m from sea-level to the world's largest lake, from 31 to 16. Previously, specially built ocean-going cargo ships 76·5 m long with a beam of 12·8 m, voyaging between the Great Lakes and Europe, had to load to less than their economical capacity so as to reduce their draught from 4·8 m to 4·2 m to negotiate the pre-Seaway canal system. The St. Lawrence Seaway opened the way for the through passage of ships with a length of 222 m and a beam of 22·8 m.

III. PORTS AND HARBOURS

Since 1900 seaports have undergone sweeping changes because of revolutionary alterations in the methods of transport, trading, materials handling, and political ownership. Elaborate passenger landing-stages and grand ocean terminals built in the first quarter of the century were redundant by 1950, their intended patrons having been lost to the airlines. In the 1920s, the oil-fired ship was making coal-bunkering plant obsolete. Within 30 years, one British port which had had facilities to hold 20 000 tonnes of coal afloat had ceased to offer any other fuel but oil. Cargo unitization, facilities for road vehicles to roll on and roll off, the falling-off in the use of railways, etc. resulted in the demand for costly re-equipment to ensure that throughput would be profitable—the aim of every port-planner and harbour engineer.

Dover, Fishguard, Tema, and Port Talbot have artificial harbours. Each is

FIG. 36.23(a). Building the lock-walls for the St. Lawrence Seaway entailed heavy excavation work and the construction of the walls in concrete.

FIG. 36.23(b). The St. Lambert Lock near Montreal, like all the locks on the St. Lawrence Seaway, enables ocean-going ships drawing up to 8·25 m to voyage between the Atlantic Ocean and the Great Lakes in the heart of North America.

tidal and each is typical of the methods of construction being used at the particular period when the port was built. Dover was sited to afford the shortest sea-crossing for passengers travelling between England and the mainland of Europe. Fishguard, in 1909, gave the Great Western Railway Company a direct route to southern Ireland and the hope of an extension to New York. The needs of war were to bring the 'instant' landing-place sheltered by an artificial breakwater into prominence at Gallipoli in 1915, and again at Mulberry harbour in Normandy in 1944. But the next permanent harbours to be built in the open sea were the Port of Tema (1962) in Ghana, and Port Talbot (1970) in South Wales.

Dover harbour. Begun in 1897 and opened by H.R.H. the Prince of Wales in 1909, Dover harbour works were acclaimed to be one of the greatest feats of maritime constructional engineering. They far exceeded the needs of the railway companies, who would have been content with 27·5 ha of sheltered water giving a minimum depth of 9·7 m. It was the Board of Admiralty who insisted on a harbour with an area of 242 ha; its members were alive to the threat of Germany's growing navy. Later, peacetime users were to benefit: there would be ample space for a train-ferry dock (1933–6) and a busy car-ferry terminal (1951–3).

In building the harbour, 3 km of wave-resisting walls (one an island breakwater) were constructed in the open sea (Fig. 36.24). They were formed of 42-tonne precast concrete blocks laid to half bond, vertically and horizontally, and keyed with 'joggles', that is cavities in abutting surfaces which were filled with canvas bags of concrete. Joints below water were innocent of mortar. Those above were mortared and pointed with quick-setting cement. The method of construction was by Goliath cranes travelling on steel gantries supported on blue gum timber piles—specially imported from Tasmania because the wood was immune to attack by the teredo ship-worm. The largest wall was 29 m high and was founded on hard chalk; it was 17 m wide at the base and 14 m at the top; upwards from 1 m below low water, it was faced with dressed granite brought from Cornwall and Sweden. The contractors, S. Pearson and Son, had successfully completed the Old Hudson River Tunnel in New York after that work had laid abandoned for 24 years. At Dover, using a diving-bell, their men dug the foundations with spades. The Portland cement was delivered to site by barge, 160 tonnes at a time; the aggregate, flint gravel from Dungeness and sharp sand from Sandwich, came by rail; and the concrete for the blocks was mixed at the rate of 4500 m³ per

FIG. 36.24. Dover Harbour under construction, 1904. The cranes that handled dredging grabs, diving-bells, and the 42-tonne concrete blocks used in building the breakwaters ran on gantries erected in the open sea.

week and matured for 28 days. Above the waves in the open sea, 20-tonne Scotch derricks travelled on the gantries and reached ahead to handle the piles and erect the steelwork. The Goliath cranes, coal-fired and spanning 30 m, followed, breaking up the seabed and grabbing out the muck, slinging the diving-bell and setting the blocks. With tides ranging from 4·5 m at neap tides to 5·75 m at spring tides, and currents so strong that work was impossible except during four hours slack water on each tide, block-setting under water averaged six blocks in an hour. In 12 months, 575 m of break-water were completed.

Fishguard harbour. At Fishguard the single breakwater is a rubble wall composed of rock blasted out of the near-by hillside. The rock was loaded

FIG. 36.25. At Fishguard Harbour the breakwater, an artificial peninsula, was formed by dumping rock spoil conveyed by railway trucks. These came direct from the hillside which was being dynamited and levelled to accommodate the harbour railway station.

into railway tip wagons by rail-mounted steam cranes and run out and dumped straight into the sea (Fig. 36.25). The wall, 100 m wide on the seabed and 21 m at the top, rises 8 m above the sea and shelters an area of 200 ha. In the total length of 600 m, above 200 tonnes of rock went into each metre of the wall. Contrasting with the laborious block-setting at Dover, the work at Fishguard achieved the same result at a very much lower cost. The hillside had had to be cut away to make room for the railway station and the rock was therefore not only readily available but had, in any case, to be dumped somewhere.

Unfortunately, Fishguard harbour suffered from a serious defect. The swell, fetching from the south-west approaches to St. George's Channel, reflected so strongly from the coastal shore opposite to the quay that it caused a continuous rising and falling of all the vessels berthed or anchored in the so-called sheltered waters. However, the harbour has sufficed for its share of the Irish traffic; for a period before the First World War, Cunard liners used it as a port of call. S.S. *Mauretania* was the first to do so, but her captain objected most strongly to the liveliness of the sea within the harbour. On that one occasion, the passengers from the U.S.A. were landed by tender. Having steamed out of New York at 10.00 a.m. on 25 August, they alighted at Paddington Station, London, at 6.40 p.m. on 30 August. The year was 1909.

The Port of Tema (Fig. 36.26). Ghana's second deep-water port, Tema, was ceremonially declared open on 10 February 1962. It is unique. Started *de novo* since the Second World War, and originally built to serve an aluminium industry being set up 65 km inland and using cheap electricity available from the Volta River Project, Tema was planned to meet the needs of a land that was shortly to develop very rapidly as a new and independent nation. Tema is only 27 km from Accra, the capital, which itself is 320 km by railway from Takoradi, the only other deep-water port on the 480-km coast of the former British colony of the Gold Coast. Instead of being built in the shelter of a river mouth, Tema was purposely sited on a shore exposed to the pounding waves of the Atlantic; the harbour is within 1600 m of deep water (13·6 m) which is unusually close on the west coast of Africa, and access is unlikely to be hindered by shoaling.

The harbour, 200 ha of sheltered water, is behind rock breakwaters which in length total 5300 m. The method of building the breakwaters in the open sea was similar to that used at Fishguard, except for two technological advances. The profile of the walls was determined by tests on hydraulic models, and the rock, gneiss quarried at a place half-way along the railway to the aluminium works, was loaded in steel skips that were lifted on to the trains at the quarry and off the trucks by crawler cranes working on the breakwaters. The rate of placing, nearly 4000 m³ every 24 hours, was enhanced through radio communication with the locomotive drivers bringing the trains of rock from up-country, and shunting the trucks so that the skips were within easy reach of the cranes unloading the rock into the sea.

Construction began in 1954. Eight years later, and with four berths in use, the annual imports and exports passing through the Port of Tema totalled 388 500 tonnes. A year after opening, there were nine berths in operation and the throughput had almost trebled. In 1966, 3m. tonnes were being handled at 12 dry-cargo berths; an oil berth was dealing with a million tonnes; another berth was importing 250 000 tonnes of bauxite and despatching 220 000 tonnes of aluminium; and plans were afoot to increase the number of berths to 20 and to carry through an expensive rock-dredging project that would ensure a minimum depth of water of 8·5 m in the harbour. The growth of industry and trade during 12 years had been remarkable. On high ground in the immediate hinterland, the new town of Tema had sprung up; it had a population of 50 000. Where, in 1954, 8 ha had been thought sufficient for a fishing harbour to be used by small trawlers, the discovery of very rich tunny areas was attracting ocean-going craft from the U.S.A., Britain, Japan,

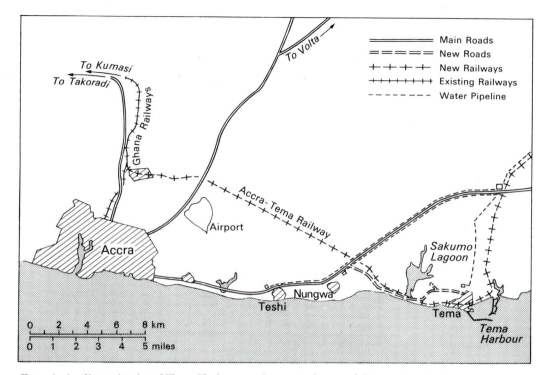

FIG. 36.26. *Above*, the site of Tema Harbour on the exposed coast of Ghana, showing the access routes; *below*, the layout of the harbour.

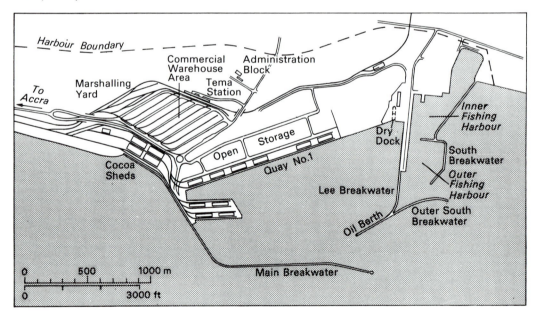

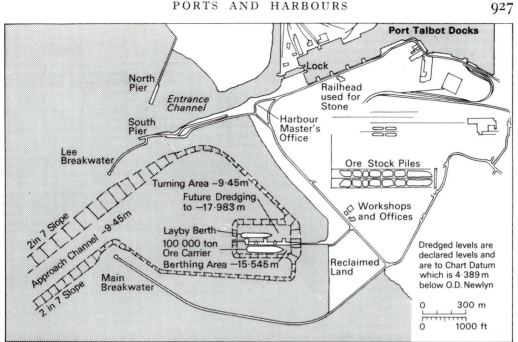

FIG. 36.27. Port Talbot Harbour.

Scandinavia, and the U.S.S.R.; by 1964 this had led to the building of another 900 m of new breakwater and the creation of a fishing harbour with an area of more than 40 ha, with 7·3 m minimum depth of water, and with extensive facilities for fish-processing plants. Tema is surely one of the world's most rapidly developing ports; it is certainly one of the newest.

Port Talbot harbour (Fig. 36.27). Port Talbot is tidal and the rise and fall can range through 10 m. The new harbour (1967–70) is outside the enclosed docks which were built in the nineteenth century. The former port could not accept vessels larger than 10 000 d.w.t. because of the restrictions imposed by the entrance lock. The modern harbour has been designed solely for importing iron ore unloaded at the rate of 3600 tonnes/h to satisfy the adjoining steelworks, whose stockyard can hold up to 620 000 tonnes of ore; but eventually it will accept single shipments of 150 000 tonnes and the annual throughput will be 20m. tonnes. It gives the British Steel Corporation the opportunity to import ore in very large, and therefore cheap, shiploads from South America and Western Australia. The length of approach channel that had to be dredged to admit the larger carriers (which have a loaded draught of 16·7 m) was less than 1·5 km. Compared with entry to most ports on the

FIG. 36.28. The *Forth Bridge*, the first ore carrier to berth at Port Talbot Harbour, brought 46000 tons of ore from Canada in March 1970.

mainland of Europe, this distance is short and for this reason Port Talbot is advantageously sited to serve the steelmaking industry.

In this harbour, ore-carriers berth alongside a finger pier that points towards the prevailing wind. They float in a dredged pocket with never less than 60 cm of water under them. With another dredged pocket for turning, a loaded carrier can berth on nearly all tides and in water sheltered by two rubble breakwaters: a short one that projects from a lee shore and another, twice as long, from the opposite shore. Combined, the breakwaters total 2100 m. They were constructed by 'tipping' outwards from the shore, and armoured with rock placed by crawler cranes. A fleet of 14 dumptrucks, travelling along a private road at speeds up to 64 km/h, transported 9m. tonnes of rock for these breakwaters in three years; a single load weighed 35 tonnes and the average haul was 14·5 km. The approach ditch and the pockets were dug out of silt, clay, sand, and gravel by suction dredgers, and their 2-in-7 slopes were stabilized by polypropylene sheeting weighted down with stone. The positioning of the dredgers was fixed by Decca Navigation Hifix, and the stone-placing on the breakwaters, which continued during fog and darkness, was accurately monitored by instrumentation. The construction of Port Talbot Harbour was one of the most highly mechanized maritime works of all time (Fig. 36.28).

BIBLIOGRAPHY

BAZLEN, K. A. *Zuiderzeeland*. N.V. Uitgevers Maatschappij Diligentia, Amsterdam (1952).

CHEVRIER, LIONEL. *The St. Lawrence Seaway*. Macmillan, Toronto (1959).

DE GLOPPER, R. J., and SEGEREN, W. A. The Lake IJssel reclamation project. *Endeavour*, **30**, 62 (1971).

FORD, S. E., and ELLIOTT, S. G. Investigation and design of the Plover Cove water scheme. *Minutes of Proceedings of the Institution of Civil Engineers*, **32**, October (1965).

HAMMOND, R., and LEWIN, C. J. *The Panama Canal*. Frederick Muller, London (1966).

HILLS, T. L. *The St. Lawrence Seaway*. Methuen, London (1959).

HOLDEN, OTTO. St. Lawrence Power Project—Hydraulic features. *Minutes of Proceedings of the Institution of Civil Engineers*, **18**, April (1961).

MacDERMOT, E. T. *History of the Great Western Railway*. Great Western Railway Company, London (1927).

McGAREY, D. G., and FRAENKEL, P. M. Port Talbot Harbour: planning and design. *Minutes of Proceedings of the Instutition of Civil Engineers*, **45**, April (1970).

ORDMAN, N. N. B. Port planning: some basic considerations. *Minutes of Proceedings of the Institution of Civil Engineers*, **37**, June (1967).

RIDGWAY, R. J., KIER, M., HILL, L. P., and LOW, D. W. Port Talbot Harbour: construction. *Minutes of Proceedings of the Institution of Civil Engineers*, **45**, April (1970).

SCOTT, P. A. Port of Tema. *Minutes of Proceedings of the Institution of Civil Engineers*, **32**, October (1965).

VAN VEEN, JOH. *Dredge drain reclaim*. Martinus Nuhoff, The Hague (1952).

37

BUILDING AND ARCHITECTURE

ROWLAND J. MAINSTONE

THE closing decade of the nineteenth century was one of great promise. The new structural material, reinforced concrete, was becoming established both in Europe and the U.S.A. Steel had superseded cast and wrought iron and, with the electric elevator, electric light, the telephone, and parallel developments in heating, it had made feasible the construction of buildings of a height undreamt-of in previous centuries except for a few special uses. In Chicago, buildings like D. H. Burnham's Reliance Building (Fig. 37.1) and L. H. Sullivan's Carson Pirie Scott Store (1899, 1903–4) had triumphantly exploited these latter developments and seemed to point the way straight forward to a new twentieth-century architecture.

The application of the new technology had, however, been very uneven, so that the new urban scene often was one of glaring contrasts. The great arched iron roof of St Pancras Station in London (Vol. V, Fig. 251) was, for instance, fronted by the massive neo-Gothic pile of Gilbert Scott's hotel. Much more seriously, in human terms, there had been an almost complete failure to apply properly even the earlier techniques of building to the housing of the vastly increased populations attracted by the new industries. Modern factory buildings were thus surrounded by crowded and insalubrious cottages or tenements built back-to-back in tight rows or round narrow, airless courts. The situation was probably worst in England—the penalty for being the first country to experience large-scale industrialization—but it was not greatly different in other countries that felt the full brunt only later. Everywhere, the cupidity of industrialists and of the speculative builders who moved in to house the new workers, the nostalgic make-believe of those who could afford to turn their backs on the industrial scene, and the general failure of those in authority to understand sufficiently and react on a large enough scale to what was happening, took their tolls.

The major achievement of the first half of the twentieth century was probably to realize fully the earlier potential and to go a long way towards applying the available technology more widely and in a more balanced manner. But the basic technology did not, in the meantime, stand still. It continued to develop, sometimes almost independently and sometimes in direct response to need, and this development must therefore also be considered. The total pattern was one of many interwoven threads and, though progress was less erratic than in the nineteenth century, its pace was far from uniform. It was interrupted, to an extent previously unknown, by two world wars and, in turn, greatly stimulated by their aftermaths. The stimulus was not merely that of widespread destruction (as in Chicago in 1871) and arrears in normal construction but, even more importantly, of major social and political upheavals. Other stimuli were provided by progress in some branches of manufacturing industry and by profound changes in the visual arts and, as a result, in the architect's creative vision.

A fundamental difficulty in the presentation of a concise account of the period 1900–50 is the length of time that has usually elapsed between the initial conception of some new way of building and its final realization. In this long time-scale the five years after the end of the Second World War were too short a period to see any major realization of some of the new forms that were then conceived. Some looking forward to the early 1950s therefore seems desirable in the latter part of this account. We shall start, though, with the more straightforward story of developments in the basic technology: in materials and components; in construction methods; in the means of servicing buildings and controlling their internal environments; and in the theoretic bases of design and their practical application and codification.

I. MATERIALS AND COMPONENTS

Developments in the principal materials of construction, considered simply as materials, are described in other chapters. Here we shall therefore make brief reference only to the more significant ones and concentrate on new uses. In doing so we shall, however, stop short of the final context of use—the complete structural form or building—leaving this for subsequent discussion.

Steel. The hot-rolled mild-steel joists and other sections which first became available towards the end of the nineteenth century continued to be used throughout the period. This range of sections was not, however, ideal for all building purposes. In particular the **I**-section joist made a very efficient beam with its relatively thick and narrow tapered flanges. But its much reduced stiffness when bent in the plane of the flanges rather than in the plane of the web made it much less suitable as a column, which may be bent and is liable to buckle in either plane. Initially this shortcoming, and any other shortcomings that arose from the limited ranges of sizes available, were made good by building up composite sections, either by riveting flat plates to the flanges of a joist or by battening or lacing together groups of channel, angle, or tee sections. All the columns of the Reliance Building (Fig. 37.1) were, for instance, made by battening together four pairs of angles, the angles of each pair being set back-to-back to give a composite tee whose stem pointed inwards. This form was then known as the Gray column. The fabrication of such composite members called, of course, for a great amount of shop riveting. A major step forward was taken when Gray introduced a wide-flange beam. This called for a more complex and costly rolling process, but this process had the further advantage that it produced flanges of uniform thickness in place of the earlier tapered ones. Wide-flange beams were first rolled in Luxembourg in 1901 and then in the U.S.A. in 1907.

Two further innovations which cannot be dated so precisely (since they did not call initially for the same large investment in new plant and were introduced more gradually) were the substitution of welding for riveting (or bolting) and the cold-rolling of lighter sections. Both became increasingly common in the 1930s, though welding made its debut for building purposes at least a decade earlier. On site it permitted much cleaner and more rigid joints to be made between members (Fig.37.2). In the shop it similarly provided a cleaner and more efficient way of fabricating composite sections to meet requirements that were not satisfied by the standard ranges of rolled sections. The basic cold-rolled sections were made by making longitudinal folds in strips of flat sheet and were thus always of uniform thickness. More complex and larger sections than could be made directly by rolling were built up by spot-welding together two or more basic rolled sections. Very efficient light box sections could, for instance, be made in this way. The wider use of cold forming was greatly stimulated by developments in the aircraft industry during the Second World War. The increased use of welding after this war for the purpose of making joints between members also then facilitated a slow but progressive re-introduction of the tube (the preferred nineteenth-century form for the cast-iron column) for structural purposes.

A different use of steel which grew rapidly and continuously was as bar, and later as high-tensile wire, to reinforce concrete—in reinforced and prestressed concrete respectively. Before turning to these, brief reference may also be made to a form of composite construction in which, typically, a reinforced concrete slab was made to act integrally with supporting steel

FIG. 37.1. Reliance Building, Chicago, 1894–5.

FIG. 37.2. Crown Hall, Illinois Institute of Technology, under construction in 1955.

beams by introducing a mechanical 'shear connection' between the two. This seems to have been first done in Germany in the 1930s, but the cost of the shear connection tended to cancel out the economy resulting from the efficient use of materials. Application, for building purposes, remained very limited up to 1950.

Reinforced concrete. Reinforced concrete is a much more adaptable structural medium than steel alone. It does not call, for instance, for large investments in heavy rolling mills capable of producing only limited ranges of standard sections. Within wide limits it can, in principle, be given any shape for which a suitable mould can be produced and, by variation of the concrete mix and the strength, quantity, and distribution of the reinforcement, whatever strength and stiffness may be required.

In the early stages of its development towards the end of the nineteenth century, its use was limited chiefly by lack of fundamental understanding of its properties—both those of the concrete and those of the composite material. In the first decade of this century its use continued to be dominated by empirically designed proprietory systems which seemed to envisage it largely as a direct substitute for steel in the columns and beams of the typical framed building.

As understanding grew, the quality of concrete was improved (chiefly by giving proper attention to the proportions of water and cement in the mix and to its compaction) and a freer approach became possible to the design of appropriate and efficient forms. In this latter respect the early work of Robert Maillart in Switzerland was particularly notable. He was one of the pioneers in the elimination of the beam as a separate entity in the floor system. He advocated and used a completely flat slab with reinforcement running only in two directions and varied in quantity in accordance with the variation in bending action. His column heads were flared out at the top to carry the vertical loads smoothly from the slab. This design may be compared with the roughly contemporary and parallel American innovation in which the ancestry of an independent beam system is still evident in the distribution of the reinforcement (Fig. 37.3) [1]. It should, however, be noted that part of the reason for the difference here is that, throughout our period, European practice usually strove much more than American for economy in the use of materials. In America, labour was relatively more costly, so that more attention was paid to simplifying forms in such a way as to reduce the labour required to build them. Subsequent developments along broadly similar

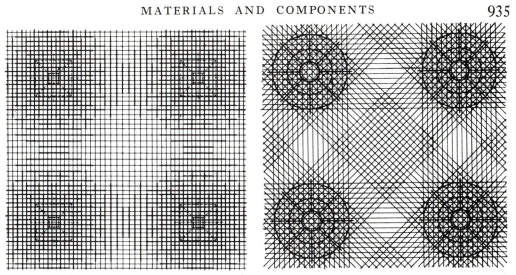

FIG. 37.3. Swiss (Maillart—*left*) and American (Turner—*right*) systems of slab reinforcement compared.

lines introduced the continuous load-bearing wall without independent columns, and a wide variety of thin-shell forms. These will be considered further below. Two other innovations that may be briefly mentioned were the introduction of lightweight concretes (which were increasingly employed after the Second World War in multi-storey construction) and of a special form of reinforced concrete known as 'ferro-cemento' invented by P. L. Nervi in Italy and consisting of a cement–sand mortar reinforced by layers of relatively fine wire mesh.

Prestressed concrete. Prestressed concrete is the one innovation to be considered here that was of major structural importance and was wholly a twentieth-century one, though the principle of prestressing was much older. It appeared explicitly at least as early as 1811, and was implicit much earlier still in the widespread use of turnbuckles and wedges to tension ties and in such practices as the shrinking of iron tyres on wooden wheels and iron hoops on wooden barrels. But the effective pretensioning of the reinforcement in concrete—to keep the concrete always in compression and thereby use it always to full advantage—was not possible until steel of considerably higher strength than normal mild steel was available. This was partly because of the additional stress that the reinforcement must continue to bear in order to keep the concrete in compression even under maximum load, and partly because it must initially bear still more stress to make good the losses that occur after the concrete is cast around it. These losses are due to irreversible contractions of the concrete as it dries and hardens and adapts itself to the compression imposed on it. Though the losses could be reduced by tensioning the reinforcement only after the concrete had set, they could not be eliminated.

Credit for the early development belongs largely to Eugene Freyssinet, who first successfully applied the principle in France in 1928 [2]. In the years before the Second World War, the idea spread to other European countries and to America and there was further rapid development after the war—notably more rapid and purposeful than the corresponding period of development of normal reinforced concrete, thanks to the much greater theoretical understanding that was available to guide it. Much of this development concentrated on devising efficient means of anchoring the stressed reinforcement. In buildings, however, as distinct from bridges and other civil engineering works, application up to 1950 rarely went beyond the fairly straightforward substitution of prestressed concrete beams for beams of normal reinforced concrete or steel. In comparison with the former, the prestressed beam had a particular advantage when it was precast in a factory, on account of both its relative lightness and its reduced liability to damage in transit and subsequent handling on the building site.

Other materials. Alongside these new or relatively new materials, most of the older ones continued in use, though the method of manufacture or manner of use usually changed significantly. Changes in brick manufacture (Ch. 25), for instance, resulted in more consistent strengths which, in turn, helped to permit the reductions in wall thicknesses that will be referred to later. Improvements in the methods of making both sheet and plate glass (Ch. 22) increased their availability and made it possible to produce larger sizes of plate. No change was possible in the basic product in the case of timber, but there were considerable improvements in methods of jointing. One was the development—chiefly in the United States during the Second World War to achieve greater economy in the use of timber but on the basis of earlier European ideas—of mechanical shear connectors. Typically these consisted of toothed plates or split rings that were interposed between the members to be jointed, which were then tightly bolted together with the bolts passing through the connectors. They made it possible, for the first time, to develop the full tensile strength of a timber tie. Another was the introduction of more durable glues which permitted a much increased use of lamination to make composite sheets or members, ranging from simple plywood to large beams and arches. (Some of the latter closely resembled the much earlier arches illustrated in Vol. V, Fig. 245.) For ceilings and internal linings generally, the now-ubiquitous plasterboard progressively supplanted wet plaster.

Closely related developments included the introduction of many new types of perforated brick; of lightweight concrete blocks for partitions and the inner leaves of cavity walls; of fibreglass for insulation; and of a variety of synthetic building boards. If, to these, are added materials like aluminium and some of the new plastics that were then coming into use, the architect in 1950 was already presented with an almost bewildering choice as compared with what had been available to his grandfather fifty years earlier.

Building components. Fortunately the architect's task was simultaneously eased somewhat by the increasing availability of standard components that he could simply order from a catalogue. He had long been able to order in this way such things as cast-iron goods and sanitary ware. But, in the years between the wars and particularly after 1945, it became increasingly possible to order also finished doors and windows to standard patterns and even complete systems for partitions and cladding. This was part of a general trend towards an increasing industrialization of the building process.

II. CONSTRUCTION METHODS

Though construction methods have received scant attention in previous volumes of this history, they have always strongly influenced design. Indeed, in the days before structural theory had developed to the point of making it possible to predict the likely performance of a finished structure, they almost certainly exerted a more direct influence than considerations of ultimate stability. By 1900, developments in theory were rapidly reversing this situation for the larger and more novel types of structure. But constructional feasibility remained an important secondary consideration.

Two trends, both traceable well back into the nineteenth century, can be identified. One was the increasing use of mechanical plant and other related aids on the building site. The other was the progressive transfer to the factory of operations previously performed on site. It is convenient to refer to them together as a trend towards industrialization, though the building 'industry' that may thus be said to have come into being remained very different from the main manufacturing industries. It adopted, in part, the organizational patterns of these industries. But it very largely remained a consumer and assembler, on individual sites, of the products of manufacturing industry proper. And, because the requirements were so diverse, it remained highly heterogeneous, with a few large organizations but a vast majority of very small firms that continued to operate in much the same way as in the past.

One classic early prototype for later developments was the building of the Crystal Palace in 1850–1 (Vol. IV, Ch. 15). This vast structure was erected in a mere nine months, very largely by the dry assembly of factory-made castings and other components. Hydraulic jacks were used on site for the proof testing of the cast-iron girders and specimens of the longer wrought-iron trusses, and various other mechanized aids were employed. Lifting, however, was still done by horse-power. By the end of the century, the steam engine had largely superseded the horse, and a considerable variety of mechanical cranes, hoists, excavators, pile-drivers, and concrete mixers was in use. Even the portable electric drill was available in Europe by 1895. Without many of these aids, the construction of buildings like the Reliance Building would hardly have been feasible.

During the first half of the twentieth century, these mechanical aids were continually improved, the improvement being stimulated, in some cases, by wartime needs. The most important single change was the replacement of the steam engine by the diesel engine and, to a lesser extent, by the petrol engine and the electric motor. This change took place largely between the two wars. Among new plant may be mentioned particularly the mobile concrete mixer, able to supply concrete ready mixed on site, and the tower crane. The first was developed in the U.S.A. before the Second World War and its use spread rapidly after the war. The second was introduced in France in 1937, but little used until after the war, and then only in continental Europe up to 1952.

Other important innovations on site were the introduction of tubular steel scaffolding in 1920 in place of the earlier rope-lashed timber scaffolds, various improvements in concrete formwork, and the use of hydraulic jacks to modify the distribution of internal forces in a structure during construction. Hand-made timber formwork could easily account for half the total cost of reinforced concrete constructed *in situ*. Steel formwork, designed for repetitive use, reduced this cost if the structure was designed to permit this repetitive use and the construction process suitably programmed. One possibility was a steel wall formwork which was progressively slid upwards as casting proceeded, being always held in place by concrete already cast and sufficiently hardened. An early English application is illustrated in Fig.

FIG. 37.4. Sliding formwork in use in the construction of Highpoint One, London, 1934.

37.4 [3]. The use of hydraulic jacks referred to here was, of course, a means of prestressing *in situ*. It was not strictly a twentieth-century innovation, but its fully controlled exploitation (involving prior calculation of the forces to be applied and their precise measurement during application) was, to a large extent, one aspect of the wider development of prestressed concrete, since its usual objective was the intimate locking together of precast concrete elements or the prestressing of concrete cast *in situ*.

Since reinforced concrete was itself an innovation of the latter part of the nineteenth century, and since there were obvious advantages in casting beams and columns in a factory (including the possibility of proof-testing them before erection), the factory casting of such elements began early. Indeed, although it was less a matter of necessity, it was closely analogous to the factory casting of iron a century earlier. Complete systems of precast construction were developed early in the century [4]. A patent drawing for one of the most widely used American systems is reproduced in Fig. 37.5.

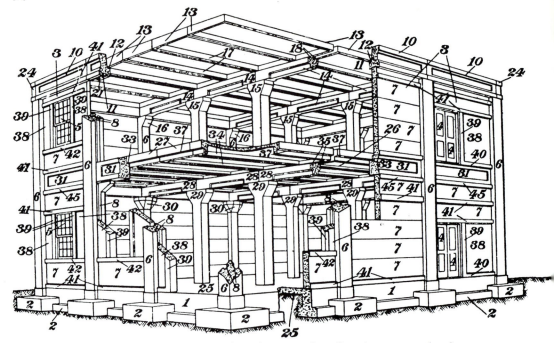

FIG. 37.5. 'Unit' system of precast concrete framed construction; Conzelman patent drawing, 1912.

The wider industrialization of the building process, in the sense of transferring work to the factory, had a more complex background. It was stimulated not only by the greater ease with which the process and the product
could be controlled, the other advantages of factory as compared with site
working, and the potential economies of mass production, but also by the
special circumstances created by the two wars. These placed a premium on
speed of construction at times when there were shortages both of traditional
materials and building craftsmen but spare factory capacity and surpluses of
some other materials. In Europe especially, and particularly for housing and
schools, both wars led to vast centrally sponsored developments of non-
traditional factory-based systems of construction and even of complete
factory-made houses. After the First World War, most of these developments
were short-lived. But after the Second World War they were mostly based on
much more careful analysis of the requirements, so that they provided a more
acceptable alternative to traditional methods. In addition, the special circumstances became, in a number of respects, more the general norm. Some of
them were therefore of more lasting significance. These included the highly
adaptable system of school construction based on a lightweight steel frame
and designed immediately after the war in close association with the Hert-

fordshire County Architect [5] and several 'large-panel' systems of reinforced concrete construction for multi-storey housing which were mostly still in the experimental stage in 1950. Alongside these directly or indirectly officially sponsored developments were the industrially sponsored systems of partitions and cladding and the like, to which some reference has already been made.

Finally some reference should be made here to what might be called the site factory. The larger building components were not only bulky but often heavy and difficult and costly to transport over considerable distances. To obviate this difficulty, it became increasingly common to precast concrete on the building site. One special way of doing this, which was applicable only to flat beamless floor slabs, was to cast all the slabs directly above one another on the ground, using each in turn as the base form for the next, and then to jack them into place up the columns. This procedure was introduced in the U.S.A. in 1948. Such a procedure imposed a severe discipline on design, of course. To a greater or lesser extent the same was generally true of most approaches to industrialization.

III. SERVICES AND FIRE PROTECTION

The principal services that, together with the steel frame, made possible the tall office buildings of the last years of the nineteenth century have already been referred to in the opening paragraph. Another, whose necessity was not fully appreciated until uncontrollable fires in the upper storeys of some supposedly fireproof buildings had shown that 'fireproof' construction alone was not enough, was the automatic sprinkler. To these services the only completely new addition in the first half of the twentieth century was full air-conditioning, apart from some relatively minor ones like the escalator, which was first demonstrated at the Paris Exhibition of 1900.

This, however, is only half the story. There were also radical improvements in the earlier services, such as the introduction of fluorescent lighting in 1938. Most importantly, in relation to building design, services generally assumed a much greater importance. In terms of total costs of building, including running costs, they were responsible for about half in the more highly serviced buildings by 1950, and might thus be considered equal in importance to the structural fabric and finishes. In terms of their accommodation within the fabric, they made greatly increased demands which were met, typically, by large vertical ducts and, for horizontal distribution, by open spaces between suspended ceilings and the floor slabs above, or even by intermediate floors devoted solely to them.

By the 1940s it was technically feasible to reduce the outer skin of a building to no more than a thin membrane to keep out wind and rain or to make it a windowless solid enclosure and still, in either case, to maintain any desired internal environmental conditions. Considerations of cost, and the psychological desirability of some visual contact with the world outside, usually prevented the adoption of these extreme approaches. But the new freedom was already exploited to a considerable extent in the use of a continuous glass curtain wall in buildings like the United Nations Building and the Lever Building (Fig. 37.6) around 1950.

To the extent that electricity replaced gas and solid fuel as the source of energy, there was a decrease in the risk of fire. But electrical faults can be a cause of fire, and the overall increase in servicing probably, in itself, increased the hazard, partly on account of the multiple paths provided by ducts and voids above ceilings etc. for the spread of a fire from one room to another. Serious fires continued to occur and continuing attention to the protection of the structural fabric and its contents and to the safety of its occupants was made all the more necessary by the introduction of so many new materials

FIG. 37.6. Lever House, New York, completed 1952.

and forms of construction. The fire-testing stations established around the turn of the century, and others added to their number, played a vital role in assessing the performances of these new materials and forms of construction —notably the performance of reinforced concrete and, later, that of pre-stressed concrete and the numerous new synthetic building boards and other synthetic materials, as well as lightweight alternatives to the heavier types of protection usually given to structural steelwork in the earlier part of the century. Since concrete is both incombustible and a fairly good insulator, reinforced concrete usually behaved well, provided that there was adequate concrete cover to the reinforcing steel and that this cover had sufficient wire binding to prevent it from spalling off as the surface temperature rose. With prestressed concrete it was also necessary to ensure that there was no prema-ture loss in stress due to heating of the steel. By the early 1930s enough tests on the development of fires in typically furnished rooms had been carried out, notably in the U.S.A., for it to be possible to standardize the testing proce-dures for building elements and then define standard grades of performance. A British Standard (BS 476) on these lines was issued in 1932. A counterpart to this definition of performances was the grading of exposures to fire to be expected for different types of occupancy.

It had however already been recognized, as noted above, that structural fire protection alone was not enough. This was true whatever the form of construction. For the safety of the occupants, if for no other reason, it was highly desirable to limit the spread of fires, and especially of smoke. Up to 1950, this was largely done on the basis of lessons learnt from actual fires, though there was some experimental work during the Second World War. The guiding principle was to divide any large building into fire-tight compart-ments using fire-tight doors for passage between compartments and to pro-vide protected stairs for escape. At the same time provisions were made for fighting a fire as near as possible to its point of origin. The extent of these provisions depended on both an assessment of the risk and likely consequences of a serious fire and the availability of, and accessibility to, external fire-fighting services. The automatic sprinkler was one answer. Where its use was not justified, the usual alternative, also introduced towards the end of the nineteenth century, was a permanent installation of stand-pipes or dry rising mains with either hose-connections or hose-reels. Increases in the size of windows, and the increased use of light claddings generally, also called for new measures to limit the risk of external spread of fire from storey to storey or building to building. In the Lever Building, for instance, the continuous

glass curtain wall was backed above and below each floor slab by a wall
0·75 m high of cinder blocks with plaster on the outer face and insulation on
the inner face. These walls show through as dark bands in Fig. 37.6.

IV. THEORY AND DESIGN

During the nineteenth century, the essential bases for the rational analysis
of the principal structural forms then in use had been well established. In
particular, methods of graphical analysis had been developed for statically
determinate frameworks—that is, frameworks with just enough members for
equilibrium—and methods of algebraic analysis had been developed for more
complex frameworks with additional members or with rigid joints equivalent
to such members. A start had also been made on the application of the basic
theory of elasticity to reinforced concrete elements. Very largely this had all
been the work of talented individual teachers and engineers with, at best,
very limited experimental facilities. In comparison virtually no theoretic work
had been done that was relevant to the non-structural aspects of building
design.

Two things especially are notable about the first half of the twentieth
century. One is the attention that then began to be given, from the scientific
point of view, to non-structural aspects of design in parallel with their increase
in relative importance as traditional forms of construction and environmental
control gave way to new ones. The other is the vastly increased part played
by planned experimental work and in the facilities provided for this. The
experimental facilities were provided in part in expanded and new university
departments and in part by specialist testing stations or laboratories such as
those established for fire testing, to which reference has already been made.
Even more significantly they were provided by new institutes with wide
briefs to conduct research into all aspects of building technology. The prototype of these was the British Building Research Station established in
1920 [6].

Despite the attention given to such subjects as lighting, heating, ventilation, and acoustics, progress therein continued to lag behind that in structural
theory. But it had become possible, by 1950, to lay down quantitative
experimental-based criteria for basic design in most of these fields and
experimental data and predictive techniques—the latter always assuming
steady-state conditions—had been made available to assist in meeting the
criteria. A notable application to acoustic design was made in the design of

the Royal Festival Hall in London in 1950–1 [7]. This involved a good deal of measurement and testing on site.

In the structural field, a vast amount of new experimental data was acquired on the properties of materials, especially concrete, and on the behaviour under load of simple elements like beams, columns, slabs, and walls, of frames and joints in frames, and even of complete buildings. Most of these data were obtained in planned series of laboratory tests carried out at full scale. But models were also increasingly used, while the tests of complete buildings were, of necessity, carried out in the field. Two notable series of such tests were those carried out on early reinforced concrete buildings by A. N. Talbot and W. A. Slater of the University of Illinois in 1910–17 [8] and those carried out on steel-framed buildings for the British Steel Structures Research Committee in 1930–5 [9].

The value of the tests and the resulting data was progressively enhanced by developments in instrumentation, particularly for the measurement of strains (from which internal stresses could be calculated). A vibrating-wire strain gauge was developed in the early 1930s in Germany and a more compact electric resistance strain gauge in the later 1930s in the U.S.A. It was also enhanced, more fundamentally, by developments in theory and analysis that both guided the planning of the tests and helped to make the data more intelligible and more widely applicable. These developments were so numerous that only a few highlights can be briefly mentioned.

Two phases can be broadly distinguished, though they are less clearly distinguishable in applications to reinforced concrete. In the first, attention was confined to elastic behaviour—or, more precisely, linearly elastic behaviour which obeys Hooke's Law, that is, stress and strain are proportional at all times. The single most significant advance here was the introduction by Hardy Cross in 1930 of a method of analysing rigid-jointed frames by successive approximations [10]. This 'moment distribution' method started with the asumption that all joints were fixed (that is, incapable of rotation), thereby making the bending moments at the ends of the beams statically determinate but usually unbalanced at each joint. The successive approximations consisted of releasing the joints and re-distributing the unbalanced moments until the lack of balance was small enough to be ignored. This method was later generalized by R. V. Southwell [11]. Other significant advances were made in the 1920s and later in the analysis of flat plates or slabs subject to bending in all directions, of thin shells, and of some of the other newer forms to be discussed below.

In the second phase, attention shifted, in part, back to behaviour near collapse and to the ultimate strengths of structures and structural elements that had been the main concern when the bases of design remained largely empirical. This phase began before the Second World War but its full fruits were not seen until after 1950. In principle a 'collapse' or 'ultimate strength' analysis had the great attraction that it obviated the computational difficulties of a rigorous elastic analysis of a statically indeterminate structure without recourse to successive approximations. It did so simply by considering a 'collapse' state in which sufficient cross-sections of the structure were acting virtually as hinges to make all the bending moments statically determinate. In practice, however, this called for certain assumptions about the rotational capacities of the virtual 'hinges' and the overall stiffness of the structure up to the point of 'collapse' that restricted direct application initially to slabs and single storey frameworks. A 'yield line' theory for reinforced concrete slabs was published by K. W. Johansen in Denmark in 1943 [12]. The corresponding theory for rigid-jointed frames was developed in England as 'plastic' design and in the U.S.A. as 'limit' design [13]. It was focused largely on steel frames, but reinforced concrete frames were also considered in the American work.

Finally, some mention should be made of the new science of soil mechanics and of two other new branches of structural theory that were coming to the fore around 1950. Soil mechanics, largely the invention of Karl Terzaghi in the 1920s, sought to place the design of foundations on a similar basis to that of superstructures [14]. Of the others, one was the application of dynamics to problems of structural response to vibration, earthquakes, and blast loads. The other was the generalized probabilistic theory of structural safety—a counterpart of the theory that had been used already for some time in aircraft design [15].

The extent to which these developments in theory affected structural design varied considerably, though the delay in application of improved methods of analysis was, on average, probably less than in the second half of the nineteenth century on account of the generally higher level of education of designers. Application was most rapid where—as in early shell design—forms or requirements were novel and there was no easy thought-saving and time-saving codified procedure to fall back upon. It took longest where—as in the design of steel frames—practice was well established, codified procedures were significantly simpler and more direct than new alternatives, and the latter neither promised marked economies in costs of construction nor obvious increases in safety. In Britain, for instance, steel frames were still almost invariably designed in 1950 according to a standard (BS 449) in which all rigidity of the joints was ignored in spite of the evidence of partial rigidity furnished by the tests carried out for the Steel Structures Research Committee, the proposals of this committee for a revision of the design procedure, and the subsequent development of plastic theory.

There was, in fact, a great deal of codification on the lines of BS 449, especially in countries like Britain where there was considerable concern for public safety and where this was sought through the regulation of design rather than through placing responsibility directly on the shoulders of designers. It was, necessarily, based partly on measurements of the loads to which structures might be subjected. Ostensibly, safe levels of response (usually in terms of stresses and deflections) to these loads were specified and procedures were given for calculating the responses. In practice, so much simplification and idealization was introduced that the calculated responses were largely fictitious. That safe structures still resulted was largely thanks to two things—the strength and stiffness of much of the structure were completely ignored in the basic simplification (notably those of the walls and floors in multi-storey framed structures) and the stress limits were usually much less critical than they were assumed to be. In the last analysis, the codes provided safe rules only for the detailed proportioning of structural forms that were already well proved in practice. These rules were more rational and powerful than the 'rules of thumb' that had chiefly been used earlier for similar purposes. But because they leant so heavily on previous practice in this way and contained no clues as to the limits of their validity, they have, since 1950, progressively had to give way to a new generation of more realistic (and inevitably more complex) codes based, *inter alia*, on more rational criteria derived from the new probabilitistic theory referred to above.

V. NEW STRUCTURAL FORMS

Despite the growth in theoretic understanding and the wealth of new experimental data, radical innovation remained hazardous because understanding was never complete. Most development in structural forms therefore continued to take place in a slow evolutionary manner. For most buildings the bearing wall or the column-and-beam frame continued to be used. These forms tended to become more efficient and lighter as understanding grew. But there was also the trend towards simplification of construction and elimination of inessential variations in member sizes and shapes for the sake of overall economy, which militated against the achievement of maximum efficiency and lightness. Three new classes of form appeared: the thin shell, the tension roof, and the space frame. These exploited not only new materials but also newly understood possibilities of three-dimensional structural action. There was also one development in foundation design that went beyond improvement of existing forms and the use of new materials.

Bearing-wall structures. The bearing wall gained a new lease of life in tall buildings from the mid-1930s onwards with the abandonment of rule-of-thumb proportioning in favour of more rational design. It was used where a relatively close and regular spacing of walls, repeating from floor to floor, was desirable for other reasons (as in multi-storey housing), and always with flat-slab reinforced concrete floors. Initially the walls were always of reinforced concrete, but later they were also constructed in brick and it was found possible, in buildings of only a few storeys, to make only the cross walls (those running from back to front) load-bearing. These developments were made possible and attractive by developments in construction technique (Fig. 37.4), by increased understanding of the structural behaviour of thin walls, and by the possibility of obtaining the increased strengths necessary for the lower storeys without increase in thickness and simply by varying the strength of the concrete or the bricks and mortar.

Column-and-beam frames and related structures. The Lever Building, like the Reliance Building, had a steel column-and-beam frame. A comparison of Figs. 37.1 and 37.6 does not suggest any great metamorphosis during the period of a little over fifty years that separated the two buildings. In their essential forms, the frames were indeed similar. During this period, however, three changes did typically take place. The hollow-tile floors used, almost without exception, in the 1890s gave way to reinforced concrete slabs. The complex composite cross-sections of the columns and beams, built up by riveting together numerous smaller sections, and the riveted joints between members, gave way to simple **I** and **H** sections and clean welded joints. And there was a corresponding marked simplification of the total form which reflected a primary emphasis in design on this total form rather than on the detailing of individual members to meet the requirements of an architect's plan. Columns in tall buildings were placed on a completely regular grid, and vertical services (including elevators) were concentrated in one or two places, usually in a 'core' with stiff reinforced concrete walls. In the Lever Building this core was placed at the rear. In an intermediate stage of development lateral stiffness (under wind load) often greatly exceeded that which was pro-vided by the frame alone by virtue partly of relatively heavy internal and external infill walls. (It did so by an estimated 350 per cent in the Empire State Building [16].) In the later, very lightly clad, form much of this bonus was lost, but the inherent stiffness of the service core made up for some of the loss.

In single-storey and other relatively low buildings, lateral stiffness was less important and it was usually reasonable to assume that it would be adequate without special provision when the frame was clad, particularly if it had rigid joints. Where long spans called for relatively heavy beams, the frame deve-loped otherwise in much the same way as the taller frame (Fig. 37.2), except that, around 1950, it was becoming possible to achieve some new economies by use of plastic theory in design. Where spans were shorter and loadings light, a lighter type of frame was introduced, for which cold-rolled sections were particularly appropriate. It was generally used with precast concrete or prefabricated lightweight claddings, and diagonal braces were used where the cladding did not contribute enough stiffness. These lighter frames were used first for multi-storey housing in France, and then in England, between 1932 and 1937 (in what was known as the Mopin system), and then much more extensively for school construction in England after 1946 (Fig. 37.7) [17].

Early tall reinforced concrete frames closely resembled steel frames with reinforced concrete floor slabs. The sixteen-storey Ingalls Building, built in Cincinnati in 1902–3, was a notable example [18]. The recognition that beams could be dispensed with if the slab was suitably strengthened and the conse-quent introduction of flat-slab floors (Fig. 37.3) led, however, to the intro-duction within a few years of a system of framing consisting only of columns and flat slabs. With the columns flared out at the top where they met the slabs, this form was widely used up to the 1930s for industrial and commercial buildings that called for large unobstructed floors (Fig. 37.8). After the Second World War, the flared column head was eliminated, sometimes with the substitution of steel columns, for buildings that called for lesser spans and were less heavily loaded. This was the form that permitted the casting of the slabs directly above one another on the ground and their subsequent jacking up the columns.

Foundations. The one addition to the late nineteenth-century repertoire of foundation possibilities—piles, spread footings, grillages, continuous rafts, etc.—was the buoyant foundation. Structurally this was just a deep basement

FIG. 37.7. Morgan's Road Junior School, Hertford, 1949.

FIG. 37.8. Boots' Factory, Beeston, Nottingham, completed 1932.

with a stiff base slab and side walls strong enough to resist the inward pressures of the surrounding ground. Placed under a tall building that might otherwise have called, for instance, for much deeper piling, it obviated the need for this by displacing a weight of earth similar to the total weight of the structure, and thereby reducing almost to nothing the net increase in vertical pressure at lower levels due to the presence of the building.

Shells. Arched roofs continued to be built, with reinforced concrete arches joining those of steel and timber. Simple arch action calls, however, for considerable depth in relation to the span, to cater for variations in loading and to avoid buckling. P. L. Nervi overcame this drawback in the 1940s in some very elegant large-span arched and domed roofs which were assembled from light precast-concrete sections, by using downward-projecting ribs or corrugations of the whole surface to give the requisite overall depth [19]. Shell action overcomes it in another way: by distributing loads in all directions around a continuous surface. When this surface is doubly curved, as in a dome, the depth can be reduced to about a tenth of that required for an arch except for some thickening near the edges. It is merely necessary to construct the shell in such a way that it can, as called for by its geometry and the distribution of the loads, distribute these loads by internal tensions as well as compressions and without excessive deformation as the tensions are developed. Reinforced concrete met the first of these requirements and pre-tensioning the second.

The first reinforced concrete domical shells were built in Jena in 1923–4, though in 1909 the crossing of the Cathedral of St John the Divine in New York had already been covered by a dome of only slightly greater average thickness constructed of plies of flat tiles and similarly reinforced near the base. E. Torroja's much flatter dome in Algeciras (Fig. 37.9) was the first in which the necessary circumferential tie at the base (encased in horizontal bands of concrete) was prestressed to control the deformations [20]. By the mid-1930s, part-cylindrical shells, saddle-shaped shells (in the form of hyperbolic paraboloids), and shells of more freely defined doubly-curved form were being built. We might also add folded-plate roofs, though these are a less clearly defined category and were not, strictly speaking, shells because all the curvature was concentrated at the folds, and the flat sections of plate between the folds were subject to significant bending.

Tension roofs. The action of a shell is predominantly compressive and arch-like curvatures predominate in the forms adopted. The inversion of these forms gives a second family capable of acting largely or wholly in tension.

Prestressing of this second family has the great advantage of making it possible to maintain tension throughout at all times and thus to reduce the structure to a thin membrane without risk, for instance, that it will flap about in the wind. In a dish-shaped form the prestress can be achieved by adding a distributed dead weight; in a saddle-shaped form by pulling along the edges in the directions of arch-like curvature. There is also the possibility of using a dome-shaped or other continuously arched form and applying the converse of a dead weight—an internal pressure. The last two possibilities had long been exploited in tents and balloons respectively. The possibility of exploiting them further for buildings arose from the development of materials strong in tension and the development of prestressing techniques and of fans capable of maintaining internal pressures.

For the inflated form a continuous membrane is, of course, essential, but for large spans much of the tension can be taken by cables or ropes slung over it. F. W. Lanchester took out patents in England in 1917 and 1919 and later proposed domes with spans up to 650 m, but the first (much smaller) domes were not built until about 1950 in the U.S.A. For the other forms a network of steel cables can be substituted to carry all the loads. Fig. 37.10 shows the first major realization, a saddle roof designed in 1950 and slung between two inclined reinforced concrete arches whose weight helped to prestress the cables [21].

Space frames. Plane trusses, like arches, continued to be built and were developed further in various ways. But the exploitation of three-dimensional structural action in slabs and shells had its counterpart in the development of three-dimensional trusses and related forms, known collectively as space frames. Alexander Graham Bell was an early pioneer at the beginning of the century, but he was more interested in structures for flight than in buildings, and aeronautical engineers probably paid more attention to him than did structural engineers. Real development for building purposes began only after the Second World War when people like Buckminster Fuller assumed Bell's mantle. Around 1950 the potentialities of forms like those seen in Fig. 37.11 were being explored and the full-scale realization of the more practicable ones (like the geodesic dome and the double-layer grid behind it) awaited chiefly the computational power of the computer (to assist in analysis) and the sponsorship of willing clients [22].

VI. ARCHITECTURAL IDEALS, OBJECTIVES, AND ACHIEVEMENTS

Innovation in building tends, initially at least, to be costly. The normal established practice is usually, *ipso facto*, the cheapest. Willing clients have,

G. 37.9. Market Hall, Algeciras, 1933.

G. 37.10. Dorton Arena, Raleigh, North Carolina, completed 1953.

FIG. 37.11. A geodesic dome and other structures exhibited at the Museum of Modern Art, New York, in 1959.

therefore, always had a major role to play. They have usually been prompted
by having new requirements to meet or by finding themselves in a new
situation. Or they have been impelled by something varying from a belief in
the value of novelty itself for the sake of the attention it attracts to a more
deeply held conviction about what is appropriate to the time.

Two major groups of clients can be distinguished in the period under
consideration: private and public. The former are taken here to include all
industrial and commercial bodies that operated to show a return on investment; the latter all governmental bodies and similar agencies that spent public
money for the public good. The former were, in general, the more important
up to 1939, and they continued to play a role very similar to that which they
had played in the nineteenth century. They were, in particular, the chief
sponsors of developments in structural forms (such as the reinforced concrete
flat slab: Figs. 37.3, 37.7) [23] and in servicing and the use of lightweight
claddings. New requirements were an important spur. But so also, one sometimes feels, was a desire for conspicuous novelty. In the years immediately
after the Second World War, public clients, at least in Europe, became relatively much more important. Even in the U.S.A., where Fuller's first client
for a geodesic dome was the Ford Company, the second was the Marine
Corps. In Europe, the priorities were housing and education and the chief
spur was a requirement, partly for political reasons, to build quickly in situations where both skilled labour and some traditional materials were in short
supply. The existence of vast programmes of building under central control
and the ability to invest in innovation on a scale that only such programmes
could justify permitted, however, some major steps towards industrializing
the building process. At the same time, the social purposes of these programmes led in some cases, notably in the British schools programme, to
radical reassessments of requirements and searches for new and more
appropriate planning concepts.

Deeply held convictions came, here, to the fore. New planning concepts
had always arisen in response to new or changed needs, but usually in a slow
and evolutionary manner. It was the radical reassessment of need as a direct
basis for design that was new. The conviction that it was necessary and a
further, less clearly formulated, conviction that a new architecture could help
bring about a better world, were fostered, from the 1920s onwards, by architects like Le Corbusier and Gropius; by Le Corbusier through his writings
[24] and by Gropius through his school of design—the German Bauhaus
(Fig. 37.12)—and the group of teachers he collected around him there [25].

FIG. 37.12. The Bauhaus, Dessau, 1925–6.

In the 1920s they were a small avant-garde preaching a new architecture—what came to be known as Modern Architecture. In the 1940s a new generation, imbued with their ideas and often with a keen social conscience, was trying to practice them more widely.

Modern architecture of the pioneering inter-war years had two other relevant characteristics, with which we must close. One was an explicit aim to use new technology to the full—to do away with the first of the contrasts referred to in the introduction and match the achievements of automobile and aircraft designers. That achievement initially fell short of this aim was less important, in the long run, than the way in which it gradually made possible a new symbiosis like those of early Imperial Rome and thirteenth-century France. The other was the very real, though less emphasized, interaction with contemporary movements in the visual arts. Le Corbusier was himself painter and sculptor as much as architect, and once defined architecture as 'the cunning, correct, and magnificent play of volumes brought together in light'. The Bauhaus was a school of design, and not just of architecture, and numbered among its teachers many of the leading abstract painters and sculptors of the time. This interaction gave the movement a new and consistent style that technology itself could not readily have provided. It also led to calls on the structural engineer to make a reality of visions of interpenetrating spaces and floating planes with minimal support, and it prepared the way for an excited acceptance, in the 1950s, of his newer three-dimensional forms.

The half-century ended with high hopes. Disillusionment, in some cases, came only later.

REFERENCES

[1] MAILLART, R. *Schweizerische Bauzeitung*, **87**, 263–5 (1926).
[2] FREYSSINET, E. *Journal of the Institution of Civil Engineers*, **33**, 331–80 (1950).
[3] *Architects Journal*, **81**, 113–19 (1935).
[4] PETERSON, J. L. *Journal of the American Concrete Institute*, **25**, 477–96 (1954).
[5] *Architects' Journal*, **110**, 431–40 (1949).
   DAVIES, R. L., and WEEKS, J. R. *Architectural Review, London*, **111**, 366–87 (1952).
[6] LEA, F. M. *Science and building. A history if the Building Research Station*. H.M.S.O., London (1971).
[7] ALLEN, W. A., and PARKIN, P. H. *Architectural Review, London*, **109**, 377–84 (1951).
[8] TALBOT, A. N., and SLATER, W. A. *Bulletin. Illinois University Engineering Experiment Station*, **64** (1913), and **84** (1916).
[9] STEEL STRUCTURES RESEARCH COMMITTEE, *Second report*, and *Third report*, H.M.S.O., London (1934 and 1936).
[10] CROSS, H. *Transactions of the American Society of Civil Engineers*, **96**, 1–10 (1932).
[11] SOUTHWELL, R. V. *Relaxation methods in engineering science*. Oxford University Press, London (1940).
[12] JOHANSEN, K. W. *Publications of the International Association for Bridge and Structural Engineering*, **1**, 277–96 (1932).
   ——. *Brudlinieteorier*. Thesis (1943); Teknisk Forlag, Copenhagen (1952).
[13] WHITNEY, C. S. *Transactions of the American Society of Civil Engineers*, **107**, 251–82 (1942).
   BAKER, J. F. *Journal of the Institution of Civil Engineers*, **31**, 188–224 (1949).
   GREENBERG, H. J., and PRAGER, W. *Transactions of the American Society of Civil Engineers*, **117**, 447–58 (1952).
[14] TERZAGHI, K. *Erdbaumechanik*. Franz Deuticke, Vienna (1925).
   ——. *Transactions of the American Society of Civil Engineers*, **93**, 270–301 (1929).
[15] FREUDENTHAL, A. M. *Transactions of the American Society of Civil Engineers*, **112**, 125–59 (1947) and **113**, 269–87 (1948).
[16] RATHBUN, J. C. *Transactions of the American Society of Civil Engineers*, **105**, 1–41 (1940).
[17] *Architect and Building News*, **141**, 230–3 (1935).
   Journal of the Royal Institute of British Architects, **44**, 765–78 (1937).
[18] CONDIT, C. W. *Technology and Culture*, **9**, 1–33 (1968).
[19] NERVI, P. L. *Structures*. F. W. Dodge, New York (1956).
[20] TORROJA, E. *The structures of Eduardo Torroja*. F. W. Dodge, New York (1958).
[21] *Architectural Forum*, **97**, 134–9 (1952) and **98**, 170–1 (1953).
[22] *Architectural Forum*, **95**, 144–51 (1951).
   MARKS, R. W. *The dymaxion world of Buckminster Fuller*. Reinhold, New York (1960).
[23] *Architects' Journal*, **76**, 125–36 (1932).
[24] LE CORBUSIER. *Towards a new architecture*. Architectural Press, London (1927).
[25] GROPIUS, W. *The new architecture and the Bauhaus*. Faber and Faber, London (1935).
   GROTE, L. *et al. 50 years Bauhaus*. Royal Academy of Arts exhibition catalogue, London (1968).

BIBLIOGRAPHY

BANHAM, R. *Theory and design in the first machine age.* Architectural Press, London (1960).

——. *The architecture of the well-tempered environment.* Architectural Press, London (1969).

BOWLEY, M. *The British Building Industry.* Cambridge University Press, London (1966).

CONDIT, C. W. *American building art. The twentieth century.* Oxford University Press, New York (1961).

COWAN, H. J. *An historical outline of architectural science.* Elsevier, Amsterdam (1966).

LEROY, J. C. *et al.* (eds.) *A half-century of French prestressing technology.* Travaux, Paris (1966).

GIEDION, S. *Space, time and architecture.* (5th edn.). Harvard University Press, Cambridge, Mass. (1967).

HAEGERMANN, G. *et al. Vom caementum zum spannbeton,* Vol. 1. Bauverlag, Wiesbaden (1964).

HAMILTON, S. B. *A note on the history of reinforced concrete in buildings.* National Building Studies, Special Report No. 24, H.M.S.O., London (1956).

——. *A short history of the structural fire protection of buildings.* National Building Studies, Special Report No. 27, H.M.S.O., London (1958).

JOEDICKE, J. *Shell architecture.* Tiranti, London (1963).

MAINSTONE, R. J. *Developments in structural form.* Allen Lane, London (1975).

MARÉ, E. DE (ed.) *New ways of building.* Architectural Press, London (1948).

MICHAELS, L. *Contemporary structure in architecture.* Reinhold, New York (1950).

OTTO, F. (ed.) *Tensile structures.* M.I.T. Press, Cambridge, Mass. (1973).

RICHARDS, J. M. *An introduction to modern architecture.* Penguin, Harmondsworth (1940).

TIMOSHENKO, S. P. *History of strength of materials.* McGraw-Hill, New York (1953).

TORROJA, E. *Philosophy of structures.* University of California Press, Berkeley (1958).

WACHSMANN, K. *The turning point of building.* Reinhold, New York (1961).

WHITE, R. B. *Prefabrication. A history of its development in Great Britain.* National Building Studies, Special Report No. 36, H.M.S.O., London (1965).

38

TOWN PLANNING

SIR COLIN BUCHANAN

ALL towns owe their existence and form to some degree of conscious planning. If the original nucleus of a town was a single building, then someone selected the site and erected the building for some purpose; someone else erected a second building on one side rather than another of the first one; and so on. But the degree of deliberate planning has varied greatly. Some towns grew, as suggested in the example already given, as the result of a series of decisions related to individual buildings governed mainly by the need to observe a street system of a rough and ready kind for practical convenience. Other towns started in accordance with conscious plans drawn up for quite large areas (for example, the Roman towns with their grid-iron street plans and areas allocated for markets, temples, and barracks (Vol. II, Ch. 14)), or the new towns developed in many parts of the world to accommodate population increase, or to act as centres for the opening up of new territory, or even to act as new capital cities (for example, Canberra, Fig. 38.1, (1908) and Brasilia, Fig. 38.17, (1960)). Then there are very many examples of cities which started with a carefully planned nucleus; then went through a period of expansion by accretion round the edges on a somewhat haphazard basis; and then had sizeable planned extensions added. A good example would be Bath, in Britain, with its planned Roman nucleus; the accretion of the Middle Ages with narrow irregular street systems; and then the grand eighteenth-century additions of squares, circuses, and terraces. To this was added a further haphazard period of expansion starting with the Industrial Revolution, and, finally, in the twentieth century the addition of very large planned housing estates round the periphery (Fig. 38.2).

In the main, however, it would be fair to say that the general pattern for urban growth in western countries up to the middle of the nineteenth century (well into the period of the Industrial Revolution, that is to say) owed far more to the play of land markets and the desire of industrialists to have workers housed close to the factories than it did to conscious efforts by public

8.1. Canberra, Australia. The plan for the Federal Capital of Australia was conceived before the First World War and, ↄ later modifications, the layout of the centre still reflects the ideas of symmetry and monumentality current at the time. ⌐r away from the centre, interesting ideas have been developed for dealing with continued growth without the strangula⌐ facilities which has characterized the haphazard peripheral growth of older cities.

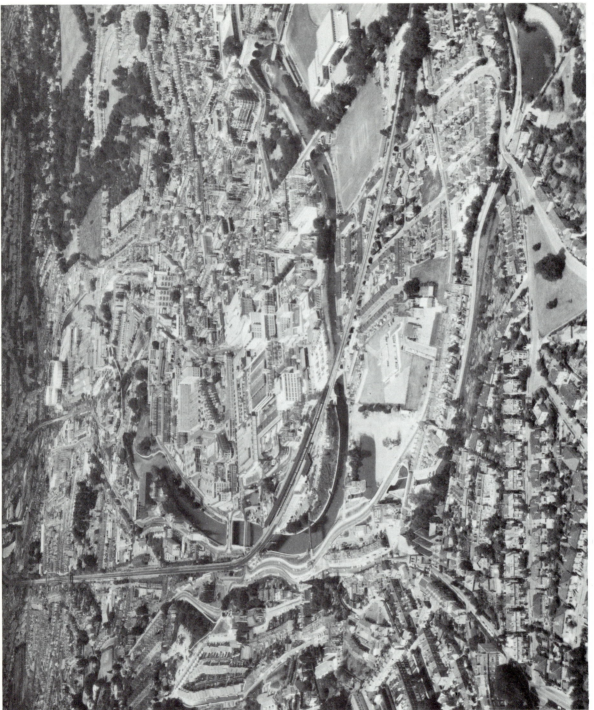

FIG. 38.2. Bath, England, an aerial view from the east. The city grew round the Roman nucleus in the loop of the River Avon. The hot spring baths still remain. The Abbey, with its surrounding narrow streets, represents the medieval development. To the north-east, at the edge of the photograph, can be seen the Royal Crescent and the Circus which are part of the great eighteenth-century extensions. Further afield, to the

FIG. 38.3. Preston, England, a typical nineteenth-century industrial town. The houses, within walking distance of the factories, are the product of by-laws prescribing minimum standards of design and layout. Note the complete absence of green space—the children played in the streets. Yet in such close-packed areas people could find friendships, loyalties, and support in distress which, it is often claimed, are absent in twentieth-century housing, whether the low-rise suburban estates or in the high-rise towers of inner-city areas.

authorities or enlightened landowners to plan towns for the convenience of those who had to occupy them. Since the period in question was one of very rapid population growth in most western countries it is not surprising that even before the middle of the century the conditions in the towns had become a source of great anxiety to thoughtful people. Cholera, typhoid, and high child mortality were the main manifestations of these conditions.

I. EFFECT OF THE INDUSTRIAL REVOLUTION

In Britain (which is a useful example to consider in the first instance because the country pioneered the Industrial Revolution and felt its impact severely in the form of a massive population explosion and headlong urban growth) conditions were bad enough to cause a Royal Commission on the Condition of the Towns to be set up. Its report, in 1844, led to the Public Health Act of 1848 and thus attention was focused on the defects of the industrial slums. The main concern initially was with sanitation—drainage, garbage and ash disposal, and ventilation—but attention soon turned to dwelling design and layout, street widths, and the prescription by government of minimum standards to be observed by public and private developers alike (Fig. 38.3). However, the housing reformers, to whom modern town planning owes so much, were not content to see the improvement of cities stop at the betterment of sanitary conditions. People like Ebenezer Howard and Patrick Geddes began asking fundamental questions about the functions and organization of cities. The Rowntree family founded a 'model' village at New Earswick near York to accommodate their factory workers, and were soon followed by the Cadbury brothers (George and Richard), who founded Bournville in 1879 (Fig. 38.5). In 1898 Howard published his book *Tomorrow: a peaceful path to social reform*. In this he advocated the acquisition of large tracts of land on which towns could be planned with full industrial facilities so that manufacturers might establish themselves and their workpeople under healthy and economical conditions. He further advocated that the land values created by the new community should be employed for commercial purposes, meeting municipal expenditure normally paid out of the rates. He also advocated the formation of closer relations between urban and rural life by the retention of a wide belt of agricultural land as part of the scheme, the town not being allowed to extend beyond a certain maximum. Further growth was to take the form of a new urban nucleus beyond this agricultural belt. In this way agriculture was to be in permanent association with the social life, business facilities, and mechanical equipment of the town.

FIG. 38.4. The outward sprawl of cities is caricatured in this drawing by George Cruickshank (1792–1878). Sprawl has been a never-ending cause for concern, and a major reason for the practice of town planning in the hope that expansion can be orderly and not too severely destructive of agricultural land and rural amenities. These hopes have not always been fulfilled.

FIG. 38.5. Bournville, England, an example of the enlightened outlook of some nineteenth-century industrialists concerned about the housing of their employees.

II. THE GARDEN CITY CONCEPT

Howard's book also advances the concept of the 'garden city', destined to play an important role in town planning thought in many countries. Here also the notion of town planning was extended to regional planning, whereby towns could be studied in the context of their areas of influence (Fig. 38.6). Howard postulated that in a national system of garden city development urban centres would be distributed evenly throughout the country. This would be to the great advantage of agriculture, and with far-reaching effects upon food production and the increase of the agricultural population. This was the first serious attempt to divert the stream of population from the big cities which Howard saw as presenting insuperable problems of government, poverty, public health, and transport. The direct result of Howard's work was the establishment in 1904 of Letchworth Garden City in a purely agricultural district in Hertfordshire on land bought by a joint stock company known as First Garden City Ltd. On this land a town for 35 000 inhabitants was planned— complete with houses, industries, shops, schools, and public buildings—and over the years the project has been carried through. Sixteen years later, in 1920, as a result of semi-official endorsement of Howard's ideas, Welwyn Garden City, with a planned population of 50 000 people, was established in pursuit of a general concept of a ring of satellite towns round London.

It could be argued against Howard and his adherents that the concept of new towns as a means of diverting the population from the large cities was

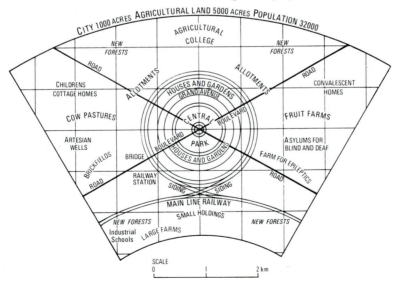

FIG. 38.6. Ebenezer Howard's concept of a 'garden city' which would avoid the evils of the industrial towns.

never a realistic policy for dealing with the problems of the cities. The 'conurbations' existed in the form of the huge mass of London; the Birmingham complex; the Liverpool–Manchester sprawl; the spread based on Newcastle upon Tyne; and the amorphous growth in the Clyde valley based on Glasgow. The teeming populations in these areas were to be numbered in many millions. No programme of little new towns of 30–40 thousand population apiece, cast realistically in terms of execution, could make more than a very small dent in the problems of these places, though they would of course provide a good life for the small number of people lucky enough to find themselves living in them. So the problems of the existing cities and conurbations continued to command attention, but with the focus of attention gradually widening from matters of sanitation and house design.

III. LEGISLATION FOR TOWN PLANNING

The term 'town planning' made its first appearance in Britain in a statutory enactment entitled the Housing, Town Planning etc. Act of 1909. This was a half-hearted piece of legislation which did little more than give local authorities optional powers to make planning schemes for parts of their areas if they believed that development was likely to take place and that control over it should be exercised in the public interest. Schemes made under these provisions were for the most part concerned with open peripheral areas of towns where the needs of expanding populations might be met. In very broad terms this was to be the pattern for town planning until the outbreak of the Second World War in 1939, although during this period the legislation was gradually becoming more sophisticated. Thus local authorities were permitted, if so inclined, to prepare 'regional planning schemes' to guide development over areas perhaps as large as a county. It should be noted that the legislation during this period was largely in response to damage already done. Vast sprawls and spreads of urban building, and 'ribbon' developments along main roads, took place during the 1920s and early 1930s, absorbing good agricultural and horticultural land; ruining the countryside; wrecking the functioning of main roads by the multiplication of points of access; and failing in any case to provide urban settlements possessing much semblance of delight or convenience. But the legislation was for the most part too late, too mild, and too much at the discretion of the local authorities, to have much beneficial effect before the outbreak of war in 1939 put a stop to the normal processes of development. There was, moreover, a fatal flaw in the legislation. Local authorities exercising their undoubted powers to restrict or prevent development which

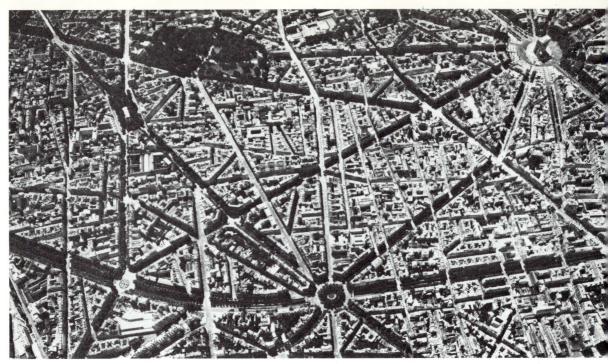

Fig. 38.7. Paris, France. In the mid-nineteenth century, Baron Haussmann (1809–91), Prefect of the Seine, initiated radical changes in Paris including a great programme of wide boulevards in geometrical patterns. The price paid in destruction of property and displacement of people must have been very great, and it may be questioned whether changes on such a scale would have been feasible in the changed climate of opinion a century later.

Fig. 38.8. New York, U.S.A. It has required many years for understanding to be reached of the quantitative relationship between the amount of building development placed on a given site and the quantities of traffic, power, sewage, supplies, pollutants, and so on which would result or be required. Manhattan is the classic case of over-building. In this illustration can be seen the older buildings of modest height and bulk, then a later phase of 'ziggurat' buildings where some attempt was made to prevent overshadowing of adjacent sites, and then the more recent phase of outright skyscraper development regardless of the consequences.

they judged to be contrary to the public interest were, nevertheless, liable to pay compensation to landowners thus deprived of their right to realize the development value inherent in their property. Local authorities were deterred from refusing permission for development for fear of having to pay out very large sums of money by way of compensation. In many cases, of course, land had become 'ripe for development' and thereby greatly increased in value, largely as a result of actions taken by the public authorities (construction of new roads, for example, or laying of sewerage systems). In spite of this, there was no means whereby the authorities could, in cases where development could reasonably be permitted, recoup all or part of these increased values which might then have been used to offset compensation claims in cases where permission for development was refused. This was the issue which came to be known as 'compensation and betterment', destined to be a nagging source of frustration in the British planning system for many years.

IV. THE WIDENING SCOPE OF TOWN PLANNING

It was the early years of the 1930s—in Britain and elsewhere years of depression, financial crisis, and high unemployment—which saw the dawn of official understanding that town planning, to be effective, must take cognizance of matters other than those relating to design and layout. More than by any other factor, this realization was brought home by the plight of the 'one-industry' towns in the northern part of Britain. Here were towns which for many years had depended fairly successfully on one staple industry—such as shipbuilding, coal-mining, or textiles—but when the markets for these industries collapsed the towns were plunged into mass unemployment, with grievous social consequencies. This process was accompanied by a tendency for the country to become separated into two parts: an impoverished and depressed northern part and a more prosperous south, or at any rate a south where there happened to be a greater diversification of employment opportunities with less dependence on the traditional heavy industries of Britain. Naturally, in these circumstances, there set in a discernible drift of population from north to south. The same phenomenon has occurred in other countries, notably Italy—except that there it is the southern part rather than the north which has tended to become impoverished.

In 1938 the British government instituted an inquiry into these matters in the form of the Royal Commission on the Distribution of Industry. The Commission reported during the Second World War and it was not until 1946 that practical effect was given to its recommendations by the passing of the Distribution of Industry Act. The main effect of this Act was to require any person or body proposing to undertake industrial development above a defined area of floor space to apply for an Industrial Development Certificate from the Board of Trade, which was the responsible department of the central government. In the exercise of its powers for granting or refusing such certificates, the Board was to have regard to the needs of the 'Development Areas', as those parts of the country were designated which had suffered severely in the recession of the 1930s. Clearly the powers bestowed by this Act were of the greatest social and economic importance, for they virtually gave the government the ability to direct industrial growth to areas where it was most needed. In effect they constituted 'regional planning'. Yet, it should be noted, they were exercisable by the Board of Trade, and not by the departments at either central or local level which were responsible for exercising planning powers. Even so thought was developing on the planning front, and the interests of the various bodies concerned were gradually converging.

Several other reports of wide significance were produced in Britain during the war. There was the Report of the Committee on the Utilization of Rural Land (1942), which drew attention to the need for husbanding valuable agricultural land against the pressures of urban development and the excavation of minerals. There was the Report of the Royal Commission on Compensation and Betterment (1942), which propounded a way to deal with this thorny issue. And there were many reports on individual cities and their replanning problems, especially the cities which had suffered air-raid damage. Probably the most important of these individual reports were the County of London Plan (1943) prepared by Patrick Abercrombie and J. H. Forshaw, and the Greater London Plan (1944) by Abercrombie (Fig. 38.9). These last were 'planning' reports in a new and much wider sense, because they attempted to analyse the social and economic problems of London before proceeding to formulate proposals for changing the physical fabric of the city. It was, for example, found that severe problems of overcrowding (of people in dwellings as well as dwellings on the ground) existed within the 'inner ring' of London. It was recommended that approximately one million people and their jobs should be 'decanted' from this area to a ring of New Towns to be established outside London beyond the Green Belt, and to other existing towns further afield. The Green Belt was itself a proposal of the Plan though it was based upon a re-validated concept of many years standing which saw positive advantage in circumscribing the outward spread of London.

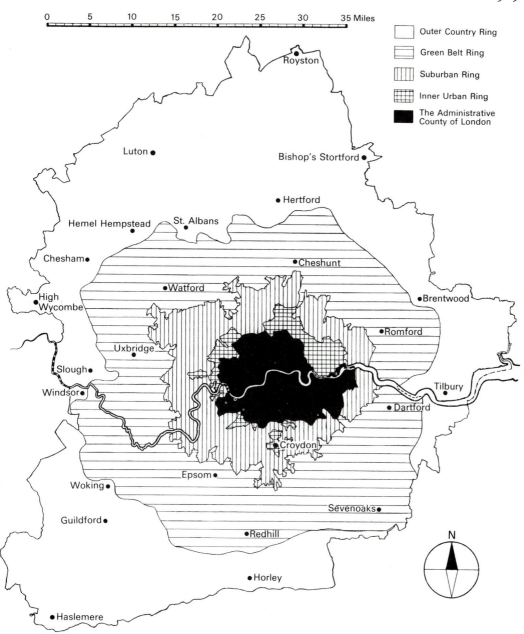

FIG. 38.9. Greater London Plan, 1944. The key element was the definition of the four rings with a policy of reducing population in the overcrowded inner areas, stabilizing it in the suburban and green belt rings, and permitting carefully controlled growth and 'overspill' in the outer country ring. From this there followed the major enterprise of the London New Towns programme.

V. BRITAIN—HISTORIC ACT OF 1947

For all this ferment of ideas and proposals to be of any practical value, however, a legislative framework was needed. This was provided by the Town and Country Planning Act of 1947 and the New Towns Act of 1946. The first of these was revolutionary. It swept away all previous planning legislation. The preparation of development plans showing the intended use of all land now became a compulsory exercise applicable to the whole surface of the country. The duties were to be exercised by the county councils and the county borough councils. Virtually all development and change of land use now became subject to detailed control by the same authorities, who, it should be noted, were larger and more powerful authorities than the urban and rural district councils which previously had the option of exercising planning powers. The Act provided that all the 'development value' in land (that is, the value which land might have for potential development over and above its existing use value) would be deemed to have been purchased by the State, and a sum of £300 millions was set aside as the total purchase price. Landowners were required to submit their claims; the money was not to be disbursed wholesale. In future, no one who had received his share of the £300m. 'cake' could claim additional compensation for being prevented from using his land for his own profit. The 'betterment' issue was dealt with by requiring payment of a 'development charge' by all persons undertaking development, the amount of the charge being assessed according to the degree of betterment obtaining. The Act also contained measures for the control of advertisements; the preservation of trees and woodlands; the designation of nature reserves, sites of scientific interest, and areas of outstanding natural beauty; and the preservation of buildings of architectural or historic interest. In all, the Act was as comprehensive a piece of planning legislation as has been enacted in any western country.

The New Towns Act was concerned primarily with the administrative machinery for planning, financing, and building new towns. These were at first conceived as new urban entities of about 60000 population, and even at this size they were considerably larger than any deliberately planned urban development previously undertaken in Britain (Fig. 38.10). In the event many (some 26 have been undertaken since the last war) have become considerably larger than 60000. The central feature of the machinery was the setting up of special bodies known as Development Corporations financed by central government, possessing powers for the compulsory acquisition of land, and authorized to establish their own professional staffs.

FIG. 38.10. Cumbernauld, Scotland. New towns, generally owing a good deal to Ebenezer Howard's ideas as developed in the garden city movement, have been a prominent feature in post-war planning to accommodate population moved out from overcrowded cities.

FIG. 38.11. The California Freeway, Los Angeles, U.S.A. Motor traffic has presented town planners with an obdurate problem. To accommodate all demands requires roads of such great width and complexity as to leave little room for the city, yet restraint policies designed to reduce the amount of traffic find little favour with the public.

FIG. 38.12. Glasgow, Scotland. High-density high-rise housing, largely dictated by inflated land values and the desire of city authorities not to lose population, has been severely criticized for its inhumanity and unsuitability for families with children.

VI. NATIONAL DIFFERENCES IN PLANNING PRACTICE

This brief account of the development of town planning in Britain up to the middle of the twentieth century is broadly representative of the experience of most western countries. Virtually without exception all countries had accepted the need for planning; the differences between them related mainly to the rigour with which planning schemes were conceived and implemented. In the U.S.A. and Australia, for example, where the pioneer spirit was still very much alive and where a man's right to do what he liked with his property was a strongly entrenched tradition, planning schemes tended to be zoning maps designed to bring some order into development which was likely to take place in any case in accordance with the land market. But in Europe, especially in Britain, where the pressures of population growth were more keenly felt, leading to conflicting demands on the use of land, the reformers were seeking, through planning, to change the social order. This involved fundamental challenges to the hitherto accepted rights of land owners and property owners.

The differences between the practice in various countries have been reflected in the organizations devised for carrying out planning. Taking the U.S.A. and Australia as examples again, planning in those countries tended to be in the hands of a multitude of small urban authorities clustered round a sizable 'centre city' which would operate its own planning scheme. This arrangement made it extremely difficult for planning to be exercised on a regional basis so that, for example, transport questions or population shifts could be viewed over a wide area. The difficulties were compounded when all the smaller authorities were intent upon their own growth programmes for the sake of prestige and rate return. For the wider view, reliance was placed upon advisory plans prepared by joint or state authorities; or by voluntary independently financed bodies (such as the New York Regional Plan Association); or upon the views expressed by research workers in universities. In Europe, the regional view was perhaps more easily promoted because the need for it was more obvious. In France, with her strong tradition of centralization, the 'overview' came almost naturally; in West Germany the State governments or *Lander* were well poised to think in regional terms; but in Britain, with her strong faith in local government, it was a good deal more difficult in spite of the obvious problems presented by the depressed areas or 'development areas' as they were later called.

VII. THE INFLUENCE OF WAR DAMAGE

It is not obvious that the destruction of towns caused in the First World War had very much influence upon the development of town planning thought, or that the rebuilding was influenced by planning ideas. But the position at the end of the Second World War was very different, with a considerable part of urban Europe lying in ruins (Fig. 38.13). Most of the countries affected found it necessary to set up research groups to study the engineering, architectural, legal, and financial problems involved in the work of reconstruction. As a consequence, urban planning thought was considerably advanced with the emergence of new techniques for controlling and financing urban change. At the same time that this work was going on, the wind of change was blowing through the rest of the world with thoughts of independence stirring in many countries, and with the first indications of urban

FIG. 38.13. Cologne, West Germany. The war-damaged cities of Europe have presented many problems as well as opportunities for town planners.

FIG. 38.14. Cologne, West Germany. The wholly enclosed air-conditioned shopping centre, usually in a suburban location, has been a feature of North American town planning. In contrast, as this example shows, the emphasis in Europe has been to retain the prosperity of existing city centres with traditional shopping streets from which traffic has been excluded.

problems of a new and desperate kind looming up in the rapidly expanding cities of the poorer parts of the world.

VIII. SOME ACHIEVEMENTS OF PLANNING

It might be said that at the mid-point of the twentieth century the need for planning in the sense of the need to control the use of land in the general public interest, and particularly to manage the change and growth of urban areas, was widely accepted throughout the world and was no longer the subject of political controversy. But acceptance of the idea was one thing: devising the machinery to put the idea into practice and making it function was another, even in a country such as Britain which by 1950 had as advanced (and onerous) a legislative system as any country outside the communist bloc. As a result, in the decades since 1950 town planning has both successes and failures to show. In Britain the bombed city centres have been rebuilt, though without architectural distinction; the New Towns have been built and must rank as a major social achievement in world terms; the countryside has been very largely protected from the worst features of urbanization and the main influence for change now undoubtedly lies with modern farming methods.

Fig. 38.15. Stockholm, Sweden. A break with tradition in a brilliant reconstruction in the centre of the city. Here shops, restaurants, and cafés are at various levels with linked terraces and walkways from which traffic is excluded.

An enormous, though still unfinished, task of slum clearance has been undertaken; the drift of population to the south has been checked; and a great though insufficient effort has been made to direct enterprise to areas in need of employments. A Herculean task of listing buildings of historic and architectural interest has been carried through; this inventory has been the basis of a sustained, though not always successful, effort to conserve this part of the national heritage. Advertising in rural areas has been brought under complete control; mineral working is now subject to strict control concerning restitution of worked-out areas; and the Clean Air Act (1956) has been remarkably successful in urban areas.

In France there have been notable achievements in regional planning, with manifest benefit to the national economy. These include the Strategic Plan for Development in the Region of Paris, of which one item is the new Charles de Gaulle airport at Roissy. In West Germany the sheer scale of the destruction wrought in the war required special measures. In the event the country, after prodigious efforts, has emerged with a great deal of her urban and industrial equipment renewed, and with her slum housing problem virtually disposed of, all to her great economic advantage. In the Scandinavian countries there is much to see in the way of imaginative city centre redevelopment,

Fig. 38.16. Stockholm, Sweden. Desirable as it is to have areas free from traffic where pedestrians can wander freely, the fact remains that it is motor traffic which supplies many of the city's needs. The price for traffic-free areas is nearly always the allocation of other areas where traffic is dominant.

as in Stockholm (Figs. 38.15 and 16), and in satellite towns built to high standards of layout and construction, as in Tapiola near Helsinki.

In the U.S.A., as though to compensate for a legislative planning system which has been slow to develop beyond the production of rigid zoning plans, there has been a ferment of activity in the voluntary field in the form of groups of people getting together to promote improvements in neighbourhood areas and to coax and cajole the public authorities into recognizing new responsibilities in connection with the improvement of the environment. This has been recognized, for example, in the setting up of the Department of Housing and Urban Development at Federal level. There has been recognition too—perhaps in advance of the rest of the world—that 'the environment' concerns much more than mere physical surroundings and must be involved with such matters as job opportunities; neighbourliness; the fruitful use of leisure time; and ease of access to facilities of all kinds. There has also been in the U.S.A. a vast, if uncoordinated, amount of research in the universities into urban problems from which the rest of the world has benefited, if not in terms of the results, at any rate in respect of the methodologies and techniques employed. Conspicuous amongst these studies have been the investigations into the relationship between the use of land and the movements of people and commodities which result.

IX. EDUCATION AND PLANNING

Town planning has opened up a new field in education. From the account already given, it could be said that planning had a sanitary origin as a result of the dismay aroused by the conditions in the industrial slums. The professional disciplines involved in the early efforts at town improvement were primarily those of the sanitary, drainage, and water-supply engineers (Vol. IV, Ch. 16; Vol. V, Ch. 23). But as attention spread to the design of housing groups and eventually to estates and garden cities, then naturally the architectural profession became more and more involved. These larger developments, however, also involved questions of land acquisition, land values, and estate management, and so the profession which in Britain is known as that of the Surveyor came also to be involved. In 1914 the three professions in Britain representing architecture, civil and municipal engineering, and surveying came to realize their common interest in town planning, and a new professional institute known as the Town Planning Institute was jointly founded. The main direction of the evolution of town-planning thought was, for a considerable period of years, controlled by the philosophies and interests of these three professions. That is to say, over-simplifying the case, the content of town-planning activity was largely constrained to matters which could be represented as designs prepared on the drawing board. There was no means nor incentive whereby social and economic issues could be introduced. Even in respect of road traffic (Ch. 30) the problems of congestion were seen essentially in 'hydraulic' terms; that is to say, traffic was seen as a fluid moving in a channel, and if the flow was obstructed then the remedy was to widen the channel. No questions were asked why road vehicles should be multiplying in numbers so rapidly nor what functions they were discharging. Thus a major social revolution—the bankrupting of railway systems by a new form of road-based transport—went on scarcely noticed in town planning circles. An important by-product of this oversight was the development in most countries of powerful professional lobbies in the form of the highway engineers, whose work has tended to dominate not only urban planning but the whole field of transport policy.

One important need which became apparent in most countries after the Second World War, when planning became an accepted activity, was the need for adequately trained staff. As planning shifted away from the drawing board to embrace social and economic issues, so the need arose for bringing in new skills. A vitally important element was the introduction of computer science, the main effect of which has been the facility to evaluate complex alternative courses of action before a choice is made. This facility, it should be noted, was not available when, for example, the plans for London were drawn up at the end of the war, upon which so much effort had been expended. It is at least conceivable that had it been possible to present the alternative possibilities for London, and to compare them rationally, quite different policies would have been pursued.

With this widening of the skills required for town planning it was not long before planning came to be recognized as a discipline worthy of attention by universities. The education of planners gradually shifted from the offices of the engineers and architects of local authorities, where young people served apprenticeships, to the postgraduate field in the universities where students with a first degree in some subject of basic relevance to planning (such as architecture, sociology, economics, or geography) could take a higher degree or diploma in planning. Later, some universities began to offer a first degree in planning, treating it as a subject in its own right. There is still much controversy concerning the best approach—whether by postgraduate training or first degree—but the answer probably is that there is ample room for both approaches and that this dual arrangement makes for a more lively and penetrating treatment of the subject.

X. URBAN PROBLEMS REMAIN ENDEMIC

In spite of the great efforts made since 1950, when planning seemed poised to make a major contribution to social and economic welfare in much of the world, the verdict after 25 years would probably amount to no more than an affirmation that things would have been even worse had no planning been invoked. Despite the huge effort, urban and regional problems continue to be a major preoccupation of government in most countries. The physical and social manifestations are to be found in besetting shortages of accommodation of all kinds (especially distressing in lack of housing); in huge accumulations of old worn-out accommodation; in drab and inconvenient environments; in transport difficulties; in pollutions of various kinds; in inadequacies in social services; in defects in the job situation, with unemployment or boring, dirty, dangerous jobs leading to bitterness and strife; in vice and violence; in a lack of worth-while things to do with leisure time; in ill-relationships of many kinds, social as well as physical; in other human problems where documentation has scarcely begun; in the sheer difficulty of financing, planning, and managing the affairs of large cities; and in the fearful 'overlay' when all these

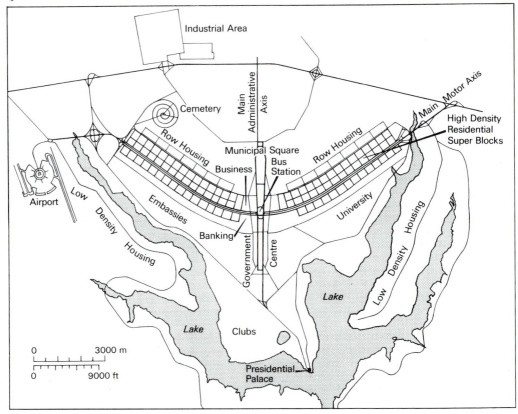

FIG. 38.17. Brasilia, Brazil. The plan for the new capital city on a desolate inland site. The rigid geometry of this 'bow-and-arrow' plan may be contrasted with the more organic layout of Cumbernauld New Town (Fig. 38.12) where contours and climate and the need for a sense of intimacy in low-rise housing have strongly influenced the design.

problems are aggravated by questions of race or religion, or both. These are the continuing problems of cities world-wide, but if they are serious in western cities they are much worse in some of the 'immature' metropolitan areas of developing countries. There growth is so rapid that it far outpaces the ability of municipal governments to provide even the most elementary services of garbage collection, let alone organize themselves to provide effective corruption-free administration.

After the euphoria of the immediate post-war years when, in Britain, the Act of 1947 seemed to promise a framework to guide the rebuilding of the whole country, and legislation elsewhere held out the same promise, town planning seems generally to have declined in public esteem. This can be attributed partly to dissatisfaction with the results of planning—an immense bureaucratic effort with many controls placed upon private effort and initiative, yet with few benefits perceivable by the man in the street—and partly to a feeling that all this work was going on and affecting people's lives in various ways but without sufficient consultation with those affected. In Britain, so often the exemplar, a sequence of incidents seemed to spark off not only dissatisfaction with the methods of planning but a sudden realization that in an overcrowded island planning was nevertheless necessary and must be made to work. The physical collapse of a block of flats in the East End of London (Ronan Point (1968)) produced an outcry against this form of housing; a new urban motorway (Westway in London (1970)) resulted in a storm of protest against the dissection of urban areas by new roads, and demands for 'integrated transport policies'; the abortive search for a site for a third airport for London (1968–70) focused attention upon a whole range of environmental questions, and even threw doubts upon the very idea of sustained economic growth as being essential to the nation's survival.

Out of this new ferment of ideas planning seems to be emerging with a new realism. Cities are now recognized as infinitely complicated places where the smallest change may set off a chain reaction of other changes. Urban problems are being studied in their totality with a more determined effort to see where the priorities should lie. Financial budgets are being framed to the same end and are kept strictly within realistic bounds of expenditure; general financial stringency has changed the emphasis from the planning of ambitious proposals to the better management of the equipment which cities already possess. Determined efforts are being made to find ways in which the public can participate in the formulation of planning policies without at the same time bringing change and development to a standstill by reason of the opposition that may be raised to every proposal. Analytical techniques are being constantly refined so that alternative courses of action may be presented and compared. Yet, when all is said and done, these are no more than changes in methods; the grand objective is as it has always been, namely to make cities better places to live in, to preserve the heritage, and to conserve resources.

Finally, we may remark that the history of town planning epitomizes the way in which social, political, and economic factors can influence technological advances. It does not suffice simply to be able to do many of the things described elsewhere in these volumes—such as building motorways, bridges, multi-storey buildings, airports, reservoirs, and sewage works. These developments are, by general consensus, increasingly controlled by various constraints imposed by society in general, acting through government. These constraints in turn affect the development of the industries concerned and thus the opportunities for employment within them. For example, the building industry at all levels—and its suppliers—is very sensitive both to local government policy and to the overall economic policy of central government. The investment of the road-building industry in the heavy plant essential for economic construction is conditioned by assessment of the likelihood of future contracts for the building of new motorways and major road reconstructions. The heavy-plant manufacturers' ability to make improved machines in turn may be frustrated by a manifest lack of a sufficient market for them. The catalogue is endless, and a reminder that technology cannot stand in isolation.

BIBLIOGRAPHY

The great bulk of planning literature is in the form of official or semi-official reports; reports of the proceedings of learned societies; university research papers; and legal enactments. The following books cover in the main the history of planning or turning points in the development of ideas.

ABERCROMBIE, PATRICK. *Town and country planning*. Butterworth, London (1933).

———. *Greater London Plan*. H.M.S.O., London (1944).

ADAMS, THOMAS. *Outline of town and city planning*. Churchill, London (1935).

BRIGGS, ASA. *Victorian cities*. Pelican, Harmondsworth (1963).

BUCHANAN, C., et al. *Traffic in towns*. H.M.S.O., London (1963).

COLLINS, G. R., and COLLINS, C. C. *Camillo Sitte and the birth of modern city planning*. Phaidon Press, Oxford (1965).

CHERRY, GORDON E. *The evolution of British town planning*. Leonard Hill, London (1974).

JACOBS, JANE. *The death and life of great American cities*. Random House, New York (1961).

LE CORBUSIER. *The city of the future*. New York (1930).

McKELVEY, BLAKE. *The urbanization of America 1860–1951*. Rutgers University Press, New Brunswick, N.J. (1963).

MERLIN, PIERRE. *Les villes nouvelles*. Presses Universitaires de France, Paris (1969).

MUMFORD, LEWIS. *The culture of cities*. Harcourt, New York (1938).

———. *The city in history*. Pelican, Harmondsworth (1966).

SHARP, THOMAS. *Town planning*. Penguin, Harmondsworth (1940).

UNWIN, RAYMOND. *Town planning in practice*. Ernest Benn, London (1909).

WEBER, ADNA FERRIN. *The growth of cities in the nineteenth century*. Macmillan, New York (1899).

39

ENGINEERING: THE SCIENTIFIC BASIS

AUBREY F. BURSTALL

THE Industrial Revolution was very largely brought about in Britain by men with little formal education. They were successful because, like the early settlers in North America, they were exploiting rich virgin territory. The momentum carried them forward to the middle of the nineteenth century but then, inevitably, the tide began to turn. Other countries wanted to share in the new prosperity that industrialization offered and recognized, as Britain was slow to do, that the basis of progress was a new class of industrial worker well versed in the scientific principles fundamental to the advancing technology of the day. The evolution of scientific education in the last half of the nineteenth century was considered in an earlier volume (Vol. V, Ch. 32) and the story is now brought up to the middle of the twentieth century (Ch. 7). This chapter on the scientific basis of engineering complements these broader studies. At the beginning of this century the professional engineer, academically qualified, was no new phenomenon, but as the century advanced his importance and status grew. Increasingly he made his contribution not as a lone inventor but as a member of a group of specialists, which might include metallurgists, chemists, and physicists. Their collaboration might be in the universities, in industry, or in one of the many national institues established in many parts of the world. Among these we may mention the National Physical Laboratory in Britain (1900) and the National Bureau of Standards (1901) in the U.S.A.

The speed of change was greatest in the U.S.A. with lavish expenditure on research and the production of more engineering graduates, followed by a large increase in productivity in industry. In aeronautics some important scientific discoveries were made in Germany, where the rate of advance in technology had been ahead of the rest of the world, and continued to be so. She led in building aeroplanes and airships; in machinery; equipment for high-pressure chemical processes; optical and other instruments; machine tools; and welding techniques. Switzerland remained a country that excelled in meticulous attention to details of design, applying scientific methods of analysis to the production of such diverse products as machine tools, turbines, and locomotives. A. Stodola of Zurich University, in his outstanding text-book (1927) on turbines [1] discussed not only the thermodynamic issues involved in design, but fluid flow, vibration, stress analysis in plates, shells, and rotating discs, thermal stresses, and stress concentrations at holes and fillets.

The use of higher pressures, temperatures, and speeds in machinery brought problems that required engineers to be well grounded in the fundamental principles of science and mathematics. Presentation became more scientific and less empirical. More use was made of mathematics and the subject of dynamics grew increasingly important. It was found that many difficult problems relating to motion in machinery could be resolved by dynamical analysis.

In Europe and the U.S.A. more graduates were being produced, often better trained than their British counterparts (Ch. 7). In Britain a belief in practical training for engineers persisted, perhaps a hangover from admiration of the achievements of the self-taught men of the previous generation. Many British engineers were still self-educated or had at best only a part-time education at a technical college. In this period many Mechanics' Institutes grew into technical colleges, providing certificate courses at a somewhat lower standard than university degree courses. Russia, after the Revolution, devised a comprehensive system of technical education and her rate of technical advance grew accordingly.

Aeronautical engineers led the way in stress analysis. The performance and safety of the machines they made depended upon the correctness of the calculations of the stressmen. The first aircraft [2] (Ch. 33) were made of wood braced with piano wire, which was the strongest steel then available, but by 1930 all-metal aeroplanes of aluminium, which had been developed on a considerable industrial scale since the First World War, were being used on regular routes in the U.S.A. [3]. From that time on aluminium alloys of a very high strength-to-weight ratio were developed for the aircraft industry.

Shortly before the First World War, at University College, London, E. N. da C. Andrade [4] began some very important researches on the long-term behaviour of metals under constant stress. This led to a clear under-standing of the physical factors involved in the phenomenon known as 'creep', a common cause of failure in engineering parts working under steady load. He recognized three components in creep: an immediate extension, a transient flow, and a constant flow. The latter Andrade called 'viscous', but it is now more generally referred to as 'steady-state' creep. In 1935, R. W.

Bailey [5] reviewed the current state of knowledge of creep, and the way in which existing data on it could be used in engineering design.

Among structures in which great stresses were encountered were the high-pressure vessels needed for such chemical processes as the hydrogenation of nitrogen, coal, and oil. Originating in Germany, these spread to Britain, the U.S.A., France, and Italy [6, 7]. Great ingenuity was displayed in devising joints and reinforcing the walls of plant working at high temperatures and pressures.

Creep is a deformation process encountered in metals subjected to steady stress. No less important, especially with the increasing speeds of machinery of all kinds, is the risk of failure in metals undergoing repeated cycles of stress. First given the name 'fatigue' by J. Braithwaite in 1854, many mechanical failures from then on were recognized as being due to this cause; most impressive was the deterioration and breakage of the wrought-iron railway axles then in wide use, numbering approximately 500 in one case and 'some thousands' in another [8]. The nature of metal fatigue became the preoccupation of many engineers and scientists [9]. The idea of an endurance limit (for example, ten million reversals of stress) and of a range of stress (for example, plus or minus 5 tons per square inch) suggested by A. Wohler in 1858 was generally accepted as a basis for design. With the advent of X-rays it was possible to show that a breakdown of crystal structure into smaller grains in a fatigue test was similar to that at the yield point in a static test. In 1917, B. P. Haigh [10] identified the related phenomenon of corrosion fatigue (p. 452).

Another factor seen in metals under stress was the residual stress remaining in the metal as a result of certain processes of manufacture. Such locked-up stresses could be dangerously large after some processes, though they could generally be resolved by suitable heat treatment. Impact and hardness tests were devised and used in specifications for metals. Tensile tests remained of the greatest importance and determined also the limit of proportionality of stress to strain (the elastic limit); the yield point, at which the material begins to stretch without further application of load; and the amount of contraction of area ('necking') of the specimen at fracture, a measure of the ductility of the metal.

The study of the science and practice of metrology was by 1940 included in courses for production engineers [12]. From 1930 onwards instruments such as autocollimators, profile projectors, gauge blocks, optical flats, the sine-bar, and improved micrometers came into regular use in workshop and toolroom [13, 14]. Production engineers with a scientific approach (Ch. 43), became responsible for the accuracy of manufacture and also with output, deciding and selecting the best arrangement for tools and operators. The evolution of new cutting steels [15, 16] and of tests for the machine tools with which they were used [17] presented many problems of an essentially scientific nature.

By 1940 welding was a generally accepted method of construction, since the conditions needed for satisfactory welds, after earlier misapplication, had been recognized. Welded vessels were subjected to various scientific tests, the most important being by X-rays or gamma rays [18, 19]. Much of the pioneer work took place in the U.S.A.; electric arc welding machines for piping, and X-ray testing, were in use there in 1930. In Europe, the oxyacetylene process was developed, both manual and automatic, but by 1940 it was mainly superseded by the electric arc for the welding of steel. Oxygen cutting of steel also came into general use.

Significant developments in machine tools took place (Ch. 42). There was a greater use of hydraulic drives and controls, first introduced in the U.S.A. by Brown and Sharpe in 1902. A new machine in the tool-room was the precision jig boring machine, used in Switzerland in watch-making, by which large castings could be machined with great accuracy, though it required a room maintained at constant temperature and humidity. Similar machines were quickly developed in England, Germany, and the U.S.A. Other innovations were the magnetic chuck (1900); centreless grinding (1915) [20]; the metal-cutting band-saw [21]; and the continuous filing machine introduced in 1933 in the U.S.A. as the DoAll machine [22].

The revolution in land transport in all civilized countries in the first half of the century was more evident in the U.S.A. than elsewhere, because there the pace of change was greatest and that country was consolidating her industrial leadership of the world. Motor transport became common, and at the same time the railways, which had reached their zenith about 1920, started to decline. The chief reason for this decline was the availability of the cheap mass-produced automobile pioneered by Henry Ford [23]. Fifteen million of his Model T were made between 1908 and 1927. He applied the conveyor belt system to car manufacture on a large scale, and other countries followed this important step towards the automatic factory and the use of automatic devices of many kinds for the control of machinery.

The gyroscope was applied to automatic control in 1903 by Otto Schlick to dampen the pitch and roll of a ship [24]. Later Elmer Sperry (U.S.A.)

fitted it to warships [25]. Another automatic device was the Crosby feed-water regulator (1912) to control the water level in steam boilers; this depended on heat transfer through a metal diaphragm. There were a variety of automatic devices to control combustion in steam boilers and their maximum efficiency rose from 70 per cent to 89 per cent between 1900 and 1931 [26]. Centrifugal governors were still used to control speed of rotation, their power being increased by an oil relay system with pressure supplied by a separate gear pump, devised by C. Parsons in England in 1917 [27].

By the 1930s the study of vibration was essential for the designer dealing with reciprocation at high speeds, such as occurred in large marine engines, high-speed piston engines for aircraft, rolling-mill machinery, and wherever the effects of vibration placed a limit on operation. Many types of vibration damper were devised, for example that for torsional vibration tried by F. W. Lanchester for his cars. In 1930 the Geiger Torsiograph became the standard instrument for continuously recording vibration on a rotating drum.

In the first part of the century, the growth of knowledge of the laws governing the motion of solid bodies through fluids was prodigious. The most important machine moving in a fluid (air) was the aeroplane (Ch. 33); the airship, too, had a relatively brief period of popularity [30] but it was virtually abandoned by 1940. Several designers developed aircraft based on rather different principles. These included aircraft with rotating wings, either rotated by power (helicopter) or by the forward motion of the traction propeller (autogyro) [43]. Data on streamlining and the effect of the boundary layer of the fluid on solid surfaces obtained from the behaviour of models in wind tunnels had a profound effect on the design of all machinery concerned with the movements of fluids at high speeds. The accumulated body of knowledge of hydraulics (Ch. 44) had been of little use to the aeronautical engineer; the mechanical engineer, accustomed to empirical formulae and factors of safety, found it hard to adapt to the exacting new requirements for aircraft design [28]. Advances made in 1920–30 resulted in hydraulics being abandoned in favour of fluid mechanics as a subject for mechanical engineers. In 1901, L. Prandtl [29] had originated this new approach, defining the theory of the boundary layer and expressing the essential features of flow problems by simple mathematical relationships based on fundamental physical laws. The same approach was followed in other countries. The acceptance of the boundary layer approach, and an analogous method of analysis, formed a basis for the study of heat transfer between flowing fluids and their boundaries, as in furnaces, boilers, evaporators, condensers, and heat exchangers generally.

From the 1920s these methods of calculating heat transfer were used by the chemical engineer, now becoming established as a specialist in his own right.

The reluctance of many mechanical engineers to accept scientific analysis in place of empirical data was often due to their having insufficient facility in the use of mathematics. Exceptions to this generalization were A. G. M. Michell (Australia) and A. Kingsbury (U.S.A.), who independently invented the tilting-pad thrust bearing at the beginning of the century [31]. The result of an elegant piece of scientific analysis, it enabled large ships to dispense with the rows of thrust collars and cooling arrangements previously needed to prevent the thrust of the propeller from disembowelling the hull, and replaced them with a single bearing. The invention was not, however, exploited until Germany used it in her battleships in 1914. Another invention, in the field of hydraulic power transmission, was the Fottinger torque converter [32], later superseded by the more efficient double helical gearing and the fluid flywheel. Germany, the U.S.A., Britain, and Sweden all took part in these developments [33]. Hydraulic couplings were commonly used to prevent vibration in piston engines along the output shaft; by 1935 very large ones were in use, as in hydro-electric plants.

Studies of the wave action in pipes were made when oil began to be used in pipe systems operating at very high pressures, as in the fuel injection systems of diesel engines. The results led to power being applied by wave action through a liquid for working rock drills and hydraulic riveters; a pioneer in this field was G. Constantinesco [34].

An important device that depended for its operation on the controlled flow of both air and liquid was the float-feed carburettor. It automatically delivered to the petrol engine the amount of fuel required for any particular opening of the throttle valve. Another machine based on fluid flow that came into general use was the domestic vacuum cleaner [35].

Changes that took place in heat engines in this period had profound effects on material civilization in all parts of the world, not through any one major innovation but rather by many small improvements. Very early in the century the hot air engine lost popularity and almost disappeared from use [36]. It had been inefficient, heavy, and expensive and its place was largely taken by the small electric motor. The gas engine [37], which was extremely efficient, also began to decline at this time, its high thermal efficiency being surpassed by that of the diesel engine, which operated at a much higher compression; in other cases it was replaced by the steam turbine which needed less space and maintenance.

Many improvements were made to the petrol engine and the high-speed diesel engine between 1930 and 1950, some arising from the work of H. R. Ricardo [38] in England, who discovered the role of turbulence in mixing the charge in the cylinder and thereby ensuring rapid combustion. He also realized that detonation of the mixture in the cylinder set a limit to the power output and economy of the engine. Later T. Midgly and T. A. Boyd, in the U.S.A., found that adding minute quantities of tetraethyl lead to the petrol suppressed the tendency to detonate. The explanation lay in the science of gas kinetics; the lead interfered with the normal process of combination of oxygen and fuel molecules. The diesel engine was improved by the so-called solid injection system. The two-stroke diesel engine became popular for small high-speed stationary engines and for large marine engines such as the Doxford engine [39] embodying opposed pistons, slightly out of phase.

The success of experiments on internal combustion engines depended on the special instruments developed to measure the engine performance, particularly the engine indicator, invented by James Watt as long ago as 1800. B. Hopkinson in England, developed a single-mirror optical indicator in 1840. This was the first of a series of similar instruments, by various designers, that appeared up to 1921 when the Farnboro indicator [40], a balanced pressure type, was developed at the Royal Aircraft Establishment, Farnborough, for exploring the performance of aircraft engines in flight. Finally, before 1940, electronic engine indicators overcame the problem inherent in moving masses at high speeds by substituting weightless beams of electrons.

Early in the century the steam turbine (Ch. 41) took first place among prime movers as the most suitable machine for producing energy in large amounts on land and sea [41]. In 1907 the thermal efficiency was 18 per cent, and by 1940 38 per cent. Efficiencies of steam boilers were also improved and forced circulation was introduced.

For many processes it was necessary to handle and treat large quantities of air, not only for boiler furnaces but for ventilating machines, mines, and buildings. Air had to be filtered, warmed, or cooled and its humidity controlled; these were all operations initiated by heating and ventilating engineers. In the field of refrigeration (Vol. V, p. 45) the compression process continued in use with improved designs and small domestic refrigerators became popular. Non-poisonous refrigerants—freons—were introduced. In the first decade a continuous absorption apparatus known as the Electrolux was put on the market by Platen and Munters, in Sweden. It needed no pump, the refrigerating fluid being circulated by the application of heat to the generator;

circulation was maintained by convection currents set up by differences in the density of the fluids in different parts of the system [42].

Up to the 1960s, the greatest of all engineering achievements was that of space flight (Ch. 35), which utilized scientific knowledge at the very limit of existing boundaries. This has been the province largely of Russian and American technology, but important associated engineering achievements have been made elsewhere. Britain's principal contribution was the construction by Sir Bernard Lovell (designer H. C. Husband) of a gigantic steerable radio telescope 250 ft (76 m) in diameter, which tracked the satellites in orbit with a tracking accuracy of 12 ft (3·7 m) [44, 45]. The framework was 2000 tons in weight and it had to be rigid. The bowl, weighing 80 tons, was mounted on a cradle of 800 tons and suspended on trunnions 180 ft (55 m) above the ground. Elevation made use of heavy gun racks salvaged from the *Royal Sovereign* battleship. The towers were connected at ground level by a diametral heavy girder system pivoted at its central point, defining the azimuth axis, and were carried on bogies moving on a double-ring track 320 ft (97·5 m) in diameter. Driving in azimuth was through four of the bogies. For elevation, the feed was supported on a 50-ft (15 m) steel tube inside a central mast. This instrument could transmit as well as receive radio signals. Since it was built, receiver techniques at shorter wavelengths have much improved, so that smaller instruments of higher surface and pointing accuracy are now made and used.

Up to the time of the Second World War it had been deemed impossible to fly above the speed of sound, but this barrier was broken when Frank Whittle [46] invented the jet propulsion engine. He filed his first patent in 1930, but jet-propelled flight was not actually achieved by him until 1941. A similar principle was used in the German V-1 flying bombs towards the end of the war. Slower modern aircraft were driven by a gas turbine through a propeller, the thrust augmented by the jet from the exhaust. These turbo-prop or prop-jet aeroplanes were typical for commercial airlines [47, 48] (Ch. 33).

After the Second World War it was generally expected that the gas turbine (Ch. 40) would supersede the steam turbine for many purposes, but this did not happen, largely because of the difficulty of operating continuously at the very high temperatures and speeds required for economic operation.

Significant contributions in the field of heat transfer were made after the Second World War—studies on flow of fluids, streamline flow, and shock waves under conditions of supersonic flow and pulsating flow [49, 50].

Greater awareness of the phenomena of fluid flow culminated in interesting mechanical devices such as the Hovercraft aeroplane which travelled slightly above ground level supported by a cushion of air [51]. Other improvements were the general use of air-lubricated bearings and the application of the vortex-flow theory to the design of turbine blading.

The development of atomic power for military and civil applications [52] is dealt with at length elsewhere in this work (Ch. 10, 11). Here we need note only that this, too, was an immense engineering project that would have been totally impossible without harnessing a great range of scientific disciplines. Indeed, the beginnings of the project are to be discerned in research on the nature of the atom that began even before the beginning of this century and was then deemed—like Faraday's discovery of electricity—to have no possible practical applications. The Second World War provided the stimulus for a great intensification of effort, and by 1942 the possibility of controlled fission reaction had been demonstrated.

Other post-war devices embodying new principles included the free-piston diesel engine that had no cranks or rotating parts [53]; this was developed originally by Pescara (France) for compressing air for construction work. It was later used as a gas generator for gas turbines. Another was the Philips Co. (Holland) refrigerator for making liquid air at atmospheric pressure [54]; this was useful in hospitals and laboratories to supply uncontaminated liquid air. In general, advances in design and construction after 1940 came about by the perfecting, and wider application, of mechanisms already known [55]. Elaborate computing machines depending on electronic components for their operation replaced the mechanical calculator machine [56]. Electric instruments recorded machine performance. Electric controllers and sensing devices replaced manual control where rapid response was needed. Machine tools were controlled by punched cards or magnetic tape, resulting in 'digital machining' and giving new standards of accuracy and speed [56].

Forming rather than cutting methods came to be preferred after 1940 for the shaping of metals. With sufficient power available metals could be worked cold—by rolling, forging, and pressing—and in a fraction of the time required by other methods. Furthermore, the metal in the finished article was usually in a better metallurgical state as a result of the cold-forming operations. Finned tubing, for example, in great demand for many purposes by this time, could be made by extrusion through a die.

Plastic materials were, of course, in use even before the beginning of the present century but their very extensive application did not occur until after the Second World War. Not only were chemically different plastics then introduced—polyethylene, polyamide, for example—but new methods of forming them had to be found, especially for the manufacture of large items. In some respects, plastics proved to have higher tensile strength, greater ductility, and better resistance to corrosion than metals then in use. Others were of interest because of special physical characteristics. Polytetrafluoro-ethylene (PTFE), for example, proved to have an exceptionally low coefficient of friction; this justified its use for special applications, despite its high cost and the difficulty of working it. Better understanding of the physical charac-teristics of plastics made it possible to introduce much larger moulding machines and totally new techniques were evolved to produce really large items. One such was the use of glass-reinforcement of quick-setting plastic on a wooden former; this was used for such items as boats and car bodies. An alternative was to use plastic sheet as a constructional material. An interesting example was the 'Dracone' barge devised by W. R. Hawthorne in 1956. This was a large 'sausage' made of rubber-proofed nylon, for the transport of oil. It was towed under water when full, but rolled up and loaded on the ship's deck for the return journey [57]. The design of the towing tackle raised con-siderable hydrodynamic problems.

The advent of plastics also made possible new techniques of stress analysis. A photo-elastic method had been proposed by Maxwell in 1850. In 1926, E. G. Coker [11] suggested a two-dimensional method, utilizing a transparent loaded model which produced a characteristic coloured pattern when examined by polarized light. This idea was taken further. Certain plastics, such as ethoxylene resin, not only have photo-elastic properties but can retain at room temperature locked-up streses previously induced in the material by subjecting it to loading at a higher temperature and then cooling under load. Thus it is possible to study the stress system in a three-dimensional specimen by the so-called 'frozen stress' technique. The specimen is cut into slices and the stress pattern in each is examined under polarized light [58]. Another advance in experimental stress analysis was the use of a special plastic paint on a metal surface. Under load, cracks appeared in the paint, their width and disposition giving a measure of the stress in the metal surface [59]. An elegant method of stress analysis, developed in the U.S.A. in the Second World War, was the use of electrical-resistance strain gauges [60]. Small pieces of resistance wire were cemented on to the surface of members under load and the working stress of any part of a design checked by noting changes in the resistance. Kelvin had shown as long ago as 1856 that metal wires carrying an electric current change their electrical resistance when subjected to a tensile load, the change being proportional to the tensile strain in the wire. Many of these innovations required considerable technical knowledge and skill for their development.

REFERENCES

[1] STODOLA, A. *Steam and gas turbines* (trans. L. C. Loewenstein). McGraw-Hill, New York (1927).

[2] GIBBS-SMITH, C. H. *The aeroplane.* Science Museum Publication, H.M.S.O., London (1960).

[3] BROOKS, P. W. The development of the aeroplane. Cantor Lecture, *Journal of the Royal Society of Arts*, January (1959).

[4] ANDRADE, E. N. DA C. On the viscous flow and allied phenomena in metals. *Proceedings of the Royal Society*, A., **84**, 1 (1910).

[5] BAILEY, R. W. Utilisation of creep test data in engineering design. *Proceedings of the Institution of Mechanical Engineers*, **131**, 131 (1935).

[6] SMITH, F. E. Plant for the production of petrol by the hydrogenation of bituminous coal. *Proceedings of the Institution of Mechanical Engineers*, **133**, 139 (1936).

[7] BARBER, A. T., and TAYLOR, A. H. High pressure plant for experimental hydrogenation processes. *Proceedings of the Institution of Mechanical Engineers*, **128**, 5 (1934).

[8] PARSONS, R. H. *The History of the Institution of Mechanical Engineers*, p. 95. Institution of Mechanical Engineers, London (1947).

[9] DOREY, S. F. Large scale torsional fatigue testing of marine shafting. *Proceedings of the Institution of Mechanical Engineers*, **159**, 399 (1948).

[10] HAIGH, B. P. *Journal of the Institute of Metals*, **18** (1917).

[11] COKER, E. G. Elasticity and plasticity. *Proceedings of the Institution of Mechanical Engineers*, No. 5, 897 (1926).

[12] SEARS, J. E. Gauging and metrology. *Proceedings of the Institution of Mechanical Engineers*, **157**, 298 (1947).

[13] CARSON, T. Gauging in machine tool manufacture. Symposium on machine tool practice. *Proceedings of the Institution of Mechanical Engineers*, **141**, 19 (1939).

[14] ROLT, F. H. *Gauges and fine measurements.* Macmillan, London (1929).

[15] STRASSMAN, W. P. *Risk and technological innovation.* Cornell University Press, Ithaca (1959).

[16] TAYLOR, F. W. *On the art of cutting metals.* American Society of Mechanical Engineers (1907).

[17] SCHLESINGER, G. Machine tool tests and alignments. *Proceedings of the Institution of Mechanical Engineers*, **138**, 59 (1938).

[18] PULLEN, V. E. X-rays in engineering practice. *Proceedings of the Institute of Mechanical Engineers*, **11**, 1133 (1930).

[19] BRAGG, W. H. The application of X-rays to the study of the crystalline structure of materials. *Proceedings of the Institution of Mechanical Engineers*, No. 3, 751 (1927).

[20] WOODBURY, R. S. *The history of the grinding machine.* M.I.T. Press, Cambridge, Mass. (1959).

[21] CHAMBERLAND, H. J. Friction cutting of metals by bandsaws. *Machinery*, **52**, No. 2 (1945).

[22] DO ALL INSTRUCTION PROGRAMS, Vol. 1. The Do All Co. (1945).

[23] POMEROY, L. E. *Engineering heritage*, p. 164. Heinneman, London (1963).

[24] INGLIS, C. E. Gyroscopic principles and applications. *Proceedings of the Institution of Mechanical Engineers*, **151**, 223 (1944).

[25] SPERRY, E. *The gyroscope through the ages*. Sperry Gyroscope Co., U.S.A. (1960).
HUGHES, T. P. *Elmer Sperry: inventor and engineer*. Johns Hopkins Press, Baltimore and London (1971).

[26] HODGSON, J. L., and ROBINSON, L. L. Development of automatic control systems for industrial and power station boilers. *Proceedings of the Institution of Mechanical Engineers*, **126,** 59 (1934).

[27] PARSONS, R. H. *The development of the Parsons steam turbine*, p. 142, Constable, London (1936).

[28] KARMAN, T. VON, and BIOT, M. A. *Mathematical methods in engineering*. McGraw-Hill, New York (1940).

[29] PRANDTL, L., and TIETJENS, O. G. *Applied hydro- and aero-mechanisms*. McGraw-Hill, London (1934).

[30] DAVY, M. J. B. *Aeronautics. Lighter-than-air aircraft*. Science Museum Publication, H.M.S.O., London (1950).

[31] BARWELL, F. T. *Lubrication of bearings*. Butterworth, London (1956).

[32] SINCLAIR, H. Problems in the transmission of power by fluid couplings. *Proceedings of the Institution of Mechanical Engineers*, **139**, 83 (1938).

[33] TOWN, H. C. Recent developments in the use of hydraulic power. *Proceedings of the Institution of Mechanical Engineers*, **143**, 129 (1940).

[34] CONSTANTINESCO, G. *The theory of wave transmission*. Haddon, London (1922).

[35] BOOTH, H. C. The origin of the vacuum cleaner. *Transactions of the Newcomen Society*, **15**, 85 (1934–5).

[36] FINKELSTEIN, T. Air engines. *The Engineer*, April (1959.)

[37] LANCHESTER, F. W. The gas engine and after. *Proceedings of the Institution of Mechanical Engineers*, **136**, 195 (1937).

[38] RICARDO, H. R. *The high speed internal combustion engine* (4th edn.). Blackie, London (1953).

[39] PURDIE, W. H. Thirty years' development of opposed piston propelling machinery. *Proceedings of the Institution of Mechanical Engineers*, **162**, 446 (1950).

[40] *Symposium on indicators*. Institution of Mechanical Engineers, London (1923).

[41] PEARCE, S. L. Forty years' development in mechanical engineering plant for power stations. *Proceedings of the Institution of Mechanical Engineers*, **142**, 305 (1939).

[42] MOYER, J. A., and FITTZ, R. U. *Refrigeration*, p. 190. McGraw-Hill, New York (1932).

[43] SIKORSKI, I. I. The transport helicopter. *Proceedings of the Institution of Mechanical Engineers*, **169**, 1183 (1955).

[44] LOVELL, B. *The exploration of outer space*, p. 8. Oxford University Press, London (1962).

[45] KUIPER, P. G., and MIDDLEHURST, B. M. (eds.) *Stars and stellar systems*, p. 197. University of Chicago Press (1966).

[46] WHITTLE, F. Early history of the Whittle jet propulsion gas turbine. *Proceedings of the Institution of Mechanical Engineers*, **152**, 419 (1945).

[47] BANKS, F. R. The aviation engine. *Proceedings of the Institution of Mechanical Engineers*, **162**, 433 (1950).

[48] WIMPERIS, H. E. Research and development in aeronautics. *Proceedings of the Institution of Mechanical Engineers*, **152**, 353 (1945).

[49] WRANGHAM, D. A. *The elements of heat flow*. Chatto and Windus, London (1961).

[50] LANDER, C. H. Review of recent progress in heat transfer. *Proceedings of the Institution of Mechanical Engineers*, **148**, 81 (1942); **149**, 117 (1943).

[51] CROOME, H. *Hovercraft*. Jarrold, Norwich (1960).

[52] GIBB, C. D. Some engineering problems in connection with the industrial application of nuclear energy. *Proceedings of the Institution of Mechanical Engineers*, **171**, 22 (1957).

[53] FARMER, H. O. Free piston compression engines. *Proceedings of the Institution of Mechanical Engineers*, **156**, 253 (1947).

[54] KOHLER, J. W., and JONKERS, C. O. Fundamentals of the gas refrigerating machine. *Philips Technical Review*, **16**, 69 (1954).

[55] GIEDION, H. L., and WATSON, H. H. *Mechanization takes command*. (2nd edn.).Oxford University Press, London (1955).

[56] Electronic digital computers for solving engineering problems. *Engineering*, p. 349, 9 September 1953.

[57] HAWTHORNE, W. R. The early development of the Dracone flexible barge. *Proceedings of the Institution of Mechanical Engineers*, **175**, 52 (1961).

[58] FESSLER, H., and ROSE, R. T. Photo-elastic investigation of stresses in the heads of thick pressure vessels. *Proceedings of the Institution of Mechanical Engineers*, **171**, 73 (1957).

[59] CLENSHAW, J. W. Measurement of strain in components of complicated form by brittle lacquer coatings. *Proceedings of the Institution of Mechanical Engineers*, **152**, 221 (1945).

[60] BRISTOW, J. R. *et al.* Use of wire resistance strain gauges in automobile engineering research. *Proceedings of the Institution of Mechanical Engineers*, **163**, 27 (1950).

BIBLIOGRAPHY

AMERICAN SOCIETY OF TOOL ENGINEERS. *Tool engineer's handbook*. McGraw-Hill, New York (1951).

AUGHTIE, F. Electrical resistance wire strain gauges. *Proceedings of the Institution of Mechanical Engineers*, **152**, 213 (1945).

BAXTER, A. D. Rockets in space. *Journal of Stephenson Engineering Society King's College, Newcastle-upon-Tyne*. 2 (No. 4), 7 (1959–60).

BARWELL, F. T. *Lubrication of bearings*. Butterworth, London (1956).

BEVAN, T. *Theory of machines*. Longmans Green, London (1939).

BOWDEN, F. P. Recent studies of metallic friction. *Proceedings of the Institution of Mechanical Engineers*, **169**, 7 (1955).

BRAME, J. S., and KING, R. O. *Fuel* (4th edn.). Arnold, London (1935).

BURSTALL, AUBREY F. *A history of mechanical engineering*. Faber and Faber, London (1963).

CARPENTER, H., and ROBERTSON, D. *Metals*. Oxford University Press, London (1939).

CONSTANT, H. Early history of the axial type of gas turbine engine. *Proceedings of the Institution of Mechanical Engineers*, **153**, 411 (1945).

CROWTHER, J. G. *Discoveries and inventions of the twentieth century*. Routledge and Keegan Paul, London (1955).

DALBY, W. E. *Steam Power* (2nd edn.). Arnold, London (1920).

DAVY, M. J. B. *Aeronautics. Heavier-than-air aircraft. Part 1. Historical survey*. Science Museum Publication, H.M.S.O., London (1949).

EWING, J. A. *The steam engine and other heat engines* (3rd edn.). Cambridge University Press, London (1908).

——. *The mechanical production of cold*. Cambridge University Press, London (1908).

FIELD, FOSTER P. *The mechanical testing of metals and alloys*. Pitman, London (1948).

FISHENDEN, M., and SAUNDERS, O. A. *Calculation of heat transmission*. H.M.S.O., London (1932).

FREEDMAN, P. *Principles of scientific research*. Macdonald, London (1949).

GARDNER, G. W. H. Guided missiles. *Proceedings of the Institution of Mechanical Engineers*, **169**, 30 (1955).

GARTMANN, H. *Science as history*. Hodder and Stoughton, London (1960).

GIBSON, A. H. *Hydraulics and its applications* (4th edn.). Constable, London (1930).

GOLDSTEIN, S. (ed.) *Modern developments in fluid mechanics*. Oxford University Press, London (1938).

GOODMAN, J. *Mechanics applied to engineering*. Longmans Green, London (1930).

HOOVER, T. J., and FISH, J. C. C. *The Engineering Profession*. Stanford University Press (1941).

DEN HARTOG, J. P. *Mechanical vibrations*. McGraw-Hill, New York (1940).

LANCHESTER, F. W. *Aerial flight: aerodynamics*. Constable, London (1907).

——. *Aerial flight: aerodonetics*. Constable, London (1908).

LARSEN, E. *Atomic energy*. Pan, London (1958).

LEA, F. C. *Hydraulics* (6th edn.). Arnold, London (1938).

MACMILLAN, R. H. *Automation, friend or foe?* Cambridge University Press, London (1956).

MCADAMS, W. H. *Heat transmission*. McGraw-Hill, New York (1933).

MORLEY, A. *Strength of materials* (9th edn.). Longmans Green, London (1940).

MOYER, J. A., and FITTZ, R. U. *Refrigeration*. McGraw-Hill, New York (1932).

NEWITT, D. M. *Design of high pressure plant and properties of fluids at high pressure*. Oxford University Press, London (1940).

NEWMAN, R. P., and HOULDCROFT, P. T. Welding—engineering and metallurgical aspects. *Chartered Mechanical Engineer*, **8**, 214 (1961).

OWER, E. *Measurement of air flow* (2nd edn.). Chapman and Hall, London (1933).

PIERCY, N. A. V. *Aerodynamics*. English Universities Press, London (1937).

PORTER, A. *An introduction to servo-mechanisms*. Methuen, London (1950).

PRANDTL, L. *The physics of solids and fluids*. (2nd edn.). Blackie, London (1936).

——, and TIETJENS, O. G. *Applied hydro- and aero-mechanisms*. McGraw-Hill, London (1934).

PYE, D. R. *The internal combustion engine*. (2nd edn.). Oxford University Press, London (1937).

RICARDO, H. R. *The high speed internal combustion engine*. (4th edn.). Blackie, London (1953).

ROLLASON, E. C. *Metallurgy for engineers*. Arnold, London (1939).

ROLT, F. H. *Gauges and fine measurements*. Macmillan, London (1929).

SOUTHWELL, R. V. *Theory of elasticity*. Cambridge University Press, London (1936).

STODOLA, A. *Steam and gas turbines* (trans. L. C. Loewenstein). McGraw-Hill, New York (1927).

TIMOSHENKO, S. P. *History of strength of materials*. McGraw-Hill, New York (1953).

WALSHAW, A. C. *Heat engines*. (4th edn.). Longmans Green, London (1956).

40

THE INTERNAL COMBUSTION ENGINE

LYNWOOD BRYANT

IN 1900 man's favourite prime mover, after the horse, was the steam piston engine. Steam power is essentially heavy, and uneconomical in small sizes, so that it never seriously threatened animal power on farms, and it was never very successful for road vehicles; but for railways, ships, and concentrated industry the steam piston engine was dominant as the century opened. By 1950 it had been displaced by another type of heat engine which is essentially simpler and lighter because the combustion is internal.

Steam power uses external combustion: the fuel is burned outside the engine, in a firebox, to heat water and steam inside a boiler. The steam is then conveyed to a separate engine, where its heat (or some of it) is converted into work when the expanding steam drives a piston (or turbine blades). In the internal combustion system the heat-generator and the engine are combined in one machine. The fuel is burned inside the cylinder where the piston is working, and the products of combustion are themselves the working fluid that drives the piston (or turbine). Such an engine can avoid some of the losses of energy in a steam plant, and it is more convenient and economical in many applications, especially for vehicles.

Three types of internal combustion engine evolved during this half-century to take the place of the steam piston engine in different sections of its power range. The petrol (gasoline) engine was the first to emerge. It operates on the Otto cycle: that is, it draws a combustible mixture of fuel and air into the cylinder, compresses it with a stroke of the piston, and ignites it, usually with a spark, near the point of maximum compression at the beginning of the power stroke. This type developed into an extraordinarily light and versatile engine, the ideal power for a vehicle the size of the family car or smaller, and it was until recently the only practical kind of power for aircraft. It is still made at the rate of millions per month and has entered into human experience in all advanced countries as no other machine has ever done.

The next type of engine to emerge, the diesel, draws in and compresses plain air rather than a combustible mixture, as in the Otto cycle, and it compresses the charge much farther, to about 1/16th of its original volume. It then injects fuel into the compressed air, which is so hot that ignition occurs without a spark. The diesel engine is heavier than the Otto and uses a different, and usually cheaper, fuel. It proved to be well adapted for vehicles larger than the family car, especially for locomotives and ships, and for some stationary applications.

In a petrol (Otto) or diesel engine, combustion is not continuous as it is in a steam system. The fuel is burnt in pulses, one flash of combustion at the beginning of every power stroke. In intermittent-combustion engines like these the charge has to be fired at exactly the right time, many times per second in a fast engine. Ignition is therefore a key problem.

The third type of internal combustion engine, the last to emerge, was the gas turbine, a rotary engine that has the advantage of continuous combustion. The fuel is sprayed steadily into a stream of compressed air passing through a combustion chamber. The hot, expanding gases drive a turbine, and the turbine drives a rotary compressor that provides the stream of compressed air. Like a steam plant it is economical only in large units, but it is much lighter than a steam plant of equal power, and it is well adapted to high speeds and high altitudes. It revolutionized air transport in the 1950s, while the diesel engine was revolutionizing rail power.

I. THE OTTO ENGINE

The petrol, or Otto, engine was already well developed by 1901. It had begun as a heavy, slow engine burning illuminating gas (Vol. V, p. 158), hence usable only for stationary power. Inventors dreamed of using it for a self-propelled vehicle, as they always do for any new type of power, but before it could be used for a motor-car (Ch. 30) a number of radical changes were necessary. In the first place, the original Otto engine was much too heavy to carry itself uphill. Its weight per horsepower was ten times what it should be for a self-propelled vehicle. Then, the gas engine had to be adapted to liquid fuel, and since the load on a road engine fluctuates, the designer had to learn how to mix the fuel and air in just the right proportion for various speeds and loads, for this type of engine is very sensitive to fuel quality and fuel–air ratio. And then, if an engine is to be light and powerful enough for a motor-car, it has to run fast at, say, 500–1000 rev/min; that is, five or ten times as fast as the original Otto engine. This was too fast for the old system of flame ignition (Vol. V, p. 159), so that a new ignition system that could be precisely controlled at high speed had to be devised. This type of engine also requires cooling, which becomes a serious problem at higher powers; and it tends to stall at low speeds, so that a motor-car needs a clutch and a variable transmission that will allow the engine to run fast while the wheels are turning at different speeds. Starting the engine was another problem, especially for motor-cars, which have to stop and start frequently. The petrol engine was notoriously temperamental about starting.

These five problems—carburation, ignition, cooling, transmission, and starting—are special problems of the internal combustion engine that do not affect the steam engine. They were all solved in time, through a prolonged evolutionary process.

The earliest automobile engines could be very simple ones designed for the modified bicycle that served as the first light, popular car, with one or two cylinders developing one or two horsepower. At the same time a wealthy sportsman would need ten times the power for his luxurious touring car or racing car (often the same car). Automobile racing was a popular sport in all western countries after 1895 and an important testing ground for engine designers. The most famous early racing engine, designed by Wilhelm Maybach for the first Mercedes (Fig. 40.1), will illustrate the state of the art

FIG. 40.1. The engine of the first Mercedes, 1900. Its four cylinders, cast in two blocks, developed 35 hp at 1000 rev/min, which gave this famous sports car a top speed of 85 km/h. The specific weight was 6·8 kg/hp, about half that of contemporary engines.

at the opening of the century. It already had the features of the mature automobile engine, mostly designed by Maybach: the variable gear transmission,
now standard; the jet carburettor, which has become the standard solution
to the problem of providing the correct mixture at varying speeds; and the
familiar honeycomb radiator that made high performance possible and reduced by half the amount of cooling water that had to be carried. The ignition
was by electric spark, but it used a make-and-break device within the cylinder
to make the spark, rather than the modern high-tension spark system, which
was not developed until 1904. When this engine first appeared at Race Week
in Nice in 1901, it won every race, and in a series of increasingly powerful
annual models it dominated European racing until 1914.

The most familiar engine of all in the early years was the one that drove
the Model T Ford (1908–27), which introduced millions of people everywhere to the new world created by the internal combustion engine (Fig. 40.2).
Sixteen million of them were built with many incremental improvements as
the years went by, but with no essential change. By 1908 the central problems

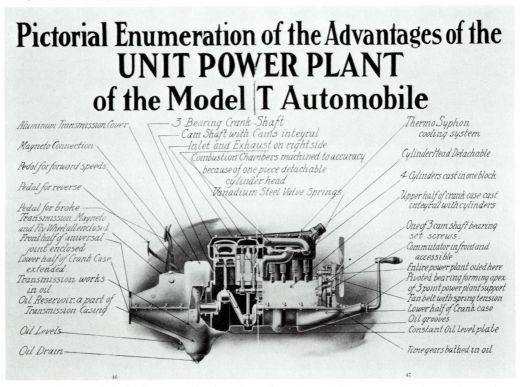

FIG. 40.2. The Ford Model T engine, simple and sturdy, with a reliable output of 20 hp at 1800 rev/
min, enough to drive the Model T at 65 km/h.

of ignition, carburation, and cooling were fairly well solved, and a simple engine like Ford's could be trusted to run reliably year after year without expert care. Ford's solution to the transmission problem was the most memorable feature of his system: he used a pedal-operated planetary transmission, hard to understand but remarkably easy to operate. It was almost an automatic transmission: once the engine was started, a driver could take off, change gear, and stop with a simple movement of a pedal (interlocked with a hand brake), requiring no skill at all. This was a decisive advantage in those days when it was thought to be difficult for a man, and next to impossible for a woman, to learn the coordinated control of clutch, throttle, and gear-lever necessary to drive a petrol-fuelled car. The Ford still had to be started by a hand-crank, and so did the Mercedes, although inventors had been working for years on many kinds of self-starters. Finally in 1910 C. F. Kettering designed a special kind of battery-powered electric motor strong enough to turn the engine over until it fired, which was quickly and universally adopted. It made the petrol engine easy to start as well as easy to run. Steam and electric power were then virtually eliminated for road vehicles.

The Otto engine was versatile and especially well adapted to its chief market, road vehicles. For this purpose it was produced in a thousand shapes and sizes, from the one-cylinder motorcycle engine to the straight-8s and V-16s that powered the classic cars of the 1920s and 1930s. At the same time it continued in use in increasing numbers for its original purpose, to provide stationary power in small units, in applications where steam would be uneconomical. A new form of very large gas-burning Otto engine also emerged after 1890, designed for industrial use in places where low-grade gas fuel was available in quantity or where it could be economically generated from coal on the spot (Fig. 40.3).

In the days before farms were electrified, power for routine farm work such as pumping, cutting, or sawing often came from simple Otto engines of 2 to 5 hp burning petrol or paraffin (kerosene), cooled by an open tank of water on the horizontal cylinder. A hundred manufacturers sold these engines in large numbers between 1890 and 1940. During the same period the heavier farm work was taken over gradually by the petrol tractor, which was the most important application of the Otto engine after the automobile. The tractor could go anywhere, and through a power take-off and auxiliary equipment could do the light work formerly done by a stationary engine, as well as the heavier work of ploughing and hauling harvesting machinery. It replaced animal power and transformed the agricultural economy from the 1920s.

The Otto engine was also a common prime mover for isolated electric plants; in the city for a factory, hotel, or office building that wished to generate its own power, and in the country where thin population and great distances retarded the extension of power networks. Later, the diesel engine took over this function, for powers larger than 30–50 hp. Smaller integrated engine-and-generator units of 1–6 hp (Fig. 40.4) brought the blessings of electricity to the farm long before power companies could reach them.

The easiest fuel to use for any of these engines was petrol, but many of them were designed for heavier oils like paraffin, which were cheaper and safer than petrol but much harder to vaporize and ignite. Such an oil engine, as it was called, often had a hot chamber where the oil could be vaporized and mixed with air before being injected into the cylinder. Some were called hot-bulb or semi-diesel engines. They did not use the high compression ratio of the diesel engine, but once started some of them could run without a spark. The Priestman and the Akroyd were two early types, already well developed in the 1890s. They were used in large numbers well into the twentieth century for stationary applications, farm traction engines, and even a good number of locomotives, but most commonly for fishing vessels and other small boats.

FIG. 40.3. A pair of Allis-Chalmers double-acting four-stroke gas engines, each driving a 750-kW generator, c.1915. The fuel was natural gas.

FIG. 40.4. A portable electric power plant of 1918 powered by a one-cylinder kerosene-burning engine and examples of its use.

11. THE DIESEL ENGINE

Internal combustion engines were invented and developed mostly by practical mechanics who did not know or care much about the scientific principles of energy conversion. The diesel engine (Vol. V, p. 163) was different: it was conceived in 1891 as a scientific engine by Rudolf Diesel, an engineer who had studied thermodynamics and believed that he could make an engine that would operate on the Carnot cycle, an ideal cycle for heat engines familiar to students of thermodynamics, which was originally described by Sadi Carnot in 1824.

In the theoretical Carnot engine the heat to be converted to work must be added at the highest temperature of the cycle, without raising the temperature further. The combustion, if it is a combustion engine, has to take place at constant temperature. Diesel thought he could achieve constant-temperature combustion, and therefore the ideal Carnot cycle, in an engine that would operate as follows. First, the suction stroke would draw in a cylinder-full of air. The next stroke of the piston would compress this air to a very high temperature (higher than the ignition point of the fuel, so that the engine would not need any special ignition device). Then, on the next stroke, as the air was beginning to expand, fuel would be introduced into the hot, expanding air at a rate carefully calculated to keep the temperature constant: combustion would tend to raise the temperature, but expansion of the gases would tend to lower it. If these two tendencies could be balanced, an approximation to the ideal engine would be possible.

Diesel faced many difficulties, theoretical and practical, when he tried to turn this idea into a real engine, and the machine that emerged was not very close to a Carnot engine. Eventually, he was able to achieve higher compressions, and hence higher efficiencies, than other heat engines, but only after many years of the most frustrating kind of development work.

The central problem was, and still is, fuel injection. In a diesel engine the fuel has to be introduced into the combustion chamber at exactly the right time, near the moment of maximum compression, in very small and precisely controlled amounts, under very high pressure; after it is inside it has to be thoroughly mixed with air in a fraction of a second, so that it will ignite early and burn smoothly. Ignition in an Otto-cycle engine is much easier, because the fuel and air are already mixed and ready to burn when they enter the cylinder. Diesel tried dozens of injection and ignition devices. The best he could find was a blast of compressed air that carried a small amount of oil into the cylinder, atomized it, and forced it through the dense hot air as a violent spray. This compressed-air system remained the standard type of fuel injection for a generation; but it was heavy and complicated, and the work of compression absorbed a good part of the engine's power. So long as the diesel engine was tied to an air compressor and air tank, it could not become the versatile engine that the inventor had foreseen. It was one of several available types of stationary oil engines, rather heavy, more expensive than the steam engine it replaced, but promising some fuel economy.

Diesel patented his engine in 1892. In five years he was able to exhibit an engine that ran; and in another five years the Maschinenfabrik Augsburg, first maker of diesels, had developed an engine that could be depended on to operate under load all day, under the expert care of factory mechanics. Fig. 40.5 shows this first successful engine, which provided power for a factory for nearly twenty years. Manufacturers in several countries joined the Diesel enterprise in the following years, and the new engine began to find a place for itself in the power economy. It usually took the place of a steam engine in a factory, a pumping station, or an isolated electric-light plant. Perhaps a thousand were in service by 1908, usually of 50–100 hp, and men were beginning to talk about diesel-powered ships and locomotives.

Diesel originally thought of his engine as a universal heat engine, which once developed could be easily adapted to larger or smaller tasks, and which

FIG. 40.5. The first successful diesel, built by Maschinenfabrik Augsburg and delivered in 1898 to a factory in Kempten, Germany. After considerable further development, it became reliable enough to replace a steam engine. It had two cylinders and delivered 60 hp at 180 rev/min. The compressed-air tank and pump required for fuel injection in all the early diesels are not shown in this picture.

could burn almost any fuel from peanut oil to powdered coal. Special forms of diesel engine evolved over the next fifty years for different purposes, but each was a separate species with its own rather long and painful development history, and in all but the largest sizes it was sensitive to fuel quality.

The earliest special type to evolve was the submarine engine. Several navies were working on the unique problems of submarine power at the very time when the diesel was being developed. Internal combustion (in comparison with steam) promised great savings in space and weight, and the diesel engine (in comparison with the Otto) offered a safe fuel and an efficiency that meant increased range for the same weight of fuel. But the submarine engine needed ten times the power of the current stationary diesel, and a much lower specific weight. By 1914 submarines of six nations were diesel-powered, with one to four engines of 500 hp each, weighing as little as 25 kg/hp. This was the first triumph of the diesel. It made possible a new mode of transport and a fearful new weapon.

The choice of power for merchant ships (Ch. 31) is determined primarily by fuel economy. The power plant is a very large one—1000–20000 hp—and it runs steadily for a large fraction of the year. From the beginning the diesel engine looked promising for this application. It released engine-room and fuel-storage space for cargo, and it reduced engine-room crew by two-thirds. A large part of this economy is due to the shift from coal to oil, which had already begun in steamships in the 1880s. Oil is easier to store and handle on the ship and offers large savings in refuelling stations ashore. A steamship-owner could afford to pay twice as much for a ton of oil as for a ton of coal, and the shift to diesel power promised large additional economies of space and labour, once it had attained reliability, which took about twenty years.

The first motorship crossed the Atlantic in 1911, and before Diesel died in 1913 he could count about 300 diesel-powered ships, most of them quite small. Early in the 1920s several large liners were diesel-powered, and by 1927 new, very large engines especially designed for marine service (Fig. 40.6) were available from German, Swiss, Dutch, and Danish manufacturers, led by Burmeister and Wain of Copenhagen. By this time engineers had learned enough about combustion, fuel injection, and design of combustion chambers to use 'direct' or 'solid' injection, as it was called, instead of compressed-air injection, and they were able to raise the output to as much as a thousand horsepower from a single cylinder. The Scandinavians were quick to adopt diesel marine power, the British and Americans much slower. By 1927 half the new ships being built were motor vessels, and by 1950 the diesel conquest

40.6. A typical marine diesel of the 1930s, an eight-cylinder, double-acting, two-stroke engine with direct fuel injection, t by Maschinenfabrik Augsburg–Nürnberg. It developed 6350 hp at 140 rev/min. The cylinders had a diameter of 600 mm a stroke of 1100 mm.

of the sea was nearly complete. Only the largest liners and naval vessels could afford the steam turbine.

At the other extreme of the power range, the small high-speed diesel engine suitable for a road vehicle was being developed during the same period, in the 1920s. A road engine needs perhaps 100 hp, and it should not weigh more than, say, 6 kg/hp; consequently it cannot afford the weight of an air compressor. Engineers worked for many years designing fuel pumps and injectors, and trying holes and nozzles in many sizes and patterns to get an effective spray of fuel for different sizes of cylinder and speeds of piston. A road engine has to run at ten times the speed of the early marine or stationary engine in order to meet the weight requirement, and at this speed ignition becomes a serious problem. In a marine engine running at 120 rev/min, in which a stroke takes a quarter of a second, the fuel has time to become well mixed with air in the first part of the stroke in, say, 1/20 second, but a high-speed engine allows only a few thousandths of a second for the same mixing. The solution that emerged was a combination of a powerful and precise pump and injector system with a special design of combustion chamber which induced a violent turbulence that forced masses of air through the spray of fuel. Hundreds of injection systems, and more hundreds of shapes of combustion chamber and ways of driving the air into a swirl, were tried in many countries, with the most significant work being done by Prosper L'Orange in Germany and by Harry R. Ricardo in England in the 1920s. By 1930 diesel-powered lorries began to appear on the highways of Europe and America and soon became common.

The small diesel engine grew steadily faster and more powerful after 1930 and found many new applications. It powered tanks, landing craft, and bulldozers during the Second World War, and the heavy construction equipment that built the great highway systems of 1950–70. By mid-century the high-speed diesel was a thoroughly reliable engine produced in large numbers in all industrial countries to meet a rising demand for light power plants. It began to look like the universal heat engine that the inventor had envisaged.

One application that Rudolf Diesel explicitly foresaw was the railway locomotive (Ch. 32). Internal combustion engines of many kinds, including diesels, were often used for small industrial and shunting locomotives, beginning in the 1890s, and especially for railcars—single self-propelled coaches designed for light traffic on branch lines. The theoretical economies offered by the diesel engine in fuel and maintenance costs were widely discussed, and in the 1920s a good number of larger experimental diesel locomotives designed to explore the possibilities in main-line traffic appeared. A dozen engine manufacturers and locomotive builders in the U.S.A. took up diesel locomotive projects, with interest rising around 1930 as growing experience with fuel injection made diesel engines reliable. General Motors had begun work on the high-speed diesel in the late 1920s, and exhibited the prototype of its famous locomotive diesels at the Chicago Exposition of 1933. G.M. had achieved a drastic reduction in weight and many incremental improvements in such matters as materials, lubrication, and cooling, but the chief contribution was the unit injector, which gave each cylinder its own precisely controlled pump and injector unit. The possibilities of the diesel engine in long, non-stop runs were first demonstrated in the articulated trains that appeared in the late 1930s, but diesel power found its true vocation as a standard locomotive for all railway traffic. It outperformed steam in power, flexibility, fuel economy, and ease of maintenance. In the U.S.A. the last steam locomotive was built in 1953, and the last main-line steam run was in 1960. Diesel would have been pleased to see this revolution, but would have been surprised that it was so late. He did not understand how long it takes to develop a reliable engine.

III. AIRCRAFT ENGINES

The aeroplane piston engine operates on the Otto cycle. It is a cousin of the automobile engine, with most of the same problems and some special ones of its own. Ordinarily it has no transmission, since once aloft it runs at steady speed, but it must be capable of a great surge of power to get off the ground and, in military aircraft, to meet battle emergencies. It also has higher reliability requirements. But what counts most in an aeroplane engine is power, or rather specific power, the amount of power that can be provided per kilogram of engine. (It is sometimes convenient to reverse this ratio and speak of low specific weight, in kilograms per horsepower, kg/hp, rather than high specific power.)

Low specific weight of engine, desirable for a motor-car, is essential for an aeroplane. In 1880 Otto engines weighed about 200 kg/hp. By 1890, after the radical redesign of Daimler and Maybach, the specific weight was down to 30 kg/hp, low enough to make it practical for road vehicles, and by 1900 it was down to 4 kg/hp. At this level it was possible to think realistically of powered flight (Ch. 33).

Power for the first flying machines came mostly from adaptations of existing petrol engines. The American pioneer S. P. Langley ordered his first engine (using public funds) from Stephen M. Balzer, a New York mechanic who had been experimenting with horseless carriages. It was to be a three-cylinder rotary engine[1] weighing 45 kg for 12 hp. Balzer had already built such an engine for a tricycle, but he had great difficulty with the weight specification. Langley and his assistant Charles Manly (the only aviation pioneer with formal engineering training) then toured England and France looking for a light engine. They liked the De Dion-Bouton motorcycle engine, bought one, and shipped it home for study. Using his experience with the Balzer and the De Dion-Bouton, Manly then developed an engine of his own, a five-cylinder radial,[1] which powered Langley's ill-fated attempt at flight in 1903, with Manly at the controls. This was the first Otto engine especially designed for flight, and it was a good one. It had the circular form that became standard for air-cooled aircraft engines, developed 52 hp at 1000 rev/min, and weighed about 2 kg/hp. It never flew.

The first engine that actually flew (a few weeks later at Kitty Hawk) was a four-cylinder horizontal water-cooled engine that gave a surge of about 16 hp for take-off and then settled down to about 12 hp at 1050 rev/min. It was a home-made engine, simple and reliable, rather heavy—about 6 kg/hp. The Wright brothers, Wilbur and Orville, built it, using their own money and their experience with a one-cylinder gas engine in their bicycle shop in Dayton. The Wrights continued to make their own engines for experimental flights during the next few years, each one a little stronger than the previous one. All told, they built some 200 engines.

After the first flight, aviation was dormant for a few years. The Wrights were quietly practising, and Glenn Curtiss, another bicycle mechanic who built his own engines, was racing motorcycles and beginning to experiment with aviation. Then, in 1908-9, the Wrights gave a series of exhibition flights in France which initiated a great wave of excitement over aviation something like the Lindbergh hysteria of 1927. France remained the world centre for the design and production of aircraft and aircraft engines until well into the First World War.

Most early European fliers used French engines. Soon new types emerged especially designed for aircraft. At the beginning the designer had two basic decisions to make, on cooling and on arrangement of cylinders. Cooling could be by air or liquid. Cylinders could be set in a row (to make an in-line engine); or in two rows set at an angle to each other (like a V); or they could be

---

[1] A radial engine has its cylinders arranged like the radii of a circle round a crankshaft that rotates with the propeller. A rotary engine has the same shape, but the whole engine rotates around a stationary crankshaft, and the propeller rotates with the engine, not the crankshaft. These forms of Otto engine have certain advantages in weight. For smooth running and good balance, they need an odd number of cylinders.

arranged in a radial pattern, like the spokes of a wheel. Two basic types emerged very early: the air-cooled type, usually radial, and the water-cooled type, usually in-line or V-type. The liquid-cooled engine was more complex and expensive and more vulnerable to enemy attack, but it gave higher performance per cubic centimetre of cylinder and lower drag. The choice between them remained a subject of controversy throughout the life of the piston engine.

By 1910 the rich French sportsman who needed power for his flying machine could choose among 37 engines offered by French manufacturers. The most popular throughout Europe was the Antoinette, a water-cooled V-8 that weighed 95 kg for 50 hp. A newer type, an elegant rotary design by Laurent Seguin called the Gnome, weighed only 75 kg for the same power, or 1·5 kg/hp (Fig. 40.7). The rotary engine, simple, light, and smooth-running, was the most common type for Allied fighters in the First World War, but the species became extinct around 1920. The whirling engine had problems with centrifugal and gyroscopic forces that became hard to cope with in the larger sizes required in the 1920s.

In 1910 flying was a sport. It became a serious business with the coming of war in 1914, and thereafter the evolution of aircraft engines was completely dominated by military urgencies. The British and the Americans were slow to appreciate the importance of the aeroplane, but the French and Germans both entered the war with several hundred warplanes—the French planes

FIG. 40.7. The Gnome, a French air-cooled rotary engine, the most popular type for Allied aircraft in the early years of the First World War. The whole engine rotated around a fixed crankshaft. In its simplest form, the 'Monosoupape', each cylinder had only one valve, used for both intake and exhaust. Castor oil was the common lubricant.

powered mostly with light Gnome-type engines, which were outclassed at first by slightly modified Mercedes and Benz automobile engines on the German side, with an output of 150 hp. The French recovered by enlarging their air-cooled engines and by adopting the Spanish Hispano-Suiza, a water-cooled V-8, 150-hp engine that was respected and imitated in all countries, designed by the great Marc Birkigt.

At the opening of the war the British had less than a hundred planes ready, powered mostly by French engines. The Royal Aircraft Factory had developed one plane and one sturdy engine, but the British were far behind the Continental powers. Actual war made these deficiencies clear, and the development job was turned over to the rapidly growing aircraft and engine industries. Eventually some new and elegant engines appeared.

America was even farther behind than Britain. The Army had bought a Wright plane in 1908, and the Navy had bought two hydroplanes from Curtiss in 1910. The Wright and the Curtiss enterprises evolved into rival corporations that became active in the early years of the European war in planning new and more powerful engines to be sold at home and abroad. Curtiss developed the 90-hp OX-5, a water-cooled V-8 designed by Charles B. Kirkham; this powered the Curtiss Jenny, the most familiar American plane in the First World War. Eventually 5000 of them were built. Wright developed its own version of the 150-hp Hispano-Suiza, and then Curtiss raised its sights to the 300-hp level with a new Kirkham design, the K-12. By this time, 1916, fighters were already attaining 150 km/h, with engines and planes of double the power and speed on the drawing-boards.

When the U.S.A. entered the war in April 1917, planners could choose from a wide range of engines. The government made the decision to concentrate on one standard engine that could be mass-produced in time to do some good in the present war. The result was the classic Liberty engine (Fig. 40.8). It was an extraordinarily successful cooperative effort. The decision on the project was made in May 1917; a test engine was ready in seven weeks; and the first production model was delivered in November. Four automobile companies made 20000 of them for the American and British air forces.

From the Gnome of 1910 to the Liberty of 1918 was a remarkably rapid development. The product, the aeroplane engine of 1918, was a much bigger thing than the automobile engine and economically a different species, ten times as powerful and perhaps a hundred times as expensive. Its design was dictated by military rather than market forces, and in peacetime it was pro-

FIG. 40.8. The Liberty, an American water-cooled V-12, designed by a committee and mass-produced by automobile manufacturers. It developed 450 hp at 1800 rev/min, and weighed only 1 kg/hp. It was used for many purposes throughout the 1920s.

duced in batches of dozens rather than millions. In fact, with all the Liberty engines left over from the war, very little production was necessary for a number of years. But development continued, at a slower pace, to get ready for the next war.

IV. RESEARCH AND DEVELOPMENT

The aeroplane emerged from the First World War as a decisive new weapon that relied for power solely on the Otto engine. Its military value—speed, range, and ceiling—depended directly on specific power. The air forces of the major powers therefore began a vigorous programme of research designed to discover ways of getting more power from each kilogram of engine. The automobile and oil industries also had a vital interest in this endless quest for power. Annual improvement of engine performance was a commercial necessity in the competitive automobile business and a military necessity in the aircraft business, also competitive.

The easiest way to get more power from an Otto engine is to raise the compression ratio. Higher compression gives economy as well as power: it raises the power output for the same rate of fuel flow, which means less fuel burned per horsepower-hour. But this way to better performance and economy is blocked by a mysterious phenomenon known as knock, or detonation (Ch. 39, p. 989), an abnormal and destructive kind of burning that limits the power of an Otto engine. Understanding knock, and finding ways of avoiding it, became the central task of engine development for the next 25 years.

The knock problem attracted technical men from many fields, experts on petroleum, combustion, and metals as well as chemical and mechanical engineers and various kinds of chemists and physicists. One approach was to find a fuel that could stand high compression without premature explosion. Another was to experiment with engine design to find a shape of combustion chamber that would minimize knock. The work went on on both sides of the Atlantic, in industrial, university, and government laboratories. In England the most significant results came from Harry R. Ricardo and his associates, who collected information about hundreds of fuels; began a basic study of combustion; and were able to raise the power of an engine by as much as 20 per cent by modifying the shape of the combustion chamber. Similar work on fuels and engines went on in the U.S.A., with one spectacular breakthrough in 1921: the discovery of the remarkable knock-suppressing property of tetraethyl lead in the General Motors Research Laboratories. A very small amount of this chemical added to petrol allowed the compression ratio to be raised enough to improve the performance of the engine by another 20 per cent. Leaded petrol was quickly adopted as an easy way of getting more power from an engine and more mileage from the fuel. Fuel and engine had to progress together. Motor manufacturers were quick to offer high-compression engines that could take advantage of the new fuel, and oil refiners were busy finding ways of raising the anti-knock quality of petrol. Octane numbers[1] and compression ratios rose together.

Average compression ratios of American car engines rose from 4:1 to 7:1 between 1920 and 1950, and octane numbers from 55 to 85, so that a litre of good petrol in 1950, if burned in a suitable engine, could provide energy for about twice as many ton-miles of road transport as a litre of petrol in 1920. This kind of progress was the joint product of several industries and a dozen technical professions working together in an evolutionary process involving hundreds of incremental improvements in engine design, as well as the occasional breakthrough in petroleum cracking or the discovery of tetraethyl lead. Perhaps half of the improvement might be attributed to progress in fuels and combustion chambers, aided by basic research on the combustion of hydrocarbons; and the rest to improvements in the details of cooling, carburation,

---

[1] The octane number is a measure of the anti-knock quality of a fuel. It is an index number that shows how much compression a fuel can stand without knocking, in comparison with a standard fuel in a standard engine.

lubrication, and the design of valves and pistons, and to the development of new materials by metallurgists.

Another essential contribution of the aeronautical engineer in this period was the supercharger, which made high-altitude performance possible. A special problem of the aircraft piston engine is that it loses power as it rises because the air gets thinner. To keep its power constant it needs a supercharger to compress the thin air and deliver it to the cylinders at sea-level pressure, or higher. One common type, called a turbosupercharger, was a predecessor of the gas turbine. It used the energy of the exhaust to drive a turbine, which in turn drove a compressor that gave the engine more air.

This research and development effort between the wars doubled the power of aircraft engines. On the American side, the Allison, a water-cooled V-12 with about the same cylinder volume as the Liberty engine, had about three times the power. The British entered the Second World War with the great Rolls-Royce Merlin powering Hurricanes and Spitfires. The Merlin engine was a water-cooled V-12 that began at 1000 hp and grew in a series of new models through the war, matching a similar steady rise in power on the German side. The air-cooled radial, the preferred form on the American side, was mass-produced by Wright and Pratt & Whitney for the great fleets of American bombers. This type also began the war in a 1000-hp size, but by 1944 the B29 bomber was using four 2200-hp Wright Cyclones (Fig. 40.9). At its peak the radial type had 28 cylinders (four circles of seven each). These

FIG. 40.9. The Wright Cyclone R3350, an air-cooled radial engine of 1944, with 18 cylinders arranged in two circles of 9 cylinders each. The specific weight was near the minimum for piston engines, 0·5 kg/hp. Four of these engines, supercharged, gave the American B29 bomber a total power of 8800 hp.

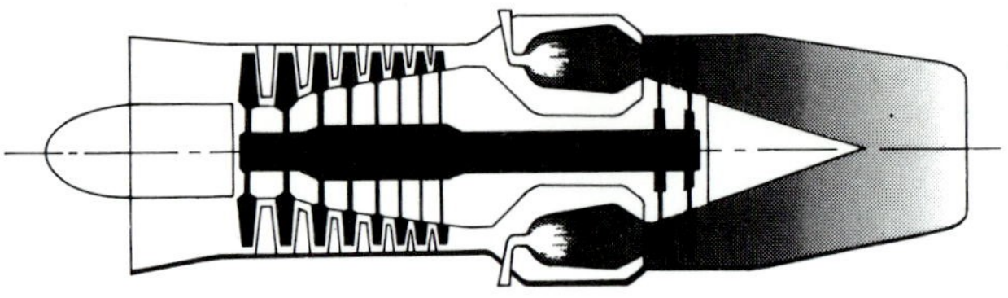

Air intake   Compressor Fuel feed Turbine   Nozzle

Combustion chamber

FIG. 40.10. The structure of a jet engine, a gas turbine for aircraft. Air enters at the front (left), is compressed in the compressor, and joins the continuously burning fuel in the combustion chamber. The fiery expanding gases pass through the turbine and out through the nozzle in the rear, which shapes the jet exhaust. In the turbo-jet all the propulsive force comes from the blast of exhaust gases, but the turbine is needed to drive the compressor. In the turbo-prop the turbine also drives a propeller.

magnificent engines, incredibly reliable for such intricate pieces of machinery, capable of delivering 3000 hp hour after hour without faltering, were rendered obsolete almost overnight by the gas turbine.

V. THE GAS TURBINE

The idea of the gas turbine was quite common in the early years of this century, and some engines were actually built, usually on the plan shown in Fig. 40.10, the plan of today's gas turbine. This type of internal combustion engine is radically different in structure from the Otto and the diesel engine, but it has exactly the same four basic functions: (1) it admits air; (2) it compresses the air; (3) it adds heat to the air by burning fuel in it, so that the air expands and does work by exerting pressure against something; (4) it expels the spent gases. In an Otto or a diesel engine these four processes all take place inside the same cylinder, one after another, intermittently. In a gas turbine the same four processes take place in different parts of the engine, and each process runs continuously. The air enters; is compressed, usually by a rotary compressor; and passes into a combustion chamber, where fuel is injected continuously and burns intensely, all the time. The expanding gases pass through and drive a turbine, which converts some of the heat energy into work, and then pass out through an exhaust jet. The turbine drives the compressor, and with any energy left over it can do such useful work as driving an electric generator or the propeller of an aeroplane.

The great advantage of this scheme for a heat engine is that the combustion is continuous. The manifold problems of intermittent combustion in cycles all simply disappear; no precise timing of ignition or control of valve is necessary, and the engine is less sensitive to fuel quality, since the combustion does not have to start and stop many times per second. Furthermore, the knock problem vanishes: there is no such limit to the specific power of the engine.

But continuous combustion does create one central problem: the turbine has to endure very high temperatures all the time, and from the point of view of efficiency, the higher the better. The combustion in an Otto or diesel engine cylinder is going on only perhaps one-fifth or one-tenth of the time, so that there is time to cool off between pulses. But the turbine runs steadily in the fiery gases without relief, so that it has to be made of special heat-resistant material, and the compressor must supply extra air for cooling. The performance of the gas turbine was then, and still is, limited by the material available for turbine blades. Another problem was the low efficiency of the rotary components, the rotary pump (compressor) and the rotary motor (turbine). The piston–cylinder system may look inelegant to a turbine enthusiast, but it was actually a very well-developed and efficient system for handling gases, with losses of hardly 1 per cent, whereas the mechanical efficiency of rotary pumps and motors handling gases at this time was very low. The turbine had so much internal work to do that it had very little energy left for useful output.

In spite of difficulties that seemed insurmountable to conservative engineers, a good many gas turbines, perhaps a hundred, were built and sold before 1940 for industrial power and for electric power generation, and there were even some experiments with ships and locomotives. The Swiss firm of Brown Boveri and Co. were the pioneers in the development of industrial gas turbines in the late 1930s.

The potential of the gas turbine for air power was also interesting to some far-seeing designers of military aircraft. Its fuel consumption would be extravagant, but its ability to handle large masses of fuel and air per second promised a thrust that might double the speed and altitude of a fighter aircraft, and the very high speed of the turbine meant a great saving of weight.

Most of the early planning assumed a turboprop system, with a turbine driving a conventional propeller, which it would have to do through a transmission system, for the turbine would have a much higher optimum speed than a propeller. But the gas turbine also opened up the prospect of a radically new mode of propulsion that would be especially attractive for aircraft, jet propulsion.[1] The thrust of a jet engine is a simple reaction to the blast of hot, expanding exhaust gases through a nozzle to the rear. The turbojet idea was attractive because of its internal simplicity—continuous combustion, no propeller, no transmission—and because it seemed well adapted to the thin air of high altitudes.

---

[1] The word jet in the early days was often used ambiguously to refer to both rocket and jet engines. In both the thrust is a reaction to an exhaust jet. As the words are now used, the rocket carries its own oxygen with it, so that it is independent of the atmosphere, but the jet relies on the surrounding air for its oxygen.

In the period 1920–35 there was some enthusiastic speculation and some serious study of both of these possibilities—the gas turbine to replace the piston engine as prime mover for aircraft and the jet to replace the propeller as a means of propulsion—but sober analysis of fuel economy and specific power was discouraging. Not much was known about aerodynamic problems at very high speeds, but the propeller was certainly a more efficient mode of propulsion than the jet up to at least 500 miles/h, perhaps higher, and the gas turbine would have a fuel consumption two or three times as high as the piston engine. An influential report to the British Air Ministry in 1920 assumed a minimum specific weight of 2·7 kg/hp for the gas turbine at a time when the piston engine was already down to about 1 kg/hp. It is not surprising, then, that advocates of the new techniques could not find military or commercial support for their development, especially in the Depression when budgets were tight. It was only in the late 1930s, with war at hand, that development of such an unorthodox engine was politically possible.

The development of the turbojet is an interesting case of parallel, independent development. It took place in Britain and Germany at about the same time, between 1935 and 1945. In Britain the story begins in 1926 with the abortive development within the Royal Aircraft Establishment of an experimental gas turbine with axial-flow compressor and turbine designed by A. A. Griffith on the basis of new aerodynamic theories. This project was dropped in 1929, and the British did no further work until 1936. In the meantime, Frank Whittle, a young cadet in the Royal Air Force with an unusual combination of practical experience and theoretical training, had become interested in the theory of aircraft propulsion. He had begun as an apprentice in the R.A.F. and was sent to an officers' training school, where in 1930 he wrote a prophetic paper that mentioned the combination of the gas turbine and jet propulsion and recognized that the gas turbine was well adapted to high altitudes. The British Air Ministry allowed Whittle to spend some of his time working on these ideas and had no objection to open publication, for the ideas were judged to be of no military significance. Whittle's patent in 1930 revealed the essentials of the turbojet, but it was not widely noticed, for such visionary patents are common. In the early 1930s, Whittle was unable to get government or industrial support for the development work he hoped to undertake, and in 1936 he was so discouraged that he did not bother to renew the patent. In the meantime the R.A.F. sent him to Cambridge to study mechanical sciences. While there he ran into two or three men with a little capital and a taste for risky ventures; with them he formed the firm of Power Jets Ltd., to exploit his ideas. They were able to put together an experimental engine that ran in 1937. The next year they got a government contract for another experimental engine, and then, on the eve of war, the Air Ministry promised full support. Research money was now plentiful.

The first British experimental flight took place on 15 May 1941, in a Gloster Meteor powered by an early Whittle engine with a thrust of 1200 lb, already twice the thrust of the first engine. Feasibility was now demonstrated, and the engineers could turn their energies to the design of the production model and to the continuing research and development of the details of compressor, turbine, and combustion chamber which would be necessary to raise the thrust and improve the reliability. Learning to understand and control a new and intense kind of combustion was an important part of this work. By 1943, half-a-dozen gas turbine projects were in various stages of development and production in Britain. The Royal Aircraft Establishment had already revived Griffith's project for a turboprop system with an axial compressor, which was more difficult to develop but promised higher efficiency than Whittle's centrifugal, or radial, compressor. The engine and aircraft firms of Rolls-Royce, Bristol, de Havilland, and Vickers were all involved in an all-out effort to put the gas turbine into combat.

The Germans began work on the gas turbine at about the same time as the British, in 1935, but they were the first to fly and the first to get a jet into combat. The story begins in Göttingen, long a centre for aerodynamic theory. Here, in the 1920s, Ludwig Prandtl, the great pioneer of fluid mechanics (p. 987), had worked out the theory of the flow of air around aerofoils, which enabled aircraft designers to raise the lift and lower the drag of aerofoils by as much as half. The same theory could also be used to improve the efficiency of turbines and compressors.

Hans Pabst von Ohain, a student of aerodynamics at Göttingen, who had never heard of Whittle and his work, designed and patented a turbojet system essentially the same as Whittle's but differing in nearly all details. In 1936 he went to work for Heinkel, an aircraft manufacturing firm interested in rocket and jet propulsion. Von Ohain had an engine running in 1937 which flew on 27 August 1939, just before the war began. This was the first jet flight anywhere. Another line of development, initiated by Herbert Wagner, a professor of aerodynamics from Berlin, took place in another firm of aircraft manufacturers, Junkers. Wagner's original proposal was for a turboprop system, which was changed to a turbojet in 1938 and eventually became the Junkers 004, the first jet engine to go into action. Some 1400 of them were built before the end of the war.

Both these developments were private and secret, internally financed

within an industrial firm, and they were both revealed to the German Air
Ministry in 1938. The German authorities took a somewhat stronger interest
in unorthodox engines than the British, and somewhat earlier. Like the
British, they chose to support half a dozen different projects in parallel:
turbojets, turboprops, and rockets—some within industry and some in
government laboratories. The Germans had difficult choices to make in
allocating scarce resources between production of conventional engines and
development of new ones, perhaps more difficult than the British, and they
were more hampered by scarcity of strategic materials and, later, more disturbed by the nuisance of air raids. But they did get one jet fighter into
combat, the Messerschmitt 262, powered by two Junkers 004 engines.

Both the British and the Germans used jets in combat in 1944. The British
used the Gloster Meteor, powered by two Whittle engines, each with a thrust
of 1700 lb, which gave it a speed of 625 km/h, somewhat more than the best
German piston-driven fighter. It was announced to the public in January,
1944, and used against the German V-1 or 'buzz bomb' (Ch. 35, p. 865),
which was used to attack London in August 1944.[1]

The Messerschmitt 262 also went into action in 1944, against flights of
American bombers, sometimes with devastating effect. It was faster than the
Meteor, with a more advanced design, but the Germans had been forced to
cut some corners in design and production and put jet fighters into combat
before they were fully developed and reliable, so that there were many difficulties with them and many accidents.

American development began later than European, but once begun, was
prosecuted energetically. One of the earliest successful installations of an
industrial gas turbine was in an oil refinery in Pennsylvania in 1937 (Fig.
40.11), and some work was done on gas turbines for locomotives and ships.
There was also some talk about the gas turbine for air power and several
specific proposals to the military, but the prevailing opinion in America was
the same as it was in Europe, namely that the gas turbine was too heavy for
use in the air and too inefficient.

The earliest American pioneer was an engineering student named
Sanford H. Moss, a machinist's apprentice who went to engineering school

[1] The V-1 engine was a new type of internal combustion engine called a pulse-jet, which is a variety of
the ram-jet. The ram-jet is the simplest possible internal combustion engine, with no moving parts at all.
It works only at a speed that is high enough for the air coming in the nose opening to be compressed
without any compressor: it is rammed into the combustion chamber, where it is burned and expelled in
a jet to the rear without the need for a turbine. The pulse-jet is the same type of machine, except that the
passage of air into the combustion chamber is controlled by flap valves so that it burns in a series of
explosions; in the V-1 about 40 per second.

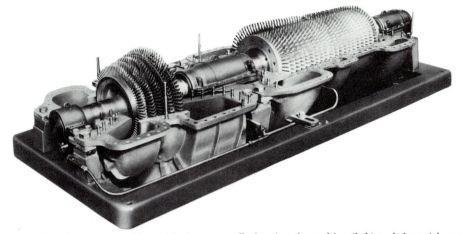

FIG. 40.11. A stationary gas turbine with the cover off, showing the turbine (left) and the axial compressor (right). This picture shows the first industrial gas turbine in the U.S.A., built by the Swiss firm
of Brown Boveri in 1937 for the Sun Oil Company to power the Houdry process in their refinery in
Marcus Hook, Pennsylvania. This type of engine has no jet. All the power comes from the turbine.
Such engines are useful in electric power plants to handle peak and emergency loads because they are
ready for service without a warm-up period.

and wrote a thesis on gas turbines at Cornell University in 1902. General
Electric was interested, hired Moss, and supported a gas turbine project for a
few years, but the best efficiency that Moss could achieve was about 3 per
cent, which was judged hopeless. The experience was not wasted, though, for
in 1918 Moss began the development of a turbosupercharger for piston
engines, which turned out to be an important project for military aviation and
a profitable one for General Electric. Work on the turbosupercharger gave
American engineers experience with a form of gas turbine and a head start in
the development of special alloys for turbine blades.

In the U.S.A. the most influential body in aeronautical affairs was the
National Advisory Committee for Aeronautics (NACA), a group of unsalaried
experts appointed in 1915 to coordinate aeronautical research and development. NACA funded research in industrial and academic laboratories and
also carried on research in its own laboratory at Langley Field, established in
1917. The topics of the gas turbine and jet propulsion came up a number of
times in their deliberations, but as war approached NACA thought it prudent
not to make a major investment in jet propulsion.

In March 1941, with rumours of German work on rockets and jets filtering
in, NACA decided that the time had come to look again at new types of engine,
and appointed a committee on Jet Propulsion, which went to work at once
under the energetic leadership of W. F. Durand and soon recommended

contracts with General Electric, Westinghouse, and Allis Chalmers for gas-turbine development. By this time the Army and the Navy were also interested and revived old proposals from Northrop, Lockheed, and Pratt & Whitney. By 1943 eight projects were under way, mostly turboprop systems, for everyone was thinking of speeds around 400 or at most 500 mile/h. NACA had also built two large laboratories, one of which, the Flight Propulsion Laboratory at Cleveland, had a jet propulsion testing facility.

No native American gas turbine flew before the end of the war, but an American version of the Whittle engine was developed very quickly and became the first American jet to fly. American visitors to Britain had got wind of what was going on behind the closed doors of Power Jets, and by 1941 the British were willing to share their experience with the Americans. The American Army asked General Electric to undertake development of the Whittle type of engine. The British sent one of the earliest engines to America, with complete plans and a team of experts, and Whittle himself visited the Lynn plant where the work was being done. The Americans in turn were able to provide the British with a superior material for turbine blades that allowed a substantial rise in turbine inlet temperature. The product of this development was the GE 140, which powered the first American jet fighter, the Shooting Star, with a thrust of 4000 lb, three or four times the thrust of the first jets to fly. Work had begun in October 1941. The engine ran in April 1942, and flew in October 1942, but this development was incomplete at the end of the war.

It is interesting to note that the development of the turbojet followed similar paths in all three countries. Both ideas—the gas turbine and jet propulsion—had been in the air for some time. Jet propulsion was visionary before the Second World War. The gas turbine was a more realistic possibility for stationary power, but the best judgement of the experts right down to 1940 was that it was not feasible for air power. In each country one or two individual engineers became convinced by prolonged theoretical work that it was feasible. These men were not enthusiastic amateurs or self-taught mechanics; they were all academic men with formal training in thermodynamics and aerodynamics. The gas turbine was a product of modern engineering science.

In all three countries the development was eventually controlled and financed by public authority, the British Air Ministry, the Reichsluftfahrt-ministerium, or NACA. These institutions had different structures and various ties to the government and the armed forces, but all had responsibility for coordinating research and development in dozens of laboratories, public and private, and for deciding which lines of development should be supported. Technological evolution of this kind is not controlled by market forces, but by men, usually in committees, who read reports, listen to testimony, balance the conflicting pressures—political, military, and economic—and look forward into the unknown as best they can. They had hard questions to answer. Should scarce resources be concentrated on the most promising engine, or scattered among a number of alternatives? How should effort be divided between production of known and development of unknown types? What sort of balance between short-run and long-run objectives could be agreed on, between production and research, between speed of production and reliability of product? Which institutions should do which kinds of work, the scientific research, the engineering development, the design of production models, and the actual production? These hard questions were answered in different ways in different countries, but all three ministries chose a pluralistic approach: they supported half-a-dozen lines of development rather than risk a premature commitment to one. Some of the most important research was done in the laboratories of the air ministry itself, the Royal Aircraft Establishment, the Deutsche Versuchsanstalt für Luftfahrt, or the NACA Flight Propulsion Research Laboratory. All the ministries also used independent academic laboratories and the industrial laboratories of major manufacturers for theoretical research as well as practical development. The gas turbine, like most technological achievements of this century, was the product of an intricate network of institutions rather than the creation of heroic individual inventors.

The gas turbine was too late to influence the course of the Second World War, but in the next fifteen years it completely transformed military aviation and the whole business of long-distance passenger transportation. In the next war, in Korea, jet fighters were standard equipment on both sides, and jet bombers were in the air, powered by four or six jets, each with ten or twenty times the thrust of the first jets. This great concentration of power, and a new knowledge of aerodynamics, made possible the first sustained supersonic flight in 1953. The gas turbine entered the civilian passenger transport business in 1952, at first in the form of the turboprop, and took over the transatlantic trade, beginning in 1957. The transatlantic liner was doomed, and railways were suddenly eager to retire from the long-distance passenger business.

The internal combustion engine in its manifold variations seems to have a way of initiating changes like this in the economy and in human experience. In one form it simply eases the task of mowing lawns; in another it halves the cost of power for railways and ships. The tank and the aeroplane revolutionize the art of war, the tractor doubles the productivity of the farmer, and the snowmobile transforms life in the Arctic. Some of these are quiet revolutions scarcely noticed by the public, such as the radical change wrought by the chain-saw and the bulldozer in the timber business. Others, such as the introduction of the motor-car into our culture, touch all our lives and raise persistent and frustrating social problems. Man's commitment to the internal combustion engine is surely a central fact in the history of this century.

BIBLIOGRAPHY

BOYD, T. A. Pathfinding in fuels and engines. *Quarterly Transactions of the Society of Automotive Engineers*, **4**, 182–95 (1950).

BRYANT, L. Rudolf Diesel and his rational engine. *Scientific American*, **221**, 108–17 (1969).

DAY, J. *The Bosch book of the motor car, its evolution and engineering development*. St. Martin's Press, New York (1976).

The development of the internal combustion turbine. *Minutes of Proceedings of the Institution of Mechanical Engineers*, **153**, 409–512 (1945).

DICKEY, P. S. *The Liberty engine 1918–1942*. Smithsonian Institution, Washington (1968).

GOLDBECK, G. Geschichte des Verbrennungsmotors. *Automobil-industrie*, No. 3, 61–9 (1971); No. 4, 47–58 (1971); No. 3, 37–48 (1972).

HARDY, A. C. *History of motorshipping*. Whitehall Technical Press, London (1955).

HOBBS, L. S. *The Wright brothers' engines and their design*. Smithsonian Institution, Washington (1971).

JANE, F. T. *All the world's air-craft*. Part C: *The world's aerial engines*. Samson, Low, Marston & Co., London (1914).

KOLIN, I. *The evolution of the heat engine*. Longman, London (1972).

LEHR, G. *La propulsion des avions*. Presses Universitaires de France, Paris (1965).

MEYER, R. B., JR. *Langley's aero engine of 1903*. Smithsonian Institution, Washington (1971).

Oil Engine Traction in 1936. *Engineering*, **143**, 45–6, 58 (1937).

RICARDO, H. R. The development and progress of the aero engine. *Journal of the Royal Aeronautical Society*, **34**, 1000–15 (1930).

RICARDO, H. R. High-speed diesel engines. *Engineering*, **143**, 136–8 (1937).

SASS, F. *Geschichte des deutschen Verbrennungsmotorenbaues von 1860 bis 1918*. Springer, Berlin (1962).

SCHLAIFER, R. Development of aircraft engines, and HERON, S. D., Development of aviation fuels. Graduate School of Business Administration, Harvard University, Boston, Mass. (1950).

TAYLOR, C. F. *Aircraft propulsion. A review of the evolution of aircraft powerplants*. Smithsonian Institution, Washington (1963).

WHITTLE, F. The early history of the Whittle jet propulsion gas turbine. *Minutes of Proceedings of the Institution of Mechanical Engineers*, **152**, 419–35 (1945).

41

THE STEAM TURBINE

A. SMITH AND T. DIXON

THE close of the nineteenth century had seen the emergence of a new form of prime mover in the shape of the steam turbine (Vol. V, Chs. 6, 7), which was to pave the way to a dramatic increase in the production of electricity (Ch. 45), giving a tremendous boost to industrial productivity and providing numerous benefits to home life. It was also applied to marine propulsion and other forms of industrial activity with considerable success. The principle of the steam turbine was not new, but it took the individual efforts of a number of outstanding engineers to develop the idea and make it a practical proposition.

Although C. G. de Laval [1] was the first of these engineers to produce a workable turbine in 1883, it was C. A. Parsons who, by introducing the reaction principle, was able to make the first practical turbine in 1884; this was directly coupled to his own design for a high-speed electrical dynamo. De Laval's original turbine was a single-stage wheel which C. G. Curtis [2] followed with a velocity-compounded wheel having two or more stages. C. E. A. Rateau [2] recognized the limitation of both de Laval's and Curtis's designs and introduced a pressure-compounded impulse design as an alternative to Parsons reaction principle.

When Parsons took out his master patent, which covered both turbines and compressors, in 1884 [3], the reciprocating steam engine had been highly developed into multi-cylinder condensing arrangements for powers of up to 750 kW (Vol. V, Ch. 6). The first Parsons turbine-driven generator produced only 7·5 kW, but at an unprecedented speed of 18 000 rev/min. By the turn of the century a 1000-kW unit had been manufactured for Elberfeld in Germany (Fig. 41.1); by 1923 a 50 000-kW machine (Fig. 41.2) had been completed; and by 1950 unit size had risen to 150 000 kW [4].

Steam turbine development, moreover, was not confined to the production of electricity in large centralized units but was applied to marine propulsion by Parsons. In 1897, at the Spithead Review to celebrate Queen Victoria's Diamond Jubilee, his turbine-driven boat *Turbinia* demonstrated a remark-

FIG. 41.1. The 1000-kW turbo-generator supplied to Elberfeld, Germany (1900).

FIG. 41.2. The 50 000-kW turbo-generator at Crawford Avenue power station, Chicago (1923).

able speed of $34\frac{1}{2}$ knots. The steam reciprocating engine was soon relegated to propelling tramp steamers.

Quite apart from its high specific output, the steam turbine, because of its purely rotary motion and consequent lack of vibration and sliding parts, quickly demonstrated its reliability over other forms of prime mover. This feature both collieries and steelworks quickly appreciated for ventilation and blast-furnace blower drives. Other uses were also found in paper mills and later in the petrochemical field. In fact, the turbine found use in those applications where bulk heating demands from pass-off steam coincided with high electrical loads. The petroleum industry, in particular, quickly appreciated that the waste combustible products from refining could be used to generate steam for cracking processes and electricity generation.

The turbine differed from the reciprocating engine it replaced by employing alternate rings of fixed and moving blades (Fig. 41.3) to convert thermal energy into kinetic energy in the curved passages between the blades. The resulting high-velocity jets are successively changed in direction through fixed and moving rows to enable work to be performed on the moving shaft; the power generated is proportional to the change in tangential momentum

FIG. 41.3. Cut-away view of turbine showing alternating rings of fixed and moving blades.

and blade speed [5]. Euler's form of Newton's second law of motion is employed to calculate the blade tangential forces which result in pressure and velocity changes across the individual blade profiles. It is these pressure differences that ultimately limit the tangential thrust from the blades. If loading is excessive, unacceptably high pressure-gradients can develop, resulting in boundary layer separation and high losses.

The basic efficiency of a steam turbine is a function of the blade to steam velocity ratio. Parsons (and later Rateau) realized that if the total energy of the incoming steam was released in a single stage, as proposed by de Laval, the resulting rotational speeds and fluid friction losses would be prohibitive. Independently, therefore, they introduced pressure compounding in which several stages were employed to reduce the pressure and heat drops so that lower blade speeds could be employed. This made it possible to keep blade stresses within limits and achieve the desired performance.

I. IMPULSE AND REACTION TURBINES

In the Rateau concept the pressure drop over each stage (one fixed and one moving row of blades) was all taken over the fixed row, and the work was done on the moving row without further pressure drop. This design became known as the 'impulse'-type turbine.

Parsons designed his turbines so that the pressure drop across each stage was split to give equal heat drops across the fixed and moving rows. This became commonly known as the reaction-type turbine because of the reaction created by accelerating the flow in the moving blade. It is, in fact, more correct to designate Parsons's concept as a 50 per cent reaction design, because reaction is usually defined as the ratio of the heat drop across the moving row to the total heat drop over the stage. The impulse design therefore corresponds to a zero reaction arrangement.

Both types of design have been developed by various turbine manufacturers over the years without either design being able to claim any clear advantage over the other on overall performance. While the potential efficiency of a 50 per cent reaction blading arrangement is better than that of an impulse arrangement, the latter has the advantage of smaller clearance losses and balance-piston leakage because of its disc-type rotor and diaphragm arrangement. The differences between the two designs were, however, gradually narrowed as the impulse turbine builders introduced varying degrees of reaction into their designs. For the last two or three stages of low-pressure blading there is now practically no difference in the designs because of aerodynamic and stressing restraints.

A design developed in the U.S.A. by Curtis about 1903, embodying a two-row velocity compounded wheel, has had only limited application because of its inherent poor efficiency, but it has been used successfully as inlet stages to many land turbines to reduce the pressure and temperature of the steam on the turbine cylinder and shaft. It is also used for the astern blading of marine turbines (p. 1033) where a compact arrangement is required for relatively large outputs without the need for high efficiency.

A steam turbine has to be capable of accommodating increases in specific volume from inlet to outlet and also of maintaining a near uniform ratio of blade speed to steam speed. The required flow area is provided by progressively increasing the mean diameter or height of the blading, or both. In condensing turbines the volumetric ratio can be as large as several hundred to one, in fact, difficulty in providing sufficient blading flow area in the last row, in order to limit the loss in energy in the exhaust, has been one of the major constraints in the rise of unit size. Initially, two cylinders arranged in line enabled the low-pressure turbine to be made double-flow, thus providing larger exhaust area without subjecting the shaft to excessive rotational stresses.

As steam conditions and outputs continued to rise, better materials had to be developed to limit 'creep' rates in the high-temperature section of the turbine and to provide adequate safety in respect of the high stresses in both blades and shafts at the exhaust end. The use of disc, drum, or welded shaft construction eased the difficulty of obtaining reliable forgings with the necessary mechanical properties, but even so last-row low-pressure blade and shaft proportions are still a major limitation.

Initially, tandem arrangements of turbo-alternators running at either 3000 or 3600 rev/min to suit the respective frequency standards in Europe or North America (Ch. 12, p. 288) were used up to the limits of prevailing materials. Still larger machines were then devised using a side-by-side arrangement with the high- and intermediate-pressure sections, running at 3000 or 3600 rev/min and the low-pressure section at 1500 or 1800 rev/min [4]. This arrangement resulted in a compact design of high- and intermediate-pressure turbines with low casing stresses. It also provided much larger exhaust areas for a given rotational stress. However, because of the need for two generators and the size of the low-pressure turbines, their cost per kW was higher than the corresponding high-speed single-line machine.

A number of novel designs have been adopted over the years to provide additional exhaust areas within the limitation imposed by blade speed. In 1926, Parsons developed a duplex exhaust arrangement in which the steam flow was divided, at sub-atmospheric pressure, into two unidirectional flows on the same shaft, each having three or four stages of blading before exhausting into a common condenser. The largest of these machines developed about 30 000 kW. Only a few were built and their use was discontinued as larger multi-cylinder designs were developed.

K. Baumann provided an alternative solution for high flow rates at the exhaust by introducing a flow system in which advantage was taken of the higher work potential at the blade tips to reduce the steam flow progressively through the last two low-pressure stages [6]. The system ultimately enabled 100 MW to be generated from an exhaust having the same tip diameter as a previous 60-MW machine, without loss in performance. By reducing blade-tip velocities, moreover, the Baumann system also reduced the relative impact velocity between water droplets formed in the expansion of the steam and the moving blades, thereby reducing the need for erosion protection necessary in conventional exhaust blading of equivalent rating.

An important variant from the axial-flow steam turbine was a design developed by F. Ljunström [7]. This employed two contrarotating shafts having 50 per cent reaction blading, delivering their power to separate generators. By admitting the steam near the axis and allowing it to expand radially outwards through concentric blade rows, the rise in specific volume of the steam could be partially accommodated by the increase in diameter. In larger turbines, however, blade stressing demanded axial flow stages, so that this type of machine ceased to be built above sizes of 40 MW.

II. CYCLE EFFICIENCY

For a given back-pressure and heat rejection temperature level, cycle efficiency is improved by raising the inlet temperature. In satisfying the reversibility requirements of the Carnot ideal engine (Vol. IV, p. 163) it is also necessary to supply and reject heat isothermally during the expansion. In the Rankine vapour cycle of the steam engine this first requirement is approached by raising the inlet pressure so that heat is supplied at as high a temperature as practicable. As a measure of the progress made it may be noted that working pressures and temperatures have risen from 11 bar and 200 °C in 1900 to 103 bar and 565 °C in 1950.

In 1918 regenerative feed heating was adopted at Carville power station[8] to avoid unnecessary heat degradation. Steam bled from the low-pressure turbine was used to raise the feed-water temperature after extraction from the condenser on its way back to the boiler. The net gain was sufficient to encourage the widespread adoption of regenerative feed heating, which was subsequently extended to high-pressure cylinders with up to six steam bleed points.

In following the second Carnot principle an important advance in cycle efficiency was achieved with the first commercial applications of steam reheat between the high- and low-pressure turbines at North Tees power station [6] and in Chicago in 1923. This was repeated at Barking, near London, in 1924, but without doubt the most successful application was at Dunston 'B' power station in 1930. The combined improvement to cycle efficiency and reduction in blade wetness losses in the low-pressure turbines was such that these 50-MW, 1500-rev/min, tandem turbines achieved an overall efficiency of 36·8 per cent, a figure not exceeded for almost a decade. Perhaps the full significance of this efficiency level can be judged by comparison with the efficiency of 15·5 per cent obtained on the 1-MW Elberfeld machines at the turn of the century. In twenty-five years efficiency had more than doubled.

In parallel with these thermodynamic developments, experiments were made in wind tunnels and turbines to optimize blade profile shapes, circumferential pitching, setting angles, and height for both efficiency and strength. Sealing the blade clearances between the moving and stationary parts has also received extensive attention.

With the heat drop being carried equally by both the stationary and moving blade rows in 50 per cent reaction blading, it became necessary to seal both stationary and moving blade rows against steam leakage past the tips of the blades. In impulse stages, however, the stationary nozzles were designed to carry nearly twice the heat drop of a reaction stage with an insignificant heat drop across the rows of moving blades: elaborate sealing of the tips of the moving blades was consequently avoided, but it was imperative to seal the stationary nozzle rows, with their high pressure drop. To achieve this, a form of rotor construction using shrunk-on discs was adopted for impulse turbines; the stationary nozzle blades were mounted in diaphragms, the inside diameter of which was kept small to reduce leakage area. This option was not, however, open to the reaction blade designer because, in unidirectional flow turbines, the cumulative axial force resulting from the pressure drop across the shaft discs would have resulted in excessive thrust-bearing load. Drum-type rotor construction was therefore retained in 50 per cent reaction turbines, the residual blade axial forces being balanced by a 'dummy piston'

FIG. 41.4. An example of a large marine turbine and single reduction gearing from the *Maheno*.

at the high-pressure end of the shaft, the pressure at the rear face of which was coupled by a balance pipe to a lower pressure belt further down the turbine expansion.

The rapid increase in flow area through the last few low-pressure turbine stages can be provided only by increasing blade height at a faster rate than the shaft diameters, and unless twisted blading is employed excessive aerodynamic losses can result. The adoption of a 1·9:1 tip-to-hub diameter ratio for the last row of a geared single flow turbo-generator for Bankside power station, London, in 1919 forced the adoption of such twisted and flattened blades to accommodate the large radial variation in blade speed and steam incidence. The degree of twist, however, was limited to maintaining a radially constant discharge angle from the blade trailing edge, in order to minimize downstream mixing losses [9].

The design treatment outlined above has been only one of many theories which have been applied to the special flow condition in low-pressure blading where, in addition to high tip-to-hub ratios, steep cylinder wall flare angles result at the outer diameters, coupled with large axial gaps between the blade rows. Design procedures to minimize radial flow movement followed recognition of the problem by G. Darrius [10]. B. Pochabradsky [11] and H. D. Emmert [12] subsequently endeavoured to improve blading efficiencies by twisting the blading to achieve radial equilibrium. These theoretical models, however, were unreliable for low-pressure turbines, making experimental approaches necessary. It was not until 1970, well past the end of the period of our present concern, that a reliable method became available.

From the foregoing remarks the reader will appreciate that the halving of fuel consumption of steam turbo-generators in the period under review has been the result of continuous development. An even greater saving in capital cost per kilowatt has also resulted from the rise in unit sizes. It was no accident that by mid-century the steam turbine supplied almost all thermal electric generation needs.

III. MARINE TURBINES

Marine turbine development differed considerably from land-based power-station practice because high torque was required at comparatively low shaft speeds (200–500 rev/min) to avoid cavitation damage to propellers. Early attempts had, in fact, been made by Parsons in his *Turbinia* to avoid this cavitation problem. He subdivided his turbines into three cylinders, each driving a separate shaft carrying three propellers in tandem. The situation was somewhat eased as powers and sizes grew; this was confirmed by the success of the 38 000-ton 'Blue Riband' Cunarder *Mauretania* (70 000 hp), but it was not until de Laval introduced high-speed double-helical reduction gearing that turbines could be effectively matched to propeller speeds.

Gearing offered exceptional compactness since the turbines could be disposed peripherally around the large central gear wheel, delivering their power through pinions sized to suit the optimum speed of the respective turbines (Fig. 41.4). Both single- and double-reduction geared steam turbines subsequently became the standard method of propulsion in larger ships throughout the world. Between 1940 and 1950, however, the development of the heavy oil-burning diesel engine put the turbine at an economic disadvantage below power ratings of 8000 kW.

Unlike turbines driving generators, mechanically coupled marine turbines have to be reversed for manoeuvring purposes. Astern power is invariably supplied by a two- or three-row Curtis velocity-compounded stage, situated in a back-to-back arrangement on the same shaft as the ahead turbine and discharging into the same exhaust. By locating these astern turbines only on the low-pressure shaft, high windage losses are avoided during ahead running because they are under vacuum. Manoeuvring is accomplished by admitting steam to either the ahead or astern turbines as required.

Because the level of stored energy in the machinery is high and the astern turbine relatively inefficient (usually about two-thirds of that of the ahead turbines) alternative drives have been sought to improve manoeuvring. The most notable perhaps was the turbo-electric machinery fitted to some U.S. battleships and to the French liner *Normandie*. This consisted of conventional turbo-generators supplying multi-pole slow-speed synchronous motors directly coupled to the propellers [13]. More recently, both hydraulic couplings and reversible pitch propellers have been considered as alternatives to reversing turbines, but mechanical difficulties have prevented designers from using them above tug-boat sizes.

REFERENCES

[1] STODOLA, A. *Steam and gas turbines*, Vol. 1, p. 1. McGraw-Hill, New York (1927).

[2] KEARTON, W. J. *Steam turbine theory and practice* (7th ed.), p. 7. Pitman, London (1958).

[3] PARSONS, R. H. *The development of the Parsons steam turbine*, p. 2. Constable, London (1936).

[4] Turbines, condensers and auxiliaries, feedwater heaters and evaporators. Edison Electric Institution Publications No. R3 49, p. 26 (1946–7).

[5] KEENAN, J. H. *Thermodynamics*, p. 148. Wiley, New York (1957).

[6] BAUMANN, K. Some recent developments in steam turbine practice. *Journal of the Institution of Electrical Engineers*, **59**, 565 (1921).

[7] CARR, T. H. *Electric power station*, p. 504. Chapman and Hall, London (1947).

[8] PARSONS, R. H. Op. cit. [3], p. 136.

[9] SMITH, A. Survey of twisted blading development in steam turbines. *Proceedings of the Institution of Mechanical Engineers*, **184**, 449 (1969).

[10] DARRIEUS, G. *Contribution au trace des aubes radiales des turbines.* Orel Fussli Verlag, Zurich (1929).

[11] POCHABRADSKY, B. Effect of centrifugal forces in axial flow turbines. *Engineering, London*, **163**, 205 (1947).

[12] EMMERT, H. D. Current design practice for gas turbine power elements. *Transactions of the American Society of Mechanical Engineers*, **72**, 189 (1950).

[13] The French liner *Normandie*. *The Engineer*, **154**, 462 (1932).

42

MACHINE TOOLS

ROBERT S. WOODBURY

DURING the first half of the twentieth century the development of machine tools centred around the increasing widespread demand for highly specialized tools of high precision, high speed, and high productivity for use in mass manufacture by the principle of interchangeable parts. In the van of this important growth was the automobile industry and later the manufacture of aircraft. These two were to become the principal customers of the machine-tool industry. Machine-tool design was therefore strongly influenced by the special needs of these manufacturing processes. However, this is not to say that they were the only factors influencing the development of machine tools in this period. The role of production engineering in effecting the maximum utilization of machine tools, is the subject of a separate chapter (Ch. 43).

The development of machine tools up to 1900 has been discussed elsewhere (Vol. V, Ch. 26). The most significant advances for the future came in several fields. There was the matter of the cutting point itself, with new materials: 'high-speed steel', carbide tips, and ceramic cutters. The grinding machine required nonmetallic wheels of synthetic abrasives. The milling machine soon had a multitude of multiple rotary cutting points. And all this led to basic research on the problem of exactly what happens to the cutter and to the work at the cutting point. Increased cutting capacity led to much greater speeds, strength, and rigidity in machine tools designed to utilize the possibilities of the new cutters. This trend is to be seen in the lathe and in the milling machine, but especially in C. H. Norton's work on the grinding machine.

The demand for higher production rates lead to hydraulic and electric drive and controls, not only for the tools designed for the special needs of mass production, but those for more conventional machining. Computer, tape, and other controls were developed to balance the advantages of specialization against those of flexibility. The result was highly complex machine tools, which, however, required less skilled labour to operate them, even at high production rates. This is a continuation of the long-range development of machine tools and other machines in which the skill required is built into the machine and less and less skill is required of the operator. Economic historians and others have here failed to note that far higher skills are required for installation and maintenance. High-precision work had been made possible by the earlier introduction at the workbench of the vernier caliper and the micrometer caliper, but one more important step was needed— precision shop standards. This step was taken with the appearance of the Johansson blocks.

A few tools entirely new to the machining of metals appeared in this period. Broaching and swaging were more widely used for certain purposes. But a really fundamental advance was the Wilkies' adaptation of the band saw to cutting metals. In this technique the excess metal is removed from the workpiece, not by reducing it to chips, but by actually cutting it off in rather large pieces, thereby not only saving time but making the scrap more valuable and useful. Die forging and casting rapidly advanced to the point at which much less had to be machined from the work. Certain techniques of mechanical drawing were introduced to make the transfer of the design into metal more rapid and precise, especially methods of indicating tolerances and symbols for surface finish.

I. THE LATHE

By 1900 the principal features of the oldest of the machine tools—the lathe —were fairly well established. Increased speeds, power, feed, rigidity, and precision were all obvious needs, as were lathes of increased complexity but requiring a decreasing level of operating skill along with increasing productivity. All these elements were to be accelerated over the next 75 years. Flexibility was built into the lathes of the early 1900s with the quick-change gearbox invented in 1892 by W. P. Norton. This device not only provided easy change of feed rate, but also a wide range of thread cutting by 1909. By 1920 electric drive and rolling contact bearings were in use, as were hardened and ground precision ways and guides. The turret and automatic lathes had become of major industrial importance by 1900. They already had chip pans, coolant sumps, electric drive, preselection of spindle speeds, and rapid traverse features. The universal cross slide appeared by 1915 and permitted multiple simultaneous cuts to be taken. These features were also appearing in the various automatic lathes—all aimed at high productivity and flexibility. Specialization is evident by 1914 in the multi-station vertical lathes introduced by E. P. Bullard jun.

However, by far the most important advance in all lathes, in fact in all machine tools, was in the cutting tool itself and in the reflection of its new possibilities in the overall design of the lathe. The new materials for cutting tools not only produced important changes in the size, rigidity, and power required to utilize them for high production rates, but they also gave rise to scientific study of the actual cutting process with the application of the theory of solid-state physics.

By 1900 practically all lathe cutting-tools were of Mushet steel, with manganese replaced by chromium. But F. W. Taylor and M. White produced tools of greatly increased stability which more than doubled the cutting speeds possible to as much as 60 ft/min (18 m/min); these therefore became known as high-speed steel (HSS). The material that they used was not new, but their heat treatment of it was. From 1900 to 1910 the allowable cutting speed increased from about 25 ft/min (7·5 m/min) to well over 100 ft/min (30 m/min), and this had an immediate and far-reaching influence on lathe development. HSS of higher quality, made possible by electric furnace melting in 1906, outran the power and speeds available in lathes until about 1920. By then the super-high-speed steels had appeared and the difficulties of working them in practice were finally overcome by 1940, by substitution of the cheaper molybdenum for tungsten.

About 1915 non-ferrous high-temperature alloy cutters were devised by Edward Haynes, and within a decade these cast alloy tools came into use for certain purposes. The first successful tungsten carbide tools appeared in Germany before 1928. These tools consisted of finely ground tungsten carbide particles sintered together with a cobalt binder (Ch. 18, p. 454). During the 1930s the use of the carbide tools greatly expanded as problems of grinding them, cratering, and brittleness were overcome. By the time of the Second World War carbide tools were widely used in lathes and in other machine tools designed to utilize the high cutting speeds they made possible.

Just on the horizon was the very important use of ceramic cutting tools, at first in Britain and in the U.S.S.R. This type of cutter was explored by the U.S. Army's Rodman Laboratory and developed to a high level for very high cutting speeds, using machines of unusual rigidity and power. The ceramic material is very closely related to the abrasive material developed earlier for grinding wheels, but here used for very heavy and large cuts, rather than the many fine but rapid cuts of the grinding wheel. The future of ceramic cutters is very promising—especially in respect of their very low cost and their independence of strategic materials.

All these new materials for the cutting tools of the lathe were very easily adapted to the cutters of other machine tools.

II. THE MILLING MACHINE

In 1900 the milling machine had already reached a high level of development and was in wide use in American and Continental machine shops. By 1925 it had responded to the need for heavier construction of the stand, knee, unit construction, interchangeable frames, overarms, and braces, much of it the work of Fred Holtz and A. L. DeLeeuw. One of the most important advances in the milling machine at this time was the constant-speed geared drive and the associated features of spindle and feed drives independent of each other and in geometrical progression. Above all these was the introduction of local electric drive. The constant-speed drive was first designed by John Parker in 1900. This mechanism made possible the electric drive by a constant-speed motor. The multiple rotary cutters used on the milling machine were the subject of very extensive and careful research by Holtz and DeLeeuw after 1908 until the design of the milling machine passed from empirical to engineering methods after 1926.

Various types of specialized milling machines appeared. These included the modification of the vertical milling machine into the jig borer, which made possible the wide use of precision jigs for high-precision work and high-production machining by relatively unskilled labour.

Very large, heavy, and powerful milling machines soon replaced the planer and shaper, even for the heaviest work, because of more rapid workings and with better surface finish, by using wide cutters. Specialized milling machines for the automobile industry were built for Ford as early as 1913. Automatic control of various types came in a flood from 1910 onward, from the work of Sol Einstein, Hazelton, and DeLeeuw. Hydraulic drive was embodied in a milling machine by 1927, and vertical milling was applied to automatic die sinking by 1932. Tracer, tape, and electronic control of machine tools were applied to electrical or hydraulic automatic controls by 1927. By the end of the half-century the M.I.T. tape-controlled milling machine had been developed for the U.S. Air Force, to give quick and easy setting up for high-speed machining of short runs with great flexibility. Soon after, the milling machine and other machine tools even had direct computer controls.

As with the lathe, we see in the milling machine the effects of demands for high speed, high precision, and high production rates, together with good flexiblity. These were all made possible by scientific analysis of the cutter; more powerful drive; greater size and rigidity and greater complexity; and the introduction of automation to reduce labour cost.

III. THE GEAR-CUTTING MACHINE

The automobile created a demand, not only for new types of gears made cheaply and in quantity, but also for precision gears hardened to withstand heavy wear and at the same time quiet in operation. This meant precision and high production rates for a very difficult form of work. At this time the basic forms of the gear-cutting machines had already evolved, and grinding of small hardened parts was widely used as means of precision production with good surface finish. But the process was slow and very expensive, even using the Fellows gear shaper to produce the unhardend gear automatically. The solution was to make the gears by using a generating grinding wheel or a formed grinding cutter. But here a special problem arose. In using a metallic cutting tool there is a certain amount of wear on the tool as it cuts, but this is small and the problem of tool wear can easily be met simply by resharpening. In the grinding process, however, the grinding tool itself wears away quite rapidly. In fact, controlled wear is the means by which the dulled, minute cutters of the grinding wheel are replaced by new sharp ones. So proper wear is essential to the grinding process. This means that compensation for the wear of the grinding wheel must be provided—and preferably automatically. In grinding gear teeth a beginning had been made by H. M. Leland and Falconer in 1899 with hardened gears for the chainless bicycle. In 1908 the crucial invention for grinding hardened gears was made by Ward and Taylor. Their device corrected for the wear on a formed grinding wheel by two diamond points; these not only maintained the correct form automatically, but the resulting wear on their formed grinding wheel was also compensated automatically.

The first machine designed especially for grinding hardened gears for automobiles was the work of J. E. R. Reinecker of Germany. At about the same time, the Oerlikon firm in Switzerland brought out a somewhat different type of gear grinder which was widely used in automobile work. In order to assure that the gear has the necessary precision for smooth running and minimum wear the technique also required application of the principle of the Hartness screw thread comparator of 1921 to the measurement of gear teeth.

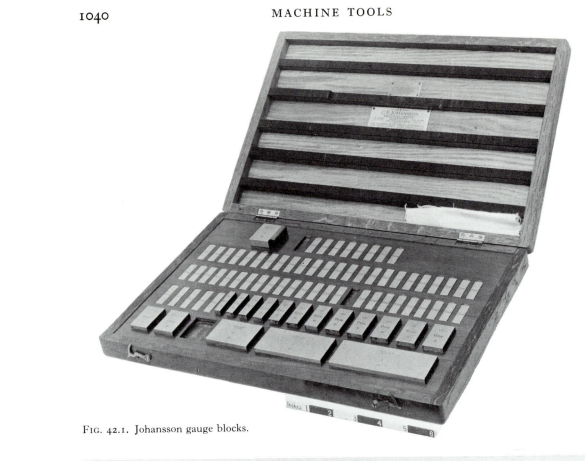

FIG. 42.1. Johansson gauge blocks.

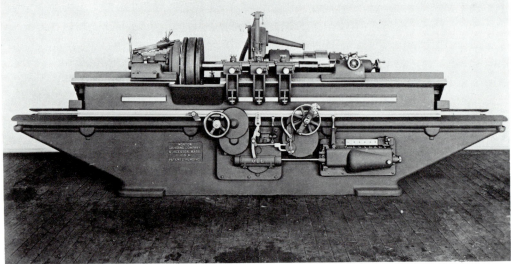

FIG. 42.2. The original Norton grinding machine (1900).

IV. SHOP PRECISION OF MEASUREMENT

All the foregoing developments in machine tools had made it possible for designers of all kinds of machines and devices to demand greater and greater precision of manufacture. The introduction of Joseph R. Brown's vernier caliper in 1851 and his micrometer caliper in 1867 had put precision measurement on the work bench of every machinist by 1890. It was evident at the turn of the century that there was a need for shop precision standards that, used in conjunction with standardized techniques of mechanical drawing, would make it possible to manufacture parts that would be interchangable throughout the world. Precision standards for use in shop calibration of micrometers was recognized by the Swedish technician C. E. Johansson, who with great ingenuity and patient skill had developed his gauge blocks by 1898 (Fig. 42.1). By 1907 Johansson had scientifically linked his gauge system to the standard metre at Paris and to the physical properties of the steel of which his blocks were made. The manufacture and the actual use of these blocks depended on obtaining absolutely plane surfaces of high surface finish, absolutely parallel to each other, and precisely of the indicated dimension. Johansson obtained these results by patient hand skill; at first his own and that of his family. Later, he trained others to do the work. Mechanical means of doing this work were developed by Major Hoke of the U.S. Bureau of Standards in 1918, but these gauge blocks are still called 'Joe blocks' by most machinists. As important as their precision is the ingenious set of dimensioned blocks by which any dimension could be obtained over a very wide range. These gauge blocks still remain the standards of precision of measurement in the shop, despite the many measuring methods—electronic, pneumatic, and hydraulic—which have been developed since.

V. THE GRINDING MACHINE

Since Henry Maudslay's (Vol. IV, pp. 423–31) introduction of the all-metal lathe with a precision lead screw and precision ways and guides, two basically new machine tools have appeared which have become of major industrial importance: Joseph R. Brown's universal milling machine of 1861, and Charles H. Norton's heavy-duty, precision, high-production-rate grinding machine of 1900 (Fig. 42.2).

Norton's machine was not only of immediate importance to the automobile industry, but his basic technique quickly gave rise to many other applications, many to very specialized work, such as the manufacture of steam locomotives.

It led also to James H. Heald's planetary cylinder grinder, to automatic ball-bearing grinders, automatic thread grinders, and to centreless grinding originating from the work of L. R. Heim in 1915. But above all, it gave birth to the science of grinding and the grinding wheel, stemming from the work of James J. Guest in 1915.

When Henry Ford decreed that his car must be light, rugged, reliable, and cheap, the only way in which his requirements could be met was to use various hardened alloy steels at certain crucial points in the design of the car. But at the same time, precision and some degree of surface finish were equally necessary. It had been possible long before 1900 to achieve these technical results by grinding, but at enormous cost, by hand skill, and the use of very light grinding techniques. To meet Ford's demands two entirely new elements had to be found: first, grinding wheels, cheap and in quantity, of known and controllable characteristics suitable for grinding in a number of different processes; secondly, a grinding machine capable of heavy, accurate, and rapid cuts on a production scale and at low cost. Both these problems were to be solved by the work of Charles H. Norton, and by the efforts of the men who followed him in this new field of grinding—principally for the manufacture of automobiles, but soon for many other important industrial uses.

The solution of the grinding wheel problem came from two developments, namely, the introduction of two artificial abrasives: silicon carbide and aluminium oxide. Silicon carbide, better known under its trade name 'carborundum', was the work of Edward G. Acheson, who discovered it independently, and almost accidentally, in connection with his attempt to produce synthetic diamonds. Acheson, however, recognized the importance of this new abrasive and its potential influence on production grinding. Carborundum grinding wheels appeared commercially as early as 1898, though they were then rather expensive. Some of their limitations were overcome over the next decade, and silicon carbide grinding wheels are important today for certain applications.

Artificial corundum, with the trade name 'alundum', had been produced on a laboratory scale by Charles B. Jacobs in 1897. Jacobs's discovery had been taken up by the Norton Emery Wheel Company,[1] which undertook large-scale experiments. By 1906 emery and natural corundum were completely replaced by aluminium oxide in Norton grinding wheels. Further experimental work by the Norton Company, using bauxite of extra high

---

[1] Named not after Charles Norton, but after a much earlier and unrelated Norton.

purity, made available by 1910 to the practical grinding machine operator the advantages of artificial abrasives in solid grinding wheels of a number of types and grades, of uniform and known characteristics. The operator also had adequate information on the way to use these grinding wheels to do the precision work inherent in this technique of machining metals. All that was then needed, was a grinding machine capable of fully exploiting the grinding procedures made possible by the use of these wheels to give precision production, especially of hardened alloy steel parts. This machine was the work of Charles H. Norton.

In his work at Brown and Sharpe and elsewhere, Norton had had extensive experience in grinding problems. On his return to Brown and Sharpe in 1896 his ideas had become clear. He wanted to use very much larger and wider wheels in both plunge and rapid traverse grinding, and also to use formed wheels. He wanted to use a very heavy and rigid machine, and (as he wrote) '. . . we could make an accurate micrometer out of the machine itself.' All this was going to require a much more powerful machine as well. He knew that such a machine would use up the grinding wheel very rapidly. He also knew that the wheels, the machines, and the power would be costly, but that their cost would be far outweighed by the saving in time and labour cost—the most expensive item in nearly all industrial manufacture. Norton's ideas met only with ridicule at Brown and Sharpe. He therefore left and went to the Norton Company, where he was given full facilities and free rein to design and build an actual grinding machine embodying his ideas of precision production grinding. In 1900 he completed two such machines, which were a great success. From then on Norton's efforts were primarily in the application of these principles to the special problems of the automobile industry. By 1905 his specialized crankshaft grinder could do in 15 minutes what had previously required 5 hours of skilful hand work. The result of Norton's plunge grinding of crankshafts was not only an enormous saving in labour and time costs, but greater precision and better surface finish. By 1910 he had a production grinder designed especially for the production of hardened camshafts for automobile engines. By this time grinding engineers were in constant cooperation with the automobile engineers for joint solutions of mass-production problems. The Norton Company established a research laboratory, one of the first industrial research laboratories, to undertake basic research on all aspects of grinding.

What Norton had done was to demonstrate conclusively that grinding could be a rapid, flexible, and economical means of production, and to establish it as one of the most important elements in the dramatic change in production from 1900 to 1915. His work and methods were rapidly applied to many production processes. Of these, we must at least mention the work of James H. Heald and his piston-ring grinder of 1904, and his planetary spindle cylinder grinder of 1905, which revolutionized the production of precision cylinders for the internal combustion engine. A far cry from Watt's troubles with the cylinders for his steam engine!

The next step in production grinding was to make it automatic and of high speed. Machine tools with these characteristics, of course, wore down their grinding wheels fairly rapidly, even at the designed rate. The basic problem of automatic, high-speed production grinding was therefore to make pro- vision for automatic size control. Grinding machines with these features were also usually highly specialized, so a number of machine-tool builders brought out various types—Bryant, Heald, Pratt and Whitney, Brown and Sharpe, and Landis machines all came into use by 1930. At the same time grinding machines for much wider uses appeared. With O. S. Walker's invention of the magnetic chuck in 1896, surface grinding machines could easily hold light work firmly, but without distortion, to meet the light touch of the grinding wheel and thus permit the high precision and fine surface finish inherent in grinding methods. Form and thread grinding speeded up produc- tion at reduced cost of gears, worms, and screws in material too hard (or too soft) for other methods, especially for the aircraft industry. High production rates at low cost in fully automatic machine for certain parts, both hard and soft, became easily achieved with centreless grinding after the work of L. R. Heim in 1915 was developed by the Cincinnati Milling Machine Company into industrial use by 1925.

The application of the grinding machine in both its standard and special- ized forms in a number of industries made work which was previously impos- sible easy and inexpensive. This is especially true of the automobile industry, which was to become the largest single branch of our metal-working industrial economy. The grinding machine has created the modern view of what constitutes high-class production machine work. It even created whole industries which would not otherwise have been possible.

We need only to point to the enormous economic, social, political, and even military influence of the automobile on our entire industrial way of life to see the influence of Charles H. Norton. Few of the millions who daily drive a car have ever heard his name. Machine tools have thus made possible methods of mass production which underlie the very high standards of living of our industrial society, but they must not be blamed for the social, economic, and political problems which seem to be inherent in such a society.

BIBLIOGRAPHY

ALTHIN, T. K. W. *C. E. Johansson 1864–1943. The master of measurement*, Stockholm (1948). [Written at Johansson's own desk and with full access to all his papers.]

BOOKER, P. J. *A history of engineering drawing*, Chatto and Windus, London (1963). [Indicates the interaction of advances in engineering drawing with the tools used to create their devices.]

FELDHAUS, F. M. *Geschichte des Technischen Zeichnens*, Wilhelmshaven (1959).

GARANGER, A. *Petite histoire d'une grande industrie*. Societe d'edition pour la mecanique et la machine-outil, Neuilly-sur-seine (1960). [Full of data on world-wide machine tool production.]

MATSCHOSS, C., and BIHL, A. *Schiess, ein Beitrag zur Geschichte des deutschen Werkzeugmaschinenbaues*, VDI-Verlag, Berlin (1942). [Contains some splendid drawings of machine tools.]

NEDOLUHA, A. Kulturgeschichte des technischen zeichens. In *Blätter für Technikgeschichte*, Vol. 21, Vienna (1959).

ROLT, L. T. C. *A short history of machine tools*. M.I.T. Press, Cambridge, Mass. (1965). Simultaneous publication as *Tools for the job*, Batsford, London (1965). [The best general introduction to the history of machine tools. Supersedes J. W. ROE, *English and American tool builders*, Yale University Press, New Haven (1916).]

ROSENBERG, N. Technological change in the machine tool industry, 1840–1910. *Journal of Economic History*, **23**, December (1963). [Economic history of machine tools.]

SHAW, M. G. Development of the lathe in the U.S.A. Unpublished paper, *c.* 1960, in the files of the Department of Mechanical Engineering, M.I.T. [Written by a distinguished engineer who played an important part in the application of solid-state physics to metal cutting.]

STEEDS, W. *A history of machine tools, 1700–1910*, Clarendon Press, Oxford (1969). [Excellent photographs and drawings of largely British machine tools.]

WAGONER, H. D. *The U.S. machine tool industry from 1900–1950*. M.I.T. Press, Cambridge, Mass. (1966). [A detailed study of the machine tool industry, principally in the U.S.A. Emphasis on the economic factors.]

WITTMAN, K. *Die Entwicklung der Drehbank bis zum Jahre 1939*, VDI-Verlag, Gmbh., Düsseldorf (1960). [A doctoral dissertation. After 1850 largely a chronicle of patents, with little anlysis or interpretation, but an invaluable source.]

WOODBURY, R. S. *Studies in the history of machine tools*. M.I.T. Press, Cambridge, Mass. (1972). The gear cutting machine; The grinding machine; The milling machine; The lathe to 1850.

43

PRODUCTION ENGINEERING

F. KOENIGSBERGER

I N the various fields covered by the term 'production engineering' it is often difficult to discern the rather complex interaction between the various factors that cause economic or technological changes over a period of time. In many cases technological progress has led to new ideas in the design and application of equipment. In others, new design ideas demand considerable technological research and development before they can be realized. The appearance of novel products often creates the need for new production methods. The economics of technological development and the sources of innovation are topics of such importance as to form the subject of separate chapters (Chs. 2, 3).

The outstanding feature that can be observed almost throughout the period 1890–1960 is the trend towards a scientifically based, or at least a systematically empirical, approach to the solutions of the various production problems which presented themselves. It is perhaps significant that the title of one of the first fundamental publications in the field of production engineer-ing [1] contains the word 'scientific', and that although the same author chose for his other classic treatise the title 'On the art of cutting metals' [2], one basis for this art was the establishment of a mathematical relationship be-tween tool-life and cutting speed, the so-called Taylor equation.[1] This is in fact a further indication of F. W. Taylor's farsighted appreciation of the need for combining the results of scientific study with the artisan's empirical understanding in order to achieve success on the shop floor. The existence of new machines and processes was not in itself sufficient to ensure progress; it was necessary to combine them into a production system that also took note of human factors.

---

[1] The tool-life (T), i.e. the time between the need for regrinds, decreases as a hyperbolic function with the cutting speed (v). The general equation is:

$$T^y = C_T/v,$$

where y depends on the materials of the workpiece and the cutting tool; C_T is the cutting speed at which the tool-life is one minute, and has been called the Taylor constant.

It must be stressed that the appearance of something new did not always mean that existing practices had to be completely abandoned. New materials, methods, techniques, or pieces of equipment enabled production engineers to arrange for certain operations to be carried out more quickly, more easily, or more efficiently. For other operations, however, there were advantages in using existing, older methods. It is interesting to note, for example, that even today high-speed steel (HSS) tools are still used for some 50 per cent of all machining operations, despite the development of materials of much higher performance.

I. FACTORS INFLUENCING PRODUCTION ENGINEERING

During the period under review developments in production engineering were caused—or at least affected—by the creation, application, and inter-relation of the following factors.

Materials used in the design and manufacture of various products. The manu-facturing properties of newly introduced materials (Table 43.1)—such as machinability, formability, and weldability—often caused problems that could not be solved by the application of existing experience and techniques. On the other hand, their application offered opportunities, both technological and economic, that could not be ignored, thus necessitating the creation of new production methods and techniques.

Tool materials. The demonstration, at the Paris Exhibition in 1900, of the cutting performance obtainable with HSS tools was 'a landmark in the history of mankind' [4]. The material for these tools had been developed by Frederick W. Taylor—acknowledged as the father of scientific management—

TABLE 43.1
Some constructional materials

	Year of industrial application
Monel (corrosion-resistant)	1905
Stainless steel	1912
Alloy steels, PVC, polyethylene	1920–45
Ultra-high strength steel (150 kp/mm²)	
Heat-resistant steels, materials produced by powder metallurgy, beryllium, zirconium, reinforced plastics	1945–60

Source: C. Ruiz [3].

in collaboration with a metallurgist, M. White, in the U.S.A. It contained tungsten and chromium, to which they later added vanadium, and it enabled cutting speeds to be increased threefold.

In the years following the introduction of HSS a cast tool material, 'Stellite'—consisting mainly of tungsten, chromium, cobalt, molybdenum, and carbon—was developed. This had a better heat resistance and an even higher cutting performance (80 per cent higher cutting speeds than for HSS). However, its cast structure resulted in brittleness and sensitivity to impact loads, resulting in tool failure during interrupted cuts; for example, when turning splined shafts, castings, etc.

The next major development was presented at the Machine Tool Exhibition in Leipzig (Germany) in 1927, when Krupp–Essen demonstrated their Widia (WIe DIAmant = like diamond) a sintered tungsten-carbide which became known as Carboloy in the U.S.A. and as 'Wimet' in Britain. With tool tips of this material, it was possible not only to double, or even treble, the cutting speeds used for HSS tools but also to cut materials which up to that time had not been machinable at all. The effect of these developments upon the design of machine tools (Ch. 42) will be considered later.

In the 1950s the introduction of cermets, that is ceramic cutting materials (alumina), showed great promise. However, their application was limited, because of their lack of toughness and poor resistance to thermal shock. They were mainly used for continuous (turning) rather than for interrupted (milling) operations, but when they were used cutting speeds could be increased still further (Table 43.2).

At the time when Taylor produced his HSS a similar development took place in the field of grinding wheel materials (Ch. 42, p. 1041). Charles H. Norton had undertaken the task of developing high-performance grinding

TABLE 43.2
Cutting speeds of cermets

| Workpiece material | Cutting speed (m/min) | |
	When material was first introduced	1960
Aluminium	150 (1915)	3000
Aluminium alloys	40 (1920)	300
Carbon steels (60 kp/mm^2)	30 (1920)	100
Titanium	15 (1950)	50
High strength steels (150 kp/mm^2)	15 (1960)	20

Source: M. E. Merchant [5].

machines, and during this work he had studied the performance of existing grinding wheels. Up to the 1880s, emery had been used as abrasive for grinding wheels, but its quality varied considerably in the natural state. Synthetically produced abrasives such as pure corundum (Al_2O_3) or silicon carbide (SiC), generally known as carborundum, were found to be more consistent. Both were produced in the 1890s. Mention must also be made of later developments concerning rubber or resin-bonded diamond wheels for special grinding operations and a new type of wheel containing synthetically produced cubic boron nitride (Borazon) which, although not as hard as diamond, is much harder than corundum or silicon carbide.

In the years up to 1904 Norton published a series of papers in which he reported on the results of some 15 years' research into the relationship between wheel grades and speeds on the one hand, and workpiece properties and requirements on the other. In 1908 F. H. Colvin and F. A. Stanley's *American Machinist* grinding book was published; this provided data similar to those published by Taylor for single point tool machining.

Manufacturing processes and techniques. Some of the many processes that were introduced into engineering manufacture during the first half of the twentieth century are:

(i) moulding and forming processes (investment casting, die casting, hot pressing, cold forging of steel, and powder metallurgy);

(ii) metal removal processes (gear hobbing, pull broaching, heavy production grinding, centreless grinding, electro-discharge machining, electrochemical machining, ultrasonic machining, and laser cutting);

(iii) welding and cutting (metal arc welding with and without coated electrodes, atomic hydrogen welding, Thermit welding, automatic arc welding under powder and with coated electrodes, CO_2 welding, inert-gas welding, spot and flash-butt welding, electro-slag welding, and electron-beam welding).

Manufacturing equipment. The high performance of the new cutting tool materials could be fully utilized only after the design of machine tools had been radically changed, so that they could transmit the required power and were sufficiently rigid under the forces acting at the cutting edge. The introduction of individual motor drives for machine tools was a further important step towards higher efficiency. Line shaft and cone pulley drives could still be found in some factories for many years (some even today!) but from 1906 onwards the greater safety, ease, and efficiency of operation of individual electric drives gained them more and more ground, especially when—through the introduction of multi-tool operations, negative rake cutting tools, and the use of very high cutting speeds—power requirements grew even further. By the 1950s even some medium-size machine tools were equipped with motor drives, of 25 to 50 kW capacity.

Industry could take advantage of the processes that had been successfully demonstrated in the laboratory only after workshop equipment had been designed and built for the purpose. The first universal gear-hobbing machine was built by Pfauter in 1897; the first pull broaching machine was produced by Lapointe in 1902; and the first centreless grinding machine by Cincinnati in 1922.

Work on cutting-tool performance had not been limited to the development of new materials. The research by A. L. DeLeeuw of the Cincinnati Milling Machine Company led to the design and manufacture of milling cutters with fewer, stronger, and more widely spaced teeth than had been previously used (1904). Together with the careful determination of optimum rake angles for particular applications and the introduction of helical cutting edges, increased rates of metal removal resulted for a given driving power.

As a result of his researches into the performance of grinding wheels, Norton had been able not only to increase the metal removal rate for a given wheel width but also to produce wider wheels, thus increasing the metal removal rate per minute. He also introduced new methods of wheel balancing and wheel dressing and in 1900 he succeeded in using grinding not only for fine finishing but also for heavier metal-removing operations. On the basis of this work he designed and had built a heavy production grinding machine (Ch. 42, p. 1041).

Progress in the field of machining equipment was not limited to increases in metal removal rates. Considerable efforts in connection with the development of both machine tools and quality-control equipment led to higher accuracies becoming practicable. The micrometer screw had been produced and used for accurate measurements ($2 \cdot 5$ μm) by H. Maudslay (1805) and later by J. Whitworth (1851), whose machines could measure $0 \cdot 025 \mu$m. The hand micrometer (measuring 10 μm) for use in the average machine shop was produced by Brown and Sharpe in the U.S.A. and brought to England by Charles Churchill around 1900. This was followed by dial gauges ($2 \cdot 5$ μm) becoming available around 1920; the mechanical comparator (1 μm) around 1930; the electronic comparator ($0 \cdot 1$ μm) in 1948; and R. E. Reason's famous

Taylor-Hobson instruments (0·025 μm), the 'Talysurf' (1940) for surface finish and the 'Talyrond' (1954) for roundness measurements.

In order to ensure accuracy in production, in particular in quantity production, the machine shop needs precision equipment, especially accurate jigs and fixtures. In order to satisfy this need the Société Génévoise d'Instruments de Physique (SIP) produced, in 1912, a machine for accurately positioning the centre-lines of holes that had to be bored. The machine marked with a centre punch the co-ordinate positions of the hole centres, which could then be checked by means of a microscope. This machine was the forerunner of the famous SIP jig borer. This, at first with table positioning along two coordinates operated by lead screws (any lead screw errors being eliminated by a cam-operated correction device) and later (1934) by hydraulic operation and optical measurement, was able to ensure accurate positioning of the axes (within 2 μm) for its boring operations.

Once the means for large-scale manufacture to a high standard were available, it was necessary to ensure that specified performance requirements were satisfied in practice.

The machine tool in the production workshop must be able to: (i) produce constantly—and, as far as possible, independently of an operator's skill—workpieces within prescribed limits of shape, dimensions, and surface quality; (ii) provide the possibility of using operational speeds and rates of metal removal in accordance with the opportunities offered by technological developments; (iii) maintain its performance under practical industrial conditions for a technically and economically reasonable period.

The assessment of performance used to be a matter of subjective judgement on the part of machine-tool manufacturers and users until the 1920s. It then became clear that certain standards had to be established in order to ensure that performance was maintained above a permissible minimum and that the cost of machine tools remained competitive. These standards had to serve the machine-tool manufacturer during the assembly of his machines and the machine-tool user before he put the machine into operation in his workshop. Many machine-tool manufacturers had established their own—confidential—standards concerning the accuracy of their products. However, the customer had no access to these and thus no yardstick as to what he should and could demand.

In 1927 G. Schlesinger published the first edition of his acceptance tests [6], which defined methods for measuring, and permissible limits of alignment errors, for most standard machine tools then in use. In order to cover also the behaviour of machine tools under a variety of operating conditions P. Salmon [7] added machining tests (*épreuves pratiques*) to the Schlesinger tests which he called *vérifications géometriques*.

The need for these developments was borne out by the eagerness with which the test specifications were received and applied. Salmon's book was reprinted in 1943. A second edition of the German version of Schlesinger's book followed the original publication, as well as translations into French (1929), Japanese (1930), English (1932), Russian (1932), and Italian (1937). The material produced by Schlesinger and Salmon now forms the basis of international and national standards.

For machine tools that have been either adapted or specifically designed for numerical control, or equipped with digital read-out devices, the Schlesinger and Salmon tests are, however, no longer sufficient, not only because the working accuracy of such machines must be obtainable without any intervention by the operator but also because the usual machining sequences necessitate greater inherent accuracy. Additional test methods and procedures were therefore developed during the 1950s and 1960s.

Design, planning and control facilities. The fast and effective utilization of new materials and machines, and of advanced processes, was facilitated by the concurrent development of new concepts, methods, techniques, and equipment which assisted design, production, management, and control.

A very important aid to efficient design and economical manufacture is standardization. The importance of variety reduction and interchangeability as a means of improving the economics of production had been recognized as long ago as the middle of the nineteenth century when Whitworth (Vol. IV, p. 433) created standards for the most common of all machine elements, the screw thread [8] and advocated minimum numbers of sizes and dimensions [9]. Large-scale standardization of sizes, dimensions, and other numerical values became possible only after Colonel Renard in the 1880s and J. Androuin in 1917 had discovered the system of preferred numbers, that is, decimal geometric progressions based on steps of $\sqrt[10]{10}$, $\sqrt[20]{10}$, and $\sqrt[40]{10}$ which contain the numbers 1 and, with reasonable accuracy, π.

Between the two world wars standardization of material properties, sizes and shapes, limits and fits, machine elements and components (screws, nuts washers, keys and keyways, shafts, gears, etc.) as well as of spindle speeds and feeds for machine tools, helped to reduce design and planning work as well as tooling and manufacturing cost. This simplified purchasing, testing, inspecting, and storage procedures.

A very important part of standardization—and one which was essential for making interchangeable production an economic possibility—was the establishment of limits and fits. In 1902 J. W. Newall published standard tables of limits which he had based on the practice of various British engineering firms. The first British Standard system of limits and fits (BS 27) was published in 1906; a German Standard (DIN 772–4) in 1921; and an American Standard in 1925.

The most important step in this direction was the establishment in 1928 of the I.S.A.[1] Committee 3 which published—provisionally in 1932 and 1938, and finally in 1942—an international system of limits and fits based on the many national and international industrial standards in use all over the world.

Standardization also contributed to the possibility of preparing handbooks and data books for designers and planners. After the German *Hütte*, first published in 1856, the first Machinery's *Handbook* appeared in 1914; both books were intended mainly for the benefit of design engineers. Handbooks giving recommendations for cutting speeds and feeds, to be used by planning engineers in the machine shop, appeared for example in Germany (A.W.F. Richtwerte[2]) and in the U.S.A. (A.S.M.E. *Manual on cutting metals*) during the 1920s and 1930s. Recommendations for welding procedures appeared in the 1940s and 1950s, as welding became more and more established as an important manufacturing process. Together with other values which became available from time to time, some of the information contained in these publications has been collected in 'data banks'. These enabled production engineers to use a new instrument, the computer, for design, planning, and control.

II. PRODUCTIVITY

The rates of metal removal made possible through higher cutting speeds and the introduction of stiffer and more powerful machine tools, together with faster processes of casting and forming, led to a situation in which the operational speed of the actual manufacturing process was not always the decisive factor in determining the 'floor-to-floor' time of manufacturing operations. Setting, handling, and checking times had to be reduced if the

---

[1] Today called I.S.O. (International Standards Organization).
[2] Ausschuss für Wirtschaftliche Fertigung (Committee for Economic Manufacture), *Guiding values*.

higher working speeds were to be of real benefit. Moreover, as these 'auxiliary' times were taken up by an operator manipulating or clamping parts, positioning tools, moving levers, and so on, the times taken for these activities could be reduced only by asking the operator to work harder and faster. This was possible up to a point, but only if it were combined with an appropriate incentive. The logical step was therefore to perform these manual tasks by mechanical devices and to provide the necessary energy for the work to be carried out as soon as the appropriate signal had been given. Mechanical drives for feed movements; electrically propelled welding carriages; mechanically operated die casting or pressing operations; casting techniques in which metal flowed straight from the furnaces into the moulds as they passed by on a conveyor, could be initiated as soon as an operator pushed a button or moved a lever. In other words, the signal was given by the operator while the energy was provided by mechanical power. In order to make this possible, any setting operation of the tools and of the locating and clamping devices of the workpiece had to be carried out before the actual operations could be started. This applied in particular to the setting of cutting tools for multi-tool operations and in the turret heads of capstan and turret lathes.

Operator-initiated mechanization by means of electrical, mechanical, or hydraulic power (Ch. 44) was used not only for setting, cutting, and feed movements but also for actuating speed changes and workpiece clamping devices. The logical next step was to replace the operator's function by providing the initiating signals with time or sequence control devices such as, for example, rotating camshafts. Because the operator was no longer required, such machines were called 'automatics'. It is, however, important to distinguish between mechanical actuation and true automatic control.

In a controlled action the signal which initiates the power supply for carrying out the actual operation can be produced and transmitted:

(i) At specified time-intervals, for example, by means of a camshaft which rotates at a given speed, as is found in most automatic screw machines and turret 'autos' (C. M. Spencer, 1873).

(ii) As a function of operational movements, for example, during or at the end of the movement of a slide, by means of stops, trip dogs, or master profiles (copy-machining, Georg Fischer, A.G. (Switzerland), 1938).

(iii) In accordance with specified conditions (cutting speeds and feeds) with a planned sequence of operations. Such a 'programme' may be contained in a plug board, punched card, or punched or magnetic tape (numerical control was developed at the Massachusetts Institute of Technology in 1947 and was first in operation about 1954). The programme can be made a function of actual operations by independent measurement of the results, for example, by measuring the length of traverse of a slide or the dimension produced by a machining operation, and by comparing these measurements with the required values as stated in the programme (feedback). In this case the signal for terminating one operation or for initiating the subsequent one is given only when the required and actual values coincide within predetermined limits. Numerical control may concern either longitudinal, vertical, transverse, or rotational movements for setting purposes (position control) or interrelated simultaneous feed movements for profiling operations (continuous path control).

The latest step in this development, known as 'adaptive' control, checks and adjusts the cutting conditions to suit the prevailing requirements of the material, surface finish, etc., thus providing real automation in the sense that it fully replaces the thinking human operator. All this has become possible by achievements made not only in production engineering but in such fields as optics (precision measurement); electronics (data transmission and processing especially by means of computers); electrical engineering and hydraulics (power supply); and the science of communication and control (cybernetics).

In the developments that took place during the first half of the twentieth century the application of mechanization and automation was not limited to single machines. The supply of materials by means of hoppers or conveyors, and the transfer of workpieces from one machine tool to the next in 'link lines' or 'transfer lines' are typical examples of wider applications.

The degree of mechanization appropriate for various applications depends upon the variety and quantity of the product. Transfer lines and special-purpose machine tools are used, for example, in the mass production of motor-cars, while link lines between standard universal machines can also be used in the manufacture of medium-size batches.

Quality of production. The importance of interchangeability to the efficiency and the economics of assembly operations had long been recognized and its achievement in mass production admired (Vol. IV, p. 438). The misconception that mass production means lack of quality and precision was disproved over and over again during the Second World War when the component quality required for the mass production of sophisticated war equipment operators carried out their work without losing time by having to move around.

While systematically planned and organized production became more or less general practice during the first half of the twentieth century, the great benefits which Henry Ford and other manufacturers obtained were applicable mainly to mass, or at least large-scale, production. This was because the initial cost of installing the necessary specialized equipment, as well as that of planning and production control, was usually so high as to be economically viable only with very large production runs. However, the increase in the demand for specialized products, and limited-life consumer goods, after the Second World War resulted in a need for small-quantity or batch manufacturing methods, which at the same time enjoyed the economic benefits of large-scale production.

The manufacture of workpiece 'groups' described before the Second World War [11, 12] seemed to be an answer to the problem. However, it was only in 1956 [13] that a scientific approach to 'Group Technology' was established. As a result of several investigations based on workpiece statistics, published in the 1960s, the concept of Group Technology meant originally that the effective size of a batch—and therefore the economic efficiency with which it could be produced—could be increased by grouping together workpieces that were similar in size, shape, or method of manufacture.

It was soon found that the idea of grouping together merely components had only limited advantages, and that the group idea had to embrace not only workpieces but also machines and operators. This led to the application of the 'cellular' concept of manufacture, in which the cells became self-contained units as far as administration, planning, and operation were concerned.

Progress in the technological and organizational fields had considerably increased the economic efficiency of production. After the Second World War it became apparent, however, that this was counteracted by losses in human efficiency on the shop floor. As the activity of the operator became a sequence of more or less mechanical actions, the turnover of labour in many factories grew because men and women whose intellectual capacity was not sufficiently utilized left their jobs and sought more interesting work. This made it necessary to train a succession of new workers, with a resulting loss in labour efficiency and productivity.

In a chapter on 'Human relations in the workshop' [14] published in 1950 A. Roberts wrote:

Industry cannot expect individuals to be one thing in their general lives and something else immediately they have entered the gates of a works. They bring their sense of necessitated high degrees of manufacturing accuracy. The development of the means for very accurate measurement and quality control was essential to enable inspectors to decide whether the manufactured parts satisfied the specified accuracy requirements. The progress in mechanization and automation had ensured that relatively good consistency of working quality had been obtainable with single-purpose machine tools; with mechanized 'automatic' lathes; and with similar machines working in mass production or on very large batches. Numerical control in automation ensured the same, if not a greater, consistency even for small and medium batch production.

III. UTILIZATION OF PLANT, EQUIPMENT, AND MANPOWER

The full benefits of the technological progress achieved were obtained only through the use of scientific, organizational, and managerial methods. Economic success in production can be obtained if the production activities are carried out with a minimum of human effort and if the raw material cost and investment in buildings, plant, and equipment are also kept as low as possible. This was the basic philosophy of the Taylor-System [1] which aims at an optimum utilization of men and machines in the factory. For this purpose Taylor departed from the practice of giving to an operator a certain task and allowing him to decide how best to carry it out. The production engineer, representing the management, had to determine the time in which the job could be carried out efficiently and the operàtor was offered a financial incentive if he achieved at least the predetermined speed. This concept of the time-study was supplemented by Frank B. Gilbreth's motion-study [10], a detailed analysis—by descriptive or visual means (ciné-photography)—of every element of activity that contributed to the performance of a certain task. On the basis of such an analysis, it was possible to determine those sequences of movements of head, body, arm, hand, leg, or foot—as well as optimum workplace lay-outs and tool arrangements—which would result in the work in question being carried out with minimum effort in the shortest possible time.

One of the first industrialists to convert Taylor's ideas into outstandingly successful practice was Henry Ford. At the beginning of the century he not only shortened individual operating times to a minimum but he also reduced overall production times by arranging machine tools and special-purpose machines in accordance with the sequences of operations needed for producing his workpieces (flow lines) and by transporting the workpieces from one machine to the next on conveyors. He applied the same principles to assembly operations by conveying the component parts to assembly points where perspective, their emotions, hopes and fears with them. Above all they want to feel that they belong to the undertaking, that that undertaking and their places in it have the respect of other men, and that their own contribution is going to be effective.

In flow production—as encountered, for example, in the motor industry—the man in the workshop has to carry out the same operation day-in day-out as the work is delivered to his work station. In cellular production not only physical but the intellectual contribution of each worker is of importance. In other words, the cellular concept is not only technologically and economically effective but it also replaces a boring and uninteresting activity by one in which responsibility for and within the group plays an important part. This in turn leads to greater 'job satisfaction' which for many—though not all—is of greater importance than a purely monetary recognition.

The fact that the efficiency of human operators cannot be assessed in the same manner as that of machines was recognized by W. Moede, who started work in the field of industrial psychology during the First World War [15]. Just as Gilbreth and his successors studied the physical conditions of man, his workplace, and his work, the industrial psychologist looked at intellectual and emotional attitudes, at aptitudes—especially their changes with environment and age—and at physiological problems, many of which are today studied under the heading of 'ergonomics'. The results gave managers a basis for selecting workers best suited for specific jobs and vice versa, as well as for creating those environmental conditions which enhance productivity.

REFERENCES

[1] TAYLOR, F. W. *The principles of scientific management*. Harper, New York (1916).

[2] TAYLOR, F. W. On the art of cutting metals. *Transactions of the American Society of Mechanical Engineers*, **28**, 31 (1907).

[3] RUIZ, C., and KOENIGSBERGER, F. *Design for strength and production*. Macmillan, London (1970).

[4] SCHLESINGER, G. Lecture to the V.D.I. Cologne, 8 April 1914.

[5] MERCHANT, M. E. *Trends in machining technology and machine tools*. International Congress for Metalworking. Hanover, September (1970).

[6] SCHLESINGER, G. *Prüfbuch für Werkzeugmaschinen*. (Testing machine tools.) Springer, Berlin (1927).

[7] SALMON, P. *Machine-outils. Réception, vérification*. (Machine tools. Acceptance, testing.) Editions Henri François, Paris (1937).

[8] WHITWORTH, J. A Uniform System of Screw Threads. Paper read at the Institution of Civil Engineers (1841).

[9] WHITWORTH, J. Address to the Institution of Mechanical Engineers, delivered at Glasgow (1856).

[10] GILBRETH, F. B. *Motion study*. Constable, London (1911).

[11] FLANDERS, R. E. Design, manufacture and production control of a standard machine. *Transactions of the American Society of Mechanical Engineers*, **46**, 691 (1924).

[12] KERR, J. C. *Planning in a general engineering shop. Journal of the Institution of Production Engineers, 18*, No. 1 (1939).

[13] MITROFANOV, S. P. *The scientific principles of group technology.* Leningrad (1956).

[14] BAKER, H. WRIGHT (ed.) *Modern workshop technology.* Part II. Cleaver-Hume Press, London (1950).

[15] MOEDE, W. *Lehrbuch der Psychotechnik.* (Textbook on industrial psychology.) Springer, Berlin (1930).

BIBLIOGRAPHY

GILBERT, K. R. *The machine tool collection* (*Science Museum*). H.M. S.O., London (1966).

ROLT, L. T. C. *Tools for the job*, Batsford, London (1965).

STEEDS, W. *A history of machine tools.* Oxford University Press, London (1969).

WITTMANN, K. *Die Entwicklung der Drehbank bis zum Jahre 1939.* (The development of the centre lathe up to 1939.) VDI-Verlag, Düsseldorf (1960).

WOODBURY, R. S. *Studies in the history of machine tools* (History of the Gear Cutting Machine; History of the Grinding Machine; History of the Milling Machine; History of the Lathe to 1850.) MIT Press, Cambridge, Mass. (1972).

ACKNOWLEDGMENT. The author would like to acknowledge the valuable assistance given to him by Mr. G. Catterall of the North Western Museum of Science and Industry.

44

FLUID POWER

LORD WILSON OF HIGH WRAY

s for water turbines (Ch. 9), the general principles of the centrifugal pump had been established by 1900, but the size, capacity, and—almost more—the wide variety of uses found for these pumps increased many hundredfold. They became amongst the most widely used machines in the world. Water-cooled motor-car engines, washing machines, and central heating systems use small pumps, with impellers perhaps only 50 mm in diameter, while large irrigation and power-station cooling water pumps may have inlet and outlet branches 3 m in diameter. Many areas in arid countries can be irrigated only by centrifugal pumps drawing from streams, springs, and boreholes, and in every sea-going ship, oil refinery, and chemical process plant pump maintenance is one of the main jobs of the engineering staff.

High-pressure boiler feed pumps can absorb so much power that they are driven by individual steam turbines, and 75-MW electric motors were specified for the pumps for the Blaenau Ffestiniog pumped storage scheme in Wales (p. 213).

I. POSITIVE, SELF-PRIMING, AND JET PUMPS

Reciprocating pumps. These have changed little in principle since Roman times. They were used extensively during the Industrial Revolution for boiler feed pumps; mine de-watering; domestic and public water supply; chemical and marine duties; and fire-fighting. They remain sturdy and reliable, and are still used for small boiler-feed pumps and certain specialized duties. One of their disadvantages is that the piston speed must be limited, and, unless very well designed, they suffer from rapid valve wear if driven too fast or against very high pressures.

High-pressure positive pumps. Fluid pressure systems can be dealt with briefly. They depend upon high-pressure pumps which enable a great force to be transmitted over a distance, though probably only for short periods of time. John and Frank Towler of Leeds did much work on the design and production of high-pressure pumps running at prime-mover speeds, and discharge pressures of over 100 kg/cm² were becoming usual for hydraulic presses during the 1930s.

H. S. Hele-Shaw and T. E. Beacham, beginning shortly before the First World War worked on a new principle, the swash-plate pump. The pump shaft drives a swash-plate, a collar which can be tilted relative to the shaft centre line at any angle from 90° to about 60° while the pump is running. From six to eight cylinders, coaxial with the shaft, contain a single-acting piston with a rigid piston rod, the end of which rests on the swash-plate. When the swash-plate is normal (perpendicular) to the shaft the pistons remain stationary, but as it is tilted the pistons at one side move inwards, discharging the fluid pumped, an oil which must have excellent lubricating properties, while those opposite move inwards, refilling the cylinder. This made available to industry a constant-speed pump with an infinitely variable delivery, absorbing little power when it was not pumping but capable of going to full discharge in a matter of seconds.

Other and cheaper designs of variable discharge pumps soon came on to the market, and provide the motive power for use with the hydraulic systems below.

Self-priming pumps. The centrifugal pump suffers from the following disadvantages:

(i) It must be filled with water[1] before it will start to pump.
(ii) It will air-lock if a substantial volume of air (or other vapour) is drawn in, and will stop pumping.
(iii) The discharge falls off rapidly if the speed drops, and it will stop pumping if the speed falls too low.

Nearly all self-priming pumps are of the side-channel or water-ring design. They work on the principle that if water can be flung to the outside of the pump casing or side-channel, a ring of air will form nearer the shaft, since water is heavier than air. The impeller comprises a disc with a number of vanes, the object of which is to 'drag' the water round; for about a quarter of the circumference the side-channel fades out, and the water is forced towards the pump centre-line down the space between the vanes. The inlet and outlet ports are near the centre (such pumps are sometimes termed centripetal as

---

[1] For convenience, the terms 'water' and 'air' embrace any fluids to be pumped together with their vapour. The problems under (i) and (ii) increase greatly when pumping hot water or volatile liquids.

opposed to centrifugal for this reason); as the impeller rotates air is forced out of the discharge and sucked into the inlet until the suction pipe is filled with water and the pump starts to deliver.

These pumps have many of the characteristics of a positive pump, since the water flowing up and down the impeller vanes gives almost a multiple piston action. There is no contact between the impeller and the casing, but clearances must be fine. Pumps of this type are most valuable as marine-engine cooling water pumps because they will handle considerable volumes of air, often drawn in when a small ship is rolling, and will operate satisfactorily over a wide range of engine speeds.

In sizes over about 100 mm inlet and discharges, the lower efficiency and larger size of these pumps tends to leave them at a disadvantage as compared with centrifugal pumps.

Eccentric helical rotor (EHR) pumps. This dseign was produced during the early 1930s. The rotor, usually made of a suitable synthetic material, is moulded in the form of a screw with a very long pitch. It is driven by a shaft through a universal joint, and rotates within a stator in which a similar 'screw thread' is turned. There is line contact between the rotor and the stator, and the pumping action is obtained by squeezing the fluid pumped along the helical passage formed as the pump rotates.

Such pumps are mainly used for pumping liquid foodstuffs such as jam, milk, and edible oil products, where the 'squeezing' action of the pump does not cause the fluid to disintegrate as it may when passed through a centrifugal pump.

Jet pumps. Jet pumps work on the same principle as the steam injector used to supply feed water to steam locomotives, but they are operated by water under a high pressure. This water is discharged through a fine jet into a chamber followed by a long, slowly divergent cone. The energy of the water is converted to velocity, and this enables water to be drawn into the ejector at the point of minimum pressure; a proportion of the inlet pressure is recovered in the divergent cone. The ejector can be used to suck water from a sump, and discharge it at or about atmospheric pressure, or, if it is placed at the bottom of a borehole, water will be entrained and delivered to the surface.

For sump clearance the ejector has the great advantage that it can deal with a proportion of dirt and solids. Many are used for bilge pumping in fishing vessels; as only clean sea-water passes through the ejector nozzle liquid muck can be sucked out of the bilge sump. For borehole pumping, usually for small domestic supplies with lifts below 30 m, the system is very inefficient, but the plant is cheap and all moving parts of the pump and motor are above ground level. When only a few hundred litres per day are required the cost of electricity for pumping is low.

II. HYDRAULIC SYSTEMS

The great change in the use of fluid power in hydraulic systems since 1900 makes it impossible to give more than a very brief sketch of the developments that have taken place. The principle of transmitting hydraulic power from central pumping stations to operate lifts, cranes, winches, lock gates, swing-bridges, etc. was well established by the end of the nineteenth century, and in large cities—particularly if they were ports—hydraulic power companies were still operating profitably in 1950. However, from about 1920 onwards the trend was towards individual self-contained systems, because the chief applications were in ships, aeroplanes, motor-cars, and tractors where each unit required its own hydraulic pump, cylinder, etc.

The Constantinesco interrupter gear. George Constantinesco came to Britain from Romania, and made a mathematical study of hydraulic transmission. During the First World War, there was a rapid development of aerial combat, and a machine gun could at first be fired only by the observer using a swivel-ling gun-mounting from his cockpit. He could fire to port, starboard, or astern, but not ahead because he would hit the propeller. (Twin-engined fighter planes had not then been built.) Constantinesco designed a hydraulic 'interrupter gear' whereby a machine gun could be mounted over the engine pointing dead ahead; when the pilot pressed the trigger, with the enemy air-craft in his sights, the gun would fire only between the propeller blades.

Gun-turret training and marine steering gear. As the size and weight of the gun turrets of warships rapidly increased, the problem of accurately training a turret weighing hundreds of tons, and holding it on a bearing within minutes of a degree, taxed marine engineers to the limit. The only answer was hydraulic operation, using a swash-plate pump which automatically locked the system when the turret had moved to the correct angle. Gun elevating was also performed hydraulically, but as only the gun barrels had to be moved, and they were counterbalanced, the forces involved were very much less.

The problem of steering big ships was similar. Steam steering engines had long been in use, but the use of steam for auxiliary purposes was steadily discouraged, particularly for naval vessels in which long runs of pressure steam and condensate piping presented problems because they could bring about disaster if fractured in action.

Great force is required to turn the rudder of, say, an aircraft carrier weighing over 20000 tonnes through 30° when the ship is travelling at, say 32 knots. The arrangement adopted in British Naval capital ships built during the 1930s was to use four large hydraulic rams, coupled in pairs fore and aft, which were connected to a crosshead on the rudder stock. Swash-plate pumps provided the motive power, and operation from the bridge, conning tower, or an emergency steering position—distances which could be well over 100 m through many bulkheads and decks—was by hydraulic servomechanisms. Provided the rudder and its operating gear were not badly damaged, and an electricity supply to the pumps could be maintained, the ship could still be steered after suffering severe damage elsewhere.

Aircraft applications. As aircraft speeds increased it was essential to reduce air resistance by streamlining, and as the monoplane with self-supporting wings replaced the biplane with its struts and wires, the undercarriage presented the greatest difficulty. In 1933 N. S. Norway was working on a hydraulically retractible undercarriage which could be folded into the body of the aircraft. The equipment, calling for a very high degree of accuracy and finish, had to be hand made, but soon George Dowty started to make standard hydraulic components, and established the vitally important business which bears his name.

With military aircraft, as with warships, the increase in size and complexity called for more power to operate ailerons, landing flaps, bomb hatch doors, etc., and complete hydraulic remote control was introduced. Even when the operating forces required were comparatively small, the hydraulic pipe was a much more convenient method of transmitting power than complicated runs of wire that called for continual inspection because of the danger of stretching and chafing.

Motor-cars. Possibly influenced by the use of hydraulic controls in aircraft, the motor industry turned from brake operation by bowden cable to hydraulic servomotors. Here the foot and leg muscles of the driver move a piston in the master cylinder and the hydraulic pressure is transmitted to cylinders and pistons connected to the brake shoes. With the general introduction of four-wheel brakes, hydraulic operation had the advantage that the correct pressure could automatically be applied to the front and rear brakes, and did not rely upon the accurate tensioning of wires.

Agriculture and civil engineering. The average man has little idea of the wide influence of hydraulic systems; he is vaguely conscious only of the fact that his car has hydraulic brakes, and that aeroplanes tuck their wheels into their bellies by some hydraulic contraption. It was largely due to the activities of the British industrialist Harry Ferguson that hydraulic systems became of major consequence in everyday life.

As early as 1923 Ferguson had the basic concept of the three-point linkage for mounting implements on agricultural tractors, and saw that their control must be by oil hydraulic servo-mechanism, using a high-pressure oil pump driven from the engine that could be connected at will. The required tool, such as a plough or harrow, can quickly be bolted on, and then set in the correct position by the hydraulic control.

The Ferguson and other similar types of tractor revolutionized farming, greatly increasing productivity and cutting down manpower. In the agricultural areas of most countries the traveller will see farm tractors at work or ready for work in the fields. The farmer must know as much about the mechanical defects of his tractors as about the physical defects of his cattle and sheep.

One remarkable feature of the hydraulic system in its agrciultural applications is its reliability under very difficult conditions. It is reasonable to expect that the delicate hydraulic equipment on a machine tool in a well-kept workshop will be carefully looked after, but the tractor spends most of its life out of doors in all weathers; the working parts become covered in mud and dust; hoses are coupled and uncoupled under similar conditions; and still the equipment works. This is a real tribute to Ferguson and those who followed him.

Since 1945 there has been a steady trend for hydraulic operation of civil engineering equipment to supersede electric drive (through a series of motors) or mechanical drive (by gearboxes and clutches). This is happening on large earth-moving equipment for dams and road construction, trench-diggers, bulldozers, and the gantries carrying pneumatic drills which have so greatly speeded up the excavation of tunnels and underground power stations (Ch. 36).

The hydraulic coupling or 'fluid flywheel'. Although the hydraulic coupling is different from the hydraulic systems described above, it should be included in this chapter. It bears some relationship to the water-ring self-priming pump, in that it depends upon the 'drag' between two rotating elements which are very much akin to the impeller of these pumps.

The purpose of the hydraulic coupling is to transmit power from the driving to the driven element in a machine with the maximum efficiency and the minimum of shock. Its place in the general field of appliances used for transmitting power from one rotating shaft to another may become clearer if the alternatives are considered:

(1) *Rigid flanged or gear type.* A permament connection broken only for dismantling.
(2) *As* (1) *but with spacing plate.* The pins and spacing plate can be removed to allow either element to rotate.
(3) *Pin type, 'flexible'.* As for (1), but space between the faces allows freedom as with (2) when pins are removed.
(4) *Dog clutch.* Each flange has four projecting 'dogs' with identical spaces between. One half is keyed to shaft, other is free to slide on a key, and can be moved to engage its dogs with the opposing spaces. Engaged only when both elements are stationary.
(5) *Multiple disc clutch.* As (4), but the dogs are replaced by spring-loaded plates covered with high-friction material as in the normal motor-car clutch. Can be engaged when one element is stationary and the other revolving. Power transmission is limited.
(6) *Hydraulic coupling.* Described below.

The coupling is often described as a pump driving a turbine, and though in basic hydraulic terms this is correct, it can be confusing. The driving and driven halves of the coupling are similar. Each comprises a shrouded disc, with a number of radial vanes which are inclined at an angle and face in opposite directions. They are not unlike half the blades of the low-pressure steam turbine, one set fixed and the other moving, blocked by a diaphragm midway between inlet and outlet. The unit is fixed in an oil-tight casing, and a small space separates the two elements.

In its simplest form, designed only to transmit power at the same speed between each element, there is no transfer of power when the casing is empty. To engage the coupling, the casing is filled with oil, and the force of the oil driven by the 'pump' to the 'turbine' causes the latter to start rotating until it is moving at approximately the same speed as the pump. Inevitably, as with a squirrel-cage motor, there must be some slip. As with a motor, the amount of slip will be only slight at low loads, and a maximum at full load. This represents a loss of power and efficiency, and cooling must be provided.

When hydraulic couplings are used for tractor purposes in motor-cars, diesel locomotives, etc., a wider space separates the turbine and pump; the casing remains filled with oil; and a movable shroud surrounds them. When the shroud is withdrawn the oil is flung outwards from the pump, and there is only a small force tending to drive the turbine. As the shroud is moved to cover the gap, the oil is contained, and pressure builds up to drive the turbine.

The hydraulic coupling can transmit very large powers, gives smooth starting, and cannot 'burn out'. In 1935, hydraulic couplings capable of transmitting 36000 hp were made for transmitting power between turbines and storage pumps at the Iterdecke hydro-electric plant. However for low powers, such as the motor-car, it is more expensive and less efficient than the multiple-disc clutch.

45

THE GENERATION, DISTRIBUTION, AND UTILIZATION OF ELECTRICITY

BRIAN BOWERS

I. POWER STATIONS, TURBINES, AND GENERATORS

THE pride of the British power station industry at the beginning of the twentieth century was the great Neptune Bank station in Newcastle upon Tyne, opened by Lord Kelvin on 18 June 1901. Neptune Bank had an installed capacity of 2100 kW and generated three-phase alternating current. The consulting engineer responsible for the station was Charles Merz of the partnership of Merz and McLellan which was to play a major role in the development of electricity supply in Britain and in several countries abroad.

Having decided that Neptune Bank was to be an a.c. station, Merz had to select the frequency of operation. He chose 40 Hz. An existing, smaller station in Newcastle generated at 100 Hz but that was rather too high for the satisfactory operation of induction motors. In the Clyde area of Scotland and in Birmingham a frequency of 25 Hz had been adopted, but that gave rise to a noticeable flicker on incandescent lamps. The choice of 40 Hz cannot be criticized, but it was unfortunate. Undertakings in the U.S.A. eventually adopted 60 Hz and the Germans 50 Hz. Most British undertakings followed the German practice so that 50 Hz eventually became the standard frequency in Britain, and indeed in most of Europe. The transmission voltage was 5500 V, which Merz considered was the highest advisable, although Sebastian de Ferranti had successfully used 10000 V transmission from Deptford into London (Vol. V, p. 199).

The first prime movers at Neptune Bank were four-cylinder slow-speed marine reciprocating engines directly coupled to the generators. Part of the reason for choosing such engines was that the company was anxious to develop an industrial load. They knew that the industrialists of Newcastle, mainly shipbuilders, would be more willing to believe in the reliability of the supply from the new station if the prime movers were the kind of machines they used themselves. Before the end of 1901, however, Merz was planning to enlarge the station and use a different kind of prime mover.

The invention which brought about the biggest change in the early electricity supply industry was not electrical but mechanical. The steam turbine is largely due to the genius of one man, Charles A. Parsons. He studied mathematics at Dublin and Cambridge, but his interest was in engineering and on leaving college he took an engineering apprenticeship and then became a partner with Clarke, Chapman and Co. of Gateshead. There he turned his attention to the steam turbine and made his first successful turbo-generator in 1884. That machine generated 75 A at 100 V d.c., running at 18 000 rev/min. It is now in the Science Museum, London.

The principle of producing power by steam issuing from a jet was not new. Parsons' achievement was in using his mathematical ability to solve the mechanical problems of shafts rotating at very high speeds and the problem of distributing the steam-pressure drop along the length of the machine.

In 1889 the partnership was dissolved and Parsons found he could no longer use the axial flow turbine because his patents then belonged to his former partners; he quickly developed instead the radial flow turbine. He formed a new firm, C. A. Parsons and Co. of Newcastle upon Tyne, and developed generators to work with his turbines. He soon obtained contracts to supply turbo-generators for three power stations. The first was at Cambridge, where he installed three 100-kW sets running at 4800 rev/min and generating single-phase a.c. at 2000 V and 80 Hz. These sets were mounted on rubber blocks, not bolted rigidly to the foundations. The quiet, vibration-free running which resulted attracted further contracts in built-up areas where residents objected to the noise and vibration of reciprocating engines. The second installation was at Scarborough. The machines were similar to those at Cambridge but a little larger, being rated at 120 kW. The third installation was of 150-kW, 50-Hz sets at Portsmouth in 1894.

In 1900 Parsons supplied two single-phase 1500-kW turbo-generator sets to Elberfeld, Germany. These were then by far the largest generators installed anywhere in the world, and they gave an impressive demonstration of the economies of large turbines: the Cambridge turbo-generators required 12·7 kg of steam per kilowatt-hour (kWh) generated, but the Elberfeld set required only 8·3 kg. The world demand for turbines was beyond the capacity of the Parsons works in Newcastle. The Swiss engineering firm of Brown Boveri acquired the European rights, and the American Westinghouse Company acquired the rights there. The further development of the steam turbine in the twentieth century is discussed elsewhere (Ch. 41).

The choice of the prime mover in a generating station imposes some constraints on the designer of the generator itself. Except for hydro-electric stations, every power station utilizes the power of steam. The fuel which heats the boiler is of little interest to the electrical engineer but the choice of the prime mover itself is of great importance because its speed determines the speed of rotation of the generator. It is true that in some early power stations the generators were belt-driven, and the drive speed could be chosen at will, but belt drives were satisfactory only for low powers. The development in the 1880s of the central-valve reciprocating steam engine by P. W. Willans was a step forward because it ran at a higher speed than conventional steam engines and a generator could be directly coupled to it. Before the advent of turbines the Willans engine (Vol. V, p. 135) had become almost universal in power stations.

For an a.c. generator the speed of rotation, the number of pairs of poles on the field magnet, and the frequency of the current generated are linked by the formula:

$$\text{Speed of rotation} = \text{Number of pairs of poles} \times \text{Frequency}.$$

The Willans engine could run at up to 500 rev/min, so that to generate at 50 Hz the generator needed six pairs of poles. The steam turbine operates at a much higher speed. The minimum number of poles for a generator is obviously two. For a 50-Hz supply this corresponds to a speed of rotation of 3000 rev/min. Steam turbo-generators in Britain and Europe are therefore designed at operate at 3000 rev/min, although a few early sets ran at 1500 rev/min. In the U.S.A., where a supply frequency of 60 Hz is usual, the machines are designed to run at 3600 rev/min.

Early generators all had the armature windings, in which the current was generated, rotating and the field magnet fixed. Brushes and slip rings were used to take the current from the rotating armature, but as larger machines were made the current-collecting arrangements proved a limiting factor. The solution was to 'invert' the machine, having the field magnets on the rotor and the armature windings on the stator. The brush-gear then has to carry only the magnetizing current for the field windings. The last large rotating-armature turbo-generator was a 1500-kW three-phase machine ordered late in 1901 to expand the Neptune Bank station. This machine had at least two other distinctions. It was the first three-phase turbine set installed for public electricity supply, though a 150-kW turbo-generator set had been supplied to Ackton Hall Colliery in Yorkshire in 1900. In 1904 the Cunard Company sent a committee to Neptune Bank to inspect the steam plant because it was the only power station in Britain with reciprocating engines and turbines working side by side. As a result of this visit, the Cunard Company adopted turbines for two new passenger liners, the *Lusitania* and the *Mauretania*.

The first rotating field generators had 'salient' poles built up on the rotor shaft. Charles Brown of Brown Boveri suggested that the field windings should be carried in slots milled in the surface of the rotor, which should be a single casting. Since the speed of rotation is fixed, the upper limit to the diameter of the rotor is determined by consideration of centrifugal forces. Brown's design led to a much stronger construction which has been adopted ever since.

Since 1903 the history of power-station development has been one of improvements in details and increases in size rather than radical changes in principles. The Carville station opened in Newcastle in 1904 had two turbo-generators designed to yield 3500 kW each, though on test it was found that they could give 6000 kW. Carville was the first station in Britain to follow the practice already established in America of having a 'system control room' with a diagram on the wall showing generators, substations, and the state of all switches in the system, with a control engineer in overall charge of the whole system. Carville used 2 kg of coal for each unit (kilowatt-hour) of electricity generated. The North Tees power station at Middlesbrough, planned during the First World War and opened just afterwards, had 20000-kW machines and consumed just under 1 kg of coal per unit generated. The steam temperature at North Tees was 370 °C. The 'B' station at Dunston opened in 1930 operated at 427 °C and required only 0·6 kg of coal per unit. The 50000-kW sets at Dunston were the largest and most efficient in Britain and generated directly at 33 kV, so avoiding the need for a transformer with each generator. The 105000-kW set installed at Battersea Power Station, London, in 1933 was for some years the largest in Europe (Fig. 45.1).

This brief summary of power-station progress can conveniently end with Blyth Power Station, only 20 km from Neptune Bank but opened 57 years later in 1958. Its four 120000-kW turbo-generators were the first of that size in Britain. The steam temperature at Blyth was 538 °C, and by that date power station efficiency had increased so that one kilowatt hour could be generated for each pound (0·454 kg) of coal consumed.

Hydro-electric power (Ch. 9) has never been very significant for electricity supply in Britain, although from its beginning the industry has had a number of small hydro stations. These have mainly been in the mountainous areas in the north of Scotland and in Wales, although there have been some

FIG. 45.1. Part of the turbine hall of Battersea A power station in 1933. Once known as the cathedral of power, Battersea A had two 69-MW generators and one of 105 MW which for many years was the largest in Europe. The station closed in 1975.

in England. In 1918 the Board of Trade appointed a Water Power Resources Committee to study the hydro power available throughout the British Empire. Their final report in 1921 concluded that Britain itself had only 210 MW of water power available which could be developed at a worthwhile cost; but other parts of the Empire, especially Canada and India, had enormous water resources. Compared with the U.S.A. and the rest of Europe the British lagged far behind in this field. In 1943 the North of Scotland Hydro-Electric Board was created to exploit the water-power resources of the Highlands of Scotland. It was responsible for most of the 200 MW of hydro-electric generating capacity in Britain in 1951; by 1972 it had 54 main hydro-electric stations with a total capacity of 1052 MW. The Board also operates a number of 'pumped storage' schemes. The first, at Sron Mor, was commissioned in 1957. In a pumped storage system electricity is used at off-peak times, when the marginal cost of generation is low, to pump water from a lower to a higher reservoir. At peak times, when additional generating capacity is desirable, the water flow is reversed and the plant operates as a hydro-electric generating station. The Sron Mor pumped storage plant had a capacity of only 5 MW, but the Ffestiniog pumped storage station in North Wales, opened in 1961, had a capacity of 300 MW initially and was subsequently uprated to 360 MW.

II. CABLES AND TRANSMISSION LINES

Early cables. From the beginning, the electricity supply industry needed cables and transmission lines to convey its product to its users. As might be expected, those manufacturers who had been supplying telegraph cables took up the manufacture of power cables. They knew that copper was the best metal to use for the conductor and that it should be stranded to give increased flexibility. Vulcanized rubber and gutta percha were the established insulating materials for telegraph cables, but they proved less satisfactory for heavily loaded power cables because they softened when the cable became warm, and the core tended to 'flow' downwards under its own weight. Many insulating materials were tried out for power cables at the end of the nineteenth century. The most successful was vulcanized bitumen (VB).

W. O. Callender, a manufacturer of road-surfacing material, had the idea that the bitumen he imported from Trinidad might provide the basis of a material for insulating cables. His son William, a chemist, carried out a series of trials that led to VB. The name is a little misleading since less than half the material is actually bitumen. VB was patented, and in 1882 the Callender Bitumen Telegraph and Waterproof Company was established at Erith, Kent. VB cable quickly became very popular in many countries, and Callenders established a factory in America as well. VB cables proved reliable, at least for low voltages.

In most countries, underground cables were much preferred to overhead wires, both on aesthetic grounds and for safety. British and European engineers usually preferred to bury their cables directly in the ground, while in the U.S.A. the use of conduits was preferred. Callenders developed an intermediate system in which VB cables were laid in an iron trough and the trough was then filled with bitumen. 'Callender's solid system', as it was called, gave the cable excellent mechanical protection, and there were many variations, such as using wooden or earthenware troughs rather than iron to save cost.

Another important insulating material for cables was jute impregnated with oil or resin. Such cables operated satisfactorily at higher voltages than were possible with VB, but the upper limit was only about 2500 V. Above that voltage the only possible insulation was vulcanized india rubber, until S. Z. de Ferranti introduced paper insulation.

The earliest cables were either single-core, with two cables laid together, or two-core with the cores running side by side in a single sheath. With the development of a.c. supplies and the increase of telephone services induction in telephone wires became a problem. An American engineer, R. S. Waring of Pittsburgh, developed 'anti-induction' cable, with concentric conductors. From 1887 such cables were made in Britain by the Fowler-Waring Company.

Conduit systems. Although most early electric power distribution was by cable there were important exceptions where bare conductors were used, supported on suitable insulators. The most important was probably Crompton's system in which copper strips were stretched across glass or porcelain insulators in a duct, usually under the pavement. The Crompton system was simple and reliable. It could be uprated by laying additional copper strips on top. Service cables to individual consumers were clamped on to the strips. Its disadvantage was that the insulator resistance was low because the insulators became dirty and the ducts were liable to become flooded. Nevertheless, Crompton copper-strip mains remained in use in London and Brighton into the 1960s. Similar systems were installed by other British engineers and were also used extensively in Paris.

Paper insulation. When S. Z. de Ferranti became engineer of the Grosvenor Gallery Company in London in 1886 (Vol. 5, Ch. 9) he took over a distribution system using rubber insulated cables working at 2400 V. When he conceived his scheme for a large power station at Deptford transmitting at 10 000 V into central London he experimented with both rubber and jute insulation. Neither was satisfactory. The rubber had too high a permittivity, so that the cable took an excessive charging current; the jute tended to catch fire. He designed a main of his own, the 'Ferranti tubular main'. This was not a cable because it was not flexible. It consisted of concentric copper tubes, separated by layers of paper impregnated with ozokerite wax, a by-product of candle manufacture (Fig. 45.2). It was a complete success.

Paper insulation had been used before. The Norwich Wire Company had been founded in the U.S.A. in 1884 to make both telegraph and electric lighting cables insulated by a helically wound paper tape. J. B. Atherton visited America in 1889, saw the Norwich Wire Company's products, and obtained the British rights. On his return to England he formed the British

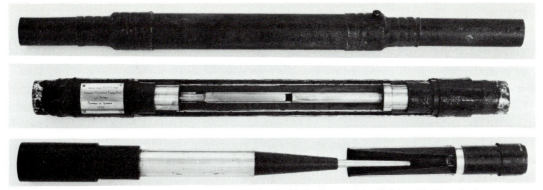

FIG. 45.2. Joints from the 10000-volt cable made by S. Z. de Ferranti for linking his Deptford generating station to central London: from top to bottom, a complete joint; a sectioned joint; and a partly sectioned demonstration joint used in training jointers. The demonstration joint shows how the ends were coned to mate accurately. The cable was the first in the world to operate satisfactorily at 10 kV.

Insulated Wire Company to manufacture paper-insulated cables, and Ferranti was invited to join the board of the new company.

Ferranti designed a flexible cable similar to his tubular main. The inner conductor was a stranded copper wire and the outer conductor was flat strips of copper arranged in a circle. Fifteen miles of this cable were supplied to the London Electric Supply Corporation in 1896.

For cables with parallel (rather than concentric) cores Ferranti pointed out the advantages of non-circular cores with a uniform thickness of insulation. Cables such as his 'clover-leaf' cable require less insulating material and are therefore smaller and cheaper than they would be if the cores were circular.

Polyphase cables and higher voltages. With three-phase cables it was recognized from the start that if each core was provided with adequate insulation for the voltage between that core and earth then the insulation between cores would be excessive. A construction was adopted in which the three cores carried only enough insulation to withstand the voltage between cores. When the three cores had been laid up together a 'belt' of insulation was put round the whole assembly to bring the core-to-earth insulation up to an adequate thickness. Such 'belted' cable became standard practice for voltages up to 33 kV.

After the First World War the power companies demanded higher-voltage cables, and manufacturers produced belted cables rated at 66 kV and designed to have the same electric stresses as the successful 33-kV ones. It soon became clear that something was wrong with the new cables, which suffered a number of breakdowns, but the cause was not at first apparent. Analysis of the electric field pattern in a three-core cable showed that the belt was carrying a component of electric stress parallel to the layers of paper, and since paper is electrically stronger through its thickness than along its surface that was at first thought to be the cause. Further research showed, however, that this was only a secondary factor. The primary cause was that in large, heavily loaded cables the cores expanded when they got warm. As they cooled and shrank spaces would be left in the insulation and, at the voltages being used, discharges would occur in the spaces and burn the insulation. Trouble arose when the maximum stress in the insulation reached about 4 kV/mm.

The solution to the problem of the 66-kV cables was to provide an earthed screen of metal or metallized paper around each core, so that the entire electric stress was borne by a homogeneous insulation. The economic advantage of belted construction had to be given up. From 1928 onwards 'screened' or 'H-type' (after the inventor Martin Hochstadter) construction was used for all cables of 33 kV and above.

Oil-filled and gas-filled cables. For even higher voltages and powers it was necessary to avoid the creation of voids in the insulation as the core expanded and contracted. In 1930 the Callender Company introduced a cable with an oval conductor. The idea was that as the cable got hot the core would change into a more nearly circular form but the cable sheath would not be stretched; on cooling the cable sheath should return to its original form, without voids forming. The real solution, however, was the oil-filled cable (Fig. 45.3), originally developed in 1920 by Luigi Emanueli, chief engineer of the Italian Pirelli Company. He used a thin mineral oil which flowed through a duct formed by a steel helix in each core. The oil permeated the whole structure of

FIG. 45.3. An oil-filled paper-insulated single-core cable rated at 380 kV, and installed in Sweden about 1952.

the cable so that any void which formed was immediately filled with oil. Oil reservoirs above the level of the cable maintained the oil pressure and took up any expansion or contraction.

The dielectric strength of oil-filled cable increases with increasing pressure. C. E. Bennett made use of that relationship for his 'oilostatic cable' introduced in 1931. By that date techniques for making long lengths of welded steel pipeline were well established. The oilostatic cable was an essentially conventional paper-insulated screened cable, without an outer sheath, drawn into a steel pipeline which was then filled with oil under pressure. The first experimental installation operated at 66 kV at Philadelphia, and in 1935 a 135-kV oilostatic cable carrying 100 MVA was installed for the Pennsylvania Railroad at Baltimore.

Some oil-filled cables were made 'self-compensating'. The sheath, which had to be specially designed for any pressurized cable, was given some degree of flexibility and the cable acted as its own reservoir, without the need for external reservoir stations.

Gas-filled cables were the subject of much experiment. There were several options: the paper insulation could be dry and no impregnating oil used or the paper could be impregnated in the conventional way and the gas used to maintain pressure. In the latter case the gas could either be in direct contact with the oil or separated from it by a flexible diaphragm. During the 1930s several gas-filled cables were laid in Britain and a few in other countries, but the lengths involved were small.

Later trends in cables. The basic construction of power cables did not change again in the first half of the twentieth century. By 1950 the introduction of cables with plastic insulation could be foreseen but they were not in service until a few years later. The impregnating oils and waxes used have been the subject of much research, the trend being to replace resin and resin oil by mineral oil products. The choice of copper for the conductor has been almost unquestioned, though for a brief period, about 1906 to 1913, aluminium was cheaper than copper and some aluminium cables were made. The choice is not only governed by the cost of the metal. The electrical conductivity of aluminium is only 60 per cent that of copper: consequently aluminium cables are larger than the equivalent copper cables and require more insulating material. Because aluminium always has a thin but tough oxide coating it is difficult to make good electrical connections with aluminium cables. However, since 1950 the price of copper has risen so much that the cable makers and the electricity supply industry have undertaken extensive research on the problem of jointing aluminium cables, and the supply authorities have used some aluminium cable in their local distribution networks.

Overhead transmission lines. The British Central Electricity Board, established in 1926, had the task of linking the supply systems of the whole country by the national grid. This required 4600 km of 132000 V circuit, which was possible only by using overhead transmission lines. The Board adopted steel-cored aluminium conductors 20 mm in diameter carried on steel pylons; each circuit could carry 50 MVA. Aluminium was used, rather than copper, because aluminium conductors are only about half the weight of copper conductors of the same current-carrying capacity.

In 1949 the British Electricity Authority decided that the capacity of the grid would have to be increased. They began planning a 275-kV system, known as the Supergrid, with a capacity of 500 MVA per circuit, which was expected to meet all requirements for at least twenty years. The first section, 66 km of single-circuit line, was brought into service in 1953. In the U.S.A., the Hoover Dam Project, in the 1930s, had utilized 287 kV on a 300-mile (480-km) transmission line.

III. SWITCHGEAR

Breaking a circuit carrying a current is a far more complicated matter than may appear at first sight. Even a domestic light switch will usually produce a small spark as the contacts open. This is because as the contacts begin to move apart the area of contact decreases, the contact resistance rises, and the last areas of contact become heated and then melt. Finally a tiny portion of the metal evaporates, forming a plasma, and the surrounding air ionizes also. In larger sizes, a switch becomes known as a circuit-breaker and the 'spark' becomes an 'arc', but the difference is one of size and nomenclature rather than physical principle.

The arc which forms when a circuit-breaker opens is an aid to the breaking of the circuit, not, as might be supposed, a hindrance. If the current were 'chopped' immediately the contacts opened, then enormous surge voltages would be induced because of the self-inductance of the circuit. The arc performs the vital function of allowing the current to continue to flow until the instantaneous value of the current falls to zero. This occurs 100 times per second in a 50-Hz system, or 120 times per second in a 60-Hz system. At the point when the current becomes zero, the arc extinguishes itself naturally;

FIG. 45.4. An early main switch showing (*left*) the open position, (*centre*) the position during opening or closing, and (*right*) the closed position. When the switch is fully closed the main contacts carry the current. When the switch is opened, the main contacts separate first and then an arc is drawn between the auxiliary contacts as they separate. Only the auxiliary contacts are burnt by the arcing, and they may easily be replaced.

for satisfactory operation, the medium in which the arc occurs must have cooled sufficiently to prevent the voltage rise in the following half-cycle from restriking the arc. A circuit breaker for d.c. is more difficult to make than an a.c. breaker because it has to depend on the arc being drawn out to a length which the prevailing voltage and current conditions cannot sustain.

The early power stations were controlled by simple knife-switches on slate or marble panels. Even the simplest such switches had main and auxiliary contacts (Fig. 45.4). The main contacts carried the current (or most of it) when the switch was closed. The auxiliary contacts were linked to the main ones by springs and they were arranged to open with a snap action after the main contacts, even if the switch were operated slowly. In this way the arc drawn between the contacts as they opened was broken as quickly as possible, and burning and pitting of the contact surfaces was confined to the auxiliary contacts, which could easily be replaced.

As voltages increased the switchgear was placed behind the panel so that it was impossible for the operator to touch any live parts. Subsequently remote control was adopted, which is totally safe for the operator and also makes it possible for the controls for switches in several different locations to be grouped in a central control room.

As currents increased switching became more difficult, and the switch became the 'circuit-breaker'. The first refinement, introduced before 1900, was the 'magnetic blowout'. This depends on the fact that an electric current —including an arc—experiences a sideways force if it passes through a magnetic field. In a circuit-breaker with magnetic blowout the conductor carrying the current is arranged so that the arc drawn when the contacts open is forced sideways. Consequently the arc takes a longer path through the air than it would otherwise do, and it is extinguished more quickly.

During the first decade of the twentieth century oil-immersed circuit breakers were introduced, in which the contacts are separated in a tank of oil. The function of the oil was first to cool the arc, thus assisting its extinction, and then to increase the insulation between the contacts so as to prevent the voltage which appears after the circuit is broken from restriking the arc.

After the First World War the developing supply industry needed circuit-breakers of ever-increasing capacity. There was no testing facility anywhere for circuit-breakers, which made it difficult to evaluate different designs. The first short-circuit testing station was established in 1929 by the switchgear manufacturers Reyrolle and Co. at Hebburn-on-Tyne. Two main types of circuit-breaker were developed during the 1920s and 1930s: the air-blast and oil-blast breakers.

In the air-blast breaker a fast-moving jet of air under high pressure is blown against the arc so as to stretch it out into a thin column which loses heat rapidly. The magnetic blowout circuit breaker can be used for circuits up to about 16000 V; a single pair of air-blast contacts can interrupt a 100000-V circuit. For higher voltages, several pairs of contacts have to be connected in series and operated by a linked mechanism.

In oil-blast breakers the contacts are enclosed in oil as in the simple oil-immersed breaker. The heat of the arc evaporates some of the oil, which then dissociates into carbon and a large volume of hydrogen at high pressure. The pressure of the hydrogen is used to draw out the arc, usually against a series of baffles. Hydrogen has a very high thermal conductivity, which makes it a good coolant for the arc. The main disadvantage of oil-filled circuit-breakers, especially the oil-blast type, is the risk of fire if a defective breaker should fail under pressure and explode.

During the 1940s the heavy, incombustible gas sulphur hexafluoride was introduced as an arc-extinguishing medium for circuit-breakers. The general construction of the breakers was similar to the air-blast breakers, but the physical properties of sulphur hexafluoride make it more suitable than air for the purpose. However, although sulphur hexafluoride itself is inert, both sulphur and fluorine are highly corrosive substances—fluorine especially so. This restricts the materials that can be used in the construction of a sulphur hexafluoride breaker. The gas has to be kept perfectly dry, and so the breaker cannot easily be opened for inspection. In addition, the gas liquefies at about 10 °C under the operating pressures used, and if the breaker is for outdoor use it must be heated. The main applications of sulphur hexafluoride circuit breakers have been indoors in situations where the reduction of fire risk is important.

Vacuum switches in which the contacts separate in a vacuum have been used for low currents since about 1930. Switches rated at up to 15 A were available in 1934, and vacuum reed switches rated at 0·5 A or less have been used extensively in telephone exchanges.

IV. TRANSFORMERS AND RECTIFIERS

The transformer for converting alternating current from one voltage to another was well understood by 1900. Ferranti made a satisfactory 110-kW transformer in 1891 (Fig. 45.5) and the practice of building up a transformer from iron stampings and pre-formed coils was firmly established. About the turn of the century Sir Robert Hadfield studied the question of the best iron to use in a transformer core to avoid energy losses, and developed the 4 per cent silicon steel which has been used ever since. Transformers have been built in ever-larger sizes as the supply industry has grown, and efficiencies above 99 per cent are usual in large grid transformers.

For conversion between a.c. and d.c., or between d.c. systems at different voltages, motor-generator sets were used. The invention of the mercury-arc

FIG. 45.5. A 10000 V to 2400 V transformer, designed by S. Z. de Ferranti and built about 1891 for a sub-station of the London Electricity Supply Corporation. This transformer remained in use until 1924.

rectifier in 1928 made conversion easy from a.c. to d.c. The 'inverted' use of the mercury arc rectifier to convert d.c. to a.c. made possible the introduction of high-voltage direct-current power transmission (HVDCPT).

For long-distance transmission, d.c. has advantages over a.c. A conductor of given cross-section and standard of insulation will carry more power with d.c., and the technical problems arising from the capacitance and inductance of long lines in a.c. systems are avoided.

Much of the development work on high-power mercury-arc rectifiers was carried out in Sweden and Germany, but the first large HVDCPT scheme was installed in the U.S.S.R. in 1950. A power of 30 MW was transmitted between Moscow and Kashira, a distance of 115 km. In 1954 the Swedish island of Gotland was linked to the mainland by an undersea cable transmitting 20 MW at 100 kV and using earth return. England and France were linked in 1961 by cables transmitting 160 MW at $\pm$ 100 kV. During the 1960s the two islands of New Zealand; Sweden and Denmark; Sardinia and Italy; and Canada and Vancouver Island were linked by HVDCPT schemes using undersea cables.

V. LIGHTING

Metal filament lamps. At the close of the nineteenth century the carbon filament lamp was in widespread use and a metal filament lamp, using osmium, had been introduced in 1898 (Vol. 5, Ch. 10). The bayonet cap lampholder used in Britain and the screw cap lampholder preferred in America had both become standard. The carbon filament lamp gave an average light output of about 1·4 lumens per watt in 1900, and had a life expectancy of 400 to 500 hours. It has been estimated that there were then $2\frac{1}{2}$ million such lamps in use in London alone.

The filament of an incandescent lamp has to retain its mechanical strength at a very high temperature. Experiments were carried out with many different metals to see which might be suitable. Osmium has been mentioned, and tantalum was also used. Tantalum had the advantage that lamps for a given operating voltage could be made for lower candle powers than was possible with carbon. Tungsten was found to be the best metal for the purpose but, initially at least, it could not be drawn into a fine filament because it is so hard and brittle. In 1908, W. D. Coolidge, in the U.S.A., produced tungsten in a ductile form by compressing tungsten powder in a mould to form a rod. After intense heating and hammering the rod could be drawn into an extremely fine wire. Because tungsten is a relatively good conductor of electricity a tungsten filament has to be longer than a corresponding carbon filament. This led to problems in the construction of the lamp, because more supports were needed for the filament, but these problems were soon overcome and within a few years virtually all incandescent lamps had tungsten filaments.

The glass bulbs of carbon filament lamps quickly became blackened on the inside by a deposit of carbon which had evaporated from the filament. This rapidly reduced the efficiency of the lamp and was a major reason for seeking alternative filament materials. The same thing happened with metal filaments, though more slowly. In 1913, Irving Langmuir suggested that filling the bulb with an inert gas would reduce the rate of evaporation. He also introduced the 'coiled' filament in which the filament is wound into a fine helix before being put in the lamp. These ideas were successfully adopted, and the gas-filled tungsten filament lamp became known as the 'half-watt lamp' because it required half a watt per candle power of light given.

Most of the energy put into a lamp is lost as heat. In 1934 the 'coiled-coil' lamp was introduced in which the filament is first wound in a helix which is then coiled on itself. This reduced both the heat loss by convection and the loss of metal by evaporation, and so raised the efficiency of the lamp.

The life of an incandescent filament lamp and its efficiency are interrelated. The efficiency can be increased by operating at a higher temperature, but the rate of evaporation of the filament will also be increased and therefore the life reduced. Typical efficiencies for new lamps would be: carbon filament 3·5 lumens per watt; tungsten filament in vacuum 8 lumens per watt; and gas-filled tungsten filament 12 lumens per watt. High-power projector lamps are usually designed to operate at higher temperatures, with twice the efficiency and a much reduced life. Since about 1920 British manufacturers have adopted a standard designed life of 1000 hours for most lamps, though some large customers prefer a different standard. The National Coal Board, for example, buys 2000-hour lamps.

The Nernst lamp. The incandescent mantle was developed for gas lighting by Auer von Welsbach towards the end of the nineteenth century. The Nernst lamp, invented in 1897, has a filament of the rare earths used by von Welsbach and produces light by heating them to incandescence. When running the filament is conducting, but an auxiliary heater is needed to start the lamp. The Nernst lamp was never widely adopted, but its attractions were

FIG. 45.6(a). Typical carbon filament lamp for domestic use (from G.E.C. catalogue of 1901). The evacuating 'pip' in the glass opposite the cap is where the bulb was sealed after the air was pumped out.

(b). Early metal filament lamps required a very long filament with many support points. This tungsten filament lamp was made about 1910.

(c) One of the first coiled filament lamps, introduced in 1913. The filament is made more compact by winding it in a fine helix.

(d) Since the 1920s lamps have been pumped and sealed from the cap end, and no evacuating 'pip' is visible. This lamp was made about 1950.

that no vacuum was required and, compared with carbon filament lamps, it had a high efficiency of about 6 lumens per watt.

The arc lamp. After the introduction of the incandescent filament lamp the carbon arc continued to be used for several decades where large-scale illumination was required, as in railway stations and for some street lighting. A number of further developments were made. The main disadvantage of arc lamps is the need to replace the carbon rods frequently. A variety of ingenious mechanisms were designed to facilitate this. In 1893 Marks introduced the enclosed arc, in which the carbons are enclosed in a glass tube. This restricts the flow of air and increases the life of the carbons fivefold.

Various fluorescent materials, such as salts of magnesium, strontium, barium, and calcium, were added as cores to the carbon rods, and these improved both the efficiency and colour of the arc lamp. In the 'flame arc' of 1897 the arc was drawn out magnetically to increase the light given.

Discharge and fluorescent lighting. Just before the Second World War another light source was developed which gave up to four times the light given by a filament lamp of the same power consumption. This was the discharge lamp which utilized the visible glow produced when an electric current passes through certain gases at low pressure. There are several varieties of gas discharge lamps, using different gases and either hot or cold electrodes. The two most important are the mercury vapour lamp, giving a bluish light, and the sodium vapour lamp, which gives a monochromatic yellow light.

The sodium vapour lamp is very popular for street lighting because of its high efficiency. The lamp runs at a high temperature and is always enclosed in a double glass envelope to reduce heat loss. At ambient temperature the sodium exists as the solid metal inside the lamp. A small quantity of neon gas is enclosed in the lamp and when first switched on the lamp runs as a neon lamp with a red light until the sodium vaporizes and takes over.

Discharge lamps cannot be connected directly to the mains. There must be some current-limiting device in the circuit, usually an inductance. The hot-cathode lamps, and some cold-cathode ones, also require special starting circuits, but the cost of these is more than offset by the reduction in running costs compared with filament lamps.

The fluorescent lamp, introduced just after the last war, is a development of the mercury vapour discharge lamp. The discharge in mercury yields ultraviolet light, as well as visible light. The inside of the glass of a fluorescent lamp is coated with materials (phosphors) that absorb ultraviolet light and emit visible light. The colour of a fluorescent lamp can be controlled by choosing the appropriate phosphors. No ultraviolet light is emitted, because it will not pass through the glass.

VI. ELECTRIC MOTORS

The direct current motor was in widespread use, mainly for electric traction, by 1900. The principles of the induction motor and synchronous motor were also understood, although these machines were hardly used before the introduction of a polyphase electricity supply, in London in 1900 and Newcastle upon Tyne in 1901. The Tyneside engineering industry was the first to use electric motors extensively. Charles Merz, the engineer responsible for much of the electrical development of north-east England, worked hard to persuade local industry to adopt electric power. He found that his customers were mainly influenced by the flexibility of electric motors, as compared with steam engines; the economics were a secondary consideration.

Induction and synchronous motors. In terms of power produced, most of the world's electric motors are induction motors. In the induction motor (Fig. 45.7), invented by Nikola Tesla in 1888, the field windings produce a magnetic field whose effective direction rotates around the axis of the machine.

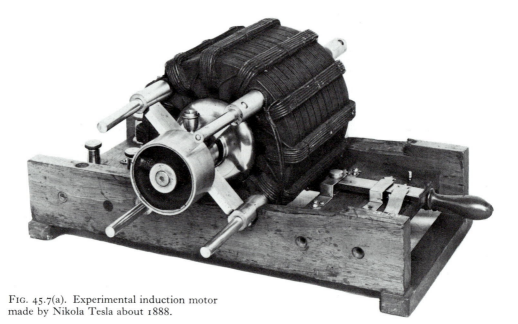

FIG. 45.7(a). Experimental induction motor made by Nikola Tesla about 1888.

Electric currents are induced in the rotor—hence the term 'induction' motor. The rotor becomes magnetized by the induced currents and is pulled around at almost the same speed as the field. The speed of rotation of the field is determined by two factors, the arrangement of the windings and the frequency of the electricity supply. For a given motor these two quantities are usually fixed, and the approximate speed of the motor is fixed also.

In the 'synchronous' motor, also devised by Tesla, the field is the same as in an induction motor, but the rotor is either a permanent magnet or an iron core with coils carrying direct current. The rotor follows the rotating field around, keeping in phase with it. Consequently the synchronous motor can run only at one, fixed speed.

For many purposes a variable-speed motor is required, but the user wishes to retain the advantages of the induction and synchronous motors, which are by far the most reliable and efficient types of electric motor. Motors have been made with two complete sets of field windings, arranged to give different numbers of poles, but the resulting machines are larger and more expensive than conventional motors of the same power rating.

The pole amplitude modulated (or 'PAM') motor was invented by G. H. Rawcliffe of Bristol University in 1957. The number of poles can be changed by a simple switch which reverses the connections of some of the field windings in a machine which is otherwise quite conventional. The windings are so

FIG. 45.7(b). The rotor of the Tesla induction motor.

FIG. 45.8. The first British-made electric drill, 1914. It weighed 23½ lb (10·5 kg) and was rated at 370 W.

arranged that rotating fields with different pole numbers are given by the two connections. The term 'pole amplitude modulation' was adopted because the reversible windings may be considered to be modulating the flux produced by the other windings. In any one phase this would give a magnetic field with a mixture of two pole numbers, but in a three-phase machine the resultant field at one pole number can be made to be zero. The PAM motor is therefore essentially a polyphase machine.

Linear motors may be considered as a development of the induction motor in which the field windings are laid out in a straight line rather than arranged around a cylinder. Although linear motors were made experimentally in the nineteenth century their practical development and commercial availability did not begin until the second half of the twentieth century, largely inspired by the work of E. R. Laithwaite.

Small electric motors. During the twentieth century a variety of small motors, known collectively as 'fractional horsepower motors', have been developed. The two most important types are the 'universal' motor and the small induction motor.

There are more universal motors in use than any other type. They are essentially d.c. motors in which the field iron is laminated so that the polarity of both field and armature can reverse at the frequency of the supply. Such motors run equally well on d.c. or 50 or 60 Hz a.c., and were popular initially for that reason. They have the high starting torque of the d.c. motor, in contrast to the low starting torque of the induction motor, and can also run faster than an induction motor. In small domestic appliances and portable tools, such as electric drills, the high-speed universal motor achieves a greater power-to-weight ratio than would be possible with any other motor. Speeds of 4000 to 10000 rev/min are commonly used and 20000 rev/min is possible. Universal motors have been used since about 1925 in vacuum cleaners, floor polishers, hair dryers, sewing-machines, and portable tools. Portable electric drills, for example, were first made in Germany about 1895 using a d.c. motor. The first British 'portable' electric drill, made by Wolf in 1914, weighed over 10 kg and had a two-pole compound-wound d.c. motor running at 350 rev/min and consuming 370 W (Fig. 45.8). The first drill to use a universal motor, made in 1925, weighed 2·5 kg, was rated at 100 W, and ran at 1500 rev/min on load. During the Second World War a drill of even lighter weight was developed for use by women working in factories. It weighed just over 1 kg, was rated at 175 W, and ran at 2750 rev/min.

The universal motor can be series or shunt wound, though in practice it is always series wound. In mass production the armature and field laminations are stamped from the same sheet of silicon steel and the windings are wound directly into the insulated slots in the laminations, not wound separately on formers and then inserted in the slots, as is the practice with larger machines. The commutator, brushes, and bearings of universal motors are all designed to give maximum life with little or no maintenance, and such machines often run for years without requiring attention.

Small induction motors have been developed simultaneously with universal motors for domestic and similar use. They may be classified by their starting arrangements, since the single-phase induction motor is not inherently self-starting. For the smallest ratings the shaded-pole motor is the most used. It is usually adopted in such devices as fans and gramophones, where the power required is very small and simplicity and reliability are paramount. The name 'shaded-pole' arises because part of one pole is surrounded by a short-circuited coil or a loop of copper strip. Current induced in that coil or loop retards the rise or fall of the magnetic field within it, compared with the magnetic field in the unshaded part of the pole. The net result is a two-pole magnetic field with a rotating component which pulls the armature round.

The shaded-pole motor is therefore a two-phase induction motor. Its efficiency is poor and its use is confined to applications where both the power required and the running cost are negligible.

The second most important group of small induction motors is the 'capacitor start' motor, which has been used from the beginning of the century. Large numbers are used in washing-machines and similar light machinery. The field winding of these motors is in two parts (hence the term 'split-field' winding which is sometimes used). One part of the field is connected directly to the supply and the other is connected through a capacitor. The capacitor produces a phase displacement so that the motor effectively runs on a two-phase supply.

BIBLIOGRAPHY

DUNSHEATH, P. *A history of electrical engineering*. Faber and Faber, London (1962).

EMANUELI, L. *High voltage cables*. Chapman and Hall, London (1929).

HENNESSEY, R. A. S. *The electric revolution*. Oriel Press, Newcastle upon Tyne (1972).

HUNTER, P. V., and HAZELL, J. TEMPLE. *Development of power cables*, Newnes, London (1956).

MELLANBY, JOHN. *The history of electric wiring*. Macdonald, London (1957).

PHILPOTT, STUART F. *Fractional horse power motors*. Chapman and Hall, London (1951).

ROWLAND, JOHN. *Progress in power—the contribution of Charles Merz and his associates to sixty years of electrical development, 1899–1959*. Privately published for Merz and McLellan (1960).

SALVAGE, B. Overhead lines or underground cables: the problem of electrical power transmission. *Endeavour*, **34**, 3 (1975).

46

ELECTRONIC ENGINEERING

J. R. TILLMAN AND D. G. TUCKER

ELECTRONIC engineering as such is a product of the twentieth century, for the electron itself was not identified and described until almost the very end of the nineteenth century. Nevertheless, the subject grew naturally out of electrical engineering and, as will be seen from this chapter, many aspects of the subject as it is now broadly recognized by engineers have their roots in the nineteenth century. It was the development of the thermionic valve that created electronic engineering; in this device electrons are emitted from a heated surface in a rarefied gas or in a vacuum and are subjected to electric forces in such a way as to provide a variety of effects which can be exploited to generate, amplify, and control electrical signals. It is the processing of signals by electronic devices which essentially constitutes electronic engineering. The thermionic valve, having created electronic engineering, has now been largely displaced by solid-state devices such as the transistor; but this development had barely commenced by 1950.

The early applications of electronic engineering were almost entirely in electrical communications, and these have been described elsewhere (Ch. 50). Subsequent applications to industry, computers, radar, etc. are also described elsewhere. This chapter, therefore, concentrates on the history of the fundamental devices, circuits, and basic systems of electronic engineering. In preparing it, we quickly found that we could not write for the wholly non-scientific layman without making the chapter unacceptable to the physicist or engineer. We have therefore assumed a little knowledge of physics. For example, it is not possible to evaluate the contributions of such pioneers as Lee de Forest and E. H. Armstrong without some explanation of the vitally important feedback principle. Readers daunted, even by this, should nevertheless be able to pick out the historically significant events in the history of electronic engineering with which we are here concerned. In the few circuit diagrams that are included we have used British Standard symbols.

1. THE THERMIONIC VALVE

When once established in triode form as a reproducible device, the thermionic valve was steadily developed to exploit more fully its ability to amplify, rectify, and modulate electrical signals, and to act in other capacities; for example as a switch, a generator of various kinds of waveform, an information store, and a logic unit in computers. But its earlier history was piecemeal, offering little prospect of wide-ranging usage. It began with observations of effects which were later shown to be manifestations of electronic emission.

Electronic emission. In 1873, F. Guthrie [1] noted effects with heated metals brought near to an electroscope, for which we now know electrons emitted from the metals must have been responsible. Ten years later, T. A. Edison [2] reported that a current could flow in one direction only between a second electrode and the heated filament in a vacuum incandescent lamp. The effect defied correct explanation until 1897 when J. J. Thomson [3] established the existence and elementary properties of free electrons. Thus he measured the ratio of the charge to the mass of the electron, and showed evidence that all free electrons, however generated, were indistinguishable from one another. In 1898, by making an approximate measurement of the charge, he deduced that the mass of the electron must be about one-thousandth that of the hydrogen atom.

Other electronic effects were discovered during the next decade, laying the foundations for electronic engineering. It became recognized that when moving electrons collided with matter, radiation was produced; X-rays, discovered by W. K. Röntgen in 1897, were a notable example. A converse effect had been investigated by J. Elster and H. Geitel (1889 onwards), following H. Hertz's observation that the discharge of a spark gap was influenced by ultraviolet illumination. They demonstrated that such illumination caused metals to emit electrons in numbers proportional to, but with emission velocities independent of, its intensity; moreover, above a limiting wavelength there was no emission. These findings, and M. Planck's quantum theory (1900) put forward to explain the failure of the classical wave theory to account for a key feature of radiation from hot bodies, led Einstein, in 1905, to propose his simple photoelectric emission equation

$$h\nu = q\phi,$$

where ν is the frequency of the longest wavelength capable of exciting emission, h is Planck's constant, q is the electronic charge, and ϕ is the work function of the metal ($q\phi$ is defined as the energy needed to remove an electron from the metal to a great distance).

Of other studies, closely related to the above results, that of O. W. Richardson [4] (1901) was of most direct relevance to the thermionic valve; using hot platinum sources, he concluded that the temperature dependence of thermionic emission of electrons was dominated by a term $\exp\left(-q\phi/kT\right)$ where k is Boltzmann's constant and T is absolute temperature.

The cathodes of the first valves used refractory metals, principally tungsten, in the form of filaments. Such metals have rather higher values of work function (e.g. 4·5 electron volts (eV)) than do other metals obtainable in wire form, necessitating a high operating temperature (e.g. 2500 K) but ensuring a sufficient margin between this temperature and their melting-points. Thoriated tungsten, first introduced by Irving Langmuir (U.S.A.) in 1914, had a work function of only 2·7 eV; running at about 1650 K, it showed a clear advantage and found use for a while. But in turn it was largely superseded by the oxide cathode, due originally to A. Wehnelt [5] in 1904 and comprizing a thin layer (about 0·0025 cm) of mixed oxides of the alkaline-earth metals, particularly strontium and barium, suitably activated by a partial reduction. The work function was sufficiently low (about 1·2 eV) to enable adequate emission to be obtained at temperatures of only 1000–1100 K, with considerable saving of power and increase of life.

The thermionic diode. Although, as we have seen, the unidirectional conductivity between a plate and the filament inside an electric filament lamp had been well explored by the turn of the century, no practical application seems to have been put forward until J. A. Fleming proposed its use as a detecting device in radio receivers in 1904 [6]. The conventional receiver of that time used a coherer or an electromagnetic detector (see Ch. 50), either of which could quite strictly be called a detector because its response to the reception of a radio signal was to bring in an auxiliary circuit of greater power. It had been known since 1898 that another way of making evident the receipt of a radio signal was to rectify it, so that either the envelope component (which was usually at an audible frequency) or the direct current (d.c.) component could be 'detected' by earphones or galvanometer respectively. It occurred to Fleming that the thermionic diode was an ideal device to perform this rectification, and he used it in a radio receiver in the way exemplified in Fig. 46.1(a). The way it worked in principle is shown in Fig. 46.1(d). The radio signal, which at that time would probably be in Morse code, consisted

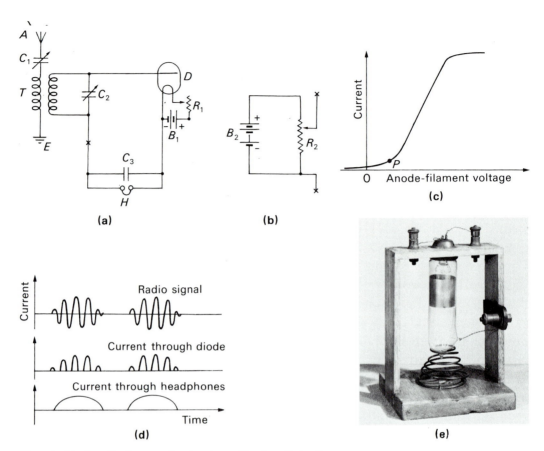

Fig. 46.1(a). A radio detector circuit using a Fleming diode, D.

(b). A bias circuit to improve sensitivity, inserted at X in (a).

(c). The current/voltage curve for a diode. P is the operating point under biased conditions,
as in (b).

(d). The principle of operation.

(e). The Fleming thermionic diode (1905), in a wooden stand.

A = aerial; B_1 = battery for filament; C_1, C_2, = variable capacitors (condensers); C_3 = capacitor to
bypass headphones, H, for radio-frequency currents; T = aerial tuning coils or transformer; E = earth;
R_1 = resistance for adjusting filament temperature; R_2 = resistance for adjusting
bias voltage; B_2 = bias battery.

of short transmissions, controlled by a telegraph key, each made up of a series
of bursts of oscillations from a spark transmitter as shown in the first line.
The diode would pass only the positive parts of the current waveform, so that
the current in the diode was as shown in the second line. The radio-frequency
components of this passed through the capacitor C_3, leaving the current
through the headphones as the enveolpe component shown in the third line.

After a time, Fleming realized that significantly greater sensitivity could be
achieved if the diode were used a little differently. Instead of relying on the
idealized concept of a device that passed current equally easily on all positive

parts of the wave, but no current on negative parts, which we see from Fig. 46.1(c) is a long way from the truth, he added a biasing battery in the diode circuit, as shown in Fig. 46.1(b), so that there was a current even when no signal was being received, as indicated by the operating point P on the curve in Fig. 46.1(c). The difference in current between positive and negative swings of the received wave is now greater than the 'rectified' wave previously obtained. This method was patented in 1908.

Thermionic diodes have been used for a wide variety of purposes over the years; in small sizes as signal rectifiers, in somewhat larger sizes as rectifiers for electric mains supplies in domestic radio receivers, in large sizes as power rectifiers. High vacuum has been needed for some applications; in others, residual gas has been tolerable or even desirable.

The thermionic triode. It was an American, Lee de Forest, who first discovered the advantages of adding a third electrode to the thermionic device [7]. There was much bitter litigation over the invention; Fleming claimed, not without considerable justification, that the triode was a modification of his diode and depended on it; de Forest claimed it was a new invention. Uncertainty as to who had the patent rights delayed the development of applications throughout the patent period. Nevertheless, the triode led to a number of vitally important new achievements.

De Forest had been working on detector systems for radio signals during 1905–6, and, allegedly without knowing of Fleming's work, had tried using a filament lamp with a platinum plate added. He went on to add a third electrode, and tried several different forms of it: a piece of foil outside the tube; a second plate inside the tube, opposite to the first plate; and, finally, a wire grid between the filament and the original plate. It was this final arrangement which became the standard triode valve or tube (Fig. 46.2). (The name 'valve', derived from the valve action of Fleming's diode, carried on in Britain as the accepted name; but in the U.S.A. the device soon became called the 'vacuum tube'.) De Forest called his device the 'audion', but the name lasted barely a decade.

For some years the audion was used only as a more sensitive detector in radio-telegraph reception. The additional electrode, which soon became called the 'grid', was connected to the signal input via a capacitor, C_4 in the typical circuit of Fig. 46.3(a), the resistor R_2 shown there being absent in these early days. With the capacitor in the grid connection, the audion could operate as a detector of telegraph signals because the grid current which flowed

FIG. 46.2. The de Forest audion valve.

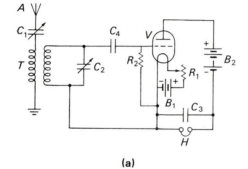

(a)

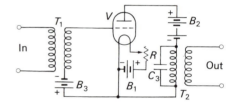

(b)

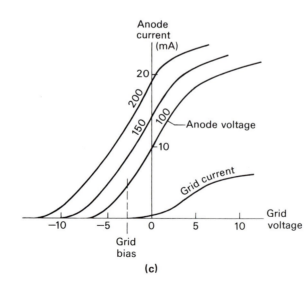

(c)

(d)

FIG. 46.3(a). A radio receiver using a triode valve, V.
    (b). An amplifier using a triode valve, V.
    (c). Typical characteristic curves of a small triode.
    (d). The French or Army 'R' triode valve, c. 1915.

B_1 = filament battery; B_2 = anode (or plate) battery; B_3 = grid bias battery; C_4 = grid condenser; R_2 = grid leak; T_1, T_2 = input and output transformers. Other symbols as in Fig. 46.1.

on each positive excursion of the incoming bursts of damped waves (for example, from a spark transmitter) drained charge from the capacitor and made the grid voltage negative with respect to the filament, thus reducing the anode current. At the end of each burst, the capacitor would recover by the reverse flow of current due to the ionization of the gas in the tube. Headphones in the anode circuit would give an audible signal from these variations of current at the repetition frequency of the bursts of waves. When 'hard' valves came into use, a grid leak (R_2 in Fig. 46.3(a)) was necessary to provide for the recovery of the capacitor charge, and this was invented by H. J. Round (Britain) in 1914.

The real importance of the triode, however, lay not in its detection capability but in its power of providing amplification of a signal. With the capacitance-coupled grid this could not be achieved because the modulation of the anode current did not even roughly follow the signal waveform. It was therefore a big step forward when F. Lowenstein (U.S.A.), in 1912, discovered the favourable effect of a negative bias of moderate voltage, applied by a battery in series with the grid circuit, as shown in Fig. 46.3(b). Then, for the first time, the valve could be worked under its best operating conditions. The signal voltage swing could be kept within the range where at the positive extremity the grid current became excessive, and at the negative extremity the valve cut off. In this way the signal power absorbed could be made very small indeed, and the power amplification comparatively large. It was later found that Round's grid-leak and capacitor arrangement (Fig. 46.3(a)) could, by suitable choice of values, give a suitable steady grid bias voltage when the signal was of the continuous-carrier kind, as in radio telephony, thus dispensing with the need for a battery in many applications.

Triode amplifiers with two or more stages, to give an amplification of perhaps 20 dB, came into use, and in 1915 were applied to the trans-continental telephone line between New York and San Francisco.

Early valves contained residual gas, and became known as 'soft'. Their performance was irregular and they could not stand more than a few tens of volts on the anode. 'Hard', or high-vacuum valves came into use in the early 1910s. Better mechanical design enabled electrode spacings to be reduced, and greater control of the anode current by the grid voltage was obtained, thus making higher amplification possible.

Although de Forest can justly be credited with the invention of the triode, it is clear from his writings that he never understood its operation or how properly to use it. The clarification of the physical principles involved was largely due to I. Langmuir (U.S.A.). The formulation of the principles of use in circuits was largely due to E. H. Armstrong (U.S.A.), whose paper of 1915 was masterly [8]. Using measured characteristic curves of the type shown in Fig. 46.3(c), he showed how the triode could be used as a rectifier, amplifier, or both together; how feedback could be applied to increase the amplification or to make a self-oscillating detector; how grid-to-anode capacitance could be exploited, and so on.

The feedback principle, just mentioned, was a vitally important one. There was much dispute and litigation as to who invented it. In the U.S.A. the main contenders were de Forest and Armstrong, but there were also several British and European inventors, all producing feedback circuits in 1913 [9]. There were two main uses of feedback, which was conceived at that time as positive feedback: first, to provide a very high amplification in a triode circuit, accompanied by increased selectivity, and secondly to provide a generator of high-frequency oscillations using a triode. These two uses are illustrated in Fig. 46.4(a) and (b). Fig. 46.4(a) shows a radio receiver circuit in which the triode has a negative grid bias and operates as a combined detector and amplifier through the lack of symmetry of the anode current–grid voltage curve about the bias voltage point. The output part of the circuit includes the winding T_F on the input transformer T, and this feeds some output signal back to the grid in phase with the input signal. Consequently a given output requires a much smaller input; that is, the receiver is much more sensitive. The feedback also makes the tuning sharper. Fig. 46.4(b) shows a triode amplifier circuit in which the output is coupled back to the input, with a coupling strong enough to sustain self-oscillation approximately at the resonance frequency of the tuned circuit LC. Such an oscillation generator was very much more satisfactory for radio transmitters than the spark, arc, and rotating-machine types hitherto used. It also lent itself much better to modulation by speech, and thus helped the advance of radio-telephony.

As valve circuits developed and became increasingly versatile, it became essential to integrate the triode into circuit theory. From the use of characteristic curves, as started by Armstrong in 1915, there evolved over the next decade a concept of valve parameters, which soon led into the use of equivalent-circuit representation for the triode, and then, later, for other types of valve. These parameters were essentially partial differentials expressing the interdependence of two variables while all others were kept constant. The three most important parameters were:

(i) The amplification factor, $\partial V_a/\partial V_g$ for constant anode current.
(ii) The mutual conductance, $\partial I_a/\partial V_g$ for constant anode voltage.
(iii) The internal resistance, $\partial V_a/\partial I_a$ for constant grid voltage.

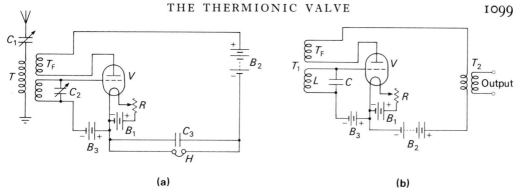

(a)   **(b)**

FIG. 46.4(a). A radio receiver with reaction or retroaction, i.e. with positive feedback.
(b). An oscillation generator. If the coupling in T_1 is fairly loose, the frequency of oscillation is approximately $f = (1/2\pi)(1/LC)^{\frac{1}{2}}$ Hz.

T_F = feedback winding or coil on aerial tuning transformer T; T_1 = the transformer that couples the feedback from the anode (winding T_F) into the grid circuit winding, which has inductance L henries; C = the tuning capacitance in farads. Other symbols as in Figs. 46.1 and 46.3.

For most purposes of circuit design and calculation, these three were sufficient, since grid current was often negligible, and inter-electrode capacitances could be considered as external added elements. (This discussion is, of course, highly simplified, being intended only to introduce the basic ideas.)

Equally it became important for valve designers to understand the characteristic curves in terms of their design parameters. Now Richardson's equation expressed the total (saturation or temperature-limited) current that could be drawn from an emitter—by applying high enough voltage to a collecting electrode. This saturation current is, however, 10 to 100 times the anode current with the recommended electrode voltages. The difference is accounted for by the charge on the electron which produces in the dense cloud of slowly moving electrons, emitted from and very close to the cathode surface, an intense negatively charged (space-charge) region. The region imposes a retarding field which decelerates these electrons so much that most of them return to the cathode. The retarding field, and hence the fraction of electrons not so returned, is, however, influenced by the voltage of the adjacent control grid and to a lesser extent by that of the anode. This leads to the basic equation relating I_a to V_g and V_a, namely

$$I_a = k \left(V_g + V_a/\mu \right)^n$$

where $\mu = \partial V_a/\partial V_g$ and is dependent on the inter-electrode spacings; k is also a geometry-dependent constant; and n is about 1·5 for indirectly heated and about 2–2·5 for directly heated cathodes. This equation and its constants

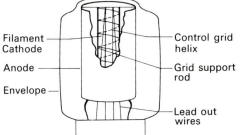

FIG. 46.5. A directly heated triode.

Filament
Cathode

Control grid
helix

Anode

Grid support
rod

Envelope

Lead out
wires

are little affected by any loss of saturation emission so long as that emission remains at least a few times I_a.

The design and construction of valves improved over the years, without however any revolutionary change in the basic structure of the essential triode (see Fig. 46.5), other than the addition of further electrodes (mostly other grids) and the substitution of indirectly heated for directly heated cathodes. In the earlier directly heated valves the cathode took the shape of one or more hairpins, heated by the passage of direct current. The control grid, closely surrounding the cathode, comprised a helix of fine wire wound on two support rods. The anode took the form of a pair of plates (or, commonly, a partially flattened cylinder) at a much greater distance, positioned to receive only those electrons which could reach it through the grid. Where necessary, small electrically insulating spacers, usually of mica, were used to maintain the electrodes at the specified spacings. The electrode structure was mounted on a pinch, integral with the well-evacuated envelope, containing lead-out wires connected to a cemented-on base with positioned contact pins. The introduction of the indirectly heated cathode in about 1930 brought two advantages. Firstly, raw alternating current (a.c.) from the mains, merely transformed to a low voltage, could be used to power it, thus eliminating the need for a battery or a rectifier and smoothing circuit. Secondly the cathode voltage (*vis-à-vis* ground) was more at the circuit designer's choice. The heater was a twisted metal hairpin coated with a refractory insulator, inserted into a cylindrical cathode; the outer surface of this cathode was sprayed with a mixture of the appropriate carbonates and binder, subsequently heated to convert the carbonates to oxides, and activated by a short period of running at a high temperature.

For long-range radio communication and for broadcasting, very high signal power was required for feeding to the transmitting aerials, and special triodes were developed for this use, calling for special materials and water-cooling of the anode or the whole valve.

The thermionic tetrode. As the construction of triode valves improved, giving higher amplification, and the use of multi-stage amplifiers became common, trouble was experienced from the capacitance between anode and grid. This capacitance limited the frequency range over which the valve could operate, and, perhaps more seriously, it caused unwanted feedback leading to self-oscillation in what was supposed to be a signal-amplifier. To overcome this latter trouble, the neutrodyne principle was introduced by L. A. Hazeltine (U.S.A.) in 1923, by which some signal was fed back by a separate path to cancel the undesired feedback due to anode-to-grid capacitance [10]. However, a better solution was a valve which had a greatly reduced capacitance. This was the tetrode valve. It had a most important influence on radio-receiver design in the 1930s.

The idea of introducing an extra grid (later called the screen-grid, or just 'screen') between the normal grid and the anode, to reduce back-coupling between the anode and the grid, was due to W. Schottky (Germany) in 1916–19 [11]. It was made effective, however, by Round in 1926. The screen-grid was maintained at a constant high voltage and so accelerated electrons from the cathode; but being of open mesh allowed them to pass through to the anode. The anode current was thus almost independent of the anode voltage; that is, the internal resistance was nearly infinite. It was a good valve for both voltage and power amplification.

There was one feature of the screen-grid valve which, while being capable of exploitation for some special purposes, limited its use in general. This was the effect of secondary electrons; that is, those emitted by the anode as a result of the bombardment by the normal, or primary, electron stream. These interfered with the amplifying function of the valve when the relative voltages of the screen and anode were such that the secondary electrons were attracted to the screen. Over a limited range of anode voltage, below the screen voltage, the anode current was actually reduced as the anode voltage was raised, giving a negative-resistance effect which could be exploited in a circuit such as the 'dynatron' oscillation-generator. When a tuned circuit was connected across the negative resistance, its resistance losses were neutralized and it oscillated spontaneously at approximately its resonance frequency.

The thermionic pentode. Although the tetrode was, in general, a good valve, and remained in production and use for some decades, the difficulty with secondary emission from the anode could be overcome by the use of yet another electrode, the suppressor grid, inserted between the screen-grid and the anode. This grid would usually be connected directly to the cathode, itself at or near earth voltage, and so repelled the secondary electrons back to the anode. Being of open construction, it did not prevent the primary electrons, accelerated by the screen, from reaching the anode. This five-electrode valve, the pentode, was the invention of G. Holst and B. D. H. Tellegen (Holland) in 1926–7 [12]. It was a most versatile and successful type of valve, and formed the active element of most electronic developments until displaced by the transistor in the 1950s and 1960s.

It is impossible to give any account here of the vast variety of circuits which were developed during the 1930s and 1940s to exploit the pentode. All that can be attempted is an explanation of how the pentode was used in some basic amplifier applications.

In Fig. 46.6(a) is shown a two-stage pentode amplifier using input and output transformers. In both valves the suppressor-grid is connected directly to the cathode, and the screen-grid directly to the high-tension positive voltage. Other arrangements were often used, but these are the simplest. The first stage develops its amplified signal voltage across the anode load resistance R_L, and this voltage is transferred to the grid of the second valve by the capacitance-resistance coupling C,R_G which prevents any high-tension direct voltage from reaching the grid. The second valve develops its amplified signal power into the load via the output transformer. Negative bias for the first, or control, grid of each valve is obtained by a method that became almost universal; namely, by the voltage drop in the resistance R_C connected in the cathode circuit. The capacitance C_C is to smooth out any signal component. This system was much more convenient than the use of grid-bias batteries. The valves are shown as having a simple cathode, indirectly heated. Small filament-type pentodes were made for use with dry batteries.

Figure 46.6(b) shows a typical set of characteristic curves for a pentode. The 'load line' has a slope of $1/R_L$ mhos[1] and terminates at the right-hand end at the voltage of the high-tension supply, since this is the voltage of the anode when the anode current is zero. The grid should normally not be swung positive by the applied signal because the consequent flow of grid current would lead to distortion. Equally, it should not be swung negative too far, for the cramping-up of the lines at the larger negative voltages also indicates distortion. So R_C is chosen to give a bias voltage of about -10 in the numerical example shown.

[1] The mho is the unit of electrical conductance, and is the reciprocal of the ohm, the unit of resistance.

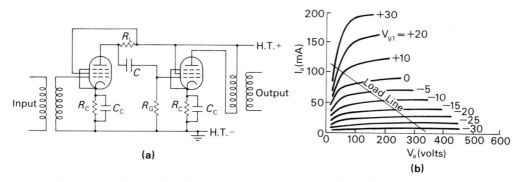

(a)

FIG. 46.6(a). An amplifier circuit with two pentodes.
(For symbols see text)

(b). Curves for a typical power pentode.
V_a = anode voltage; I_a = anode current;
V_{g1} = control-grid voltage.

In the output stage, the operation is slightly different. Here, assuming an ideal transformer, the mean, or 'quiescent', anode voltage is equal to the high-tension voltage. The signal voltage from the first stage then causes the anode voltage to swing above and below this high-tension voltage. For a power stage, this is evidently a much more efficient way of working the valve.

Other types of valve circuit. In the preceding discussion of thermionic valve circuits the range of operations involved has been confined to the three very basic ones of rectification, amplification, and oscillation-generation, the last being intended to provide a substantially sinusoidal waveform. These operations provided for most of the electronic requirements of communications, and the very few industrial applications, up to the early 1930s. Other early needs had arisen, however, as exemplified by the time-base circuits of cathode-ray oscilloscopes. During the 1930s the growing development of television and military electronics (for example, radar) put a new emphasis on the need for valve circuits to perform functions such as time-bases with a strictly linear sweep; generators of very short pulses; triggers which could change the state of a circuit from one condition to another on receipt of a suitable pulse signal; circuits which could multiply or divide the frequency of a wave or pulse train by given factors; circuits which could radically change the waveform of a signal in a specified manner; etc. A whole range of new kinds of circuits emerged which is far too complex to be discussed in any breadth or depth here.

Since it is so important, the time-base with linear sweep will be considered as an example of new ways of using valves. It is based on the relaxation oscillator, known in the 1920s. In essence, this simple device is as shown in

Fig. 46.7(a), where N is typically a small neon lamp, and not a thermionic valve. When the battery B is first connected, current flows through the high resistance R to charge the capacitance C, and the rise of voltage is as shown in Fig. 46.7(b). If N were absent, then in a time $t_1 = RC$ the voltage would rise to $V_B[1-\exp(-1)]$, which is approximately 0·63 V_B. However, the neon lamp has the property of being an open circuit until the voltage across it reaches a certain value V_1 at which the gas ionizes, a glow discharge results, and the lamp provides a very low resistance—a short-circuit in comparison with R. So when V_C reaches V_1, the capacitance begins to discharge very rapidly through the lamp; at the voltage V_2, however, the glow can no longer

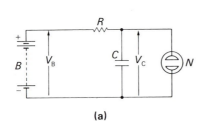

(a)

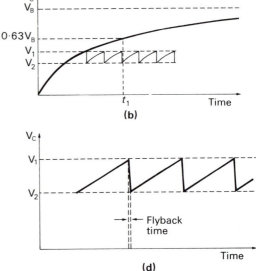

(b)

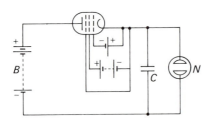

(c)

(d)

Fig. 46.7(a). A circuit for a simple relaxation oscillator.
(b). The variation of V_C with time.
(c). The use of a pentode valve to give linear sweep of voltage.
(d). An expanded portion of the sweep waveform for a circuit with pentode valve.

(For symbols see text)

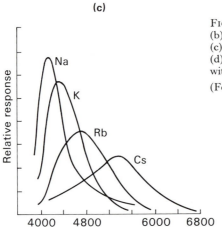

Fig. 46.8. The photoemissive response of the alkali metals.

be maintained and the lamp returns to the open-circuit condition and C begins to charge up once more. The process is repetitive as shown in Fig. 46.7(b), so that the voltage V_C has a succession of gradual sweeps upwards with rapid 'flyback'. These sweeps can be used for the time-base deflection in a cathode-ray oscilloscope, but they have the disadvantage of not being linear. The reason for this is clearly the fact that the rate at which C charges is a function of V_C because the current in R is given by $(V_B - V_C)/R$, and V_C is proportional to the charge acquired.

To obtain a linear sweep, as is so obviously desirable both for instrumental and television purposes, it is necessary to force C to charge at a constant rate; that is, to make the charging current independent of V_C. A method of doing this was invented by L. H. Bedford (Britain) in 1933, using a property of the pentode valve. The typical pentode curves shown in Fig. 46.6(b) indicate very clearly that for a fixed grid voltage, once the anode voltage is above a certain level the anode current is almost independent of it. This is just what is required. If R in Fig. 46.7(a) is replaced by a pentode connected as in Fig. 46.7(c), then C is forced to charge at a rate practically unaffected by the charge acquired. The sweep is then as shown in Fig. 46.7(d).

11. OTHER DEVICES USING ELECTRONIC EMISSION

Photoelectric devices. An early finding of Elster and Geitel, when studying photoemission, had been that the two alkali metals, sodium and potassium, responded well in a vacuum to the shorter wavelengths of the visible spectrum. By 1920 the responses of the other alkali metals had been measured, extending to longer wavelengths for those of rubidium and caesium. These results (Fig. 46.8) stimulated the development of photoemissive cells. The commonest types employed photocathodes of caesium (partially oxidized) on silver, giving a response throughout the visible spectrum and into the near infrared. Straightforward vacuum photodiodes with anode voltages as low as 10 V responded with negligible delay to incident radiation. Their sensitivity could be increased by up to ten times by the admission of an inert gas, at low pressure, and the use of higher voltages (of the order of 100 V), but at the expense of considerable loss of speed of response.

To increase sensitivity, with little loss of speed, the photomultiplier was developed (V. K. Zworykin, G. A. Morton, and L. Walter, 1936) [13]. In it, the primary electrons emitted by the photocathode are accelerated to a first anode (here called a dynode) whose surface is specially prepared to maximize the emission of secondary electrons, which in turn are accelerated towards a second dynode at a higher voltage, where a second multiplication of current takes place. Up to 10 such dynodes might be included before the final anode collects the output current, which could be 10000 times the primary (and even a million times in modern versions).

A more important device (the iconoscope) had earlier been conceived and demonstrated (1929) by Zworykin [14]. It was an image detector, giving more than merely a measure of the total useful optical flux falling upon its photosensitive electrode. An image of an illuminated scene could be focused on to this electrode, which was made up of a mosaic of very small, closely packed globules containing silver and coated with caesium. Light falling on these globules caused them to lose a proportional charge through the emission of electrons. An electron beam, of diameter several times that of a globule, was scanned across the electrode, line by line, in a manner now familiar in television. Each globule restored its charge by extracting electrons from the beam as it passed over it; the sequence of contiguous current pulses thus produced was sensed by a conducting backing plate on the electrode. The iconoscope, and some early developments of it, found increasing use, and were the forerunners of the vidicons, plumbicons, and other television camera tubes so widely used after 1950.

Cathode ray tubes. The development of electronics required new analytical instruments, none more so than one to display the waveforms of electric signals, such as those produced by a microphone when spoken into. Early attempts to meet this need used lightweight pens or galvanometers, but the speed of response, and the bandwidth of the signals satisfactorily handled, were severely limited. F. Braun's earlier work (1897) on deflecting an electron beam [15] led to the recognition that such a beam alone possessed the negligible inertia necessary to allow very high writing speeds, and spurred the efforts to design a suitable cathode ray tube (c.r.t.). The term 'cathode ray' was widely used before 1900 to denote the emission—now known to be a stream of electrons—from the cathode of a gas discharge tube when bombarded by the positive ions of the gas. It survived solely in the context of the c.r.t. and oscilloscopes using it, though no gas discharge is now implied.

The tube has several sections (see Fig. 46.9). The electron beam is produced by the gun, consisting of a thermionic cathode; a sleeve-shaped 'grid' to control the intensity of the beam, with one end closed except for a small central aperture; and a first anode (A1), also sleeve-shaped with diaphragm ends, providing the initial acceleration and the main focusing (on to the final

FIG. 46.9. A cathode ray tube with electrostatic focusing and deflection.

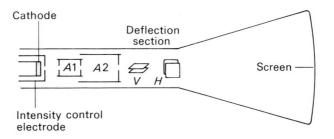

screen) of the beam. Further acceleration is provided by the second anode (A2). The beam then enters the deflection section where the horizontal and vertical deflections are effected separately, the means being either two suitably wound coils producing magnetic forces or two pairs of plates (V and H) producing electrostatic forces. The horizontal deflection is usually a linear time-base repeated regularly, while the vertical deflection represents the amplitude of the signal under observation. The deflected beam finally strikes the luminescent screen, which consists essentially of a thin layer of fine particles of a phosphor exhibiting fluorescence (an instantaneous effect) or phosphorescence (with a delay peculiar to the material used, ranging up to seconds)—or both—under the impact of the beam. Early c.r.t.s used willemite (a zinc silicate containing a manganese impurity) for yellow-green emission, or calcium tungstate giving a blue emission more easily photographed. The needs of radar systems led to improved screen materials, with silicates, sulphides, and fluorides predominating.

Microwave devices. Although conventional thermionic valves met the needs of early radar systems, there soon arose a demand for high peak powers at microwave frequencies, lasting about 1 microsecond (μs) every millisecond (ms) or so, which these valves could not supply. The magnetron, first studied by A. W. Hull in 1921 as a low-power diode using a magnetic field at right angles to the electric field between cathode and anode, was developed, largely by J. T. Randall and H. A. Boot during the early years of the Second World War, to the pitch where it was capable of delivering peak powers of more than 100kW at a frequency of 3 GHz. In this device, the emitted electrons, under the influence of the two fields, pass close to the openings of a series of cavities in the copper block making up the anode (Fig. 46.10). The cavities, together with the remainder of the structure, are of such size as to be resonant at the frequency of the microwave oscillation required. There is complex interaction between the energetic electron stream and the fields

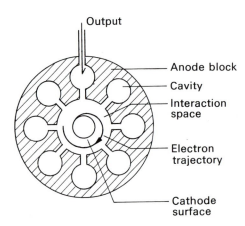

created in the cavities, allowing microwave power to be extracted. The inter-connection of alternate segments of the anode by fine wires can improve the performance.

Another promising source of microwave power was the klystron, which owed its origin to studies initiated in 1929 and renewed in the late 1930s. But the development of the magnetron as a high-power source tended to limit the role of the klystron to low-power applications—for example, as a local oscillator in radar receivers—though high-power units were successfully developed after 1950. In the klystron, a broad beam of electrons, already accelerated in a triode section, is passed in turn through an input cavity (called a buncher), a field-free space, and an output cavity (called a catcher) to a collector; the two cavities resonate at the same frequency. The buncher is so called because, for some interval in each cycle of oscillation and relative to electrons entering at the mean time of that interval, its electromagnetic field retards electrons entering earlier and accelerates those entering later, though the actual bunching becomes more pronounced as the beam passes through the field-free space. In the catcher the bunched stream excites an electromagnetic field which can extract more power from the beam than was given it in the buncher, so that suitable coupling together of the two fields leads to oscillation and extractable power at the resonant frequency. This principle of velocity modulation of a stream of electrons offers some advantage over crossed-field operation, as exploited in the magnetron, and many designs of klystron have resulted. A notable example is the reflex klystron, in which one cavity serves as both buncher and catcher, the electron beam being reflected after its first passage through the cavity by a negative-voltage electrode, called a repeller, to return through the cavity.

III. NONLINEARITY AND MODULATORS

It is clear that many, if not most, electronic elements have parameters which depend on the amplitude of the signal applied, because the graphs of response versus stimulus are not straight lines; that is, they are nonlinear. The thermionic valve, for instance, shows this well. From the typical non-linear characteristic curve relating anode current to grid voltage in a triode (Fig. 46.3(c)) it is easy to see that the mutual conductance $\partial I_a/\partial V_g$ is different for different grid–bias voltages. This was sometimes exploitable and sometimes an undesirable effect. The early use of the triode as an amplifying-detector maximized this effect to give rectification of the signal. In the early telephone and other audio amplifiers, it was realized that distortion in the form of spurious frequency components (that is, harmonics and inter-modulation products), was produced, and so the effect was minimized by suitable choice of grid bias; and after about 1930, by compensatory arrangements such as 'push–pull' circuits in which two valves were used to balance out the even-order distortion, as shown in Fig. 46.11.

In radio-telephony it was necessary to modulate the amplitude of a carrier wave by the speech waveform; this was amplitude modulation (A.M.). A good way of doing this was to use the nonlinearity of the triode valve. In

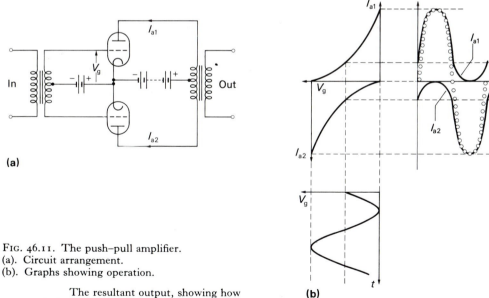

(a)

(b)

FIG. 46.11. The push–pull amplifier.
(a). Circuit arrangement.
(b). Graphs showing operation.

         The resultant output, showing how symmetrical waveform is obtained.

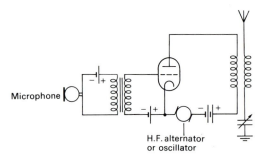

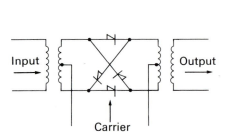

FIG. 46.12. The triode valve used as modulator in radio transmitter.

FIG. 46.13. A ring modulator using solid-state rectifiers.

experiments in the early 1900s a carbon microphone had been used directly in the aerial circuit; its varying resistance, which followed the variations of sound pressure, modulated the instantaneous transmitted power by varying the proportion of aerial power absorbed in the resistance of the microphone. Microphones could not, however, absorb large amounts of power. Consequently, when radio-telephony later came into service with transmitters of higher power, a triode valve was used as the modulating resistance; one arrangement is shown in Fig. 46.12. This relies on the fact that the internal resistance $\partial V_a / \partial I_a$ of the triode depends markedly on the grid voltage. Other early methods of modulation included the direct modulation of the amplitude of oscillation in a triode-valve oscillator by applying the speech signal to the grid of the valve. There was much distortion in these early modulators, but improved circuits were rapidly developed. Modulators using saturable iron-cored inductors were also used, but not widely.

In carrier telephone systems (originally on lines, but later also on radio links), and in single-sideband systems generally (Ch. 50), a different kind of modulator came into use in the 1930s. This was based on solid-state rectifiers, at that time of the copper-oxide type. In principle, thermionic diodes could have been used; later, from the 1940s onwards, germanium and silicon rectifiers were used. There were many different circuit arrangements, but one of the most widely used was the 'ring' modulator, shown in Fig. 46.13, so called because the rectifiers pointed round a ring. The operation of the circuit is most usefully described by assuming that each rectifier is a perfect switch, opening when the voltage across it is negative, closing when positive. The carrier-wave voltage is high with respect to the input signal voltage and so controls the 'switches', which thus reverse the polarity of the signal twice in each carrier cycle. The output thus comprises the sidebands of the modu-

FIG. 46.14. A valve reactor circuit for frequency-modulation.

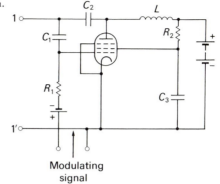

L = high frequency choke; C_2 = coupling capacitance; C_3 = smoothing capacitance; R_1 = very small compared with reactance of C_1 at carrier frequency; R_2 = fairly high resistance.

Modulating signal

lated signal, but not the carrier itself. Rectifier modulators of this family have been used in millions in telephone systems and many other electronic systems.

Frequency modulation (F.M.) became an important process in the late 1930s, although as a concept it was much older [16]. Its principle was to carry the signal information by modulating, not the amplitude, but the frequency of the carrier. To effect this, one method was to connect a circuit called a 'valve reactor' (Fig. 46.14) across the tuned circuit of the carrier oscillator. This circuit produces an effective capacitance between terminals 1,1′, which is made up of two components: C_1, plus another approximately equal to the product of $R_1 C_1$ multiplied by the mutual conductance of the valve. The modulating signal, applied to the grid circuit with suitable bias, modulates the mutual conductance and hence the effective capacitance across 1,1′. Since this is connected across the tuned circuit of the carrier oscillator, the frequency generated by the latter is modulated by the signal. At the receiver, the F.M. wave is applied to a circuit which has an amplitude response varying very sharply with frequency, thus converting the F.M. to A.M. which can then be detected in the normal way. Later, more sophisticated ways of forming and detecting F.M. signals were developed.

IV. CIRCUIT AND SYSTEM THEORY

The development of electronic and communication engineering has depended not only on the provision of suitable electronic devices and passive components but also, perhaps *a fortiore*, on the development of circuit (or 'network') theory, which towards the end of the first half of the twentieth century started to extend rapidly into system theory. While much, perhaps most, of the design work in communications up to the 1920s was done on an empirical basis, relying on a knowledge of the physical behaviour of the devices and components, yet there can be little doubt that the rapid progress of the 1930s and 1940s was due to the more general use of mathematical formulation in the conception and design of new circuits and systems.

Circuit and system theory is so abstruse and mathematical that its history can be presented properly only in terms which require a high degree of specialized knowledge. An excellent history in that class was given by V. Belevitch in 1962 [17]. Here we must be content with a history in broad terms with elementary examples. Four stages of development may be identified:

(i) The mathematical statement of the properties of individual circuit elements and of simple combinations of elements.

(ii) The formulation of the properties of complex circuit structures in which each simple combination of elements is represented by a mathematically-defined impedance or admittance function.

(iii) The use of this knowledge and special procedures to synthesize a complex circuit that will have a prescribed performance within stated tolerances.

(iv) The extension of these ideas to systems in which the various parts are complex circuits, each represented only by a mathematical function defining its behaviour as observable externally between one pair of terminals and another.

Simple combinations of elements. The basic passive circuit elements are resistance (R (ohms)), inductance (L (henries)), and capacitance (C (farads)), and a simple series combination of all three is shown in Fig. 46.15(a). The term 'passive' is used to distinguish these elements from 'active' elements such as valves, in which voltage and/or current sources operate notionally within the element (see below).

The differential equation for the *RLC* circuit of Fig. 46.15(a) was first set up by William Thomson (later Lord Kelvin) in 1853 [18]. He was concerned with the discharge of a capacitor (for example, a Leyden jar) through a conductor which had resistance and a property which he called 'electro-dynamic capacity', that is, inductance. In more specifically circuit terms, the equation was restated by J. Clerk Maxwell in 1868 [19]; in modern symbols:

$$E \sin \omega t = L \frac{di}{dt} + Ri + \frac{1}{C} \int i \, dt,$$

where i is the current and $E \sin \omega t$ the applied voltage. Maxwell pointed out that the current would be a maximum when $\omega L = 1/\omega C$. This knowledge was not put to much practical use, however, until work began on radio, with H. R. Hertz in 1887 (he called the effect 'resonance') and Oliver Lodge in 1890 (who called the effect 'syntony'). Electrical power engineers were also conscious of the effects of L and C about this time, although they were concerned with the much lower frequencies of a.c. power supplies.

As early as 1882, F. van Rysselberghe (Belgium) used a capacitance and inductance to separate a telephone and a telegraph channel working on the same wire [20], as shown in Fig. 46.15(b)—the forerunner of the high-pass and low-pass filter pair—and in 1883 he was using the circuit of Fig. 46.15(c). for the telegraph channel: a low-pass filter of the type normally associated with the 1920s. However, he did not examine this circuit mathematically.

The equation given above, and all calculations on more complex circuits, used the basic laws enunciated by G. R. Kirchhoff in 1845–7, that the voltage drops round a closed-loop circuit must sum to zero, and likewise the currents flowing into a junction of several conductors (that is, into a 'node'). Maxwell, in 1873, extended these laws to provide a means of solution for circuits with any number of interconnected nodes; his mesh and nodal equations, as they are now usually called, remain the fundamental method of circuit calculation.

Around 1890, O. Heaviside introduced the idea of an operational calculus for circuits; the use of vector (now called 'phasor') diagrams for the calculation of impedance and the application of the j operator (where mathematically $j = \sqrt{(-1)}$), were introduced in the 1890s. We thus see that the whole basis for circuit calculations was available before 1900.

When the thermionic triode valve came into general use in amplifiers, it

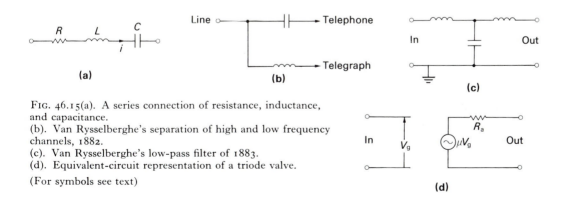

FIG. 46.15(a). A series connection of resistance, inductance, and capacitance.
(b). Van Rysselberghe's separation of high and low frequency channels, 1882.
(c). Van Rysselberghe's low-pass filter of 1883.
(d). Equivalent-circuit representation of a triode valve.

(For symbols see text)

was found useful to have the equivalent circuit shown in Fig. 46.15(d) to represent it in circuit calculations. Here μ is the amplification factor $\partial V_a / \partial V_g$, and R_a the internal resistance $\partial V_a / \partial I_a$. Grid current and inter-electrode capacitances could be allowed for by inserting extra elements. Since there is here a built-in source of electromotive force (e.m.f.), the valve is termed an 'active' circuit element.

Complex circuit structures. The beginning of the next stage of circuit theory dates from the work on loaded lines by G. A. Campbell and M. I. Pupin (U.S.A.) in about 1900 [21]. Calculations on cables and lines had, from the days of long telegraph cables, been based on distributed resistance and capacitance and, later, leakance and inductance. However, the introduction of loading coils at regular intervals in a line introduced a 'lumped' element into the system, and the idea of a recurrent circuit or network structure (Fig. 46.16(a)) developed. Here R, L, G, and C are the resistance, inductance, leakance, and capacitance of a line collected into a 'lumped' circuit to represent a given length of line. From the point of view of transmission between terminal pairs (or 'ports') 1,1' and 2,2', the 'unbalanced' tee network of Fig. 46.16(b) is equivalent; equally so is the pi network of Fig. 46.16(c) if the length represented is very small. From this developed the generalized networks of Figs. 46.16(d), (e), and (f), where Z_1, Z_2, and Z_3 are impedance functions expressed mathematically; equally well they could be admittance functions Y_1, Y_2, and Y_3.

Networks of these kinds (and of other kinds, too) can be connected in a chain, each two-port section having different responses if desired, so that specified overall transmission properties may be achieved. One very important early use was in 'electric wave filters'.

The idea of an electric wave filter as a formal network structure which will pass signals of some frequencies (in the 'pass-band') while giving a high loss to others (in the 'stop-band'), as indicated in Fig. 46.16(g), appears to have been due to G. A. Campbell in 1915 [22]. A formal system of such network structures giving a very large degree of control over their characteristics, based on the matching of so-called 'image' impedances at the junctions of the tee, pi, or L sections, was invented by O. J. Zobel (U.S.A.) and published in 1923 [23]. The Zobel system of filters was widely used for carrier telephone systems for many years. In practice, abrupt cut-off as shown in Fig. 46.16(g) was not realizable, and methods of optimizing pass-band and stop-band responses were introduced by W. Cauer (Germany) and others in the early

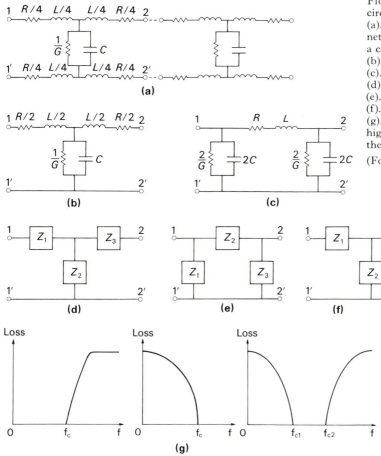

FIG. 46.16. The development of complex circuit structures and filters.

(a). The recurrent 'ladder' circuit or network, derived from representation of a cable or line.

(b). The Tee or T network.

(c). The Pi or π network.

(d). A generalized Tee network.

(e). A generalized Pi network.

(f). The L network.

(g). Loss/frequency curves for low-pass, high-pass, and band-pass filters (f_c is the cut-off frequency).

(For symbols see text)

1930s, leading to formal mathematical synthesis of networks to give a specified performance by S. Darlington (U.S.A.) in 1939 [24].

As electronic systems extended in frequency into the microwave region (centimetric wavelengths, frequencies of thousands of megahertz), the concept of lumped circuits had to be extended to wave concepts: waveguides, cavity resonators, etc.

With the introduction of pulse and waveform-transmission systems, for example, television, the determination and specification of performance in terms of amplitude or loss or gain versus frequency was not always adequate, and performance in terms of time-response had to be considered. The foundation for this had been laid in the work of J. A. Carson, E. A. Guillemin (both U.S.A.), and others during the 1920s and 1930s.

V. SOLID-STATE DEVICES

The thermionic valve, in its triode and later forms, had no serious competitor as an amplifying device until the junction transistor was developed; but it had several as a diode. Two such competitors, distinguished particularly by their geometries, were metal rectifiers and crystal detectors. Both exploited the unidirectional flow of current between a metal and a semiconductor (a class of material with electrical conductivity intermediate between metals and insulators). Metal rectifiers belonged to electrical engineering generally, for example, for battery charging, electroplating, and copper refining. Crystal detectors were initially specific to early radio receivers, a passing application that did not lead to elucidation of the rectifying property that was used. A later application, which valves could not satisfactorily meet, demanded fuller studies, from which sprung the transistor.

Metal rectifiers. L. O. Grondahl's work (1926) on the copper–cuprous oxide interface [25] led to reproducible and stable rectifiers, in contrast to earlier studies of metal to oxide (or sulphide) interfaces. Production, begun in the U.S.A., was simple though empirical. Discs of high-purity copper, about 1 mm thick, were oxidized at about 1000 °C. If this process, or any subsequent annealing, produced a surface film of cupric oxide (CuO), as well as the required layer of cuprous oxide (Cu_2O), it was removed chemically or mechanically. The second (counter) electrode, making good contact to the oxide layer, evolved from lead washers through colloidal graphite to sputtered metals. The direction of easy flow of current was from oxide to copper. Because current blocking in the other direction became unsatisfactory when the applied voltage exceeded about 10 V, many applications required multiple units, series-connected. Units of large area, for heavy current use, also incorporated cooling fins. Applications were as power rectifiers, modulators, and simple switches.

The copper oxide rectifier had a rival in the selenium type, developed a little later, though first studied much earlier by Fritts (1883). In production, a pure powdered form of selenium was spread thinly on plates of steel or aluminium (preferred for its better thermal conductivity, for larger units), and heat treated just below its melting point (217 °C), converting it to the required crystalline form and making good electrical contact with the plates. The rectifying interface was then prepared by spraying the exposed selenium surface with an alloy of low melting-point, for example, of bismuth and cadmium with lead or tin, serving also as the second electrode. Forming, by the passage of current in the 'non-easy' direction of flow (from the second electrode to the plate), much improved the performance. The maximum usable inverse voltages, though higher than for the copper-oxide type, were still insufficient to avoid the necessity for stacking for most applications.

Crystal detectors. A crystal detector was essentially a fine wire with pointed tip (called a cat's whisker) pressed flexibly, with a force of about 1 gram, on to the surface of a small crystal (or one in a polycrystalline piece) of a semiconductor. Several minerals (for example, galena) were used as suitable semiconductors for this purpose. The whisker acted as one electrode and a metallic clamp for the crystal as the other. Variations in the ratio of forward to reverse conductivity were considerable as the whisker tip was moved over the crystal surface. Units for early radio receivers allowed for such movement, permitting a search for a sensitive spot. Unfortunately, usage or shock could quickly spoil the performance, necessitating a further search.

A later application, in radar receivers of the Second World War and primarily for a 'mixer' (modulator) rather than a detector, demanded a much better controlled and reliable unit. Efforts concentrated on silicon with low levels of added impurity as the semiconductor, and wires of tungsten or molybdenum. Empirical searching gave way to (rather less) empirical tapping which could much improve performance, though lightly welding the wire tip to the silicon was sometimes practised. The maximum withstandable reverse voltage—before breakdown and permanent damage occurred—was low.

Because the element germanium resembles silicon in being tetravalent and crystallizing with the same (diamond) structure, attention was given to germanium point-contact diodes. Units with much higher peak inverse voltages became possible, allowing use in many valve switching and logic circuits such as were used in early electronic digital computers. With its lower melting-point, facilitating the preparation of single crystals, and a higher mobility for conduction electrons, germanium received more study in the late 1940s (and indeed the early 1950s) than silicon. The discovery of transistor action, launching a new era in electronics, was thus brought forward.

The transistor. Scientists had long speculated on the possibilities of adding a third electrode either to a solid-state rectifier to modulate the current–voltage relationship or to a piece of semiconductor to modulate its conductivity, with the object of achieving amplification or controlled switching.

Thus J. Lillienfeld had sought patents in 1925, 1927, and 1928 for three different structures. The most notable was the third, an insulated-gate field-effect device resembling the metal-oxide–silicon transistor (MOST) of the 1960s; copper sulphide was cited as the semiconductor with an aluminium foil as the gate electrode insulated from the semiconductor by having been anodized. But no demonstration was given; the necessary materials technology was lacking. Twenty years later, both the preparation of semiconductors and understanding of their properties, had much advanced with the work on silicon and germanium point-contact diodes. One fact, in particular, had been fully established. Semiconductors could conduct in one of two ways: either by 'free' electrons (electrons surplus to those needed to bind together the atoms in the crystal, and normally present in silicon and germanium if a pentavalent impurity has been added) when it is labelled n-type ('n' for negative), or by 'holes' (deficiencies in the binding electrons, normally present if a trivalent impurity has been added) when it is labelled p-type ('p' for positive). The holes do indeed respond to electric fields as if positively charged. Although the properties of the barrier to current flow at the contact of a metal and a semiconductor—which is lowered when a voltage of one polarity is applied and raised for the other polarity—were not wholly predictable, the possibility of efficient rectification at the junction between an n region and a p region integral in one crystal was emerging.

A series of experiments, backed by relevant theoretical studies, at the Bell Telephone Laboratories revealed and explained new findings. Thus J. Bardeen and W. H. Brattain (1947), using a second whisker to probe the surface of n-type germanium close to (within 0·1 mm of) the point of contact of a whisker which was carrying a forward current (I_E), discovered that when the second whisker was reverse biased it passed an abnormally high current (I_C) approximately proportional to I_E [26]. Indeed dI_C/dI_E could exceed unity, but—most important of all—because the first forward-biased contact presented low impedance and the second, reverse-biased, a high impedance, power gain could be obtained. Here, therefore, was a solid-state amplifying device, to be called a point-contact transistor (Fig. 46.17(a)). Its electronic behaviour was explained as follows. The first point contact (the emitter) injected holes into the n-type germanium (the base); under the influence of the voltage of the second contact (the collector) the majority of the holes travelled to that electrode undiminished despite the presence of the free electrons in the base. That presence, it had hitherto been assumed, would destroy holes instantaneously; that is, make good any deficiencies (holes)

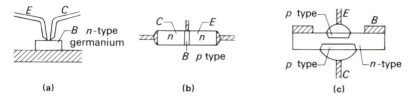

FIG. 46.17. The earliest transistors. (a). Point contact. (b). Germanium *n–p–n* grown junction. (c). Germanium *p–n–p* alloyed.

E = emitter; *B* = base; *C* = collector; hatched areas are metallic connections.

occurring in the binding (valency) electrons. The current gain at the collector turned out to be of less importance.

W. Shockley, encouraged by his colleagues' findings, then postulated a junction transistor, in which a piece of monocrystalline semiconductor comprised three regions (emitter, base, and collector) respectively of *n-*, *p-*, and *n*-types [27]. He predicted very promising electrical behaviour for it, involving electrons being injected from the *n*-type emitter into the *p*-type base, and diffusing to the collector. Efforts to fabricate the structure followed—a formidable task. Success came in 1950 (W. Shockley, M. Sparks, and G. K. Teal [28]) with a structure grown by adapting the Czochralski technique already in use for pulling monocrystalline ingots from a melt held close to its freezing-point. The conventional seed crystal was dipped into *n*-type molten germanium, but after a few millimetres of solid had been grown on, the melt was over-doped to *p*-type by the addition of a suitable impurity; when an additional length of up to 0·05 mm had been grown the melt was over-doped in the opposite direction, reconverting it to *n*-type, and a further short length grown. The ingot was cut lengthwise into bars, each containing the three regions (*n*-type collector, *p*-type base, and *n*-type emitter), and wire connections made to each region of a bar (Fig. 46.17(b)). The performance of the grown junction transistor confirmed Shockley's predictions completely. The device proved reproducible, and offered a power gain higher than that of the point-contact transistor which quickly lost favour, the more so when R. R. Law [29] and, independently, J. S. Saby (1952) [30] developed a method of making junction transistors well suited to large-scale production. They started with small wafers of *n*-type germanium of thickness about 0·1 mm, and alloyed pairs of small pellets of indium—a trivalent element of low melting-point—to the pairs of faces. Hence *p-n-p* structures resulted (see Fig. 46.17(c)). Contact-making was straightforward.

Although the good performance of early junction transistors was largely confined to frequencies below 100 kHz, their electrical characterization was simple, presenting few problems to circuit designers. They could be used with input signals applied to the emitter and output taken from the collector (with grounded base), or have input to the base with output from collector (with grounded emitter) or from emitter (with grounded collector). Their potential as low-power switches and as logic elements was quickly seized upon for many applications.

Further developments concentrated on reducing the base width—the major factor restricting bandwidth—from 0·025 mm to 0·001 mm and less, and on methods of processing silicon to make similar devices, thereby to benefit from the smaller leakage currents inherent in silicon devices and their ability to perform better than germanium counterparts at higher ambient temperatures. But the resulting predominance of silicon stemmed as much from the excellent electrical, and chemically passive properties of its thermally grown oxide (a vitreous silica), permitting the mass production of wideband devices by a planar technology. All that, however, belongs to the second half of the twentieth century.

VI. PASSIVE COMPONENTS

The most common passive components used in electronic circuits were resistors, capacitors, inductors, and transformers. Electrical engineering had made available examples of all four types by 1900. Electronic engineering began by using the same general designs, but from around 1920 made demands for specific improvements, to which research and development responded, generally successfully.

Resistors. The resistance (R) of a conductor depends on its geometry and the resistivity (ρ) of its material. For a wire of length L and cross-sectional area A, $R = \rho L/A$. Electronic engineering requires resistors having R in the range from about 10 to 10^6 ohms. They must also have the ability to dissipate the heat produced by the current flowing, a small temperature coefficient of resistance, and specified tolerances of resistance.

By 1900 both wire and carbon-composition resistors were available. For the former, pure metals had generally too low a resistivity and too high a temperature coefficient (typically 4000 p.p.m./°C). Alloys were developed with more suitable values. German silver (copper, zinc, and nickel) and Constantin (copper and nickel) had resistivities some twenty times that of copper, and coefficients around one-twentieth. Manganin (copper, manganese, and nickel) had a coefficient less than 20 p.p.m./°C at 20 °C. The wire was wound on a former, but even the best designs introduced enough self-capacitance or self-inductance to upset performance at frequencies above about 1 MHz. Carbon-composition resistors greatly extended the frequency range, enabled high values of resistance (for example, 1 megohm) to be easily produced, and were cheap; but manufacture to close tolerances proved impracticable and their temperature coefficient was large and negative, typically −1000 p.p.m./°C. By 1930 they were in large-scale production, with wire types restricted to special uses.

Carbon-film resistors, developed in Germany in 1928, represented a major advance, and later found much use. The film was deposited on a ceramic rod by the pyrolysis of a hydrocarbon and a thin spiral cut in it to make what was effectively a long narrow strip of film. Tolerances on nominal values could be finer than ±1 per cent; the temperature coefficient was typically −250 p.p.m./°C.

Thermistors (that is, resistors with very pronounced sensitivity to temperature, making them suitable as temperature sensors, regulating elements, etc.) were developed before 1950; they used oxides of manganese and nickel.

Small-sized variable resistors and potentiometers were in continuous demand, for example as volume controls of radio receivers. Wire and carbon-film types, on circular formers with a sliding contact attached to a rotatable central spindle, generally met the demand.

Capacitors. Circuit needs for discrete capacitance (called capacity until about 1950) were met by capacitors (previously called condensers), deriving from the Leyden jar (1745). The late nineteenth century saw more compact forms, but all comprised essentially a pair of conducting plates, parallel to one another and separated by an insulating gap filled with gaseous, liquid, or, more usually, solid material possessing suitable dielectric properties. The capacitance (C) is approximately proportional to the area of the plates, inversely proportional to their separation, and proportional to the permittivity (k) of the dielectric (called the specific inductive capacity in the nineteenth century and later the dielectric constant).

The first dielectric of industrial importance was wax-impregnated paper ($k = 1.2$ for paper, but 3 for waxed paper). The capacitor would be made up of a strip of tinfoil, two sheets of the paper, another strip of tinfoil, and two more sheets of paper, all rolled up together to make a very compact component which could have capacitances of up to 10 microfarads (μF) and be able to withstand direct voltages of 100 V or more.

Dielectric loss in a capacitor introduces a resistive component in its imped-ance. Although paper capacitors were acceptable for most uses, lower loss and smaller size could be obtained—at greater cost—with mica as the dielectric ($k \simeq 6$). Other materials also found applications, culminating in the 1940s with rutile (TiO_2), and some titanates, having $k \simeq 100$.

Where large capacitance (for example, 25 μF) was required in a small volume, without the need for precision or low loss (for example, in smoothing power supplies), dry aluminium electrolytic capacitors became important. Evolving from an earlier wet type (demonstrated in 1892), they used a strip of absorbent material saturated with (usually) a borate, sandwiched between an anodically oxidized aluminium foil and a plain foil. The voltage across this capacitor had to be of stated polarity.

Variable capacitors, for example, for tuning radio receivers, almost always comprised a set of fixed vanes with rotatable cam-shaped vanes interleaved, with air as the dielectric (Fig. 46.18).

Inductors and transformers. An inductor is essentially a closely wound coil of copper wire, with inductance (L) proportional both to the area and the square

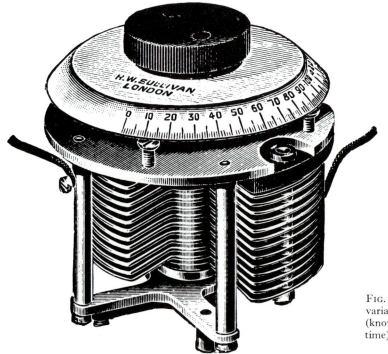

Fig. 46.18. A continuously variable air capacitor, *c.* 1920 (known as a condenser at that time).

of the number of turns. When the coil is immersed in a material of magnetic permeability μ, L increases μ times. In practice a magnetic core is used, filling the cross-section of the coil and forming a loop of its own, achieving much the same increase. Air-cored coils found some favour in early radio receivers, but more latterly only at higher frequencies.

A transformer closely resembles an inductor in construction, except in having more than one coil. It offers transformations of impedance, voltage, and current between the circuits connected to its separate coils.

Coil winding changed little effectively between 1900 and 1950, beyond being mechanized; inductor and transformer development consequently centred on improved core materials.

In 1900 the electricity supply industry was already seeking materials better than soft iron for its transformers. R. A. Hadfield had led the way, with alloys of iron with a few per cent of silicon; production of bulk material began in 1903 followed a few years later by laminations which, stacked with thin insulation between, much reduced the power losses due to the eddy currents induced in the core.

Electronics used this family of alloys ($\mu \simeq 5000$) for its power transformers and smoothing inductors (familiarly called 'chokes'), but sought still higher values of μ for components handling signal frequencies. G. W. Elmen (1917) showed the promise of alloys of nickel (80 per cent) with iron (20 per cent) [31]. Several families were developed, with small additions of other metals; two, mumetal and permalloy, offered values of μ up to 100 000. They found wide use. But, even with lamination thickness reduced to 0·025 mm, their eddy-current losses were unacceptable at the higher radio frequencies. Attention turned to the use of insulated particles (the dimensions of which were to be measured in microns) of iron or nickel-iron mixtures, compressed together and fired, to form 'dust' cores. Despite their considerable sacrifice of permeability, they found use from about 1920. Then, around 1935, the magnetic properties of ferrites—first reported on by S. Hilpert in 1909 [32] —were re-examined with marked success, leading to production and many applications. Ferrites have the generic formula $MO.Fe_2O_3$, where M is a divalent element, as in nickel ferrite, $NiFe_2O_4$, or a mixture of two such elements, as in zinc manganese ferrite, $ZnMnFe_4O_8$. They are insulators, thereby minimizing eddy current loss, and the various compositions offer a range of values of μ up to about 1000. Both dust and ferrite cores were frequently offered in toroidal shape, necessitating coil-winding directly on to them, instead of on to bobbins or formers into which earlier cores fitted.

REFERENCES

[1] GUTHRIE, F. *Philosophical Magazine* (4th series) **46**, 257 (1873).

[2] ANON. *Engineering*, **38**, 553 (1884).

[3] THOMSON, J. J. *Philosophical Magazine* (5th series), **44**, 293 (1897).

[4] RICHARDSON, O. W. *Proceedings of the Cambridge Philosophical Society*, **11**, 286 (1901).

[5] WEHNELT, A. *Annalen der Physik*, **14,** 425 (1904).

[6] FLEMING, J. A. British Patent 24 850; 1904.

[7] DE FOREST, L. *Transactions of the American Institute of Electrical Engineers*, **25**, 735 (1906).

[8] ARMSTRONG, E. H. *Proceedings of the Institute of Radio Engineers*, **3**, 215 (1915).

[9] TUCKER, D. G. *Radio and Electronic Engineer*, **42**, 69 (1972).

[10] HAZELTINE, L. A. *Proceedings of the Radio Club of America*, **2**, No. 8 (1923).

[11] SCHOTTKY, W. *Archiv für Elektrotechnik*, **8**, 1 and 299 (1919).

[12] HOLST, G. and TELLEGEN, B. D. H. U.S. Patent 1 945 040; filed 1927.

[13] ZWORYKIN, V. K., MORTON, G. A., and WALTER, L. *Proceedings of the Institute of Radio Engineers*, **24**, 251 (1936).

[14] ZWORYKIN, V. K. *Proceedings of the Institute of Radio Engineers*, **22**, 16 (1934).

[15] BRAUN, F. *Annalen der Physik*, **60**, 552 (1897).

[16] TUCKER, D. G. *Radio and Electronic Engineer*, **40**, 33 (1970).

[17] BELEVITCH, V. *Proceedings of the Institute of Radio Engineers*, **50,** 848 (1962).

[18] THOMSON, W. *Philosophical Magazine*, **5**, 393 (1853).

[19] MAXWELL, J. C. *Philosophical Magazine*, **35**, 360 (1868).

[20] VAN RYSSELBERGHE, F. British Patents 2466, 1882; and 5503, 1883.

[21] BRITTAIN, J. E. *Technology and Culture*, **11**, 36 (1970).

[22] CAMPBELL, G. A. U.S. Patents 1 227 113 and 1 227 114; filed 1915.

[23] ZOBEL, O. J. *Bell System Technical Journal*, **2**, 1 (1923).

[24] DARLINGTON, S. *Journal of Mathematics and Physics*, **18**, 257 (1939).

[25] GRONDAHL, L. O. *Physical Review*, **27**, 813 (1926).

[26] BARDEEN, J. and BRATTAIN, W. H. *Physical Review*, **74**, 230 (1948).

[27] SHOCKLEY, W. *Bell System Technical Journal*, **28**, 435 (1949).

[28] SHOCKLEY, W., SPARKS, M., and TEAL, G. K. *Physical Review*, **83**, 151 (1951).

[29] LAW, R. R. *Proceedings of the Institute of Radio Engineers*, **40**, 1352 (1952).

[30] SABY, J. S. *Proceedings of the Institute of Radio Engineers*, **40**, 1358 (1952).

[31] ELMEN, G. W. Canadian Patent 180 539; filed 1916.

[32] SNOEK, J. L. *Philips Technical Review*, **8**, 353 (1946).

BIBLIOGRAPHY

CRUFT LABORATORY, HARVARD UNIVERSITY. *Electronic circuits and tubes*. McGraw–Hill, New York (1947).

FLEMING, J. A. *The thermionic valve*. Wireless Press, London (1919).

GUILLEMIN, E. A. *Communication networks*. Wiley, New York (1935).

HEAVISIDE, O. *Electrical papers*. Macmillan, London (1892).

LATHAM, R., KING, A. H., and RUSHFORTH, L. *The magnetron*. Chapman and Hall, London (1952).

LUBSZYNSKI, H. G. Photocells for the visible and ultra-violet, in *Electronics* (ed. B. LOVELL), pp. 53–95. Pilot Press, London (1947).

MAXWELL, J. C. *Electricity and magnetism.* Oxford University Press (1873).

REICH, H. J. *Theory and applications of electron tubes.* McGraw–Hill, New York (1939).

ROUND, H. J. *The shielded four-electrode valve.* Cassell and Bernard Jones, London (1927).

SAY, M. G. (ed.). *Cathode-ray tubes.* Newnes, London (1954).

SCOTT-TAGGART, J. *Wireless vacuum tubes.* Radio Press, London (1922).

SHIVE, J. N. *The properties, physics and design of semiconductor devices.* Van Nostrand, New York (1959).

SHOCKLEY, W. *Electrons and holes in semiconductors.* Van Nostrand, Princeton (1950).

TERMAN, F. E. *Radio engineers' handbook.* McGraw–Hill, New York (1943).

TORREY, H. C. and WHITMER, C. A. *Crystal rectifiers.* McGraw–Hill, New York (1948).

TUCKER, D. G. *Modulators and frequency changers.* Macdonald, London (1953).

TURNER, L. B. *Wireless telegraphy and telephony.* Cambridge (1921).

ZWORYKIN, V. K. and RAMBERG, E. G. *Photo-electricity.* Wiley, New York (1930).

47

DOMESTIC APPLIANCES

G. B. L. WILSON

THE domestic appliance as we now know it was essentially a product of the nineteenth century, when for the first time in man's history iron and brass were in good supply and there were craftsmen and inventors in abundance. Before that time the life of the common man differed little from that of his forbears for many centuries before. His wood fires burned in brick recesses in the wall, his food was cooked in metal pots slung over them, and his water for all purposes heated over the same fire in cauldrons. Domestic baths scarcely existed and lavatories, outside the house, were little more than holes in the earth or buckets beneath a wooden bench. A man of the Middle Ages had little less in the way of creature comforts than a man at the end of the eighteenth century. Indeed, pots and pans, pokers, and pot-hooks were all that either had.

But in the nineteenth century, with the systematic mining of coal and the advent of the machines of the Industrial Revolution (and all the tools and accessories which they required), men's minds turned to inventing devices which could make their living conditions a little less primitive and miserable, could economize in the use of effort, which was fully extended in the weary toil of the factories, and could save money when food and fuel had to be bought in shops instead of being freely culled from the woods and fields around them.

With one or two exceptions, nearly all the domestic appliances which we have today were invented during the nineteenth century but not fully developed or exploited until the twentieth. The reason was that in those days there was an abundance of domestic servants to do all the work of the household. The first pieces of household equipment to receive the inventors' attentions were the open fireplaces in the sitting room, burning coal or wood, and the huge open-sided roasting fires in the kitchen. Both were extremely wasteful (most of the heat going up the chimney) but there were plenty of servants to keep them well fed with fuel. Their reformation was largely the work of the American social scientist Benjamin Thompson, who later became Count Rumford. He redesigned the wasteful open fireplace with its iron basket of burning coal set beneath a huge chimney opening, by installing a compact iron grate in the bricked-up recess with a comparatively small outlet to the chimney. This was the 'Rumford Fireplace'. He also built the first kitchen range by enclosing the coal fire in a square brick setting with a flat top on which stood the pots and pans. These two appliances, the scientifically designed fireplace and the kitchen range, might well be considered to be the first 'domestic appliances'; they date from 1800 and just before. Many others had also tackled the problems of making the burning of fuel more efficient in the house, notably Benjamin Franklin. The 'Franklin Stove' of 1745 was widely used in America and it is interesting to note that many stoves of this pattern are still in use in the Tessin, the Italian-speaking part of Switzerland, where they are still called 'Franklins'. Rumford also invented the infuser-type coffee pot (almost identical with those in use today) to provide an alternative beverage for the citizens of Munich, whose drunkenness was causing concern to his employer, Maximilian I, Elector of Bavaria.

The application of plumbing (used by the Romans) and the provision of a piped water supply to cities was another achievement of the nineteenth century, but it was not until a proper system of sewers and drains existed that this water could be used to its full extent in lavatories (Vol. IV, Chs. 15 and 16; Vol. V, Ch. 23). This, too, was a nineteenth-century achievement. By the end of the century the water-closet (invented by Sir John Harington in 1596 but not put into general use until the water-closets of Cummings (1775) and J. Bramah (1778) were being installed in wealthy households) was universal in most city dwellings. From 1889, when the washdown closet was introduced, there has been little improvement in home sanitation—the design remained the same.

When coal-gas was first introduced (in London in 1812) it was considered only as a source of light, and as such it transformed the living and working conditions of all town dwellers. Its use as a source of heat, for cooking and warming, came later (Vol. IV, pp. 273-4)—with the gas cooker, the geyser, and the gas fire as the outstanding examples of domestic appliances of the nineteenth century.

Whereas the invention of most of the domestic appliances took place in England, and to a less degree on the Continent, it was in America that they were developed more quickly. There was good reason for this: Britain and the Continent always had cheap supplies of coal and labour for domestic work. The need for domestic appliances, in consequence, was not as great as it was in America where the pioneers of the nineteenth century were fully occupied in building, hunting, mining, and prospecting and had little time for the amenities of living. Anything that reduced the labour of domestic washing, cleaning, water heating (even dishwashing and apple peeling) was seized on and used to the full. As Siegfried Giedion wrote: '. . . in England servants were a *class* and a *profession*'. In America they never were, except for the Negroes.

I. THE INTRODUCTION OF ELECTRICITY

Although electricity had been introduced as a public service in the last two decades of the nineteenth century, its progress in the household was slow, for two reasons. First, it was an expensive form of energy and not many houses had a supply installed; secondly, coal gas was very firmly entrenched for lighting, heating, and cooking, and was capable of strongly resisting any opposition—a virtue which became a necessity in the twentieth century and which has served it well.

The first Electric Lighting Acts in Britain were passed in 1882 but the competition with gas did not begin until 1892. Almost the only use proposed for electricity in the early years was for lighting, for which it had obvious advantages in the ease with which it could be switched on and off. Gas lighting at that time was by flat-flame burners which were almost comparable with the comparatively feeble carbon-filament electric bulbs then in use. In 1887, however, Auer von Welsbach's incandescent gas mantles were introduced (Vol. IV, p. 274) and by 1900 were in general use. Electricity found it hard to compete. Furthermore, in the 1890s the gas companies introduced the coin-in-the-slot gas meter (invented by Thorp and Marsh in 1889) and this put gas within the reach of the working classes and greatly increased the clientele. Gas was, however, suitable only for lighting, cooking, and heating; electricity could be turned to other uses: the saving of labour with the application of the electric motor.

All the mechanical devices in the nineteenth-century household were operated by hand: the washing-machines, the mincers, the apple-parers, the knife cleaners, the mangles, and even the ice-making machines. But the twentieth century saw the development of the small electric motor, and this gradually took over all the hand-operated gadgets. The first use of the small electric motor in the house was to drive a fan. The Westinghouse Company in America took up the small motor developed for them by Nikola Tesla, fitted it to a small rotary fan in 1889, and offered it for sale for use in offices and houses in 1891.

11. THE VACUUM CLEANER

The second device to use the electric motor was the vacuum cleaner, invented and patented by H. Cecil Booth in 1901. It was an entirely new domestic appliance: nothing like it had been seen before among the myriad of nineteenth-century inventions.

Booth was a civil engineer occupied in designing bridges and most of the Big Wheels which were then a popular feature of fairgrounds and international exhibitions; the Big Wheel at the Earl's Court Exhibition in London was his and also that in the Prater in Vienna—the only one surviving. One day he was invited by a friend to the St. Pancras Hotel, London, to witness a demonstration of an American machine for cleaning the seats of railway carriages by blowing compressed air on to them to drive out the dust. It occurred to Booth that it would be more efficacious if the dust were sucked out of the fabric, and on his return to his office he placed his handkerchief on the carpet, knelt down and sucked through it. As he expected, the underside of the handkerchief was impregnated with dust. That was the essence of the invention. He immediately bought an electric motor and ordered a vertical-reciprocating pump—and sent out to the Army and Navy Stores (near his office in Victoria Street in London) to buy some cloth. With these he made up his first 'vacuum cleaner'. It was wholly and immediately successful and he started a company, the British Vacuum Cleaner Co. (now the Goblin Co.), and carried out cleaning operations in properties in London. A notable success was the cleaning of Westminster Abbey for the coronation of King Edward VII in 1902.

In the early days the vacuum equipment was mounted on a horse-drawn cart. Uniformed officials passed long suction tubes through the windows of the house and cleaned the rooms. In 1904 the company began to manufacture small domestic cleaners in which the motor, pump, and collecting canister were mounted on a small wheeled trolley, which was plugged in to the domestic electric supply in the room and operated by the servants (Fig. 47.1). Booth's patent was challenged many times in the courts but he was always successful, not only in protecting his invention of the cloth bag to trap the dust but also in establishing that his invention was indeed the first vacuum cleaner. His original vacuum cleaner (called the 'Puffing Billy') with its 5-hp electric motor first went to work on 25 February 1902; it is now preserved in the Science Museum in London.

Sir Hiram Maxim (inventor of the Maxim Gun (1884)) produced a hand-powered vacuum cleaner in 1909, the 'Little Giant', and avoided infringing

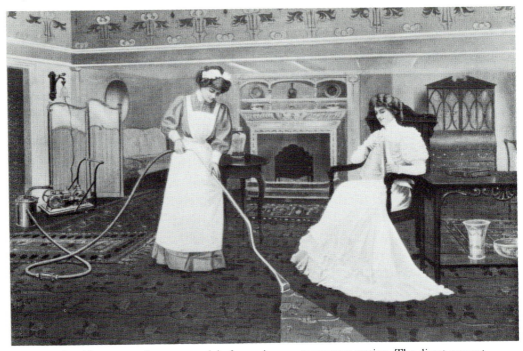

Fig 47.1. Booth's vacuum cleaner, a model of 1904 in a contemporary setting. The direct-current electric motor and vacuum pump are mounted on a trolley and plugged into a light-fitting. The dust is collected in the metal canister.

Booth's patent by sucking the dust into a canister full of sawdust, which filtered it out. Many other hand-operated vacuum cleaners were sold by Booth and others during the first decade of the century; the 'Daisy' of 1908 was very popular. It is indicative of the state of society at that time that most of them required two servants to work them: one to work the wheel or handle and the other to pass the nozzle over the carpet.

The First World War changed all that. Not only were there fewer households which could afford the luxury of keeping two servants, but it became a normal situation—even a necessary one—that women went out to work in factories and offices during the day and did the housework in the few hours that they had at home. This affected the design of some domestic appliances (notably vacuum cleaners) and made them necessities rather than luxuries.

Among the early vacuum cleaners were models which could just be operated by one person. In some, the wheels worked a bellows when the machine was pushed over the carpet; others were constructed like giant bicycle pumps which sucked up the dust when the handle was drawn up. But these lacked power and were poor substitutes for cleaners which used an electric motor for creating the vacuum. Consequently cleaners were developed which could be pushed by one person and had a powerful electric fan mounted over the wheels.

A pioneer of the small electric vacuum cleaner was the 'Hoover', which began in America in 1908 but conquered the world after the war and gave its name to the very word for carpet sweeping. An American, James M. Spangler, patented a form of vacuum cleaner which had a vertical-shaft electric motor mounted on a pair of wheels and delivering the dust into an external dust-bag. This patent was taken over by the Hoover Company. The machine proved such a success that they turned their business—originally the manufacture and processing of leather—over to making vacuum cleaners only. In 1936 they brought out their Hoover Junior. This also incorporated a rotating brush, driven by the fan motor, which helped to dislodge the dust from the carpet. The company marketed it with the catch-phrase 'It beats as it cleans'.

When Booth's vacuum cleaner was introduced it met with considerable opposition from the servant class, who not only regarded it as threat to their livelihood but were frightened at having to control such a novel machine; it must be remembered that this invention was almost the first machine to be put into the hands of simple, uneducated people. Booth discovered this to his cost: he invited the most famous poster artist of the time, John Hassall, R.I., to design his advertisement in 1906. His poster 'Help' (Fig. 47.2, *left*) gravely offended the susceptibilities of the housemaids and made them more determined than ever to have nothing to do with his invention. Realizing his mistake, Booth asked Hassall to design him another poster in 1909. The result, 'Friends' (Fig. 47.2, *right*) mollified the opponents and saved the day.

One must not forget the simple carpet-sweeper, however. It evolved from Sir Joseph Whitworth's patent horse-drawn Street Sweeping Machine of 1842 in which a chain of brushes, moved by the wheels of the advancing cart, swept the dirt from the streets up into the body of the cart. The carpet sweeper, which works in exactly the same way, was developed in America by the Grand Rapids Carpet Sweeper Co. in Michigan in the 1860s. It remains almost unchanged (and as useful) to this day. Indeed, in the period we are discussing it was the principal method of carpet cleaning: the vacuum cleaner was still gathering strength.

FIG. 47.2. Two early vacuum cleaner advertisements by John Hassall.

III. ELECTRIC FIRES AND COOKERS

Apart from the fan and the vacuum cleaner, little domestic use was made of the electric motor for appliances for the first quarter of the twentieth century, but electricity did begin to serve the household for cooking and heating. In 1891 an Electric Fair was held at the Crystal Palace in London, and R. E. B. Crompton, the pioneer of the electricity supply industry, showed what were probably the first electric cookers and heaters. In 1894 his firm was offering them for sale.

The heaters ('electric radiant panels') made use of the Lane Fox system of embedding bare iron heating wires in a layer of enamel on cast-iron studded plates about twelve inches square. These panels were secured to walls; they were used for heating cabins in warships and, set in highly ornamental wrought-iron screens, made into room heaters (Fig. 47.3). Although it was the first application of electric heating, it was not very satisfactory because, the coefficient of expansion of the iron wires differed from that of the enamel and breakages were frequent. Crompton's electric cookers resembled the square cast-iron gas cookers of the period but had no hot-plate on the top. They merely had an oven with electric heating elements along its bottom.

In America the impetus for the adoption of electricity for heating and cook-

Fig. 47.3. Crompton's original electric fires of 1893. These were the first to be offered for sale. The heating wire is embedded in a layer of enamel on studded cast-iron panels (Lane Fox's patent).

ing came from the Columbian Exhibition in Chicago in 1893. In this there was a 'model electric kitchen' in which were shown an electric cooker (above which was mounted a large ventilating hood) and numerous electric kettles, saucepans, and food warmers, all standing on a wooden sideboard. At that time America was ripe for electricity, for it had few gasworks to provide an alternative source of power, whereas Britain was already served by over a thousand of them. Consequently the Chicago Exhibition sparked off an interest in domestic electricity throughout the country which was not matched by the effects of the Crystal Palace Fair and the appliances of Crompton.

After the lack of success of Crompton's heating panels, others took up the challenge. In 1904 H. J. Dowsing developed a fire in which the heaters were large sausage-shaped electric light bulbs with carbon filaments (Fig. 47.4). Two or three of these bulbs were mounted vertically in an ornamental stand. Though they gave out little heat, they looked warm (the bulbs were sometimes yellow or red) and were widely sold. However, it was not until a reliable heating wire could be developed that the electric fire could come into its own.

This was done in 1906 when A. L. Marsh in England patented a nickel-chrome alloy wire which fulfilled all conditions (p. 445). This could be raised to high temperatures and yet not oxidize or lose its strength. It was adopted in

FIG. 47.4. The two-bulb electric fire, on a wooden base, made by the General Electric Company, c. 1914. The bulbs have carbon filaments and glow; the glass is coloured red or yellow and the bulbs are set in an Art Nouveau polished reflector (Dowsing's patent, 1904).

most electric fires. One of the first was the Belling fire introduced in 1913 and still in production—the standard type of electric heater. An interesting 'sport' was the Bastian fire of 1909 in which the heating wire was threaded through a horizontal tube of quartz (six of these elements on a single fire). The tube protected the bare wire and prevented it from causing a fire if it broke. In 1926 some electric fires were developed in America which had as the heating element a thick rod of silicon carbide. This had a high electric resistance and glowed when the current flowed: hence the name, the 'Globar'. But the stability and ease of construction of the hot-wire heating element won the day and the Belling radiant-type fire, with its heating wire wound round a ceramic former, remained little changed up to the middle of this century. With a consumption of 1 or 2 kW it was sufficient to heat a medium-sized room and its direct radiant heat and bright, cheerful look made it an acceptable substitute for the old coal fire. It was, however, generally more expensive to run than a gas fire, though the actual difference depended on local variation in tariff.

The invention of the tangential fan in 1953 by Bruno Eck of Cologne led to a further development of the electric fire. In the 1960s electric fires began to be sold in which the horizontal bare heating wires were set behind an electrically driven tangential fan. This fan served a double purpose. In the first place, the heating wires could carry a higher wattage of electricity because the fan cooled them and prevented them from overheating. Secondly, the hot air was driven into the room so that the heat was convected over a wider area instead of being radiated from the fire in a direct beam.

IV. THE FIRST WORLD WAR

The First World War was a watershed in social habits and conditions and greatly affected the design and adoption of household objects. During and after the war servants effectively vanished for ever—and in any case comparatively few families were left who could have afforded them. Also young girls and housewives who had worked on the land or in factories during the war no longer felt that their place was in the home: they went out to work in offices and shops. Consequently anything which would help to keep the house clean and reduce the labour of housework was welcomed.

Even the design of kitchens changed. Gone was the huge black kitchen range (swallowing tons of coal) with the kitchen table in front of it, round which the cook and the maids would sit, and the separate scullery with its tiled floor and coal-heated built-in 'copper' for the washing. The new kitchen was built for the housewife. It had flat-topped equipment, a small compact gas stove and wash-boiler—all easily fitted into a small room.

In America the idea of 'kitchen design' had begun much earlier. As long ago as 1869 Catherine Beecher in the *American Woman's Home* had suggested a rational layout for kitchens and the provision of working surfaces, and in 1912 Christina Frederick wrote a series of articles on 'The New Housekeeping' in the *Ladies Home Journal*. At the German Bauhaus in 1923 was erected a specimen 'house of the future' which pointed the way to the changes which soon came. In Britain the year 1927 seems to have heralded the new era.

V. GAS COOKERS AND FIRES

When the twentieth century began gas cookers and fires held an unchallenged position in the house—a position which they kept until the end of the First World War. The cookers were of heavy black cast iron with an oven ventilated at the top and with its burners at the sides near the bottom. The hot-plate had its usual array of bunsen burners, with a grill or toaster just beneath it—exactly as they had been throughout the latter half of the preceding century.

The gas fires, too, were little different, with their vertical refractory radiants, black cast-iron surrounds, and flue leading directly into the chimney. But one interesting feature has always distinguished the gas fire. Standing as it does literally in the focus of the room, it has always been decorative, and its form and design have always reflected the art in vogue at the time of its construction. The heavy Victorian style (bringing out miracles of technique in the art of iron-founding) temporarily assumed, in the 1870s, the light Japanese patterns which were first revealed to the Occident in 1865. This was followed by art nouveau at the turn of the century, and succeeded by 'modern' and art deco in the 1930s. Unique among domestic appliances, a gas fire can be dated within a few years at a glance.

Slight improvements were made in the twentieth century in the design and shape of the radiants to make them more efficient and more robust. Automatic methods of igniting them were also introduced: successively the flint-lighter type, the electric hot-wire igniter and, finally, the spark from a piezo-electric crystal. However, it has always been realized (as it had by Rumford about 150 years before) that the best improvement which could be made to any fire was to prevent the heat from going up the chimney. In the 1950s gas fires began to be made which took air from the room and passed it over the hot parts of the fire, passing it back into the room without contact with the products of combustion. These 'convector' fires are now standard practice and it is of interest to note that such fires were made by the firm of Fletcher Russell and sold as long ago as 1882; but they did not then catch on.

In 1923 a very important improvement was made to the gas cooker: the introduction of an oven thermostat. Hitherto cooking in the gas oven was similar to that in a kitchen range: the heat of the oven was inexact and the process of cooking had to be judged by repeated inspection. The first employment of the new device in Britain was in 1923 on the Davis 'New World' cooker fitted with a 'Regulo' (Fig. 47.5): an expanding rod thermostat at the top of the oven which controlled the gas supply. A calibrated dial on the side of the cooker altered the setting. The Davis Co. produced cookery books in which the setting of the dial was given for every dish. To accomplish this the oven was lagged for the first time and the oven flue was moved from the top to a position at the bottom. Apart from improving the cooking the device enabled the housewife to leave the house and return to find the meal properly cooked. It was ten years later that a thermostat was applied to electric cookers. The first cooker to have one was the Creda cooker in 1933; their thermostat was called the 'Credastat'.

FIG. 47.5. A gas cooker of 1923, with 'Regulo' oven thermostat, by the Davis Gas Stove Co. This was the first cooker to use the lagged oven, with thermostatic control of heat—the most important improvement to be made to the gas cooker. Note that the cooker is made of heavy cast-iron, but with enamelled iron panels attached to the door and sides—a practice introduced in the 1920s.

FIG. 47.6. The all-enamelled 'Mainservor' gas cooker of the early 1930s, by Mains. In this period all domestic appliances lost their black, grimy and heavy appearance as a result of a satisfactory process of enamelling in colour, and kitchens acquired a new look. Little change has taken place in cookers since then, apart from some streamlining and much lighter and less durable construction.

Domestic appliances have always tended to be massively designed—rightly so, for they are worked incessantly, often by unskilled hands. Black cast iron was the metal most favoured for kitchen ranges and gas and electric cookers and fires. These had to be polished with black-lead, a very dirty task and one to which the housewife after the First World War was disinclined. In 1920 black gas cookers were first fitted with white enamelled iron panels on the sides and oven door, but the hot-plate remained of black cast iron. The great innovation came in the 1930s when it was found possible to enamel the entire

FIG. 47.7. A free-standing, solid fuel, enamelled room heater, the 'Courtier' by Smith and Wellstood, *c.* 1955. Designed to stand in existing fireplaces, this stove burned coke or other solid fuel under closely controlled conditions (the circular valve in front regulated the air for combustion of the totally enclosed fuel bed). Air from the room also circulated through the louvres at the side and top of the stove and was heated out of contact with the fuel. A flue at the back led the products of combustion to the chimney.

cooker or fire (gas or electric) (Fig. 47.6) so that it could be cleaned with a quick rub of a damp cloth. All domestic appliances therefrom were enamelled in white or light colours and kitchens took on a new aspect (p. 599).

VI. SOLID FUEL APPLIANCES

The use of solid fuel declined steadily throughout the first half of this century. The introduction of coke, coalite, and other smokeless fuels was encouraged to reduce smoke pollution—and it led to the death of the kitchen range and the ordinary living-room fire. But a good fight was put up by the manufacturers of special fuels on behalf of the domestic fireplace. Special boxed-in living-room heaters were designed to burn coalite and the like very efficiently under very strictly controlled conditions (Fig. 47.7). However, the wider use of central heating systems and the development of gas and electric fires nearly

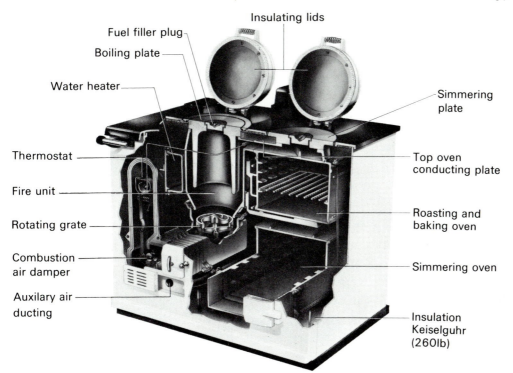

Insulating lids

Fuel filler plug

Boiling plate

Water heater

Simmering plate

Thermostat

Top oven conducting plate

Fire unit

Roasting and baking oven

Rotating grate

Combustion air damper

Simmering oven

Auxilary air ducting

Insulation Keiselguhr (260lb)

FIG. 47.8. The 'Aga' solid fuel cooker of 1946. The sectioned view shows the construction of this very efficient and popular cooker. The deep central fuel bed is provided with a thermostatically controlled supply of air. The enamelled cast iron stove is fully lagged and heat can only escape through the two heating plates—one for boiling and the other for simmering. When not in use the hinged lids, also lagged, are folded down.

brought the solid fuel fire to an end by mid-century. Many British cities made the use of all but smokeless solid fuel illegal—and pea-soup fogs disappeared completely.

The one solid fuel appliance which remains and flourishes is the Aga Cooker (Fig. 47.8). Invented in 1924 by a Swede, Gustav Dalen, a blind Nobel Prize winner (1912), it is a cast-iron kitchen range in which a totally enclosed fire of a smokeless fuel burns under completely controlled conditions. The whole range is thermally lagged and the only way the heat can escape is through two circular apertures on the top surface, on which the pots and pans are placed. Heavily insulated hinged lids cover these holes when no cooking is being done. There is also an oven, and arrangements can be made to heat water for domestic use. It is unrivalled for cooking and remarkable for its economy: a household's annual fuel bill can be accurately estimated in advance. Models are now also made for gas and oil firing.

VII. STORAGE HEATERS

As electricity, unlike gas, cannot be stored efforts were made, in Sweden and elsewhere in the 1920s, to ease the peak load of power stations by making electric heaters which would take electricity during the night (at cheap rates) and store the heat produced in large blocks of concrete or brick. This high-temperature heat would be used to warm the house throughout the day, when the electricity would be turned off by a time-switch.

This system was introduced in Britain in Watford in 1930, with storage heaters imported from Sweden; these consisted of a block of soapstone in which electric heating wires were embedded. The reduced night charge for the electricity used was called, in consequence, the 'soapstone tariff'. The scheme was eventually given up and it was not until the 1960s that there was a massive campaign in Britain to instal storage heaters to reduce the peak loads. The storage heaters were of concrete and encased in an enamelled box, heavily lagged so that they were not too hot to touch. Many of them contained small electric fans to assist the flow of air through the heater and so control its output.

VIII. WASHING-MACHINES

The work of washing clothes depends almost entirely on mechanical effort —the churning up of the clothes in soapy water. This was an obvious use for the newly developed electric motor, but curiously enough it was slow in being adopted for this purpose. This was probably because up to the First World War households without servants rarely had an electricity supply, and those with servants did not need washing-machines.

The old wooden tub with hand-operated dolly was the standard type of machine at the beginning of the century. The water had to be heated over a fire and poured into the tub. In the 1920s and onwards a very popular appliance was the gas-fired wash-boiler, a light copper cauldron on legs with a gas burner under it to heat the water. There was no dolly and the parboiled clothes were swirled by hand.

However, in the 1920s wooden-tub washers (with a wooden dolly on a vertical shaft) were manufactured (mostly in America and especially in Canada). An electric motor bolted to the underside of the tub oscillated the dolly. By engaging gears it could also operate a mangle fitted above the tub (Fig. 47.9). Unfortunately, water trickling on to the motor often caused short-circuits and electric shocks.

FIG. 47.9. A wooden washing-machine by Beatty Bros. of Canada, electrically driven, *c.* 1920. The wooden tub and reciprocating wooden dolly were the standard features of nineteenth-century washing-machines. After the First World War mechanical washing-machines such as this were sold having an electric motor (beneath the tub) and a belt drive for the dolly which would also drive the mangle. The water had to be heated externally and poured into the tub.

FIG. 47.10. An electric washing-machine by Parnall-Radiation, 1960. By mid-century the washing-machine had become fully automatic. The water is heated by an electric immersion heater, thermostatically controlled, and in some models the whole process of filling, agitation, flushing, and emptying can be controlled by time-switches. The mangle is also electrically driven, and the whole machine is designed with a streamlined look for ease of cleaning.

Later in that decade the true electric washing-machine was redesigned—all in metal and with waterproof motors. In all these early machines the water had to be heated externally and poured into the tub; it was not until the 1950s that machines were made which heated the water in the tub electrically. The final improvement in the 1960s was in the installation of automatic control of the washing process, with time-switches to turn the mechanism on and off, change the water, empty the tub, etc. at predetermined moments (Fig. 47.10). Spin dryers came into use in America in the 1920s but it was not until the 1960s that they were adopted in British households—an unaccountable delay of some forty years.

IX. DOMESTIC HOT WATER

In Victorian times hot water was a very great luxury indeed. For a hot bath the water had to be heated in kettles over a kitchen range and carried in cans by servants upstairs to the bathroom. Even now older people will recall staying as a guest in a country house and being wakened in the morning by a knock on the door heralding the boy with the hot water for washing and shaving. By the end of the century most large households had hot water piped to the bathroom from a back or side boiler built into the kitchen range.

In the first quarter of the twentieth century hot water became a first priority for any household, rich or poor, and nearly all but the cheapest houses built in that period had this mode of supply or, where the kitchen range had already been abandoned and cooking done by gas, drew its hot water from a small free-standing coal or coke boiler of the 'Ideal' type. This was a cylindrical iron stove with a water-jacket; the hot water circulated by a thermo-siphon effect, with a storage tank in the linen cupboard.

The gas geyser had been invented by Benjamin Waddy Maughan in 1868, and it was he who first called the appliance a 'geyser'. These and similar models (Fig. 47.11) were used in many small houses but they were, in the early days, capricious and dangerous—occasionally exploding and at other times asphyxiating or at least singeing the eyebrows of the careless user.

Geysers supplied water only to one point—the bath—but in 1889 the firm of Ewart (already makers of geysers) introduced their 'Califont' which, mounted in the scullery, supplied hot water to taps all over the house. The burners lit up (from a pilot light) when a tap was turned on anywhere in the house. The drop in water pressure when the water began to flow caused a diaphragm valve to turn on the full gas-supply to the appliance. In 1925 their 'Vivo', a more compact model, had a great vogue in the smaller houses built between the wars. However the greatest progress in instantaneous water heating came from Germany. From the firm of Junkers, Bernard Friedman came to England and in 1932 began making and supplying gas water-heaters, the 'Ascot', which used multiple jets instead of the flat-flame non-aerated burners used in geysers. This very efficient multi-point instantaneous water heater captured the market and the word 'Ascot' became synonymous with a water heater, as 'Ewart' had been before. This heater was not, in fact, the first of its type to reach England, for the 'Progas' (also German) was introduced in 1930 and manufactured in Leiston, but it did not survive the Second World War.

FIG. 47.11. A geyser by Fletcher Russell and Co., 1914. The gas-fired instantaneous water heater in polished copper has been a serviceable and popular method of heating bath water ever since Maughan invented it (and the title 'geyser') in 1868. This illustration from a contemporary catalogue is a social document, with its unruffled long-skirted girl, just back from hockey, being attended by her maid. It was an era which ended with the First World War.

On account of its mild climate, Britain was slow in adopting central heating for houses, but after the First World War it began to be accepted, and after the Second World War it developed apace until by mid-century it was usual in most houses. At first, coal or coke were the universal fuels for this, but with the gradual phasing out of solid fuels in the 1960s gas and oil took their place. Some of the old coke-fired boilers had oil or gas burners fitted into them, with oil taking the lead on account of its cheapness until the 1970s, when gas overhauled it in economy.

Some systems were expressly designed to burn gas. Potterton's boilers (cast-iron beehive-shaped vessels with a water-jacket) were used to heat Sandow's Institute of Physical Culture in London as early as 1904, but in general gas could not compete with solid fuels in those days. By the mid-century gas-fired central heating boilers had become much more compact and elegant, culminating in the early 1960s in the 'Servotomic' system in which the gas flames are concealed within a slim master-radiator (in the hall or a corridor) and the hot water is circulated throughout the house in small pipes. The 'small-bore' system, with an electric motor to circulate the water, was introduced in the 1950s.

Electricity has never been an important fuel for heating water in bulk, partly because of its price and also on account of the difficulty of supplying enough power to the appliance to raise its temperature quickly without blowing fuses. Consequently most of the electric water heaters are of the storage type, of which the Bastian 'Quartzalite Storageyser' of 1924 was a pioneer. This consisted of a lagged water tank (with ball-valve to control the water supply) under which was an ordinary hot-wire electric heating element. In later years large storage tanks with immersion electric heaters and thermostats became popular.

The electric kettle has a much longer history and is now one of the more important domestic appliances. Electric kettles were among the electric appliances offered in Crompton's catalogue in 1894, but it would be idle to pretend that in the early days that appliance was a satisfactory one. In all these early models the electric heating coil was merely attached to the underside of an ordinary kettle. Less than half the heat generated by the coil could be transferred to the water by this method—and since electricity was already an expensive fuel it is not surprising that the electric kettle could not hope to rival the kettle on the gas-ring.

In 1921 the Birmingham firm of Bulpitt and Sons marketed their 'Swan' kettle in which the heating element was totally immersed in the water, giving almost 100 per cent efficiency. This was a major improvement and thenceforth electric kettles began to find favour with the public, not least because they were portable and did not carry a risk of fire. By 1950 automatic cut-outs were added, which switched off the current automatically when the water boiled. Previously this had been the great disadvantage of the electric kettle; the water could boil away and the heating element would then be exposed and burn out.

X. REFRIGERATORS

When the century opened ice-boxes were to be found in some wealthy households, but for the most part the spacious and shaded larder or pantry with its good ventilation and heavy stone shelves was regarded sufficient for the protection of food.

The ice-box was a cabinet lined with zinc with a heavy wooden casing which formed an insulator against the entry of heat. A block of ice was placed in a compartment at the top of the cabinet, and the air which it cooled descended through holes on to the food placed on the shelves in the chamber. The condensed water was collected in a tray at the bottom. Heavy, lagged doors sealed the chamber. The blocks of ice were sold from horse-drawn carts which patrolled the streets weekly.

Although the vapour-compression type of refrigerator had been fully exploited in ships and in meat stores since the 1850s (Vol. V, p. 45), it was not until the early 1920s that domestic refrigerators were made for sale (in America first); by 1923 no fewer than 20 000 were in use. The first household refrigerators were offered for sale in Britain in the mid-1920s; among the pioneers were the 'Frigidaire' and the 'Kelvinator'. These employed an electric motor to drive the compressor. In the early days it was sometimes necessary to connect the equipment to a water supply to provide additional cooling. Some models, for example the B.T.H. machine much used in Britain during the 1930s, had a large radiator mounted on the top of the refrigerator (Fig. 47.12).

FIG. 47.12. A refrigerator, by B.T.H., 1932. Some domestic refrigerators in the early days, electrically driven and working on the vapour-compression system, required additional cooling in the form either of a supply of running cold water or, as in this case, a large radiator mounted on the top.

At first ammonia was used as the refrigerant, but in the late 1920s synthetic refrigerants were developed. These halogenated hydrocarbons, which are now universally used, are less objectionable in the event of a leak and are non-toxic. 'Freon' was the name given to one of the earliest synthetic chemicals used for this purpose.

In 1922 the Swedish firm of Electrolux bought from two young students Carl Munters and Balzer von Platen, the patent for a refrigerator working on the absorption principle. In this, a small flame or an electric heater evaporates the refrigerant vapour from an ammonia–water solution, forcing it into a condenser. The resulting liquid expands and its temperature is lowered. The Electrolux refrigerator, having no moving parts to wear out, is widely used in households and especially in places where there is no electric power, for it works well on an oil or gas burner. This type was introduced into Britain in 1925. By the 1960s refrigerators were to be found in most households.

XI. IRONING

The early Victorian flat-irons (in America, sad-irons) were in the form of heavy iron boxes, with wooden handles, into which were dropped a red-hot slug of iron which had been heated in the kitchen fire and removed with a pair of tongs. Later, they were made in the familiar shape we know now and were heated on top, or in front, of an open fire, or on special flat-iron stoves in laundries or large country houses. Later in the nineteenth century they were heated on the hot-plate of the gas-cooker; and this continued during the first quarter of the twentieth century, after which gas and electric irons were mostly favoured by housewives.

Irons were among the first domestic appliances to be electrified. They were shown in the catalogue of the Crompton Co. in 1894 together with a variety of electric kettles, food-warmers, hot-plates, and curling tongs. Gas irons, with a flexible tube supplying a gas-burner within the iron, were also in use when the twentieth century started and they are still supplied. Slight improvements were made during the first thirty years of the century: gas and electric irons were enamelled in the 1930s; thermostats were fitted to electric irons; and later 'steam-irons' were developed which sent tiny jets of steam on to the cloth from holes in its base. But after these innovations little change has occurred in the design.

XII. MISCELLANEOUS APPLIANCES

Apart from the vacuum cleaner and the refrigerator, the twentieth century brought very few appliances to the home which had not already been introduced by the Victorians. The apple-parer died completely but the mincers, coffee-grinders, food mixers, and tin-openers were merely electrified, though the majority were still worked by hand. The old rotary knife cleaner, in which the steel table knives were rubbed with a polishing powder, lasted until stainless steel was introduced for cutlery after the First World War. But wherever electricity could be used to heat or to operate a gadget, it was employed. Between the wars the firm of Landers, Frary, and Clark of New Britain, Conn., U.S.A. were great manufacturers and electrifiers of domestic appliances.

During the twentieth century electric hair dryers gradually came into use, first as square boxes resting on the dressing table from which hot air emerged from a small square hole, and then, in the 1920s, the pistol-shaped appliances of the present type. Entirely new to the house was the pneumatic 'corkscrew' of the 1950s, which consisted of a thin hollow steel spike set on the end of a small gas cylinder, such as is used in a domestic soda siphon. The spike is driven through the cork and the gas passes through it (or air is pumped by hand in another model)—and the cork is forced out. Electric carving knives were also introduced in the 1960s (the blade oscillated by an electromagnet) and also automatic waste disposal units which, fitted into the sink waste pipe, macerated the solid kitchen waste and allowed it to pass into the domestic drain.

The dish-washer (a cabinet into which the dirty crockery is put and then subjected to jets of hot water) was invented in 1865 in America but although much used in liners and hotels has not been widely adopted by any but the larger households. By contrast, electric blankets have been eagerly adopted. Although unsafe when they were first introduced after the Second World War, they are, thanks to new safety regulations, a great boon to many and they have almost ousted the old hot-water bottle (even though this, too, has been electrified).

One invention new to the century is the automatic morning-tea maker. The first made for general sale (Fig. 47.13) was patented by a Birmingham gunsmith as early as 1904. It was set in motion by an ordinary alarm clock. At the appointed hour the clock triggered off a mechanism which first struck a match and lit a spirit stove under a kettle. When the water boiled the bubbling water released a catch which allowed the kettle to tilt over and fill the teapot standing alongside—and struck the bell of the alarm-clock to wake the sleeper (if he was not awake already, in an agony of apprehension). An electric tea-making device was not marketed until 1932 when the Hawkins 'Teasmade'

FIG. 47.13. An automatic tea-making machine, 1904. This ingenious machine for making the early-morning cup of tea, marketed then for £1. 5s. to £3. 10s. (£1.25 to £3.50) at the beginning of the century, strikes a match to ignite a spirit stove and pours out the water when the kettle boils. Some thirty years later the application of electricity to this domestic appliance, as with most of the appliances of the previous century, greatly simplified it.

appeared. This was a simple bedside appliance in which an electric clock switched on an immersion heater in a kettle and automatically poured out the boiling water.

The social changes of the twentieth century—the disappearance of the servant class, the levelling of incomes, and the universal employment of women in offices and factories—were the principal factors in the speedy application of domestic appliances in the period under discussion. New materials have also helped in their adoption: the enamelling of iron, the use of stainless steel and aluminium, the discovery of new chemicals (as for non-stick pans and detergents for washing), and, above all, the use of plastics for making smooth working surfaces and in the manufacture of appliances and crockery.

A most remarkable concentration of all these new materials and appliances was in the manufacture in Britain of the prefabricated houses of 1944. On account of the destruction by bombs of so many houses in the preceding years, and the curtailment of the normal building programme, the government had designed a simple bungalow type of house which could be transported on a lorry and erected in two pieces on the simplest of foundations. They were installed in thousands in 1945 and designed to last 10 years; hundreds were still in use over thirty years later. They had every possible convenience: central heating by air-ducts, constant hot water from a smokeless fuel stove, wash-boiler, refrigerator, gas or electric cooker, etc.—all built into a single unit. It was the first time that the working classes had been provided with all the comforts and facilities available to the middle and upper classes —a landmark in British social history.

Thanks to copious advertising throughout the twentieth century and to universal hire-purchase selling (which was instituted in the 1930s for such appliances as gas cookers, geysers, and fires) domestic life became more sybaritic, albeit fraught with complications.

BIBLIOGRAPHY

BERNAN, W. *Warming and ventilation*. London (1845).

EDWARDS, F. *Our domestic fire-places*. London (1865).

GIEDION, SIEGFRIED. *Mechanization takes command*. Oxford University Press, New York (1948).

JOLY, V. C. *Traité pratique du chauffage*. Paris (1873).

STEWART, E. G. *Town gas*. H.M.S.O. London (1958).

WRIGHT, LAWRENCE. *Clean and decent*. Routledge and Kegan Paul, London (1960).

——. *Home fires burning*. Routledge and Kegan Paul, London (1964).

Much relevant information will be found in the following periodicals: *Gas World*; *Gas Journal* (especially the centenary issue in 1949); *Ironmonger*; *Electrical Times*; and *Electrical Review*. The Science Museum in London has an extensive collection of all kinds of domestic appliances.

48

COMPUTERS

T. A. MARGERISON

O F all twentieth-century technological developments, the digital computer has had the most universal and far-reaching consequences. The arrival of an automation that could mimic the arithmetic and logical problem-solving capability of the human brain was well overdue. The demand in science, the applied sciences, and commerce for some means of reducing the labour of arithmetic, sorting, counting, indexing, and classifying had become urgent, not only because of the enormous number of people engaged in these tasks, but because human frailty faced with monotonous and repetitive paper work generated errors which could be not merely inconvenient but occasionally disastrous.

Although our particular concern in this chapter is the first half of the twentieth century, the devices of this period were direct descendants of much earlier ones. Since these have not been described in earlier volumes of this work we must necessarily preface our account with a summary of the early history of calculating machines.

Before the introduction of any effective computing aids, the preparation of tables of logarithms, for example, involved the organization and control of large teams of human computers. When the French Government decided in 1784 to have new tables of logarithms of numbers and trigonometric functions prepared, they set up a team of six mathematicians (including the eminent A.-M. Legendre) to devise the methods to be used and to supervise the work. Seven or eight calculators with some mathematical knowledge, acting as foremen, handed out the work to seventy or eighty computers, and checked the results. Every calculation was double checked. The work took two years, and the result was two copies of tables in manuscript. The manuscripts, known as the *Tables de Cadastres*, were each bound into seventeen folio volumes. They were never printed, since this would have introduced many errors.

Most of the available tables, even in the nineteenth century, contained inaccuracies. The British *Nautical Almanac*, which had been founded by the Astronomer Royal Nevil Maskelyne (1732–1811) and had acquired a high reputation for its accuracy, fell into disrepute after his death. The 1818 edition was found to contain 58 errors, and there were a similar number in that of 1830. Charles Babbage (1791–1871) who about 1840 worked out a design for a mechanical computing machine with many of the characteristics of the modern electronic computer, was motivated by an awareness of the urgent need for accurate computation. Some time in 1812 (or so the story goes) Babbage and John Herschel (later Sir John, the astronomer and physicist (1792–1871)) were sitting in Babbage's room in Cambridge checking some calculations which had been done for them, which they suspected contained many errors. 'I wish to God these calculations had been executed by steam,' remarked Babbage. 'It is quite possible,' replied Herschel, and so started Babbage thinking about the design of an automatic calculating machine.

Babbage's machines were, as we shall see later, extremely ambitious, and quite beyond the scope of the technology then available to manufacture them. It was the same lack of engineering technology that prevented other simpler machines, which had been invented in the seventeenth and eighteenth centuries, coming into common use. These were not automatic, but involved the continual intervention of the operator, as in the present-day desk calculators. The first adding machine was invented by the French philosopher and mathematician Blaise Pascal (1623–1662) in 1642 when he was 19, and is said to have been used in his father's work as a tax collector. Some thirty years later the German mathematician Gottfried Leibniz (1646–1716) improved on the original idea, and made a machine which could add, subtract, multiply, and divide. The mechanism he designed was still in use in many mechanical calculators in the twentieth century, but it was too complex to be reliable and to be manufactured in quantity in his day.

During the seventeenth century, no less than the nineteenth century, the demand for a machine to do arithmetic was very great. Mathematics and science had been growing rapidly and their application to navigation and commerce created a demand for arithmetic skills. Grown men struggled to learn their multiplication tables, and to master the intricacies of long division. Samuel Pepys, when he was 29 years old and already a senior civil servant, records in his diary the efforts he was making to learn the multiplication table so that he could do arithmetic.

It was not a machine but the mathematical invention of John Napier, Baron of Merchiston, near Edinburgh in Scotland (1550–1617), which eventually came to the rescue of the seventeenth-century calculator. Napier was very much aware of the difficulties that many people had with arithmetic, and had

FIG. 48.1. Napier's bones.

devised a new method of multiplication, which he called, somewhat ostenta-
tiously 'rhabdology'. It is better known as 'Napier's bones' (Fig. 48.1). The
'bones' were really a movable multiplication table, built out of a number of
separate square-section rods to match a particular multiplicand. Each rod was
divided into a ladder of nine compartments, the uppermost containing a digit,
the second that digit multiplied by 2, and so on, so that the lowest compartment in the ladder contained the digit multiplied by 9. A selection of rods or
'bones' was contained in a box, and one, with the appropriate digit, was
selected for each digit of the multiplicand. The rods were placed touching one
another on the table so that the row of digits along the top corresponded with
the multiplicand. Suppose the multiplier is 679. The user looks at the ninth
(bottom) row across the 'bones' which contains the products of 9 and the
individual digits in the multiplicand. Starting with the right-hand 'bone' he
writes down the unit value of the ninth row. He then adds the tens value of
that 'bone' to the unit value of the ninth row of the one on its left, and so on.
In this way he obtains the product 9 times the multiplicand. He now does the
same thing for row 7 and writes down the product 70 times the multiplicand.
And again, using row 6, he can write down the product 600 times the multiplicand. The
answer is obtained by adding the three partial products together. Napier's
'bones' are valuable only for people who do not know their multiplication
tables by heart. But multiplication by means of a 'look-up' table of this kind
has been embodied in a number of twentieth-century calculators and computers.

More important than the bones, however, was Napier's discovery of the logarithm, which he described in 1614. The original table he produced consisted of the logarithms of the sines of angles. The idea was taken up enthusiastically by Henry Briggs (1561–1631), Professor of Geometry at Gresham College, London, who, when he read Napier's account wrote 'Napier, lord of Markinston, hath set my head and hands at work with his new and admirable logarithms.' Briggs recognized that he could use the logarithm to transform multiplication to addition, and division to subtraction. He saw the value of logarithms to the base 10, and spent his whole life computing and publishing tables of logarithms.

It was only towards the end of the nineteenth century that mechanical aids to computation began to play an important part. The first effective calculating machine, built on the same principles as the Leibniz machine, was made about 1820 by Charles Xavier Thomas de Colmar. It won a medal at the International Exhibition in London in 1862, and about 1500 seem to have been manufactured over the next thirty years under the name 'Arithmometer'. Major-General J. Hannyngton used two arithmometers for calculating a table of haversines he produced in 1876. But the machines did not gain universal acceptance. 'On the whole, mathematicians have not much to expect from the aid of calculating machines,' wrote Edward Sang in a paper, Mechanical aids to calculation (1871). 'We must fall back on the wholesome truth that we cannot delegate our intellectual functions and say to a machine, to a formula, to a rule or to a dogma, I am too lazy to think; do, please, think for me.' Cornelius Walford, author of the *Insurance Cyclopaedia*, responded (1871) '. . . the "arithmometer", clever as it is admitted to be by all those familiar with its use, has not attained the *ultima thule* of our calculating appliances. We believe those great mechanical powers, foreshadowed and demonstrated by Babbage, will be yet brought into practical use.' [1]

However, it was another seventy years before the kind of machine which Babbage had designed was eventually built, using not mechanical but electro-mechanical, and later electronic, technologies. The demand was almost immediate. It burst upon the world and was applied with extraordinary promptness, not simply for government and scientific work, but in the ordinary commercial world. In the 1930s a certain amount of important theoretical work on computers had been published, particularly by Alan M. Turing in Britain [2]. But even in 1940 no digital computer had been built. All calculation was still carried out by mechanical calculators, differing little from the Leibniz machine. In commerce, punched-card machines, which were capable of sorting data, carrying out simple arithmetic operations and printing the results were used by larger firms, and accounting machines, which combined the functions of typewriter and calculator were fairly widely used. Some mathematicians, such as L. J. Comrie, had discovered how such machines could be used as difference engines to compute tables. A number of mechanical analogue computers had also been built, based on Vannevar Bush's differential analyser [3] (1931), and these were used for a wide variety of scientific and defence problems involving the solution of differential equations.

By 1950, partly as a result of the rapid growth of electronics and communications techniques during the Second World War, digital machines had been built in Germany (1941); the U.S.A. (1944); Britain (1948); and Sweden (1950). The earliest machines were electromechanical rather than electronic, and did not store their own program of instructions, but had to be set by hand for each problem either by means of a patch board, or by a fixed sequence of instructions contained on punched cards or tape. In this respect, and in other ways, they were considerably less ambitious than Babbage's original plan for a mechanical computer. 'Had Babbage lived 75 years later,' said H. H. Aiken, who built the first computer in the United States, 'I would have been out of a job.'

By 1951 the first commercial electronic computer, the UNIVAC 1, was installed at the U.S. Bureau of Census, and in 1952 it was used to predict (correctly, as it happens) the result of the U.S. Presidential election. The following year a British computer, LEO, based on the design of the Cambridge University computer EDSAC, was at work handling orders for bread and cakes in the J. Lyons bakery chain in London. This was the first application of a computer in commerce.

The demand for computers grew so quickly that by 1960 a thriving industry had been built, with 26 firms in the U.S.A., seven in Britain, three German, two Dutch, one French, and one Italian all engaged in designing, building, and selling computers. By 1965 the new industry was in the world class, with about $10 000m.-worth of equipment installed; a growth rate of almost 50 per cent per year; an army of employees; and another third of a million people engaged in operating and maintaining the machines. The U.S.A. showed itself a clear leader by this time, with more than 20 000 computer installations, compared with 5000 in western Europe and less than 2000 in the Soviet Union and eastern Europe [4].

The pattern of use was different in the United States from that elsewhere. Most of the American machines were used for accounting and commercial calculations, whereas in Europe the majority were used for scientific and defence purposes. The reason for the difference, which gave one American firm (IBM) almost three-quarters of the world computer market by 1965, was due partly to economic conditions, and partly to the entry into computer manufacture of two American firms, Remington Rand and (a little later) IBM, which had long experience of selling punched card systems to industry. A combination of the selling skills of these companies, which tailored their computer systems to handle commercial accounting procedures, and the willingness of American company management to install new machines which promised to improve speed and reliability and to reduce labour costs, caused such a dramatic lift-off for the American computer industry that other countries found it difficult or impossible to compete.

The earliest applications of electronic digital computers were concerned with exploiting their arithmetic capability, but it soon became clear that they had much wider use as logical machines for information handling, storage, and retrieval. The machines could carry out all the logical processes foreseen by Leibniz in his seventeenth-century 'laws of thought' and worked out in detail in the mid-nineteenth century by George Boole (1815–64). These processes were carried out with such rapidity that although the individual steps were trivial, the totality of many million such operations provided an entirely new dimension of capability. Many applications, ranging from finger-print searches, to linguistic studies, to stock control suddenly came within the reach of detailed analysis using the computer.

The high speed of operation also made it possible to conduct data searches or to carry out computation on demand, using what have become known as 'real-time' systems. For example, by 1964 Project MAC was in operation at Massachusetts Institute of Technology allowing users direct access to a computer through a teletypewriter terminal in such a way that although the facilities of the computer were being shared by many, each had the impression of being the sole user. Both 'time-sharing' operations of this sort, and other 'real-time' applications (of which the earliest industrial example was airline seat reservations) continue to develop rapidly.

The first electronic computers, designed during the 1940s and early 1950s made use of electronic valves or vacuum tubes as their switching elements. Most electronic equipment built at that time contained a dozen or so valves, and was regarded as reliable if its mean time between failures exceeded a few thousand hours. This level of reliability was quite unsatisfactory for a computer with between a hundred and a thousand times as many components.

IBM's 701, built in 1953, had 4000 valves. The UNIVAC 1103 of the same date had nearly 2000 valves. These machines were close to the reliability limit of the day. Had they been much larger, the probability is that they would never have remained in operation long enough to do useful work. Not only were the 'first-generation' valve-operated machines unreliable, but they consumed large quantities of electric power, which made them physically large and heat had to be removed by a forced-air cooling system.

As the new computer industry grew, its needs began to be reflected back on to component manufacturers. In particular it encouraged the development of the switching transistor, designed specifically to operate in two states, on and off. These transistors began to be used in computers towards the end of the 1950s. The first experimental transistorized computer, the Leprechaun, was built in 1956 by Bell Telephone Laboratories, where the transistor (p. 1117) had originally been discovered in 1947. Philco, IBM, and General Electric followed quickly and offered transistorized computers for sale in 1958. These new machines offered many advantages, but in particular they were much more reliable, and consumed much less power.

Computers made from discrete components including transistors are regarded as 'second generation', and span the years 1958 to about 1964. But semiconductor manufacturers were able to offer the computer industry a further major improvement in reliability by incorporating on a single 'chip' of silicon, all the components—transistors, resistors, and capacitors—for a particular logical operation. These new building blocks, or 'integrated circuits' removed many of the uncertainties from computer manufacture, since the integrated circuits were manufactured in quantity to tightly controlled specifications, and could be built together with the same confidence that a mechanical engineer uses standard nuts and bolts. The first of these new 'third-generation' machines were introduced in 1964.

The new technology now made it possible to build computers much more cheaply, and within a few years low-cost, yet powerful small computers were being manufactured in large numbers, particularly by the Digital Equipment Corporation in the U.S.A. More recently, still more components have been included in integrated circuits, so that a single 'chip' may now contain virtually all the electronics of a complete processor. Computers using 'large-scale integration', or LSI, known as 'fourth generation', started to come on the market around 1970. However, it now appears that the very rapid technical development of computers is stabilizing.

One effect of the development of the integrated circuit for use in computers has been its adoption by control engineers and others who now find it more convenient and cheaper to design their systems to use integrated circuits in place of the relays and electromechanical devices they previously used. Thus, most traffic lights, lifts, and machine-tool controllers now incorporate integrated-circuit logic originally designed for the computer industry.

We have so far discussed the technologies used in the design and building of the computer itself (called the 'main-frame'), but it soon became clear this was only part of the total requirement. Equipment was needed to get information into the computer, and to return it to the user. This 'peripheral equipment' was originally borrowed either from the telegraph industry, as for example the teletypewriter, or from the punched-card accounting machine. Gradually, as the computer industry grew larger, special computer peripherals, such as high-speed printers, magnetic tape decks, and magnetic discs were designed. As the new integrated circuits were developed and applied in the computer main-frame, the peripherals came to represent an increasing proportion of the total cost of systems.

The same was also true of the cost of preparing the program of instructions for the computer to do a particular job, which is now usually the highest cost in any new computer system. Computer manufacturers have attempted to reduce programming ('software') costs, by providing standard programs for their machines which undertake frequently required 'housekeeping' tasks, such as the control of particular pieces of peripheral equipment, or the scheduling of the use of the various parts of the computer to different programs. This became known as 'basic software' of which the most important part was the 'operating system' responsible for the supervision and control of the computer's operations.

In addition, auxiliary software, also normally supplied by the manufacturer, was designed to make it easier for the user to write his own programs, using a 'language' embodying a mixture of commonly used mathematical symbols and a kind of pidgin English. The auxiliary software enabled programs written in such languages to be translated automatically into the form recognized by the machine. Such translation programs are known as 'compilers'. The development of programming languages, which was started in the late 1940s by Grace Hopper of the U.S. Navy, resulted in two great advantages. The first was that the task of writing programs for a computer was simplified, so that the time taken and the number of errors made by the programmer were reduced. Secondly, it made it possible, in theory, for a program written for one machine to be used on another, provided that it also had a compiler for that particular language. Unfortunately this promise was not fulfilled, owing to lack of complete standardization of the major languages.

In spite of these developments, the relative cost of the software associated with a computer system steadily increased as new technologies and increased production reduced the cost of the 'hardware'. In the early 1950s, software costs were 5 to 10 per cent of total system costs. By 1970 they amounted to about 70 per cent of the total. With the continuing steady decline in the cost of computer hardware it seems likely that extremely inefficient hardware utilization may be merited if it results in cheaper software.

The most interesting aspect of the 'information revolution' which the development of the electronic computer brought about was the evolution towards decentralization and an ability to respond to individual requirements. In this respect it was a move in the opposite direction from mass production, which lowered prices by the manufacture of standardized items in large numbers. In principle, the computer allowed so close a degree of control over a manufacturing process that each individual item could be made to special order. This applied not simply to manufacturing industry, but also to services. 'The invasion of computers into education,' said an O.E.C.D. report, *Electronic computers* [4] (1969), 'shows that the same result might be obtained in the education system as was obtained in certain manufacturing industries. Computer-aided instruction, and the development of teaching machines, are making an individually "tailor-made instruction" theoretically possible. All school-children and students could possibly some day benefit from the advantages which in the distant past were reserved to the few privileged who had their own tutors . . .'

I. THE CALCULATING MACHINE

The earliest form of calculating machine was the *abacus*, which was an *aide-mémoire* for calculators, like a sheet of paper and pencil, rather than a true machine. It is worth remarking, however, that the Chinese abacus or *Souan-pan*, and the Japanese version, the *Soroban*, which work on the biquinary system of numbers, can be used with extraordinary speed. On 12 November 1946 Private T. N. Wood, who had been selected as the most skilled electric desk calculator operator with the American troops in Japan was beaten on speed and accuracy in a contest with Kiyoshi Matsuzaki of the Ministry of Postal Administration using a Soroban. 'The abacus, centuries old, dealt defeat to the most up-to-date electric machine now being used by the U.S. Government' said an American newspaper report [5]. In fact, the German Post Office had conducted trials and considered introducing the Soroban in 1927 because of its accuracy, high speed, and low cost.

As we have seen above, the first true calculating machine, although it was capable only of adding, was built by Blaise Pascal in 1642. 'I submit to the public a small machine of my own invention' he wrote, 'by means of which you alone may, without any effort perform all the operations of arithmetic, and may be relieved of the work which has often times fatigued your spirit when you have worked with the counters or with the pen.'

Pascal's machine consisted of a series of spurred setting wheels, each of which was geared on a 1:1 ratio with a results wheel or drum. The results wheels lay behind a cover in which there were openings through which a numeral on each was displayed. As the setting wheel revolved and turned the results wheel the digits appeared in turn in the window. Each setting wheel was surrounded by a fixed ring engraved with the digits from 0 to 9. The setting wheel was used like a telephone dial. Using a small stylus each number was dialled into the machine by pulling the stylus down to a stop. Pascal devised a special method for propagating a 'carry' so that when one results wheel passed zero it automatically incremented by one the value of the results wheel on its left. He recognized the special difficulty of multiple carry propagation, where, for example 1 is added to 99 999 999. His method was to arrange a mechanism (Fig. 48.2) such that as the results wheel turned from 0 to 9, a cam gradually lifted a claw against the pull from a weight. When the results wheel passed zero, the cam released the claw, which was pulled down by the weight and turned the next results wheel one position. Thus the energy needed to propagate the carry was accumulated gradually as each results wheel turned from 0 to 9. The principle is still used (although with a spring to store the energy) in some modern mechanical calculating machines. Pascal wrote: 'It is just as easy to move one thousand or ten thousand dials all at one time, if one desired, as to make a single dial move, although all accomplish the movement perfectly.'

The Pascal machine was not taken up immediately, because of difficulty in manufacturing it. It also suffered from lack of positive action. The setting wheels could be turned in error part way between digit positions. It was probably these faults which led the encyclopaedist Dionysius Lardner (1793–1859), when explaining Babbage's inventions in 1834, to remark about the Pascal machine that it was 'subject to all the chances of error in manipulation: attended also with little more expedition (if so much) as would be attained by the pen of an expert computer' [1]. Pascal's machine was imitated by others.

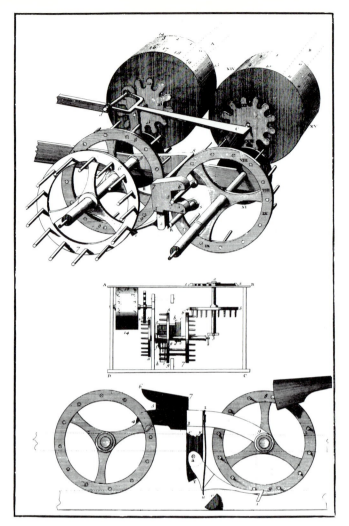

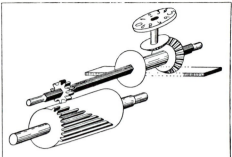

Fig. 48.2. The carrying mechanism used by Pascal for his calculating machine.

Fig. 48.3. The Leibniz stepped wheel.

Fig. 48.4. Arrangement of the mechanism in the Leibniz calculating machine.

In 1666 Sir Samuel Morland built a simple pocket adding machine capable of handling sums from a farthing up to £10 000, but it did not include automatic carry propagation. Another simple stylus-operated adding machine, based on the Morland principle, but using flat slides in place of wheels was designed by G. Troncet in 1889, and versions were still being sold in 1950.

It was Gottfried Leibniz who made the next major step towards the development of the automatic calculator, with a truly remarkable machine, the first model of which was built in 1671. The principles embodied in Leibniz's machine have been used in almost every subsequent mechanical calculator. Leibniz recognized the weaknesses of the Pascal machine, particularly when it was used for multiplication, and saw that it was necessary, if multiplication was to be done by successive addition, to store the multiplicand in a register, from which it could be introduced successively to the adding section of the machine. He also recognized that, as in manual 'long' multiplication, means must be provided to find the partial products of the multiplicand with each figure in turn of the multiplier, and to add these partial products to obtain the final result.

Leibniz took the principle of the Pascal adding machine and devised a means of rotating the setting wheels the required amount, as indicated by the multiplicand register, by a single turn of a shaft. He considered gears with retracting teeth (which were re-invented later) and other mechanisms before settling for a cylinder with stepped teeth, now known as the Leibniz wheel (Fig. 48.3).

One Leibniz wheel was provided for each place of the largest multiplicand the machine was designed for, and all of them were geared to a main shaft, so that a single turn of the shaft rotated all the wheels. Each Leibniz wheel carried nine teeth on half its circumference, the first tooth running nine-tenths of the length of the cylinder, the next eight-tenths, and the last, or ninth tooth, only one-tenth of the length of the cylinder. The 'setting' wheel of the adding part of the machine had ten teeth and was free to move along a square shaft with its axis parallel to that of the stepped wheel. This shaft drove the results wheel. According to its position on the square shaft the ten-tooth wheel engaged with different numbers of teeth on the stepped wheel from 0 to 9.

Thus, when the stepped Leibniz wheel made a complete revolution, the ten-tooth wheel (and hence the results wheel) would rotate by a variable amount, depending on the ten-tooth wheel's position on the shaft, and hence the number of teeth on the stepped wheel which engaged with it. Each digit of the multiplicand was set on a knob which slid the setting wheel along its shaft to a position where it would engage with the appropriate number of teeth on the stepped wheel. When the mainshaft was rotated through a whole turn the number set on the multiplicand register was thus added to the total. A further turn of the main shaft added the multiplicand again, and the results wheels showed the product 2 times the multiplicand.

However, there was one complication. The carry mechanism in the Pascal machine required the least significant digit to be dialled into the machine first, so that any carry could be propagated through the results wheels from right to left as far as was required. Leibniz made his machine do the same. He arranged that the nine stepped teeth on each wheel occupied only half of its circumference, the other half being blank. He then set the relative phases of the stepped cylinders so that on turning the main shaft the addition of the least significant digit of the multiplicand was made first, followed by the others in succession, with each carry being transmitted to the results wheel on its left without conflicting with the addition of the digit to that wheel.

In the form described a rotation of the main shaft was required every time the multiplicand was added to the results register. To multiply numbers of two or more places without having to turn the shaft an impracticably large number of times, a simple device enabled the multiplicand raised to a power of 10 to be added to the result. This was done by a carriage which shifted the ten-tooth wheels with respect to the results wheels. Thus if the carriage was moved one place to the left the ten-tooth wheel representing the least significant digit of the multiplicand now engaged on the tens digit of the results register, and so 10 times the multiplicand was added to the result. By turning the handle more than once, 20, 30, 40 . . . 90 times the multiplicand could be added to the result. To allow room for the product to appear in the results register, it was necessary, of course, to provide more results wheels than ten-tooth wheels.

Using a machine of this sort, the main shaft need never be turned more than 9 times for each digit of the multiplier. Leibniz, intent on making the machine as automatic as possible, then attempted in one of his machines to arrange to turn the main shaft the appropriate number of times, as indicated by a multiplier digit set on the machine, for a single turn of the operating handle. This he did with nine wheels connected to the main shaft by sprocket chains, so arranged that the gearing between them was 1:1, 1:2, 1:3 . . . 1:9. The wheels, on a common axis, were turned by an operating handle. The selection of the digit required for the multiplier clutched the appropriate 'wheel of the multi-

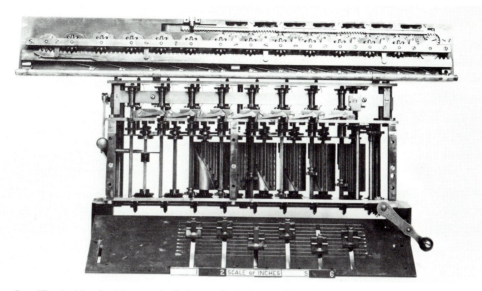

FIG. 48.5. The inside of a Thomas de Colmar calculating machine showing the stepped wheels. These machines were made until about 1930.

plier' to the main shaft, which turned the number of times required when the operating handle was turned once.

Not surprisingly, this ambitious machine (Fig. 48.4) proved too complex to be manufactured in the seventeenth century, although, as we shall see, the principles it pioneered were exploited during the nineteenth and twentieth centuries as precision engineering advanced. Leibniz did succeed, however, in making several machines, one of which is preserved at Hanover, where he spent the last forty years of his life looking after the library of the Brunswick family, and hatching grandiose schemes for reuniting the Catholic and Protestant churches.

The first calculating machine to be manufactured in quantity and used widely was designed by Charles Xavier Thomas de Colmar in Alsace, probably around 1820. Its use, first in France and Germany, seems to have developed slowly because of manufacturing difficulties. This 'arithmometer' (Fig. 48.5) continued to be made until the 1930s. The design was similar to that of Leibniz, but with some refinements and some simplifications. Special cams were provided to lock the ten-tooth wheels except during that part of the cycle when they might be acted upon by the teeth of the Leibniz stepped wheels. Another set of cams made the action of the results wheels positive so that they would come to rest only when the indicated digit was central in the window. Thomas also dispensed with Leibniz's 'wheels of the multiplier' so that the operating handle had to be turned up to nine times for each multiplier digit. However, to prevent the operator losing count of the number of turns he had given the handle he provided a 'multiplier register' arranged just below the results or product register. This register simply counted the number of turns of the operating handle which had been made in each position of the carriage. When the operation was complete the setting register thus contained the multiplicand; the multiplier register the multiplier; and the results register the product.

A refinement to the machine was a special gear which reversed the relative motion of the setting wheels and the results wheels, so that the results register was decremented by the multiplicand, thereby allowing the machine to perform subtraction and division. A leaflet published about 1870 gives an idea of the range of users of the arithmometer.

> The machine renders the greatest services to astronomers, geometricians, architects and all scientific men engaged in mathematical searches.
>
> The commerce in general, and particularly Bankers, Brewers, Stockbrokers, Public mints, corporate companies, etc. will find in its use the greatest assistance, if we judge the daily services it renders to most of the railway companies, to the Imperial mint, and the Imperial Bank of deposit and consignations in Paris, to the Creuzot iron works, and to a vast number of large public and private establishments.

The arithmometer was claimed to multiply two eight-figure numbers in 18 seconds; to divide a 16-figure number by an eight-figure one in 24 seconds; and to extract a square root of a 16-figure number in 1 minute. It had a virtual monopoly for many years, but in the latter part of the nineteenth century, as the problems of manufacture became less severe, there were many imitators, and some entirely new designs were introduced.

An alternative to the Leibniz stepped wheel was invented by Frank Stephen Baldwin in the U.S.A. in 1872. Machines based on Baldwin's design were made by W. T. Ohdner a few years later, and the device is now usually known as the Ohdner wheel. The machine was provided with one Ohdner wheel for each digit of the largest multiplicand. All the wheels were fixed to the main shaft of the machine and turned with it. Each individual wheel consisted of two concentric rings, the inner one being able to turn within the outer one, which was fixed to the main shaft. The position of the inner ring could be moved by means of a setting lever, which extended beyond the outer ring. This inner ring carried a profiled slot, as shown in Fig. 48.6, so that, according to the relative positions of the inner and outer ring, different numbers of

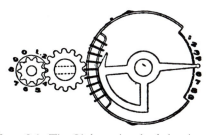

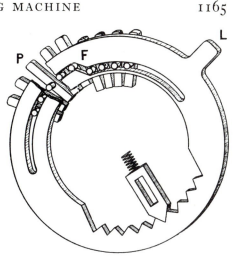

FIG. 48.6. The Ohdner pin wheel showing principle of construction.

FIG. 48.7. The construction of the pin wheel of the Brunsviga machine.

teeth, between 0 and 9, protruded through the outer ring. The setting lever was provided with spring-loaded location devices which were numbered to indicate the number of teeth protruding when the setting lever was in that position. When the main shaft, with the Ohdner wheels, was rotated one turn, the teeth meshed with ten-toothed wheels, similar to those in the Liebniz and Thomas machines, and thus added the multiplicand as set on the setting levers to the results register. A multiplier register, similar to that on the Thomas machine was provided.

The main advantage of the Ohdner-type machine, which was also made under the name Brunsviga (Fig. 48.7), and many others, was a much improved carry mechanism. Each Ohdner wheel was provided with two additional teeth, which performed the carry operation directly on the ten-tooth wheels, one when the main shaft was rotated clockwise in the addition direction, and one which operated when the shaft was rotated counterclockwise for subtraction. These teeth were not in the same plane as the extending teeth and therefore did not normally engage the ten-tooth wheel. However, each was provided with a snap-action hinge so that the tooth could be displaced to engage with the ten-tooth wheel. The carry teeth were pushed into the carry position by a lever operated by the immediately less significant ten-tooth wheel as it passed from the 9 to the 0 position. As the carry was effected, rotation of the main shaft returned the carry teeth to their inoperative position.

The chief advantage of this ingenious carry operation was that the main shaft of the machine could be turned in either direction, and this meant that a skilled operator could work much more rapidly than with an Arithmometer, by arranging his work to minimize the number of turns of the handle required. For example, to multiply by 199, he could multiply by 200 and subtract 1, requiring three turns of the handle and two carriage shifts. On an Arithmometer 19 turns of the handle would be needed, or alternatively a gear change into reverse.

The Ohdner-type machine had the further advantage that it was cheaper to make and more compact than the Arithmometer. The main shaft was turned directly by a handle, and the ten-tooth wheels, which were mounted on the carriage, were fastened directly to discs on the edge of which the digits representing the results were engraved. This type of machine was in widespread use, particularly for scientific calculations, until the introduction of the electronic calculator in about 1960.

Although, as mentioned above, the Arithmometer had disappeared by about 1930, an ingenious small calculator based on the Leibniz wheel, known as the Curta, was sold until it was displaced by electronic pocket calculators. The machine was built in the form of a drum with a single Leibniz wheel. The ten-tooth wheels clustered round the central drum, and were set by slides on the outside of the drum parallel with its axis. The result was displayed on dials viewed through windows arranged in a circle on the top of the machine.

Another machine of interest, developed in 1887 by Otto Steiger of Zürich, based on an original design by Leon Bollée, used a mechanical 'look-up' table and was thus effectively an automatic version of Napier's bones. The machine was rather cumbersome, but proved popular and 2500 had been sold under the name 'Millionaire' by 1912. From 1910 onwards electrically operated versions were available.

The machine had a carriage with results and multiplier registers rather similar to the Arithmometer. The multiplicand was set, as on the Thomas machine, by knobs sliding in grooves, which moved ten-tooth setting wheels along splined shafts. However, the ten-tooth wheels were turned by toothed racks in place of the Leibniz wheels. The racks were acted on directly by the 'look-up' table, which was called the 'multiplication table block' (Fig. 48.8). It consisted of a vertical plate in which were set rows of horizontal rods or tongues of varying length. Each row could contain 18 rods, arranged so that alternate rods lay in line with the ends of the racks. Each row of rods corresponded with one of Napier's bones. The lowest row represented the 'one times' table, the next the two times table, and so on to the top row, which represented the nine times table. Each of the products in the table was

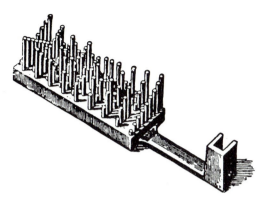

FIG. 48.8. The multiplication table block of a Bollée calculating machine. The various lengthened tongues represent the multiplication tables and are a physical representation of Napier's bones. The look-up table approach is still used in many electronic computers.

represented by a pair of adjacent rods, one representing the units, and the other the tens. All the rods were an exact number from 0 to 9 centimetres long (measured from the plate).

The machine was set up by placing the multiplicand on the slide knobs controlling the setting wheels, and moving the multiplier handle to the least significant figure in the multiplier. This raised or lowered the multiplication table block so that the row of rods corresponding to the digit set on the multiplier handle came into line with the racks. As the operating handle was rotated the first quarter-turn the multiplication table block moved forward 9 cm, and the 'units' rods pushed the racks a distance equal to the length of each rod. A movement of 1 cm of each rack was designed to move the corresponding results wheel one place. This first quarter-turn of the handle thus added the units given by the table to the result, and propagated whatever carries were necessary. The next quarter-turn of the handle disengaged the racks from the ten-tooth wheels and returned them and the multiplication table block to their original position. The carriage was then moved automatically one step to the right, and the multiplication table block was moved forward to align the 'tens' rods with the ends of the racks. The third quarter-turn repeated the sequence of the first quarter-turn and thus added the tens value of the table to the result. The final quarter-turn disengaged the racks again, and returned them and the multiplication block to their original positions. The block also moved back to align the units rods with the racks once more. The operation could then be continued without moving the carriage by setting the multiplier handle to the next most significant figure in the multiplier. The machine had a reversing gear, like the Thomas design, for subtraction and division. Addition and subtraction required the multiplier handle to be set to 1.

The Millionaire (Fig. 48.9) was considerably faster than the Arithmometer and the hand-operated version enabled two eight-figure numbers to be multiplied together in 6 or 7 seconds. A six-figure number could be divided by a three-figure one in the same time. The square root, to five places, of a nine-figure number could be found in 18 seconds.

II. KEYBOARD MACHINES

With the development of the typewriter in the early 1870s (Vol. IV, p. 689) there was a demand, particularly in the U.S.A., for a calculating machine which used keys to enter the numbers, in place of slides or setting levers. An attempt had been made to build such a machine as early as 1850 by J. M. Parmelee, but it would add only a single column of digits and was not a success. The first successful keyboard machine was designed by an American, Dorr Eugene Felt when he was in his early 20s and was built in an old cigar-box. Within two years he had developed a practical machine called the Comptometer (Fig. 48.10), which was in production by 1887. The Felt machine could only be used for adding, and was of the 'full keyboard' type, with ten keys numbered from 0 to 9 for each digit position. The registers were driven directly by the keys through a mechanical linkage. The early machines required that only one key at a time was pressed, to allow the tens carry to work without conflict. In 1903 Felt developed an epicyclic gear arrangement which allowed a carry to propagate at the same time that the next key was being pressed, and all keys representing a number could be operated simultaneously if desired.

The chief problem with key-driven adding machines lay in designing mechanical linkages which would result in each key moving through about the same distance and requiring the same pressure to operate it whether a carry propagation was required or not. The keys had to be so arranged that a partial depression did not produce a false result, and locking mechanisms had to be provided to stop sharp depression of a key causing the results wheels to spin and overshoot. The majority of these machines were based on the key depression turning a toothed quadrant through an appropriate angle. The quadrant engaged a ten-tooth wheel which was coupled to the results wheel. An important extension was made by Felt in 1889, when he introduced the first practical adding-listing machine, which printed the results on a tally roll.

About the same time William S. Burroughs, who had been a bank clerk, was working on the design of an adding machine which was driven, not by the keys themselves, but by a separate handle. The number was first set on the

48.9. The Millionaire calculating machine based on the Bollée
inciple. These machines were still being sold in a motorized
sion at the time of the First World War.

48.10. One of the first Comptometers
1890) built in a wooden case.

keyboard, those keys which had been pressed remaining down. The operator was thus given the chance to check that the number entered was correct. When the handle was pulled the number was added to the results register. The machine also printed the numbers entered, and was thus also an adding–listing machine. The first 'key-set' machines of this type were manufactured in 1890, but they were not reliable until a year or two later. By 1909 their popularity had grown and 15 000 machines a year were being manufactured. The key-set principle was easily adapted to motor drive, and the first motor-driven machines were introduced in 1906. It was from machines of this type that the accounting machine, the mainstay of banks and medium-sized businesses until it was displaced by the electronic computer, was developed in the years following the First World War. These machines were effectively adding–listing machines built with a typewriter carriage and tabulators. They were thus able to print columns of figures across a page, rather than a single column on a narrow 'tally' roll. A number of adding registers could be fitted on the carriage, to keep a total of figures entered into particular columns.

A different approach to entering numbers in an adding machine was developed by Oscar and David Sundstrand in 1914. Their keyboard contained only 10 keys, one for each digit, and a number of control keys, whereas Felt and Burroughs had provided a full set of nine keys for each digit place. The Sundstrand keyboard required the operator to enter the number digit by digit, starting with the most significant. A setting register on a carriage moved step by step as the numbers were entered and could be read by the operator. When the number was complete an add button was pressed, so the machine was of the key-set rather than the key-driven variety.

The use of the new key-set technique pioneered by Burroughs was quickly extended to calculating machines which would perform all the arithmetic functions. Among the first was the TIM Arithmometer built just before the First World War, which replaced the multiplicand-setting slides of a Thomas-type machine with a full keyboard. About the same time Jay R. Monroe and Frank S. Baldwin designed an entirely new full keyboard calculator, which was in production by 1922. A rather similar machine was introduced a little later which was essentially an Ohdner calculator with a ten-key keyboard to load the multiplicand register.

All these machines still required the operator to turn a handle, or, where they had been fitted with an electric motor, to press a motor bar for each step of addition which made up a multiplication although a multiplier register kept count, as in the Arithmometer, of the number of addition operations. They were thus less advanced than Leibniz's original concept, or Otto Steiger's Millionaire which was semi-automatic. It was only in the 1930s that the mechanical desk calculator reached its ultimate form in which multiplication or division of two numbers, each entered via the keyboard, was carried out entirely automatically. This final step required the addition of a further register to the machine, known as the control register. A number was entered on the keyboard into the setting register (which on simpler machines contained the multiplicand). This could then be transferred into the control register and became the multiplier. The multiplicand was now entered into the setting register. When the multiplier knob was pressed the two numbers were multiplied together, the machine making automatically the correct number of main shaft revolutions and carriage shifts. The majority of these machines used a full keyboard, but Facit produced a design with a ten-key keyboard and 'invisible' control register (not displayed to the operator) which was operated in almost exactly the same way as modern electronic pocket calculators.

The electronic calculator. It was with machines of the mechanical types described above that virtually all computational work (except that suitable for punched-card machines described below) was carried out until the 1950s, when the universal digital electronic computers began to come into general use. However, the new computers were extremely expensive and few people had access to them, so that mechanical machines continued to be used for some considerable time. But the new electronic techniques were gradually applied to the design of calculators. One of the earliest, known as the Anita, was developed largely by N. Kritz who had worked at the National Physical Laboratory in Britain on the development of the ACE electronic computer. The new electronic calculators benefited also from the development during the war (in connection with the atomic bomb programme) of numerical display devices for nuclear radiation counters. The Anita used neon digital displays for its results register. It was manufactured by the Sumlock Comptometer Company Ltd. and introduced in 1961, not long after the launch of the last of the mechanical calculators. The development of electronic calculators continued during the 1960s. By the early 1970s the new large-scale integrated circuit technology, which had been brought about by the computer industry, became available, and the development of light-emitting semi-conductor diodes made it possible to mass-produce electronic calculators of great speed and flexibility at extremely low cost.

III. AUTOMATIC MACHINES: THE COMPUTING ENGINE

All the machines described above have been concerned with aiding a human operator to carry out a calculation. Even the most advanced forms needed human intervention to enter numbers and to instruct the machine to carry out the next step. Where tables of any kind have to be computed, whether by hand, or through the use of a calculating machine, it is common practice to make use of numerical methods which enable one value in the table to be calculated by a repetitive process from the preceding one. One of the commonest such methods is by 'differencing'.

Suppose a table has been made of the value of a function for different values of x, the interval between successive values of x being constant. The difference between the value of the function for two successive values of x is known as the first-order difference. That between two successive first-order differences is called the second-order difference, and so on. Now, it can be shown that if the function is a polynomial of the nth degree the nth-order difference is a constant. The third-order difference is constant for a cubic function, the fourth-order for a quartic, etc. Thus, given the value of the constant difference and the first few terms in a table, it is possible by simple addition to construct the next term. And having done that the operation can be repeated to create the complete table step by step.

The example displayed in Table 48.1, calculated for the expression $y = x^2+x+41$, should make the method clear.

It follows that the value of y for $x = 8$, and as many further terms as we wish, can be calculated by adding the constant second-order difference to the

TABLE 48.1
Calculation by differencing of $y=x^2+x+41$

x	y	First-order difference	Second-order difference
0	41		
1	43	2	
2	47	4	2
3	53	6	2
4	61	8	2
5	71	10	2
6	83	12	2
7	97	14	2
etc.			

last first-order difference. We then add this new first-order difference to the last value of the function to obtain the new value:

2+14 = 16 and 16+97 = 113, which is the next value to be entered in the table. Although the method is only mathematically valid for polynomials, any function approximates as closely as required to a polynomial over a restricted range of values of x. Thus differencing can be applied to the calculation of a wide range of tables.

Charles Babbage recognized that this was so, and since the method of differences required only a hierarchical series of additions, he started to design a multiple adding machine, which he called a 'difference engine'. The first machine, which took two years to build, was a pilot model. He described it in a paper read to the Royal Astronomical Society in 1822, when he was just 30. 'I have taken the method of differences as the principle on which my machine is founded, and in the engine which is just finished I have limited myself to two orders of difference. With this machine I have repeatedly constructed tables of square and triangular numbers, as well as a table from the singular formula x^2+x+41, which comprises among its terms so many prime numbers.' A little later he wrote to Sir Humphry Davy, then President of the Royal Society, suggesting that his machine should be used to remove the 'intolerable labour and fatiguing monotony' of repetitive calculations, and so to replace 'one of the lowest occupations of the human intellect.'

Babbage's lobbying was successful, and the British Government, which was greatly concerned by inaccuracies in existing tables, and the labour involved in preparing new ones, agreed to support a project to build a full-scale difference engine, which would compute six orders of difference, each of 20 places. The engine would not only compute the values of the function required, but would set them in type, thereby avoiding compositors' errors, which were even more numerous than computation and copying errors. The work started in 1823. It was an extraordinarily ambitious venture, undertaken fifty years before either typesetting machines or typewriters had been invented. At a time when Thomas de Colmar was having great difficulty in manufacturing his relatively simple Arithmometer, Babbage was setting about designing a machine with seven 20-digit registers, each of which added its contents in turn to the next above it in the hierarchy. And finally, the contents of the last register, which contained the new value to appear in the table, had to be set in type.

For fourteen years (with a standstill of five years) Babbage worked on the design of his great machine at a cost to the country of £17 000. Gradually the

Government lost patience, in spite of its eagerness for the machine, and Babbage himself became more and more engrossed in a still more ambitious dream: an 'analytical engine' which would be a truly universal automatic calculating machine, instead of being limited to differencing. We shall return to that machine later.

A description of the Babbage difference engine was published in the *Edinburgh Review* in 1834 and aroused the interest of George Scheutz, a printer and editor of a technological journal in Stockholm. Three years later he and his son Edward Scheutz, a student at the Royal Technological Institute, Stockholm designed a difference engine of their own, complete with printing apparatus. It was capable of calculating functions to five places, using two or three orders of difference: it found no buyers. Meanwhile Scheutz designed a bigger machine working to 15 places and four orders of difference. It could calculate either in the ordinary denary (or decimal) system, or it could be adjusted for the mixed senary system (degrees, minutes, seconds, and decimals of seconds) used for many navigational, astronomical, and trigonometric tables. The whole machine was about the size of 'a small square pianoforte'. It

exhibits the numbers or answer resulting from the calculation of 15 places of figures, the first eight of which the machine stereotypes . . . While the process is going on the argument proper to each result is at the same time stereotyped in its proper place; nothing more being required for that purpose than . . . to place a sheet of strip lead on the slide of the printing apparatus; then by turning the handle (to do which requires no greater power than that which is exerted in turning that of a small barrel organ), the whole table is calculated and stereomoulded in lead. By this expression is meant that the strip of lead is made into a beautiful stereotype mould from which any number of sharp stereotype plates can be produced ready for the working of an ordinary printing press.

The Scheutz machine worked at a speed of 120 lines an hour, and the eight-figure results that it stereotyped were rounded. It was demonstrated in England in 1854; won a Gold Medal for its inventors in the Paris International Exhibition of 1855; and was then installed at the Dudley Observatory, Albany, New York, where it worked for many years. A second Scheutz machine (Fig. 48.11) was built by Bryan Donkin of Bermondsey and is now in the Science Museum, London. It was used for some of the computations for a life table based on the British Registrar-General's records of births and deaths for the years 1838–54. In a foreword to the completed table, published in 1864, William Farr wrote:

Several of the series were calculated by Scheutz's machine . . . It gave us the opportunity of testing its working powers in England, where Mr. Babbage explained the

FIG. 48.11. The Scheutz difference engine, showing the printing mechanism. This machine was used to calculate life tables.

principles, and first demonstrated the practicability of performing certain calculations and printing the results by machinery . . . The idea had been as beautifully embodied in metal by Mr. Bryan Donkin as it had been conceived by the genius of its inventors; but it was untried. So its work had to be watched with anxiety, and its arithmetical music had to be elicited by frequent tuning and skilful handling in the quiet most conducive to such productions. This volume is the result.

In fact, the Scheutz machine seems to have been unreliable, but at least it was built, whereas only parts of Babbage's difference engine (now also in the Science Museum, London) were completed. Scheutz had the advantage of having set himself a somewhat more realistic target. He also understood much more of the problems of printing. Babbage had not only attempted a much larger machine, but devoted much of his energy to designing a faster and more effective method of carrying tens than the usual digit-by-digit propagation.

In any case, by 1832 Babbage's attention had turned to his 'analytical engine'. Most of the rest of his life was devoted to designing and seeking support for this machine, which, like the difference engine, was never built. After Babbage's death in 1871, his son Major-General H. P. Babbage succeeded in building part of the machine, which also is now in the Science Museum in London.

The analytical engine included most of the essential features of the modern electronic digital computer expressed, of course, in mechanical terms. But, as with his other projects, Babbage was far too ambitious. The analytical engine was designed to operate with 50-digit numbers throughout. It had a method of anticipating carry digits which allowed all the pairs of corresponding digits in the two 50-place numbers to be added simultaneously. Babbage estimated that the machine would require 1 second for the addition of two 50-place numbers, and 1 minute for multiplication of two similar numbers, or division of a 100-place number by a 50-place one.

However, the main significance of the analytical machine lay not in the ingenuity of its mechanical arrangements, but in the structural concepts involved. The machine was to be divided into two major parts, the mill (Fig. 48.12) in which the arithmetic processes were carried out, and the store which contained the data to be worked on, and intermediate results. The store was to consist of 1000 registers, each containing a 50-digit number. Thus, numbers could be selected from the store, operated upon (for example by adding them together), and the result returned to another location in the store. The control of the whole process was to be carried out through a set of punched cards (Fig. 48.13), similar to those used in the Jacquard loom (Vol. IV, p. 317) invented in 1801 and used for the weaving of elaborately patterned fabrics. The pattern of holes on each card was read by plungers which passed through them. Babbage proposed to use the cards in different ways, both to specify the operation to be carried out, and to give the address of the operand in the store.

There are therefore two sets of cards: the first, to direct the nature of the operations to be performed—these are called *operation cards*; the other, to direct the particular variables on which those cards are required to operate—these latter are called *variable cards*.

Under this arrangement, when any formula is required to be computed, a set of operation cards must be strung together, which contain the series of operations in the order in which they are required to be acted on. Each operation card will required three other cards, two to represent the variables and constants and their numerical values on which the previous operation card is to act, and one to indicate the variable on which the arithmetic result of the operation is to be placed . . . Whenever variables are ordered into the mill, these figures will be brought in, and the operation indicated by the preceding

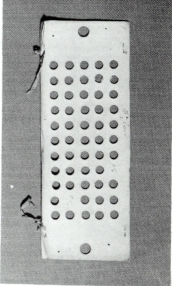

FIG. 48.12. The mill of Babbage's analytical engine as built by his son H. P. Babbage about 1910.

FIG. 48.13. One of the cards used by the Babbage analytical engine. Cards were strung together by the tapes to make a complete program.

card will be performed upon them. The result of this operation will then be replaced in the store.

Every set of cards made for any formula will at any future time recalculate that formula with whatever constants may be required. Thus the Analytical Engine will possess a library of its own.

Babbage also envisaged using another set of cards, the number cards, as a means of feeding data into the machine, although it appears that he expected the store registers to be set up by hand with the constants required, and would use his number cards only for selecting a particular value from a table which was too large to store. The selection of the card required would have been made by an operator. If the card was the wrong one the machine would ring a loud bell and display a sign 'Wrong number card'.

Still more important, although missed by most of the contemporary enthusiasts for the analytical engine, was the understanding shown by Babbage and his friend Lady Lovelace of the importance of what would now be called the conditional jump. In the normal way, control was exercised by the cards being read in sequence. But mechanical means were to be provided to allow the band of cards to be advanced or backed, thereby jumping some cards, or alternatively repeating them. The control of such a jump in sequence was to have been exercised by the sign of the difference between two numbers subtracted in the mill. In current computer language:

> Subtract B from A
> Jump if negative to XXX

Ada Augusta, Countess of Lovelace, daughter of Lord Byron, translated a paper describing the analytical engine written by General L. F. Menebrea after discussions with Babbage when he visited Italy in 1840–1, and in doing so added extensive translator's notes (in total more than twice the length of the original paper) which amounted to an explanation of the manner in which the machine would be programmed. Lady Lovelace recognized that in many calculations there would be recurring patterns of instructions, and pointed out that by using the conditional jump facility proposed for the Analytical Engine, it should be possible to prepare only a single set of cards for the recurring instructions. In this way many fewer cards would be required. She called the recurring sequence of operations a cycle and saw that a group of such cycles could itself recur to form a cycle of cycles. She thus described what we would now call a 'loop' and a 'sub-routine'.

Unfortunately for Babbage, his thinking was a hundred years ahead of his times. His mechanical machines could probably have been made at the beginning of the twentieth century, but it was not to be. Lord Moulton, speaking at the Napier Tercentenary in Edinburgh in 1914, described a visit to Babbage as an old man, probably about 1870.

In the first room I saw the parts of the original Calculating Machine, which had been shown in an incomplete state many years before and had even been put to some use. I asked him about its present form. 'I have not finished it because in working at it I came on the idea of my Analytical Machine, which would do all that it was capable of doing and much more. Indeed the idea was so much simpler that it would have taken more work to complete the calculating machine than to design and construct the other in its entirety, so I turned my attention to the Analytical Machine.' After a few minutes' talk we went into the next workroom where he showed and explained to me the working of the elements of the Analytical Machine. I asked if I could see it. 'I have never completed it', he said, 'because I hit upon the idea of doing the same thing by a different and far more effective method, and this rendered it useless to proceed on the old lines.' Then we went into the third room. There lay scattered bits of mechanism but I saw no trace of any working machine. Very cautiously I approached the subject, and received the dreaded answer, 'It is not constructed yet, but I am working at it, and will take less time to construct it altogether than it would have taken to complete the Analytical Machine from the stage in which I left it.' I took leave of the old man with a heavy heart.

IV. PUNCHED-CARD MACHINES

In spite of total failure in his lifetime to build a working machine larger than the original model difference engine, Babbage's work was widely known, and—thanks to General Menebrea and Lady Lovelace—well documented. But the next development towards the modern computer came from an entirely different direction. The U.S. Census Bureau, which was set up under a law of 1879, took on a statistician, Herman Hollerith the following year, in preparation for the analysis of the 1880 census. The work took $7\frac{1}{2}$ years to complete, and the final volumes were published only shortly before the next census in 1890 was due. The population of the U.S.A. was growing rapidly, and it was clear that manual tabulation of census results was inadequate. Hollerith undertook to mechanize the census operations, and decided, as Babbage had done, to make use of punched cards as used on the Jacquard loom. His first machine, built in 1887, used a continuous paper strip with holes punched in it in place of individual cards. This first attempt was abandoned in favour of separate cards 3 inches by 5 inches, with one corner chopped off in order to face them.

The cards were read by placing them in a 'pin press', which contained a mercury cup beneath each position where a hole might occur in a card. The card was read by closing a hinged lid which carried a spring-loaded 'pin' or plunger corresponding to each mercury cup. If a hole had been punched the pin passed through it to make electrical contact with the mercury in the cup below: if there was no hole the card held back the pin, and no contact was made. Hollerith borrowed the electromechanical technology that had been developed for the electric telegraph (Vol. IV, p. 656) and used electro-mechanical counters to count the number of cards with a particular perforation, and an electromagnetically controlled sorting slot to separate the selected cards. The equipment was tested on 10 000 returns, and it was shown that the enumeration time was three-quarters of that taken by the best manual system, and the tabulation time one-sixth. Between 50 and 80 cards a minute could be passed through the pin press. As a result the machine was used to analyse the 1890 census, and proved satisfactory (Fig. 48.14). Although the population of the U.S.A. had grown since the 1880 census from 50 million to 63 million, the whole analysis was completed in $2\frac{1}{2}$ years, one-third of the time taken for the previous census.

FIG. 48.14. Mechanizing the 1890 census. The cover of the *Scientific American* shows the various machines in use, including the pin press card punch, and sorter–counter.

Herman Hollerith recognized that his machine could have other applications and in 1896 set up the Tabulating Machine Company to exploit the idea. He also developed improved machines, including a card punch operated from a numerical keyboard (1901). Various other new machines were developed shortly afterwards, and the Hollerith system was used for the analysis of the British Census of 1911. In that year Hollerith's company merged with the International Time Recording Company, which made time-recording clocks, and the Dayton Scale Company, to form the Computing-Tabulating Recording Company. In 1914 Thomas J. Watson became President of the new company, and in 1924 its name was changed to International Business Machines Corporation.

Meanwhile, the U.S. Census Bureau, recognizing that still higher speed and accuracy were desirable for the 1910 Census, appointed a New Jersey statistician, James Powers, as director of a new laboratory set up to develop

FIG. 48.15. A Powers tabulator of 1910. The stack of cards was fed one by one through the reading point where plungers passed through any holes. The plungers operated cables (like bicycle brake cables) which passed up the funnel-shaped section to operate the five counters at the top. Different funnel-shaped sections were available to route the motion to whichever counter was required.

improved equipment. Powers took a different approach from Hollerith and decided to build machines which were entirely mechanical, rather than electromechanical. In 1908 he introduced the 'simultaneous punching' concept in which all the data to be placed on a 20-column card were entered on a keyboard, and then, on pressing a punch key, all the holes required were perforated at once. This avoided the difficulty that partially perforated cards might enter the system, and allowed operators to check the contents before operating the punch. It was the equivalent of the Burroughs key-set adding machine keyboard. Powers also developed, still on mechanical principles, sorters and tabulators (Fig. 48.15). The machines proved very reliable and 300 punches and corresponding quantities of sorters and tabulators were built and used in the 1910 Census. Powers, like Hollerith, recognized the commercial value of the machines on which he had been working and formed, in 1911, the Powers Accounting Machine Company. In 1927 Powers, Remington (the typewriter company), and other office equipment and supply companies merged to form Remington Rand, which in 1955 became the Sperry Rand Corporation. Thus the companies started by the two punched card pioneers, Hollerith and Powers, were to become the two most significant electronic computer manufacturers from 1950 onwards.

The two companies developed the punched card system in parallel. The tabulator, which had originally simply contained counters (electromechanical in the Hollerith, mechanical in the Powers) which were read at the end of a run, and the numbers transferred manually to a permanent record. But within a few years printing tabulators were developed working on the same principles as the key-set adding and listing machines described above (Fig. 48.16).

The Hollerith company soon replaced the pin press with its mercury cups with a metal brush, which made contact through holes in the card to a metal roll beneath it. The contact wires from the brushes led to a plug-board, like a manual telephone switchboard, which enabled a brush to be connected to any of the electromagnetic counters. Each counter or register consisted of a set of number wheels mounted on a constantly revolving shaft. The number wheels normally remained still, but when a hole was sensed by the brush, an electromagnetic clutch was energized and the number wheel was locked to and turned with the shaft. All the clutches were disengaged at the same moment, when the card had passed. The extent to which the number wheel was turned thus depended on the time at which the brush found the hole in the card. The holes were arranged in columns and so spaced that the hole representing each digit caused the number wheel to be turned by the appropriate amount. Suitable arrangements were made for tens carry between number wheels.

FIG. 48.16. The Great Northern Railway's punched-card department at Peterborough in 1920. Most of the girls are perforating cards. In the background are sorters and a printing tabulator. In the foreground is a Comptometer.

The next step in the development of the punched-card machines was the ability to take two or more numbers from the same card, to operate on them, for example by adding them together, and both to punch the result back on to the card and to print it out. By 1926 Powers had introduced their listing multiplier and calculator, which enabled numbers and their products to be listed. In 1932 IBM brought out a still more flexible machine which allowed the summation of partial products. And in the 1950s, towards the end of the punched-card machine era, a variety of electronic calculators were being offered as components of punched card systems. Some of these had their own internal memories for constants and could be programmed by plug-board to carry out a predetermined sequence of operations, which might consist of additions, subtractions, multiplications, and divisions in any order.

V. THE FIRST COMPUTERS

By 1937 interest in automatic computation, which had been dormant since Charles Babbage's death in 1871, began to revive. Alan Mathison Turing, working in Britain, had published a paper [2] in which he defined very precisely, and in abstract terms, the generalized conception of a universal com-

FIG. 48.17. A general view of the Automatic Sequence Controlled Calculator (ASCC), designed by Howard Aiken. The photograph was taken at Harvard University about 1945. On the left are the switches used for setting values of constants. Each bank contains 30 rows of 23 ten-position switches. To the right of these switches are the banks containing the counting-adding units which are the machine's main storage. To store 72 numbers, 1656 counters had to be provided. To the right again are the multiplying and dividing units. Behind the control desk are the four input tape readers, which used broad tape like a pianola roll. On the extreme right are the two electric typewriters on which results appeared.

puter. He then used this definition to express the criteria for computable problems, and discussed the possibility of machines teaching themselves through a process of trial and error. In the same year, in the U.S.A., Howard Aiken of Harvard University had the idea of applying the engineering principles used in the punched-card machines, and the relays and similar components used in automatic telephony (see p. 1244) to build an automatic calculator of the kind that had been envisaged by Babbage. Because the Hollerith-derived machines were most suitable for his purpose, Aiken approached International Business Machines Corporation for their assistance. Over the next seven years he and a group of engineers built the Automatic Sequence Controlled Calculator (or ASCC). It was presented to Harvard University in August 1944.

ASCC was very similar to the Babbage machine in concept, although entirely different in engineering realization. It was also much smaller and less ambitious. Babbage had decided on a store containing 1000 numbers of 50 places. Aiken contented himself with 72 of 23 places, plus a sign. In addition he provided storage for 60 constants which were set up by hand on switches. The

machine also had an arithmetic unit, or mill (to use Babbage's term), but this
was used only for multiplication and division, the distinction between mill and
store being less clear-cut than in the Analytical Engine. Addition and subtraction were performed directly on the 72 store registers, using the same
electromagnetic clutch system that was used on the punched-card tabulator
registers. Aiken used what Babbage called the 'anticipating carriage' method
of tens carry, which allows all the digits to be added into the register simultaneously, followed by all carry digits. When a number wheel passed zero, a
lever was automatically set closing a contact. Immediately after the digit add
had been completed, the clutches were operated again to add 1 to all number
wheels immediately to the left of those with the tens carry contact closed. All
the contacts were then reset to the open position. However, the arrangement
as described so far, would not work where a tens carry was made to a number
wheel already set to 9, since that would create a further carry. An additional
contact was therefore provided which closed on all number wheels set to 9.
The way the 'anticipating carriage' worked may be seen in the following
example (C denotes a closed contact, O an open contact):

| Current setting of register | 4 | 9 | 9 | 9 | 9 | 5 |
Addend	o	o	o	o	o	6
Sum of digits	4	9	9	9	9	1
Tens carry contact	O	O	O	O	O	C
Nines contact	O	C	C	C	C	O
Final result	5	o	o	o	o	1

The tens carry contact on the least significant digit causes the digit to its left
to be incremented by 1. But because the nines contact is closed, the carry is
passed on to the next digit, and so on until a digit is reached which is not a 9.
Here the anticipatory carry stops.

The multiply–divide unit of ASCC worked like Napier's bones by building
up a table of 1 to 9 times the multiplicand (or divisor). In multiplication the
required partial products were selected, shifted to the appropriate position,
and added to produce the result. In division, the process was similar to
manual 'long' division, the remainder at each stage being compared with the
table to find the highest value which would give a positive remainder.

Whereas the punched-card tabulator could read only data provided on
cards, ASCC needed to be able to read back into itself the values set in its
registers. To do so, each number wheel was provided with a brush and a ten-

contact commutator switch, the value to which the number wheel was set determining which of the switch contacts was closed. The contacts were connected with nine timing cams, which produced a clutch-engaging pulse representing the digit required in the same way as in the Hollerith tabulator described above. Two numbers were added together simply by setting up, through relays, an electrical pathway to route the signals representing the addend, read out from one register, to the clutches of the register in which the partial sum had been stored. Subtraction was carried out in the same way, but by adding the complement. Numbers stored in registers could be automatically complemented by a suitably connected relay.

Data were fed into the storage registers from punched cards. Operating instructions, which were carried out sequentially, were provided not on cards, but on a continuous roll of perforated paper, like a pianola roll. The tape had 24 positions where holes might be punched, and each row represented a single instruction identifying the operation to be performed, the location of the data to be operated on, and the location or destination for the result. Output was printed on two electric typewriters or punched on cards. There was no facility, as Babbage had planned, for stepping out of sequence of instructions to repeat a loop, or to make a conditional jump.

The ASCC (or Harvard Mark I as it is often called) was an enormous machine, weighing 5 tons, 51 ft long, 8 ft high, and containing 800 000 parts and 500 miles of wire. Its performance was rather slow. An addition of two numbers took 0·3 second; multiplication 3 seconds; and division about 10 seconds. However, it was the first general-purpose digital computer, and it is preserved at Harvard University where it laboured night and day for 15 years on a variety of scientific and engineering calculations. Aiken and his team subsequently built three further computers (Mark II, III, and IV) for various laboratories, using specially designed relays in place of the Hollerith electro-magnetic-clutch mechanical counters. The Mark II was delivered to the U.S. Naval Proving Ground at Dahlgren, Virginia in 1947. It handled only 10-digit numbers in place of the 23 digits of ASCC. Its add time was 200 milliseconds and multiplication time 700 milliseconds. Aiken also went some way towards making the machine more flexible by providing three program input mechanisms, each loaded with a sequence of instructions punched on standard Teletype paper tape (in place of the pianola-roll). When a condition set in the instruction sequence being used was fulfilled, the machine could be programmed to switch for its next instruction to one of the two other input tapes. An instruction contained in this sequence could then return control to the first sequence. In modern computer language this would be known as a 'conditional call and return'.

The use of relays as logic elements for computers had been stimulated by a paper published in 1937 by Claude E. Shannon, a research student in electrical engineering at Massachusetts Institute of Technology, on A symbolic analysis of relay and switching circuits [6] which applied Boole's symbolic logic to the analysis of switching circuitry and showed how logical algebra could be performed by relays. In 1939, George R. Stibitz of Bell Telephone Laboratories, who was aware of the large amount of time communications engineers spent calculating the products of complex numbers, set about designing a machine using relays to perform automatically the logical processes involved in these calculations. The machine accepted data in standard teleprinter code, and provided the result in the same form, so that engineers anywhere in the U.S.A. could communicate with the machine over a standard teleprinter circuit. At the first demonstration in 1940, the machine, which was in New York, solved problems fed into it from a teleprinter in Dartmouth College, New Hampshire, and replied by printing out the answer. This was the first example of tele-computing, a technique which was to become extremely important from the middle 1960s.

The complex number machine was followed by other special-purpose computers, including two military fire-control computers which were used during the Second World War, and an interpolator. It soon became clear that these special-purpose machines could be used for other jobs, and in 1944 Bell Telephone Laboratories received a contract to build two general-purpose machines working on the same principles. One was delivered in July 1946 to Langley Air Field, and one in February 1947 to the Ballistics Research Laboratory at Aberdeen, Maryland.

The Bell machines had several unusual features. They worked in the bi-quinary code (as used in the Japanese abacus, the Soroban) instead of the normal denary system which was used by Aiken. In the biquinary system 7 relays were used to store each digit. Five of them represented the digits 0 to 4, and two represented 0 and 5. Any digit was thus represented by the operation of two relays, one selected from the set of five, and one from the set of two. The fact that every digit required two relays, one from each set, was used as an error-checking feature. All the functions of the machine were performed by relays, which were used both as registers to hold data and in the adding unit, which could also be used for multiplication by repetitive adding. Addition was performed by a 'look-up table' built into the machine by the pattern of interconnections between the various relay contacts. The principle was not dissimilar to the mechanical look-up table devised by Leon Bollée and used in Steiger's Millionaire calculator described earlier. The Bell machines had one other novel feature: all numbers were held in floating point form, $\pm x \times 10^{\pm y}$, where x was a seven-digit number not greater than 1 and y was any integer less than 20. The operation times for the Bell machines were: addition, 300 milliseconds; multiplication, 1 second; division, 2·2 seconds; square root, 4·3 seconds.

Several other large-scale relay-operated machines were built in the 1940s, including the B.A.R.K. machine in Stockholm, and the Imperial College Computing Engine, in London.

VI. THE ELECTRONIC COMPUTER

The success of relay-operated automatic calculating machines was short-lived, for by 1946 the first electronic machine had been built and demonstrated, working at a thousand times the speed of the best relay machines. From that time the whole weight of development effort centred on the electronic computer. In a way, it was surprising that it had taken so long to arrive. The triode valve had been invented by Lee de Forest in 1906 (p. 1095) and W. H. Eccles and F. W. Jordan had shown how to connect two triodes in a circuit which had two stable states as long ago as 1919. During the 1920s and 1930s the electronic valve had been enormously improved and circuitry had advanced through the development of broadcasting and the application of mass-production techniques to manufacture of valves and components (Ch. 46). In fact, the characteristics required from thermionic valves and circuits in use at that time for broadcast receivers were far more stringent than those that would have been needed for the simple on–off switching requirement of an electronic computer. The only application for electronic valves in this switching role was the development in 1930, by C. E. Wynn-Williams and others at Cambridge University, of electronic circuits for counting nuclear particles.

The first electronic computer owed its existence to the U.S. Defense Department's wartime need for extensive ballistic tables. In the early 1940s John W. Mauchly recognized the advantage of speed that would be obtained from a calculating machine using electronic counting circuits, especially in applications—such as the reduction of weather data—where the volume of calculation required was beyond existing machines. He and J. Presper Eckert, working in the Moore School of Electrical Engineering at the University of

Pennsylvania, designed and built the machine under a U.S. Government contract for the Ballistic Research Laboratory at Aberdeen Proving Grounds, Maryland. It was completed in 1946, only two years after Aiken's relay machine ASCC.

The new machine (Fig. 48.18) was called ENIAC, an acronym meaning Electronic Numerical Integrator and Calculator. In principle, it worked in a manner very similar to ASCC, but in place of the timed electrical impulses from the cams, a train of electronic pulses was generated every 0·2 milliseconds. The clutch of ASCC was replaced by an electronic gate which allowed the required number of pulses to pass to represent the digit. And the mechanical counter of ASCC became a decimal 'ring counter'. The ring counter was a circuit developed for nuclear particle counting and was the electronic equivalent of the number wheel. It consisted of 10 interconnected electronic valves, only one of which conducted current at any time. When this circuit was pulsed the conducting valve was 'turned off' and the next one in the ring conducted. Small lamps were usually included in the valve circuits to show which one was conducting current, so that the counter could be read by eye. As the count caused the valve representing zero to conduct, a carry pulse was passed to the next counter.

In many ways ENIAC was less ambitious than ASCC, since it had only 20 electronic counters or 'accumulators', and of these four were required for multiplication, two to hold the factors, and two to accumulate the partial products. There were thus only 16 locations available for storage, each of 10 digits and a sign. In addition, hand switches were provided to enable 104 values of any function to be set up by hand, a long and laborious process. Multiplication was carried out in a special unit which was wired with a multiplication table, similar in principle to the mechanical 'look-up' table designed by Leon Bollée.

Input and output to ENIAC was by punched cards. Since card reading and punching were (and still are) slow operations, the throughput of the computer was limited by the time taken to read data and to output the results. In the later development of computers much effort was used to overcome this problem of mismatch between peripherals and processing unit. Once information was contained in the accumulators, ENIAC was able to operate on it at high speed. A number contained in one accumulator could be added to another in one machine cycle of 0·2 milliseconds. Two 10-digit numbers could be multiplied together in 2·3 milliseconds (compared with 3 seconds for the ASCC).

FIG. 48.18(a). The original ENIAC electronic computer. Among the first tasks given to the Electronic Numerical Integrator and Calculator was a problem in nuclear physics. In two hours it produced an answer which would have taken 100 engineers, using conventional methods, a year to solve.

FIG. 48.18(b). Henry H. Goldstine (*left*, in uniform), who later worked with John von Neumann on the Princeton stored program parallel computer, and J. Presper Eckert, one of the designers of ENIAC, are holding one of the machine's shift registers and counters. Within 20 years the circuitry they are holding had reduced in size to a silicon chip a millimetre across.

However, partly because it was originally designed for the special purposes of the Ballistics Research Laboratory, the method of programming ENIAC compared poorly even with ASCC. 'Programs' to carry out a particular calculation were set up by interconnecting the various accumulators and other parts of the machine by switches and manual plugging of connecting leads. Each of these units was quiescent until it received a 'program pulse', or what would now be called a 'strobe'. When its operation was completed it produced a further strobe (obtained by gating the master pulse train) and this was routed by switches and plugs to provide the program pulse to activate the next unit. In addition, a 'master-programmer' allowed a choice to be made by ten six-position electronic 'stepper' switches of sequences of pre-plugged programs. This decentralized control and the need to adapt the machine by replugging the units to perform particular calculations was much less advanced in concept than the complete universality and central control of the Babbage analytical engine.

ENIAC was a vast machine 100 ft long, consuming over 100 kilowatts of electrical power in 18 000 electronic valves, difficult to maintain and cumbersome to program. But in spite of all its limitations it represented an enormous advance. ENIAC could do in a day what a man using the latest desk calculator available in the mid-1940s would have taken a year to achieve. Its speed made it possible to perform computations that were so tedious and time-consuming they could not have been undertaken previously. It was in continuous use from 1946 to 1956, when it was placed in the Smithsonian Institution. ENIAC, and another machine of rather similar construction, the Selective Sequence Electronic Calculator (SSEC) built by IBM and installed at their New York headquarters marked the end of the first period of experimental machines, all of which were less ambitious in design than the original analytical engine. Douglas Hartree, the British mathematician who had worked on ENIAC wrote in 1949: 'The machines of the future will be considerably different in principle and appearance; smaller and simpler, with numbers of tubes or relays numbered in thousands rather than tens of thousands ... faster, more versatile, easier to code for and to operate.' [7]

VII. THE BINARY STORED PROGRAM MACHINES

The summer of 1946 saw not only the completion of ENIAC at the Moore School of Electrical Engineering, but a course of lectures given there by John von Neumann on 'The theory and techniques of electronic digital computers' which led directly to the computer architecture which we know today. Von

Neumann swept up a number of concepts which went back to Gottfried Leibniz's 'laws of thought' which he described in what he called his 'schoolboy's essay' *De arte combinatoria* published in 1666, when he was 20 years old. He explained how he was attempting to create 'a general method in which all truths of the reason would be reduced to a kind of calculation. At the same time this would be a kind of universal language or script, but infinitely different from those projected hereto; and errors, except those of fact would be mere mistakes in calculation'. Leibniz saw the advantages of the binary, as compared with the usual denary scale, for reducing his laws of thought to their simplest form and conducting the arithmetic manipulations he required. The binary scale is one in which numerals are represented by only two different symbols (for example, 0 and 1) instead of the ten symbols or digits used in denary arithmetic. 'Leibniz saw in his binary arithmetic the image of creation', wrote the French mathematician, Pierre-Simon de Laplace about a century later. 'He imagined that unity represented God and zero the void; that the Supreme Being drew all beings from the void, just as unity and zero express all numbers in the system of numeration.'

Leibniz's ideas had been taken up and extended in the mid-nineteenth century by George Boole, and now both men's work was applied by von Neumann in his consideration of how a computer should be designed. He saw the advantages of the binary system, not simply because it underlined the equivalence of arithmetic and logic machines, but also because the two states needed to perform binary operations were readily provided in electrical and electronic terms by the opening and closing of a switch, the presence or absence of a voltage or current. Still more important was von Neumann's recognition of the enormous importance of what Babbage had called 'judgement'—the ability of the machine to modify its course of action according to the results that it obtained. He realized that if the store was sufficiently large to contain the program of instructions, the machine could operate on its own instructions [8] and change them during the course of a calculation. Von Neumann explained:

Indeed the machine, under the control of its orders, can extract numbers (or orders) from the memory, process them (as numbers!), and return them to the memory (to the same or to other locations); i.e. it can change the contents of the memory—indeed this is its normal *modus operandi*. Hence it can, in particular, change the orders (since these are in the memory!)—the very orders that control its actions. Thus all sorts of sophisticated order-systems become possible, which keep successively modifying themselves and hence also the computational processes that are likewise under their control.

The von Neumann concept of the stored program machine immediately demanded much larger storage capacity than had been available on the early automatic calculators. He calculated that a machine which could store both the numbers it was working on and its program would need a capacity of 1000 numbers or more. The problem was how to provide this storage. It was necessary to be able to read from the store, to write to it, and to have access to any particular location in it with as little delay as possible. The development of improved stores (or memories as they are often called) has formed a major part of the subsequent development of electronic computers.

Some of the features of the von Neumann concept had been anticipated by Alan Turing in his 1937 paper referred to above, and by Konrad Zuse whose work with H. Schreyer in wartime Germany on the design of a relay calculator, and later on an electronic machine completed in 1941, went unnoticed until 1947. Zuse clearly recognized the advantage of binary machines, and the equivalence of logical and arithmetic operations.

Before ENIAC was completed a group of engineers at the Moore School of Electrical Engineering were working on a machine designed according to the von Neumann principles, using a mercury delay line as the storage medium. However, this machine, the Electronic Discrete Variable Automatic Computer (EDVAC) was not the first stored program computer to be built, for three other projects which had been started in Britain in 1946 were completed first. The first of these was a minimal machine, designed by F. C. Williams and Tom Kilburn at Manchester University as a test-bed for the Williams cathode-ray tube store. It operated successfully in June 1948 and is referred to again below. Close behind it was the Electronic Delayed Storage Automatic Computer (EDSAC) built under the direction of Maurice V. Wilkes in the Mathematical Laboratory of the University of Cambridge. It was completed early in 1949.

EDSAC stored 512 words, each of 34 bits (a bit is the binary equivalent of a digit, and consists of one 'place' which may have value 0 or 1) in a mercury delay line. This consisted of a long tube of mercury with a quartz transducer at either end. An electrical pulse applied to the input end was converted by the transducer into a sonic pulse, which travelled through the mercury in the tube with the velocity of sound. When this pulse reached the transducer at the far end, it momentarily compressed the quartz crystal, which converted it back into an electrical pulse. This output pulse could be amplified, 'reshaped', and applied to the input again, so that the pulse circulated continuously, appearing at the output transducer periodically at intervals equal to the transit time. The pulses were used to represent the bits of the words stored. Thus, at any time the EDSAC mercury delay lines contained 512 trains of pulses, each train representing a 34-bit binary number. The selection of a particular number was made by timing its arrival at the receiving transducer with a master clock, and gating out the pulses which represented it during the next 34 beats of the clock.

Because the storage medium was of a serial kind, and the numbers coming from it were represented by trains of pulses, the arithmetic and logical processes of EDSAC were also carried out on the serial numbers. EDSAC added two 34-bit numbers (corresponding in decimals to a maximum of 17 180 million) in 70 microseconds (a microsecond is one-millionth of a second, or one-thousandth of a millisecond). Multiplication of two numbers took 8·5 milliseconds. The most significant feature of EDSAC, however, was not its speed, but the great flexibility in programming that it achieved by storing both the program and the working data in the same store, thereby allowing the computer to exercise 'judgement' in jumping out of normal sequence, as Babbage and Lady Lovelace had envisaged, or to modify its own programs, as von Neumann had imagined. EDSAC also fulfilled Hartree's prophecy of smaller size, since it had only 3000 electronic valves. Input to the machine, both of program and data was from five-hole Teletype paper tape, using ordinary teleprinter codes as the Bell relay machines had done. Output was to a paper-tape punch or to a teleprinter.

The third project was started at the National Physical Laboratory at Teddington near London in 1945 under the guidance of A. M. Turing. The first version of the N.P.L. machine, called the Automatic Calculating Engine (and known as the ACE (Pilot) to distinguish it from the larger ACE completed eight years later) is now in the Science Museum in London. It had storage capacity for 512 words of 32 bits in a mercury delay line; an addition time of 32 microseconds; and a multiply time of about 1 millisecond. ACE (Pilot) was carefully designed for reliability and contained only 1000 valves. A major difference between this machine and EDSAC was its method of storing program instructions. EDSAC moved automatically through its store in sequence, each instruction being held in the location after the preceding one. Only if a jump away from the sequence was necessary was an instruction taken out of order. A separate register, called the program counter, kept track of where the next instruction was to be found. In ACE (Pilot) a different approach was used, called the 'two-address method' in which each instruction also contained the position in the store (its 'address') where the next instruction had been placed.

Thus the program was not in sequence but might be dotted randomly all over the store.

Delay-line storage had the advantage that few electronic components were required, but it was bulky, sensitive to changes in temperature (and therefore the mercury columns had to be kept in thermostatically controlled enclosures), and to noise or vibration. An alternative was the magnetic drum, which was first used by Andrew D. Booth in a relay-operated machine he designed in 1947. It consisted of a nickel-plated cylinder rotating at high speed fitted with recording heads which could magnetize a strip or 'track' around the cylinder. The technology had been developed before and especially during the Second World War in Germany for sound recording. Pulse trains were supplied to the recording head corresponding to the bit pattern of the numbers to be stored, and these were converted into magnetized patches of nickel around the track. The recording head could also be used to replay the tracks, since as each patch passed under the head it induced a current in it. Booth built several electronic computers using drum storage from 1950 and Aiken used them for his Mark III and Mark IV machines at the Harvard Computation Laboratory.

The magnetic drum had three advantages over the delay line. It was small; had a large storage capacity; and was 'non-volatile'. That is to say, the information stored was preserved unchanged even when the power supply was turned off. However, both drum and delay line suffered one major disadvantage. It was always necessary to wait until the particular piece of information required arrived at the reading head or transducer, which could be anything up to the full transit time.

Efforts were therefore made to find stores with much more rapid access. Several investigators attempted to store information as patches of electric charge on a dielectric sheet. The presence or absence of the electric charge could be detected by a narrow beam of electrons which was aimed at the part of the dielectric to be tested. A similar beam could be used to place the charge on the dielectric in the first place. The advantage of these stores was that the electron beam could be steered to any spot on the dielectric sheet extremely rapidly. Much of the required technology had already been provided by the development of radar display tubes during the Second World War.

The first of these dielectric stores was devised by Jay W. Forrester and Andrew V. Haeff at the Massachusetts Institute of Technology in 1947, using a specially developed cathode ray tube. It was subsequently incorporated into a very fast computer called Whirlwind, which was built at the Servomechanisms Laboratory at M.I.T. in 1949. It had storage for 1000 16-bit words, used 6000 valves; had an add time of 5 microseconds; and a multiply time of 40 microseconds. Another rather similar device, called the Selectron, was developed for the Radio Corporation of America by J. Rajchman.

But the most practical solution came from F. C. Williams of Manchester University, who developed in 1948 a cathode ray tube store with no special parts within the glass envelope, and which could therefore be built from cheap, mass-produced tubes. The information to be stored was arranged in 32 lines on the tube face, each of which corresponded to one 'word'. ('Word' is used instead of 'number' for the pattern of bits stored since, as we have seen, a bit pattern may represent a number or an instruction, or any other piece of information.) Any required word could be selected at random, without waiting for a complete cycle, simply by directing the electron beam to the beginning of the line containing the word to be read. The bit pattern was stored along the line by patches of electric charge on the glass face of the tube. As the reading beam passed over the pattern of charges, a varying current, characteristic of the charge pattern, flowed from the electron beam into a metal plate placed externally over the face of the tube.

The charge pattern was 'written' by the same electron beam operated under different conditions chosen so as to leave the glass face of the tube with a patch of positive charge where the beam had struck it. Different charge patterns were used to indicate binary 1 and 0. The charges so generated gradually leaked away, and so the pattern had to be continually 'refreshed', which was done sequentially line by line by the same electron beam when it was not being used for reading or writing.

F. C. Williams and Tom Kilburn of Manchester University incorporated the store in a small computer MADM, which, as mentioned above, was the first stored-program computer to be built. Work was immediately started on the design of larger machines and two of these were operating by 1949. The Williams store was also used in machines built by the Telecommunications Research Establishment at Malvern, England; the Institute of Numerical Analysis in California; the University of Illinois; and in Sweden and the U.S.S.R. It was short-lived, and by 1956 had been ousted by the magnetic core store; but it was the first step towards a new revolution in computer design.

That revolution was started by John von Neumann, and again harked back to some of Babbage's original ideas, particularly his understanding of the importance in arithmetic operations of being able to operate on all digits at once. Von Neumann's team, in a series of classical reports beginning in 1946,

analysed the design of computers and pointed out the advantages of 'parallel'
machines in which each computer word appeared not as a train of pulses on a
single wire but as voltages on a group of wires, one wire representing each bit
in the word. Such a machine would not require the delicate timing necessary
to identify the presence or absence of a pulse in a train. It should, therefore,
be simpler to construct and faster in operation. The principles were embodied
in the new machine which the von Neumann group built at the Institute of
Advanced Study in Princeton University. The machine was completed in
March 1952, using a modified Williams cathode ray tube store of 1024 words
of 40 bits. It had an add and subtract time of 10 microseconds, and a multiply
time of 300 microseconds, making it easily the fastest machine of its time.
From that time on the serial machine gradually disappeared.

Its end was hastened by the development of the magnetic core store, which
had all the advantages of rapid access of the dielectric store, but was cheaper,
simpler, more reliable, had much greater storage capacity, and could output
a complete 'word' at a time, with each bit appearing on a line of its own. It was
thus ideally suited to the von Neumann concept of a parallel binary computer.

The development of the core store involved many people. Jay Forrester of
the Servomechanisms Laboratory at the Massachusetts Institute of Technology was among the first to see how a matrix of magnetic rings could be
used as a store. Each magnetic ring represented a bit, its value depending on
whether it was magnetized clockwise or anticlockwise. The store was non-
volatile because once the rings had been magnetized in a particular direction
they retained that magnetization until it was changed, even if the power supply was switched off. The only problem was that the direction of magnetization
of a ring could be determined only by changing it; thus each time a piece of
information was read from the store it was destroyed, and had to be introduced again if it was required for further reference.

The economy of the magnetic core store came from its matrix structure.
The magnetic rings were arranged in a lattice pattern of rows and columns.
A wire which could carry a current pulse passed down each column. A second
set of wires passed along each row. To select a particular ring a current pulse
was placed on the wire passing along its row, and that which passed down its
column. These pulses were insufficient on their own to change the magnetization of the ring. But when they arrived together, as they did at the selected
ring, their joint effect could change the direction of magnetization. In effect,
each ring acted as an 'and' gate, operating only when an input occurred on
both the column line and the row line. A third wire which passed through all

the rings detected when a magnetization change in any ring occurred and thus provided the output. Thus, in any matrix of n rings it was only necessary to provide one pulse generating circuit for each row and column, a total of $\sqrt{n}$. But since the information was required a word at a time, rather than a bit at a time, a separate matrix (or 'plane' as it is usually called) could be provided for each bit in a word. Corresponding columns and corresponding rows on each plane could then be interconnected, with further economy in the number of circuits needed. The output circuits from each plane had, of course, to remain separate.

This extremely attractive form of store became possible only as a result of the development of new magnetic materials, called ferrites, which could change their direction of magnetization suddenly, very quickly, and easily. Ferrites had been known since about the turn of the century, but their magnetic properties were systematically investigated only from 1933 by J. L. Snoek of the Philips Laboratories, Eindhoven, Holland [9]. Work at the Lincoln Laboratory, Massachusetts Institute of Technology, revealed that magnesium ferrites had ideal properties for a core store. The new store offered so many advantages that it was quickly taken up by computer manufacturers, and was first used in the Remington-Rand UNIVAC 1103A in 1956. Until the development of the large-scale integration (LSI) dynamic semiconductor memories in 1970, magnetic core stores became the standard computer memory offering access times of under one microsecond. The successful development of this store was followed within four years by the change from logic units based on thermionic valves to the use of transistors.

As the number of computer applications increased, so it became clear that the equipment taken over from the punched-card accounting machines and the telegraph industry was inadequate as a means of supplying information to, and outputting the results from, an electronic computer. Even the ENIAC had been limited by data input and output. It took between 2000 and 3000 addition times to imput the data on a single punched card. Von Neumann's high-speed parallel machine at Princeton needed 20 minutes to have its 1024-word store loaded from paper tape. There were thus strong pressures to develop faster input and output 'peripheral' equipment. UNIVAC made use of magnetic tape in place of paper tape, using the technology developed in Germany and Japan for recording sound. In Britain, the Cambridge University EDSAC group developed a high-speed paper-tape reader in the mid-1950s using photoelectric sensing of the holes, and a special braking system to clamp the tape and stop it immediately. In France, the Compagnie des

Machines Bull, made an important contribution in 1954 with the development of the 'line-at-a-time' high-speed drum printer which was to become a standard output device.

VIII. THE DEVELOPMENT OF PROGRAMMING TECHNIQUES

The preparation of instructions for the early electronic computers was exceedingly laborious. Countess Lovelace had, in the notes to her translation of Menabrea's description of the Analytical Engine [10] pointed out that a large calculation might contain many repetitions of the same sequence of instructions. This idea was extended by Turing in his 1937 paper and later by von Neumann [8] (1946). These principles were applied by M. V. Wilkes and the EDSAC team at Cambridge University Mathematical Laboratory, who published in 1951 their early experiences under the title: 'The preparation of programs for an electronic digital computer with special reference to the EDSAC and the use of a library of subroutines' [11]. The concept of subroutines enabled programs written for commonly used purposes, such as the calculation of a square root, interpolation between two values in a table, or the control of a peripheral such as a card reader or printer, to be prepared only once, and to be incorporated in all subsequent programs that required them. Wilkes and his team had designed EDSAC with a form of instruction code designed to make it easy to assemble programs from a collection of routines and library programs. A special program, known as the assembly program or assembler, was provided to allocate storage to the various segments of program; to keep track of all cross-references between them; and to fill in the addresses which had been allocated. The use of assemblers grew rapidly during the 1950s and was extended to provide means of translating mnemonics, which programmers found easier to remember than the often clumsy sequence of digits used to represent the machine instructions. Thus the bit pattern representing the instruction 'multiply' might be replaced in the assembly language by the mnemonic MULT, which was translated into the machine form by the assembly program.

An entirely different, but still more significant development was the attempt by the Manchester University team to develop an 'Autocode' for the MADM computer. The aim was to describe in ordinary mathematical notation the problem which was to be solved, and then to use a program which would convert the programmer's description of the problem into instructions for the computer to solve it. Similar developments were taking place in the United States, where Grace Hopper, working for the U.S. Navy, wrote the first of these problem-oriented 'languages'. She was followed, two years later, by J. Backus of IBM, who, working with the IBM Computer Users' Association (SHARE) defined an algebraic language, and wrote a 'compiler' for the IBM 704 to enable the machine to accept a problem described in the new language and to translate it into a form in which it could subsequently process it. The new language was called FORmula TRANslator (FORTRAN) and the compiler took 18 man-years to write. FORTRAN subsequently became an international standard. Other languages followed, including ALGOL (ALGOrithmic Language) which was a bold attempt at an international and universal computer language. In 1958, at a conference in Zurich, representatives of the American Association for Computing Machinery and the European Association for Applied Mathematics and Mechanics agreed on the form of a language, and the first compiler for it was written by E. W. Dijkstra of the Netherlands. ALGOL was adopted by a number of manufacturers for use on their computers, but became more widely used in Europe than in the United States. The third of the major computer languages, COBOL, was developed in the U.S.A. by a committee representing government users and computer manufacturers. The Committee started its work in 1959 and published a specification of the language, which was oriented towards the type of problem found in commercial rather than scientific or mathematical applications of computers. Since that time the original languages have been improved and updated in various ways, and a host of new languages, many of them for special applications, have been developed.

IX. THE START OF THE COMPUTER INDUSTRY

In 1948, J. P. Eckert and J. W. Mauchly, recognizing, as Hollerith and Powers had done before them, that the machine they had developed could be exploited commercially, set up the Eckert–Mauchly Computer Corporation and succeeded in obtaining orders for two machines. One, the BINAC, was a relatively small machine with a mercury delay line store, whose main interest lay in having all its major units duplicated. Every computation was performed separately in the two halves of the machine, and the results compared to check them. The other machine, called UNIVAC (Fig. 48.19), was delivered to the U.S. Census Bureau early in 1951, and was the first stored-program computer to be manufactured commercially. It was a serial machine, using mercury delay-line store, and an unusual binary-coded decimal system known as the 'excess three' code, which offered certain advantages in designing the arithmetic unit. UNIVAC had many novel features. Because the census required

FIG. 48.19. The UNIVAC 1 was the first commercial electronic computer. It was installed at the U.S. Bureau of Census in 1951 and successfully predicted General Eisenhower's success in the 1952 Presidential election. The machine was built by the Eckert–Mauchly Computer Corporation. It used magnetic tape input and output (on the right) and was the first machine with a centralized operator's control console.

the handling of very large quantities of data, UNIVAC used magnetic tape as an input and output medium in place of cards or paper tape. It was also the first machine to provide the operator with a console which allowed him to stop at any particular point in the program, and, if he wished, to substitute the word contained at that point in the store for another. It was UNIVAC, particularly as a result of its successful prediction that General Dwight D. Eisenhower would win the 1952 U.S. Presidential Election, that aroused public interest in computers, and sparked off lay discussion about whether machines could think. As it happens, Lady Lovelace had dealt with that question too, 110 years earlier, when she wrote: 'The Analytical Engine has no pretensions whatsoever to originate anything. It can do anything that *we know how to order it* to perform.' [10] Unfortunately, the Eckert–Mauchly Computer Corporation was beset with financial troubles throughout its short life, and in 1950 was absorbed into Remington Rand (which had, of course, previously digested the Powers Accounting Machine Company).

Meanwhile, IBM, which had supported Aiken's ASCC, seemed to regard that project simply as a showpiece. Apart from bringing out a relay calculator for use with standard punched-card systems. IBM was slow to appreciate

FIG. 48.20. The first IBM data-processing system (1952).

the commercial possibilities of computers. The first IBM commercial machine was the 701 built in 1953 (Fig. 48.20), but thereafter the company's progress was very fast. By 1956 IBM machines were outselling the UNIVAC, and although IBM was not a leading innovator it succeeded in gaining an increasing share of the world market, reaching about 70 per cent by 1960.

In Britain, the industrial development of computers followed the research groups at Manchester and Cambridge Universities and at the National Physical Laboratory. Academic work on computer design had started around the winter of 1946–7. Ferranti Ltd. built a computer to a design by the Manchester University team in 1951, only a few months after UNIVAC. The company had received an order for seven of the machines, known as the Ferranti Mark I, through the National Research Development Corporation. English Electric followed with a machine called DEUCE, based on the National Physical Laboratory's ACE (Pilot) design. J. Lyons and Company, the London-based bakery chain, set up a team of engineers to work with the Cambridge University group, and built a computer similar to EDSAC, which was called LEO (Lyons Electronic Office). It was completed in 1951 and was the first computer used for purely commercial data handling. Later a company, Leo Computers Ltd., was formed to design and sell machines. Finally, the British Tabulating Machine Company Ltd., which had sold the original Hollerith punched-card machines in Britain, brought out a small computer (HEC) in 1954 using magnetic drum storage and based on A. D. Booth's Birkbeck College machine APE.

Within the next few years many other firms decided to manufacture computers, both in the U.S.A. and Europe. But for most the venture was disastrous, and as the technical designs stabilized, the number of companies involved in building computers declined dramatically.

REFERENCES

[1] WALFORD, CORNELIUS. *Insurance Cyclopaedia*. London (1871). (Article on Calculating machines.)

[2] TURING, A. M. *Proceedings of the London Mathematical Society*, **42**, 230 (1936).

[3] BUSH, V. *Journal of the Franklin Institute*, **212**, 447 (1931).

[4] *Electronic computers: gaps in technology*. O.E.C.D., Paris (1969).

[5] HOLLINGDALE, S. H. and TOOTILL, G. C. *Electronic computers*, p. 18. Penguin, Harmondsworth (1965).

[6] SHANNON, C. E. *Transactions of the American Institution of Electrical Engineers*, **57**, 713 (1938).

[7] HARTREE, D. R. Foreword to *Calculating instruments and machines*. Cambridge University Press (1950).

[8] GOLDSTINE, H. H. and VON NEUMANN, J. *Planning and coding of problems for an electronic computing instrument*. Institute of Advanced Study, Princetown (1947).

[9] SNOEK, J. L. *New developments in ferromagnetic materials*. Elsevier, New York (1947).

[10] MENEBREA, L. F. *Scientific Memoirs*, Vol. 3, p. 666. London (1842).

[11] WILKES, M. V., WHEELER, D. J., and GILL, S. *The preparation of programs for an electronic digital computer*. Addison Wesley, Cambridge, Mass. (1951).

BIBLIOGRAPHY

Automatic digital computation. H.M.S.O., London (1955).

BABBAGE, C. *Passages from the life of a philosopher*. Longmans, London (1864).

BABBAGE, H. P. *Babbage's calculating engines*. Spon, London (1889).

BOOTH, A. D. and BOOTH, K. H. V. *Automatic digital calculators*. Butterworth, London (1953).

BOWDEN, B. V. *Faster than thought*. Pitman, London (1955).

COUFFIGNAL, L. *Les machines à calculer*. Paris (1933).

——. *Les machines à penser*. Paris (1952).

ECKERT, W. J. *Punched card methods in scientific computing*. Columbia University Press, New York (1940).

Electronic computers: Gaps in technology. O.E.C.D., Paris (1969).

HARTREE, D. R. *Calculating instruments and machines*. Cambridge University Press (1950).

HORSBURGH, E. H. (ed.) *Modern instruments of calculation*. Bell, London (1914).

Machines and appliances in government offices. H.M.S.O., London (1947).

MONTGOMERIE, G. A. *Digital calculating machines*. Blackie, London (1956).

MORRISON, E. and MORRISON, P. (eds.) *Charles Babbage and his calculating engines*. Dover Reprints, New York (1961). [Reprints Babbage's papers and Menebrea with Lady Lovelace's comments.]

WILKES, M. V. (ed.) *Report of a Conference on high speed automatic calculating machines*. Cambridge University Press (1950).

49

INSTRUMENTS

FRANK GREENAWAY

THE manufacture and use of scientific instruments and their role in the advancement of technology has been repeatedly stressed in earlier volumes of this work (Vol. I, Chs. 30, 31; Vol. II, Ch. 21; Vol. III, Ch. 23; Vol. IV, Ch. 13; Vol. V, Ch. 19). In these present volumes, covering the first half of the twentieth century, the availability of appropriate instruments has been tacitly assumed as a prerequisite for technological achievement in many, indeed most, fields. Many instruments—as diverse as navigational aids for aircraft, stethoscopes for medical diagnosis, and echo-sounders for plumbing the ocean depths—have been explicitly referred to and the general principles of their action explained. New technology required not only new kinds of instruments but instruments in numbers far greater than ever before. Motor-cars, for example, required instruments for measuring speed and distance; oil pressure; battery-charging current; radiator water temperature; fuel volume; and so on. The manufacture of instruments became a major industry in itself, though one necessarily fragmented because of the great diversity of its products. The manufacture of optical instruments such as cameras, microscopes, and binoculars would be separate from, say, the manufacture of time-keepers or gas-meters. In this chapter we will briefly consider how the instrument industry fitted into the general pattern of technology, both by providing for immediate requirements and, no less important, by making possible new technological advances. Many of the new instruments originated in scientific laboratories as an aid to fundamental research, but in many cases this industrial potential was quickly realized. The gradual disappearance of a distinction between science and technology is nowhere better illustrated than in this field.

The change in the industry is exemplified by catalogues issued in 1914 and 1962 respectively by one manufacturer, J. Griffin (1914) and its successor firm Griffin and Tatlock. The title-page of the 1914 catalogue reads *Griffin's scientific handicraft*. By contrast the 1962 title is backed by pictures showing a large factory and a well-organized warehouse. The manufacture and supply of laboratory instruments alone is thus seen to have grown in scale and changed in method. There were other aspects, however, than the consequences of mere growth. Instruments are no longer primarily laboratory equipment as they were in 1900. By the 1950s they were to be found everywhere in the new industry-based society, not only in factories but in the home. Industrial processes began to make greater and greater use of instrumental controls, and it is now impossible to think of any large-scale manufacture which does not have many, if not all, its stages controlled by highly sophisticated testing or measuring devices. Although assembly lines may be manned by operatives carrying out routine repetitive tasks, not only will their actions have been defined by measured investigations at the research and development stage, but the inspection and final issue of their products will depend on measuring instruments, some of which may themselves have been specially designed as part of the overall project for the product. Apart from instruments in fairly common use, we must not forget those of massive size such as radio-telescopes (p. 990) with their great steerable bowls; the giant optical telescopes used in astronomy; and the big accelerators designed to measure the properties of subatomic particles.

The change was not a sudden one; the origins of the modern instrument industry can be discerned in the instrument makers of the eighteenth century, when specialist craftsmen who were not themselves investigators supplied instruments for research and for routine purposes. For example, Lavoisier purchased special apparatus for use in his research laboratory; Dalton was just one of many who purchased thermometers and barometers for daily meteorological observation.

At the beginning of the nineteenth century many industries were affected by the growing recognition that the laws of nature are quantitative and not merely qualitative; notably was this so in the chemical industry, in which chemical analysis began to play a steadily increasing role. Growing chemical and medical knowledge made it possible to identify impurities in foods and drugs sufficiently well for laws to be enacted in many countries putting such substances under controls based on analytical procedures (p. 1402). A striking instance of the interaction of science, industry, and social welfare was the (British) Alkali Act of 1863, which brought the effluents of the heavy chemical industry under control—under threat of heavy penalties—through the application of analytical chemistry. Such laws could not have been made effective without the wide availability of analytical apparatus manufactured in standard forms for standard procedures.

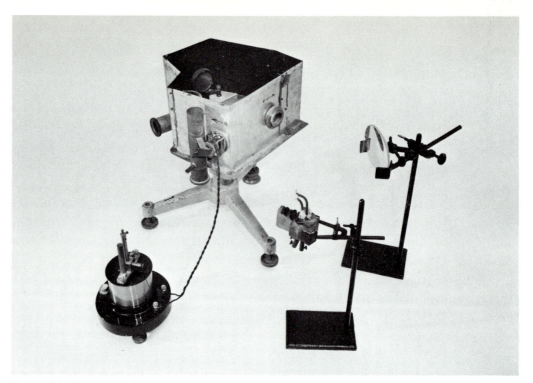

FIG.49.1(a). The infra-red spectrophotometer of H. W. Thompson constructed in 1941, and based on the Hilger spectrometer of 1934. This is typical of the laboratory-assembled individual instrument used for personal research. It was used for the study of hydrocarbon mixtures.

Scientific research establishes new principles which are embodied in new instruments. The instruments become widely used and in turn stimulate some other technological service or manufacture. The demand for the instrument results in its manufacture being put on an industrial basis and the extent to which instrument manufacture is industrialized reflects the state of industry as a whole. In a way, instrument-making has become an index of industrialization, and in this sense may be compared with the machine-tool industry. The early supply of tools required a large number of craftsmen, but from the time of the first successful multiple manufacture with mechanical tools (the Portsmouth block machinery (Vol. IV, p. 427) the demands of a mechanized industry have been such that machine tools had to be created which cannot be considered as mere extensions of manual skills or power. The same considerations apply to the manufacture of instruments, which grew in complexity and by the twentieth century were required in such large numbers that the craft approach could no longer serve the demand.

Another aspect of the growth of the demand for instruments is the way in which service industries have made use of instruments for control and costing. This is a truism in the simple social sense: the grocer weighing a pound of

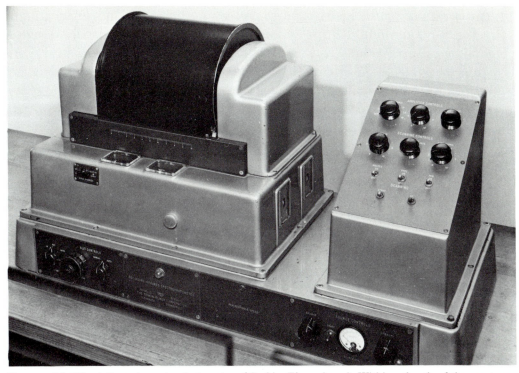

FIG. 49.1(b). The infra-red spectrophotometer of Perkin–Elmer (1950). Within a decade of the construction of the instrument in (a) this type was available in numbers large enough for many laboratories to use it for routine multiple analyses and for programmes of research on large numbers of specimens. Comparison of results was also aided by the use of identical instruments.

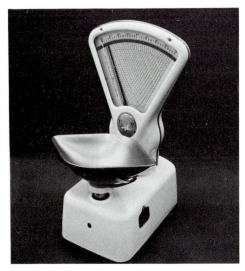

FIG. 49.2. A grocer's scale, a design current from 1950. The basic principle, that of a pendulum with associated levers, was, however, first sketched by Leonardo da Vinci and applied soon after.

FIG. 49.3. A general purpose electric meter (1975). Unlike the older generation of meters based on the galvanometer, this has no moving parts. Response is electronic and display is by light-emitting diodes.

butter uses a scientific instrument to convey to the user a measured amount of a desired commodity. But the development of service industries based on technological innovations had begun already in the nineteenth century, and by the beginning of the twentieth century urban societies in all industrialized countries were heavily dependent on them, electricity and gas supply in particular. Motorists had to be supplied with measured volumes of petrol. Electricity supply was totally dependent on meters for its economic operation. Most meters had been devised, in principle at least, in the early years of the discovery of electromagnetic induction.

It was in the electric supply industry that there was the largest development of industrial manufacture, based on principles established in the nineteenth century and widely applied in the twentieth. The methods of measuring voltage, current, and power consumption were all clearly understood by the time the industry began to extend from supply for a single factory and its surroundings to supply for areas the size of a whole city. The revolution in repetitive work demanded by the First World War could not have been brought about without small electric motors; consequentially the control of electric installations increasingly became an essential managerial responsibility of many, if not all, factories. The demand for meters was enormously expanded, and companies developed whose principal product was measuring instruments.

By the mid-1920s electric supply systems in many parts of the world (Ch. 12) had passed far beyond the scale of generation and consumption within the bounds of one small municipality. Generation systems began to be linked up to provide for the balancing of loads and consequent economies of production. A new call was made on instrument designers for central control and recording. While the individual components of these systems might not be novel, there were new problems in the planning of the whole central system, which might be observed not by an individual but by a central control team. Many examples of such systems will be found elsewhere in the work, but we may perhaps mention here the development of automatic train control on the railways (p. 783). There is an analogy here with the team controlling service instruments in large laboratories. The most recent developments have brought in electronic communications systems and computers so that the idea of an 'instrument' in the older sense of a single observed meter has been largely superseded.

The gas industry supplied a material commodity even though it was really transmitting energy, just as did the electricity supply industry. The measure-

FIG. 49.4. The control desk of the Anglo–Iranian Oil Company's refinery, Kent. This complex of instruments was designed to give an immediate overall picture of the refinery's steam and power generation and utilization. It is typical of the development in the means of controlling highly automated installations through remote observation and metering of production processes which took place in the post-1950 period.

ment of the supply of a material substance seems elementary but in fact the metering of gas flows demanded considerable ingenuity, both for the large meters intended for industrial installations (including gasworks themselves) and the small meters needed for domestic installations. These minor devices are not to be despised in estimating the progress of technology. They often showed a grasp, on the part of their inventors, of the fundamentals of instrument design. We have become so accustomed in recent times to the separation of the several factors in instrument design—namely, the detection of a signal, its conversion to transmissible information, the conversion of that information to display on record, and to the use of electrical or electronic means at each stage—that we tend to forget the ingenuity formerly shown in doing the same things mechanically. In the case of gas meters measurement was based on the rotation of a vaned wheel under a pressure differential.

In gas measurement the basically mechanical approach survived on into the period of natural gas supplies—essentially post-war in Europe, though much earlier in North America—only at the domestic or low-pressure end of the supply system. It was already evident in the 1930s that the supply of gas could not rely on the distillation of coal, and methods of converting other substances, such as petroleum, to gases capable of being sent into the existing supply system were studied. The gas industry thus became more closely associated with the chemical industry, to which it had long been an important supplier of raw materials, and began to adapt its sophisticated methods of control.

With the revolutionary change in industrial chemical methods typified by the thermodynamic and engineering successes of Fritz Haber and Carl Bosch (p. 523) the range of temperatures and pressure used, the increase in quantities handled, and the development of more and more continuous processes entailed a virtually complete elimination of individual judgement from the manufacturing system. Oil refineries are the most obvious example of the new type of plant which came into being, but in the manufacture of heavy inorganic chemicals as well the continuity of the processes could be guaranteed only by instrumental control.

The interplay between science and industry is well exemplified in the field of electrochemistry, with the concept of hydrogen-ion concentration (pH) as a measure of acidity. This idea was first put forward by biochemists working on enzymes of interest to brewers, where improvement of the product demanded a knowledge of the conditions of enzyme action. Hydrogen-ion concentration was found to be critical. New theories were developed which rapidly influenced analytical chemistry and became significant in biochemistry and physiology at large. The methods of determing pH were at first dependent on classical electrical methods (using simple potentiometers and bridges), but from about 1935 onwards the utilization of vacuum-tube methods so improved sensitivity as to render several things possible. One was the achievement of greater sensitivity through the amplification of extremely small signals. The other was rapid and automatic operation. Hydrogen-ion concentration is so important as a condition of chemical reaction that its measurement has become an essential technique in all analytical work connected with manufacture entailing aqueous solutions, which may range from brewing to the manufacture of explosives.

The measurement of hydrogen-ion concentration has developed steadily since the beginning of the century, but the usefulness of some other discoveries were not so immediately apparent. An outstanding example is that of chromatography. The observation of M. S. Tswett in 1903 that colouring matters of plants could be separated by a solvent extraction process conducted by passing a solution through a powder was largely overlooked until revived in a different form (partition chromatography) by A. J. P. Martin and R. L. M. Synge in 1941. The apparatus used in their work was of the simplest character, utilizing silica gel as the basis of separation. The paper chromatography of

FIG. 49.5. A gas–liquid chromatograph (*c.* 1950) used for the separation for analytical purposes of mixtures of compounds of closely similar characteristics. The separation relies on the exaggeration of minute differences in the degree of absorption of components of a mixture by conveying them in a mobile carrier (e.g. an inert gas) over a stationary absorbent (in this case a liquid held on a solid base). This is only one of many devices exploiting differences in physical properties inaccessible to the users of older analytical methods.

1944 was even simpler. More elaborate devices were developed for gas chromatography (also in 1944) in which the differential separation of complex vapour systems is achieved.

The techniques became more and more widely utilized in the laboratory because of their power to separate species of chemical compound so similar as to defy traditional separation. They were also very valuable for isolating very sensitive substances, such as penicillin, which might be destroyed by conventional methods. In their later stages modifications of the chromatographic process used standardized preparations and apparatus which could be manufactured with relative ease to satisfy a large worldwide demand. Gas chromatography required apparatus of some complexity, but since it could be applied to the analysis of intractable mixtures such as perfume components or petroleum distillation products, the market for apparatus became considerable,

FIG. 49.6. The Thornbridge transmitter, a pendulum-controlled electric clock system (1909). This master clock drove a number of 'slave' clocks by impulses emitted at intervals, in this case, each half a minute.

FIG. 49.7. *Below*, parts of the first quartz-crystal clock system (Bell Telephone Laboratories, 1927). The oscillation frequency of the quartz crystal is used to drive a conventional synchronous motor. *Left*, a complete crystal oscillator with mounted crystal. *Right*, a 1000-cycle synchronous motor geared to the clock.

especially as the technique could be applied for the on-line control of chemical manufacturing processes. The development of an instrument industry is not just a matter of multiplication of traditional instrument making.

In the later years of the nineteenth century the making of scientific instruments was a sophisticated handicraft, and although certain types of instrument, such as microscopes, electric meters, and gauges, were wanted in large numbers they were still made and assembled by craftsmen who individually did the whole job, or the greater part of it. By the 1950s the demand for routine recording instruments was enormous. Every citizen in the advanced countries made continuous use of meters and recording devices in situations so familiar that he probably did not think of himself as using scientific instruments at all. These everyday devices were all developments of instruments which at the turn of the century had barely emerged from the laboratory. We must distinguish, however, between the meters and gauges which formed part of the new equipment of a consumer society, and the instruments which were used by scientifically or technically trained men in the course of their professional work.

The importance of time measurement in science and society is enormous. Great inventiveness has gone into the design of mechanical clocks, high accuracy generally depending on the property of the pendulum. Progress to the most accurate time measurement, however, entailed the introduction of electrical devices, intermittent electrostatic attraction being applied experimentally to the maintenance of a clock pendulum as early as 1814. Later, electromagnetic attraction was used, notably by Alexander Bain in Britain and Mattheus Hipp in Germany. Eventually Shortt (1921) produced a free-pendulum electric clock surpassing in accuracy the best mechanical clocks, and so qualifying for use in observatories throughout the world, until itself superseded by the quartz clock.

Electrical drive also made possible clock systems, giving uniform recording throughout a large office block or ship, for example. On a national scale, the standardization of mains frequencies made possible the use of synchronous-motor-driven clocks, of high accuracy but vulnerable to faults in the mains system.

A new epoch in constancy was introduced by the use of the vibrating quartz crystal, determining the frequency of an amplifier driving a clock (Morrison, the U.S.A.; W. D. Dye and L. Essen, Britain), all were active in the early 1930s. This has itself been superseded by standardization using the vibrations of the atom of caesium (Essen 1957). Domestic and personal time-keeping benefited from the transistor (1956) and in 1972 a clock without moving parts was made possible by the use of light-emitting diodes to give a digital display.

Many other remarkable developments in twentieth-century instrumentation arose from an area of science which emerged as a total novelty in the mid-nineteenth century. Current electricity was studied first in solids, then in liquids (solutions), and finally in gases. From the behaviour of current in gases came a good deal of the information which led to the modern theory of the structure of the atom. Many devices of crucial importance in twentieth-century technology were implicit in nineteenth-century discoveries, notably the unidirectional flow of current in a gas; the unidirectional flow of current carried by free electrons in a vacuum; and the control of the direction of the path of an electron stream by means of a magnetic or electrostatic field. The mode of propagation of electromagnetic waves was also established. The applications of all these to radio is described elsewhere (Ch. 50). What is important in the present context is that the diode valve (1904) and later the triode (1907–11) made possible first the rectification of an alternating current and second the control of a large current by a small signal. These had both been basic problems in electrical instruments, attempts to solve them by classical electrical or mechanical means having stimulated much ingenuity.

The introduction of the vacuum tube into physical instrumentation took a long time. There is no mention of it for example, in R. T. Glazebrook's *Dictionary of applied physics* of 1922. However, with the devising of the valve voltmeter (1935) many uses were found for the vacuum-tube wherever the fundamental control or amplification facility of the triode could be used. The industry manufacturing vacuum tubes for the radio industry was able to supply the instrument industry with anything it needed, but this market was still small. The stimulus to growth was the Second World War, which found innumerable new uses for vacuum-tube instruments in addition to the obvious ones in communication. The growth of the computer (Ch. 48) is outside the scope of this chapter, but it is worth remembering that it parallels that of the automobile industry in its virtual dominance of some aspects of the life of communities to which its products should have been subservient. This growth has been made possible by the revolution in electronic fabrication consequent on the reduction in size (of many orders of magnitude) of the essential elements of operation made possible by the availability of the transistor; the functions of vacuum tubes formerly occupying very much space could be carried out within a volume of the order of a cubic millimetre or less. Even more effective in respect of size reduction has been the various means devised for storing information magnetically or electronically. It has also followed from progress in solid-state electronics that reductions in size, with increases in flexibility of the equipment needed for all manner of operations entailing signalling or computation, has altered very many instrumental functions, but this falls into the most recent period of technology and industry, beyond the middle of the century.

This area of technology exemplifies another historical change. The early work on the application of vacuum tubes to the control of electric signals was largely academic. By mid-century however, the main effort in this field was exerted in the research laboratories of large industrial concerns which had grown up around the exploitation of the new discoveries. The new instruments which could be developed around vacuum-tube technology were, to some extent, dependent on the existence of a mass-market for products which were utilized in non-scientific devices. The same industrial research effort in electronics produced in the third quarter of the century the solid-state devices referred to above. The dependence of the instrument industry on industrial

FIG. 49.8. The control panel of a Svedberg ultra-centrifuge 1936–9. Between 1924 and 1933 Svedberg developed a high-speed ultra-centrifuge for the determination of high molecular weights by sedimentation under high centrifugal forces. The control panel of this ultra-centrifuge, installed at the Lister Institute in London 1936–7, is an early example of the instrumentation necessary for the management of the very large scale apparatus which was to become commonplace in physical and chemical laboratories. Note the oscilloscope (added in 1939), an early adaptation of this device for instrument display.

growth generally is also exemplified in microscopy. Following the work of
Ernst Abbe, considerable industrial organizations were created which were
dedicated to the production of high-precision instruments in large numbers.
Microscope design developed as far as optical ingenuity would allow. Resolving
power was increased, for example, by the use of ultraviolet light or by phase
contrast, but it was appreciated that some new principle was needed to go
further.

This new principle, providing a radical change in the basic method of
microscopy, derived from an initially unrelated field, that of electron-ray
diffraction. The theory of the microscope had been elaborated in the nineteenth century and it had long been known that higher resolution would
theoretically be obtainable by the use of radiation of higher frequency (or
shorter wavelength) than that of the visual spectrum. Some success had been
obtained with ultra-violet light but the logical extension into X-rays was
impracticable because no means were known of refracting them. However, the
wave theory of matter introduced by L. de Broglie made it appear that a beam
of electrons could be diffracted by a crystal atomic lattice if it behaved as a
wave system like X-rays. The reality of the phenomenon was established by
G. P. Thomson. It was then shown that as the electron beam is charged, it
could be refracted by electrical or magnetic fields analogous with a lens
system. That is to say, a microscope was possible in which the observing
radiations had a frequency many orders of magnitude higher than that of
visible light. The instruments made following this discovery were beyond the
capacity of traditional craftsmen to contruct. From the point of view of the
history of technology what is significant is not only the application of the
instrument to industrial purposes but the fact that the instrument was not
the product of a single craftsman or a small group, but a measuring and
observational device produced by a collaboration of scientists and engineers.
Moreover, in common with the other instruments referred to in this section,
it is commonly installed in a laboratory as a service, not as the personal
instrument of an individual investigator. The manufacturers of electron
microscopes are not small firms of specialists, as the producers of optical
microscopes were, but branches of very large industrial organizations manufacturing electrical and electronic equipment—such as radio and television—
for the mass consumer and industrial market.

On a larger scale, instruments have been developed out of researches into
the fundamental structure of matter. One striking instance of this is in the
field of nuclear magnetic resonance (n.m.r.). The magnetic properties of the

FIG. 49.9. Part of an electron-density map of vitamin B_{12}. It was constructed from a succession of electron density contours arranged as a multilayer glass sandwich by Dorothy Hodgkin in 1958. The interpretation of X-ray crystallographic data has entailed the construction of a wide variety of molecular models which may be considered a necessary adjunct to the instrumental techniques.

atom and its nucleus had been studied since the inception of modern atomic theory at the turn of the century. After many studies of the absorption of electromagnetic radiation by matter it was perceived in the late 1940s that the characteristic absorption frequency of a nucleus depended to a small, but measurable, extent on the molecular environment of the nucleus; in other words, nuclear magnetic resonance gave an indication of molecular structure. The method proved rapid and effective, but required apparatus of some size and complexity. However, some electronics firms, encouraged by the potential market for rapid organic analysis offered by large chemical and oil companies, persevered and by the 1960s commercial instruments were well established. One company (Varian) records that it sold several thousand instruments at prices ranging up to $250 000 in the decade 1960–70. It is clear that the development of this elaborate and expensive instrument could not have taken place unless it was manufactured on an industrial scale to serve investigations also carried out on an industrial scale. At the same time, it

FIG. 49.10. Fifty years of development of the instruments in the cockpit of a long-range aircraft.
(a). The Vickers Vimy flown by Alcock and Brown on their transatlantic flight in 1919. The instruments show air speed, height, levels, and state of engines.

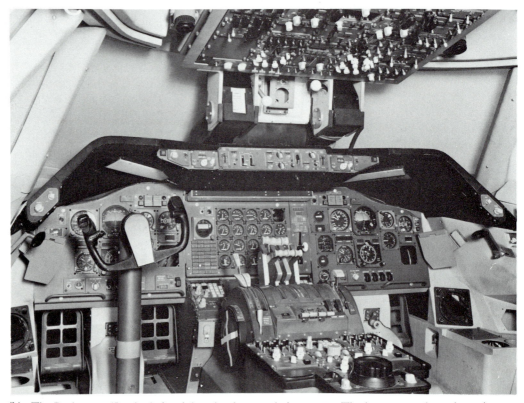

(b). The Boeing 747 'Jumbo jet' training simulator cockpit, c. 1971. The instruments here show air speed, Mach number, height, levels, state of all controls and services, state of engines, with a complex of radio equipment mainly for navigational purposes.

became available for academic research workers, concerned primarily with the advancement of fundamental knowledge, which in turn would serve to advance technology.

Similar remarks could be made about other instruments, like the mass spectrograph, originally created in laboratory workshops as one-off devices for personal research but later manufactured in considerable numbers as service instruments. The development of medical technology is dealt with elsewhere (Ch. 54) but we may remark here that by the middle of the century surgeons and physicians called for the provision of machines and apparatus of a size and complexity comparable with those of their colleagues in science and engineering. The apparatus used in cardiac surgery, or the dialysis apparatus used as substitutes for malfunctioning kidneys, were beginning to match the mass-spectrometers, polarographs, and so on of the physical chemistry laboratory and like them, were dependent on design and manufacture in industrialized organizations.

The history of scientific instrumentation cannot be complete without consideration of its economic aspects. In the early years of the century the cost of instruments was not a major part of the total budget of any research activity except in the case of astronomy or of special expeditions (such as eclipse or transit observations) which had to be specifically and comprehensively equipped. The gradual growth in complexity and specificity of instruments, and of dependence on them, has changed the pattern of budgeting entirely. In much research work the planning of work had to begin with consideration of the capital elements, the recurrent costs in man-power being left to be argued as a separate issue, almost as if the men were there to service the machine. Indeed, it was not unknown for the purchase of an instrument to be deferred, even though the money was available, because there was no provision to pay for the specialist staff required to use and service it. However, this raises issues beyond the scope of the present chapter.

BIBLIOGRAPHY

GLAZEBROOK, R. *Dictionary of applied physics.* 5 vols. London (1922–3).
Instrument manual. United Trade Press, London (1949, 1953, 1960).
COOPER, H. J. (ed.) *Scientific instruments.* 2 vols. London (1946, 1948).
COCHRANE, R. C. *Measures for progress: History of the National Bureau of Standards.* Washington (1966).
BRADBURY, S. *Evolution of the microscope.* Oxford (1967).
SZABADVARY, F. *History of analytical chemistry.* Oxford (1966).
JACKMAN, L. M. *Applications of nuclear magnetic resonance.* London (1959).
HOPE-JONES, F. *Electrical time-keeping.* London (1949; reprinted 1976).

50

ELECTRICAL COMMUNICATION

D. G. TUCKER

I. TELEGRAPHY

THE nineteenth-century developments in telegraphy have been previously described in this work (Vol. IV, Ch. 22; Vol. V, Ch. 10) and there is not a great deal to add now. By the end of the nineteenth century there was an efficient inland telegraph system in all developed countries, together with a world-wide network of submarine cables and other international lines. The only subsequent developments we have space to mention here, other than radio which is dealt with separately, are the general adoption of the teleprinter (a telegraphic typewriter) in place of other telegraph instruments; the spread during the last two decades before 1950, and even more since then, of the telex service whereby teleprinters operate over ordinary local telephone lines and through an international system of switching centres; and the general adoption of carrier transmission whereby telegraph signals are modulated on to carrier tones for transmission over telephone channels.

In the following account of the history of electrical communication we shall have occasion to refer to certain basic devices—such as valves, capacitors, resistors, and inductors—which are normal components of the circuits involved. The history of the development of these devices has already been discussed (Ch. 46).

II. THE BEGINNINGS OF TELEPHONY (1876–c. 1915)

Origins. The invention of the telephone is generally credited to the Scottish-born inventor Alexander Graham Bell who emigrated to the U.S.A. in 1871. It was on 10 March 1876 that he first obtained good clear articulation from his experimental system. There had been much earlier attempts at electric telephony but they were hardly successful. More importantly, there was an almost simultaneous rival inventor, Elisha Gray (U.S.A. [1]), who filed a caveat in the U.S. Patent Office on his design of a telephone system on the same day (but later in the day) that Bell had filed a patent application for his system. Both Bell and Gray had been working on harmonic telegraphs which could transmit and respond to a number of simultaneous tones, and an extension of this idea to the transmission of the human voice was a logical step. Gray did not think telephony was important and did little more work on it; Bell followed it up for a while and his sponsors made a commercial success of it. Bell was in advance of Gray experimentally, but used at first an electromagnetic transmitter, rather similar to his receiver, the general principle of which still forms the basis of modern telephone receivers. This transmitter caused a piece of iron to vibrate under the influence of the sound waves in the field of a magnet with coils on it, and thus to induce voltages in the coils and corresponding currents in the line extending from them to the receiver. It was Gray, however, who invented the variable-resistance transmitter, in which the voice waves, through the medium of a wire attached to the diaphragm and dipping into a conducting solution, varied the resistance and thus the current (established by a battery) in the line and receiver. This was (and is) a far more powerful method and, in the form of a cell of carbon granules where the pressure of the diaphragm varies the resistance through the cell, is the basis of the modern telephone transmitter. Here the power is provided by the current obtained from a battery, not from the voice, which merely modulates the current.

Bell was undoubtedly aware of the importance of having in his instruments a relatively strong unidirectional magnetic field (produced either by a battery giving a standing current in the coils, or by the use of a permanent magnet as the core), but the fundamental nature of the requirement appears to have been first set out by Oliver Heaviside (Britain), as early as February 1887 [2]. He showed that if the permanent field in a receiver is H, and this varies from $H+h$ to $H-h$ under the influence of the speech currents, then the force on the diaphragm, which is proportional to the square of the field, varies from $(H+h)^2$ to $(H-h)^2$, a variation of $4Hh$, ignoring the constant of proportionality. That is to say, the variation is proportional to the permanent field H provided H is larger than h. If there is no permanent field, then $H = 0$ and the force on the diaphragm does not reproduce correctly the current waveform.

Late in 1876 Bell offered his patent to the Western Union Telegraph Company for $100 000. Western Union then saw no future in the telephone and refused the offer. Bell continued his developments with support from the company he himself founded, and a year later the obvious success of the telephone showed Western Union the greatness of their error of judgement. They entered the telephone field on the basis of Gray's patent (Gray was

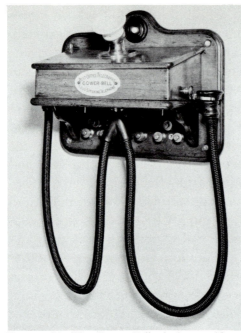

FIG. 50.1(a). The Gower–Bell telephone, 1880–2.

(b). National Telephone Company's telephone instrument, type No. 1 for Central Battery Exchanges, c. 1910.

associated with them through their subsidiary Western Electric Manufacturing Company, which Gray had virtually founded) and with commissioned development by Thomas A. Edison (U.S.A.). Edison developed an improved variable-resistance transmitter in which the speech waves acted upon a loose contact between pieces of carbon, and a rather unsatisfactory receiver in which the speech current produced a varying drag on a stylus conducting it into a rotating chalk cylinder moistened with potassium iodide; this varying drag produced vibrations in a diaphragm coupled to the stylus. Western Union went ahead commercially, and fought the Bell Company over patents, but eventually sold out to Bell in return for 20 per cent royalties for the duration of the patents.

The beginning of telephone service [3]. Commercial development of the telephone began quite soon after the initial inventions of Bell and Gray in 1876. Bell's company started in 1877, changing its form rapidly at first, and became well established in the U.S.A., with subsidiary companies in Britain and elsewhere, by 1879. Independent telephone companies which Edison had set up in London and elsewhere amalgamated within a further year or two with the

Bell or other suitable companies in their locality. Nevertheless, there were numerous inventions of new or modified forms of telephone transmitter and receiver, and numerous companies were set up to exploit them (Fig. 50.1).

The concept of the telephone providing a public service on a basis rather different from that provided by the telegraph sprang up quickly. Individual telephone renters, or 'subscribers', would require to be connected to another subscriber on demand, and to provide this service telephone 'exchanges' were introduced; by Bell from 1878 and by Edison from 1879. At first, of course, the service was entirely local, but as exchanges became more numerous, the need for interconnecting them became apparent. Thus an inter-urban telephone network started to grow; its growth and usefulness were considerably restricted by the fact that in many areas each exchange, or small group of exchanges, belonged to a separate company using different technical and commercial methods. Since also many governments actively discouraged the development of inter-urban links from fear of competition with state-owned telegraphs, it is not surprising that it was only in the U.S.A. that a significant telephone network had developed by 1884. Statistics published in 1885 showed the U.S.A. to have 140 000 subscribers with 800 exchanges, while for the rest of the world the list was topped by Britain with a mere 10 000 telephones; inter-urban lines in the U.S.A. numbered over 800, while there were only about 80 in Britain. It is probable that the U.S.A. had more than twice as many telephones and inter-urban lines as the rest of the world put together. In spite of disparities in telephone densities in different countries, proportional growth rates represented by a doubling of numbers and wire mileages every two or three years were maintained almost everywhere.

Telephone exchanges. The idea of connecting one subscriber, on request, to another by means of a flexible switching system had, on a very small scale, been applied to local telegraph subscribers in the U.S.A. and Britain before 1877. During 1877 one or two very small private telephone exchanges had been tried in the U.S.A., but the first commercial telephone exchange was that at New Haven, Connecticut, opened on 28 January 1878. In this, eight lines (with 21 telephones connected) could be connected in pairs by means of a direct cord with a plug at each end; calling 'annunciators' were provided, operated by d.c. from the subscriber's battery. A 20-line exchange was fitted six months later at Bridgeport, Connecticut. During the same year, the American District Telegraph Company opened an Edison exchange in Chicago, also using direct interconnection by a single cord. Calling for sub-

FIG. 50.2. The Jones telephone switchboard, 1879, made by C. E. Jones & Brother, Electricians, Cincinnati, Ohio, U.S.A.

FIG. 50.3. The Edison crossbar telephone exchange unit, 1879.

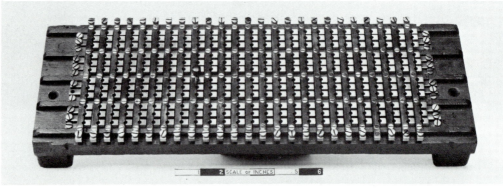

scribers who already had a telegraph instrument was by telegraph; for others, calling relays were used. This switchboard grew rapidly and several boards were needed, with interboard connections and two operators involved in most calls. It was here that the 'jack-knife' switch, forerunner of the well-known 'jack', was introduced by C. E. Scribner, engineer of the Western Electric Manufacturing Company.

The year 1879 might well be regarded as the year of the telephone exchange, for it saw the introduction of double-cord interconnection via intermediate connecting bars which could run the length of a whole suite of 25-line boards; of the 'multiple' whereby outgoing access to subscribers' lines was repeated throughout the suite so that each operator had direct access to every subscriber; of several line-engaged testing arrangements; and of the first exchange in Britain. This last was opened by the (Bell) Telephone Company in August 1879 at Coleman Street in London, and had calling indicators, jacks, cords, and connecting bars.

It could fairly be said that the manual telephone exchange of the form which became so ubiquitous in the first half of the present century arose directly out of the developments just described. Many technical and operating improvements were introduced, of course, such as making the engaged signal a click when the operator touched the tip of her calling plug on the outer ring of the jack, the use of small lamps as calling and supervisory signals, etc. But this type of switchboard was not the only one. The National Bell Telephone Company in the U.S.A. in 1880 introduced a board using an array of horizontal and vertical bars—one of the latter for each line—so that interconnections could be made by inserting plugs at each crossing of any one horizontal bar with the two lines to be connected together. In Britain, the Edison Telephone Company used a similar arrangement (Fig. 50.3). It was, however, not suitable for expansion by the 'multiple' method (Fig. 50.4), and so died out.

FIG. 50.4. A multiple-type telephone switchboard, 1925 (Post Office type CB1).

The reliance on batteries at each subscriber's premises was obviously undesirable. Common battery signalling, with a central battery at the exchange, was introduced at Boston as early as 1880, and the use of a central battery for both speaking and signalling first came into commercial service at Lexington, Mass., in 1893.

For many decades there was no economic incentive to try to use automatic exchanges, for operators were cheap and equipment was expensive. Nevertheless, A. B. Strowger of Kansas City began the development of his automatic switching system in 1889 (Fig. 50.5); the first commercial automatic exchange was working by 1897; and by 1898 the U.S.A. had 22 such exchanges. The first one in Britain was at Epsom in 1912.

The growth of inter-urban telephone networks. As the number of telephone exchanges grew, so did the demand for links between the exchanges in neighbouring places. Subscribers' lines were usually of the single-wire type, with earth return, so there was no difficulty in linking them by means of single-wire inter-exchange lines. In the U.S.A. there was no obstacle other than transmission and commercial considerations to the growth of inter-exchange networks. In Britain, however, there were legal difficulties imposed by the licensing system. In granting a licence to a company, the Post Office restricted the area to be served under the licence to a radius of four or five miles. It was thus impossible for a company to develop a network which could be classed as inter-urban. This disability was removed in 1884, and thereafter there were a few notable inter-urban networks built up, an outstanding example

FIG. 50.5. The Strowger automatic telephone switch of 1897–8.

being that of the Lancashire and Cheshire Company which by 1886 had about 3000 km of inter-urban lines.

Long-distance telephony. The main obstacle to the achievement of effective long-distance telephone communication was the interference due to telegraph signals on adjacent wires. This 'induction', as it was called, could seriously interfere with telephony even over very short distances, and it entirely prevented telephone communication from taking place over distances greater than about 50 km except at night when the telegraphs were quiet. It was appreciated that the trouble was largely due to the use of single-wire lines with earth return, and as early as 1877 the use of 'metallic', that is two-wire or loop, circuits without an earth connection had been suggested. In such circuits the lateral induction would be opposite in the two wires and would therefore tend to cancel out, especially if the wires were run on a twist system so that each wire had the same average spacing from the source of interference. In spite of this early knowledge of the technical cure for induction, however, the use of single wires continued because of the great expense of providing metallic circuits. It was not until the turn of the century that metallic circuits became more or less universal, although there were some notable examples of their use in the early 1880s—for example, the line between Boston and Providence, U.S.A., about 80 km, opened in 1882 between special switchboards at each end, which had metallic-loop extensions to special subscribers. Another major exception was the whole of the telephone system operated by the Post Office in Britain from its very beginning in 1881, including trunk lines in South Wales extending to 130 km, over which speech was said to be good.

Induction was not the only problem in long-distance telephony; another was the poor quality of speech transmitted over iron wires. The use of iron wire in telephony was only slowly abandoned, but most long-distance lines were of copper or phosphor-bronze from the middle 1880s.

To enable single-wire telephone lines to operate in the vicinity of telegraph wires, François van Rysselberghe (Belgium) introduced some special anti-interference methods. Realizing that the interference from telegraph to telephone circuits was largely due to the transients caused by the rapid rise and fall of the telegraph impulses, he showed early in 1882 that suitable chokes connected in the telegraph circuits could reduce interference to a satisfactory level on adjacent telephone lines. From there it was a short step to showing that the telephone circuits could actually be superimposed on the telegraph

FIG. 50.6. The trunk telephone network in Britain in 1896, distinguishing between the lines constructed by the Post Office and those taken over from the National Telephone Company.

lines by means of capacitance couplings. Thus a technical and economic solution of the long-distance telephony problem was available, and was immediately taken up by the Belgian authorities and, before long, by many others. Telegraph lines existed over Europe and in other countries on an extensive scale, and it was attractive to be able to work telephony over them at low cost. By mid-1887 there was a long-distance telephone network in Europe amounting to over 17000 km, all on the van Rysselberghe system; there were many similar lines in many other parts of the world, including South America, China, and Japan.

Britain was markedly behind in the provision of trunk lines owing to the Government's anti-telephone policy, but the amalgamation of the numerous telephone companies into the National Telephone Company in 1889 led to a considerable improvement. Mounting public pressure led to the establishment of a proper trunk telephone network (see Fig. 50.6) by the Post Office in 1896, incorporating also the trunk lines of the National Telephone Company which had been compulsorily purchased (leaving the Company with only its local systems and subscribers). The network of trunk lines on the Continent of Europe had by then grown into a largely interconnected system (Fig. 50.7). With the availability of lines, demand grew quickly, and these

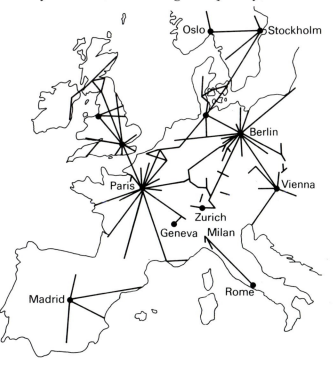

FIG. 50.7. The trunk telephone network in Europe in 1896. N.B. this map is a modern compilation and may well have inadvertently omitted some important links of which records have not been found.

networks were rapidly extended and consolidated. By this time, metallic-loop working of independent telephone lines was becoming normal everywhere, and the van Rysselberghe system gradually went out of use except for some special cases.

In the U.S.A., interest in long-distance telephony arose even earlier than in Europe. There were a number of experiments in long-distance working from 1879 onwards. The Southern New England Telephone Company opened in 1884, for public service, a metallic-loop circuit (claimed to be the first metallic long-distance telephone line ever built) between New York and Boston, approximately 450 km in length. This proved very satisfactory. In 1886 the newly formed American Telephone and Telegraph Company (A.T. and T.), generally referred to as the 'Long Distance Telephone Company' and a subsidiary of the Bell Company, embarked on a programme of long-distance lines, several routes being opened in 1887–9 over distances up to about 700 km. The success of these led to the construction in 1892 of a through metallic-loop circuit from New York to Chicago with copper conductors of No. 8 gauge (121 kg/km), a substantial increase in conductor size over the previously-used No. 12 gauge (48 kg/km). The lines could be extended at each end to give through speaking between Boston and Milwaukee, about 2100 km, but this was considered rather beyond the limit of satisfactory transmission. Normally special soundproof booths were used at New York and Chicago.

By the early years of the twentieth century, the A.T. and T.'s network had linked all major towns in the eastern half of the U.S.A. The first trans-continental line, from New York to San Francisco, was opened in 1915. This, however, depended for its operation on the use of coil loading and, most important of all, telephone repeaters or amplifiers.

III. THE BEGINNINGS OF RADIO (NINETEENTH CENTURY–c. 1910)

Origins. There were, from 1838 until the end of the nineteenth century, numerous attempts at communication by electrical signals without the use of wires to connect the two communicants—thus introducing the concept of 'wireless' communication. These mostly relied on conduction, generally through water, or on inductive coupling between what were effectively coils of wire with transmitted signals in the same form as on lines; they gave some useful practical results in communicating across estuaries or relatively narrow sea-channels. Their potentiality for communication over long distances was, however, negligible; inductive coupling gives, for a constant transmitted power at the frequencies of telegraph or telephone signals where the wavelength is several hundred kilometres, a received signal power inversely proportional to the sixth power of the distance, provided the distance is large compared with the dimensions of the coils and small compared with the wavelength. They were thus necessarily short-range systems and almost irrelevant to the modern 'radio' method of communication, which owes its importance to the use of radiated electromagnetic waves whose power at a distant point is inversely proportional to only the square of the distance.

The concept of electromagnetic waves was due to James Clerk Maxwell who, in 1864, set out a mathematical statement of their properties; showed that light was an example of an electromagnetic wave; and predicted that waves could be radiated at longer wavelengths with the same velocity of propagation as light. Electromagnetic waves (in free space, remote from their source) are characterized by electric and magnetic fields of equal energy density, with the vibratory electric and magnetic fields mutually at right angles and also at right angles to the direction of propagation. Following Maxwell, many people made experiments and put forward ideas on the subject [4], but it was the work of Heinrich Hertz which in 1887–8 demonstrated clearly that electromagnetic waves could be produced by a sufficiently rapid disturbance (that is, a spark discharge) in an electrical system; that the wavelength (in his experiments between 0·5 and 10 m) was a function of the electrical circuit parameters; that resonance response was exhibited; that the waves were polarized; and that they could be reflected by plane and curved mirrors made of conducting material, and refracted by a dielectric (non-conducting) material. The foundation for radio communication had been laid, but the potentiality for communication was largely overlooked by scientists who followed Hertz, until it was brought to notice by the work of Guglielmo Marconi.[1]

Another important development, made between the Hertz and Marconi periods, was the coherer, a device for the detection of electromagnetic waves. Hertz had used for detecting the reception of a wave a rather insensitive device, namely the observation of a small spark between small spheres fixed to the ends of an incomplete loop of wire. The coherer was in essence a non-conducting tube containing a large number of very small conducting particles (typically metal filings) between two metal contact wires or plates. Normally the resistance of the device was high, because of the loose contact between

---

[1] In passing, it is interesting to note that A. G. Bell in 1878, and others soon afterwards, were able to demonstrate telephony over a modulated-light link, using selenium as the detector; this was a form of electromagnetic-wave wireless communication, but was, of course, irrelevant to the development of radio.

particles, but when an electrical discharge occurred in its vicinity, or a voltage of the high frequency associated with electromagnetic waves was applied to the wires at its ends, the particles to some extent stuck together or cohered, and its resistance fell dramatically. This fall in resistance could be detected by a local battery circuit with some sort of indicator in it. The coherer had then to be tapped mechanically to loosen the particles and thus restore the high resistance.

The coherer had a long prehistory, but in its practical form was due largely to Edouard Branly (France) in 1890–1, although Oliver Lodge also claimed to have developed it, and had undoubtedly done much along similar lines.

Marconi and other pioneers. As early as 1894 the young Marconi, who had little scientific training, had seen the potentiality of Hertz's work for commercial telegraphy, and started experimenting in his home at the Villa Griffone near Bologna in Italy. He had soon tried an elevated aerial with its lower end connected to an earth plate; he used an induction coil to generate sparks under the control of a telegraph key; and he used a coherer for detection, improving its design by the use of nickel filings with an admixture of 4 per cent of silver filings and by exhausting the air from the tube. He was able to achieve a range of 2·4 km.

The Italian Government was not interested in taking up Marconi's ideas, and so in February 1896 he took his apparatus to Britain. Before long, and with the support of the Post Office, he was able to demonstrate radio telegraphy over several kilometres on Salisbury Plain and across the Bristol Channel. He also had valuable contacts with the Admiralty and War Office, and a friendly relationship with H. B. Jackson, a senior naval officer who was himself also a pioneer of radio, particularly for naval use. The friendly relationship with the Post Office terminated, however, in 1897 as a result of the formation by Marconi of a commercial company to exploit his patents, which the British Government had declined to pay for. His experiments continued; in May 1898 he demonstrated telegraphy over a sea path of 23 km from Alum Bay to Bournemouth, and in March 1899 over 50 km across the English Channel from Wimereux near Boulogne to the South Foreland lighthouse near Dover.

On 12 December 1901 Marconi's long-planned attempt to transmit a radio message across the Atlantic Ocean resulted in partial success; he claimed to have heard at his station at St. John's, Newfoundland, signals comprising a series of the letter *S* in Morse code—each letter being three dots—transmitted by prior arrangement from the station in Cornwall, over 3500 km away. There was no instrumental record to support his claim, which has thus always been suspect; however, a recent reassessment in the light of modern knowledge shows that there is now no scientific case against it [5]. At the time nobody suspected the existence of reflecting layers in the earth's upper atmosphere which would divert back to earth some of the energy in the transmitted signal, which probably encompassed the range of wavelengths from 600 m down to 30 m (the frequency range 0·5–10 MHz). However, whatever the real facts of the Newfoundland experiment, there was no disputing Marconi's achievement of a range of about 2500 km between Poldhu and the ship *Philadelphia* in February 1902, for on this occasion, with much better equipment, he obtained inked-paper records of genuine telegraph messages. Only six years later Marconi was able to establish a commercial radio telegraph service across the Atlantic.

There were undoubtedly several quite independent workers in the practical application to radio communication of the scientific matters demonstrated by Hertz, Lodge, Branly, and others. Priorities have been difficult to determine, but it now seems generally agreed that Marconi was slightly ahead of—and was certainly more successful than—Jackson (already mentioned), A. C. H. Slaby (Germany), and A. S. Popov (Russia); these three were his closest rivals.

The beginning of radio technology and radio service. Marconi's early experiments in Italy and Britain were made with transmitters which were still recognizably based on those used by Hertz; Fig. 50.8(a) shows the arrangement. When the telegraph key K is depressed to make a 'mark' signal, the break-and-make contacts of the induction coil IC vibrate. Each time the contacts break or make there is a sudden change of current in the primary winding and of magnetic flux in the iron core; there is thus induced a large electromotive force (e.m.f.) in the secondary winding which has many times the number of turns of the primary. Now the aerial A_1 forms, with the earth, effectively a capacitor (then called a 'condenser'), and the e.m.f. from the coil causes electric charge to flow into it. As it charges up, a voltage develops between A_1 and earth. Eventually (after a time-interval, short compared with the period of vibration of the contacts of IC) this voltage is sufficient to cause a spark between the metal balls of the spark gap G, and the charge stored in the aerial capacitance is suddenly discharged through the conducting path of ionized gas produced by the spark. This provides the energy for the production and radiation of electromagnetic waves in a short decaying burst, of

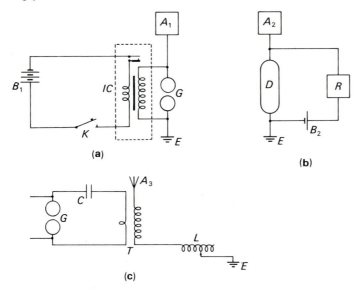

FIG. 50.8. Early radio circuits used by Marconi.
(a). Transmitter, 1896–7.
(b). Receiver, 1896–7.
(c). Transmitter tuning arrangement, 1900; a similar circuit was used in the receiver.

A_1 = plate-type transmitting aerial; A_2 = plate-type receiving aerial; A_3 = antenna-type aerial; B_1, B_2 = batteries; C = capacitor (condenser); D = detector, i.e. coherer; E = earth connection; G = spark gap; IC = induction coil with iron core and magnetic break-and-make; K = telegraph key; L = tuning inductance coil with adjustment; R = receiving instrument (Morse sounder, inker, or telephone receiver); T = transformer, or coupled coils.

duration much less than the period of vibration of the contacts of IC, and of frequency and wavelength determined by the capacitance and inductance of the aerial–gap circuit.

The receiver in these early experiments was typically as shown in Fig. 50.8 (b). A_2 is an aerial similar to A_1. When the burst of waves is received, the resistance of the coherer D falls, and the battery current through the receiving indicator R rises and operates it. The resistance is then automatically restored to its high value by a mechanical tapper on the coherer. The telegraph key K is kept depressed for the duration of a mark signal, and this greatly exceeds the period of vibration of the contacts of IC; the telegraph signal thus comprises a train of short bursts of electromagnetic waves.

In these simple circuits there is no very definite natural frequency, and so, in Marconi's early work, the transmitted waves covered quite a wide spectrum. This meant that neighbouring radio links would interfere with one another; the difficulty was particularly marked when trying to operate radio telegraphy between ships of a naval fleet. The potential solution of this problem was to apply the principle of tuning (then called 'syntony' (p. 1113)) which had been developed by Lodge during several years before 1897; this principle involved resonating both transmitter and receiver circuits to the same frequency, so that a more limited band of frequencies was transmitted and the receiver was much more sensitive to this band than to any other. Marconi could not use Lodge's patent, but eventually designed a circuit arrangement, shown for a transmitter in Fig. 50.8(c), which achieved the desired result without infringing Lodge's patent—although there was a dispute over this. Here the aerial A_3 (by now a wire antenna replacing the old plate aerials) was tuned to the frequency of the tuned spark-gap circuit by means of the adjustable inductance L, the relatively loosely coupled transformer T making the aerial tuning and the spark-gap tuning largely independent. The receiver had a similar double tuning. This system proved successful.

Many improvements in transmitters and receivers were made in very rapid succession in the years following 1900. We can here mention only a few. Although spark transmitters continued to be used, particularly in marine equipment, for several decades, they had serious disadvantages, and for point-to-point communication were largely displaced by either arc-generators or high-frequency alternators. The former was first used by W. Duddell (Britain) in 1900 as a simple direct-current arc with a resonant circuit connected across it. The negative-resistance characteristic of the arc (that is, the negative slope of the voltage–current curve) enabled an oscillation to be generated at the frequency of resonance of the circuit, the power being drawn from the direct current. The improvements made by V. Poulsen (Denmark) in 1903, which included the use of a water-cooled copper anode and an enclosed atmosphere of hydrogen, together with a strong applied magnetic field to extinguish the arc for a part of each cycle, resulted in a much higher efficiency, and such devices were used for important radio stations for some decades. The high-frequency alternator was a special design of rotating machine which could generate an alternating current of frequency up to about 100 kHz, and is particularly associated with E. F. W. Alexanderson (U.S.A.), who built a successful one in 1907. Both the Poulsen arc and high-frequency alternator eventually provided transmitter powers up to about 500 kW.

In reception, the coherer tended to be displaced at first by the electromagnetic detector of E. Rutherford (Britain). In 1896 he demonstrated the effect of an electromagnetic wave on the magnetism in an iron wire, and Marconi developed the idea in 1902 into a device (Fig. 50.9) with a clockwork-driven soft-iron wire or band which passed continuously through a permanent magnetic field and a coil carrying the aerial current to be detected. The receipt of a wave demagnetized the wire suddenly, thus inducing a click in a telephone earpiece connected in a secondary winding on the coil. In the long-term

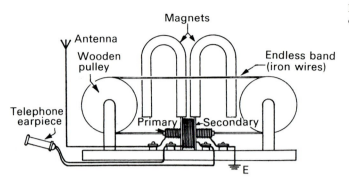

Fig. 50.9. Marconi's second electromagnetic detector, 1902.

aspect, the most important innovation of the early years was the crystal detector or receiver discovered by H. H. C. Dunwoody (U.S.A.) in 1906, but the idea of using a non-linear circuit element as a detector seems to have been due to M. I. Pupin (U.S.A.) in 1898; he used an electrolytic rectifier. Possibly the greatest importance of the rectifier-type of detector was that it could be used as well for radio-telephony as for radio-telegraphy.

The idea that speech might be transmitted by radio had occurred to several of the early workers and ideas of modulating a high-frequency current by speech signals had been put forward as early as 1886 by M. Leblanc (France). However, it was R. A. Fessenden (U.S.A.) who first demonstrated the transmission of speech by the modulation of a radio wave in 1902. For this purpose he used a continuous alternating wave generated by an alternator, and although he developed several methods of modulation, the most successful seems to have been the simplest, namely the direct modulation of the transmitting aerial current by a microphone in the same way that a direct current is modulated in a normal telephone transmitter. Speech could also be transmitted on a wave generated by a Poulsen arc, or even by a spark. However, radio-telephony made only slow progress before the general use of the thermionic valve.

Radio-telegraphy entered successfully into commercial service after 1900. We shall consider its world-wide applications later.

IV. TECHNOLOGICAL DEVELOPMENTS IN ELECTRICAL COMMUNICATIONS

Having in previous sections described the origins of telephony and radio communication and the main inventions and developments which initially established them as vital means of rapid communication, we now turn to the major technological developments which led electrical communications into the modern era.

The impact of the thermionic valve. There is no doubt that the biggest influence in the development of electrical communications into the modern pattern was the introduction of the thermionic valve. Yet its effect was at first very small and slow to emerge.

The history of the thermionic valve (or 'tube' in the U.S.A.) is outlined elsewhere (Ch. 46). Although originating as a diode rectifier, it had little impact in that form. The triode valve or 'audion' invented by Lee de Forest (U.S.A.) in 1906 was a crude device, little understood—even by its inventor —and therefore not very effectively used for some years. It was used to some extent as an amplifier, but the real breakthrough came in the years 1912–15 when three important steps were made. First, the use of the triode as an oscillator, or generator of radio-frequency oscillations, using positive feedback from the output to the input circuit. Secondly, the use of the triode as an amplifier of very high amplification and high tuned-selectivity, also by means of positive feedback, carefully adjusted to avoid the oscillatory condition. Thirdly, the understanding of triode valve operation and the quantitative design of valve circuits through the use of characteristic curves relating anode–cathode current to anode–cathode and grid–cathode voltages. E. H. Armstrong (U.S.A.) contributed more than anyone else to these matters, but the invention of positive feedback was strongly disputed [6]. It now became possible to obtain relatively pure radio-frequency power at frequencies which were readily adjustable and controllable, thus making radio-telephony satisfactory for the first time; it became possible to make extremely sensitive receivers with high selectivity. Because of these factors, together with the hastening effect of the First World War, radio communication—and soon radio broadcasting—made a rapid leap forward.

Many other inventions based on the thermionic valve led to significant advances in radio. One of the most important was the superheterodyne principle, which improved receiver design greatly. The idea of forming a low-frequency 'beat' note between the incoming radio signal and a local oscillation-generator of frequency near to that of the signal was due to Fessenden in 1902, but its development as the superheterodyne, based on valves, was due to Armstrong in 1919. The advantages of the system were that, since the incoming signal was effectively changed to a much lower frequency on reception, the amplification and selectivity could be readily provided at the lower frequency, thus permitting the use of radio frequencies above the range at which effective amplification could then be provided directly. Moreover, selectivity could be better when carried out at the fixed intermediate frequency; this was particularly important when radio broadcasting got under way in the mid-1920s.

Even though the application of the thermionic valve to radio was surprisingly slow, its application to line telephony was quite remarkably laggardly. The problems of long-distance telephony in the U.S.A. had led to the idea of using amplifiers in telephone lines as early as 1900, and electromechanical 'repeaters' based essentially on the coupling of a telephone receiver to a microphone were developed by 1903 [7]. Yet such amplifiers were never introduced on any large scale. They were used initially on the first transcontinental telephone line, opened between New York and San Francisco in 1915. However, the telephone engineers had at last caught up with the thermionic valve, and valve amplifiers replaced the electromechanical type almost immediately, giving much better results. Thereafter, long-distance telephone systems were planned on the basis of valve amplifiers, which permitted the use of much lighter wires, underground cable, and much better quality of transmission. After some years of experience of trying to operate amplified circuits using the same pair of wires for both directions of transmission, it became standard practice to use a separate pair of wires for each direction.

Modulation, sidebands, carrier telephony. The rapid growth of the long-distance telephone network in the last two decades before 1950 was not only responsible for the development of new ways of providing trunk circuits but was to a large extent created by the availability of new methods and the economies achieved by them. Although, as we shall see later, the invention of negative feedback was the main trigger for the trunk explosion, the basic concepts had been laid down during the preceding half-century.

The main feature of the 1930s development was the use of a wide spectrum of frequencies on a line, this spectrum being divided up into bands typically of about 4 kHz, each to carry a speech channel. This system is called 'frequency-division-multiplex' (f.d.m.). All the incoming speech signals from subscribers have to be translated in frequency to the bands allotted. This is done by a process of modulation with, or of, a 'carrier tone'. The use of the radio spectrum had, of course, been similar from the early years of the century, and had involved the same basic process of modulation when speech or programme material was transmitted. This process originated at least as early as 1886 [8]. In that year, M. Leblanc (France) described a way of transmitting speech from a microphone which was combined with a self-maintained tuning fork in such a way that the sound waves impinging on a diaphragm controlled the amplitude of vibration, and therefore of the electrical oscillation sent to a telephone line from a pick-up coil on the fork. The envelope of the waveform sent on the line thus reproduced the sound waves. Leblanc's receiving device was not so clear in its operation. However, about five years later Leblanc, in conjunction with M. Hutin (France), put forward a system using electrical resonance and a dynamometer type of receiver, with different carrier frequencies allocated to different telephones, so that a proper f.d.m. system was produced. It is believed that no practical use was made of the system at that time, but it was undoubtedly the forerunner of modern systems.

Amplitude modulation (A.M.) for radio seems to have been developed quite separately around 1900 by R. A. Fessenden (U.S.A.). In neither line nor radio work, however, was there any understanding of sidebands until around 1915, although Lord Rayleigh had fully discussed them in the context of acoustics in 1894. Yet an understanding of sidebands was essential for progress in f.d.m. telephony, whether on line or radio. If the speech signal is represented by a single tone $e_s \cos \omega_s t$, and the carrier tone (that is, the tuning fork note in Leblanc's system) as $e_c \cos \omega_c t$, then the modulated signal is

$$e_c \cos \omega_c t \ (1 + m \ e_s \cos \omega_s t),$$

where m is the depth of modulation; this can be expanded as

$$e_c \cos \omega_c t \ [\text{carrier tone}] + \tfrac{1}{2} m \ e_c \ e_s \cos (\omega_c + \omega_s)t \ [\text{upper sideband}]$$
$$+ \tfrac{1}{2} m \ e_c \ e_s \cos (\omega_c - \omega_s)t \ [\text{lower sideband}].$$

No speech information is contained in the first, carrier, term, and all speech information is contained in each of the sidebands. There is, therefore, no point in transmitting anything more than one of the sidebands without the carrier. If only one sideband is transmitted for each speech channel, the maximum use is made of the available power and the available frequency spectrum. The problem was, of course, to separate the sidebands. This was solved from 1915 by the invention of electrical filters (Ch. 46). There were many early f.d.m. line telephone systems using one carrier channel in addition to the normal direct speech ('audio') channel on each line. Their importance was small, however, until the use of negative feedback made multi-channel working possible.

Towards the end of our period two other kinds of modulation attracted interest and have become important. First, frequency modulation (F.M.) invented in 1902 but first seriously developed in the early 1930s, in which the information is carried by variations of the frequency and not the amplitude of the carrier [9]. Secondly, pulse modulation, in which information is carried by variations in amplitude, timing, or coding of sequences of short pulses. F.M., although extravagant in spectrum width, has the advantages of being relatively unaffected by fading in radio systems and in usually giving good discrimination against noise; it is, therefore, much used for important high-quality radio work. Pulse modulation has the attraction that it can be digital in form and thus compatible with data-transmission requirements, and it lends itself to another kind of multiplexing—time-division-multiplex (t.d.m.)—where signals from different channels are sampled in sequence. T.d.m. for speech was first demonstrated by W. M. Miner (U.S.A.) in 1903, but for practical application had to await the modern electronic era; the principle had been used in telegraphy from the mid-1870s.

The impact of negative feedback on telephony. We have pointed out earlier how ideas on modulation and frequency-division-multiplex in relation to the trunk telephone network had origins in the nineteenth century, and how greatly the introduction of the thermionic valve had speeded progress in electrical communication generally. Techniques of 'carrier-telephony', as the f.d.m. system was usually called, had been developed, and during the 1920s and early 1930s had been applied to open-wire trunk lines without intermediate amplifiers, and also as two-channel systems on amplified lines. In the latter case, one channel was the normal audio channel, and one carrier channel was placed above it in the frequency range of, roughly, 3–6 kHz. Further progress was limited by the difficulty of intermodulation in amplifiers. Owing to the fact that the instantaneous output voltage of a thermionic-valve amplifier was not exactly proportional to the instantaneous input voltage, but had a non-linear relationship, there was a distortion of any signal waveform applied to the amplifier. For a single speech channel this was generally not serious. However, when two or more channels were worked through the same amplifier, this distortion involved the formation of new frequency-components produced by the interaction of the signals in the different channels, and thus elements of the speech in one channel were transferred to another. Although this 'intermodulation' crosstalk was generally unintelligible, it formed a serious limitation to the extension of the system.

The breakthrough came with the invention of negative feedback by H. S. Black (U.S.A.), and its general application following his publication in 1934 [10]. The term 'negative' is not now generally retained, and indeed it is not strictly quite correct, but it is useful to use it here to avoid confusion with the other type of feedback—positive feedback—which was so extensively used in the early valve period. What negative feedback does, in its simplest conception, is to feed some of the output signal back to the input in opposition to the input signal. If the voltage–amplification ratio of the amplifier is A, and the feedback ratio, determined for instance by a network of resistors, is B, then the overall amplification with the feedback is reduced from A to $A/(1 + AB)$; if AB is much greater than 1, this amplification is approximately $1/B$. In other words, the overall amplification becomes practically independent of A. Thus, if the original amplification was non-linear, the new amplification is practically linear; and if the original amplification tended to fluctuate, the new amplification is practically constant. Thus negative feedback could reduce intermodulation crosstalk between channels to any desired level, and by stabilizing amplification could permit much more amplification to be provided in any long trunk route.

So from 1934 there was no further fundamental obstacle to the extension of the trunk telephone system by the use of very wide spectra on the lines, with numerous channels on each pair of conductors. It became common practice to use basic groups of 12 speech channels in the frequency range 60–108 kHz, thus allowing 4 kHz spacing of channels. Several, or many, such groups could be assembled in a wide frequency range as super-groups, and so on. By thus reducing the line costs per speech channel, it became practicable to offer cheap trunk calls; to meet an ever-increasing demand for long-distance telephone service; and eventually to provide an automatically switched, on demand, subscriber-dialling service.

Not only have special types of cable been introduced to transmit the very wide frequency bands involved, but 'microwave' radio links are also commonly used, with wavelengths of the order of 10–30 cm. Wideband cables do not naturally have a loss which is constant over the frequency band, and it is necessary to provide 'equalizing' circuits to correct this.

One could justifiably refer to the trunk 'explosion', for the number of channels provided between important towns, once numbered in single figures, had by 1950 reached thousands. Although, as shown above, the most obvious result of the invention of negative feedback was the revolution in telephone trunk circuits, yet numerous other important improvements in electrical communications—and indeed in electronic technology generally—also arose from the use of negative feedback. Precise amplification, good frequency response, low distortion, etc. became not only available, but calculable and designable.

Cables. Telegraphs had been worked over long submarines cables, and over short lengths of land cable, for some decades before telephony began (Vol. V, Ch. 10). It was, however, appreciated from the beginning that telephony had requirements for transmission rather different from those of telegraph signals, but the nature of the requirements was not understood. Early telephone cable schemes, such as that at Newcastle upon Tyne, England, in 1882, where the City Corporation would not permit overhead wires, demonstrated clearly that telephone transmission on cable was difficult. With the gutta-percha-insulated cable then available, 6–7 km was the maximum attainable distance over which intelligible speech was possible. It was appreciated that, whatever other requirements there might be, it was essential to reduce the capacitance of the cable. Lead-covered cable with cotton insulation was made in Philadelphia in 1884, and in 1889 the use of paper insulation started the kind of cable that remained standard throughout our period. For local telephone distribution, such cables with relatively fine wire (eventually, for example, 5–10 kg/km) were very satisfactory. For trunk lines, however, cables became possible at first only with the use of very heavy conductors. An important early example was the first Anglo–French telephone cable of 1891 (still gutta-percha insulated) which provided two telephone circuits between London and Paris. The land extensions used open wires weighing about 150–200 kg/km, and the 35-km cable itself had conductors weighing about 50 kg/km.

The understanding of the principles of telephone transmission, which were clearly set out by Oliver Heaviside in 1887 but not appreciated for another decade, led to the introduction of loading coils from about 1901 [11]. These made an immense improvement in transmission, and made it possible to use cable for trunk lines up to perhaps 200–300 km. The principle involved was that the natural electrical constants of the cable—resistance (R), capacitance (C), leakage (G), and inductance (L), per unit length—did not have the right relationships for good transmission. Heaviside had shown that for distortion-less transmission it was necessary to have $R/L = G/C$, but in cables L was far too low. A good cable would have low R, G, and C in order to keep the attenuation low, but even so it was necessary to add inductance to achieve the relationship specified. Coils were added in series with the conductors at intervals calculated from the new formulae of Pupin. (Open lines normally met the Heaviside condition fairly well, the wide spacing of the conductors giving a lower capacitance and higher inductance than in cables; but even so, some American open lines had coil loading to improve their transmission.)

The real development of telephone trunk networks based on cable came with the introduction of the thermionic-valve amplifier. It then became possible to use comparatively light and cheap cable, with 'repeaters' (amplifiers) inserted at regular intervals, to achieve very long lengths of route, eventually providing a global network. As modulation and carrier techniques developed, enabling many channels to be operated on each pair of conductors, inductance loading became a restriction, for it had bought improved audio transmission at the expense of a rapid cut-off above the audio range. Thus by about 1950, coil-loading had disappeared from the trunk network.

Crosstalk between pairs of conductors in cables has always been a problem. Twisting of the wires in various ways helped, but for modern requirements, special crosstalk-cancelling or balancing networks have proved useful. One of the most important cable developments has been the use, since about 1935, of 'coaxial' cables in which one conductor of each circuit is encircled by the other. This construction is particularly suitable for use with very wide frequency bands, as in modern carrier-telephone or television transmission. One of the most exciting cable developments is the use of trans-ocean telephone cables with built-in amplifiers and other equipment. These are discussed below.

Radio aerials or antennas. The theory of radio aerials (usually called antennas in the U.S.A. and elsewhere) is very complex, and it is understandable that early aerials were designed by trial and error. As we have seen, the early radio workers appreciated that the wavelengths radiated depended on the resonant tuning (if any) of the transmitting aerial, and Marconi found that larger, higher aerials led to radiation at longer wavelengths, and that these led to greater ranges of reception. As early as 1898, A. Blondel (France) had produced a theoretical treatment of the vertical wire aerial, laying the basis of the long-wave aerial theory using the concept that the earth produces an image of the aerial. The concept of 'effective height' (h_e) of a simple wire aerial (for example, straight vertical wire, inverted L, or T configurations) came into use, the effective transmitted power being proportional to $h_e^2 i_A^2 / \lambda^2$ where i_A is the aerial current and λ is the wavelength of the radiated wave. It was realized that aerials of this type used at wavelengths of about 15 000 m, even when made several kilometres long and some hundreds of metres high, were very inefficient, the power radiated being only a few per cent of the total power fed to the aerial. Much effort was made to improve this efficiency by devices such as multiple tuning and extensive ground-wire systems which by the early 1920s brought efficiencies up to 20–30 per cent. The aerials radiated more or less uniformly in all horizontal directions.

In the late 1910s Marconi and his colleagues, C. S. Franklin and H. J. Round, were experimenting with short waves, with wavelengths in the range 2–15 m. It was known (as Hertz had known) that such waves could be propagated directionally by means of reflectors, made of a network of wires, which could be large compared with the wavelength and thus give a radiation in the preferred direction some hundred times greater than if the power had been uniformly radiated in all directions. The actual radiating element could be half-a-wavelength in principal dimension and much more efficient than a long-wave aerial. Such a system was used successfully by the Marconi group over relatively short paths of about 100 km and then in 1923–4 with a wavelength of the order of 100 m over paths up to nearly 20 000 km. The story of the exploitation of this 'beam' system is told elsewhere in this chapter. Franklin went on to design short-wave aerials on the array system, where a large number of individual half-wave aerial elements were suspended in front of reflecting wires in a huge assembly, separated horizontally and vertically by the right distance to keep all elements in phase. Such a system radiates effectively only in a limited angular cone; the larger the array for a given wavelength, the smaller the angle of the cone. The diffraction theory on which it is based was already well known, especially in optics, and the system had been put forward for radio telegraphy as early as 1903 by A. Blondel [12].

Numerous other kinds of aerial were developed over the years and there were many significant improvements of detail. Moreover, whereas the aerials of 1895–1920 were designed largely empirically, a much greater extent of theoretical design became apparent in later years; the introduction of the electronic computer led to aerials being designed theoretically almost down to the smallest detail. However, the principles discussed above remained the foundation of aerial operation, which extended during the 1940s into the range of wavelengths between 1 m and 3 cm. At the lower end of this range the feeders to the aerial were waveguides in place of the wire-line and coaxial-cable feeds used at the longer wavelengths, and reflectors and horns of metal sheet were used in place of wire structures.

For broadcast receivers and mobile-communication radio, special small aerials have been used, often without directivity, although small directional arrays are normally used for reception of VHF and UHF sound and television broadcasts (wavelengths in the range 0·1–10 m).

Telephone exchanges; automatic switching; trunk dialling [13, 14]. We have earlier mentioned that automatic telephone exchanges originated in the

U.S.A.; Strowger's system was the first to be put into practice, in 1897. In 1900 an exchange with a capacity of 10 000 lines, on this system, was brought into service at New Bedford, Mass. Subscribers still had local batteries for speaking, but common-battery working became normal within a few years. The subscriber's dial, for generating the impulses which govern the switch movements, was introduced in 1896. Each train of impulses, corresponding to each digit of the telephone number dialled, stepped a selector switch at the exchange. If the subscriber dialled 763, for example, the switch connected to his own line would step to the seventh set of contacts, which would lead to another selector switch which would step to its sixth set of contacts, which would lead to a final selector switch which would step to its third set of contacts: that is, the required subscriber's line. This became known as the step-by-step system.

These early Strowger exchanges were uneconomic in having to allocate an expensive selector switch to each subscriber's line. A much cheaper method was introduced; this was the line switch, where a contact arm would rotate and search a bank of contacts, each set of contacts being the termination of a subscriber's line, to find the set corresponding to a calling subscriber. By this system, only as many selector switches needed to be provided as the traffic density warranted. Thus arose the concept of telephone traffic planning. This had been dealt with in a very empirical way in manual exchanges, but now started to become a mathematical study of some precision. By using the methods of mathematical statistics, coupled with actual observations of the incidence of calls in exchanges, it became possible to calculate the number of switches to be provided at each stage in order to give a specified grade of service, defined in terms of the probability of an incoming call finding a free selector switch for each digit dialled. This flexible approach greatly reduced the cost of automatic exchanges. The mathematical methods improved over the years, and did not reach some sort of finality until around 1950.

Whether telephone switching should be manual or automatic was essentially a matter of economics. In places where the average number of calls per subscriber per day was high it might be cheaper to use an automatic exchange. And since in early systems—and, indeed, in some cases, throughout our period—it was necessary to route calls for other exchanges through a manual switchboard, another criterion was the proportion of calls which could be handled automatically, that is, which were within the one exchange area. These considerations may account for the relatively rapid introduction of automatic exchanges in the U.S.A., compared with a much slower development in Britain and Europe. There had been demonstrations of automatic exchange systems in Britain before 1900, but the first operational installations were in 1912 at Epsom and at the Post Office Headquarters in London. Other systems for automatic exchanges were developed and used elsewhere, but the Strowger system was standardized for Britain.

As the number of automatic exchanges increased, the problem arose of how to deal with large areas. The solution adopted was to make each area one large system, often with a central large exchange and outlying satellite exchanges, all on the same numbering scheme. Calls for subscribers on the same satellite exchange as the caller were routed locally; all other calls went through the central exchange, which had the one manual switchboard for the whole area. In very large and dense areas such as New York, London, Birmingham, etc., a more complex system was necessary, with a complicated pattern of inter-exchange links. Here the 'director' system was used. All subscriber's numbers were of seven digits, although the first three were commonly represented by letters related to the name of the local exchange. When a subscriber dialled a number, the impulses were stored in his own exchange; the first three digits, indicating the desired exchange, were then automatically translated into a routing code of up to six digits in the 'director'. This new set of impulses operated selector switches which connected the call either directly or via intermediate exchanges to the called exchange. The last four digits (being the called subscriber's number within his local exchange) were then transmitted to operate selector switches in the normal way. The first director exchange in Britain was that at Holborn, London, in 1927.

In all these automatic exchange areas the system had to allow for some (initially often most) of the exchanges remaining manual for many years, since it was not economic to replace manual exchanges of recent type until some return had been obtained on their capital cost. The solution in smaller areas was that subscribers on automatic exchanges had to call the operator for connection to manual exchanges; but in director areas subscribers on automatic exchanges were allowed to dial any number in the whole area. In this case, when the called exchange was manual, the first three digits took the call to an operator at the called exchange, to whom the final digits were visually displayed so that she could complete the connection without having any verbal contact with either calling or called subscriber.

The direct dialling of calls over trunk lines from one area into the automatic exchange system of another area began only at the end of our period, around 1950. It had to be preceded by a period of development of alternating-current (a.c.) signalling over trunk lines. The reason for this was that, whereas the old trunk lines had used one pair of wires for each speech channel, thus providing an individual conducting circuit for direct-current (d.c.) signalling, the newer trunk lines worked on the frequency-division-multiplex (or carrier) principle, and no longer provided a d.c. path for each channel. Once sufficiently sophisticated a.c. signalling was available, dialling over trunk lines was possible by sending trains of pulses of a.c. tones. Initially only operators dialled calls, but eventually an almost universal and international subscriber-trunk-dialling system came into use; it began, in Britain, at Bristol in 1958.

Since 1950 a great deal of work has been done on the theory and design of electronic automatic exchanges—a natural application of principles developed in electronic computers (Ch. 48), but with some very special and difficult problems, and with solutions which bear little or no relation to methods used in the conventional exchanges. New methods of electromechanical switching have also been introduced, and partially electronic exchanges are satisfactory; but the economic advantages of all-electronic exchanges are not obvious. However, this development was barely started before 1950.

Theoretical and mathematical developments. It must be obvious that electrical communications could not have developed to the state of sophistication attained by 1950 without a very sound background of theory and mathematical methods. There can, indeed, be few branches of technology so much influenced by, and so dependent on, mathematical treatment. Kelvin's theory of telegraph transmission on cables (1855) and of elementary electrical circuits (1853), Clerk Maxwell's theory of electromagnetic waves (1864), Hertz's development of Maxwell's theory, and Heaviside's electromagnetic theory (1887 onwards)—to mention only the most outstanding work—laid a sound theoretical and mathematical foundation for electrical communications. Few of the engineers of those days understood this theory, and its immediate impact was therefore not as great as its importance warranted. Initial progress was undoubtedly retarded by this, but education in electrical engineering was well established on a sound basis by the end of the nineteenth century, and theory took its proper place. Much of the theoretical work was the application of established scientific theory and established mathematics to the engineering problems, but there has been, all through, a strong element of new theory and new mathematics developed for the problems of electrical communications. Heaviside's 'operational calculus' for solving circuit problems was one example. A more recent case has been the development of a general theory of communication by C. E. Shannon [15] (1948 onwards), based on an understanding of the fundamental nature of the background 'noise' in an electrical system as first set out by J. B. Johnson [16] in 1928, and on the limits set by bandwidth as first explored by H. Nyquist [17] and R. V. L. Hartley [18].

Johnson showed that there was in all electrical systems a basic noise composed of random variations in the potential of any point in a conductor due to the random motion of electrons in the conductor. He showed, too, that the mean power was uniformly distributed over the frequency spectrum passed by the circuit, and was proportional to the absolute temperature of the conductor and to the bandwidth (that is, the width of the spectrum passed by the circuit). However well a communication system might be protected from external interference, such as crosstalk from other circuits, its background noise level could never be reduced below this basic level. Communication theory introduced formally the idea of signal-to-noise ratio as a criterion of performance and related to this the rate at which information could be communicated. This involved a basis for the measurement of information; it was postulated that information, however complex, can, fundamentally, be broken down into a series of binary, or yes–no, decisions. Each elementary decision was a binary unit, or 'bit', of information. A complicated speech sentence may involve some thousands of bits, in some ways analogous to the way it could be transmitted by telegraphy using, for example, the Morse code. The rate at which bits could be transmitted through a communication system with a specified proportion of erroneous detections of the 'yes' or 'no' content of the bits could be precisely related to the bandwidth and to the signal-to-noise ratio. The effect of this theory and its ramifications has been profound since 1950, but it was discernable before then, particularly in the new kinds of communication equipment developed during the Second World War, especially those using pulse modulation, and in radar and sonar systems.

V. GLOBAL COMMUNICATION

Radio versus cable. The first commercial transatlantic radio telegraph service was opened by the Marconi Company between Clifden (Ireland) and Glace Bay (Canada) in October 1907, and the charges for messages were substantially lower than those of the cable companies. The Company's experience from this operation enabled them to propose to the British Government, in 1910, a radio-telegraph chain linking up the whole of the then very extensive

British Empire. Unfortunately, the attitude of the British Government to the problem of the monopoly such a scheme would give the Company in terms of traffic and also of available wavelengths, together with the opposition of the cable companies, resulted in the proposal being repeatedly deferred. A hesitant start in 1914, providing the British terminal at Leafield, was nullified by the First World War. Government opposition to the Marconi Company led, after the war, to a new plan for a Post Office radio network with relay stations at intervals of up to 4000 miles, although the Company had already demonstrated its ability to communicate directly, without intermediate relay, between Britain and Australia. There were further delays, and in 1922 the various Dominions made independent arrangements with the Marconi Company for direct links to Britain. But still the British Government could reach no agreement with Marconi.

The breakthrough occurred in 1924. Until then the plans had always been for long-wavelength (that is, wavelength greater than 1 km) systems, which transmitted and received in all directions. But for some years Marconi had been experimenting with 'short waves' (that is, with wavelengths of about 30 m) which permitted the aerials to be made directional, so that transmissions could be 'beamed' towards the equally directional receiving stations. Moreover, very long distances could be obtained by using reflection from the ionized layers in the upper atmosphere. This development was decisive; a contract with the Marconi Company was speedily signed by the British Government, the work went ahead, and by 1928 there was global radio-telegraph communication, linking Canada, South Africa, India, Australia, and other Dominions to Britain and to one another (Fig. 50.10).

The existing global cable telegraph network, which had by then been established for nearly three-quarters of a century (Vol. V, Ch. 10), was severely challenged by the beamed-radio network, which could offer greatly reduced charges for messages. Cable charges fell, but so also did cable traffic. After negotiations, started in 1928, the British long-distance radio and cable interests—that is Marconi's Wireless Telegraph Company, the Eastern Telegraph Company, the Eastern Extension Telegraph Company, and the Western Telegraph Company, including the Marconi Company's very extensive long-wave network—were amalgamated into Cables and Wireless Ltd. in 1929. This was a holding company which had an operating company, Imperial and International Communication Ltd., over which there was a measure of government control through an official Advisory Committee. In 1934 the operating company took the name Cables and Wireless Ltd., the

FIG. 50.10. Marconi Company's 20-kW short-wave transmitter Type SWB1, installed at Dorchester in 1927, showing water-cooled valves.

holding company being distinguished by the parenthetic addition of (Holding) to its name. The companies were nationalized after the Second World War.

The ascendancy of telephony over telegraphy. As we have seen, the transmission and reception of telephony on radio links had been established before the general availability of thermionic valves, but it was the valve which made radio telephony suitable for long-distance services. As early as 1915 A.T. and T. had demonstrated the transmission of speech from the U.S.A. to France. By the early 1920s, special high-power triode valves with water-cooling could be used in parallel-connected banks of 20 or 30 to give transmitted powers of up to 300 kW at long wavelengths (5–10 km), that is, at frequencies around 30–60 kHz. An experimental one-way transatlantic telephone link was set up for long-term evaluation by the A.T. and T. in association with the Radio Corporation of America, between Rocky Point, U.S.A., and New Southgate, England, early in 1923 on a carrier frequency of 60 kHz, using single-sideband transmission at 60 kW [19].

The British Post Office decided, as a result of these trials, to set up a commercial two-way link between Britain and the U.S.A., using its Rugby longwave radio telegraph station, which was being established to provide a worldwide telegraph service on a wavelength of 40 km as a rather expensive addition to the beam service already discussed. Aerials for telephony could readily be added, and radio-telephone equipment was provided by Standard Telephones and Cables Ltd., the British subsidiary of the A.T. and T. Both telegraph and telephone transmitters at Rugby were completed in 1926 [20]. The telephone link comprised two separate one-way links, well spaced geographically and operating on different frequencies, in the range 50–65 kHz. The service was successful, although because of the propagation fluctuations and interference it was necessary to have technical operators manually regulating the link all the time speech was in progress. The charge was £15 for a three-minute (effective) call.

Similar telephone services were subsequently provided to Australia and South America, and many other places. The short-wave beam system, so successful with telegraphy, was also exploited for telephony, and it could be said that from the 1930s there was global telephony as well as telegraphy.

As with inland communications, telephone business increased while telegraph business declined. It was evident that provision must be made for the expansion and improvement of telephony on inter-continental services. The concept of the oceanic telephone cable with electronic amplifiers embedded in it arose in the U.S.A. in the 1930s and was developed after the Second World War, leading to a limited installation between Key West and Havana in 1950. From this experience was gained of a system using separate cables for each direction of transmission, each with three built-in repeaters operating in depths up to 1700 m; 24 speech circuits were carried. The repeaters were mechanically flexible, electrically simple, fed with power over the cable. In the meantime, experience had been gained in Britain with submerged repeaters of more complex type. These gave operation in both directions on a single cable, attached to, rather than embedded in, the cables, operating in relatively shallow water on the Continental Shelf. The first such repeater was laid on the route between Holyhead and the Isle of Man in 1943, providing 48 speech circuits. Techniques for making reliable, long-life thermionic valves were successfully developed. This successful experience on both sides of the Atlantic led to the planning and provision of a transatlantic cable telephone system which was successfully inaugurated in 1956 and provided 35 high-quality telephone circuits between Europe and America. Subsequently the demand grew so enormously that by the mid-1970s several thousand telephone circuits were available, by cable and by satellite-radio links, not only across the Atlantic, but all round the world.

Although there is no doubt that Britain played the leading part for more than a century in global communication, and the role of the U.S.A. has latterly been dominant, nevertheless many other countries, and particularly Germany, have been very active.

VI. COMMUNICATION WITH SHIPS AND VEHICLES

Marine radio. Several of the early Marconi experiments involved lighthouses and lightships, and it seemed clear that radio offered a solution to the problem of communicating with ships at sea in all weathers. Marconi and Jackson were much concerned in the years before 1900 in trials which showed the value of radio communication in the Royal Navy, which by the end of 1900 had 51 sets installed. The Marconi Marine Company was formed in 1900 to exploit the Marconi patents in marine applications. It quickly became apparent that the Company itself would have to build the shore stations, hire out the ship-board apparatus, and control the marine communications service. There was soon much competition from other firms, and in Britain also from the Post Office, which in 1909 took over all the coast stations in Britain. The situation in the world generally was far from satisfactory, but eventually all organizations agreed to handle messages from whatever equipment they originated. By March 1915 there were altogether 706 coast stations and 4846 ship-board installations.

The loss of the liner *Titanic* in the Atlantic in 1912 stimulated a demand for compulsory provision of radio on ships. It gradually became obligatory for ships to carry radio; legislation to this effect was introduced for the different classes of ships in the U.S.A., Britain, and other countries from 1914 onwards. The early ship-board transmitters all used spark generators. As valve transmitters became available they were commonly adopted in both naval and merchant ships. In 1927 it was internationally agreed that spark transmitters over 300 watts should be abolished by 1940 because their impure transmissions caused interference problems.

Other important marine radio developments were direction-finders as an aid to navigation (Ch. 34), mainly after the First World War; ship-to-shore telephony from the early 1920s; and automatic distress-call alarms, also in the 1920s. Although single-sideband working was well established in fixed point-to-point radio systems during the last two decades before 1950, it had little influence on marine systems, which remained double-sideband until after 1950.

Vehicular and pedestrian communication [21, 22]. Radio communication with land vehicles lagged far behind marine radio. There had been early attempts to provide communication with railway trains by inductive methods, but these did not come into general use. Radio was the only feasible method for road vehicles, but the problems of effective service with very small aerials and very compact equipment, and with difficult propagation conditions, held back development until the 1930s.

Early systems used frequencies around 2 MHz, mainly with Morse signalling. In the late 1930s police systems in Britain moved to the frequency range 30–100 MHz, with fixed station power of 100 W and mobile station power of 10 W; good telephone communication was generally possible up to about 25 km. Over the world the use of mobile radio in this frequency range, and later, after 1950, in the range around 400 MHz, spread to many private as well as official uses, and equipment became very small and convenient.

The main fundamental problem was, and remains, that of fading owing to the phasing in and out of signals travelling to or from a moving vehicle by different paths involving reflection from buildings and other objects, fixed or moving. These fluctuations are different for different frequencies and for different positions on the vehicle, and 'diversity' methods have often been used in which the outputs from transmissions at different frequencies or from several aerials have been combined to give less serious fading.

Communication with pedestrians, which also started in the 1930s, followed the same lines as for vehicles, but with greater emphasis on compactness and convenience.

The early development of radio communication between the ground and an aircraft followed the same line as marine radio, using medium frequencies (300–3000 kHz). The Second World War led to the use of much higher frequencies (30–300 MHz) as for land mobile radio, giving effective communication over line-of-sight paths.

VII. RADIO BROADCASTING

The beginnings. Radio broadcasting, in the present-day sense of the broadcast transmission of radio sound programmes and messages for reception by anyone who has access to a suitable receiver, had its origins in many experiments in several countries before the First World War, and in several local broadcasting programmes during the years 1914–20 in Belgium, Holland, and Germany. Its genesis as a regular public service may be said to date from 1920. From 23 February 1920 until the licence from the Postmaster-General was withdrawn on 23 November that year, the Marconi Company transmitted regular news broadcasts from its 15 kW transmitter at Chelmsford, England, on a wavelength of 2·8 km. From April 1920, Frank Conrad of the Westinghouse Company broadcast entertainment privately from his home in Pittsburgh, U.S.A., and the Company's official broadcasting station opened in Pittsburgh on 2 November 1920. Two years later there were an estimated million listeners and nearly 600 broadcasting stations in the U.S.A. In Britain, the Marconi Company engaged in further experimental broadcasts early in 1922, and opened the famous 2LO broadcasting station in London on 11 May that year, operating on a wavelength of 360 m. By the end of the year the British Broadcasting Company had been formed and represented the end of commercial competition in the broadcasting field in Britain; the Company became a public corporation in 1927, by which time there were over two million receiving sets in Britain. In the U.S.A., broadcasting has remained commercial, with some Federal supervision; and in the world generally some degree of government control or supervision can be found in every country.

The provision of receivers for radio broadcasting has been a competitive commercial matter in almost all countries, and led to much patent activity and an emphasis on well-engineered, cheap, mass production. There has, however, always been a keen amateur interest in receiver construction; this was particularly marked in the early days when a simple receiver with no thermionic valve and only a 'catswhisker' (crystal) detector was often adequate for use with headphones. A typical circuit arrangement of such a type is shown in Fig. 50.11. The addition of even one valve permitted a loudspeaker to be used. Loudspeakers using a conical metal diaphragm, vibrated by a small magnetic

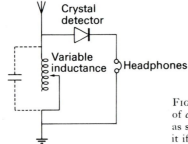

FIG. 50.11. A typical circuit arrangement of a simple 'wireless set' of c. 1923. It was generally unnecessary to add a physical capacitor as shown; self-capacitance of the inductor was sufficient to resonate it if suitably designed.

reed in the field of a coil through which passed the audio current from the radio receiver, became available from 1920; the horn loudspeaker followed very quickly. The performance of studio microphones, headphones, and loudspeakers, in terms of frequency response and non-linear distortion, was rather poor at first; constant research and development led to the condenser microphone and moving-coil speaker and eventually to the superb quality required by 'hi-fi' (high-fidelity) enthusiasts.

Developments in broadcasting. The range of the medium-wave transmitters which were first set up, with wavelengths in the range 300–500 m and powers of about 3 kW, was not reliably more than about 40 km. In Britain, 'relay stations' were therefore set up to transmit programmes, received from the main stations, in limited local areas outside the effective range of the main stations. Many countries, including the U.S.A., relied entirely on medium-wave broadcasting. but in some European countries long-wave transmitters were set up with higher powers and the ability to give good coverage of a whole country. The British long-wave station at Daventry, with a wavelength of about 1·5 km and a power of 25 kW, opened in 1925, was the first of these.

The use of relay stations in Britain, and the frequent need for all stations to transmit the same programme, led to the development of a line network to carry programmes from one centre to another. At first, ordinary telephone lines were used, but to ensure acceptable technical quality only open-wire lines could be used, the frequency response of loaded cable being too restricted. Special amplifiers were used, and national networks grew up. As the use of cables with amplifiers became more general for telephony, the provision of special circuits for programme material within telephone cables became common. This started, it is believed, in Denmark and some other European countries about 1927, and in Britain in 1931, when four pairs in the centre of a new London–Birmingham cable were separately screened to prevent interference, and very lightly loaded (15 mH coils at intervals of about 3 km) to give a good frequency response up to almost 8000 Hz. Various means of providing even higher quality were introduced in later years.

An important development in broadcasting, introduced in the mid-1920s, was the use of short-wave transmission (wavelengths in the range 10–100 m) which could be directional if desired, and with quite modest powers of perhaps 10 kW could attain ranges of many thousands of kilometres, relying on reflection from ionized layers in the upper atmosphere.

The development of broadcasting on even shorter wavelengths of 1–10 m (the so-called VHF or very-high-frequency range, 30–300 MHz) started after the Second World War. The object here was not to transmit over a long range, but to provide a better coverage of a region with high-quality reception. This was achieved largely because of the use of frequency modulation (F.M.). In this process the audio signal is carried by variations in the frequency, not the amplitude, of the radiated signal. It is thus relatively unaffected by variations in propagation; it is also less susceptible to interference. Because it requires a much wider bandwidth in the transmitted signal it is not a suitable method of modulation for transmission at lower frequencies, that is, on longer wavelengths.

An important aspect of broadcasting technology is the design of studios and the technical control of programmes. To obtain suitable acoustic performance of studios for different types of programme and to arrange the adjustment and mixing of the signals from arrays of microphones is a highly specialized matter which has been the subject of much research and experiment.

Developments in receivers. In general appearance radio receivers changed considerably in the decades after 1920, but in general principle there were few significant changes. The two most important were probably the introduction of the superheterodyne system of reception, which provided greatly increased selectivity, and the use of automatic volume control.

We have already described the principle of the superheterodyne system (p. 1237). In broadcast-radio receivers it came into use in the early 1930s. The intermediate frequency (I.F.) is usually set at 465 kHz, so that high selectivity can be obtained by fixed and precisely adjusted tuning at this frequency. To tune in to a signal at, say, 1000 kHz, the local oscillator is set at 1465 kHz, so that the image frequency—that is, the frequency which can also enter the I.F. stages along with the wanted signal—is 1930 kHz, which is within the ordinary radio band. It is therefore usual to have some variable tuning, which need not be very sharp, in the amplifier stages which precede the frequency-changer; this is conveniently 'ganged' to the oscillator-frequency control, thus permitting single-knob tuning. Superheterodyne receivers were, of course, considerably more complex than the older 'straight' receivers, and used more valves, typically six or seven, although in Britain and a few other countries several valve units were often combined in the one envelope structure with a common heater.

Automatic volume control also came into use in the early 1930s; it was a system whereby a direct voltage proportional to the amplitude of the carrier signal at the output of the I.F. stage was used to control the gain of the amplifying valves, thus greatly reducing the variations in the output of the receiver when the input signal fluctuated owing to fading, etc. Its operation depended on the 'variable-mu' valve, introduced in the late 1920s; this is a thermionic valve in which the grid is designed with unequal spacing of the mesh-wires so that the negative-grid characteristic of the valve is greatly prolonged along the negative voltage axis. By this means the amplification of the valve is gradually reduced as the grid bias is made more negative. When the direct control voltage, mentioned above, is fed negatively to the grids of the several valves in the receiver, their overall amplification is reduced by a factor many times greater than that by which the output has increased. Thus a hundredfold fluctuation of amplitude in the input leads to a fluctuation of audio output of perhaps only two or three times. The superheterodyne and automatic volume control methods survived into the 1970s, merely with the replacement of thermionic valves by transistors.

VIII. TELEVISION [23]

Origins. The desire to transmit pictures rapidly to a distant place by some electric-telegraphic method was evinced almost from the beginning of electric telegraphy. As early as 1850, F. C. Bakewell (Britain) constructed a system which could transmit hand-written messages (and therefore presumably also line drawings) written in non-conducting ink on a metal plate which was then scanned by a series of styluses each connected in an electric circuit. At the receiving end the currents in each stylus-circuit (directly, or through relays and a local circuit) caused marks on a rotating drum covered with chemically prepared paper; the original message or picture was thus reproduced by white lines. There were several other developments of this idea, and a public picture-transmission service existed in France as early as 1863.

Methods of this kind could not deal with pictures other than line drawings. For transmitting pictures with tones, something having an electrical response dependent on light intensity was needed. When Willoughby Smith (Britain) discovered in 1873 the light-sensitive property of selenium, by which its conductivity was increased when light fell on it, it seemed that the necessary device was at hand, and many proposals for picture transmission were put forward, notably by M. Senlacq (France) in 1878; W. E. Ayrton and J. Perry (Britain) in 1880; G. Carey (U.S.A.) in 1880; and Shelford Bidwell (Britain) in 1881. In some schemes the picture was projected on to a mosaic of selenium

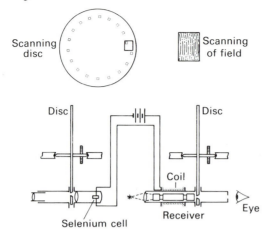

Scanning disc

Scanning of field

Disc   Disc

Coil

Selenium cell

Receiver   Eye

FIG. 50.12. Nipkow's patent, 1884; a redrawing of the diagram published in the original patent specification showing his scanning disc with apertures on a spiral track. A selenium cell was proposed as the light-sensitive element at the transmitter, while rotation of the plane of polarization in a magnetic field was proposed as the light-control at the receiver.

cells, each connected by a separate wire to the receiver (which might be of the electrochemical type); others used the scanning of the picture by a single selenium cell, the transmission over one telegraph line of the sequence of signals corresponding to each scan, and a receiver presumably synchronized. P. Nipkow's scheme of 1884 used a method of scanning that remained important for a long time: viz, a large rotating disc with a spiral series of small holes in it (see Fig. 50.12). Mirror-drum scanning was also proposed at about this time.

It became apparent during these years that selenium had a fundamental limitation to its suitability for picture transmission; its response to variations of light intensity was too slow for there to be any possibility of its serving for the transmission of moving pictures. While it remained a suitable material for the slow transmission of still pictures over telegraph and telephone lines, and was indeed widely used for this purpose as late as 1930–40, it clearly had no future for television. The development of television lapsed for a couple of decades, until the possibilities of the cathode-ray tube became evident in about 1907–11.

The cathode-ray tube had been introduced in 1897. The idea of using it as the means of reproducing the picture at the receiving end was due to B. Rosing (Russia) in 1907, but he still used mechanical devices for scanning at the transmitter, with a photocell of some kind. A. A. Campbell Swinton (Britain) in 1908 specified the nature of a successful television system in terms of cathode-ray tubes at transmitter and receiver:

... two beams of kathode rays (one at the transmitting and one at the receiving station) synchronously deflected by the varying fields of two electromagnets placed at right angles to one another and energized by two alternating electric currents of widely different frequencies, so that the moving extremities of the two beams are caused to sweep synchronously over the whole of the required surfaces within one-tenth of a second necessary to take advantage of visual persistence . . .

The real difficulties lie in devising an efficient transmitter which, under the influence of light and shade, shall sufficiently vary the transmitted electric current . . . and further in making this transmitter sufficiently rapid in its action to respond to the 160 000 variations per second that are necessary as a minimum.

The transmitter, he proposed three years later, should have a special cathode-ray tube with a mosaic screen of photoelectric elements on which an image of the scene to be transmitted was projected, and the consequent charges stored on the elements were scanned by, and modulated the current in, the cathode-ray beam. This quite accurately describes the modern television system in its basic principles, but could not be implemented with the technology of 1911, as Campbell Swinton took care to explain.

It was during this period at the beginning of the twentieth century that photoelectric (as opposed to photoconductive) cells were developed; instead of varying their conductivity under the influence of light, they generated a voltage or current, and proved to be much faster in operation, thus permitting fast scanning.

Practical systems: the low-definition interlude. In the mid-1920s determined efforts to launch television were made by a number of workers, especially D. von Mihály (Hungary); C. F. Jenkins (U.S.A.); H. Ives (U.S.A.: Bell Telephone Laboratories); and J. L. Baird (Britain). Of these, the last-mentioned attracted most attention. Starting work in 1923, he gave frequent public demonstrations of his sytem from 1925 onwards. He used a Nipkow disc, with lenses in the holes, for scanning the scene, which had to be very brightly lit. The picture had 30-line scanning at five frames a second. At the receiver another Nipkow disc, driven in synchronism with the transmitter, rotated between the observer's eye and a neon lamp modulated in brightness in proportion to the current from the photocell at the transmitter. This was, of course, now the era of electronics, and Baird used carrier waves and valve amplifiers as necessary. Although the picture was small (about 5 cm by 4 cm) and dull, and flickered badly, it was just possible to recognize faces.

Improvements came gradually, including the flying-spot scanning system, in which the scene was illuminated by an intense spot of light caused, by a revolving mirror-drum, to scan the scene in 30 vertical lines; and in 1929 the British Broadcasting Corporation allowed Baird's company to start public television broadcasts, still with 30-line scanning but now at 12·5 frames a second; in 1932 the B.B.C. took over the broadcasts themselves. Suitable receivers were marketed from 1930. The service continued until 1935.

Baird's work, more than that of anyone else, showed that television had a future worth working for; but it also showed that the future did not lie with his system. Much higher definition was essential for success, and this could not be obtained satisfactorily, if at all, by mechanical scanning. Campbell Swinton's proposals were now technologically realizable and it was in this direction that development took place.

Practical systems: the high-definition era. From about 1931 the development of high-definition television was aided by a number of important technological advances; it is also arguable that these advances were stimulated by the desire for good television. Some developments proved to be mere interludes, others led directly to post-1950 television practice. The more significant of the advances were four in number.

(i) The improvement of cathode-ray tubes from the older 'gas-focused' tubes where the focus could not be preserved over a range of intensity, to the high-vacuum type with electrostatic focusing.

(ii) The development of electronic circuits as 'time-bases', that is, circuits which generated an output voltage which in each cycle varied linearly from one value to another and then returned rapidly—the 'fly-back'—to the first. Applied to the new cathode-ray tubes these circuits provided the voltage waveform required to scan the beam over the face of the tube: one time-base for the horizontal scan and one for the vertical scan. The time-bases at the receiver could be synchronized with those at the transmitter by the transmission of synchronizing pulses at the start of each cycle.

(iii) The development of a transmitting-type cathode-ray tube (as specified by Campbell Swinton in 1911) by V. K. Zworykin (U.S.A.) from 1925 onwards, and first put forward publicly in 1933. Called the 'iconoscope', later developed to the much more sensitive 'image orthicon', it had a mosaic of photoelectric elements which stored charge produced by the incident light until scanned by the cathode-ray beam.

(iv) The development, a few years later, by J. D. McGee and others of the British E.M.I. Company, of the 'emitron', a device with the same functions as the iconoscope, but somewhat more sensitive. Both these types of tube compared well in sensitivity with photographic film used under the same conditions.

With these developments, picture definition improved rapidly; by 1935

E.M.I. was able to offer the B.B.C. a television system with 405 lines per frame, 50 frames a second, with alternate frames interlaced. This was adopted as standard in Britain, but then the Second World War interrupted public television services in most countries. In America and in other countries in Europe progress was similar, although uniform standards and international television were not provided until after 1950.

Some of the interesting interludes to which reference was made earlier deserve further mention.

(i) The use of velocity modulation. Before the new cathode-ray tubes were developed with their suitability for varying the light intensity on the receiver screen by varying (or 'modulating') the intensity of the cathode-ray beam, the idea of obtaining varying illumination on the screen by varying the speed of scan of the beam was developed by L. H. Bedford and O. S. Puckle of the British Cossor Company. Naturally, the same velocity variations had to be applied at the transmitting tube.

(ii) The use of intermediate film. The Baird Company adopted a 240-line standard when they abandoned the original mechanical system, and developed a flying-spot scanner suitable for scanning 35-mm film. When a live programme was to be transmitted, it was first filmed, the film was processed in about 60 seconds, and then immediately scanned for television transmission.

(iii) Large-screen television. A British firm, Scophony, believed that there was a demand for large-screen viewing, especially in cinemas. They developed a technically successful system, which by 1938 could give a picture about 4·5 m by 4 m with the B.B.C. standard 405-line definition. The demand was, however, only short-lived.

One of the effects of the new standards of picture definition was the need for a wide frequency bandwidth in transmission. The very rapid scanning of the picture gave rise to very rapid changes of voltage, which required a frequency range up to 4 MHz. To modulate this on to a medium-wave carrier of around 1 MHz was clearly quite impossible, and so radio frequencies around 40 MHz (wavelengths around 7 m) had to be used—the so-called VHF band. Later, after 1950, much higher frequencies also came into use—the UHF band.

Public television service. The phenomenal growth in demand for television and its world-wide provision is too obvious to need description here. The introduction of colour television and the superb technology of the production of both equipment and programmes are great achievements. But the importance of television lies not in these matters, but in the ambiguity of its effect on society. With nuclear technology it stands at the head of the league table of technological developments of greatest importance to mankind. Like nuclear technology, television can have vast beneficent influences on life—in its case these include education, entertainment, and the raising of moral and material standards—but also like nuclear technology, it can destroy—in its case the soul and spirit of man. It needs just as careful handling as nuclear weapons, but unfortunately its dangers are more subtle, insidious, and sinister.

IX. SOUND RECORDING AND REPRODUCTION

Origins. Undoubtedly sound recording and reproduction has for over half a century been a part of electrical communications; in contrast, the first half-century of the art had practically no connection with electricity.

Since reproduction of any sound recorded is an essential feature of any useful system, the beginning of the art may be taken as 1877; however, the idea of recording sound waves on a solid medium covered with lamp-black, by means of lateral undulations of a line, is attributable to L. Scott, who described his 'phonautograph' in 1856. In 1877, C. Cros (France) described a system in which the recording was to be made by Scott's method on a disc with spiral traverse, from which a steel copy was to be made by photoetching; this could be used for reproduction by a stylus coupled to a diaphragm. In the same year, T. A. Edison (U.S.A.) made his 'phonograph' (Fig. 50.13), using metal foil fastened to a rotating cylinder to record sound waves by variation of the depth of impression—the 'hill-and-dale' method; recording and reproduction used the same stylus and diaphragm.

During the subsequent fifty years the purely acoustic (or mechanical) system made some progress. The term 'gramophone' was introduced by E. Berliner (U.S.A.) in 1887; he soon introduced the mass production of disc records from a permanent master with lateral undulations on a spiral groove, the system which became standard thereafter.

Disc recording in the electronic era. The availability of electronic amplifiers in the 1920s meant that voice power was no longer necessary for cutting the master record. A microphone of good quality could be used, generating very little power. Amplifiers provided the power for cutting. This method of 'electrical recording' was used from about 1926. With other acoustical improvements, the frequency range of the recording was improved to 100–5000 Hz. Electromagnetic 'pickups', converting the vibrations of the stylus (or

FIG. 50.13. Edison's phonograph, 1877.

'needle') into electrical signals for amplification and use with a loudspeaker, quickly followed. They were rather heavy: about 100 g. In the late 1930s, 'crystal' pickups, of about 25 g weight using piezoelectric elements, became available; by 1950 effective masses of only a few grammes were achieved. This was important for the long playing (LP) type of record that was introduced just before 1950. With a playing speed of $33\frac{1}{3}$ rev/min instead of the 78 rev/min which had been standard for so long, they achieved not only long playing times (20 minutes or more) but also much higher quality of reproduction. The 'hi-fi' age had arrived.

In order to reproduce the spatial effects of music, especially when played by large orchestras spread over a large area of a hall, stereophonic recording and reproduction had been considered from the 1920s onwards. Using two channels (from two suitably placed microphones), techniques largely due to A. D. Blumlein (Britain) for recording and reproduction using a single groove were developed before 1950, but were not generally available until after that date.

Film recording. Early 'talkies', or motion pictures with synchronized sound, introduced in 1927, used disc recording for the sound (Ch. 53). The complications of synchronizing the film and the sound led to the development of direct recording of the sound on a narrow track at the edge of the picture film. For studio work it was found better to record the sound initially on a separate film. Optical systems were used at first. The earliest equipments used a deposit of variable density on the film, produced by modulating the intensity of a narrow light beam. Reproduction was by scanning the film with a narrow light beam, the modulation produced in it by transmission through the film being picked up by a photocell. Later, a variable area system was found preferable to the variable density system. Still later, around 1948, magnetic recording was applied to film work.

Magnetic recording. The recording of sound on magnetized tape or wire came into general use only a few years before 1950, but its history is much longer. The idea was first introduced in a practical form by V. Poulsen (Denmark) in 1897–8. His 'telegraphon' used a steel wire wound spirally on a drum, with a magnetic recording and reading head traversing longitudinally as the drum rotated. The sound to be recorded was converted by a microphone into an electrical current which, flowing through a coil in the magnetic head, varied the magnetization of the wire and was thus recorded until wiped out by demagnetization.

Development of magnetic recording was slow until, in the 1940s, a new magnetic medium was produced: a flexible plastic tape coated with fine magnetic particles. Good dynamic and frequency response became possible and progress became rapid. Since then tape recorders have become commonplace for entertainment, research, and office purposes. Techniques have been developed to the point where even television picture signals, with a frequency range up to 4 MHz, are recorded on videotape.

Microphones. The purpose of a microphone is to convert the sound wave into an electrical signal of corresponding waveform. This it can do in one of two ways: either by generating an electrical signal directly, or by modulating a current or a voltage, or both, already existing so that the amplitude variations of the current or voltage follow the variations of instantaneous amplitude of the sound. The latter method is the more powerful and, as seen under the heading 'Telephony', is the one almost universally used in telephone systems, where carbon-granule microphones are used. In these, the sound pressure varies the contact resistance through a cell of close-packed hard-carbon particles and thus varies the line current. This provides a powerful microphone giving effectively a high amplification, but it is noisy and unsteady. It is difficult to use this type of microphone for high-fidelity work, where electrostatic or capacitance microphones came into use before 1920. In this kind of microphone, the diaphragm forms one plate of a capacitor, the other plate being the solid back-plate, with a spacing of perhaps 2×10^{-5} m. A static voltage, applied between the two plates, is therefore modulated as the diaphragm vibrates under the varying sound pressure.

The class of microphone which generates an electrical signal directly from the sound wave is represented by the electromagnetic microphone which Bell used in 1876, which was thereafter little-used as a microphone but was universally used in reverse as a telephone receiver; by the moving-coil and ribbon microphones, also electromagnetic; and by the piezo-electric microphone which came into use for special purposes in the 1930s.

Loudspeakers. In very general terms, loudspeakers are based on devices for converting electrical signals back into sound waves, which are merely those used in microphones in reverse. The carbon-granule microphone is not reversible in this way, but most other types are. These devices are coupled to a sound-radiator, typically a paper cone, but in the early years of radio broadcasting and electrical gramophones, more usually a metal horn. The acoustical problems of loudspeakers have always given great difficulty, and the contribution of mathematical theory in this field has been large. The performance of early loudspeakers was very poor, but by 1950 'high fidelity' was commercially achievable.

X. SIGNIFICANT TRENDS DISCERNABLE BY 1950

During and after the Second World War progress in electrical communication was rapid, and trends for the future became apparent. The story of their development belongs to the post-1950 period, but some of them, not discussed elsewhere in this work, must be mentioned here [24].

The development of radar stimulated the opening up of the frequency ranges above 300 MHz, generally known as the microwave region, where wavelengths are below 1 m. In this region there are many attractions for communications. Aerials can be highly directive and efficient for point-to-point communication; propagation can be along lines of sight and relatively free from fading and interference over distances of, say, 50 km; long links can be built up by using intermediate relay stations; and very wide bandwidth can be available, for example, 100 MHz when the radio frequency is, say, 6000 MHz. This gives spectrum space not only for the thousands of telephone channels required on major inter-urban links by 1950, but also for television transmission links. The further development of world-wide communication by microwaves reflected or relayed from artificial satellites in space, although not begun until after 1950, was foreseen as early as 1945 [25].

The growing importance of pulse transmission, using pulses shorter by several orders than the conventional telegraph signal elements, heralded the possibilities of time-division-multiplex systems and data-transmission systems, which by 1960 were already being accepted as the communication systems of the future.

Perhaps the most spectacular changes of the post-1950 era have been associated with the replacement of the thermionic valve by the transistor (Ch. 46) as the basis of what are now called 'active' circuits and systems. The trend was hardly noticeable in 1950, for the transistor was then only two years old as a commercial device.

REFERENCES

[1] HOUNSHELL, D. A. *Technology and Culture*, **16**, 133 (1975).

[2] HEAVISIDE, O. *Electrician*, **18**, 302 (1887).

[3] TUCKER, D. G. *Proceedings of the Institution of Electrical Engineers*, **123**, 561 (1976).

[4] SUSSKIND, C. *I.E.E.E. Spectrum*, **5**, 90, August (1968); **5**, 57, December (1968); **6**, 69, April (1969); **6**, 66, August (1969).

[5] RATCLIFFE, J. A. *Electronics and Power*, **20**, 320 (1974).

[6] TUCKER, D. G. *Radio and Electronic Engineer*, **42**, 69 (1972).

[7] GHERARDI, B. and JEWETT, F. B., *Transactions of the American Institution of Electrical Engineers*, **38**, 1287 (1919).

[8] TUCKER, D. G. *Radio and Electronic Engineer*, **41**, 43 (1971).

[9] TUCKER, D. G. *Radio and Electronic Engineer*, **40**, 33 (1970).

[10] BLACK, H. S. *Bell System Technical Journal*, **13**, 1 (1934).

[11] BRITTAIN, J. E. *Technology and Culture*, **11**, 36 (1970).

[12] BLONDEL, A. *Mémoires du Côngrès de l'Association française à Angers*, 538 (1903).
——. *Compte rendu hebdomadaire des séances de l'Acadamie des sciences, Paris*, **147**, 673 (1908).

[13] SCOWEN, F. *Transactions of the Newcomen Society*, **47**, 35 (1977).
FLOWERS, T. H. *Exchange systems*. Wiley, London (1976).

[14] WILLIAMS, M. B. and IRELAND, J. C. *Electronics and Power*, **22,** 173 (1976).

[15] SHANNON, C. E. *Bell System Technical Journal*, **27,** 379 and 623 (1948).

[16] JOHNSON, J. B. *Physical Review*, **32**, 97 (1928).

[17] NYQUIST, H. *Bell System Technical Journal*, **3**, 324 (1924).

[18] HARTLEY, R. V. L. *Bell System Technical Journal*, **7**, 535 (1928).

[19] NICHOLLS, H. W. *Journal of the Institution of Electrical Engineers*, **61**, 812 (1922–3).

[20] OSWALD, A. A. and DELORAINE, E. M. *Electrician*, **96**, 572 and 666 (1926).

[21] DRYBROUGH, D. A. S. *Proceedings of the Institution of Electrical Engineers*, **122**, 953 (1975).

[22] BRINKLEY, J. R. *Radio and Electronic Engineer*, **45**, 551 (1975).

[23] GARRATT, G. R. M. and MUMFORD, A. H. *Proceedings of the Institution of Electrical Engineers*, **99**, Part 3A 25 (1952).
[24] HALSEY, R. J. *Engineering*, **184**, 432 (1957).
[25] CLARKE, A. C. *Wireless World*, **51**, 305 (1945).

BIBLIOGRAPHY

BLACK, H. S. *Modulation theory*. Van Nostrand, New York (1953).

FAHIE, J. J. *A history of wireless telegraphy, 1838–1899*. Blackwood, Edinburgh and London (1899).

50th anniversary number of *Proceedings of the Institute of Radio Engineers* (1962).

HEAVISIDE, O. *Electrical papers*. Macmillan, London (1892).

HUNT, F. V. *Electroacoustics*. Wiley, New York (1954).

JOLLY, W. P. *Marconi: a biography*. Constable, London (1972).

MARLAND, E. A. *Early electrical communication*. Abelard–Schuman, London (1964).

MONCEL, COUNT DU. *The telephone, the microphone and the phonograph*. Kegan Paul, Trench and Co., London (1884).

PALMER, L. S. *Wireless principles and practice*. Longmans Green, London (1928).

PAWLEY, E. L. E. *B.B.C. engineering, 1922–1972*. British Broadcasting Corporation Publications, London (1972).

POCOCK, R. F. and GARRATT, G. R. M. *The origins of maritime radio*. H.M.S.O., London (1972).

RHODES, F. L. *Beginnings of telephony*. Harper, New York (1929).

RUHMER, E. *Wireless telephony*. Crosby Lockwood, London (1908). [First published in German, 1907.]

SNEL, D. A. *Magnetic sound recording*. Philips, Eindhoven (1958).

STURMEY, S. G. *The economic development of radio*, Duckworth, London (1958).

Symposium on the trans-atlantic telephone cable, special volume of the *Proceedings of the Institution of Electrical Engineers*, **104,** Part B, Supplement 4 (1957).

Transistors—the first 25 years, 1948–1973. Special volume of *Radio and Electronic Engineer* (1973).

51

PRINTING

JAMES MORAN

B Y the end of the nineteenth century the technique of relief printing had reached its zenith, at a point where photography was just beginning to emerge in an ancillary role (Vol. V, Ch. 29). The technical history of the first fifty years of the twentieth century is therefore one of extension of nineteenth-century methods, co-existing with a gradual application of photographic techniques. Because of this the period may now be seen as the final flowering of conventional relief printing and of metal type; but only a few could even faintly see what lay ahead in film, electronics, and computer work which were to transform radically the face of printing in the last two decades of the twentieth century.

The three main printing processes, relief, intaglio, and planographic had all by 1900 established their more advanced forms: rotary letterpress, photogravure, and metal plate lithography—but in the first half of the new century letterpress was dominant (see explanatory note (1)).[1] Associated with it was the photo-mechanical method of making relief printing plates. Nevertheless, there was a gradual development of photogravure and photolithography. Although photography had thus been harnessed to all processes, the setting of text was almost entirely from metal type, and only just as the half-century was coming to an end did small advances in photographic composition take place.

For the fifty years under survey the great mass of printing designed to be read, rather than merely looked at, was produced by letterpress and from type. The significant changes after 1900 were in the means of setting type and in the size and speed of printing presses. It was the era of the composing machine, which in the 1920s and 1930s coincidentally ushered in a typographical renaissance.

By the turn of the century, process engraving—the etching of relief metal blocks from line negatives—was known, but the transformation of photo-

---

[1] For the convenience of the reader certain technical terms commonly used in the printing industry are defined in explanatory notes at the end of this chapter.

graphs into so-called halftone blocks (explanatory note (2)) was not satisfactorily resolved until the development of the Levy halftone screen in Philadelphia in the 1890s. The screen was made from two sheets of glass automatically engraved with parallel lines, which were etched and filled with black pigment, the two plates being bound together at an angle of 90°. When this screen was interposed between the sensitive plate in the camera and the original photograph the effect was to translate the photograph into dots; on the final block the heavier the concentration of dots the darker was the printed result. The *Daily Mirror*, when it was founded in London in 1904, was the first daily newspaper to be illustrated exclusively from mechanically made blocks.

The substitution of metal plates for stone in lithography had been proposed at an early stage, and by 1860 zinc plates were being used. As early as 1891 aluminium was also being considered as a lithographic printing metal, and by 1904 machines were in being for printing from such plates. But the idea of using the offset process for printing on paper was some four years away. In Nutley, New Jersey, Ira Rubel re-discovered, by accident, the advantages of indirect printing. This had been known for fifty years in tinplate printing, having originally been patented by Robert Barclay in 1875. The hard, unsympathetic printing surface was replaced by a resilient one of rubber on to which the image was impressed or 'set-off' and from which it was transferred to the tin plate and later to paper (explanatory note (3)). Owing to Rubel's death his machine was not continued, and the American firm of Harris and the British one of George Mann and Co. moved into the making of rotary offset lithographic presses. They were followed by other firms in the U.S.A., Britain, and Germany. At Leipzig, in 1912, VOMAG built the first web-fed offset press, which produced at a rate of up to 7500 impressions an hour. Printing from stone began to die out except for artistic work.

A simplified version of the offset litho process was launched in Germany in 1923 when the first 'small offset' press—the Rotaprint—was made in Berlin. An agency was formed in Britain and the machine gradually improved, so that it was no longer merely a rival to the office duplicator, but one which could be used for commercial printing on a larger scale. An American machine—the Multilith—introduced a competitive spirit, but it was not until after the Second World War that small offset litho began to have a significant effect. Then, in conjunction with text produced on special typewriters, the machine began cutting into the markets of the conventional printer, who having regarded the small offsets as office machines now realized how they could be used for·jobbing and specialized work, and began to instal them himself.

Another technical advance in offset lithography was the step-and-repeat machine for multiple copying on offset plates, first used in New York in 1920. The machine considerably encouraged the printing of labels and similar smaller pieces of printing in the packaging field.

Most lithographic printers during this period prepared their own plates, but the popularity of small offset machines led to the introduction of presensitized plates. Early experiments were made by Kalle of Wiesbaden in 1938, who introduced the first diazo-coated presensitized plate nine years later. In the meantime experiments had been going on in the U.S.A., and by 1950 a number of firms were moving into this new market (explanatory note (4)).

I. THE TYPEWRITER

The typewriter, as an invention, dates back to at least the early nineteenth century, but manufacture did not start until 1873 when the Scholes and Glidden machine was produced in the Remington factory in New York. Thereafter typewriters were developed by a wide variety of firms (some 400 eventually) in different parts of the world. It was not, however, until the first decade of the twentieth century that the demand became really significant. Techniques differed from machine to machine, but eventually the 'front strike' machine with a four-bank keyboard, based on the 'Qwerty' arrangement of keys, finally dominated the market.

The typewritten message could be reproduced by lithography but since the result was clearly from a typewritten original it was unable to compete with printing from type, particularly if there was a poor impression from a cheap or worn ribbon. But there were other drawbacks. Only one typeface could be used, and the single-spacing principle—which allows the same space for all characters regardless of their width—and the fact that the lines did not justify, did not appeal (explanatory note (5)).

James Hammond from 1881 visualized a typewriter on which type could be changed and which had a system of uniform impression which did not depend on the force with which keys were struck. After Hammond's death, Ralph C. Coxhead in the 1930s made those changes which saw the machine emerge as the world's first 'cold composing machine', named the VariTyper. By 1933 the changeable type system was adopted; in 1934 the carbon ribbon was added to give the type a better impression; in 1937 automatic justification enabled margins to be squared up as in conventional typesetting; and in 1947 differential spacing at last overcame the objection to the typewriter single-spacing principle.

Electric typewriters have a history going back to 1871, but in 1923 an American firm, North Eastern Appliances Co. began their manufacture. For ten years few electric typewriters were in use but the firm which ultimately merged with the North Eastern Appliances Co.—International Business Machines—invested a million dollars in the making of a safe electric typewriter. In 1941 IBM also went into research to overcome some of the drawbacks of the conventional typewriter, producing a mechanism which would measure each alphabetical character in units. In 1944 they announced the first IBM Executive typewriter with proportional spacing. Owing to the war it was not marketed until 1946. The path was laid for the later development: the IBM 'Selectric' typewriter, with its interchangeable 'golf-ball' printing head, but this did not occur until 1961.

II. PHOTOGRAVURE

Modern photogravure derives from the development by Karl Klic of earlier work which entailed the copying of image and screen on a carbon tissue; transferring to a cylindrical surface; etching the latter through the layer; and printing by the rotary method, using a thinly flowing liquid ink and removing the surplus with a doctor-blade knife. In 1895, Klic suggested the formation of the Rembrandt Intaglio Printing Company to the Storey Brothers of Lancaster (calico printers). They used reel-fed textile gravure presses for the production of art prints.

The Rembrandt company managed to maintain a monopoly for some ten years, and it was nearly another ten years before effective competition emerged. Presses for printing on paper were made and photogravure was used to print art reproductions, wallpaper, postage stamps, and eventually journals. On Easter Day, 1910, the *Freiburger Zeitung* appeared with two special sections, which carried gravure pictures on the pages. These had taken a long time to prepare and the lengthy preparatory work on copper cylinders was for a long time a drawback in producing a topical newspaper by photogravure. In fact, the printing of the *Freiburger Zeitung* was on a hybrid press: a gravure press connected with a newspaper letterpress machine. In England, the *Southend Standard* similarly printed from 1913 on a gravure press attached to a newspaper press.

The *Illustrated London News*, on the other hand, produced from 1913, a magazine in gravure, in which pictures and text were printed simultaneously.

In the U.S.A., the first edition of the *New York Times* carrying a gravure supplement appeared on 5 April 1914 and then became a regular feature. By 1915, ten magazine printers and eight newspapers were running gravure departments. Large-scale photogravure arrived in Britain in the 1930s and was used for long run magazines. It remained a popular process and did not run into severe competition until the 1970s—outside the period of this review.

III. TYPESETTING

In 1900 the square-based Linotype (Vol. V, p. 686), invented by Ottmar Mergenthaler, was just giving way to the lighter 'star-based' model. Mergenthaler began working on a slug-casting machine as early as the 1870s, but not until 1885 was the independent matrix Linotype ready. Basically, the Linotype stores a large number of single matrices in a sloping magazine. These are released by keyboard action and assembled in words, separated by space bands. The completed justified line is brought to the orifice of a mould and then cast into a type-high 'slug', or solid bar of metal. For the next sixty years the Linotype was improved until it could set and cast fifteen newspaper lines a minute. There were other line-casting machines, but the only real rival to the Linotype was the Intertype, launched in 1913 and first installed at the New York *Journal of Commerce*.

The other machine which was to have, coincidentally, the greatest effect on typography was the Monotype, a single-type composer governed by a per-forated tape, itself punched by action of a keyboard. This had been invented by Talbot Lanston in 1887 but the modern concept was not launched until 1890 and put on the market in 1894. The Monotype machine consists of two units: the keyboard (Fig. 51.1) and the caster (Fig. 51.2). The perforated ribbon is used to control the caster, which carries a matrix case; this moves to different positions in accordance with the perforations, and molten metal is pumped into the appropriate matrix. Cast types are ejected singly and assembled in a channel until the line is completed. The first advanced model was installed by Cassell and Co. in London in 1900. Over the years refinements and developments brought the Monotype to a high standard of performance. There were rival machines which utilized the perforated ribbon but they did not succeed.

Although hand-setting of type for text continued until at least the First World War, from the 1920s onwards most text was set on one of these three machines—Linotype, Intertype, and Monotype—and if printing was to be by

FIG. 51.1. A battery of Monotype keyboards in the early 1920s.

FIG. 51.2. Monotype casters at work.

photogravure or lithography it was necessary to take a proof and photograph it first.

Although the private presses, following William Morris, had been producing their own typefaces, with a few commercial typefoundries following, the composing machine manufacturers had mainly concentrated on copying the types already produced by the typefoundries. A few of these, particularly American Type Founders, had, in the early part of the century, taken a step forward by bringing out new designs. When the composing machines began to offer new and attractive typefaces, the gradual decay of the typefounder set in. By 1950 the small number still in existence could not have survived by producing type alone; they had other business interests, including, for example, the making of matrices for composing machine manufacturers.

In 1913 the British Monotype Corporation brought out not only its Plantin but also Imprint, the first typeface specifically designed for a composing machine. But it was not until after the rigours of the First World War had passed that the various companies began to look out for historical models, and the 1920s and 1930s saw the issue of many of the famous text faces which were to improve the look of books and magazines. They were followed by a wide range of display faces, particularly from the German typefoundries. Up to 1940, with the amount of excellent typographical material available, there was a veritable typographical renaissance. Fortunately there were by this time printers who were able to take full advantage of the changes, and typography became an acceptable part of a printer's armoury. The word 'typographer' ceased to refer to a letterpress printer and took on the modern meaning of a planner of printed work.

Setting type by remote control had been envisaged as early as 1905 but it was not until 1928 that a successful device—the Teletypesetter—was first demonstrated in New York. Essentially the Teletypesetter is an electromagnetic device which operates linecasting machines by electrical impulses over telegraph wires. An example of typesetting by remote control was the apparatus installed in the House of Commons to send text of Parliamentary reports to *The Times* newspaper, but teletypesetting was also used internally to increase composing-room output. Linotype and Intertype machines were specially designed for teletypesetting.

In the early 1920s, the rising interest in offset litho printing led to requests to the composing-machine manufacturers and typefounders to produce special type so that printing could be in reverse, and thus save an operation in getting the transfer to the litho plate. Some typefounders responded, but found that the amount of business did not justify their efforts. The machine manufacturers said it showed want of intelligent anticipation to expect those who made type and process blocks to reverse their method of manufacture in order that a single process might be simplified. The 'intelligent anticipation' referred to in 1922 was to shine light through the blank portion of a well-printed sheet of transparent paper; but offset litho was really awaiting photocomposition.

IV. OFFSET PRINTING AND PHOTOCOMPOSITION

However, the printing industry was preoccupied with metal type during the first fifty years of the twentieth century and tended in the main to ignore the experiments which were being made to dispense with type for the composition of alphabetic characters. Nevertheless, the inventors were at work. It was not until 1946 that photocomposition became a commercial proposition, but the idea went back to 1876. From then onward a number of photocomposing devices were patented but none were completely successful.

The suggestions took a number of forms, utilizing white on black characters on strips of film, on glass discs, on keybars, and on the matrices of line-casting machines. This last idea was the one that was ultimately adopted as the basis of the first commercially successful machine just before the 1950s came to a close: the Intertype Fotosetter (Fig. 51.3). This was an adaptation of the Intertype hot-metal machine and used by the then well-known circulating matrix system. A negative character was inserted into the side of the matrix, which was known as a 'Fotomat'. The machine was an automatic photographic line-composing machine, producing justified composition in galley form directly on film or photographic paper in one operation. It was possible, by the operation of a dial which selected an appropriate lens, to produce enlarged or reduced type sizes without changing magazines. Two founts of Fotomats covered a range of sizes from 4 point to 36 point. Other photocomposing machines which were in the process of development came to fruition in the next two decades, but they are part of the technical history of the last half of the twentieth century.

By 1900 the flatbed cylinder printing machine had advanced to a high level of performance, but the desire for a completely automatic machine had not been fully met. In 1897 an automatic paper sheet feeder had been invented in the U.S.A. but it took many years for automatic feeding to become universal. By 1914 the first flatbed cylinder press was designed with an integrated feeder, employing a combination blast and suction device.

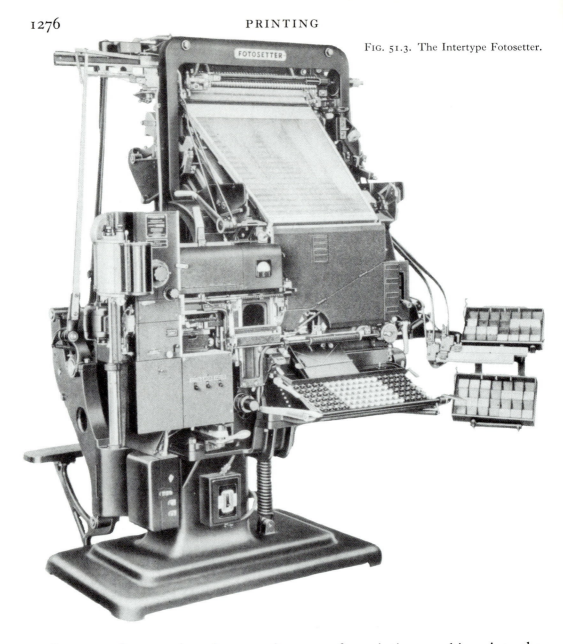

Fɪɢ. 51.3. The Intertype Fotosetter.

Steam engines continued to supply power for printing machines into the twentieth century, but gradually gave way to gas engines and then to electrical power. Static electricity caused sheets of paper to cling to metal and wood, but from 1910 static eliminators became available. The various problems arising from set-off—originally tackled with 'set-off' sheets and 'slip-sheets'—were from 1904 counteracted with anti-set sprays and specially formulated inks.

FIG. 51.4. The Goss Comet reel-fed flatbed press, *c.* 1910.

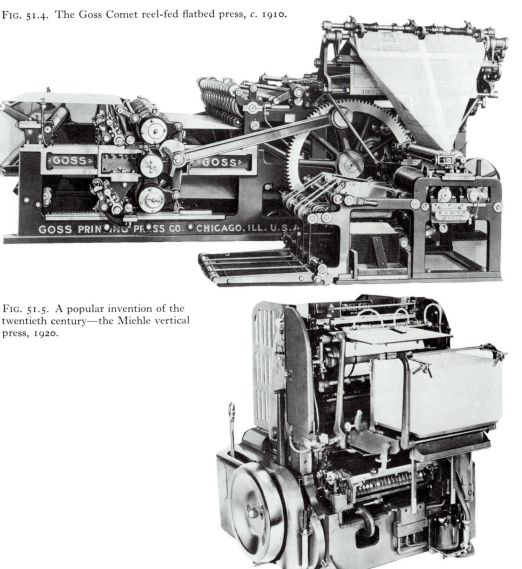

FIG. 51.5. A popular invention of the twentieth century—the Miehle vertical press, 1920.

One new invention in the field of cylinder presses was the vertical press—in effect a flatbed cylinder machine stood on end, with feeding and delivery carried out horizontally. Invented by Edward Cheshire, of Milwaukee, in 1920, it was made by the Miehle Company of Chicago, which was also responsible for one of the leading flatbed cylinder machines. By 1940 the Miehle Vertical (Fig. 51.5) could produce at the rate of 5000 impressions an hour.

The rotary letterpress printing machine developed most rapidly in newspaper production. Productivity was improved in two ways: by improving the working parts, and by multiplying the number of printing units. Rotary printing both developed and grew. The letterpress rotary machine consisted of revolving cylinders (one of which carried the printing surface) between which was fed a continuous reel of paper. On the printing cylinder was a curved stereotyped plate, which had been cast from a matrix known as a 'flong'. This was for some years a wet paste mixture into which a forme of type was pressed. Allowed to dry, it could then be curved into the requisite shape for the cylinder. During the early 1900s the dry flong was gradually adopted by newspapers. This was a pliable sheet made from paper pulp into which a type forme was pressed, after which it was used to cast a curved plate in an automatic casting box, invented by Henry Wise Wood in New York in 1900.

The expansion in output of the rotary press by increasing the number of printing units began in the U.S.A., and by 1902 the Hoe Octuple was printing from four reels, each four pages wide, with a running speed of 96000 an hour for four-, six-, or eight-page newspapers. Presses grew in length and in the number of decks in which printing units were arranged horizontally. In 1925 Hoe's 24-cylinder multicolour press was advertised as the world's largest newspaper press.

Later, from 1920, newspapers began to instal a multiple low construction press and folder unit all in one line on one floor level. Developments by both American and British manufacturers allowed the changing of a reel of paper while the press was running, and for tension to be applied to the web automatically. In 1927 the 'flying paster' came into operation, permitting the splice to be made while the press was at full speed.

The reel-fed rotary system applied from the beginning to photogravure, but in lithography the flatbed machine took some time to give way, first to the direct rotary machine, and then, by the 1920s, to the web-fed offset litho rotary, which began to be used for the printing of illustrated magazines, particularly in Germany.

Not all newspaper printers in the period under review needed large rotary presses, with their additional commitment to a stereotyping department. The small newspaper printer was not, however, unaware of the benefits of printing several formes up together, or of feeding from a reel of paper. The reel-fed flatbed press was the answer to this requirement, and was made from 1889 onwards when the Duplex was invented by Paul Cox of Battle Creek, Michigan. Competition was soon forthcoming and a number of manufacturers, British and American, brought out their machines. Perhaps the best known in Britain was the Cossar, which was developed in 1900. These presses continued to be used in the second half of the century but by then were being replaced by web offset litho presses, as local newspapers turned to the other printing process.

While photocomposition was obviously beneficial to lithographic and gravure printers its combination with photolithography stimulated advances in relief printing, the major one being the development of thin, flexible 'wraparound' relief printing plates, which could be made by process engravers from photo-set originals. But this development, like that of 'powderless etching', belong to the next decade, although its roots were in the 1930s and 1940s. Indeed, this applies to those other developments which were to make the 1970s the watershed between conventional printing techniques and the new processes based on scanning and electronic image forming. The pace of change so quickened that it is easy to understand how the period 1900–1950 has now entered into technical history.

EXPLANATORY NOTES

(1) *Relief*, or *letterpress*, refers to printing from raised surfaces so that ink is deposited only on these—printing from type or blocks, however made. *Intaglio* denotes printing from plates on which the image is incised or etched, surplus ink being wiped off, leaving the ink only in the engraved parts. *Photogravure* is a development in which, by the action of light, the etched image is divided by means of a screen into small cells which hold the ink. Surplus ink is scraped off by a flexible 'doctor' blade. *Planographic printing* is from level surfaces in which the parts to be printed accept ink while non-image areas reject it. The best known form is *lithography*, in which a greasy image is surrounded by a water-attracting area on a stone forme. Modern lithography is derived from metal formes or plates with photography used to place the image on the plate.

There are subdivisions into flat and rotary processes: in the first the printing forme is flat and in the second it is on a curved cylinder. Printing can be either direct or indirect. Paper supply can be either sheet or web (i.e. from a reel). Offset refers to indirect printing and mainly to lithography; so that web offset lithography, for example, is a method of indirect printing by planographic means on a machine fed from a reel of paper.

The offset technique could be applied to other processes, and the method of feeding the paper is not exclusive to one or other type of printing: web fed and sheet fed can apply to either rotary or flat-bed machines.

(2) According to William Gamble, editor of the *Penrose Annual*, in the early days of the process it was advertised as reproducing all the delicate half tones of photographs and thus was shortened to halftone process. An article, 'Wonderful process', by the Editor in *The Process Year Book* (later the *Penrose Annual*) 1901 describes the history of the halftone process.

(3) The complicated progress of Barclay's patent and the development of the offset press is dealt with by Alec Davis in 'Towards a history of tin-printing' (*Journal of the Printing Historical Society*, No. 8 (1972)). The word set-off or offset—the accidental transfer of ink from a freshly printed sheet to another—thus took on an additional meaning.

(4) See MERTLE, J. S. Presensitised lithographic printing plates, in *Penrose Annual*. Lund Humphries, London (1953).

(5) The word 'justification' has undergone change. In setting from individual types every line must be 'justified' or made the normal length and the last line in a paragraph containing perhaps not more than one word, must be justified equally with the full-length line with quadrats which fill up the line, but being lower than the type do not print. Typographers tended to use 'justification' to refer to lines of equal length, and with the coming of photocomposition this meaning has taken hold.

BIBLIOGRAPHY

BEECHING, WILFRED A. *Century of the typewriter*. Heinemann, London (1974).

GLAISTER, G. A. *Glossary of the book*. Allen and Unwin, London (1960).

LILIEN, OTTO M. *History of industrial gravure printing up to 1920*. Lund Humphries, London (1972).

MORAN, JAMES. *The composition of reading matter*. Ernest Benn, London (1965).

——. *Printing presses*. Faber and Faber, London (1973).

——. *Printing in the 20th century*. Northwood Publications, London (1974).

52

PHOTOGRAPHY

HELMUT GERNSHEIM

THE first sixty years after the introduction of photography on metal and paper saw a rapid evolution from the slow light-sensitive materials that the photographer had to prepare himself—which entailed exposures measured in minutes—to factory-produced dry plates on glass and film four hundred times faster. Cumbersome apparatus with accessories amounting to a hundredweight had been reduced to a camera loaded with film sufficient for a hundred exposures that almost fitted into the pocket (Vol. V, Ch. 30, Pt. I). By comparison with the early period the epoch-making inventions in the first half of the twentieth century were few. It was remarkable more for the progressive refinement of existing foundations than for the laying of new ones.

Modern photography started in 1880 with the mass production of fast gelatine dry plates; the introduction of hand cameras; and the possibility of enlarging the small negative on to fast bromide paper. With the Kodak, nine years later, there arrived the modern system of making a large number of exposures on a long band of celluloid film rolled up on a spool and inserted into the camera. The light-sensitive, but originally colour-blind, emulsion had been made sensitive to certain colours, and though in 1885 the term 'orthochromatic' (that is, reproducing the colours correctly) was prematurely applied, once the principle of colour sensitizing had been established it was only a question of time before the emulsion became panchromatic, that is sensitive to all spectral colours (1906).

In optics the ultimate degree of lens correction had been achieved in the anastigmat (1889), so that the photographer had at last a lens free from all aberrations. The next step lay in creating a greater lens opening or aperture to increase its speed. Thus all the basic elements of monochrome photography were firmly established by the turn of the century. X-rays had been discovered in 1895, but understanding of their numerous applications in medicine and dentistry was acquired only gradually in the early decades of this century (Ch. 54).

Even if the inventions that transformed the technical evolution of photography in the first five decades of the twentieth century seem less startling than those of the preceding six, they nevertheless provided the final and logical solution to a number of important problems that had engaged scientific minds for a long time. The twentieth century saw the production of panchromatic material; the introduction of colour photography; the establishment of miniature photography; and the Polaroid system of obtaining instant prints.

I. THE PRODUCTION OF PANCHROMATIC MATERIAL

The silver bromide–gelatine emulsion with which the negative material is coated underwent a number of considerable improvements with several aims: (*a*) extending the sensitivity of the emulsion to all colours of the spectrum (a precondition for colour photography and for the accurate reproduction of paintings); (*b*) increasing its light sensitivity (to reduce exposures under poor light conditions and to permit the photography of fast-moving objects); (*c*) reducing the size of the silver grain—a drawback of high-speed material; and (*d*) to find an equally transparent, but non-inflammable, film base to replace the highly inflammable cellulose nitrate.

Despite its name, the orthochromatic negative material which came on the market in 1885, and still manufactured in the 1970s, was—and is—oversensitive to blue light and largely insensitive to red. For most technical work these shortcomings do not make themselves felt; indeed, the steeper gradation of the negative image is often in fact preferred to one on softer panchromatic material. Moreover, the oversensitivity of the emulsion to blue light can easily be corrected by the use of a yellow filter, and orthochromatic film thus serves most purposes in the photography of landscapes, architecture, and sculpture. However, red is rendered too dark in the reproduction of paintings and considerable retouching on the negative is required to give a true tone rendering in monochrome.

By the addition of ethyl red Adolf Miethe and his assistant Arthur Traube, both of the Technical University of Berlin, succeeded in 1903 in extending the sensitivity of the orthochromatic emulsion to yellow and orange. Yet it was only after the new dyestuffs pinachrome and pinacynol had been discovered at the I.G. Farben works in 1905–6, by Ernst Koenig and Benno Homolka respectively, that the sensitivity of emulsions could be extended to red and infrared. The first truly panchromatic plates were placed on the market by Wratten and Wainwright Ltd., London, in 1906. The successful conclusion of Hermann Vogel's pioneer work on colour sensitizing, begun in 1873, at last made possible the correct reproduction of all colours in nature and art, and was an essential step in colour photography.

Stepping up the light-sensitivity, or speed, of the photographic material by cooking the emulsion at higher temperatures and for a longer period brought in its wake a coarsening of the silver grain through partial decomposition of the gelatine in which the silver is embedded. This put a serious check on miniature photography in the first six years of its existence (1925–32) for the 35-mm negative required a considerably greater magnification than the conventional negative sizes (then 6×9 cm and 9×12 cm). The problem caused much concern, but was eventually overcome by the action of special fine-grain developers, such as paraphenylenediamine, at a low temperature ($18°$ C) and over a comparatively long period (20 minutes). To facilitate the control of time and temperature of development special developing tanks came on the market in which the film lay spirally in grooves. By about 1932 leading manufacturers also introduced fine-grain film of a lower speed rating.

The increase of accidents in cinemas through overheating of the highly inflammable cellulose nitrate film base led to its replacement in about 1930 by non-inflammable cellulose acetate. This safety measure was also extended to the 35-mm cine-film used in miniature cameras and to roll film and cut film.

II. SENSITOMETRY

A vital factor in calculating the exposure is the degree of sensitivity or speed of the negative material used. To this end a standardized system of photo-sensitometry had to be established, as well as agreement among the various manufacturers of a country to apply it. In Britain the speed rating in force until 1960 was given in H & D numbers, so named after the founders of the first scientific method of photosensitometry, Ferdinand Hurter and Vero Charles Driffield. In 1890 they determined the speed of a photographic plate by exposing it to a series of lights of known intensities and measuring the densities obtained on development (the gamma curve).

On the Continent another system was introduced in 1894 by Julius Scheiner of Berlin. A plate was mounted behind a rotatable disc with numbered segments which were graduated in a certain ratio from light to dark and was exposed for one second to a standard candle flame at a distance of 1 m. The last number which was legible on the developed negative when placed on white paper indicated the speed of that negative emulsion. Each packet of plates or film was marked in Scheiner degrees until the system was replaced in 1936 by the *Deutsche Industrie Norm* (DIN) scale which added the figure ten to every Scheiner degree (15 Sch = 25 DIN).

In the U.S.A. the Weston scale was replaced in the 1930s by a norm established by the American Standards Association (ASA). In 1960 methods of speed measurement of photographic emulsions were internationally revised, and the main producer countries, Britain, Germany, Japan, and the U.S.A., agreed to mark thenceforward all negative material in ASA and DIN only, 80 ASA being equivalent to 20 DIN.

III. EXPOSURE METERS

The exposure time depends upon a number of factors—apart from the speed rating of the sensitive material—such as the light intensity, the focal length of the lens, and the aperture used. Apart from simple exposure tables and time-consuming calculators on which the exposure could be read off when all the data had been set, there had existed since 1880 more accurate instruments by which the actinic intensity of light was measured by the time (in seconds) needed to darken a strip of silver chloride paper to a given standard tint. By the First World War actinometers were gradually being superseded by visual or optical light meters in which the subject to be photographed was observed through a small tube held to the eye. It contained a blue glass with numbered gradations of tone from light to dark. From the last still-visible number the exposure could be read off when the instrument had been set for a number of known data. The first of these optical exposure meters had been introduced by C. P. Goerz in 1888.

The electrical conductivity of selenium, which was discovered in 1930, changes under the influence of light—a property that naturally invited utilization for photographic exposure meters. Weston in the U.S.A. and Gossen in Germany marketed the first photoelectric light meters based on selenite cells two years later. The Contaflex (1935) and the Contax III (1936) both of Zeiss Ikon manufacture, were the first and only cameras before the Second World War to incorporate a selenium exposure meter in the camera body.

After the Second World War several miniature cameras had built-in light meters, usually near the viewfinder window. They measure the light reflected from the subject, and incident light falling on the photocell therefore affects the accuracy of the reading. In fact, the only reliable measurement is that of the light passing through the lens to form the image. The first behind-the-lens exposure meter was incorporated in the Pentax Spotmatic introduced in 1964 by the Japanese manufacturer Asahi. Two highly sensitive cadmium sulphide sensors measure the light and activate an exposure pointer. Having pre-set the film and shutter speeds, the photographer has merely to adjust the diaphragm until the pointer is in a horizontal position and then expose. The behind-the-lens light measurement revolutionized camera design. Most high-class miniature cameras with interchangable lenses now incorporate this or a similar semi-automatic exposure-meter arrangement. The cheaper ones with fixed lenses continue to measure reflected light.

IV. SHUTTERS

The gelatine dry plate and the small negative sizes coming into vogue after 1880 reduced exposures to fractions of a second and called for quick-acting shutters of variable speeds. Such shutters were either in the form of concentric metal segments or revolving discs set by springs and released by a pneumatic bulb, or they were pneumatic guillotine or roller-blind shutters with speeds variable from 1 second to 1/100 second, according to the pneumatic pressure or spring tension. They were all fixed in front of the lens. After 1900, these unwieldy drop and flap shutters were superseded by diaphragm or sector shutters incorporated between the lens combinations, a form pioneered as a front-lens shutter by Bausch and Lomb of Rochester, New York, in 1888. The Compound and Koilos sector shutters introduced by Friedrich Deckel in 1902 and Alfred Gauthier in 1904 respectively proved superior to most and were fitted to most of the German lenses. The shutter speeds were controlled through air pistons. To achieve exposures down to 1/250 second Deckel of Munich adopted the gear-wheels of a watch mechanism for his Compur shutter (1912). This shutter was, and still is, almost universally fitted to the more expensive hand cameras from 1935 onwards with speeds down to 1/500 second. The cheaper brands of amateur cameras usually have the simpler Prontor shutter of Gauthier, limiting speeds to 1/200 second.

All press and miniature cameras requiring speeds down to 1/1000 second have a focal-plane shutter incorporated behind the lens. The focal-plane shutter with variable slit was invented by William England in 1861, long before a real need for high-speed shutters existed. It is often mistakenly ascribed to the German photographer Ottomar Anschütz, who used it for his studies of storks in flight in 1883 and included it in his camera patent of 1888. C. P. Goerz subsequently fitted the popular Goerz–Anschütz press camera with this shutter. The first British camera to have a focal-plane shutter was the Cambier Bolton, designed by the press photographer F. W. Mills and manufactured by W. Watson and Sons, London, in 1898. It was a single-lens reflex. Electricity entered the shutter industry in 1942, when Ilex introduced the first flash-synchronized shutter.

V. LENSES

Between 1900 and 1950 exposures were many times reduced not only by the constantly increased light-sensitivity of the negative material and the further reduction of negative formats requiring lenses of much shorter focal length, but by the gradually increased apertures of high-class lenses. While the original Dagor double anastigmat of 1893 had an aperture of f 6·8, the first Tessar lens of 1902 had an opening of f 4·5, and the Leica's Elmax in 1925 was f 3·5. The most powerful lens before the Second World War was the Ernostar of the Ermanox (1925) with f 1·8. Since then anastigmats with a maximum aperature of f 1·4, and even of f 1·2, have been designed, both Takumar lenses for the Asahi Pentax. Considering that each successively greater aperture opening halves the exposure of the next higher-rated stop number or smaller lens opening, and that the Tessar was already four times faster than the Dagor (because it jumped the f 5·6 rating which lies between f 4·5 and f 6·8), the Takumar f 1·4 lens is roughly 32 times faster than the Dagor, if used at full aperture. Actually its speed is even greater, for since about 1950 all lenses have been 'bloomed' or coated with a thin film of magnesium fluoride to eliminate flare caused by air-to-glass surface reflection, which in a lens composed of a number of elements could reduce the light transmission by as much as 50 per cent.

While the greatest aperture openings are required for work in poor light, speeds beyond 1/250 second are also rarely needed by the majority of amateur photographers. Yet both have greatly extended the scope of the miniature camera, making it a universal instrument for almost any subject, and under the most divergent conditions. The same applies to the introduction of zoom lenses, that is, lenses of variable focal length allowing an object to be photographed from the same standpoint at different magnification. The zoom lens was originally developed for motion picture cameras in the 1930s, to avoid a break in the continuity caused by changing lenses. In still photography it makes the camera more versatile, avoiding the need for additional lenses. The first zoom lens, the Zoomar, was introduced by Voigtländer in 1958 and had a focal length variable from 36 to 82 mm. In the 1970s, the focal length of a zoom lens for a 35-mm camera usually extended from 70 to 150 mm, though the zoom Nikkor has the unusual range of 50 to 300 mm. To maintain sharp focus throughout the zoom range these lenses require a far greater number of lens elements than an ordinary lens; the Takumar zoom has 14; the Nikkor zoom just mentioned has 20. The disadvantage of zoom lenses has been their great weight and relatively small aperture.

The range of lenses available in the 1970s for use with any of the Japanese miniature cameras is eight to nine times greater than for any of the German ones made before the Second World War. The Pentax outfit, for instance, comprises 24 lenses, from the 1000-mm telephoto lens for wild-life photography to the fish-eye wide-angle of 18 mm. The latter is one of the widest wide-angle lenses ever to have been designed, extending the angle of vision to 180°. Previously, the Goerz Hypergon, introduced in 1900, extended the angle of vision to 135°. Most readers will be acquainted with the curvilinear distortion that is unavoidable in fish-eye pictures.

VI. APPARATUS

The simplification of photography with factory-produced dry plates attracted a constantly rising number of amateur photographers who created a new and highly important market. Their fascination with equipment and their credulity that each novelty was of necessity improving the quality of their pictures knew no bounds. Their clamour for utmost simplicity and compactness of design led on the one hand to 'detective' cameras that were amusing toys rather than useful instruments, but on the other hand also to high-precision miniature cameras, now in universal use. By 1900 every tenth person in Britain—four million people—was reckoned to own a camera. The proportion was probably about the same in the U.S.A., but considerably lower on the Continent. By the 1970s the U.S.A., with over forty million amateur photographers, was the largest camera-owning country, followed by Germany, Japan, and Britain.

The new amateurs were mainly happy-go-lucky Sunday snapshooters whose requirements differed widely from those of the serious amateur and professional. In Europe, the latter continued to employ until about 1939 plate cameras 9×12 cm and 13×18 cm for portraits, landscapes, architecture, and advertising, making enlargements for their clients and occasionally for exhibitions. In the U.S.A. the desire for extreme sharpness and realism became a national obsession after the formation of the f 64 group in 1932. In consequence all the leading photographers worked until about 1950 with an 8×10-inch ($20 \times 25 \cdot 5$-cm) view camera, making only contact prints from their negatives. Despite the obvious advantages of the miniature camera for press and reportage work, even *Life* refused to accept miniature work until forced to do so by shortage of material during the Second World War. The editors of the leading fashion magazines *Vogue* and *Vanity Fair* insisted on un-cropped 8 × 10-inch contact prints for another ten years. The universally used press camera in America remained for several decades the Graflex, a single-lens reflex camera of large dimensions, made in Rochester, but fitted with a Tessar lens.

By contrast, the average amateur in the U.S.A. and in Europe used a hand camera either of the box type or the lightweight metal folding or strut type for 9 × 12-cm plates or 6 × 9-cm roll film until about 1930. None of these required a tripod. He was satisfied with contact prints, made by the local chemist or one of the many developing and printing (D & P) firms. Gaumont of Paris introduced in 1903 a vest pocket camera, as the 4·5 × 6-cm film or plate camera came to be called. This was the smallest size from which a con-tact print was considered acceptable for pasting into the photographic album.

Despite the fact that from 1880 onward enlarging on fast bromide paper was quite a simple procedure, requiring only a few minutes' exposure by artificial light (compared with several hours' continuous sunshine with the former albumen paper), it remained the exception until the introduction of the first miniature camera, the Leica, in 1925. For all users of 35-mm film and other small-picture cameras that began to come on the market about the same time, such as the Ermanox and the Rolleiflex, enlarging was a *sine qua non*.

VII. THE MINIATURE AND OTHER SMALL-PICTURE CAMERAS

The mass production of 35-mm film for the cinema industry (Ch. 53) made it economical for still photography, the perforation being an essential require-ment for a uniform film transport. It is not surprising, therefore, that more than one camera designer should have been struck by the practicability of the idea and constructed a miniature camera incorporating such film. The first was George P. Smith of Missouri in 1912. Two years later Levy Roth of Berlin brought out the Minigraph, taking 50 pictures 18 × 24 mm in size. The lens aperture, f 3·5, and the external dimensions of the Minigraph (5 × 6 × 13 cm) were identical with those of the later Leicas, the prototype of which had been constructed in 1913 by Oskar Barnack, a microscope designer at Leitz in Wetzlar; it was for his own use as an exposure checker for ciné cameras.

Owing to the First World War and the subsequent inflation in Germany it was eleven years before the Leica went into production. The first 500 models made their debut at the Leipzig Fair in 1925, where the compactness of the camera and the excellence of the Elmax lens, designed by Max Berek, giving first-rate definition at the full aperture of $f\,3\cdot5$, impressed novelty-hunters and dealers alike. Fitted with a focal-plane shutter with speeds extending from 1/20 to 1/500 second some misgivings were voiced about the missing longer speeds from 1 second to 1/20 second. To satisfy the demand, Leitz brought out another model the following year; this had the Elmax set in a Compur shutter with speeds ranging from 1 second to 1/300 second. Other novel features introduced in later models were of more lasting value, such as the interchangeability of lenses in 1930 and coupled rangefinder focusing two years later.

With the Leica began the era of miniature photography, for it not only raised the miniature camera to a scientific precision instrument, but it was also the first apparatus planned as the basis of a photographic system to cover most fields of photography by an extensive range of accessories and specialized equipment, all manufactured by Leitz. The most important was an enlarger for the 35-mm negatives which, as far as is known, had not existed for the previous miniature cameras mentioned above. Miniature negatives and subsequent enlarging had been advocated by Adolphe Bertsch and others in the 1860s as the ideal procedure, but without an artificial light source in the enlarger and fast bromide paper the system was doomed to find few supporters.

The Leitz Focomat (1931) was the prototype of a whole new range of vertical enlargers that came on the market in the 1930s for 35-mm negatives and the somewhat larger film sizes then coming into vogue (4×4 cm, 6×6 cm). In these, an opal electric bulb provided the light source and a condenser, or double condenser, spread the illumination evenly over the negative, which was projected on to the baseboard by the enlarging lens. By raising or lowering this entire unit on a vertical tube the desired magnification was achieved. Enlarging proved so simple that from 1930 onward it became a standard practice for the serious amateur, converting the kitchen or bathroom into a darkroom. With the widespread use of colour film since 1960 this trend was of necessity reversed, for no private darkroom in occasional use can provide the scientifically controlled conditions of temperature and the equipment for professional work.

Nevertheless, the undoubted advantages of miniature photography were offset for the first few years by considerable drawbacks. In particular, the high resolving power of the Elmar lens was by no means matched by the resolving power of the films of the time. The coarse grain that could be seen

FIG. 52.1. The Ermanox camera, 1924.

in a 24 × 30-cm print did not add to its attraction and resulted in a general softening of line. Like the fading of prints eighty years earlier, coarse grain was a serious problem much discussed and written about. A temporary solution was found in the time-and-temperature method of development, using so-called fine-grain developers introduced about 1931–2, but the real answer lay in the manufacture of slower fine-grain films; these came on the market in about 1933–4.

Meanwhile a small plate camera had captured the imagination of many, for even the 4·5 × 6-cm plate of the Ermanox was several times larger than 35-mm film and did not therefore suffer from the disadvantage of 'grainy' enlargements. Moreover, plates could be developed individually directly after exposure without having to wait for the completion of a 36-exposure film. While these were important considerations for anyone working for the press, the Ermanox had a further advantage over the Leica in the Ernostar *f* 2 lens (Fig. 52.1), which was twice as fast as the Elmax. For photo-journalists, often having to work in poor light conditions, this was the greatest asset of the Ermanox, tipping the scale in its favour. Fitted with a focal-plane shutter extending to 1/1000 second, this camera had been put on the market by the Ernemann Works, Dresden in 1924, one year before the Leica, with the bold slogan: 'What you can see you can photograph with the Ermanox'. This photographer's dream was not in fact realized then, nor with the Ernostar f 1·8 lens introduced the following year. However, the Ermanox did make possible—for the first time in the one-hundred-year history of the art—snapshots of stage productions, political meetings, and indoor social functions where the available light was poor and the use of flash prohibited.

Another popular instrument with press photographers favouring a still larger negative size was the Makina 6×9 cm with the Anticomar f 2·9 lens, also introduced in 1924 by Plaubel of Frankfurt. The majority of the amateur cameras in the 1930s took pictures on 6×9-cm roll film. The more renowned were either single- or twin-lens reflex cameras in the 6×6-cm format, using the same roll film size. Reflex cameras have the advantage that the subject can be focused and observed up to the moment of making the exposure by means of a mirror, fixed behind the lens at an angle of 45°, reflecting the image on to a ground-glass screen. The twin-lens reflex has a viewing lens above the taking lens with a static mirror, and the image appears in a special compartment in the top of the camera. In the single-lens reflex the mirror is automatically removed to a horizontal position in the camera roof on making the exposure. In larger formats both camera types had already existed in late Victorian days. Their re-introduction as compact hand-cameras created prototypes of apparatus that remained popular until the 1970s. Some leading makes deserve to be singled out for special features.

The Rolleiflex—put on the market in 1929 by Franke and Heidecke, Braunschweig—was the precursor of numerous similar twin-lens reflex cameras in the 6×6-cm size. It had a Tessar f 4·5 lens set in a Compur shutter ranging from 1 second to 1/300 second. From the end of the 1960s there was a marked decline in the production of these cameras in favour of the single-lens reflex using 35-mm film. The first of these was the Kine Exacta of Ihagee, Dresden, in 1936. It had an f 3·5 Tessar lens, a focal-plane shutter, and interchangeable lenses. The same firm also built a single reflex for 4×6·5-cm pictures on 6×9-cm roll film. Another well-known single-lens reflex camera in the 6×6-cm format was the Reflex Korelle with a Xenar f 3·5 lens, brought out by Kochmann in 1936.

A miniature camera that enjoyed an international reputation hardly less than the Leica was the Contax of Zeiss Ikon. It made its first appearance in 1932 when all the teething troubles of the early 35-mm film had been overcome; it had a Zeiss Sonar f 2 lens and a focal-plane shutter. Mention should also be made of a sub-miniature camera that held its own from 1937 to the 1970s. This is the Minox, taking 50 pictures 8×11-mm on special film.

Originally produced in Riga, Latvia, manufacture was continued after the Second World War in West Germany.

All the apparatus mentioned above underwent considerable modifications in later pre- and post-war models, in so far as production was continued. After having led the world for fifty years the German camera and optical industry received a crippling blow by the division of the country in 1945. Much of it had been situated in what became the Eastern Zone. What remained standing there after the holocaust was dismantled and taken to Russia. A number of leading firms, like Zeiss, restarted in the Federal Republic from scratch, divorced from the Schott–Zeiss optical glass factories at Jena that had enjoyed a virtual monopoly for all German and many foreign lens makes.

In this state of affairs the Japanese camera industry rose in the post-war period to a dominant position, aided by generous government export subsidies and the unrestricted import into the U.S.A. which accounts for about one-third of the total Japanese photographic exports. In the 1960s other countries relaxed their tariff and quota barriers against Japanese equipment, for the simple reason that there was little of European manufacture of comparable quality and price. Whereas before the Second World War, and directly after it, the Japanese camera manufacturers had the reputation for producing excellent imitations of leading German camera makes, in the mid-1950s their own research departments got into their stride and made significant advances in the design and production of high-class lenses and in camera technology generally. Japanese photographic equipment subsequently became the most advanced in design and of the highest quality. Nothing demonstrates more clearly the decline of the German hegemony in this field than the fact that the famous Zeiss Contax camera is now produced by Yashika in Japan (another version being produced in East Germany), and that a Swiss firms holds a 50 per cent interest in Leitz. By the 1970s the six leading Japanese camera manufacturers—Canon, Yashika, Asahi, Nippon, Minolta, and Olympus—gave employment to nearly 20000 people. In the ten years from 1959 to 1969 the value of the Japanese production of photographic goods trebled. Of every three single-lens reflex cameras sold today two are of Japanese manufacture. The Pentax Spotmatic of Asahi was the smallest of these and the most popular.

VIII. PROFESSIONAL STUDIO EQUIPMENT

Professional work in portraiture, advertising, architecture, industry, and reproduction ('repro') work called for specialized equipment, usually in

FIG. 52.2. The Kühn–Stegemann camera, 1925.

the 9×12-cm and 13×18-cm plate formats. These cameras have certain features that are often required in this work, such as a long bellows extension, a swing front with rising and interchangeable lens panel, and a swing back holding the plate. The square format has the additional advantage that the ground-glass frame and plate-holder can be moved from vertical to horizontal pictures without changing the position of the camera body. The greatest versatility is achieved in those cameras in which front and back can be moved separately on an optical bench. Such a universal 9×12-cm studio camera was custom-built by the Berlin cabinet maker Stegemann from 1925 to 1940 from a design by the Austrian photographer Heinrich Kühn (Fig. 52.2). Copied from the first optical bench camera constructed by J. Petzoal in 1857, it was made of teak and the optical bench consisted of a prism-shaped piece of wood 50 cm long, strengthened with metal. The square bellows had the same 50-cm extension, essential for photographic magnification of small objects.

From September 1948 onwards the Sinar camera, produced by Carl Koch of Schaffhausen, Switzerland, incorporated the features of the former Kühn–Stegemann, but light metal replaced all the wooden parts, and the

FIG. 52.3. The Sinar camera, showing optical bench system, 1948.

optical bench consisted of a light metal tube (Fig. 52.3). There has also been a further extension in versatility by additional movements. Apart from this apparatus, which in the larger format is used for still photographs in the motion-picture industry, the Technika, made by Linhof of Munich before and since the last war, also enjoys international reputation. Yet compared with the optical bench principle, the Linhof is more restricted in its versatility and movements by its static back and a baseboard which limits the bellows extension. For use with wide-angle lenses the baseboard can be lowered to avoid getting it into the picture—a precaution unnecessary in the optical bench where camera back and front can be screwed to its extremity.

IX. THE POLAROID SYSTEM

For amateurs and professionals desiring an instant picture, the American Edwin H. Land invented in 1947 a special camera, produced since 1948 by the Polaroid Land Corporation of Cambridge, Massachusetts. On a special film, manufactured by the same company, a positive was obtained within 60 seconds of the exposure (later reduced to 10 seconds). The production of pictures works on the same principle as in the original photocopying machines: the unexposed and undeveloped silver salts are transferred by diffusion from the negative paper to the positive paper. The lower roll in the camera holds the light-sensitive negative paper; the upper roll the non-sensitive positive paper. After exposing the image on the negative paper it passes with the positive paper between rollers which press them into contact and spreads a film of jellied processing reagent between them for development. The negative image then develops in the negative layer while the unexposed silver salts diffuse into the positive layer to form the positive picture. The finished black-and-white positive can then be removed. Extremely simple in operation, the system has the disadvantage of producing only one print, for the negative cannot be re-used. In 1963 the Polaroid Corporation introduced a colour film for use in this camera, delivering by a similar process a colour print within one minute of making the exposure.

X. COLOUR PHOTOGRAPHY

In the 1890s a number of methods and instruments were introduced that promised to bring to a successful conclusion the age-old aspiration to reproduce nature in colour—a problem that had engaged scientific minds from the earliest days of the daguerreotype. In particular, the Kromograms of the American Frederic Eugene Ives—diapositives copied from three separation negatives taken in quick succession by means of a repeating back (1893) through red, green, and blue-violet filters, and from 1900 onward simultaneously in a one-shot colour camera—left nothing to be desired in the rendering of colour when laid on his Kromscop viewing instrument. And this despite the fact that only orthochromatic negative and positive material was available at that time. Yet the expensive equipment required for taking and viewing the pictures precluded Ives's system from becoming popular, and for the same reason his other ingenious inventions in this field were denied the success they deserved. These included the Stereoscopic Kromscop camera and viewing instrument (1895); the Projection Kromscop (1895) containing red, green, and blue-violet filters in which the three diapositives were superimposed on a screen by means of an ordinary magic lantern; and, finally, the Diffraction Chromoscope (1900) in which each diapositive had superimposed on it a different diffraction screen: 2000 lines per inch for red, 2400 for green, and 2750 for blue. The three positives were then printed together in register to form the final picture which is perfectly transparent and merely consists of a diffraction screen with variable spacing. When this transparency is viewed in the Diffraction Chromoscope, designed by Ives for R. W. Wood of Wisconsin, the light waves pass through the corresponding lines and form a perfect colour picture.

Ducos du Hauron's Mélanochromoscope (1899), a combined taking and viewing instrument for three-colour photographs, 35 mm × 35 mm, did not find much favour either. The light rays passing through the lens were reflected by a mirror and split into three beams of light, passing through the same number of lenses and coloured filters—blue, magenta, and green—on to the sensitive plates. When viewing diapositives from these in a reversal of the arrangement, the picture was seen in colour. Yet the results obtained by this simplified method were less brilliant than with Ives's Kromscop.

It was obvious that to attract the amateur photographer—far more progessive than the professional, and since 1900 forming approximately 90 per cent of the fraternity—the colour process had to be extremely simple and the apparatus convenient and cheap. These requirements were met by the Auto-chrome process of the brothers Auguste and Louis Lumière (1907), who had already become famous a dozen years earlier as the inventors of the *Cinemato-graphe* with which cinematography and cinema shows to paying audiences made their debut. Their colour-screen plate called for no new equipment. All one had to do was to expose in the existing camera an Autochrome plate, manufactured at the Lumière factory at Lyons.

These glass plates were coated with microscopically small grains of potato-starch dyed green, red, and blue, about $8000–9000/mm^2$. Over this coating lay a thin film of panchromatic emulsion. (In fact, the invention, dating back to 1904, had been purposely held up until panchromatic emulsion was available.) The exposure was made through the glass side of the plate, that is through the colour-grain base acting as colour filters. After development, the plate was re-exposed to light and redeveloped (reversal process), resulting in a transparency composed of small specks of primary.colours giving the effect of mixed colours, as in a *pointilliste* painting. Autochrome plates were manu-factured in all standard sizes, but the pleasure of seeing a picture in colour was fraught with certain inconveniences: the exposure time was about forty times longer than with black and white material, and the transparencies were rather dense, owing to the starch-grain screen. Nonetheless, the Lumière process proved the least complicated and most popular of several additive and subtractive colour methods introduced before the First World War. In 1913 6000 Autochrome plates were manufactured daily at the Lumière factory at Lyon. Well-known *fin-de-siècle* pictorialists and numerous other amateurs produced excellent portraits and landscapes, as will be seen from Charles Holme's pioneer work *Colour photography and other recent developments of the art of the camera* (London, 1908).

Before giving a resumé of some of the better-known colour processes intro-duced before 1935, which fall into two distinctive groups, a brief explanation of the meaning of 'additive' and 'subtractive' in this context is called for. In the additive colour-mixing methods (synthesis) light is added to light. When the whole spectrum is transmitted, the result is white light. In the subtractive colour-mixing methods (analysis) the pigments of the colour filters absorb or subtract from light all colours except their own, which they reflect. When the whole spectrum is absorbed, i.e. all the light suppressed, the result is black.

Additive processes include Lumière Autochrome screen plate (1907); Dufay Dioptichrome screen plate, introduced by Louis D. Dufay (1908); Agfa colour screen plate (1916), introduced in film form as Agfacolor (1932); Finlay screen plate, introduced by C. L. Finlay (1929).

Subtractive processes are all based on the production of three colour separation negatives and the combination of colour positives in colours complementary to those of the negatives, such as Sanger–Shephard (1900); Pinatypie, introduced by Ernst Koenig (1904); Uvachrom, introduced by Arthur Traube (1916); Duxochrom (Herzog, 1929); Autotype carbro process (1930); Vivex colour (D. C. Spencer, 1932); Kodak Wash-off relief (1934).

Some of the subtractive processes were still in use up to the Second World War, for the production of either transparencies or colour prints. The main demand for colour photography came from advertising firms, art galleries, and leading industrial concerns. It lay in the hands of a few specialists, working for a very restricted market, on account of the great expense and the frequently poor colour reproduction in print. They generally produced three separation negatives by means of a one-shot colour camera, such as the Bermpohl (1934) or Jos Pé (1924) or one with a repeating back, and had the enlarged colour prints or transparencies produced by one of the few laboratories catering for this highly specialized work.

In the mid-1930s the two largest manufacturers of photographic materials introduced almost simultaneous subtractive colour films that were based on the same principle of using multi-layer film plus dye couplers, the latter invented by the German chemist Rudolf Fischer in 1911 and fundamental to all colour films in use today. The three layers of emulsion were coated on film support, each layer sensitive to only one colour. The top layer was sensitive to blue light; the middle layer to green; and the bottom layer to red. After development, the residual silver bromide in each layer was re-exposed and independently developed in so-called coupler developers which deposited dye of predetermined colours wherever silver bromide was converted into silver. In the Kodachrome film (1935), devised by two American musicians Leopold Godowsky and Leopold Mannes, different coupler developers were used for each layer. After dissolving away the positive silver image a subtractive colour photograph of yellow, magenta, and cyan dyes remained.

In the new Agfacolor film, perfected in 1936 by Gustav Wilmanns, the three coupling components were incorporated in the three emulsion layers during manufacture. After developing to a negative and bleaching out the silver image, the reversal positive image was produced by a single colour-forming developer in the required subtractive colours.

With both Kodachrome and Agfacolor, film transparencies (diapositives) were obtained, suitable for projection and for reproduction. The natural desire, especially of the amateur, is however, to have colour prints, even though they are, by and large, inferior to transparencies on account of their much greater light absorption. The same applies also to monochrome prints as compared with diapositives. Agfa tried to fulfil this need by creating an Agfacolor negative–positive process, but war intervened and the film did not become available until 1949. Meanwhile Kodak had in 1942 brought out the Kodacolor negative–positive film in which the first part of the process was analogous to the procedure described above under Agfacolor. However, instead of converting the negative into a positive transparency, a negative dye image in the complementary colour was left and then printed on to paper coated with a set of emulsions similar to those on the original negative. After similar processing a positive print in the primary colours was obtained.

After 1950 leading manufacturers in many parts of the world marketed colour films under their own trade names. They are all more or less based on the Agfacolor patent of 1937 which, as an enemy invention, had after the war become available to the Allied Powers. Only one American, English, and Japanese manufacturer brought out colour film on the Kodachrome principle. A further exception is the Polaroid colour film introduced in 1963.

The pre-war colour films were rather slow (8 DIN) and expensive by later standards, and hence were in comparatively small demand. The popularity of colour photography began only with the economic expansion and prosperity that set in about 1960. By that time, all the practical difficulties of working with colour film had been solved. In the industrially developed countries a large number of processing firms had been established; the speed of colour film was about four times faster than ten years previously; and a considerable reduction in its price and the cost of processing had taken place. As a consequence, eight out of ten amateurs subsequently went over from monochrome photography to colour, Kodacolor being the most favoured film. Figures available for West Germany may be indicative for the taking of colour pictures in other developed countries; the number of exposures rose from 380 million in 1969 to 2000 million in 1976.

XI. RADIOLOGY

The discovery of 'A new kind of rays' in November 1895 by Wilhelm Konrad von Röntgen of Würzburg University proved to be one of the greatest scientific discoveries of the age. The full importance of Röntgen rays, or X-rays as they are called in Anglo-Saxon countries, to medicine (Ch. 54) began to be realized, however, only in the first two decades of the twentieth century and is the reason for deferring their consideration to the present volume.

Though early in 1896 a Viennese physician detected a gallstone by X-rays and part of a needle was found in a woman's finger at the Royal Free Hospital in London at the beginning of March 1896, radiographical examination of fractures, location of foreign bodies, and other uses did not immediately become general. This was mainly for three reasons: the harmful nature of the

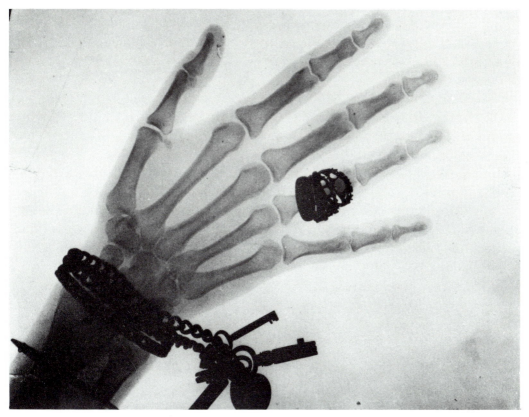

FIG. 52.4. A very early X-ray photograph of a hand, 1896–7.

rays, causing dermatitis through frequent and prolonged contact with them; the lack of safe apparatus; and the non-existence of trained radiologists.

Röntgen's discovery was made accidentally while experimenting with a vacuum tube of a type invented by William Crookes. Filled with neon gas such a tube produces the well-known neon light. The rays produced by the discharge of a high voltage through this tube being invisible, Röntgen investigated their action by their effect on a photographic dry plate. He also found that they have the property of rendering certain substances—such as calcium tungstate and barium platinocyanide—fluorescent. If, say, a hand or a purse is placed between a screen coated with such a substance and the tube, the denser parts—the bones in the hand or the coins in the purse—appear as black shadows in a grey background (Fig. 52.4).

X-rays penetrate all substances to some degree, but least of all lead, which is therefore used as a protective shield. Apart from surgery and radiotherapy X-rays are extensively used for the detection of flaws in metals, the examination of old paintings, in dentistry, and in crystallography. In the 1930s the better shoe shops had one or more X-ray boxes, by means of which customers could examine the fit of a new shoe. Yet because too-frequent examination was found to be potentially harmful, this device was abandoned again after the Second World War.

X-rays cannot readily be brought to a focus; so the images produced on the photographic emulsion are merely shadows of the objects. Nowadays, radiography is no longer conducted in a dark-room. The specially produced contrast films of low sensitivity are packed in light-tight envelopes and placed behind the object to be photographed, the film side facing the tube. Development and fixation are the same as with ordinary photography. For the purpose of shortening the exposure, intensifying screens have been introduced. The apparatus containing the tube is lined with lead to shield both operator and patient from harmful radiation, except for a small window through which the beam emerges.

BIBLIOGRAPHY

GERNSHEIM, H. and GERNSHEIM, A. *The history of photography*. Oxford University Press, London (1955).
—— ——. *A concise history of photography*. Thames and Hudson (1965).

G. 52.5. An early news photograph of 1904: King Edward VII and Queen Alexandra at the Royal Agricultural Show, held at
Park Royal.

53

CINEMATOGRAPHY

DAVID B. THOMAS AND JOHN P. WARD

I. THE GROWTH OF THE CINEMA

THE first half of the twentieth century presents a period during which the cinema grew from a little-known curiosity to become one of the important communications media. In 1900 cinematography was a newly invented novelty (Vol. V, Ch. 30, Pt. II). There were no cinemas, but films were to be seen as items on music-hall bills, in sideshows at fairgrounds, or in converted shop premises. The growth of the industry is linked to the development of both the art and the technology of cinematography.

The industry began to mushroom after 1905 when the narrative possibilities of the medium were first appreciated. Around that time the first 'nickelodeons' appeared in the U.S.A. and the first purpose-built cinema was constructed in London. Within only a few years many thousands of cinemas were in operation and the industry had become big business, with the American industry becoming increasingly dominant. At the beginning of the First World War there were about 3500 cinemas in Britain, but nearly all were quite small.

Vigorous competition in the second decade of the century produced longer and better pictures with a greater range of subject-matter. Audiences, which before the war had come mainly from the working classes, now included a cross-section of the population—nearly everyone began to go to the 'pictures' or 'movies'. The medium acquired this new stature with the appearance of film-makers who exploited the artistic potential by skilful editing, montage, and composition; foremost among these new innovators was the director D. W. Griffiths. The camera was now freed from its tripod and moved to follow the action in front of it. Audiences began to identify with individual players and the star system became firmly entrenched.

In the 1920s the cinema was a feature of nearly every town of the industrialized countries. The introduction of 'talkies' at the end of the decade further stimulated takings at the box office. The industry, particularly in Hollywood, acquired a self-confidence and an expertise which produced escapist entertainment which characterizes the age. The cinemas built during the inter-war years were large, lavishly decorated, and thickly carpeted. Even if economic times could be hard, the cinema provided an escape from harsh reality.

The growth of television in America in the 1940s, a growth even more rapid than that of the cinema thirty years before, was the first indication that the popularity of the cinema had reached a peak and was about to have its supremacy in entertainment challenged by another offspring of developing technology. In Britain the peak was reached in 1946 when there were nearly 5000 operating cinemas with a total seating capacity of 4·3 million. In that year there were 1635m. admissions, about 35 for each man, woman, and child [1]. The new competition from television initiated work on a number of technical innovations, including wide-screen and three-dimensional films. In the U.S.A. a feature of the post-war era was the introduction of 'drive-in' cinemas. About 4000 were opened in the years 1945–54. Some had a capacity of over 1000 cars with screen widths of 120 ft [2]. Nevertheless, by mid-century it was clear that the cinema was in decline.

II. FILM STOCK

In the average cinema the image on the film is magnified about 350 times during projection on to the screen. Any defects in projection equipment, graininess in the film, or lack of precision in the camera, result in flaws, jerkiness, scratches, etc. The manufacture of the film stock, and of the taking and projection equipment, is a demanding and precise operation..

At the beginning of the century there was a multiplicity of film gauges in use but the predominant one was the Edison 35-mm film with four perforations per frame and 16 frames to the foot. The precise dimensions of this gauge, which for the whole half-century was the one most used by professionals, were first standardized at an international conference in 1909. For reasons of economy, both in cost and in bulk, a number of narrower gauges have been employed, particularly for the amateur market. The most successful of these narrow-gauge films was the 16-mm safety reversal film introduced by Eastman Kodak in 1923. Around the same time Pathé brought out a 9·5-mm amateur gauge. Eastman Kodak introduced the 8-mm gauge in 1932.

Until the mid-1920s the film stock available was sensitive only to blue light, giving a false rendering in black and white of the colour tones, but producing sharp, clear images of high contrast. Panchromatic stock, which began to be produced in 1919, but was used in large quantities only after 1925, produced a softer graduation of tones. With the introduction of talking pictures panchromatic film became essential for optical sound-track printing. The dis-

FIG. 53.1(a). Film-developing on pin frames, *c.* 1910.

covery of new sensitizing dyes increased the speed of panchromatic film in the 1930s and improvements in emulsion-making technique produced faster film with a lower graininess.

Cellulose nitrate was used as the base for professional film stock for virtually the whole of the period from 1900 to 1950. This material is extremely inflammable and, for this reason, is unsuitable for use by amateurs. The film base used for making amateur motion-picture film is the slow-burning cellulose acetate.

III. FILM STUDIOS

In the early days, motion pictures were shot either out-of-doors or in 'glasshouse' studios. Sunlight, sometimes augmented by reflectors, was the illuminant. As the art progressed, artificial light, often from enclosed arcs, came increasingly into use. The use of incandescent tungsten lamps was limited by the low sensitivity of the film stock to light from the red end of the spectrum. The introduction of panchromatic film in the mid-1920s made possible a great increase in the popularity of incandescent bulb equipment. The introduction of sound recording necessitated silent light sources (the early arcs were noisy) and this also produced an increase in the use of incandescent light sources. However, with an improvement in carbon arcs, they were again used in studios, in particular in shooting the early Technicolor

FIG. 53.1(b). Film drying rooms, *c.* 1910.

films in the mid- and late 1930s. Incandescent lamps needed colour filters when used for colour work. The introduction of sound recording also meant that film studios needed to be completely enclosed in large soundproof, warehouse-like structures known as 'sound stages' fitted with huge sliding doors big enough to permit entire walls of sets to be brought in. Adjacent to the sound stages were the ancillary buildings—housing stores, workshops, projection theatres, offices, and, sometimes, laboratories (Fig. 53.1).

Studio cameras used for shooting feature films have increased in complexity and precision over the years, but the basic intermittent transport mechanism, the heart of the camera, has remained basically the same. The very earliest of cameras employed many different ingenious intermittent mechanisms, but all were rejected in favour of the claw mechanism used on nearly all later cameras. Projectors for 35-mm film, on the other hand, move the film intermittently by means of a sprocket wheel activated by a 'Maltese cross' and cam. For many years the standard projector illuminant in 35-mm projectors was the carbon arc.

IV. COLOUR CINEMATOGRAPHY

Motion pictures in colour could be seen in 1896, soon after the birth of the cinema. They were hand-coloured films lasting at most a few minutes on the screen. Hand-colouring was practicable only when small numbers of copies of relatively short films were required. By 1907, when films were much longer and there were many more cinemas, a method of colouring films was devised by Pathé Frères which employed machine-made stencils through which the colours were applied mechanically. The method was used until the 1920s. Colour was also introduced on to the screen by tinting and toning; a fire scene would be tinted red or a night scene blue.

The first presentation of a motion picture in natural colour took place in London in 1909. The process used was Kinemacolor, a two-colour additive method developed by George Albert Smith. Black-and-white film stock was exposed at twice the normal rate in a specially modified camera which was fitted with a rotating disc of red and green filters. The developed negative consisted of alternate frames of red record and green record (Fig. 53.2). In the cinema the processed black-and-white print was then projected, again at twice normal speed, through similar filters. The eye combined the rapidly alternating red and green images perceiving an image with the wide range of colours possible with a two-colour process. The result was good enough to ensure that Kinemacolor was commercially viable for several years. Films made by the process were seen in a dozen countries. Its greatest success was a $2\frac{1}{2}$-hour film of the Delhi Durbar of 1911. The several feature films made using the process were much less successful. The disadvantage of the process was that, as the two-colour records were not taken simultaneously, on projection a moving object appeared surrounded by a coloured fringe. Like all additive colour processes it needed a special projector. The process ceased to be exploited during the First World War [3].

The successful colour processes which appeared after 1920 were subtractive processes in which a coloured image is carried on the film itself in the form of a dyed image instead of the colour being introduced by coloured filters. Such processes have the advantage that prints can be shown in conventional projectors running at normal speed without modification. The early two-colour subtractive film processes used double-coated film stock, that is, film stock coated on both front and back. The film carried two coloured images, one red and one blue-green, one on each side of the film base. There were several such processes operating from about 1920 until about 1950, some quite successfully. None, however, achieved the success of Technicolor and many were rendered obsolete by Technicolor.

The Technicolor Motion Picture Corporation originated in 1915 and used a two-colour system up to 1930 [4]. In its early days, Technicolor prints were made by cementing together two thin positives back to back, each side of the film carrying an image coloured by a dye mordanting process. To avoid the

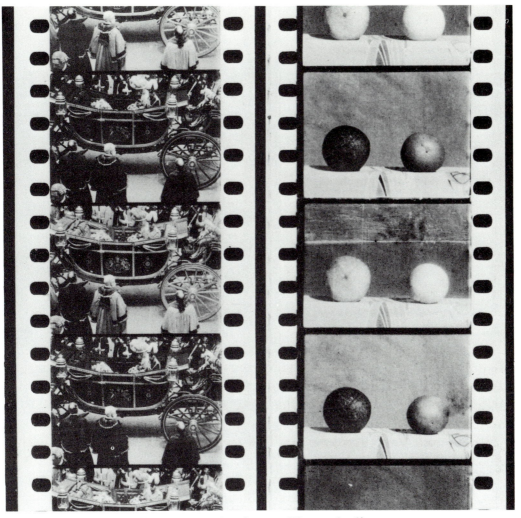

FIG. 53.2. Samples of 35-mm Kinemacolor film.

colour fringes of the Kinemacolor process a camera was designed to obtain both red and blue-green records simultaneously by splitting up the beam of light into two portions within the camera. However, it was the three-colour process which the company developed in the 1930s that made Technicolor a household word synonymous with 'brighter-than-life' colour rendition. Using this process, three colour records (red, blue, and green) were obtained on three separate films in a specially developed beam-splitting camera (Fig. 53.3). After passing through the lens light was split up into two portions by a partially transmitting mirror. Light reflected at the mirror formed an image on a

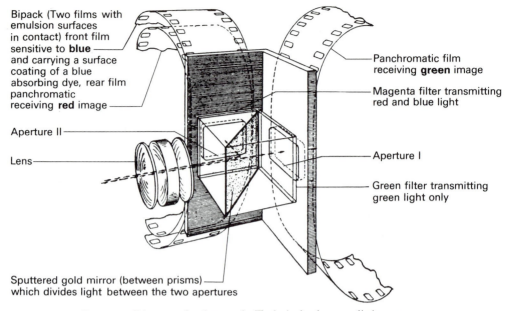

Bipack (Two films with emulsion surfaces in contact) front film sensitive to **blue** and carrying a surface coating of a blue absorbing dye, rear film panchromatic receiving **red** image

Aperture II

Lens

Sputtered gold mirror (between prisms) which divides light between the two apertures

Panchromatic film receiving **green** image

Magenta filter transmitting red and blue light

Aperture I

Green filter transmitting green light only

FIG. 53.3. Diagram of a three-strip Technicolor beam-splitting camera.

bipack, the front film of which was sensitive only to blue light (so giving the blue record); the rear film was panchromatic and provided the red record. Light transmitted through the mirror, after passing through a green filter produced the green record. The first of these cameras was produced in 1932 and they were in use until 1950.

Having prepared these three negative colour records in the beam-splitting camera the next step was to prepare from them three positive relief prints of hardened gelatine. These were then dyed to the appropriate colour, yellow, cyan, or magenta. These three sets of images were used as matrices and the dye was transferred from them on to blank film stock by a method known as imbibition printing. The process is similar in some ways to the colour printing of a book or magazine illustration, except that in the case of a Technicolor print the final image must stand magnification of several hundred times. The development of equipment sufficiently precise for such a demanding requirement was possible only after much research.

The Technicolor dye-transfer three-colour process was first used for a Walt Disney cartoon film in 1932. This was followed by many other Technicolor Disney cartoons. The first full-length Technicolor three-colour film was *Becky Sharp* (1935). Some of the most successful films ever made used the process, including *The Wizard of Oz* (1938), *The Four Feathers* (1939), and the longest and most memorable of colour films made before the Second World War *Gone with the Wind* (1939).

The appearance of a multilayer integral tripack (also called monopack) colour film in the late 1930s provided an opportunity of replacing the bulky, inelegant, beam-splitting camera by a conventional cinematograph camera which could obtain the three colour records on one film, such as Kodacolor. From this one negative film three sets of positive colour separation matrices could be made by optical printing through filters. This method was used for sequences of Technicolor film as early as 1942 but the first full-length Technicolor film made on an integral tripack was *Thunderhead, Son of Flicker* (1948). By 1950 the Technicolor beam-splitting camera was obsolete.

The success of Technicolor after 1935 derived partly from the ease and cheapness with which a large number of prints could be made by the process on blank uncoated stock and partly from the excellent colour reproduction which could be achieved by a three-colour subtractive process which afforded a large degree of control in its execution.

V. SOUND IN THE CINEMA

The conception of 'talking pictures' dates from the earliest days of cinematography. Yet over thirty years passed before successful sound systems appeared in the late 1920s. The failure of many promising attempts in the intervening period (Fig. 53.4) was partly due to a lukewarm response by the film-makers, who were producing very successful silent films and saw little reason to change their methods. But it was also a reflection of the inadequacy of associated technology. The evolution of talking pictures is a classic example of the new development made possible only by scientific and technical advances in apparently unrelated fields and was intimately bound up with the development of the phonograph, the photoelectric cell, and the thermionic valve. Motion-picture sound systems grew up in the shadow of the giant radio and telecommunications industries and benefited accordingly.

During the early experimental period of sound films, efforts to produce a practical system were channelled into two distinct fields. The method which seemed the most immediately promising involved harnessing and synchronizing the ciné camera and projector with the phonograph. The alternative was the more complex problem of reproducing sound captured photographically on film.

The idea of marrying the phonograph to the cinematograph occurred to a number of pioneers, including Edison (Vol. V, p. 743). The claim of Dickson to be the first talking picture star, as early as 1889, is open to doubt but certainly by the late 1890s he and Edison had combined phonograph and Kinetoscope to produce at least fifty talking 'peep shows'. In 1902 Léon Gaumont gave the first public demonstration of his synchronized talking picture experiments which were based on work by M. G. Demeny. Later demonstrations of these 'Phono-Scenes' were given in both England and the U.S.A., as were a number of similar disc systems that appeared prior to 1914 [5]. In all cases, commercial success was limited and brief. Interest revived after the First World War and some impetus was given by the promise of electrical recording and amplification. In 1925 the newly formed Vitaphone Company of the U.S.A., produced *Don Juan*, a converted silent picture which made a great impression within the industry. There were no speaking parts but an orchestral accompaniment was produced from centre-start, one-sided gramophone records of 16 inches diameter which rotated at $33\frac{1}{3}$ revolutions per minute. Each record carried the sound for one reel of film. The Vitaphone Company was sufficiently encouraged to produce their first film conceived from the outset as a talking picture, *The Jazz Singer*. This was a gamble, for only a hundred cinemas were wired for sound when it was released in October 1927. But *The Jazz Singer* captured the imagination of both industry and the public and is now popularly accepted as the film that ushered in the talking-picture era.

Sound-on-film has a long history which in part pre-dates the cinema. The many and varied lines of development which make up this history were gradually brought together and resolved into translating sound waves from a microphone into a variable light signal, which then produces the photographic image. Many systems were evolved which made this possible, but all produced images which, when developed and printed, either gave a sound track in which the opacity (density) of the photographic image varied, or alternatively, gave a continuous dense serrated track of variable width. In both variable-density and variable-area systems, sound is reproduced by projecting a narrow beam of light through the film sound track (Fig. 53.5). As the film moves along, the intensity of the light transmitted varies rapidly and continuously. By means of a photoelectric cell the light is converted into electric current which, when amplified, drives a loudspeaker.

Some of the most significant early work on sound-on-film was carried out by Ernst Rühmer, who published his first account in 1901. His 'photographophon' has been likened to a sound camera [6]. Although his system was never developed commercially, he produced a variable-area film, samples of which were later acquired by the Fox Film Corporation of America.

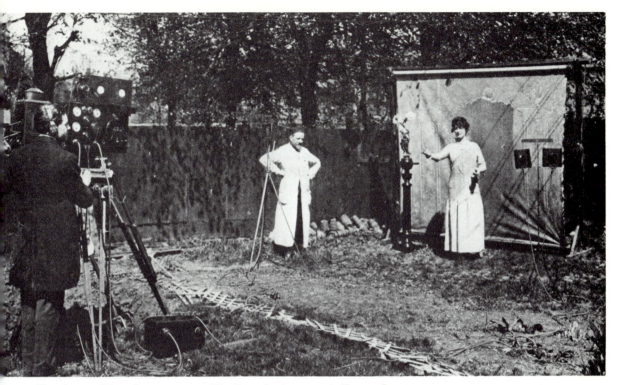

53.4. Shooting a talking picture, *c.* 1910. The figure in the centre is Eugene Lauste.

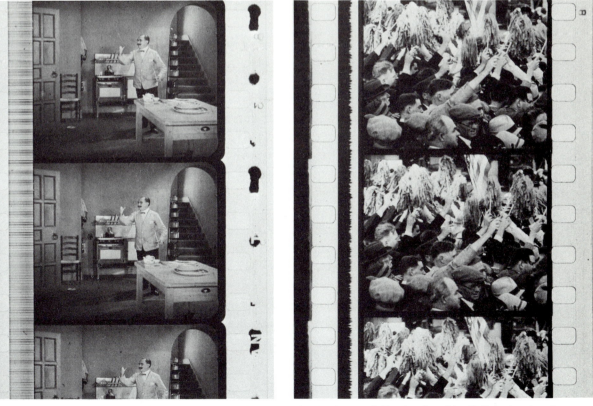

53.5(a). Early sound film developed by Western Electric ~~sh~~wing the variable-density sound track.

(b). Early sound film developed by R.C.A. showing the variable-area sound track.

Eugene A. Lauste may have been the first to suggest putting sound track and picture on to the same strip of film. Lauste had originally worked for Edison but moved to England in 1904. By 1907 he had succeeded in photographing sound and picture simultaneously, each image occupying half the film. But despite successful demonstrations of his methods on both sides of the Atlantic, he achieved no commercial success. His efforts were finally brought to a halt by the First World War. In 1918 the German Tri-Ergon group began developing a variable-density system using a variable intensity light modulator for recording and a photocell for reproducing. Although a practical system was demonstrated, the group failed completely to overcome the difficult technical problems of recording and reproducing distortion-free sound at a full dynamic range with the relatively primitive equipment available at the time. In 1926 items of Tri-Ergon equipment were transferred to the U.S.A., where William Fox acquired the American rights a year later. Fox also bought an interest in the 'Aeolight', a glow-discharge modulator lamp developed by T. W. Case, which was later used in the Fox Movietone News system [7]. Case in turn had cooperated closely with the inventor of the triode valve, Lee de Forest, supplying him with photoelectric cells and primitive sound cameras. De Forest claimed to have dreamed of sound film as early as 1900. Although he did not begin work until much later, he eventually devised his own variable-density sound system, using a glow-discharge modulator, the 'Photion'. By 1926, de Forest's 'Phonofilm' had been successfully demonstrated in over fifty theatres and this system became the basis of 'Movietone' [8]. A further sound-on-film system was introduced by Western Electric, despite their interest in the sound-on-disc 'Vitaphone' system. They developed a light valve as an alternative to the glow-discharge modulator for variable density recording. In the light valve, the light rays are projected on to the film through a slit formed by two minute metallic strips vibrating in sympathy with a magnetic field induced by microphone currents. The system was used to produce *Showboat* in 1928. The light valve later displaced the Aeolight in the production of variable density sound-on-film. In the same year, R.C.A.–Westinghouse and the General Electric Company in collaboration announced their own variable area sound system; the first picture with 'R.C.A. Photophone' sound, *The Perfect Crime*, was released on 17 June 1928. R.C.A. Photophone was partly derived from the early work of Lauste and partly from a sound recorder incorporating a mirror galvanometer, the 'Pallophototone', completed by C. A. Hoxie in 1921.

At the end of the 1920s, the talkies suddenly became accepted and established, despite reservations within the industry. Indeed, in March 1929, William Fox ceased production of all silent pictures. At the beginning of 1930, over 8700 theatres were equipped for sound in the U.S.A. alone, and this had risen to 13 500 by the end of the year. Of films under production at Hollywood, 95 per cent were now talkies and by 1931 the Academy of Motion Picture Arts and Sciences claimed to have given instruction in sound to some 900 men [9]. With successful films being produced using both sound-on-disc, variable-area, and variable-density sound-on-film systems, the theatres temporarily found themselves in a difficult position regarding projection equipment. But although the Vitaphone Company confidently prophesied a bright future for disc recording, it became increasingly clear that the future lay with sound-on-film and the system that had initially popularized the talking picture became one of technology's dead ends. Variable-area and variable-density systems continued to be developed side by side. The lack of standardization caused only minor inconvenience to the industry, for equipment was soon evolved which would accept both types of sound track.

The introduction of sound caused a revolution in techniques and in technology of the film industry. The recording engineer found it necessary to develop microphone baffles, filters, wind gags, directional devices, and booms. He was forced to learn the mysteries of mixing, dubbing, and re-recording. The new technology demanded a means of synchronizing sound and vision and one solution was the simple clapper board which was first used in the early days of the talkies. A troublesome problem was the elimination of unwanted sound. The development of a camera that was silent in operation proved difficult, and for a short while it became the practice to enclose cameras and operators in sound-proof booths or boxes on wheels (Fig. 53.6). In many situations these were impractical and so cameras were commonly enclosed in sound-proof packing or bags—the so-called 'blimps', still sometimes used today. Rubber-tyred, battery-operated camera dollies were introduced, facilitating rapid and silent changes of camera angles.

The arrival of sound films marked the end of professional hand-operated cameras and projectors. Nominally, silent films had been filmed and projected at the same speed, 16 frames per second or 60 ft per minute. In practice, projection speeds had risen over the years to around 85 ft per minute. This was partly to reduce picture flicker but also for the more dubious commercial reasons of cramming more shows into a day, and perhaps also to give what one writer described as a 'kick' to the performance. Whatever the motive, the public had been conditioned to accept the slightly unnatural movement

FIG. 53.6. Cinema sound stage, c. 1928.

shown in the cinema. With sound pictures it soon became apparent that not only must recording and reproducing speeds be matched but, as the human ear is particularly sensitive to pitch variations, the projection speed must be constant throughout a performance. Electric motors with specially developed governors were introduced to drive the projectors and, as a superior high-frequency response with a reduced margin of speed fluctuation could be obtained with a higher speed, the 90 ft per minute (24 frames per second) system chosen by Western Electric eventually became standard.

Continuous improvements in sound quality took place in the 1930s. Noise reduction was achieved by applying bias and by the development of push-pull variable-area recording by R.C.A. Experiments with multi-speaker systems and stereophonic sound met with some success but no concerted effort was made by the industry to exploit this commercially. Disney's 'Fantasound' was an exception; used in *Fantasia* (1941), it was enthusiastically received by the public. But the system, produced by multiple-track recordings, was expensive and complicated both in the studio and the cinema, very few of the latter being suitably equipped. Stereophonic sound was not generally used until the widespread use of magnetic sound tracks in the 1950s.

The principles of magnetic recording had been established in 1909 by Valdemar Poulsen and developed by Bell Telephone Laboratories and A.E.G. in Germany in the 1930s. Samples of German magnetic tape taken to America after the Second World War inspired intensive development, but it was not until the late 1940s that the studios began to use magnetic recording. Optical methods of sound production were applied to the sub-standard 16-mm and 9·5-mm gauges in the 1930s and 1940s, although not without considerable technical difficulties. The 8-mm gauge posed particular problems which were solved satisfactorily only by magnetic recording.

REFERENCES

[1] Figures provided by the British Film Institute Library.
[2] *Journal of the Society of Motion Picture and Television Engineers*, **64**, 386 (1955).
[3] THOMAS, D. B. *The first colour motion pictures*, H.M.S.O., London (1969).
[4] KALMUS, H. T., *Journal of the Society of Motion Picture Engineers*, **31**, 564–85 (1938).
[5] FORD, P., History of sound recording, *Recorded Sound*, **2**, 146–54 (1963).
[6] SPONABLE, E. I., *Journal of the Society of Motion Picture Engineers*, **48**, 275–303 and 407–22 (1947).
[7] KELLOGG, E. W., *Journal of the Society of Motion Picture Engineers*, **64**, 291–302 and 356–74 (1955).
[8] DE FOREST, L., *Journal of the Society of Motion Picture Engineers*, **10**, 64–76 (1926).

[9] COWAN, L. (ed.) *Recording sound for motion pictures*. Academy of Motion Picture Arts and Sciences, McGraw–Hill, New York (1931).

BIBLIOGRAPHY

BROWN, B., *Talking pictures*, Pitman, London (1931).

CORNWALL-KLYNE, A. *Colour cinematography* (3rd edn.). Chapman and Hall, London (1951).

FIELDING, R. *A technological history of motion pictures and television; an anthology from the pages of the Journal of the Society of Motion Picture and Television Engineers.* University of California Press, Berkeley (1967).

LOW, R. *A history of the British film.* Vol. 1: *1896–1906.* R. Low and R. Manvell (1948); Vol. 2: *1906–1914.* R. Low (1949); Vol. 3: *1914–1918.* R. Low and R. Manvell (1950). George Allen and Unwin, London.

MEES, C. E. K. *From dry plates to Ektachrome film.* Eastman Kodak Company, New York (1961).

WHEELER, L. J. Principles of cinematography, a handbook of motion picture technology (3rd edn.). Fountain Press, London (1963).

ROBINSON, D. *The history of world cinema.* Stein and Day, New York (1973).

54

MEDICAL TECHNOLOGY

AUDREY B. DAVIS

ALTHOUGH certain aspects of technology relevant to medicine, such as the development of the microscope, the making of steels capable of taking a very keen cutting edge, the manufacture of chemicals having anaesthetic or antibacterial properties, have been treated in earlier volumes of this work, the history of medical technology as such has not been explicitly considered. Although this chapter is concerned primarily with the first half of the present century we shall therefore necessarily have to pick up the threads of the story somewhat earlier.

A year before the turn of the twentieth century, Charles Truax, a Chicago manufacturer, summed up the extant literature on the technology of surgical instruments:

The practitioner who desires information relative to any particular surgical instrument or appliance, and searches in the standard text-books for descriptions and recommendations, is soon lost in a maze of unsatisfactory and confusing suggestions. Accurate descriptions are few, differentiations of patterns are almost unknown and definite reasons for preferring one model rather than another are often absolutely wanting. If the practitioner, still in doubt, resorts to a surgical instrument catalogue, he finds only illustrations, often inaccurately designed, and as a rule poorly executed, which convey no information other than the name and price. In despair, he usually chooses whatever instrument seems on a cursory examination to be the best adapted to his purpose, but has only a vague idea of the merits.

Following in the grand tradition of Johannes Scultetus, Lorenz Heister, Giovanni Alessandro Brambilla, John H. Savigny, Réné Jacques Croissant de Garengeot, Justus Arnemann, Albert W. H. Seerig, and Jean Jacques Perret, who had written technical accounts of surgical instruments in 1674, 1718, 1772, 1780, 1796, 1798, and 1838, Charles Truax sought to classify the vast numbers of instruments manufactured for surgeons and physicians in the last half of the nineteenth century. Confused by a terminology which labelled some instruments with a variety of names, medical practitioners welcomed Truax's attempt to simplify this nomenclature followed by an explanation of the construction, uses, and merits of each instrument.

Until the nineteenth century, the blacksmith, silversmith, and cutler were among the chief craftsmen who made the tools used by barber-surgeons, surgeons, dentists, and apothecaries. To meet the increasing demand of the surgeons in the nineteenth century, the cutler began to employ a specialist in surgical instruments and to represent himself as 'Cutler and Surgical Instrument Maker' where formerly he advertised as 'Cutler and Scissors Grinder'. The adaptation of the cutler to surgical instrument maker has been seen as extremely unfortunate for the evolution of surgical instruments.

In 1964, Pedro Curutchet of Brazil studied the design of surgical instruments and concluded that there did not exist 'another trade with such primitive, clumsy instrumental fingering as Surgery' [2]. An American dental manufacturer recognized the inferiority of surgical tools even earlier, in 1926, when he declared: 'No surgical instruments are to be had which in adaptation to the use intended, in temper or in finish, are at all comparable to the dentists' [3]. The design was fundamentally inappropriate. Since the hand is not anatomically symmetric, the instruments used by the surgeon should be asymmetrical, which generally was not reflected in the type of instrument manufactured. Curutchet classified instruments into two categories: axis-manual and crucimanual. In the axis-manual instrument, the longitudinal axis follows the same direction as the hand that is holding it, whereas in a crucimanual tool, its longitudinal axis lies across the hand's axis. Axis-manual instruments cannot be the result of a geometric, extra-manual, theoretical design, but are the consequence of an anatomic, functional modelling. Thus, the early surgeons who accepted tools similar to the barber's shears (crucimanual) set a precedent which condemned surgeons to the use of instruments which are difficult to manipulate. Their early mode of manufacture largely accounts for the minimal design changes in basic surgical instruments for many centuries.

It is primarily to the publications and patents of tradesmen and craftsmen that one must look for technical details concerning medical instrumentation. J. Arnemann in 1796 was among the first to compile an international instrument catalogue arranged according to their use, a system later adopted by most manufacturers in the design of trade catalogues. The twentieth century, which witnessed a great upsurge in technology in the service of medicine, stimulated the publication by medical professionals of classic compendia and reviews on the advances in the specialized sciences and technologies of medicine.

One problem which the reviewers tackled regularly was the mechanical and material deficiencies in manufactured instruments. A proportion of surgical instruments of poor quality continued to be manufactured throughout the twentieth century. Needles which snapped after they were injected into the body; rusting and flaking metals; and instruments that were liable to damage in the sterilization process were some of the dangers. Max Thorek, a Chicago surgeon, called for a governing body with direct power to oversee the instrument industry in 1959. After discussing in detail the numerous faults found in surgical instruments, he suggested that a quality control group be formed within the framework of one of the major surgical organizations. It would be the organization's responsibility to act as a bureau of standards in drawing up a standard set of tests to apply to all manufactured instruments and supplies. By supporting reliable manufacturers and censuring poor workmanship, Thorak believed that the instrument would become the central issue in a field where advertising, salesmanship, and company reputation were over-important factors [4].

Medical technology had to meet the unique standards created by the special demands of medical practice; patient need and response; medical theory; and cultural bias. Equally critical was the ease with which instruments could be understood and used. A. E. Fossier stated in 1923 that 'the value of a method of diagnosis is to be assessed not by the success with which it is employed in special trained hands, but by its success when employed by the average medical man' [5]. The average practitioner who administered most of the medicine and surgery bought most of the necessary instruments and assured their commercial success. This was especially true of basic instruments like the stethoscope and sphygmomanometer.

The individual demands and idiosyncracies of physicians, stemming from the precision they sought and the relatively small numbers of any type of instrument produced and sold, combined to encourage a more customer-responsive industry. One result was the proliferation of instruments designed to perform the same function, many of them receiving the names of the physicians and surgeons who suggested their design or added a special feature to an existing implement. This pattern increased throughout the twentieth century until changing economics and rapidly shifting materials forced the modern manufacturer to limit the time he spent in making instruments to individual specifications.

Surgical and medical instrument construction, unlike that of many other classes of manufactured items, requires a good knowledge of intended use for the instrument as well as how to construct it. Thus, the forging, turning spinning, soldering, and general working of metal and other materials have to be carefully done, and the surface finish must appear unblemished and not shelter bacteria easily. Springs, screws, threads, and other complicated mechanics have to be avoided whenever possible. The instrument separable into its component parts seemed to overcome the difficulties of sterilization, but it was also prone to fall apart while in use, a problem that continued throughout the twentieth century. Thus, screw-locks and male and female joints became practical substitutes in the compromise between very intricate parts and those replacements too easily separated under operating conditions. To avoid mixing up the parts of an instrument taken apart for cleaning, each part of one instrument was stamped with an identifying number.

Twentieth-century instruments lost much of their aesthetic appeal when they were streamlined so that they could be sterilized in hot water. Decorative handles of ivory, bone, wood, and intricate patterns worked into the metal were no longer permissible. Instead, hard rubber would be baked on to bladed instruments making it possible to sterilize them. With so many individual specifications to produce, and the modest demand for any single instrument, the manufacturer was discouraged from making and using dies, stamps, and other equipment to mass-produce surgical instruments. Except for the initial roughing out of shape, polishing, and the finishing of many tools, hand labour was essential and remained the rule rather than the exception throughout most of the first half of the twentieth century.

The materials used to make surgical instruments include English crucible steel for quality of the edge and highly polished finish; softer steel such as 'Bessemer' and 'open-hearth' steel for blunt instruments, forceps, and braces; brass for constructing specula, retractors, catheters, cases, and blunt instruments; copper for making uterine sounds, probes, applicators, compressed air cylinders, and sterilizers; silver, both flexible and rigid, for probes, catheters, caustic holders, and eye syringes; German silver (not much used in the U.S.A.) for catheters, cannulated instruments, spring forceps, and pocket cases; gold for tubes of eye syringes and styles; platinum for caustic holders and applicators, inter-uterine electrodes, electrolytic needles, cautery electrode parts, and thermo-cauteries; hard and soft rubber for tubing and catheters; and glass used in mirrors, bottles, jars, and some tubes [6].

Pure silver is extremely flexible and useful for catheters, which require a frequent change of curvature. Tempered steel instruments are not easily produced, for the process is not entirely controllable. The ease with which some of these materials—such as brass, copper, German silver, rubber, and other light substances—could be worked led to a moderate price for the instruments produced from them. Hand-forged steel articles, on the contrary, were far more expensive. Nickel plating made it possible to protect instruments against corrosion, although it was necessary to coat the metallic instrument with copper before applying the nickel, which would scale or peel off when applied directly to other metals. Some instruments such as chisels and osteotomes served best when made of steel, since the manner of their use exposed them to chipping. Silver-plated instruments reacted unfavourably in contact with rubber to become discoloured and oxidized; silver was therefore not applied to instruments which contained rubber components [7].

Plastics, which began to be employed for medical instruments and hospital supplies only after the Second World War, were to revolutionize hospital practice. Plastic bags for blood transfusion, catheter sets, enema, douche and drainage sets, etc. required no preparation or sterilization by nurses and technicians. Packaged individually, each was disposed of after use.

The explicit movement just prior to the Second World War to bring physics into medicine resulted in greater awareness of the mechanical details of a multitude of devices engineered for diagnosis and therapy. To summarize and bring the various scientific and technological elements together a series of texts entitled *Medical physics*, edited by Otto Glasser of Cleveland, appeared in 1944, 1950, and 1960. These volumes combined the features of an encyclo-pedia, textbook, and a 'working instrument' containing the data required for the application of the principles of physics to medicine. They provide many details of the design and construction of the significant tools and machines used in twentieth-century medicine. Previous texts were Adolf Fick's *Die medicinische Physik* (Germany, 1856) and Fred J. Brockway's *Essentials of physics arranged in the form of questions and answers prepared especially for students of medicine* (U.S.A., 1892). These early texts were more concerned with scientific principles than technological applications and medical con-sequences, while Glasser's books drew upon the special knowledge of many experts which appealed to a more technologically sophisticated physician and surgeon.

I. INDUSTRY

Medical and surgical industrial centres were concentrated in or near large cities in western Europe and the eastern U.S.A. Established firms in France, England, Germany, and Belgium provided most of the instruments used in western medicine and surgery until the First World War. Leading manufacturers, most of whom started in business in the nineteenth century, included: John Weiss; Arnold and Sons, Allen and Hanburys Ltd., John Bell and Croyden, Theodore Hamblin Ltd., Hawksley and Sons Ltd., Down Bros., Matthew Bros., S. Maw and Son, all of London; Colin et Cie., successor to Maison Charrière, L. Mathieu, and Luer, of Paris; H. Windler and Reiniger, Gebbert and Schall, of Berlin; Carl Zeiss, of Jena; C. W. Bolte, of Hamburg; B. Braun, of Melsunger; Hermann and Georg Haertel, of Breslau; Jetter and Scheerer of Tuttlinger, in Germany; and Joseph Leiter, of Vienna, Austria.

American instrument companies were primarily dealers and distributors who imported and sold instruments except for a few firms which manufactured some equipment like George Pilling of Philadelphia, W. F. Ford of New York; Codman and Shurtleff of Boston; J. H. Gemrig of Philadelphia; A. S. Aloe of St. Louis; Max Wocher and Son of Cincinnati; D. W. Kolbe and Son of Philadelphia; and a few artificial limb manufacturers like J. E. Hangar and Sons, of Richmond, Virginia; and A. A. Marks of New York.

France enjoyed a superb reputation for the quality of instruments produced based on the renown of firms like the surgical instrument maker, Charrière. Responding to surgeons and clinicians in Paris hospitals, these makers were still considered 'le bijouterie des instruments de chirurgie' by the 1920s.

Germany, England, and France remained large exporters of medical and surgical goods until the First World War. By 1927, France continued to export three-fifths of her production to Spain, Portugal, Italy, and South America. German industrial resources and workmanship ensured leadership in the worldwide market until the First World War. The U.S.A. relied almost entirely on German-made surgical instruments and English quality steel instruments. Belgium, Italy, Austria, and the U.S.A. produced instruments, but not until after the Second World War did the U.S.A. become almost self-sufficient in the quality and quantity of her production of medical and surgical instruments [8].

A leading centre of medical instrument production in Russia during the twentieth century was established in Leningrad on Apothecary Island. With a heritage of instrument production from about 1700, when Peter the Great established a shop, it was called the Red Guard after the 1917 Revolution. The factory began to specialize about 1850 when it manufactured ophthalmological, obstetrical, and genito-urinary instruments. In 1922, a committee made a survey of instruments and suggested changes which required new manufacturing techniques. By 1933, two hundred new surgical instruments were being made in a year. After the Second World War, the Red Guard changed its emphasis radically and restricted production to very technical and complicated medical appliances and apparatus. From this factory in 1950 came the semi-automatic devices for the mechanical suturing of blood vessels, tissues, and internal organs, one of the most celebrated Russian contributions to medical technology [9].

Scientific apparatus, such as blood-counting equipment, chemical reagents, microscopes, etc. required in conducting diagnostic tests on blood and other fluids, was manufactured in ever larger quantities as the private commercial laboratory developed in response to increasing medical demands throughout the twentieth century. Established as early as 1883 in the U.S.A., laboratories grew into the hundreds by the first quarter of the twentieth century.

II. DENTAL INDUSTRY

Dental instruments, particularly hand tools and dentures, were produced in most countries. The U.S.A. had risen to eminence in these areas by the end of the nineteenth century. American-made dentures by such firms as S. S. White and H. D. Justi of Philadelphia were admired internationally. The extensive demand for artificial teeth, and the specialized skills necessary to make teeth from metals and synthetic materials, resulted in the establishment of the American Dental Laboratory. This industrial institution, which accepted the challenge of constantly improving the quality of artificial teeth, was first organized in Boston by W. H. Stowe in 1887. The laboratory evolved from a simple workshop at the turn of the century to an organized industry of thousands of laboratories by 1950.

The technicians who worked in these laboratories were not dentists. Initially characterized as tooth carpenters, next as mechanical dentists, then prosthetic dentists and, finally, dental technicians, these terms mirrored their increasing competence and the complexity of their tasks. In 1917, 97 per cent of dentists made their own prostheses, whereas by 1957 97 per cent of restorations were undertaken by commercial laboratories.

Faced with costly problems like the repeated restoration of dentures, the most skilled technicians introduced methods to improve both the manufacturing techniques and the prostheses. One of the most spectacular technical innovations reduced the price of a tooth from $1·75 to $1·00 in 1900. In the 'Twentieth Century' tooth, nickel or German silver was substituted for the expensive platinum used in the pins for holding the tooth in the denture.

By 1906, the Dentists Supply Company, which engineered these teeth, was the largest tooth factory. The company further pioneered in a system for manufacturing teeth according to the shape of the face. These teeth were marketed as the Trubyte (called Anatoform in Europe) System in 1914. They had been designed by Leon Williams, who believed that artificial teeth should be as much the result of artistic endeavours as of mechanical dentistry. Other milestones were the introduction of New Trubyte teeth in 1930; Trubyte New Hue Teeth, which were more naturally coloured, in 1939; and Trubyte Acrylic Teeth in 1947, the first of a series of plastic teeth.

Having established a good working relationship with most dentists by the third decade, the laboratories found it expedient and commercially sound to exchange ideas on basic processes. Weichert Laboratories, Inc. was one of the first laboratories to process chrome and gold partial dentures for other laboratories in 1939. Coe Laboratories of Chicago shared the work of Polk E. Akers on improved partial dentures with other laboratories.

One of the most useful metallic materials to be introduced by the dental laboratory was vitallium, produced in 1932 by Austenal Laboratories of New York and Chicago. Beginning as a modified cobalt–chromium alloy used in constructing dentures, it was applied in 1936 to the manufacture of artificial body parts, such as bone and joint replacements, because it was chemically inert, resistant to tarnish and corrosion, strong, tough, and of a desirable weight. By 1958, after training by Austenal staff, 300 authorized American, and foreign, laboratories produced vitallium dentures.

Laboratories organized themselves regionally, beginning in 1914. The American Dental Laboratory Association, a national organization, was founded in 1920 by the larger laboratories. The second American Dental Laboratory Association was formed in 1947 [10].

Dental practice in the twentieth century was shaped by the electrification of basic dental tools including the dental drill, mouth lamp, tool sterilizer, cautery, mallet, and X-ray machine (Fig. 54.1). The earliest devices were powered by batteries, but these provided only limited power, required much storage space, and were unreliable. The struggle to keep batteries functional required some technical knowledge and skill and left frustrated dentists ill-prepared for using commercially supplied electricity when it became available. After it was generally recognized by 1900 that public generators were reliable sources of electricity, dentists found they need only learn to coordinate the touching of a lever or pushing of a button to activate the bur, to soften gutta-percha, to anneal gold, to fuse procelain, and to sterilize their implements.

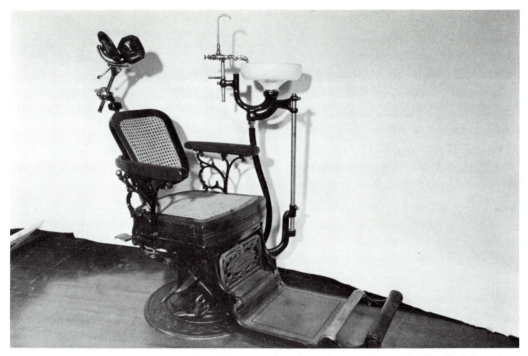

FIG. 54.1(a). The dental chair with adjustable seat and suction spitton, suggested by Dr. C. Edmund Kells, the pioneering dentist, in New Orleans, Louisiana, U.S.A. (1893).

FIG. 54.1(b). The Ritter dental unit model B (1929).

FIG. 54.1(c). The X-ray apparatus used by Dr. Kells.

Small motors specific for each instrument could be used, instead of one large machine which ran all surgery appliances. After the First World War, alternating current devices appeared as standard equipment in dental surgeries, making difficult operations easier and complex ones simpler.

The most notable improvement stemming from the use of electrically powered instruments was the aesthetic change brought about by a quieter and less cluttered surgery. The electric motor raised the tone of the profession. Instead of appearing as an organ grinder or mechanic using the pedal engine, the dentist took on the appearance of a medical professional. For the patient, faster methods of drilling teeth and of preparing the amalgams used in filling cavities provided some relief [11].

Electric light bulbs mounted on the tips of small pencil-shaped units were used to search for occluded sinuses. With radiography, the dentist could visualize surrounding tissues rarely seen before. Generally, this was the diagnostic and therapeutic function of the otolaryngologist. Dentists who had long realized the close relationship, and sometimes direct penetration, of the maxillary sinus by the roots of the upper molars found a convenient tool in the antral light. Tension between the dentist and the medical specialist grew over the issue of who should treat dentally induced sinus disease. A tooth which extended into the sinus could lead to serious local and systemic infections. The accepted practice was to call in an otolaryngologist when a tooth penetrated into the sinus; however, some dentists felt obliged to treat infected sinuses by draining and curetting them [12].

III. PHARMACEUTICAL INDUSTRY

Among the earliest pharmaceutical firms to supply synthetic substances were two American firms, Sharp and Dohme and Pfizer which produced ether and chloroform anaesthetics in the 1840s. Anaesthetics provided an early and constant bridge between the pharmacist and the surgeon. Through anaesthetics the synthetic products of the organic chemist were first applied to the care of the sick [13].

The rise of the synthetic drug industry after Pasteur's researches in the 1880s was to be the cornerstone of twentieth-century developments. Until the First World War Germany was the main source of synthetic drugs. Up to 1910 most synthetic drugs did not eliminate the cause of disease but rather reduced the discomfort caused by it. Paul Ehrlich's discovery of Salvarsan (606) to treat syphilis was a tremendous stimulus to the synthetic drug industry, which however, did not forge ahead until 1935 when Gerhard Domagk found a red dye to cure bacterial infections. By the 1930s various automatically controlled devices aided in the efficient production of synthetic drugs, including better temperature gauges, photoelectric eyes, electronic controls, and spectrographic analysis. In this period the era of the 'shot-gun' or multiple ingredient prescription ended [14].

IV. RADIOLOGY

On 8 November 1896 William Röntgen discovered that a new type of radiation was released when he activated a Geissler tube shaped according to the design of William Crookes. In the Crookes tube, cathode rays (electrons) were aimed at a target (usually the anode) composed of a metal, usually aluminium. This process required the presence of a small amount of gas, leading to the name 'gas tube'. The unknown rays from the tube Röntgen called X-rays. Out of this simple laboratory demonstration with an evacuated glass tube developed the most revolutionary and hazardous diagnostic and therapeutic tool of the twentieth century. Immediately designers, engineers, and manufacturers began to create ever more sophisticated, ingenious, and expensive equipment that made it possible to direct X-rays to designated parts of the body for revealing internal structures and healing diseased tissues.

The assorted technologies necessary for experimenting with, defining, and applying X-rays existed at the time of their discovery, a coincidence unmatched in the history of the technology of medicine. Basic equipment for the production of X-rays—including the tubes and their power sources, such as the induction coil (Ruhmkorff coil), static machine, and Tesla apparatus which supplied high voltages—were already available in laboratories and physicians' surgeries (Fig. 54.2). Lead shields, aluminum filters, high-voltage power supplies, photographic plates, and fluorescent screens are the primary devices which were soon added to enable X-rays to be more sharply focused; given sufficient power to penetrate organic and inorganic substances; and recorded. As these components were altered repeatedly to meet the shifting requirements for the generation and control of X-rays the ideal of a rapid, safe, and effective exposure became reality [15].

Diagnostic radiology developed on the basis of improved contrast densities recorded on X-ray film. The early glass plates, films, and chemicals which were used did not provide sharp and distinct images. The first plates made specifically for X-rays appeared in 1896. Steady progress in the development of X-ray sensitive films began with the need for X-ray film created in the First World War. By 1925, a highly sensitive nitrate-base film with good con-

FIG. 54.2(a). The Kelley–Koett X-ray machine
(1904)

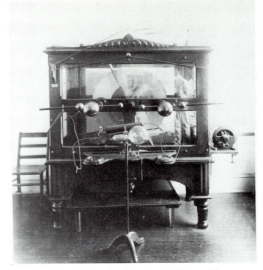

FIG. 54.2(b). A static electric machine with
X-ray tube (1900). The motor on the right
started the glass plates revolving which in turn
produced static electricity.

trast was manufactured by George Eastman of Rochester, New York. The
Eastman Company continued to improve X-ray films, beginning with the
change to an acetate-base film in the late 1920s. Then, in 1938, the developing
time was reduced from $4\frac{1}{2}$ minutes to $1\frac{3}{4}$ minutes and improved with the
introduction of successively faster films. A special lead foil film packet was
introduced for dental radiography in 1918, to reduce secondary radiation
striking the film. With bite wing packets, designed by Howard R. Raper in
1926, and improved films, the time of exposure for dental X-rays was greatly
reduced, thus finally achieving the goal of the prescient American dentist
William Herbert Rollins. Rollins was among the first to insist on using the
smallest possible dosage for dental or other diagnostic X-rays. He devised
various methods of achieving this goal, as well as anticipating other technological improvements in X-ray equipment such as placing an X-ray plate
between two intensifying screens [16].

Opaque materials to outline organs and to bring out contrasting densities
were effectively demonstrated by Walter Cannon of Boston. In 1897 he fed
a bismuth salt to a cat to emphasize its gastro-intestinal tract. Barium sulphate was found to be the most satisfactory opaque material for outlining the
human digestive tract.

Among the various effects X-rays produce are blackening of photographic plate or paper, fluorescence of certain substances, and other chemical changes. X-rays also caused biological effects such as loss of hair and reddening of the skin, to the extreme of burning, when given in dosages above a certain minimum. Only the energy which is absorbed by the specific tissues of the body will produce these effects. Recognition of the biological effects of X-rays led to their therapeutic application. The measurement of X-rays then became essential in order to control and predict their effects.

A number of attempts to designate dosages appeared earlier, but in 1937 the unit dosage for roentgen and the related gamma rays was established by the Fifth International Congress of Radiology in Chicago as the roentgen (r). This is the quantity of radiation such that the associated corpuscular emission per 0·001293 grams of air produces, in air, ions carrying one electrostatic unit of electricity. No practical method of determining the amount of energy absorbed by the tissues had evolved by mid-century although 0·3 r per week was established as the maximum permissible dosage. In the late 1930s a substitute method of gauging the amount of radiation delivered to deep-lying tissues was devised. This measuring device, called a phantom, 'is a volume of material comparable in composition, mass and dimension with a portion of the human body' which absorbs and scatters radiation in the same manner. The most satisfactory phantoms were composed of compressed cellulose.

Treatment of deep-lying cancers was undertaken using two types of implants as radiation sources. A permanent implant usually consisted of gold seeds 0·3 mm thick and 4 mm in length. At the end of three weeks, the radon in the seed had lost 99 per cent of its activity. Removable implants or needles containing radon or radium were enclosed in platinum, or in earlier versions sheathed in steel or monel metal [17].

The superficial application of X-rays to the body began c. 1900 when skin tuberculosis (lupus vulgaris) and skin cancer (epithelioma) were treated by Philip Mills Jones of San Francisco. A few early trials on the treatment of skin cancer and for the removal of excess hair began in 1896. The treatment of lupus by ultraviolet light from artificial sources such as the Finsen light (Fig. 54.3)—named after its inventor, Niels Finsen of Copenhagen—was popular after 1894 when he announced its discovery. Finsen won the first Nobel Prize in Medicine in 1903 for this form of treatment. He concentrated sunlight, or that from an arc lamp, by powerful condensing lenses and directed the rays to the lesion by pressing rock crystal against the skin; this drove the blood away, permitting the 'actinic' or ultraviolet rays to penetrate deeper. The treatment appeared successful but was expensive, because of the cost of

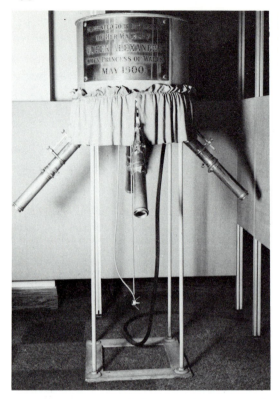

FIG. 54.3. This apparatus, pioneered by Niels Ryberg Finsen for the treatment of skin conditions by ultra-violet light, was presented to the London Hospital in 1900 by Queen Alexandra when Princess of Wales. It was in use for over 30 years.

the equipment and the need for trained staff to operate it. Light institutes and clinics soon sprang up internationally with the special lights recommended by Finsen.

The X-ray dosages required for therapeutic success with skin diseases are relatively small. American dermatologists used dosage formulae worked out by J. S. Shearer as early as 1915 and revised by P. H. Romer, W. D. Witherbee, and W. Mackie in 1946.

During 1896 X-ray treatment units were installed in the Presbyterian Hospital in New York City and the surgical department of Columbia College. The first X-ray laboratory specifically set up in an American hospital was introduced into the Philadelphia General Hospital in 1899. Into a room measuring 12 ft by 15 ft, of which a section 3 ft by 12 ft was separated off as a dark room, was placed a carriage stretcher, a Ruhmkorff induction coil, and a self-regulating tube manufactured by Queen and Company of Philadelphia. This tube, designed by Henry Lyman Sayen would generate sparks between a second pair of electrodes when the vacuum became too high. These sparks heated the potassium carbonate lodged in their path, released some gas, and started up the tube again. This tube became very popular. The first tube to receive a patent in the U.S.A. was that of Elihu Thomson of General Electric (26 June 1897) even though it was not an original design.

In Chicago, Wolfram C. Fuchs, a German-born engineer who died of cancer induced by over-exposure to X-rays, ran the first successful and respected commercial X-ray laboratory. He took over the practice started in 1896 by F. C. Harmisch and Otto L. Schmidt when it became too demanding. At the end of the first year, Fuchs had taken over 1400 shadowgraphs [18].

H. Clyde Snook, an electrical engineer, founded the Radio Electric Company in 1903. With several partners, Herbert White and Edwin Kelly to direct its development, the company grew and became known as the Roentgen Manufacturing Company of Philadelphia. It was a pioneer in manufacturing the interrupterless transformer with an induction coil and high-frequency coil for X-ray machines used in medicine. Snook's paper in 1907 explained the engineering principles of the first machine installed in the Jefferson Hospital of Philadelphia in that year. Snook laid the foundation for the medical X-ray equipment industry, which was to become one of the most lucrative medical supply industries after the First World War. The Snook machine at this time was rated at 110 000 volts and 200 milliamperes, which was far greater than existing coils [19].

X-ray tubes of higher voltage to make use of this power were being prepared in the General Electric Company (G.E.C.) Research Laboratory, Schenectady, by Irving Langmuir, who was developing the necessary high vacuum techniques. Concurrently, the target of the tube was changed to tungsten, which emitted electrons at a higher temperature.

The gas tube era terminated when William David Coolidge in 1913 devised a high-vacuum, high-voltage tube supplied with a ductile tungsten filament. Working at the G.E.C. Research Laboratory, Coolidge drew on the research efforts of colleagues who produced some of the first practical low-cost electric light bulbs. The Coolidge tube was patented in 1916 and became the prototype for X-ray tubes used in medicine and dentistry throughout the twentieth century. Some of the initial tungsten targets were mounted in tubes made by the Macalaster-Wiggen Company of Boston. Some of these were used by Francis H. Williams, one of the first physicians to use X-rays systematically in medical practice, and, therefore, the first radiologist.

An early commercially available X-ray unit for dental radiography was marketed by the Victor Electric Company around 1908. Previously Victor had supplied basic equipment to the dentist, including an electrical dental engine, a dental air compressor, and a variety of dental lathes. By 1910 Victor stopped producing all these units to specialize in X-ray equipment.

Dental X-ray procedures required that the X-ray tube and power supply should be placed close to the head and shoulders of the patient and dentist while in use. As the X-ray power supply began to deliver higher and higher voltages, which reduced the time of exposure, the potential for electric shock increased and remained even after the X-ray tube was enclosed in a glass or wooden jacket. To improve the angle of delivery of the X-ray for dental purposes a right-angle Coolidge tube was devised in 1917.

The first entirely shockproof unit was Coolidge's oil-immersion CDX unit, in which the X-ray tube and all its energizing elements were placed in an earthed oil-filled steel tank. A few of these units were distributed in 1921 and they became widely available in 1923.

A supervoltage X-ray tube was first used successfully to treat rectal cancer in 1930 by Albert Soiland of Los Angeles, California. This tube, supplied by C. C. Lauritsen of the California Institute of Technology, delivered 600 000 volts at 4 milliamperes current. The unit cost between $30 000 and $50 000. In 1935 G.E.C. introduced a model rated at 400 000 volts for general distribution. These early models were clumsy and expensive to install. In 1939, E. E. Charlton of G.E.C. reduced the size of the high-voltage units by placing them in tanks filled with a pressurized gas like freon. An early one-million-volt unit measured $7\frac{1}{2}$ ft long and 4 ft in diameter.

The next major advance in high voltage radiation was the betatron developed by D. W. Kerst of the University of Illinois in 1940, following earlier experiments by M. Steinbeck (1936) in Germany. Like the cyclotron, this compact device accelerated particles in circular orbits between the poles of an electromagnet. A 20m.-volt model for radiation therapy was described in 1943, but commercial development was interrupted by the Second World War.

By 1949, 31m.-volt betatrons were in clinical use in Europe and two 31m.-volt synchrotrons—after the principle conceived by the Russian physicist V. Veksler in 1944 and independently by E. M. McMillan of the Los Alamos Laboratory in New Mexico—were being installed in England. In 1946, F. K. Goward and D. E. Barnes, in England, converted a 4-MeV (mega-electron-volts) betatron to yield 8-MeV electrons. The synchrotron produced more voltage (70m. volts) from a smaller and lighter unit.

Robert Stone of the University of California Hospital arranged for G.E.C. to install a 70m.-volt synchronotron in 1951. It took until July 1956 to prepare it for the treatment of patients.

The source of the large budgets needed to install and operate these powerful units grew in stages from the contributions of wealthy donors like W. K. Kellogg; private foundations; the U.S. Public Health Service; and other governmental agencies, especially the U.S. Atomic Energy Commission, which supports most high-voltage clinical radiology in America.

Radiation from radium and other naturally occurring radioactive elements became clinically significant after the discovery of artificial radioactivity in 1934 by Frederic Joliot and Irène Curie. George Hevesy had suggested the technique of using radioisotopes as tracers in plants and animals in 1923. By 1936, eighteen radioisotopes of biologically significant elements were being manufactured at the Lawrence cyclotron in California. In this year the first therapeutic trial of an artificial radioisotope was undertaken. In 1951, Bruce K. Wiseman, after a decade of experience, reported that radioactive phosphorus was the treatment of choice for polycythemia or excess red blood cells. Beginning in 1946, medically useful radioisotopes were produced at Oak Ridge, Tennessee, which produced over 300 radioactive elements of which approximately 20 were used in medicine [20].

Twentieth-century X-ray machines may be classified into three types based on size, capacity, and the purpose for which they were developed. The smallest units produce a maximum of less than 30 milliamperes of current with a maximum voltage of 65 000–85 000 volts. These have a single function such as dental radiography. The medium-size units are used for general diagnosis in small institutions and physicians' surgeries. They have a capacity of 100 milliamperes current and a maximum of 100 000 volts. The largest and most complex units have the greatest capacity, 125 000 volts and 300 milliamperes. They are placed in the largest institutions and the clinics of radiologists [21].

The apparent superiority of the instrument-machine to the physician's unaided diagnostic skills elicited excessive patient cooperation, which led to patient domination. Many clamoured for X-rays in the early decades of the twentieth century, to reassure themselves that the physician had not underestimated or missed incipient disease.

The development of X-rays as a unique diagnostic aid brought some of the most spectacular technological devices and problems into medicine. It was brought into almost all specialities, including orthopaedics, internal medicine, neurology, gastroenterology, and cardiology in which it dramatically quickened the pace of discovery and therapy. A new specialty called radiology was instituted whose practitioners, the radiologists, were more dependent on their equipment than other medical specialists.

Medical examinations, medical treatment, and background radiation were the primary sources of concentrated X-ray exposure for many individuals during the first half of the twentieth century. Since then, greater background radiation and wider use of X-ray and radium treatments for a larger number of individuals has forced manufacturers, physicians, dentists and surgeons to reassess the maximum levels of medical X-rays to which a person should be exposed.

V. ANAESTHESIA

Delivering anaesthetic gases such as ether, nitrous oxide, and chloroform and maintaining them at a proper level of pressure in the lungs was the goal of several successful methods, and a variety of apparatus was introduced in the twentieth century. In 1909 S. J. Meltzer and J. Auer of the Rockefeller Institute devised an apparatus for insufflation endotracheal anaesthesia. Gases were blown into the lungs through a tube introduced deep into the trachea and returned naturally or artificially through a second tube placed in the trachea, thus minimizing respiratory movements. The technique was applied in 1910 by the surgeon, Charles Elsberg, of New York, and was widely adopted over the next five years. The initial difficulty of inserting the tube was overcome by Chevalier Jackson's improved endoscope and technique for direct-vision laryngoscopy in 1913. Jackson's laryngoscopes and bronchoscopes were among the first important endoscopes manufactured in the U.S.A.

Under the necessity of anaesthetizing thousands of patients for operations on the mouth and chest, the anaesthetists Ivan Magill and E. S. Rowbotham, assigned to the British Army Plastic Unit at Sidcup, England, in the First World War, changed the apparatus until it effected anaesthesia by the inhalation endotracheal method. They engineered the return to the older to-and-fro or inhalation method in which the gases passed through one wide-bore tube. It could be inserted through the nose or mouth, or by laryngotomy or tracheotomy. By the 1930s, inhalation anaesthesia was the superior method. The apparatus of J. T. Gwathmey and E. I. McKesson in the U.S.A. and H. E. G. Boyle in Britain were most desirable for this form of anaesthesia.

Closed-system anaesthesia—originally employed by the Englishman, John Snow, on animals in 1850—was accepted for human use in 1924 after R. M. Waters argued convincingly that this method conserved anaesthesia gas; helped retain body heat and moisture; and was both simple and economical to employ. Chemicals like caustic potash or soda lime absorbed the carbon dioxide, and air leakage was eliminated after A. E. Guedel and R. M. Waters designed an inflatable cuff trap in 1928, thus paving the way for the widespread success of closed-circuit apparatus in America beginning in the 1930s [22].

In 1916 H. E. G. Boyle of St. Bartholomew's Hospital, London, imported from America the first Gwathmey machine for inhalation anaesthesia. It was used to administer nitrous oxide, ether, carbon dioxide, and oxygen. Boyle suggested modifications to prevent leakage at the tube joints and arranged for the English firm of Coxeter to manufacture the improved machine. The first Boyle machine was encased in a heavy wooden box with two metal crossbars from which were suspended two nitrous oxide cylinders and two oxygen cylinders. The 'bubble bottle' or water bottle and ether container were placed above the gas cylinders. The bubble bottle, devised in 1910 by W. M. Boothby and Cotton, was inserted so that the gas bubbles could be observed and their rate of flow regulated by adjusting a fine adjustment valve in the cylinder. From the sight-feed bubble bottle the gases reached the patient through a narrow rubber tube which ended in a reservoir bag connected to the face-piece by a three-way stop cock. Fifteen years later, a pressure-reducing valve—which had been in use industrially since 1888—was applied to the machine. It changed the pressure from 1500 lb/ft^2 in the cylinder to 50 lb/ft^2 at delivery.

The chloroform bottle had been in use since 1910. In 1926 controls for regulating the amount of ether and chloroform vapour were added. By the early 1930s the metal controls were replaced by controls made of bakelite, since the metal wore with continual use, permitting gases to leak into the atmosphere. Between 1931 and 1933, a 'dry' flowmeter and a pressure-reducing regulator were introduced. The Coxeter bobbin meter which was used throughout the Second World War was not accurate but was more precise than the sight-feed bubble bottle. Richard Salt introduced a Rotameter bobbin in 1937. This more sensitive meter, which had been used to measure industrial gases like ammonia, was installed on anaesthesia machines only after the Second World War. It was made of duralumin with diagonal slots so that while rotating the bobbin would not touch the walls of the tube, thus eliminating wear by friction [23].

Local anaesthesia. Attempts to deaden sensation in specific locations, without making the patient unconscious, were made before the twentieth century.

European clinics used local anaesthetics for routine operations like the removal of tonsils, but some individuals suffered from 'psychic shock' induced by being conscious during the surgical procedure. Types of local anaesthesia include surface application; infiltration or paralysis of nerve endings at the site of the operation; and nerve block of the lower part of the spinal cord, introduced in 1896 by August Bier, who used cocaine.

Procaine, discovered in 1904 by Alfred Einhorn, was the forerunner of all important local anaesthetic agents. Less toxic drugs such as stovaine, tropococaine, and percaine, later called by the American name nupercaine, were used when the method came into general use. Drugs used for surface anaesthesia of the mucous membranes include cocaine, nupercaine, and xylocaine.

Spinal anaesthesia lost its popularity toward the middle of the century because of the complications to which it led and the fact that relaxing drugs induced similar anaesthesia. Physicians employing spinal anaesthesia found that insurance companies refused to pay for damages resulting from its use. The most serious hazard was the breaking of the needle used to inject the anesthetic into the spinal area below the second or third lumbar level; this had been reported as early as 1889. By 1939 sixty-three needle accidents had been recorded by 91 American anaesthetists. By the 1950s the recommended needle to minimize an accident was one designed by Howard Jones, made of stainless steel. Its bevelled tip gave better control of the puncture. To pierce thick skin more easily a 'Sise' introducer was manufactured by Down Bros. of London. A fine hardened gold needle (21 gauge) could be passed through it, directly to the dura of the spinal cord.

Dentists had from the nineteenth century administered local anaesthetics by injection to eliminate or reduce pain during extractions and while working in deep cavities and root canals. Cocaine and eucaine B in low concentrations were recommended as local anaesthetics around 1900, although toxic side-effects were a recognized problem. Dentists did not administer local anaesthetics readily since the misuse and abuse of these drugs had discredited their value. By the 1930s a solution of 2 per cent novocaine and one in 100 000 parts adrenaline was generally used for local anaesthesia, injected into the gum. General anaesthetics, such as nitrous oxide, were advised for the extraction of molars or several teeth simultaneously. For major dental surgery ether was the preferred anaesthetic. Special equipment for dental anaesthesia included the early nitrous oxide units and the simple face masks upon which ether or chloroform was dropped [24].

Anaesthesia with gases and vapours. Ethylene, acetylene, and propylene gases were all used as anaesthetics by the 1920s. These gases are similar to nitrous oxide in their effects, although nitrous oxide is the weakest anaesthetic gas and therefore must be used in the greatest concentration. They had to be delivered pure to the patient because they explode when mixed with oxygen or air. Ethylene was used only sporadically in the U.S.A., and not at all in Britain, by the 1950s. Acetylene was used widely in Germany under the name Narcylen, and to a lesser extent in the U.S.A., beginning in the 1920s and continuing to 1950. Ethyl chloride was used extensively as an anaesthetic and for brief operations on children. It was portable, safe, and rapidly soporific.

Chloroform, which had been used in at least three-quarters of all cases until the end of the Second World War, was rarely given alone by 1930. Usually, it was mixed with nitrous oxide and oxygen. It was given by dropping it on a lint cushion placed over the face of the patient, a method originated by J. Mills. A serious toxic effect was the instigation of ventricular fibrillation. Its asset is that it does not burn or explode in a mixture of air, oxygen, or nitrous oxide.

Ether, too, produced toxic effects which were mitigated by using lesser amounts of it. It was added to nitrous oxide and oxygen mixtures.

The need to heat ether vapour given to the patient was an issue raised by 1883. One device for warming ether was described in 1916 by F. E. Shipway and used throughout the Second World War. Ether or chloroform vapour is passed through a U-tube immersed in a vacuum flask filled with hot water. Other ether-warming devices include K. B. Pinson's ether 'bomb' described in 1921.

The value of rebreathing in inducing anaesthesia by ether has been recognized since the mid-nineteenth century. An early apparatus for providing ether in a closed system was invented by J. T. Clover in 1863. It was not necessary to remove all the carbon dioxide, which is a valuable respiratory stimulant. J. B. S. Haldane and Yandell Henderson described the scientific basis for this effect of the gas. Normally, carbon dioxide constitutes 0·04 per cent of inspired air. If 5 per cent carbon dioxide is present an immediate increase in depth of respiration occurs. Carbon dioxide was supplied in cylinders in ready-made mixtures of 5 per cent carbon dioxide and 95 per cent oxygen ('carbogan') in the 1930s. Other containers include a small portable 'sparklet' and a larger unit called 'Carbetha' for varying the ratio of carbon dioxide from 3 per cent to 7 per cent and the oxygen correspondingly.

Carbon dioxide provides a dual control over respiration, acting as both a stimulant and aid to narcosis in the administration of ether. Irregularities of breathing and surgical shock are some of the post-operative emergencies which were treated with carbon dioxide.

Cyclopropane, discovered in 1928 by G. H. W. Lucas and V. E. Henderson and first used in 1933, and thiopental sodium, introduced in 1934, showed the most promise of those substances introduced for general anaesthesia in the twentieth century. Their use was promoted by the discovery that a less profound anaesthaesia was satisfactory for many operative procedures, and the fact that these chemicals did not irritate the mucous membrances. Administered intravenously, thiopental sodium's greater muscle-relaxing qualities made it an especially useful anaesthetic. Curare, introduced into clinical anaesthesia in 1942, was a very effective muscle relaxant. Muscle relaxants were a highlight of the technical advances achieved in twentieth-century anaesthetics, many of which were introduced in the 1950s.

Safety problems in anaesthesia. A variety of problems in handling and applying anaesthetic gases plagued the profession throughout the twentieth century. Patient safety was threatened by the fact that uniform rubber tubing made it possible to interchange gas cylinders containing the various anaesthetic gases and oxygen. Some of these accidents occurred in base hospitals erected in Britain during the First World War in which emergency conditions prevailed. To eliminate the problem of mixing gases, specific colours were adopted for each gas cylinder assembly unit; nitrous oxide was black, carbon dioxide was green, and oxygen was white. This simple and foolproof solution required much effort to put it into force. By international agreement in 1953 the colours of the gas containers were regulated as follows: nitrous oxide, blue; oxygen, black with a white top; carbon dioxide, dark grey; cyclopropane, orange; ethylene, violet; and helium, brown. The name or symbol of the gas was painted on the shoulder of the cylinder. American and British manufacturers, technicians, and anaesthetists experienced a trying period while these standards were being phased into use, since some of the colours differed between the two countries. Two years later the British Ministry of Health required that non-interchangeable couplings between different gas cylinders and flowmeters be used in National Health Service Hospitals.

Standardization of colours and the arrangement of fittings so that anaesthetic gases could not be mistakenly administered is an example of a technical difficulty leading to a safety hazard which physicians and the medical industry could not overcome without the stimulus of a crisis and assistance from the government to suggest and enforce equipment changes [25].

Another hazard, the explosion of ethylene, acetylene, cyclopropane, ethyl chloride, and the ethers, was a threat which demanded continued technical supervision in the twentieth century. Sources of accidental ignition of these gases included static electricity and sparks from electric motors driving bone saws, suction pumps, etc. There was also the risk of spontaneous ignition, especially of ether and nitrous oxide, which provides their own source of oxygen when they decompose.

The introduction of high-frequency current for cutting and burning tissues posed the greatest danger, especially when the mouth or upper thorax were undergoing surgery. This surgical technique permitted more effective operations, but demanded much more careful control of the highly explosive anaesthetic gases.

Ethylene–oxygen accentuated the problem of explosion when it was introduced into the Presbyterian Hospital, New York City, in March 1923. After several non-fatal explosions, the Commonwealth Edison Company studied the operating room and suggested that earthing the floor underneath the staff and equipment in the operating room would prevent electrostatic sparks from igniting this gas. In about 1950 a statometer or staticator instrument was developed in the U.S.A. to give warning of dangerous charges before they sparked. This instrument was important in dry climates which promote static electricity discharges. A conducting type of rubber developed for aircraft tyres during the Second World War was introduced into the tubing on anaesthesia machines by the Dunlop Company in 1947. Conducting rubber diminished the risk of accumulating charges of high potential which could then spark in the vicinity of a gas.

Up to 1929 there were at least ten explosions in 332 721 administrations of ethylene in the U.S.A. By 1953, ether, ethylene, and cyclopropane produced two to four explosions per 100 000 anaesthesia cases in America, resulting in one fatality per 1 150 000. In Britain, on the other hand, it was estimated that about a hundred cases of burns occurred from anaesthetic explosions. An American-made instrument, the Vapotester, which was essentially a Wheatstone bridge with a balanced circuit, was designed to detect an inflammable or explosive gas mixture before it reacted [26].

By 1955, one of the greatest dangers lay in cutting off the oxygen supply owing to an empty or jammed cylinder. A device positioned to make a warning sound when the cylinder gas pressure was lowered alerted the anaesthetist to impending danger [27].

Those who administered the anaesthesia gases evolved into the medical specialists called anaesthesiologists. The growth of this specialty was slow and developed more rapidly in Europe. Nurses and medical students frequently gave anaesthetics in American hospitals through the first half of the twentieth century. One of the first full-time anaesthetists in the U.S.A. was Griffith Davis of Baltimore, who took up his post in 1904; he was followed within the next decade by about six physicians who specialized in anaesthesiology.

VI. THE ELECTROCARDIOGRAPH

An electrocardiograph machine detects and records the electrical potential variations of the heart. Willem Einthoven of Holland described the first successful machine, a string galvanometer, in 1901 and 1903. Others previously had associated the heart beat with electrical phenomena and used instruments to measure it. The capillary electrometer devised by Gabriel Lippmann in 1872 was used successfully by Augustus Waller in 1877. Einthoven's clear and accurate records made with the capillary electrometer and string galvanometer convinced clinicians of the value of these recordings. Einthoven received the Nobel Prize for Medicine in 1924. In his Nobel lecture, he credited Sir Thomas Lewis with the promotion of the electrocardiograph among the medical profession, to which he attributed the success of the instrument. Eventually, the string galvanometer was used to measure action potentials of the retina of the eye; the skeletal muscles; smooth muscles; and nerves.

The original Einthoven string galvanometer consisted of a silver-coated quartz fibre suspended between the poles of an electromagnet, which provided a constant magnetic field. Current from the heart, obtained from the body surface, was conducted through the quartz fibre and created a variable magnetic field around it. The interaction of the two magnetic fields produced a deflection of the string at right-angles to the field of the electromagnet. The shadow of the moving string cast by a strong light beam directed through small holes drilled through the electromagnet poles was focused on to a uniformly moving photographic glass plate. Investigations in Britain, Germany, Austria, France, and the U.S.A. brought about a demand for the instrument.

Disappointed with his business arrangements with Edelmann and Sons of Munich, Germany, Einthoven asked Horace Darwin, the youngest son of Charles Darwin and founder of the Cambridge Scientific Instrument Co. Ltd. of London, to manufacture the instrument. With Einthoven as consultant, until his death in 1927, the company produced smaller and more saleable string galvanometers. Its first model appeared in 1908 and its first table model in 1911. By the outbreak of the First World War, 35 instruments had been supplied to clinical and research institutions.

Alfred S. Cohn brought the first instrument, made by Edelmann, to America; it was installed in the Rockefeller Institute for Medical Research in New York in 1909. The first galvanometer to be made in America was ordered by Cohn in 1914. It was designed by Horatio B. Williams and produced in 1914 by Charles F. Hindle, a mechanic in the workshop of the College of Physicians and Surgeons in New York City. Hindle formed his own company, the Hindle Instrument Company, and from 1914 to 1921 he manufactured three models of electrocardiographs. In 1922, the Hindle Company was joined to the Cambridge Instrument Company in New York, and became the Cambridge Instrument Company of America.

Technical changes, such as the progressive reduction in size of the electromagnet, led to the development of a much smaller, and therefore portable, electrocardiograph in 1929 by Cassidy and Hall. A 30-lb unit manufactured by the Cambridge Instrument Company in 1928 succeeded the 80-lb unit. Thus the original Einthoven string galvanometer, which had weighed 600 lb, had been reduced to 1/18 its original weight; this was due in large measure to the use of special magnetic steel.

Changes in the electrodes placed on the body to pick up the current also took the form of smaller units. Einthoven's original electrodes consisted of large cylinders filled with electrolytic solutions, these were in use until the 1930s. Cohn introduced the first changes in 1920, using electrodes made of metal foil covered on the outer surface by rubber straps for attaching them to the surface of the body. Another type, by S. L. Barron, consisted of a flexible copper mesh strap enclosed in a flannel jacket saturated with an electrolyte solution. The electrode presently in use is the direct-contact plate type made of German silver, which has been produced by the Cambridge Instrument Company of New York since 1930. To lower the natural impedance of the skin, gauze saturated with saline solution was wrapped around the point at which the electrode was applied. When electrodes began to be applied to the chest regularly in 1931 (precordial leads) it became necessary to find other methods such as rubbing the skin with green soap (potassium oleate and glycerin), water, and powdered pumice.

Amplification of the small current generated by the heart is necessary to record its characteristics. Valves (vacuum tubes) for this purpose appeared in the 1920s. These permitted the replacement of the string galvanometer by the more robust, but less sensitive, d'Arsonval galvanometer. Siemens and Halske of Germany in 1934 developed one of the first amplifying electrocardiographs; they were followed by G.E.C. in America, which produced an instrument that amplified the current 3000 times.

Along with the amplifying instrument came the pen-writing or direct-writing instrument. The first one was designed by P. Duchosal and R. Luthi of Switzerland in 1932, and was produced by the Hellige Instrument Company. Although direct-writing electrocardiographs distort the electrocardiogram, they have become acceptable since the Second World War. The cathode ray tube when added to the electrocardiograph enables the electrical activity of the heart to be continuously monitoried in the laboratory, operating room, cardiology ward, clinic, and classroom. In 1950, the Cambridge Instrument Company of New York constructed an operating room cardioscope for keeping track of the electrocardiogram during surgery.

The first attempt to put an electrode at the tip of the cardiac catheter in order to record an electrocardiogram from within the chambers of the human heart *in situ* was made by the French investigators J. Lenigre and P. Maurice in 1945.

The report of a patient that quinine would stop his heart from beating irregularly led K. F. Wenckenbach of Vienna to have his patient's heart recorded by the electrocardiograph before and after taking the drug. The electrocardiogram showed atrial fibrillation before the ingestion of quinine and a normal sinus rhythm afterwards. Thus, the electrocardiograph effectively demonstrated the beneficial effect of quinine in treating this cardiac disorder [28].

Electrokymography of the heart. Of the combined methods employed later in this century—such as fluoroscopy, roentgencinematography, and roentgenkymography—only fluoroscopy was widely used clinically by 1950. The electrokymograph was designed as an attachment for use with the roentgenscope and electrocardiograph in 1945. Its purpose was to 'permit the graphic registration of the movements of the heart and large blood vessels in a patient'. Its three units and their functions were: the roentgenoscope to observe the cardiovascular silhouette and to position the electrokymographic pick-up unit over a selected area; the electrokymograph to convert the motion and density changes of these areas to corresponding current variations; and the electrocardiographic galvanometer to record the variations on moving bismuth paper to make an electrokymogram.

Actual exposure to radiation, during approximately 10 minutes examination yielding 12 records, was less than 5 minutes and was believed to be below the margin of safety. The clinical applications of the electrokymograph were uncertain by 1950. Its value for studying the physiology of the cardiovascular system was proved but more records were required to assess its clinical applications.

About 1950 the Cambridge Scientific Instrument Company, and the Sanborn Company of Massachusetts, manufactured units for electrokymography. Its other uses included recording the motions of the digestive and respiratory systems, as a photoelectric plethysmograph and a recorder in ballistocardiography [29].

VII. POLYGRAPHS

Instruments designed for medical purposes were applied in fields other than the diagnosis and treatment of disease, such as crime detection.

From the instruments developed to make continuing recordings of respiration and blood pressure was constructed a polygraph, commonly called the 'lie-detector'. The Keeler Polygraph—principally developed by the Americans, W. M. Marston, John A. Larson, and Leonard Keeler—was described by Fred E. Inbau of the Northwestern University School of Law in 1935. It consists of three units: one for recording respiratory changes; another for continuously recording the pulse wave and blood pressure; and a third for recording a duplicate blood-pressure curve or for recording muscular reflexes of the arm or leg.

For obtaining these bodily reactions, a rubber tube (pneumograph) is placed around the chest, and a blood-pressure cuff, of the type ordinarily used by physicians, is fastened about the upper arm and then inflated to a pressure about mid-way between the systolic and diastolic blood pressures. Hollow rubber tubes of approximately one quarter of an inch in diameter lead from both the pneumograph and the cuff into metal tambours to which are attached styluses. At the tip of each stylus is a small cup which is kept filled with ink and which feeds the pens as they fluctuate with each pulse beat or respiratory movement. The recordations are made upon slowly moving graph paper driven by a small synchronous electric motor.

This polygraph was used by law enforcement agencies. The 'lie-detectors' employed in psychology laboratories contained additional units including a galvanometer and a Wheatstone bridge to form a complete polygraph. The Wheatstone bridge was used to detect changes in the skin resistance by an imperceptible current of electricity flowing through the body.

Physiological abnormalities in the processes measured are compensated for

during the 'control' period, during which irrelevant questions are asked of
the person being tested. The accuracy of the polygraph in providing physiological data associated with individuals who have committed crimes depended
upon the skill of the examiner in asking the relevant questions and interpret-
ing the physiological records [30]. To purely technological problems were
added others of a legal nature, concerning the admissibility of evidence.

VIII. BLOOD-PRESSURE MEASUREMENT

Pulse irregularities had been noted since antiquity, but they were not studied
systematically with the aid of instruments until the nineteenth century. From
its beginning in 1733, when Stephen Hales measured the blood pressure of a
horse by inserting a 9-ft tube directly into the crural artery, instruments for
measuring blood pressure evolved into the units that are now a standard part
of the physician's equipment. To measure blood pressure routinely it was
essential to find an indirect method, or one involving contacting the beat of
the artery from the surface of the body.

One of the early instruments, named a sphygmograph, consisted of a rubber membrane stretched tightly over a small tube (tambour) containing air or
a liquid. The motions of the membrane which reflected the pulsations were
magnified and transmitted through a system of levers. It was introduced
around the middle of the nineteenth century. The most widely used one was
the Dudgeon sphygomograph which was later modified by James MacKenzie
and became known as the 'clinical ink writing polygraph'.

The first to succeed in developing a practical clinical procedure for taking
indirect blood-pressure readings was the Viennese physician Samuel Siegfried
Karl Ritter von Basch. In 1876 he constructed an apparatus consisting of a
pelote containing a glass funnel covered with an elastic membrane attached to
a reservoir and a mercury manometer (Fig. 54.4(a)). The funnel and tubing
were filled with water from the reservoir. To use it the membrane of the pelote
is applied forcibly to an artery lying directly upon the bone (the temporal or
radial). The pressure exerted on the artery is transmitted through the water-
filled system to the mercury manometer. Feeling the pulse with a finger just
beyond the point of compression, the manometer is read when the pulse first
disappears or when it first returns as the pressure is decreased. This is the
systolic pressure.

The next advance, by Scipione Riva-Rocci of Padua in 1896, became the
forerunner of the modern sphygmomanometer or instrument to measure
arterial pressure. Riva-Rocci introduced a rubber tube or bag to encircle the

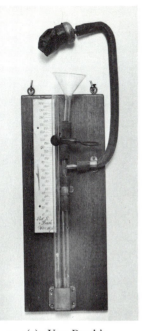

Fig. 54.4(a). Von Basch's sphygmomanometer (1876) was the first blood-pressure instrument that could be used in medical practice. Using a mercury manometer it was possible to measure the pressure necessary to collapse an artery by compressing it with a water-filled bag.

(b). Riva-Rocci's sphygmomanometer (1896) introduced the inflatable armcuff, the last essential component of sphygmomanometers used today.

(c). Von Recklinghausen's tonometer (1908) was a further development using a wider armcuff than that used by Riva-Rocci. It was very accurate and reliable, suitable for research, but too large for convenient use in everyday medical practice.

upper arm which was inflated by a hand bulb (Fig. 54.4(b)). The rubber bag was connected to a mercury or anaeroid manometer. 'The cuff with its rubber bag was placed around the upper arm, air was pumped into the bag with the rubber bulb and the pressure was raised until the pulse was obliterated at the wrist. When the air was released, the mercury fell in the manometer and the point on the scale when the pulse reappeared gave the Systolic blood-pressure.' In 1901 H. von Recklinghausen substituted a wider cuff which gave more accurate readings (Fig. 54.4(c)) and in 1905 the Russian N. S. Korotkoff suggested that a stethoscope be applied over the artery below the cuff instead of palpating the radial artery in the wrist.

With the stethoscope four distinct phases of sound can be distinguished. When phase one appears, the reading on the manometer provides the systolic pressure and at a later phase the diastolic pressure is indicated. The systolic reading corresponds to the contraction of the heart expelling blood into the aorta, which is measured by the amount of mercury displaced in the mano-meter. The diastolic pressure is the force at the time the heart muscle expands to receive blood from the pulmonary vein.

Medical investigators, beginning in 1903 with H. W. Cook and J. B. Biggs of the Johns Hopkins University, who wrote the first extensive article in English on the measurement and clinical interpretation of blood pressure, called for the establishment of the normal and abnormal limits of blood pressure readings. The normal limits of the systolic and diastolic pressure was to be based on life insurance data collected on vast numbers of men, women, and children between 1910 and 1950. One of the earliest publications of this data based on the blood pressure readings of 19339 individuals was by J. W. Fisher of the Northwestern Mutual Life Insurance Company of Milwaukee, Wisconsin in 1914 [31].

IX. STETHOSCOPES

The stethoscope remained the symbol for the clinician during the first half of the twentieth century. To make it more useful for detecting a wider range of sounds, continual refinement in the materials from which it was constructed and the arrangement of its components was essential. Interplay between the design and construction of the stethoscope and awareness of the significance of a variety of chest and abdominal cavity sounds characterized the evolution of this instrument.

René Laennec made the conception of a stethoscope practical in 1816; he first used a cylinder of paper compactly rolled. A more substantial model which he adopted was made of a cylinder of wood 3·6 cm in diametre, 28·8 cm long with a funnel, 3·6 cm deep at one end. Models also were made of metal, vulcanite, papier-maché, and other materials in combination.

The monaural stethoscope was used well into the twentieth century. A wooden model, with a detachable earpiece so that the instrument would lie flat in the pocket, was inexpensive and therefore widely used by students. A model made with a flared nickel-plated brass tube and a hard rubber ear-piece was used up to the 1950s in Europe.

Binaural-type stethoscopes began to appear before 1850 in Paris and London. The physician, A. Leared, exhibited a double stethoscope at the International Exhibition in 1851. It was made of two gutta-percha tubes attached to the chest-piece and ear-pieces. The elasticity of these tubes kept them in position.

George Camman, American physician living in New York, designed and produced one of the first practical binaural stethoscopes in 1853 and described it in 1855. The early commercial models were fitted with chest-pieces made of carefully turned ivory in various sizes. The flexible tubing was made of spiral spring wire covered with silk cloth and treated with gum elastic. The tubes were held together with a spring. Curved metal ear tubes were fastened to a hinged crosspiece and bore ivory tips for insertion into the ear. Among the early types were stethonoscopes, phonophores, hydrophones, and phonendoscopes, a forebear of the diaphragm stethoscope, which was first described as a 'resonating stethoscope.' The simple steel chest-piece used with a non-folding head-frame and rubber tubes became the standard type. The bell chest-piece was often made with a finger-rest. Early bell chest-pieces were made of polished wood, ebony, ivory, metal, rubber, china, and other materials.

Diaphragm chest-pieces were introduced by R. C. M. Bowles, who received a patent in 1898 and produced a rigid membrane diaphragm in 1901. Originally it was shaped like a flatiron and then was changed to the circular pattern in use today. About 1910 a dome-shaped chest-piece appeared which could be easily slipped under the clothing or between the patient and the bed. A chest-piece with a bell and diaphragm was devised at Guy's Hospital, London. It requires a rubber anti-chill cushion, as do other metal pieces.

A modern and widely used stethoscope is the Capac stethoscope, which became available in 1935. Two versions of this make it very versatile. Type A is for the visiting physician and Type B is for use during surgery. Type A contains a light-weight metal chest-piece with concave and conical screw-in ends which are fitted with rubber anti-chill cushions and connected to light-weight rubber tubes. Type B has a feature unique to the Capac instrument. It incorporates an annular interior diaphragm which is fully protected against damage. This stethoscope gives a good volume of sound which is clear and free from 'hair crackle'. The head-frame is a rigid self-adjusting model, giving a desired pressure in the ears.

Chest-pieces are distinctive for the sounds that may be heard with them. A bell chest-piece, provided it has a fairly small capacity, will pick up most heart sounds, especially lower frequencies as heard in the mitral diastolic murmur. A diaphragm will bring out high-frequency sounds such as the early diastolic murmur of aortic incompetence. The sounds through the bell are purer than those heard through the diaphragm; therefore it is ideal to have both types of chest-pieces.

Howard Sprague, of Boston, first described in 1926 a modern combined bell and diaphragm chest-piece which was manufactured by George P. Pilling and Son Company of Philadelphia. The chest-pieces were interchanged by turning a valve. The Meredith twin model possesses a revolving chest-piece in which the bell and diaphragm are opposite one another and revolve about a central chamber to which the stethoscope tubing is connected. The latest diaphragm is composed of rigid plastic about 0·38 mm thick. As a result of the recommendation of M. B. Rappaport and Sprague in 1951 that the volume of air in the system be kept to a minimum, the bore in a stethoscope tubing such as the St George's Hospital or A. Leatham's 1958 model is 3 mm. W. W. Mushin's diaphragm is slender and fitted with a bakelite piece. Bells may be obtained in nylon and aluminium.

Head-frames vary as much as chest-pieces. The fixed-spring type was among the earliest and may still be obtained. Folding head-frames vary. The short binaurals are more comfortable than the wide aural type. Double-folding head-frames are practical for those who wish to carry a stethoscope in a small bag. Earpieces or nibs are made of metal, ivory, and wood. Those made of plastic tend to chip. The most comfortable type is made of self-threading nylon. Stethoscope tubing is usually made of rubber, although early models, such as one from 1918, were made with corrugated metal tubing. Most popular models have a tube bore of 3–5 mm [32].

The compound or double stethoscope for lateralization and comparison of sound, successfully introduced by William J. Kerr in 1936, was a notable advance. Unlike the binaural stethoscope, in which the sound is heard as if it arises from a point directly in front of the listener, the sound comes from two distinct points. The symballophone is composed of two metal diaphragm chest-pieces attached to two equal-length rubber tubes suspended from a metal cross-piece and direct tubes. On the other end of the cross-piece are two short rubber tubes which connect to the metal earpieces. It is essential to have good hearing to make proper use of this instrument.

The stethoscope stands supreme for the detection of heart disease. Techniques, like electrocardiography, radiography, phonocardiography, ballistocardiography, angiocardiography, and cardiac catheterization are ancillary and confirmatory procedures [33].

X. HEARING

Accurate standardized measurement of hearing was realized when the audiometer was developed about 1920. Previously, hearing was tested by

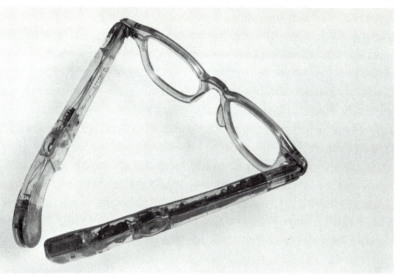

FIG. 54.5. Spectacles with temple hearing-aid, the 'Otaxion', *c.* 1957.

means of a tuning fork, the ticking of a watch, the Galton whistle, the acoumeter, or the voice. The audiometer is superior to all other devices because it presents a sound source which is defined for frequency and intensity over wide ranges, for instance from 64 to 16384 Hz (cycles per second) in one model [34].

Cordia C. Bunch and Lee W. Dean at Iowa State University developed the pitch range audiometer in 1919. Others included valve hearing testers of K. L. Schaefer and G. Gruschke, and B. Griessman, demonstrated before the Berlin Otological Society the same year, which were the laboratory forerunners of the commercial models developed by the Western Electric Company Research Laboratory. The first one, Model 1-A was presented in 1922 by Harvey Fletcher and Edmund P. Fowler. It was soon followed by a portable model 2-A and then the 3-A, 4-A, and 5-A models.

Minimal requirements for acceptable audiometers were set in 1939 by the Council on Physical Therapy of the American Medical Association. The normal threshold of audibility is the modal value of the thresholds of audibility of a large number of normal ears in persons between the ages of 18 to 30 years [35].

Hearing aids. Two types of individual electric hearing aids are the carbon and valve instruments. These consist of a microphone which converts sound pressures into electrical energy; an amplifier which increases the intensity of the electrical energy; and a receiver which converts the amplified electrical energy back into increased sound pressures. Miniature radio valves were used in the construction of hearing aids from 1936. Usually Rochelle salt crystals were used to make the microphones and the miniature earphones. The valve instruments reproduced speech more clearly and with less extraneous noise. In 1948, hearing aids were improved further by the use of transistors allowing them to be made much smaller and yet more effective (Fig. 54.5) [36].

Inspection of the ear is made with an otoscope. This instrument is held in the hand by a handle, which contains the battery, and is inserted into the auditory canal by the funnel-shaped specula made of plastic or of a metal. The head contains a two- or threefold magnifying lens, and the light bulb. Careful attention to hygiene is essential in using otoscopes [37].

XI. MICROSCOPY

The microscope provided essential confirmation of disease through the study of bacteriology and pathology in the twentieth century. Electron microscopy began to be practised during the 1940s. Its main clinical importance by mid-century was the visualization of antibodies in combination with the surface structures of bacteria and viruses, and the differentiation of closely related viruses [38]. Its technical advantage over the well-established optical microscope was that as electrons act as if they are waves of very short wavelength it could achieve very much higher magnification with satisfactory resolving power.

In 1931 the editor of a text, *Recent advances in microscopy*, wrote: 'The use of the microscope is so essential a method in medical practice and research that recent advances consist mainly in improvements in technique and in new observation of fine structure' [39]. In this same year the electron microscope was born, an instrument which would reveal the finest structures yet seen by medical researchers. On 30 May 1931 Günther Reinhold Rudenberg, the research director of a German Company, Siemens–Schuckert, filed a patent application on the subject of combining several electron lenses, magnetic or electrostatic, to use in combination as an electron microscope.

The electron microscope is a device for obtaining optical images by a beam of electrons focused by a system of electromagnetic lenses to supply the illumination. Accurate images of details as small as 0.2 μm (micrometre) were obtainable with the light microscope by 1950. With the electron microscope, organic particles of o·oi μm diameter and dense particles of 2 nm (o·oo2 μm) diameter could be seen.

Technological solutions to the problems inherent in focusing electrons with electromagnetic fields led to L. L. Marton's functional electron microscope at the Université Libre in Belgium in December 1932. Marton described the microscope as follows: 'the main body was a brass tube about 2 in. in diameter and about 1 ft in length. The single lens consisted of a wire-wound coil that could be slid along the brass tube. The electron source was a flat tungsten coil, with the brass tube serving as an anode. At the opposite end a fluorescent screen was used either for visual observation or for external photography. Inside the brass tube a specimen mount was placed with means for positional changes.' The instrument had to be opened to change specimens or their positions.

Marton made the first micrograph of a biological specimen on 4 April 1934 with his second microscope illustrated in Fig. 54.6(a). With a third one, in 1937, he observed and published a micrograph of a bacterium [40].

Special techniques for making sections of dehydrated substances suitable for viewing by the electron micrscope were essential. Early ones included osmium-impregnated tissue culture preparations; 'electron staining'; and shadowing techniques, such as metallic shadow casting for greater contrast and three-dimensional images. To prepare the exceedingly thin sections necessitated by the low penetrating power of the electron beam, a high-speed microtome which cut sections down to o·i μm thickness was developed by members of the Research Laboratories of Interchemical Corporation of New York in 1944–5. The thickness of the section is inversely proportional to the speed at which it is cut. Previous microtomes moved at the rate of 100 inches per minute. A motion of 356000 inches per minute produced good sections of organic material, although even higher speeds were obtainable with the new microtome. The specimens to be sectioned were embedded in substances such as collodion, paraffin, or a variety of plastic films. Substances subsequently easily volatilized by sublimation were the most suitable. One especially satisfactory embedding mixture was composed of camphor and naphthalene, added to a liver specimen fixed with osmium tetroxide. Sections were collected by letting them settle like dust on coated slides or screens placed in the bottom of the box containing the microtome. Before viewing the specimen the paraffin had to be completely removed from the section with xylol [41].

The first commercial manufacturing of electron microscopes began with

FIG. 54.6(a). The second electron microscope of L. L. Marton in Belgium.

the leading electrical concerns. Metropolitan-Vickers in Manchester, Britain, made an abortive attempt in 1936, which it followed up nine years later. By this time Siemens and Halske, of Germany, followed by A.E.G. of Germany, and Radio Corporation of America (R.C.A.), had produced models. To be commercially feasible, the microscope needed to be robust and able to withstand the handling of someone not trained to appreciate its delicate components and yet respond flexibly to a skilled microscopist. By mid-century the commercial models were capable of resolution greater than 5 nm and some, under favourable conditions, reached 2 nm. Spherical aberration remained the chief limitation of both magnetic and electrostatic lenses.

One of the early successful electron microscopes produced in America came from R.C.A. Under the direction of James Hillier in 1941, the type B model microscope (Fig. 54.6(b)) possessed a good alignment system and A. W. Vance's excellent power supplies [42]. Several of these early series microscopes are preserved in the collections of the Smithsonian Institution.

The microscope and surgery. At first clinicians used the microscope to observe tissues in the eye and ear. Operations employing the stereomicroscope began in 1922 with L. Holmgren's fenestration operation on the middle ear. Richard Perritt of Chicago in 1946 became the first ophthalmologist to operate on the human eye using a modified stereomicroscope. With the greater precision and finer detail which is made possible with a stereomicroscope, surgical intervention results in less trauma to the tissues. It remained until 1953 when Zeiss introduced the colposcope so that microsurgery could be attempted in other fields. The ease of use of the instrument induced other specialists to invent techniques like microvascular surgery (1960). This refinement advanced surgical techniques to a new peak of excellence at a time when surgical treatment was subject to renewed questioning and criticism.

FIG. 54.6(b). The R.C.A. Type B electron microscope. L. L. Marton is on the right demonstrating to students, *c.* 1950.

Stereoscopic microscopes for observing specimens in three dimensions were discussed in the nineteenth century, and Carl Zeiss, the famous lens maker, produced a successful one in 1897. Horatio S. Greenough, an American living in Paris, wrote to Ernst Abbé and his assistant Siegfried Czapski in 1892 suggesting ideas for a microscope able to show three-dimensional objects such as the developmental stages of eggs, seeds, and other organisms in which he was interested. Greenough's name was applied to the famous low-power, large-field stereomicroscope designed and developed by Czapski, although Greenough, unsatisfied and frustrated, disowned it in 1907. The Greenough model remained essentially unchanged until 1919 when Leitz improved the instrument by adding wide diameter, well-corrected eyepieces and larger objectives. The Greenough microscope, when mounted horizontally, became a corneal microscope for inspection of the cornea in 1899. The combined Czapski microscope and by 1911 Allvar Gullstrand's slit lamp provided the basis for the ophthalmologist's tool which revolutionized diagnosis and some types of treatment [43].

XII. SURGERY

The advance of general surgery in the twentieth century made the hospital the centre of medical care and education. The extensive and costly equipment potentially available—such as the electrified operating theatre, which included special lighting, electrically controlled operating table, air conditioning, television and other teaching aids, and outlets for various instruments —was displayed in 1933-4 at an international health exhibition held in the U.S.A. [44]. Designed for the future, this type of equipment was in fact in use by the 1950s.

Improved anaesthetics and the virtual elimination of risk of infections provided the conditions necessary for specific techniques essential to effective surgery. When these fundamentals were achieved, an incredible variety of specialized surgical tools and post-operative equipment for the home and hospital appeared. General surgical tools, however, remained essentially like those produced in the last decades of the nineteenth century.

We may consider first the successes achieved in the prevention and control of infection. Henry Drysdale Dakin and Alexis Carrel, working in a Paris military hospital in 1914, tested hundreds of germicidal substances until they found an effective chlorine compound—a neutralized sodium hypochlorite solution which became known as 'Dakin's solution'. When applied daily, it killed bacteria and dissolved dead tissues so well that it remained a staple in the treatment of injuries and surgical wounds for several decades until it was replaced by the red dye discovered in Germany by G. Domagk (prontosil and neoprontosil) in 1935 and one year later by its active ingredient, sulphanilamide. Finally, there was the revolutionary antibiotic, penicillin. Discovered in Britain in 1927 by Alexander Fleming and developed in the early 1940s by H. W. Florey and E. D. Chain, penicillin was mass produced for the first time in 1944 in the U.S.A. for use by the Allied Forces in the Mediterranean. A host of other antibiotics soon followed [45].

Sterilizers for medical and surgical instruments, dressings, hospital garments, and linen began to be in demand during the last quarter of the nineteenth century as the fundamental significance of bacteria came to be generally understood. The earliest pressure sterilizers were manufactured in France and Germany as a direct outgrowth of the work of Lister, Pasteur, and Koch. An early American company was founded by J. E. and George Hall in 1894; this became the American Sterilizer Company of Erie, Pennsylvania, in 1902. Government contracts for portable bulk disinfectors and field sterilizers for the armed services stimulated the company's growth during the First World War. By 1943, 85 per cent of the company's production was in response to government contracts. By 1945, with a reorganized distribution system which included direct sales, the American Sterilizer Company was the leading supplier of medical sterilizers, employing 670 people by 1950 [46].

The demand for sterilized dressings created by the First World War expanded this industry. Older materials like sphagnum moss came back into use in England as a highly absorbent material in both the First and the Second World Wars. A dressing called 'Tulle gras,' which is made of cotton material coated with paraffin to prevent the dressing from adhering to the wound, was revived during the First World War and came into general use in the late 1930s. By 1950, new materials, such as plastics, improved the dressing of wounds. Dressings on surgical incisions were made of waterproof, non-absorbent plastic; while covering the sutured area its transparency permitted regular visual inspection and facilitated keeping the surrounding tissues clean [47].

The most common material for suturing wounds was composed of twisted strands of the submucous cellular coat of the sheep's intestines, traditionally, though inaccurately, known as catgut. Employed since antiquity for a variety of objects, its use to hold the edges of a wound together until it healed presented a special problem when it had to be sterilized. Among the chemicals used to sterilize the catgut were phenol; formalin; a solution of iodine in aqueous alcohol introduced in 1902; and, later, the most effective sterilizing chemical, chromic acid. The commercial suppliers of catgut were responsible for the purity of the material because it could not be boiled, like silk, under the supervision of the surgeon. The surgeon received the catgut in a sealed glass vial at the operating table. Other suture materials included refined cotton and, after the Second World War plastic substances such as nylon, dacron, and teflon [48].

The growing incidence of cancer and the limited control provided by X-rays, gamma rays, and radium encouraged the surgical removal of tumours. By estimate, in the U.S.A. there were 48 000 cancer deaths in 1900 and 216 107 in 1950. Many of these patients became candidates for surgery, especially of a type which required extensive removal of cells and tissues.

Real success lay in the control and cure of cancer by early detection of the primary tumour. Biopsy by needle puncture and aspiration was introduced in 1930 by H. E. Martin and E. B. Ellis. Many instruments were developed for these procedures, which enabled the surgeon to remove and examine cells suspected of being malignant. Examination of exfoliated cells brushed off with a rough-edged instrument developed and popularized by George N. Papanicolaou as the 'pap' smear came to the fore in the 1950s as a simple method of obtaining cells from accessible sites for study or cancer detection [49].

Cardiac surgery. The quintessence of surgical achievement in the twentieth century is thoracic surgery, which developed between 1930 and 1950 to the point of showing the future line of development in cardiac surgery. To permit deep chest surgery for extended periods at a minimal risk to the patient, suitable anaesthesia; accurate blood typing; an adequate supply of blood; proper instruments; a method of reducing the body temperature (hypothermia) (Fig. 54.7); and a temporary blood-pumping device or heart–lung machine were all essential. These were all available in the early 1950s.

One of the chief causes of heart failure in the twentieth century was the occlusion of small blood vessels within the heart muscle, leading to oxygen starvation and death of the muscle. Claude Beck in the 1930s developed a technique for supplying these deprived muscles with a new blood supply by grafting vascular tissues on to the myocardial region of the heart.

Maintaining the blood supply by transfusion depended on the discovery of the blood groups A, B, O, and AB by Karl Landsteiner, for which he received

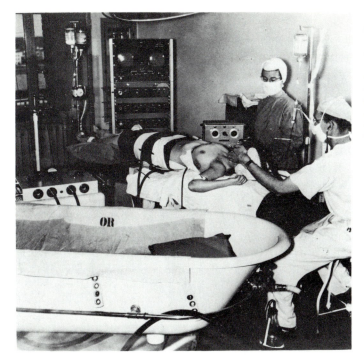

FIG. 54.7. Hypothermia apparatus (*c.* 1953) developed by Henry Swann of Lakewood, California, and used for open heart surgery. The patient, after removal from the freeze bath tub, has a heat-coil attached to bring the body temperature to normal. The oscilloscope in the background is used for monitoring temperature and heartbeat.

the Nobel Prize in 1930. By taking into account their properties of mixing without clotting, it was possible to match properly the blood of a donor with a recipient. Blood storage or banking became feasible during the Second World War (1943) when citric acid and trisodium citrate–glucose solutions were added to preserve the blood.

To keep the blood oxygenated while diverting it from the heart during open-heart surgery, the heart–lung machine was designed. As early as 1885 internal organs were perfused in such devices. The first operation on man was performed with a Forest Dodrill machine in 1952. After 1955 the DeWall bubble oxygenator became the safe and inexpensive heart–lung machine used in open-heart surgery [50].

At the time that an endoscope (cardioscope) was devised for looking directly into the mitral valve in the 1920s, cardiac catherization assumed importance in humans. Catherization was a routine procedure with laboratory animals by the 1880s and was first first applied to man by Werner Forssman in 1929, when he passed a tube into the right atrium of his own heart [51]. His purpose, and that of André Cournaud and Dickinson Richards of New York, who perfected and popularized the technique between 1937–40, was to pour medication directly into the heart through the catheter. By injecting a radio-opaque dye into the atrium, viewing the heart, pulmonary arteries, and catheter by X-rays was facilitated.

Heart valve replacement was accomplished with the aid of a valvuotome. Artificial valves were first experimented with by Charles Hufnagel of Boston operating at the Peter Brent Brigham Hospital in the 1940s. The first patient received a valve made of a hollow plexiglas ball from Hufnagel at the George-town Medical Center in 1952. As the blood flowed past the orifice, it made a clicking sound which could be heard by and beyond the patient. Soon, a hollow nylon ball coated with silicone rubber eliminated this noise [52].

Neurosurgery. Neurosurgery has largely been practised with the aid of general surgical instruments. Specialized instruments were primarily deve-loped after the First World War, except for L. Gigli's wire saw of 1898, which enabled the surgeon to remove the skull bone more safely. Other specialized tools include spinal tap devices; electroencephalographic devices developed by Hans Berger in 1929 and manufactured by the Grass Company of Boston; and stereotaxic devices for precise human cerebral localization in 1947. Electrocoagulation or electrosurgery, which is 'the application of high-frequency electric currents for the destruction and removal of diseased tissue or for cutting through normal tissues with diminished bleeding' promoted and taught successfully by the neurosurgeon Harvey Cushing, of Yale, in the 1930s, was crucial to brain surgery. Accidentally discovered by J. A. Revière, who cured an ulcer on the hand with the spark from a D'Arsonval apparatus in 1900, electrosurgery frequently replaced the scalpel, ligature, and hand contact with wounds by 1950 [53].

Obstetrics. From the seventeenth century, obstetrical forceps evolved over the centuries into hundreds of types. The main function of the instrument is to grip the head of the infant still in the womb without compressing it and leaving it free to rotate, flex, and extend during birth and to draw it in the proper direction. Various models of obstetrical forceps became fashionable on a national and regional basis.

A model designed by Arthur C. Jacobson of Brooklyn, New York in 1905 embraced the goals suitable for all instruments, although attained only in part by most of them. He claimed to have 'substituted steadiness for un-steadiness, mathematical precision for inexactness, measured traction for guesswork'.

The proliferation of models led to complex designs which hampered their effectiveness. In reaction to this trend, simplified models began to appear in the twentieth century. One example is W. Leipmann's axis-traction apparatus introduced in 1910. He replaced the metallic lever used for traction with a double cord looped over the base of both blades of the forceps [54].

Urology. In 1902, when the American Urological Association was founded in New York, the urologist was exploring the possibilities of the cystoscope developed in the mid-nineteenth century. Significant improvement in this endoscope was the result of J. F. McCarthy's design of a foroblique optical system and panendoscope in 1923. It provided a visual field of 55° deflected from the axis of the instrument and became the forerunner of many examining and operating instruments.

The most generally used urological instruments were catheters for the removal of stones and for drainage. Until the 1930s almost all catheters used in the U.S.A. were imported from France and Germany. Then the American Cystoscope Makers Corporation of New York developed an improved type in 1939. Made of nylon with a synthetic resinous coating, these instruments could be sterilized by boiling or autoclaving without deteriorating.

The most dramatic innovation in urological practice was the artificial kidney or kidney dialysis machine, which was introduced in 1943 by the Dutch physician Willem Kolff. In its original form it consisted of a large rotating metal drum wrapped with Cellophane coils, through which the patient's blood was circulated for the removal of wastes. Modified in 1950 and called the Kolff–Brigham machine, which was used extensively, the machine was refined until it became a small portable unit used twice a week by thousands of kidney disease patients in the 1970s [55].

XIII. ARTIFICIAL LIMBS AND ORTHOPAEDICS

Among the most individualized medical equipment manufactured were artificial limbs and orthopaedic devices. The First World War presented the first concentrated opportunity in the twentieth century to study amputations and the fitting of artificial limbs. The types of limbs manufactured in each country differed, but all craftsmen coped with the problems of the bearing points on a leg, proper alignment, and the mechanisms of the knee and ankle joints. The 'American leg', made of willow wood, reinforced with brass wire, covered with rawhide, and coated with enamel was the model preferred internationally [56].

American industry responded to the increasing demand for artificial limbs among the civilian population created by injuries in factory and railway accidents. In France, the orthopaedists who made corsets, braces, and trusses out of leather were called upon to produce artificial limbs during the First

World War. The expected form of rehabilitation influenced the type of limb supplied. In Europe, a manual worker who lost an arm was expected to return to his original job; hence, mechanical arms for this purpose were produced. In the U.S.A. a change of occupation was possible and amputees could wear other types of limbs [57].

Orthopaedic treatment combined surgery and the fitting of supportive and corrective appliances to direct the growth of bones and muscles (Fig. 54.8). Devices, such as the Thomas splint, originally designed in 1888; the Knight and Taylor braces introduced in 1884 and 1899; and the Sayre plaster jacket (1877) were applied carefully. The use of X-rays improved their application. although by the mid-twentieth century disillusionment with extant treatments was widespread [58].

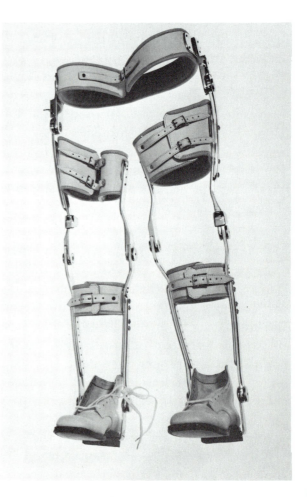

FIG. 54.8. Paediatric cerebral palsy braces.

REFERENCES

[1] TRUAX, C. *The mechanics of surgery*, p. 7. Truax, Chicago (1899).

[2] CURUTCHET, P. D. *The origin, evolution and modification of surgical instruments*, p. 19. Buenos Aires (1964).

[3] WHITE, S. S. *Eighty-two years of loyal service to dentistry*, p. 9. S. S. White, Philadelphia (1926).

[4] THOREK, M. *Surgical errors and safeguards*, pp. 19–23. Philadelphia (1958).

[5] FOSSIER, A. E. *New Orleans Medical and Surgical Journal*, 541 (1923).

[6] TRUAX, C. *Op. cit.* [1], pp. 15–18.

[7] TIEMANN, G. *The American armamentarium chirurgicum*, p. xvi. New York (1889).

[8] SALKIN, R. E. H. *Archives de médecine et de pharmacie militaires*, **86**, 334, 341–2 (1927).

[9] SELIVANOR, V. I. *Sovetsk Zdravookh*, **30**, 62–7 (1971).

[10] ROTHSTEIN, R. J. *History of dental laboratories and their contributions to dentistry*, pp. 16, 18, 22, 23, 32, 41, 70–4, 112. J. B. Lippincott, Philadelphia (1958).

[11] CUSTER, L. E. *Dental Cosmos*, **41**, 1007, 1008, 1010 (1899).

[12] DAVIS, A. B. *Texas Reports on Biology and Medicine*, **32**, 146–54 (1974).

[13] BEECHER, M. D., and FORD, C. In *Fifty years of surgical progress* (DAVIS, L. (ed.)) p. 225. Franklin H. Martin Memorial Foundation, Chicago (1955).

[14] TAINTER, M. L. and MARCELLI, G. M. A. *Bulletin of the New York Academy of Medicine*, **35**, 393, 396, 397, 399, 401, 403 (1959).

[15] BRECHER, R. and BRECHER, E. *The rays: a history of radiology in the U.S. and Canada*, pp. 48–54. Williams and Wilkins, Baltimore (1969).

[16] FUCHS, A. W. In *Classic descriptions in diagnostic roentgenology* (BRUWER, A. J. (ed.)) vol. I, pp. 92, 108, 109. Charles Thomas, Springfield (1964).

[17] QUIMBY, E. H. In *Medical physics* (GLASSER, O. (ed.)) p. 1166. Year Book Publications, New York (1944).

[18] BRECHER, R. and BRECHER, E. *Op. cit.* [15], pp. 64, 111, 138, 154.

[19] TROUT, E. D. *Journal of the Ontario Dental Association*, **35**, 33, 34, 35 (1958).

[20] BRECHER, R. and BRECHER, E., *Op. cit.* [15], pp. 343, 352, 379–384.

[21] RHINEHART, A. *Roentgenographic technique* (4th edn.), pp. 54–60. Lea and Febiger, Philadelphia (1954).

[22] JOHNSON, S. L. *The history of cardiac surgery 1896–1955*, pp. 56–8. Johns Hopkins Press, Baltimore (1970).

[23] WATT, O. M. *Anaesthesia*, **23**, 104, 105, 107, 109, 111 (1968).

[24] HEWER, C. L. *Recent advances in anaesthesia and analgesia*, pp. 19, 20, 51–3, 55, 93, 102, 113, 114, 137. J. and A. Churchill, London (1932).
For a detailed history of anaesthetic equipment up to the twentieth century see DUNCUM, BARBARA M. *The Development of inhalation anaesthesia*. Wellcome Historical Museum Medical: Oxford University Press (1947).

[25] WATT, O. M. *Op. cit.* [23], pp. 112–14, 117.

[26] HERB, I. C. *Journal of the American Medical Association*, **83**, 1788–90 (1925).
HEWER, C. L. *Journal of the American Medical Association*, 90 (1932).

[27] SALZER, M. *Journal of the American Medical Association*, **76**, 2096 (1929).

[28] BURCH, G. E. and DE PASQUALE, N. P. *A history of electrocardiography*. Year Book Medical Publications, Chicago (1964).

[29] BOONE, B. R., ELLINGER, G. F., and GILLICK, F. G. *Annals of Internal Medicine*, **31**, 1030, 1031 (1949).

[30] INBAU, F. E. *Scientific Monthly, N.Y.* **40**, 81, 82, 85 (1935).

[31] MASTER, A. M., GARFIELD, C. I., and WALTERS, M. B. *Normal blood pressure and hypertension: new definitions*, pp. 11, 27, 28, 31, 45. Lea and Febiger, Philadelphia (1952).
FISHER, J. W. *Journal of the American Medical Association*, **63**, 1754 (1914).

[32] MORRIS, S. *Practitioner*, **199**, 675–9 (1968).
MORRIS, S. *St Mary's Hospital Gazette*, **75**, 223 (1969).

[33] KERR, W. J. In *op. cit.* [17] (GLASSER, O. (ed.)) pp. 1480, 1484, 1490 (1944).

[34] REGER, S. N. In *op. cit.* [17] (GLASSER, O. (ed.)) p. 9 (1944).

[35] DAVIS, A. B. and MERZBACH, U. C. *Early auditory studies*, pp. 27, 28. Smithsonian Institution Press, Washington, D.C. (1975).

[36] BERGER, K. W. *The hearing aid: its operation and development*, pp. 23, 34, 51–55. National Hearing Aid Society, Detroit (1970).

[37] STOOL, S. E. and ANTICAGLIA, J. *Clinical Pediatrics*, **12**, 426 (1973).

[38] MUDD, S. *Annals of Internal Medicine*, **31**, 573 (1949).

[39] PINEY, A. (ed.) *Recent advances in microscopy: biological applications.* Blakiston, London (1931).

[40] MARTON, L. *Early history of the electron microscope*, pp. 9, 16. San Francisco Press (1968).

[41] MUDD, S. *Op. cit.* [38], p. 577.
FULLAM, E. F. and GESSLER, A. E. *Review of scientific instruments*, **17**, 25, 30 (1946).

[42] MARTON, L. *Op. cit.* [40], pp. 28, 29, 31, 39.

[43] PERRITT, R. A. *Internal Surgery*, **59**, 333 (1974).

[44] CAREY, E. J. *Medical science exhibits: a century of progress*, pp. 127, 128. Chicago (1934).

[45] MELENEY, F. L. In *op. cit.* [13] (DAVIS, L. (ed.)) p. 9.
CHAIN, E. B. Thirty years of penicillin therapy. *Journal of the Royal College of Physicians*, **6**, 103–31 (1972).

[46] FISH, H. E. The development and growth of the American Sterilizer Company. (typescript) pp. 6, 9, 13, 14 (1961).

[47] ELLIOTT, I. and ELLIOTT, J. R. *A short history of surgical dressings*, pp. 22, 23. The Pharmaceutical Press, London (1964).

[48] BULLOCH, W., LAMPITT, L. H., and BUSHILL, J. H. *The preparation of catgut for surgical use.* pp. 14, 20, 25, 32, 45, 98. H.M.S.O., London (1929).

[49] PACK, G. T. and ARIEL, I. M. In *op. cit.* [13] (DAVIS, L. (ed.)) p. 69.

[50] JOHNSON, S. L. In *op. cit.* [22], pp. ix, x, 42, 65, 66, 147, 156, 157.

[51] BENATT, A. J. *The Lancet*, 1, 746 (1949).

[52] JOHNSON, S. L. *Op. cit.* [22], pp. 106, 107, 129, 136.

[53] KELLY, H. A. and WARD, G. E. *Electrosurgery*, p. 1. W. B. Saunders, Philadelphia (1932).

[54] DAS, K. *Obstetric forceps: its history and evolution.* C. V. Mosby, St. Louis (1929).

[55] HIGGINS, C. C. In *op. cit.* [13] (DAVIS, L. (ed.)), p. 186.

[56] BROCA, A. and DUCROQUET, C. *Artificial limbs* (trans. ELMSLIE, R. C.), pp. xv, xvi. University of London (1918).

[57] FARIES, J. C. *Limbs for the limbless*, pp. 39, 40. Institute for the Crippled and Disabled, New York (1934).

[58] BICK, E. M. *Source book of orthopedics* (2nd edn.), pp. 431, 433, 441. Williams and Wilkins, Baltimore (1937).

55

WATER SUPPLY AND WASTE DISPOSAL

F. E. BRUCE

PART I: WATER SUPPLY

B Y the end of the nineteenth century, the main technical problems of providing adequate public supplies of good quality water had been solved (Vol. V, Ch. 23). Fundamental scientific knowledge in the realms of meteorology, geology, and hydrology had advanced sufficiently to enable reasonable estimates to be made of the available water resources of an area, even if there was still a great need for the collection of data on rainfall, runoff, and groundwater. Engineering techniques permitted great quantities of water to be stored behind massive earth or masonry dams and to be transported by aqueduct for hundreds of miles, if necessary, to the areas of demand. Powerful steam pumps could raise water from deep wells and boreholes and ensure distribution to all parts of a city. The hazards of the principal water-borne diseases were at last understood. The filtration of public water supplies through sand was becoming more generally adopted, and disinfection by chlorine or ozone had already been practised in a few limited instances.

Technically, therefore, it was possible in 1900 for almost any town to be supplied with adequate quantities of clean, safe water. In fact, this desirable state of affairs was still a long way off. The works required were usually very large and costly, requiring several years for planning and execution. In a period when cities were expanding, and their populations and industries increasing rapidly, it was only with the utmost difficulty that available sources could be brought into use to match the demand. Indeed, many major cities throughout the world have continued to the present day to struggle along with incomplete and often unsafe water supplies.

I. TRENDS IN WATER MANAGEMENT

During this period, water supply practice began to be affected by changing attitudes to the question of water resources as a whole. At the beginning of the century, the provision of public supplies of potable water could be looked at as a self-contained problem. A source of water, whether on the surface or underground, was sought, and appropriate works of collection, storage, treatment, and distribution were devised. In areas like the industrial north of England there was competition between different communities for the right to make use of the waters of a selected catchment. Competition also came from industry, whose demands were no longer to provide direct motive power through water-wheels, but were increasingly for steam-raising, cooling water, and process water.

Such competition was nothing new, but as the twentieth century progressed, other uses of water assumed more importance. Irrigation schemes, often of great magnitude, were initiated in many countries (Ch. 36), while hydro-electric power generation (p. 195) increased rapidly. Adequate river flows were necessary for navigation, the dilution of sewage and industrial effluents, recreation, and amenity, but these flows might also be subject to control to avert flooding. Not all of these often conflicting demands for water, or for its control, were necessarily present at any one place, but water supply had, more and more, to take its place among other uses, and to cope with increasing problems of pollution.

In some countries the management of water under such circumstances was effected by establishing a controlling body for a whole river basin, examples being in the Ruhr and other valleys in Germany, and the Tennessee Valley Authority in America.

The principle of unified river basin control of water resources was not accepted in Britain until 1948, when 32 River Boards, in addition to the existing Thames and Lee Conservancies, were set up in England and Wales. The idea had in fact been advocated for more than a hundred years, but had made no headway against the firmly established local government structure.

Public water supply in Britain was very much a local concern. Although Parliament had stepped in occasionally to create Joint Water Boards where competition for sources would have meant excessive waste and inefficiency, there were still, in 1935, only 48 such boards in England and Wales, compared with 790 separate municipal undertakings, 284 companies, and about a thousand private systems [1]. Proposals for a more unified control of water resources were repeatedly put forward by a variety of bodies: a Joint Select Committee of both Houses of Parliament in 1910; the Water Power Resources Committee, in 1920; and a Joint Conference of water undertakings and engineers, in 1935, among them. Some progress was made by the appointment of a Central Advisory Water Committee in 1935, while in the same year an Inland Water Survey Committee was formed to co-ordinate and stimulate the collection of records of surface water runoff and groundwater resources— an essential foundation for what was then being put forward as a 'National Water Policy'.

Such a policy was at last formulated in the Water Act 1945, which, while leaving water supply as a local function in the hands of the existing under-takings, gave the Minister of Health considerable responsibility for the con-servation and proper use of water resources, including the designation of areas in which the abstraction of groundwater should be controlled. Among other things, he was authorized to promote the amalgamation of undertakings into larger units, preferably by agreement, but compulsorily if he thought fit. This process of streamlining the water supply industry was barely under way by 1950, but it subsequently gathered momentum so that the number of statutory undertakings in England and Wales had been reduced from nearly 1200 in 1945 to fewer than 200 by the 1970s.

II. INTERNATIONAL ASPECTS

There had always been an international element in water supply, since it was incumbent upon countries with overseas territories to see that both native and expatriate populations were adequately supplied. This form of development led to some notable examples of waterworks in India, Hong Kong, and other areas.

After the Second World War, international cooperation developed in two ways. First, there was the closer communication and exchange of ideas between water authorities and engineers in various countries, exemplified by the foundation of the International Water Supply Association in 1947. Secondly, there was the increased concern of the more developed nations for the poorer countries which were still developing national and local organiza-tions and lacked money, materials, and trained personnel to design and build safe water supply systems (among their many other needs). This concern arose from many causes, among which a powerful one was the realization that, with more and speedier international travel, diseases like cholera and typhoid could be rapidly conveyed across the world, and even those countries which were making good progress in freeing themselves from these diseases were still threatened from outside.

The World Health Organization, established in 1948, quickly saw that environmental sanitation, including adequate and safe water supplies, was a necessary foundation on which health programmes could be built. In its early years it tended to emphasize assistance to rural areas, but in 1959 it began a Community Water Supply programme which, with the help of funds from international agencies, initiated major projects to improve water supplies in cities like Calcutta, Accra, and Istanbul.

III. DEVELOPMENT OF SOURCES

The search for, assessment, and development of all forms of water sources, which had gathered momentum during the latter half of the nineteenth century, continued throughout the following fifty years, checked only by wars and periods of economic stringency.

The water engineer owed much to the steady accumulation of geological knowledge, which helped him to find underground water and to locate and design dams. Increased numbers of rain gauges, including recording gauges, and of stream-flow measuring stations provided records which, when analysed by statistical methods, allowed more accurate estimates to be made of the reliable yields of catchments and hence of the volume of storage and size of dam required. Better knowledge of the frequency and magnitude of flood flows made for greater safety, particularly in the design of earth dams, many of which had failed because of inadequate spillway capacity to carry flood waters. The fact that dams were required for hydro-electric power schemes, irrigation, river regulation, and flood control, as well as for water supply, was also of assistance in stimulating the search for more scientific methods of design (Ch. 36).

Surface water supplies. The great majority of dams built during the nineteenth century had been earth embankments with central, vertical, clay (or occasionally concrete) core walls, continued as cut-off walls down to the solid rock or impervious stratum. This form continued to be generally used until the 1940s. The choice of material for the body of the dam was governed by what was available within easy reach, but the properties of the materials were not well understood until the researches of K. Terzaghi and others placed the new science of soil mechanics (officially christened as such in 1936) at the disposal of engineers.

As a result of this improved knowledge, the cross-sections of earth dams became more complex, with zones of material of carefully graded permeability, allowing free drainage of water from the outer zones, while maintaining a thoroughly watertight core. The control of seepage under a dam by such devices as an upstream blanket of impervious material or a partial cut-off

FIG. 55.1. Compaction of a rolled clay core-wall.

trench made it possible in suitable situations to dispense with a complete watertight cut-off wall where this would have been particularly deep and expensive. The value of such measures can be seen by considering the depths to which cut-off trenches have sometimes had to be excavated: up to 78 m at the Ladybower Dam (1935–45) of the Derwent Valley Water Board, nearly twice the height of the dam itself [2].

The development of heavy mechanical equipment for the excavation, transport, and consolidation of the fill material made it possible to build larger dams and led to some modifications in design. The traditional puddled clay core wall of about 2 m thickness, heeled into a compact solid mass by the treading of many workmen, was sometimes replaced by a mechanically rolled core of increased thickness (Fig. 55.1).

Rock-fill dams, made of coarse broken stone, and widely used in the U.S.A., were more economical in material than earth dams since they could be built to steeper slopes. The Shing Mun Dam, formerly known as the Gorge Dam, built between 1933 and 1936 for the water supply of Hong Kong, with a maximum height of 84 m, was unusual in having a massive concrete thrust-block designed to transmit the pressure of water to the rock fill behind it. The thrust-block itself supported a watertight concrete diaphragm forming the water face of the dam (Fig. 55.2) [3].

Dams built entirely of masonry were firmly established by 1900 (Fig. 55.3), but concrete played an increasing part in dam construction. Most 'masonry' dams built after 1900 were in fact concrete dams faced with stone for appearance's sake. Dams built entirely in concrete became more generally adopted as the quality of concrete work improved and masonry work became more expensive. A late example of a masonry-faced concrete dam is the 58-m-high Claerwen Dam built in mid-Wales for Birmingham, completed in 1952 with the help of skilled masons brought from Italy (Fig. 55.4).

The gravity type of dam continued to predominate. Design was still based on the principles enunciated by the early French engineers and by W. J. M. Rankine (Vol. V, pp. 556–7) and a celebrated controversy—mainly between Karl Pearson and W. C. Unwin, lasting from 1904 to 1908, during which serious doubts were cast on the accepted theories—eventually died down without affecting the procedures adopted by most engineers [4]. However, several of the arguments put forward were based on experiments on model dams made of wood, jelly, and rubber, and thereafter the testing of models became a recognized method of checking theoretical analyses of the stresses in a dam.

This technique was especially useful when applied to arch dams with their much more complicated stress patterns. Concrete arch dams were increasingly used where the necessary site conditions occurred—that is, in steep-sided valleys with solid rock to take the thrust of the arch. They offer an appreciable economy in the quantity of concrete required, an advantage which they share with buttress dams, such as the Haweswater Dam (1934–41) built to raise the level of Haweswater Lake by 29 m to augment Manchester's water supply (Fig. 55.5). In America many large buttress dams were built, some of them of the multiple-arch type, the dam face being formed as a series of arches supported by the buttresses.

By comparison with the impressive works required for impounding rivers in their upper reaches, the abstraction of water direct from a river is a relatively simple matter. However, it continued to be of great importance, and nowhere more so than in London, where more distant sources had been repeatedly rejected by nineteenth-century Royal Commissions. As London's thirst grew, the continued use of the Rivers Thames and Lee as the main sources was made possible only by the construction of a series of large storage reservoirs in both valleys. Being built on flat ground they were formed of a complete encircling embankment of similar cross-section to a normal earth dam, with a central clay core-wall keyed down into the natural bed of London clay.

Groundwater supplies. The collection of groundwater benefited from the improvements in rotary drilling equipment and techniques which resulted

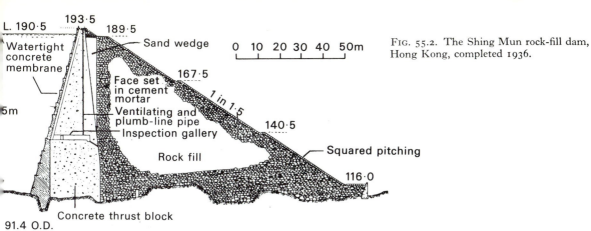

L. 190·5
193·5
189·5
Watertight concrete membrane
Sand wedge
167·5
Face set in cement mortar
1 in 1.5
Ventilating and plumb-line pipe
Inspection gallery
140·5
Rock fill
Squared pitching
5m
116·0
Concrete thrust block
91.4 O.D.

0 10 20 30 40 50m

FIG. 55.2. The Shing Mun rock-fill dam, Hong Kong, completed 1936.

55.3(a). The Howden Dam, of the Derwent Valley er Board, under construction in 1905.

(b). The Derwent Dam, of similar construction to the Howden Dam, completed 1916.

55.4(a). The Claerwen Dam for Birmingham under truction, 1949. A contrast with the construction methods n in Fig. 53.3(a).

(b). The completed dam, 1972.

FIG. 55.5. Haweswater Dam under construction, 1936. This is a mass concrete buttress-type dam.

from the growth of the oil industry. This method was gradually adopted for water wells from about 1900, but the percussion method, with a bit operated by cables or rods, continued in use, especially in softer strata. Fewer wells were constructed by digging, but the diameters of drilled wells tended to become larger, quite commonly up to 1 m, and sometimes as much as 3 m. Steel linings were in general use, but where there was much risk of corrosion cast-iron was still preferred, and occasionally more resistant materials such as stainless steel, bronze, or asbestos-cement were chosen.

Greater attention was paid to ensuring the best yield from a borehole, either by steps taken at the time of construction, or by subsequent development. From about 1930, many boreholes incorporated gravel packs, that is, a thickness of gravel placed around the well-lining as a transitional high-permeability layer between the water-bearing stratum and the well-screen. Methods of post-construction improvement, which had been in use for much longer, included surging, by forcing water alternately into and out of the well-screen by the use of a plunger; the application of acid to enlarge fissures in chalk or limestone formations; and the firing of an explosive charge at the foot of the bore.

The use of boreholes as sources of water supply was helped by the introduction of electrically driven centrifugal pumps. Steam-driven reciprocating pumps, with their massive moving parts, were to some extent replaced in the early years of the century by air-lift pumps, but by 1914 multi-stage centrifugal borehole pumps, driven by motors on the surface, had come into use. In the early 1930s completely submersible sets of pump and motor were introduced, doing away with long drive shafts and making the task of repair or replacement much easier.

IV. CONVEYANCE, DISTRIBUTION, AND PUMPING

Cast-iron pipes, which served the water engineer so well throughout the nineteenth century, continued to provide the principal means of conveying water, and the caulked lead joint remained the usual form, though many designs of mechanical joints, for example, bolted collars sealed with rubber rings, were introduced, some of them to become permanently popular. The main advance was the introduction, by Lavaud in France in 1914, of centrifugal casting of iron pipes ('spun-iron pipes'), a process resulting in sounder and stronger pipes than those produced by static vertical casting. Steel pipes were more widely adopted from the 1920s, especially when spun cement or bituminous linings became available.

Asbestos-cement pipes, first produced commercially in Italy in 1916, were laid by many water undertakings, their great assets being their relative lightness, smooth bore, and freedom from corrosion. By the late 1940s flexible polyethylene pipes of small bore were being used for some building services. Copper was making headway for this purpose, but lead plumbing was beginning to drop out of favour.

Major aqueducts requiring more than standard sizes of pipe were built as open channels, concrete conduits, or pressure tunnels, and in the U.S.A. wood-stave pipes of large diameter were not uncommon in areas where timber was easily available. New York made remarkable use of pressure tunnels in bringing water from its Catskill and Delaware catchment areas [5]. The Catskill aqueduct, built between 1907 and 1917, was a tunnel about 150 km long and 4·5 m diameter driven through solid rock. At its deepest point, where it passed under the Hudson River, it was nearly 340 m below sea-level. The Delaware aqueduct, built in the 1940s, was a similar pressure tunnel.

The long reign of the beam engine as a reliable, imposing, and dignified form of motive power for raising water was drawing to a close by 1900 when it was superseded by more compact types of steam engine or by gas or oil

FIG. 55.6. A Glenfield and Kennedy 170-hp compound beam engine, one of four installed between 1902 and 1905 at the Blagdon Pumping Station of the Bristol Waterworks Company.

FIG. 55.7. The Sir William Prescott, one of two triple-expansion pumping engines installed in 19 at the Kempton Park Works of the Metropolita Water Board. Each was of 1008 hp and capable pumping 12m. gallons a day (0·63 m³/s) to Nor London.

engines. However, some beam engines were still being built (Fig. 55.6), and the last to be installed in Britain, and probably in the world, was a 112-hp engine, made by Glenfield and Kennedy, at the Eastbury Pumping Station of the Colne Valley Water Company in 1919.

For many years most water pumps continued to be driven by steam engines of various types—horizontal or vertical, simple or compound. On larger works the vertical triple-expansion engine was a popular prime mover until the 1930s (Fig. 55.7). Diesel engines played their part, though their use as direct drivers of pumps gave way to the indirect process of generating electricity to drive centrifugal pumps.

The continuous smooth operation of the centrifugal pump, its adaptability, compactness, and wide range of sizes and types ensured that throughout the whole of this fifty-year period it would gradually oust the reciprocating pump. In the early years it was driven by steam—both reciprocating engines and turbines were used—but wherever electricity was available, or could conveniently be generated, this became the normal type of motive power.

V. WATER TREATMENT

The broad principles of treatment to convert a raw water into one fit for drinking had emerged by the early 1900s. The central process was filtration through a bed of sand by one of two distinct methods: slow or rapid sand filtration.

Slow sand filtration. The slow sand filter, depending for its great purifying powers on the physical and biochemical actions of the biological community which developed on the top surface of the sand bed, had been established for more than fifty years, and had proved its value in London, Altona, and many other cities as a barrier against the germs of cholera and typhoid. Its design remained unchanged in principle over the next fifty years, though concrete construction tended to replace brick or stone, and various designs of under-drainage systems appeared. In an attempt to avoid laborious hand cleaning, a device for washing the sand *in situ*, without draining the bed, was designed by M. Sivade in Paris about 1942. It was reported to be working satisfactorily ten years later [6].

Many cities, including London, used rapid sand filters as primary or roughing filters so that their slow sand filters could be operated at higher rates than normal. In this way the output of a works could be increased without a proportionate increase in the land required. However, pressures on land area, as well as an increasing experience of the capabilities of rapid sand filters

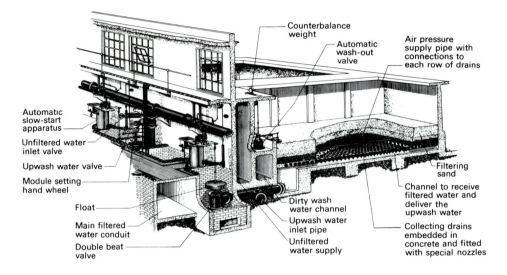

FIG. 55.8. Rapid gravity sand filters installed at the Walton-on-Thames Works of the Metropolitan Water Board, 1923–6.

and chemical coagulation, meant that by the 1940s fewer slow filters were being built for new treatment works.

Rapid sand filtration. The rapid sand filter, treating water at about fifty times the rate of the slow filter, depended almost entirely on the physical straining of suspended solids from the water (though it was later shown that some bacterial oxidation of ammonia could occur). It could take one of two forms: the gravity filter in which the water surface was at atmospheric pressure, or the pressure filter enclosed in a boiler-type shell of wrought iron or steel. Nearly all of the earliest filters of either type were built as small units in circular shells. Pressure filters necessarily continued to be limited in size, but later gravity filters were usually built in larger rectangular open tanks of reinforced concrete (Fig. 55.8).

Sand, being easily available in most parts of the world, has always been the natural material for use in filters, but other materials have been used. From 1884, the Candy Company in Britain made numerous filters containing a layer of polarite, or magnetic oxide of iron, which contributed to the oxidation of organic matter and was also useful for the removal of iron. The same company patented in 1910 its De-Clor system in which a bed of polarite or charcoal was used to remove excess chlorine following superchlorination with bleaching powder, a process in use at Reading from 1910 to 1912.

Coagulation. With coarser sand and much higher rates of filtration, the rapid filter, when used alone, was no match for the slow sand filter in removing bacteria. However, its introduction coincided with a period when the use of aluminium sulphate as a coagulant for the clarification of water was being discussed and tried in many countries. In 1885 coagulation was used by the Somerville and Raritan Water Company in New Jersey as a preliminary to rapid sand filtration and this use was adopted in many new American plants built from 1900 onwards [7]. The precipitate produced by the coagulant enabled the rapid filter to retain fine suspended solids, including bacteria, just as the biological film did on the slow sand filter. The combination of chemical coagulation followed by rapid sand filtration had by 1950 become the most usual form of water treatment.

Aluminium sulphate remained the most common coagulant, but ferrous sulphate and ferric chloride, which had been frequently used for the precipitation of sewage during the nineteenth century, were also employed. Sodium aluminate was introduced during the 1920s as an aid to coagulation by aluminium sulphate, and in 1937 John R. Baylis developed the use of 'activated silica'—a freshly prepared solution of sodium silicate which, in conjunction with aluminium sulphate, produced a tougher floc which was easier to remove from the water.

Preliminary treatment. Settling basins had been used from an early date to reduce the load of solid matter to be removed by slow sand filters, and when coagulation became a normal method of treatment a sedimentation tank gave time for the growth of the chemical flocs as well as for their settlement. Many tanks were built with baffles to provide the mild turbulence which helped this process of flocculation, while in America mechanical flocculators —usually slowly-rotating paddles—became popular.

Flocculation is also assisted if the newly formed colloidal particles come into contact with older, larger flocs. This principle was incorporated in a softening patent granted to William Paterson in 1902 [8], but it was not fully developed until the Infilco 'Accelator' (Fig. 55.9) and the Spaulding 'Precipitator' were introduced in the mid-1930s. Both included provision for the addition and mixing of chemicals, whether for normal coagulation or for lime-softening.

Sedimentation occurs naturally in impounding reservoirs, and in 1909 A. C. (later Sir Alexander) Houston reported on the great improvement in water quality, by settling and by the death of bacteria, which occurred in

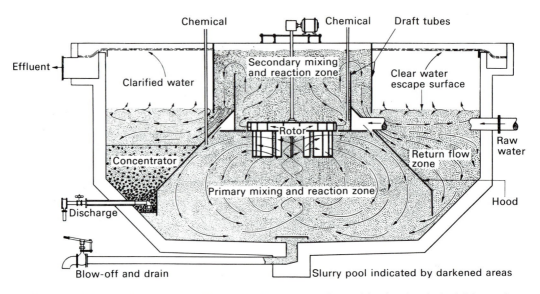

FIG. 55.9. The Accelator introduced by Infilco Inc. in 1936. It provides for chemical addition and mixing, sludge-contact flocculation, upward-flow clarification, and sludge removal.

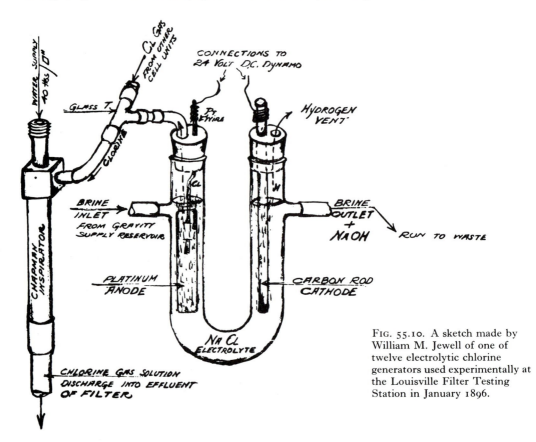

FIG. 55.10. A sketch made by William M. Jewell of one of twelve electrolytic chlorine generators used experimentally at the Louisville Filter Testing Station in January 1896.

London's Thames-side storage reservoirs. However, such exposed bodies of water, if they contain the breakdown products of organic pollution, are liable to develop heavy seasonal crops of algae, leading to serious filtration troubles and objectionable tastes and odours. M. N. Baker [7] recounts in detail the harrowing experiences in this respect of some American cities. It was shown in 1904 by G. T. Moore and K. F. Kellerman [9] that small doses of copper sulphate applied to the surface waters of a reservoir were effective in killing algae, and this treatment became the most common method of controlling the problem.

The physical removal of algae from water was made possible by the micro-strainer introduced in 1945 by Glenfield and T. Kennedy. This was a rotating-drum screen carrying a specially woven stainless steel wire mesh with apertures as small as 20 μm.

Disinfection. The increasing filtration of water supplies before and after 1900 contributed greatly to the reduction of water-borne disease. Filtration, however, was not infallible, and early experience of disinfection by hypo-chlorites in combating outbreaks of typhoid (Vol. V, p. 567) led to the idea of disinfection as a final safeguard after filtration. Solutions of bleaching-powder or other hypochlorite mixtures were used in all the earlier examples, but because of storage and handling difficulties they were not convenient for large works.

Gaseous chlorine was an established product of the chemical industry, and in 1896 it was applied experimentally to filtered water at Louisville, Kentucky by W. M. Jewell (Fig. 55.10) [7]. The wider use of the gas became possible when it was compressed to a liquid for storage in steel cylinders, in which form it was apparently used by V. Nesfield of the Indian Army Medical Service to disinfect tanks of water during a march from Lucknow to Delhi in 1908 [10]. This was an improvisation, but permanent full-scale use required precise measuring and pressure-control instruments such as were introduced by C. F. Wallace and M. F. Tiernan in America in 1913 (Fig. 55.11), and by the Paterson Engineering Company in Britain in 1917. One of the first Paterson chlorinators installed for the Metropolitan Water Board in 1917 was still in use more than fifty years later.

The addition of an alien chemical to public drinking water supplies met with considerable opposition, both from the general public and from some members of the medical and other professions. Its value was demonstrated in the treatment of doubtful sources of water for troops in the field during the

First World War, but opposition yielded only slowly during the 1920s. In Britain, there was a sharp reminder of the importance of disinfection when 43 people died of typhoid at Croydon in 1937 as a result of contamination of well water at a time when the chlorination equipment was being by-passed.

Problems of taste from the chlorine, or from its combination with other substances, were tackled at many works either by the use of ammonia in conjunction with chlorine, following the example of J. Race at Ottawa in 1916, or by superchlorination followed by dechlorination, as used at Reading in 1910. Neither process could be carried out with full understanding until the work of K. Holwerda, A. E. Griffin, and others had elucidated the phenomenon of the 'break-point'—the destruction of chloramines by higher doses of chlorine—and analytical methods had been developed to permit close study of the chemistry of chlorine and its compounds.

In 1929 Wallace and Tiernan installed at Little Falls, New Jersey, the first instrument for the continuous measurement and recording of residual

FIG. 55.11. The first gas chlorinator, installed by Wallace and Tiernan at Boonton, New Jersey, in February 1913 for the water supply of Jersey City.

chlorine. Improvements, using electrolytic instead of colorimetric measurement, led subsequently to automatic control of the dose of chlorine added to water so as to maintain a predetermined residual. The first commercial installation was at the Egham works, near London, of the South West Suburban Water Company in 1951.

The alternative disinfection process, the use of ozone, continued to be popular in France, but did not find much favour elsewhere. By 1937 the Compagnie des Eaux et de l'Ozone had provided 101 installations on public supplies in France and there were probably about thirty ozone plants in other countries (Fig. 55.12).

Among the objections to the use of ozone were its much greater cost than chlorination; the inconvenience of having to generate it at each site; difficulties in measurement; and lack of persistence. On the other hand, it is a powerful bactericide; does not produce taste problems; and leaves the water free of any extraneous chemicals. It is fair to add that ozone has attracted renewed attention outside France since 1950.

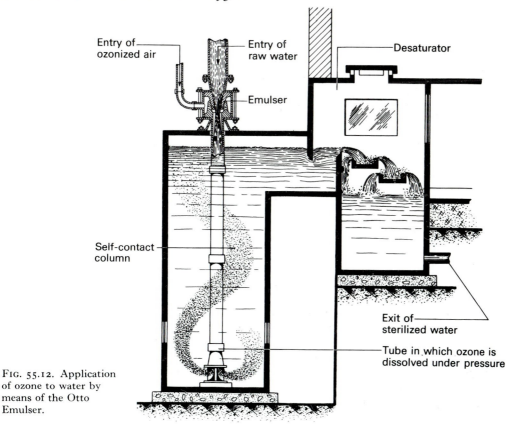

FIG. 55.12. Application of ozone to water by means of the Otto Emulser.

Other treatment processes. The ion-exchange process of softening water, patented by R. Gans in 1906, was widely adopted during the following years for both municipal and, particularly, industrial supplies, though it did not supplant the lime or lime-soda processes.

The capabilities of ion-exchange were greatly enhanced in 1935 with the production of new synthetic resins and sulphonated carbonaceous materials which had greater exchange capacities, and were physically more durable, than the earlier natural or artificial silicates. It was now possible to produce materials which could be used in a two-stage process of demineralization to give water of a purity comparable to that of distilled water—a process with many industrial applications.

As the chemistry of water treatment became better understood, other processes received more attention, particularly those of economic significance. They included the removal of iron and manganese and the adjustment of acidity and related properties to eliminate tendencies of the water to form scale on the one hand or to be corrosive on the other.

Finally mention may be made of the significant date of 25 January 1945 when the first experimental addition of fluoride to a public water supply was begun at Grand Rapids, Michigan, to be followed shortly afterwards by similar experiments at Newburgh, N.Y. and Brantford, Ontario. The object was to adjust the level of fluoride in the drinking water to around 1 mg/litre—the level at which the incidence of both dental caries and discoloration of the tooth enamel is at a practical minimum. Fluoridation has since spread to most countries where water treatment is practised, and favourable results have been repeatedly reported, but the process continues to be vigorously opposed by those who regard it as 'mass medication'.

VI. CONCLUSION

It is difficult to think of the years around 1950 as marking an end-point in the story of water supply, but it is easy to see this period as the threshold of a new era of progress. Partly as a result of the war stimulus, scientific knowledge, and technological development were forging ahead in many new directions, affecting both the problems facing water engineers and chemists and the means available for their solution.

Industrialization was spreading throughout the world, bringing greatly increased demands for water and at the same time polluting the sources of supply. There were new forms of pollution—radioactivity, pesticides, detergents, and other synthetic chemicals—while changing patterns of disease brought viruses into greater prominence and placed suspicion on many substances as possible carcinogens.

On the credit side, the post-war years brought forth the computer and the modern electronics industry, making possible the automatic control of treatment works and other equipment; the rapid analysis of flows in complicated pipe networks as well as stresses in structures, including dams; and the solution of many problems in management. Chemical analysis became more rapid, complete, and precise by the use of instrumental instead of time-consuming manual methods, and the membrane filter speeded up bacteriological examination. Several processes of desalination of brackish water or sea-water held out the prospect of a solution to the pressing need for new sources, with nuclear energy as the driving force.

Even so, the benefits of a safe and adequate water supply were available to only a very small proportion of the world's population in 1950, and the formidable task of extending these benefits required—as it still requires—many years of hard work on well-established lines, together with sensible planning and international co-operation and financing, with judicious use of advanced technology only where it was clearly appropriate.

REFERENCES

[1] DRACUP, S. B. Water supply in Great Britain 1690–1950: A brief history in six parts. *British Water Supply*, Nos. 1–6 (1973).

[2] HILL, H. P. The Ladybower Reservoir. *Journal of the Institution of Water Engineers*, 3, 414–33 (1949).

[3] BINNIE, W. J. E. and GOURLEY, H. J. F. The Gorge Dam. *Journal of the Institution of Civil Engineers*, 11, 179–222 (1938–9).

[4] PIPPARD, A. J. S. The functions of engineering research in the university, Unwin Memorial Lecture. *Journal of the Institution of Civil Engineers*, 33, 265–84 (1949–50).

[5] BLAKE, N. M. *Water for the cities*. Syracuse University Press, New York (1956).

[6] LAVAL, M. A method of washing filter sand. *Journal of the Institution of Water Engineers*, 6, 155–59 (1952).

[7] BAKER, M. N. *The quest for pure water*. American Water Works Association, New York (1948).

[8] SKEAT, W. O. (ed.) *Manual of British water engineering practice* (4th edn.). Heffer, Cambridge (1969).

[9] MOORE, G. T. and KELLERMAN, K. F. *A method of destroying or preventing the growth of algae and certain pathogenic bacteria of water supplies*. Bulletin No. 64, Bureau of Plant Industry, U.S. Department of Agriculture, Government Printing Office, Washington, D.C. (1904).

[10] NESFIELD, V. The sterilization of drinking water by chlorine. *Journal of the Institution of Water Engineers*, 16, 217–22 (1962).

BIBLIOGRAPHY

[1] above is mainly concerned with policies, legislation, and administration in Britain during the nineteenth and twentieth centuries.

[5] above is a detailed history of water supplies to the cities of Baltimore, Boston, New York, and Philadelphia, from a political, rather than a technical, point of view.

[7] above is a very thorough technical survey of water purification from the earliest times up to about 1940.

[8] above is an authoritative manual on current British practice in all aspects of water supply, and contains an historical review of mainly British developments.

The following will also be of interest.

Books

DICKINSON, H. W. *Water supply of Greater London.* Newcomen Society, London (1954).

METROPOLITAN WATER BOARD, *London's water supply, 1903–1953.* Staples Press, London (1953).

SMITH, N. A. F. *A history of dams.* Peter Davies, London (1971).

TWORT, A. C., HOATHER, R. C., and LAW, F. M. *Water supply* (2nd edn.). Arnold, London (1974).

WALTERS, R. C. S. *The nation's water supply.* Ivor Nicholson and Watson, London (1936).

WORLD HEALTH ORGANIZATION, *Urban water supply conditions and needs in seventy-five developing countries.* Public Health Papers No. 23, W.H.O., Geneva (1963).

Journals

Aqua, the quarterly bulletin of the International Water Supply Association; *British Water Supply* (formerly *Journal of the British Waterworks Association*); *Journal of the American Water Works Association*; *Journal of the Institution of Water Engineers and Scientists*; *Proceedings of the Institution of Civil Engineers*; and *Water Services* (formerly *Water and Water Engineering*).

PART II: SEWERAGE AND SEWAGE DISPOSAL

By 1900 most of the larger cities of northern Europe and North America, and many in other parts of the world influenced by European practices, possessed some degree of urban sewerage, though in few, if any, was the whole of the population served (Vol. IV, Ch. 16). The main principles of design had been established; appropriate materials and equipment were available; and the need had been clearly demonstrated by the health statistics of the nineteenth century. Progress during the next fifty years therefore consisted more in the construction of new and the extension or improvement of old systems than in the development of new techniques.

The removal of wastes from the immediate vicinity of dwellings is a considerable contribution to the protection of health, but the crowded populations of modern cities require further protection in the form of adequate purification of sewage and other effluents before they are released into the environment. The art-cum-science of sewage treatment was just being placed on a sound footing in 1900, and considerable progress was made in the course of the next half-century.

I. URBAN SEWERAGE SYSTEMS

When the water-closet began to come into general use in the early nineteenth century the existing cesspools were unable to cope with the increased flow of water-borne sewage, and it became permissible for house drains to be discharged into the surface-water sewers which had been based largely on culverted streams and ditches. In this way foul sewage from houses came to be carried in the same sewers as the intermittent and widely variable flow from rainfall and discharged direct into rivers, causing the well-known problems of river pollution in the mid- and late nineteenth century.

This system of 'combined sewerage' was maintained in J. W. Bazalgette's great interceptor scheme of 1859–74 in London (Vol. IV, p. 510), in spite of vigorous opposition by many who thought it far more sensible to keep the foul sewage and surface-water separate and send 'the rainfall to the river, the sewage to the land'. The cost and complication of two sets of sewers and house connections were enough to deter not only the Metropolitan Board of Works, but also many other towns, from adopting the 'separate system', except where there were plentiful points of outlet for surface-water direct to watercourses or soakaways.

The main disadvantage of the combined system was the necessity for overflowing part of the heavier flow in wet weather direct to a river, in order to avoid prohibitively large and costly main sewers and treatment works. These overflows caused pollution, which became more noticeable over the years as the construction of sewage treatment plants reduced the former main sources of pollution. For this reason the separate system of sewerage grew in favour. In the early years of the twentieth century, many towns converted their existing combined sewers to carry surface water only, and built new separate foul sewers. New areas of development on the outskirts of towns have usually been served by separate sewers, though many older central areas, and sometimes whole cities, including London, have continued to use combined systems.

FIG. 55.13. Shone ejectors installed in 1886 under the Speaker's Green, at the Palace of Westminster. Two of the three are still in use.

The only alternative to the familiar gravity-flow water-carriage system of sewerage to have made any progress was the pneumatic or suction system developed by Charles Liernur in the Netherlands between 1866 and 1873. The system was operated for more than thirty years in a large area of Amsterdam and was also installed in parts of Prague, St Petersburg, and other European cities. A small installation was in use in England at Stansted, Essex, for several years from 1902. The pneumatic system, however, was inherently more expensive and less reliable than gravity sewers, and fell into disuse until the principle was revived in the 1950s by Joel Liljendahl in Sweden.

A more limited application of pneumatic power was made in the Ejector patented by Isaac Shone in 1878. This was used as a low-lift pump and consisted of a chamber which, after filling with sewage, was emptied automatically by compressed air into a higher-level sewer. Numerous Shone Ejectors have continued to give reliable service all over the world. Three were installed in 1886 in the Palace of Westminster (Fig. 55.13) to prevent the bad smells caused by backflow of sewage from Bazalgette's interceptor into the Palace drains, which were said to have made Members of Parliament 'sleepy and seedy'. One was later replaced by a pump of larger capacity, but the other two were still in use ninety years later.

For the pumping of sewage where the natural gradients of the land were not sufficient for complete gravitational flow, the steam-driven reciprocating pumps in use at the beginning of the century gave way in most situations to centrifugal pumps, driven usually by electricity. Special designs of 'unchokeable' pumps were introduced which could handle crude sewage without becoming blocked by solids.

II. PROGRESS IN DESIGN

In the design of sewerage systems the estimation of the amount of foul sewage to be carried from buildings is relatively straightforward, but the calculation of surface water flows is more complicated.

Most nineteenth-century designers assumed for design purposes a continuous uniform rate of rainfall over the whole area drained, the chosen rate varying inversely with the size of the area. In 1889 E. Kuichling [1] in America showed that the maximum flow at a given point in a sewerage system resulted from a storm whose duration was equal to the time, known as the time of concentration, required for flow from the most distant part of the drainage area to reach the point under consideration. A longer storm would have a lower average intensity of rainfall, while a shorter storm would have ended before all the catchment area was contributing flow. This general principle (which requires modification in some circumstances) was the basis for the design of surface-water sewers on the 'rational' method, in which the rate of runoff at a given point was taken as the product of three items: the contributing area; a runoff coefficient depending largely on the impermeability of the ground surface; and the intensity of rainfall corresponding to the estimated time of concentration. The rational method was introduced into Britain in 1906 by D. E. Lloyd-Davies [2] but was adopted there more slowly than in Germany and America.

A weakness of the method was the use of an average intensity of rainfall which was assumed to apply throughout the duration of a storm. By the 1920s the accumulation of rain-gauge records enabled more typical 'design storms' to be used, in which rainfall intensity rose to a peak and then died away. One method for the use of such storms in design was that used by M. T. M. Ormsby [3] and C. A. Hart [4], while in America the unit hydrograph principle, as developed in surface-water hydrology, was used in a few instances before 1950.

By the 1930s formulae relating rainfall intensity and duration were extended by many observers to include a term for the frequency of occurrence of specified storms, an example being that of E. G. Bilham [5], which was applicable to the British Isles. Such knowledge permitted the selection of a design storm according to the extent of flood damage which might be tolerated in the event of inadequacy of the sewers.

III. MATERIALS AND CONSTRUCTION

Throughout the whole of this period there was little change in the design and construction of the smaller sewers. They were normally laid as circular pipes of salt-glazed 'stoneware' (more accurately, clayware) or concrete, with cast-iron pipes available where special strength was needed. They were in nearly all cases rigidly joined with spigot and socket joints sealed with cement mortar, and the many more complicated patent joints, some with a certain degree of flexibility, were not widely used.

Few other pipe materials were used for sewers to any great extent until after the Second World War. Asbestos-cement pipes, originally devised by A. Mazza in Italy in 1913, began to be manufactured in England and America in the late 1920s. They were used for many years as pressure pipes for water distribution before being adopted for gravity sewers.

Pitch-fibre pipes, made of cellulose fibres impregnated with coal-tar pitch, although used as early as the 1850s in Germany, did not become widely known until about 1900, when they were used in America principally for cable conduits, but also for small drains and gas mains. Their manufacture in Britain began in 1953.

In the early part of the period, larger sewers were built in brickwork, either to a circular cross-section, or in an egg-shape with the narrow end downwards to ensure a reasonable depth and velocity at times of low flow (Fig. 55.14). Since the 1930s sewers have rarely been built entirely in brickwork, though bricks have continued to be used as a durable lining over the lower parts of concrete sewers. Concrete, either plain or reinforced, and, since the 1940s, sometimes prestressed, provides a cheaper and more rapid form of construction, whether in the form of large-diameter precast pipes, or placed *in situ*.

The early history of clay pipe sewers had shown very frequent failures by crushing, yet, apart from some experiments by Bazalgette and W. Haywood in 1855–6, little attempt was made for very many years to relate the strength of buried pipes to the earth loads imposed on them. In 1913, Anson Marston,

FIG. 55.14. Junction of an egg-shaped brick sewer and one with vertical sides, photographed in 1951—a relic of the days of the separate Commissions of Sewers in London.

at Iowa State College, published a theory [6], based on the earlier work of W. J. M. Rankine and on his own experiments, which permitted calculation of these loads. The theory was further developed by Marston and his colleagues in the following years, but little use was made of this work in the practical design of sewers until the 1940s. It was only in the post-war period that its use spread beyond the U.S.A.

At the same time, the former concept of a sewer pipe-line as being necessarily a rigid construction, requiring massive concrete support in many situations, began to give way to the idea of a more flexible line, made possible by new designs of flexible joints and a more enlightened approach to the techniques of laying and bedding the pipes.

IV. SEWAGE TREATMENT

The last two decades of the nineteenth century had seen a major revolution in the approach to the purification of sewage. The key factor was the new knowledge which had come from the researches of Pasteur, T. Schlösing and A. Muntz, R. Warington and others into the nature and activities of bacteria. The role of bacteria in breaking down and oxidizing organic matter of all kinds was now appreciated, if not fully understood, and great efforts were directed to devising means of harnessing the labour of this vast army of microscopic workers so as to concentrate natural processes into the small compass of an artificial treatment plant.

Biological filtration. The main interest in the period around 1900 was centred on the filtration of sewage through solid media. This had progressed from unsuccessful attempts at physical straining in the 1850s, through Edward Frankland's intermittent downward filtration of 1868, to W. J. Dibdin's fill-and-draw contact beds of 1892 and many forms of aerobic and anaerobic filters in the 1890s. It was then realized that the essential feature of aerobic biological filtration was, as expressed by the Lawrence Experiment Station in Massachusetts, 'very slow motion of very thin films of liquid over the surface of particles having spaces between them sufficient to allow air to be continually in contact with the films of liquid'. This permitted the growth of an active film of bacteria and other organisms which were kept amply supplied with the necessities of life: the varied organic sources of energy and food in the sewage, plus atmospheric oxygen and moisture.

The main engineering requirement of this form of biological filtration, a means of spraying the sewage on to the surface of the bed, was soon developed by various manufacturers. Patents were taken out from 1894 onwards for distributors for both circular and rectangular filters. They were made to rotate or to travel by the jet reaction of the sewage, by the flow of sewage over a water-wheel, or by oil engine or electric motor [7].

The contact bed, comprising a watertight basin containing coarse coke, stone, or other material, which stood full and empty of sewage for alternate periods of one or more hours, continued to provide a rival method of biological treatment. The Royal Commission on Sewage Disposal, appointed in Britain in 1898 under the Chairmanship of Lord Iddesleigh, made an exhaustive study of the performance of both methods and concluded in their fifth Report, published in 1908 [8], that, volume for volume, the filter could purify sewage at twice the rate of the contact bed, and that it was, in almost all respects, a preferable form of treatment. The contact bed thereafter fell gradually from favour, though a few examples continued in use at municipal works until after 1950, for example, at Leicester and Carlisle. In Germany in the early part of the century a compromise was introduced in the form of an aerated contact bed in which air was blown through a bed carrying a continuous, instead of an intermittent, flow of sewage.

The Royal Commission established satisfactory principles of design and rates of operation which have continued ever since to guide the practice of what is now known as normal or low-rate filtration. Their recommendations were related to the production of a final effluent which could satisfy their own proposed standards (p. 1396). In America, where larger rivers were usually available to dilute effluents, such high-quality effluents were not always necessary, but attempts to operate filters at higher rates led to their being blocked by excessive biological growth. However, in 1935 it was found that this could be overcome by diluting the sewage with some of the effluent which had already passed through the filter. The application of a larger volume of diluted sewage resulted in a more uniform biological growth throughout the depth of the filter. Sewage could be treated at very much higher rates on the same volume of filter, though as the rate increased the quality of the effluent was reduced.

The principle of recirculation was rapidly taken up, and several variants of the process were patented. The use of large numbers of these plants at military installations in America during the Second World War enabled the National Research Council to produce a comprehensive report [9] analysing their performance and giving guidance for the future design and operation of high-rate biological filters.

In 1935, also, the Water Pollution Research Laboratory in England developed the method of alternating double filtration to treat milk-processing effluents which, with their high fat content and organic load, were not amenable to normal treatment [10]. This method, using two filters in series, but in alternating sequence, was subsequently found to be capable of treating domestic sewage at about twice the normal rate without deterioration of the effluent, and was adopted by many municipalities as a means of increasing the capacity of existing plants.

The activated sludge process. Just as biological filtration of sewage developed from attempts to concentrate and accelerate natural processes which occur in the soil, so the activated sludge process grew out of the observation that similar oxidation processes occur naturally in rivers. Early efforts to concentrate these processes in open tanks consisted of various forms of forced aeration to ensure ample oxygen to meet the requirements of undiluted raw sewage.

Experiments of this kind did not bear fruit until 1913, when Gilbert Fowler [11], who had worked on the aeration of sewage since 1897, suggested to his colleagues, Edward Arden and William T. Lockett, at Manchester,

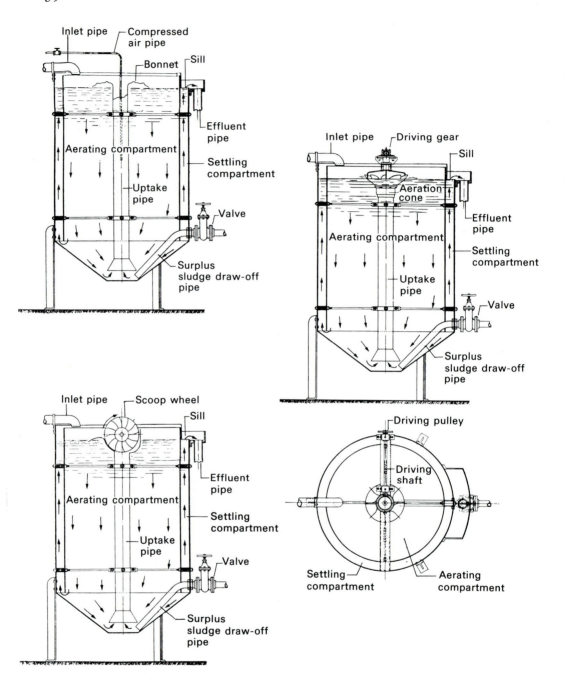

FIG. 55.15. Experimental equipment used by Joshua Bolton in developing the Simplex surface aeration system, 1916–20. The design on the right shows the form of cone finally adopted.

that when aerating sewage in batches they should retain the solids which settled out after the aeration of one batch and mix them with the next batch. The suggestion was based on his observation of some similar experiments at the Lawrence Experiment Station, Massachusetts, in 1912, but he was also aware that as long ago as 1886 J. M. H. Munro had noted that the retention of nitrifying organisms from one experiment on the oxidation of ammonium chloride enabled a succeeding experiment to proceed much more rapidly. E. Arden and W. T. Lockett followed the suggestion and found that by building up the solids through several successive aeration experiments, the time required for the stabilization of a batch of raw sewage could be reduced from five weeks to less than twenty-four hours. The solids, consisting of vast numbers of living bacteria, were named 'activated sludge' and the success of this method of treatment was announced in 1914 [12].

Further experiments on a larger scale led to the development of the continuous activated sludge process, in which the sludge was settled out in a separate tank and returned to be mixed with the incoming settled sewage in the aeration tank. Early continuous-flow plants were built at Worcester, England, in 1916; Manchester in 1917; and Houston, Texas, also in 1917. By the early 1920s several methods of aeration had become established: the diffused-air process, using porous diffuser-plates in the bottom of the tank; the surface-aeration method in which a partly submerged rotor on a vertical shaft agitated and circulated the contents of a square tank (Fig. 55.15); and the Haworth or 'bio-aeration' process, using large paddles to propel the sewage along a series of narrow channels—a kind of artificial river—first used at Sheffield in 1920. In 1925 the Kessener brush system, another surface aeration method, was introduced in the Netherlands.

Part of London's sewage was given biological treatment for the first time in 1930, using a modification of the Haworth system (Fig. 55.16). A bold step forward was taken with the construction, between 1931 and 1935, of the largest activated sludge plant in Europe at Mogden to serve a population of one million in west Middlesex (Fig. 55.17). This works, using the diffused-air process, replaced twenty-eight existing small works, and produced an effluent of very high quality for discharge into the River Thames [13].

Other treatment processes. To prepare sewage for biological treatment a large proportion of the suspended solids must first be removed by sedimentation, by allowing the sewage to flow slowly through a large open tank. The earlier practice of using chemicals to precipitate the solids was gradually

FIG. 55.16. Activated sludge plant, Northern Outfall Works, London County Council. Under construction (*left*), 1930. The unusual arrangement of under-and-over channels can be seen. In operation (*right*) in 1972, shortly before demolition.

FIG. 55.17. Mogden Purification Works, West Middlesex Main Drainage, 1936.

abandoned in most places and plain sedimentation became the rule. Besides rectangular tanks, other shapes were adopted, including circular radial-flow tanks and deep tanks of conical, pyramidal, or cylindrical section in which the sewage flowed upwards at a velocity just less than the settling velocity of the solids.

The accumulated sludge from the flat-bottomed rectangular tanks had to be removed manually every few days, after the supernatant liquid had been drawn off over a telescopic or floating weir. Perhaps the earliest attempt to remove sludge without emptying the tank was that of Joseph Corbett at Salford, near Manchester in 1894, shown in Fig. 55.18. Generally, however, the manual method persisted until the Mieder scraper, having a blade suspended from a travelling bridge, was introduced in Germany in the 1920s and to Britain in 1934.

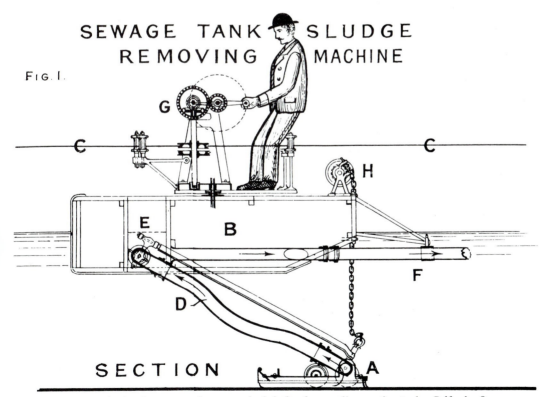

FIG. 55.18. Corbett's pontoon for removal of sludge from sedimentation tanks, Salford, 1894.

Rotating scrapers for circular tanks had already been in use for many years. The preliminary treatment processes of screening and grit removal had also long been mechanized to some extent, at least on the larger works, but mechanized equipment was much more generally adopted during the period around 1930 [14].

Sludge digestion. The sludge removed from sedimentation tanks, being essentially a more concentrated form of raw sewage, was always troublesome to deal with, since it was putrescible, odorous, and greasy and contained up to 98 per cent water, much of which was difficult to remove.

The septic tank principle, used in L. Mouras' 'Automatic Scavenger' in France from 1860, and by D. Cameron in Britain at Exeter in 1895, provided a clue to an improved method of treating sludge, for it was noticed that the sludge which had been digested or fermented by anaerobic bacteria in a septic tank was of uniform consistency and inoffensive. Moreover, the gas produced during digestion, mainly methane, was a useful fuel, which had been used by Cameron to illuminate his works. In 1907 C. Carkeet James used the gas from a septic tank to drive a $1\frac{1}{2}$-hp gas engine at a leper asylum near Bombay, and at Parramatta, in Australia, the sewage was pumped with power derived from the gas produced.

About 1904 Karl Imhoff, the German pioneer of sewage treatment, patented a two-storey sedimentation tank in which the sludge was digested in the lower compartment out of contact with the liquid part of the sewage (Fig. 55.19). These Imhoff or Emscher tanks became popular in Germany, Holland, and America, and the gas was commonly collected for use. They were not used much in Britain, but J. D. Watson in 1909 succeeded in digesting sludge, after its separation from sewage, by pumping it into a large lagoon at Minworth, Birmingham. This process was introduced on a large scale in 1911, and in 1927 special sludge-digestion tanks, with floating gas-holder roofs (Fig. 55.20), were built, the gas being used in a 150-hp engine to generate electricity [15]. In very cold weather, live steam was injected to heat the raw sludge before it was added to the tanks. The value of maintaining a high temperature in digesting sludge was emphasized by Imhoff, and from 1927 it became common practice to digest separated sludge in enclosed tanks whose contents were maintained near the optimum temperature (about 35 °C) by burning a proportion of their own gas. The improved yield of gas enabled many plants to be quite self-supporting in their energy requirements for pumping and air-compression.

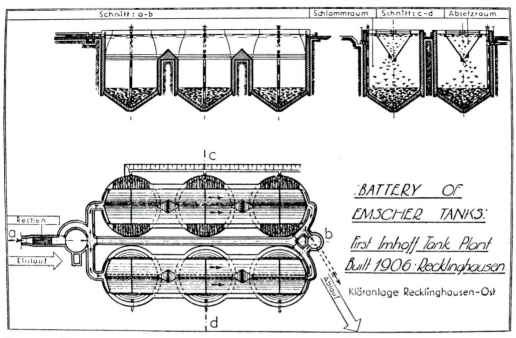

FIG. 55.19. The first Imhoff tank, 1906.

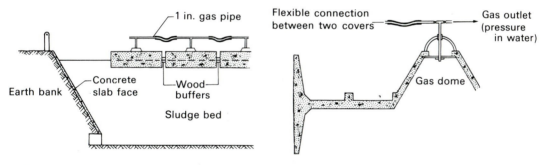

FIG. 55.20. Floating concrete covers for collecting gas from open sludge digestion tanks, Birmingham, 1927.

V. WATER POLLUTION

The widespread construction of sewerage systems meant that large amounts of polluting matter were transferred from the vicinity of dwellings to the rivers, frequently without treatment, or with only partial treatment. The same applied to industrial effluents, which were increasing in numbers, volume, and variety.

The resulting pollution of rivers called for both technical investigation and legislative and administrative action. In Britain, the technical need was met in the early years by the Royal Commission on Sewage Disposal, which sponsored many studies of treatment processes and the phenomena of water pollution. It standardized analytical procedures, notably the five-day test for biochemical oxygen demand (BOD) and recommended standards of quality for sewage effluents [16]. These widely quoted 'Royal Commission Standards,' selected as being suitable under most circumstances for effluents discharged into British rivers, were adopted as the usual basis of effluent standards by pollution control authorities in Britain, and in some other countries, for more than half a century. The fact that they were attainable by both biological filtration and the activated sludge process, as long as a plant was properly operated and not overloaded, provided an incentive to works managers.

Valuable contributions to the understanding of water pollution were also made by many individual chemists and biologists in government and local authority departments and in universities. However there was a gap in official research in Britain following the disbandment of the Royal Commission in 1915 until the Water Pollution Research Laboratory was established in 1927.

Legislatively things moved slowly. The Rivers Pollution Prevention Act, 1876 continued in force until 1951, but it was largely ineffective because its good intentions were not matched by an adequate administrative structure. Not until 1948 was the idea that drainage and pollution control should be based on natural river basins instead of artificial boundaries, an idea mooted for over a hundred years by many people, brought to partial fruition by the creation of thirty-two River Boards (plus the existing Thames and Lee Conservancies) in England and Wales. It still required the Rivers (Prevention of Pollution) Act, 1951 and later legislation to give adequate powers to the River Boards and their successors to work towards positive improvements in river conditions.

In the meantime the Public Health (Drainage of Trade Premises) Act, 1937 had regularized the discharge of industrial effluents in Britain into public sewers for treatment with domestic sewage, with a consequent reduction in the number and severity of discharges direct to rivers.

In Germany, particularly severe industrial pollution in the Ruhr District was met by the formation of special river associations with responsibility for river regulation and quality control, including the construction and operation of sewage and industrial effluent treatment plants. The first of these, the Emschergenossenschaft, was set up in 1904 [17].

American legislation on water pollution was for most of this period in the hands of individual States, with some coordination by interstate agencies where rivers crossed State boundaries. Some of these, such as the Ohio River Valley Water Sanitation Commission (ORSANCO), established in 1948 and involving eight States, were empowered to control pollution for complete river basins. The Federal Government made some progress towards a more uniform nationwide control when its Water Pollution Control Act of 1948 was passed.

Other nations, especially in Europe, were also suffering from the increasing sewage and industrial pollution of rivers and each in its own way responded by research, construction, and legislation [18]. It cannot be said, however, that these efforts, in general, did much more than keep pollution at bay. The progress which was gathering momentum during the 1930s was in many countries brought to a standstill by the Second World War and it was some time after 1945 before the forward movement could be resumed. By 1950, however, the future needs were being assessed and, with greater international exchange of knowledge and ideas, the methods of abating water pollution were more widely understood and being put into effect.

REFERENCES

[1] KUICHLING, E. The relation between the rainfall and the discharge of sewers in populous districts. *Transactions of the American Society of Civil Engineers*, **20**, 1–56 (1889).

[2] LLOYD-DAVIES, D. E. The elimination of storm-water from sewerage systems. *Minutes of the Proceedings of the Institution of Civil Engineers*, **164**, 41–67 (1905–6).

[3] ORMSBY, M. T. M. Rainfall and run-off calculations. *Journal of the Institution of Municipal Engineers*, **59**, 889–94 (1933).

[4] HART, C. A. Rainfall and run-off (Correspondence). *Journal of the Institution of Municipal Engineers*, **59**, 978 (1933).

[5] BILHAM, E. G. Classification of heavy falls in short periods. *British Rainfall, 1935*, pp. 262–80, H.M.S.O., London (1936).

[6] MARSTON, A. The theory of loads on pipes in ditches. *Iowa Engineering Experimental Station*, Bulletin No. 31 (1913).

[7] STANBRIDGE, H. H. The introduction of rotating and travelling distributors for biological filters. *Water Pollution Control*, **71**, 573–77 (1972).

[8] ROYAL COMMISSION ON SEWAGE DISPOSAL. *Fifth Report*, Cd. 4278, H.M.S.O., London (1908).

[9] NATIONAL RESEARCH COUNCIL. Sewage treatment at military installations. Report of the Sub-Committee on Sewage Treatment in Military Installations of the Committee on Sanitary Engineering. *Sewage Works Journal*, **18**, 787–1028 (1946).

[10] DEPARTMENT OF SCIENTIFIC AND INDUSTRIAL RESEARCH, *The treatment and disposal of waste waters from dairies and milk products factories*. Water Pollution Research Technical Paper No. 8, H.M.S.O., London (1941).

[11] FOWLER, G. J. *An introduction to the biochemistry of nitrogen conservation.* Arnold, London (1934).

[12] ARDEN, E. and LOCKETT, W. T. Experiments on the oxidation of sewage without the aid of filters. *Journal of the Society of Chemical Industry, Lond.*, **33**, 523–39 (1914).

[13] WATSON, D. M. West Middlesex main drainage. *Journal of the Institution of Civil Engineers,* **5**, 463–568 (1936–7).

[14] CARGILL, J. D. A history of sewage works' machinery. *Water Pollution Control*, **74**, 430–54 (1975).

[15] WATSON, J. D. Presidential Address, *Journal of the Institution of Civil Engineers*, **1**, 15–34 (1935).

[16] ROYAL COMMISSION ON SEWAGE DISPOSAL. *Eighth Report*, Cd 6464, H.M.S.O., London (1912).

[17] FAIR, G. M. Pollution abatement in the Ruhr district. *Journal of the Water Pollution Control Federation*, **34**, 749–66 (1962).

[18] WORLD HEALTH ORGANIZATION. *Control of water pollution, a survey of existing legislation.* W.H.O., Geneva (1967).

BIBLIOGRAPHY

(a) *General*

SIDWICK, J. M. and MURRAY, J. E. A brief history of sewage treatment. *Effluent and Water Treatment Journal*, **16**, pp. 65, 193, 295, 403, 515, and 609 (1976).

STANBRIDGE, H. H. *History of sewage treatment in Britain.* Institute of Water Pollution Control, Maidstone (Published in parts from 1976).

[Eleven parts published up to October 1977: Introduction of the water-carriage system; Preliminary treatment and treatment of storm sewage; Chemical treatment; Removal of suspended matter; Land treatment; Biological filtration; Activated sludge process; Tertiary treatment; Anaerobic digestion of sewage sludge; Preliminary treatment and conditioning of sewage sludge; Dewatering and drying of sewage sludge.]

(b) *Particular aspects*

CARGILL, J. D. A history of sewage works' machinery. *Water Pollution Control*, **74**, 430–54 (1975).

STANBRIDGE, H. H. The development of biological filtration. A series of articles starting in *Water and Sanitary Engineer*, **4**, 297 (1954) and concluding in *Water and Waste Treatment Journal*, **7**, 352 (1959).

Symposium on the evolution and development of the activated sludge process of sewage purification in Great Britain. *Journal and Proceedings of the Institute of Sewage Purification*, Part 3, 174–272 (1954).

Historical aspects of sewerage and sewage treatmemt are also covered in many contributions to the journals of the following bodies, among others: Institute of Water Pollution Control (formerly Institute of Sewage Purification); Institution of Civil Engineers; Institution of Public Health Engineers (formerly Institution of Sanitary Engineers); Society of Chemical Industry; and Water Pollution Control Federation (U.S.A.).

56

FOOD TECHNOLOGY

J. B. M. COPPOCK

PART I: THE SCIENTIFIC BACKGROUND

I. THE NINETEENTH-CENTURY LEGACY

THE treatment of food to make it more palatable, or to preserve it from times of plenty to times of scarcity, is virtually as old as civilization itself. Indeed, the transition from a nomadic way of life to the urban communities of the ancient world would have been impossible without the stability conferred on daily life by the development of food technology. It is, therefore, a subject that has been repeatedly touched on in earlier volumes of this work. Although our present concern is food technology in the first half of the present century, which saw the emergence of a large and highly organized food industry, we cannot altogether omit reference to the practices of earlier times, and especially of the latter part of the nineteenth century, for it is from these that modern techniques have directly evolved. Grinding and pulverizing; heat treatment; dehydration; biological treatments involving enzymes; addition of chemical preservatives; the avoidance or elimination of natural toxins, are all still an essential part of the processing of food. The two world wars of this century have provided powerful stimuli, as did many of the major wars of the past. Old results may be achieved by new methods: refrigeration replaced the ancient use of natural ice, drying in the sun by sublimation of water from the frozen state or other processes of dehydration. Greater concern for public health led to the enactment of much legislation to protect the consumer. So far as the nineteenth century is concerned these new developments have been discussed at some length in an earlier volume of this work (Vol. V, Ch. 2) and we need here recapitulate only those which served as stepping-stones to twentieth-century practice, which is the concern of this present volume.

On the manufacturing side, the variety of products and the quantity in which they were produced were such that by the end of the century a food industry was firmly established. Nicolas Appert's methods of preserving foods by enclosing them in glass vessels and then hermetically sealing these after heat treatment were quickly taken up outside France. The most important development was the substitution of tin-plate cannisters (cans) for glass jars, first in Britain (*c.* 1814) and later in the U.S.A., where they were introduced in 1817 by an Englishman, William Underwood. Fish was soon being canned in New York and in 1819 Underwood was canning meat in Boston. Cans were not, however, widely used in America until the late 1830s. In 1848, canning was introduced into New South Wales. A century later, 10 000m. cans were being used annually in America alone; the canning industry had become the world's biggest consumer of steel and tin; and the new industry had significantly affected the whole pattern of agriculture.

From France, too, developed another important form of food manufacture —the making of margarine. This was a consequence of the offer, by the government of Napoleon III, of a prize for a process for making a fat as stable, appetizing, and nutritious as butter. It was intended primarily for the use of the army and the poorer members of the community. Margarine was invented, between 1868 and 1870, by Hippolyte Mège-Mouriés. A factory was established in 1870 at Poissy, near Paris, and shortly after the Société Anonyme d'Alimentation was formed to work the process. Basically, this consists in emulsifying animal fats with milk, and colouring it with annatto. An important development, at the turn of the century, was the discovery that unsaturated oils, too fluid for margarine manufacture, would be hardened by reducing them with hydrogen, in the presence of nickel as catalyst, by the Sabatier–Senderens reaction. Like canning, this industry grew rapidly. By the middle of the present century world production exceeded £5000m. annually, and by that time it was general practice to improve the nutritional value by adding vitamins A and D.

We must recall, also, another major development in food technology—the large-scale preservation of food by refrigeration. About 1870, chilled meat was successfully imported into Britain from the U.S.A. by the use of mixtures of ice and salt. Apart from inherent disadvantages, this method was unsuitable for the much longer voyages from the new major centres of meat production such as Australia, New Zealand, and South America. For this, mechanical refrigerating plant was necessary. In 1877, Charles Tellier imported frozen meat into France from South America, after a voyage lasting 104 days. Three years later, 40 tons of frozen beef and mutton arrived in London from Australia. The importance of chilling for the preservation of fish—which spoil very rapidly—had long been recognized. By the middle of the nineteenth century fish was being kept fresh in transport from the fishing grounds to the markets by packing it in ice (Ch. 14).Other products, too, began to be refrigerated, including eggs, from about 1890, though in bulk and not in the shell. The freezing of fruit and vegetables presented difficulties which were not overcome until the present century; we shall return to this subject in the following chapter.

Milk is another basic commodity which spoils rapidly. Well before the end of the century the manufacture of both condensed and dried milk was well established, the first originating in Switzerland and the second in Britain. The manufacture of cheese, one of the oldest of all methods of preserving the nutritious content of milk, was at the same time being transformed from a small-scale farmhouse process to one carried out in factories. Factory-made cheese was already well known in North America and Australia in the 1880s.

Alongside these practical developments was growing a better understanding of the basic principles of food preservation and of human and animal nutrition. The work of Pasteur, had, of course, opened the way to recognition of the role of micro-organisms in the spoilage of food and provided a logical explanation for traditional methods of preservation. These discoveries were turned to practical use in, for example, the cheese industry. Before the end of the century R. J. Drummond and J. R. Campbell, at the Glasgow and West of Scotland Technical College, found that discoloration in the ripening of cheese could be avoided by using pure cultures of lactic acid ferments. In the nutritional field it had been established that human muscle derives its energy not from nitrogen, as Liebig had supposed, but from the oxidation of carbohydrate. By the turn of the century, in Britain, nutrition had even been incorporated in school courses on Domestic Science.

These technological developments, all generally conducive to feeding a rapidly growing population, especially one increasingly concentrated in urban areas, were unfortunately accompanied by other developments not at all in the interests of the consumer. While certain forms of treatment could be used to improve and preserve foods, others were harmful; and in the nineteenth century the adulteration of food—whether from ignorance or avarice —became an increasingly serious problem. It was not, of course, a new one: for example, in the late Middle Ages the Grocers' Company in London was entrusted with ensuring that pepper and other spices were not contaminated (Vol. II, p. 128).

By the nineteenth century, with the balance of food production beginning to shift from the home to the factory, adulteration became an increasingly disturbing problem. In Britain, early legislation to prohibit the adulteration of food was embodied in Acts of Parliament introduced in 1822 and 1836, but these contained inadequate provision for enforcement. An important factor in their introduction was the influence of Frederick Accum, who in 1820 published his *Treatise on the adulteration of food, and culinary poisons*: it was aptly prefaced by the Biblical quotation 'there is death in the pot'. Of the hundreds of illustrations he gave, we may instance: pickles coloured with copper ('boil them with a halfpence') to make them green; vinegar rendered sharp with sulphuric acid; and the leaves of the poisonous cherry laurel used as a flavouring. Ignorance, rather than avarice, prompted a hazardous recommendation to store olive oil in lead or pewter vessels to prevent its going rancid. Lead shot was sometimes added to port to create a sediment indicative of age.

In 1850 the editor of the British medical periodical *The Lancet* commenced a campaign against food adulteration, boldly naming specific cases. After a commission of inquiry in 1855, the Adulteration of Food and Drink Act came into being (1860). This made it an offence in Britain to sell food containing an injurious ingredient. It also permitted—but did not make obligatory—the appointment of analysts by certain local authorities. However, in 1872 the Adulteration of Food and Drugs Act made the powers compulsory and extended the right of appointing analysts to boroughs having separate police establishments. This was followed in 1875 by a consolidating Act which is internationally regarded as the foundation of modern food legislation.

This appointment of public analysts was an extremely important stage in the development of food technology, for it led many food manufacturers to employ chemists of their own to ensure that the required standards of purity were maintained in raw materials and finished products. It drew attention, too, to the need for improvements in analytical methods. Thus in Britain the Sale of Food and Drugs Act (1899) required that butter fat introduced into margarine should not exceed 10 per cent. Unfortunately, methods of analysis then current did not give unequivocal results and local analysts found themselves in disagreement with Government analysts based at Somerset House in London. Sir Edward Thorpe, professor of chemistry in the Royal College of Science, was instrumental in establishing the office of Government Chemist, eventually with an independent laboratory, and was the first holder of this office (1894–1909) before returning to academic life. The Government chemist was also much concerned with analyses made for revenue purposes. In the U.S.A., many states passed anti-adulteration laws before 1900—mainly in relation to dairy produce—but the first comprehensive law was the Food and Drugs Act of 1906. As this included 'other animals' as well as man, it was applicable also to feeding-stuffs.

II. SCIENCE AND PRACTICE IN THE TWENTIETH CENTURY

In the twentieth century, as in the nineteenth, the needs of war stimulated food science and technology. This was particularly so in Britain, which depended heavily on the importation of food in the face of an increasingly severe enemy blockade. In 1917 the Food Investigation Board was set up with Sir William Hardy as its first director, whom many regard as the father of food science. As an immediate outcome, the government set up the Low Temperature Research Station, first at Billingsgate (1918) and later at Cambridge (1922). In 1919, the laboratories of J. Lyons and Company Ltd. large-scale bakers, confectioners, and caterers were established. In the same year, the first cooperative research association, sponsored jointly by government and industry, was set up; this was the British Association for Research for the Cocoa, Chocolate, Sugar Confectionery, and Jam Trades; it was followed in 1923 by the Research Association of British Flour Millers. In addition the now world-famous fish research centre had been started, the Torry Research Station, at Aberdeen. In addition, two Agricultural Research Council establishments had been instituted, the Hannah Research Institute in Scotland and the National Institute for Research in Dairying at Shinfield, near Reading. Thus by 1920 the evolutionary process in food science and technology had changed, certainly in Britain, from an emphasis on food law and standards to active research on food, and in particular its biochemistry and nutritional value. It was still some years before the study of the nature of foods became a science in its own right, comprising chemistry, physics, biology, physiology, nutrition, and, to a certain extent, psychology. Sir William Hardy and Leslie H. Lampitt, the head of the J. Lyons Cadby Hall laboratories, even then recognized that the food technologist required much of the training and qualities of a food scientist, food technology being essentially the application of food science to food processing, including the development of new techniques and processes.

The significance of bacteria and other micro-organisms in the production of safe canned foods was by now well recognized; of equal importance was the realization that food poisoning, or ptomaine poisoning, was due to toxins formed during the growth of pathogenic bacteria. The hygiene of food production became of great importance in the years from 1920 onwards. The dangers were recognized of infection arising from bad handling; cross-infection from poor personal hygiene; and infection arising from animal feeds that were not heat-treated. The latter, for example, could cause salmonellosis in poultry. Modern food-handling processes have reduced such hazards to a minimum. The influence of food hygiene laws in many countries contributed to this result, and in the U.S.A. the recognition of 'good housekeeping' in promoting hygienic practices was helped by the so-called 'filth' laws, which imposed severe penalties on those offering for sale food containing rodent hairs (a measure of faecal contamination), and insect fragments (associated with insect contamination), both of which are measures of poor housekeeping. Hygiene practices in slaughter-houses greatly improved. Two such improvements in the 1960s were the bleeding immediately after slaughter of beef cattle vertically hung instead of lying on the floor in their own blood (and often mucous), and automatic dehiding (Fig. 56.1) in the hung position, the skin being pulled off avoiding cutting round the anus, the seat of much bacterial contamination. In regard to carcase quality, recognition that stress and conditions during transport, or in the lairage immediately preslaughter, can have severely adverse effects, particularly in pigs, did much to improve meat quality, both hygienically and texturally. It is interesting to note that good packaging arose from food wrapping as a hygienic measure. Now it is used for product identity; for attracting the customer; for conveying information as to the nature of the product, as required by law in many countries; and additionally, in America, to give, at present voluntarily, information on nutritive value.

The period from 1920 to the outbreak of the Second World War was marked particularly by the discovery of the role of vitamins and certain minerals in animal and human nutrition. A second development in biochemical and nutritional work was that of feeding experiments, now an everyday tool to the nutritionist or the toxicologist interested in the safety of food additives. In the 1930s much was learned about man's requirements of vitamin A; the B complex, particularly thiamine (B_1) riboflavin (B_2), pyridoxine, and nicotinic acid; vitamin C; and vitamin D and its relation to calcium deficiency.

The differing behaviour of the various vitamins to heat (and light) stimulated much research into nutrient losses during food processing, particularly of vitamins B_1 and C, both of which are thermolabile. Clearly canning is a process where nutrient loss may be expected, although with modern methods they can be small. Up to 40 per cent of thiamine and vitamin C can be lost in

FIG. 56.1. Automatic de-hiding, showing the vertical hanging of carcasses.

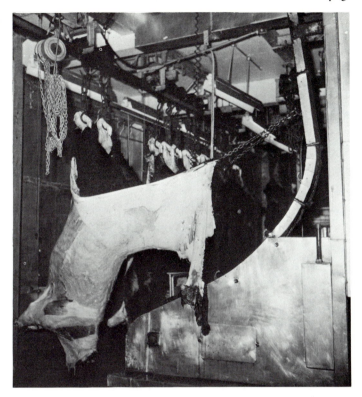

canned vegetables; vitamin C can be lost similarly in the production of potato crisps. Restoration of lost nutrients is often employed, although the method used is important. For example, if the housewife pours away the supernatant liquid from fortified canned new potatoes and then heats them in ordinary water, the value of added vitamin C is completely lost.

The new long-life milks, introduced in the late 1960s, were prepared by ultra-high-temperature (UHT) sterilization for not less than 1 second at a minimum of 135 °C, followed by filling in flexible packs under aseptic conditions, giving rise to little or no nutritional loss, including thermal damage to the milk proteins. These flexible packs, unlike glass bottles, have the advantage of being opaque, so that vitamin losses due to action of light do not occur. This light effect, nearly always accompanied by off-flavours, proved to be a general problem as brightly illuminated display cabinets became popular in shops and supermarkets.

The examples just quoted are from relatively recent history, but they illustrate the general importance of maintaining the nutritional value of foods to avoid nutritional deficiency diseases. This emphasis resulted considerably from the value attached to nutrition by the Ministry of Food in Britain in the Second World War. This included addition of vitamins A and D to margarine. Just before the war Professor (later Sir Charles) Dodds had suggested the restoration of certain nutrients partially lost during milling—principally thiamine, iron, and nicotinic acid—to 72 per cent extraction white flour. It was fortunate that before 1939 T. Moran and his colleagues at the Research Association of British Flour Millers had determined the location of the various vitamins in the wheat grain, so that when war came it was possible to devise a milling procedure to produce about 80 per cent extraction flours which retained an adequate amount of the B group vitamins essential for good nutrition. From these beginnings, and similar nutritional studies in America, came the information necessary to advise the public on appropriate daily intakes of energy and nutrients for the maintenance of good health. The dissemination of basic information on food and nutrition was much assisted by the establishing, immediately after the Second World War, of the Food and Agriculture Organisation (F.A.O.) and the World Health Organisation (W.H.O.). Both these United Nations bodies exist to improve the nutritional, food, and agricultural status of the various peoples of the world, with great emphasis on the undernourished and the developing countries where malnutrition is rampant, particularly kwashiorkor—a protein deficiency disease —in children.

The Second World War also had dramatic effects on the scale and nature of food processing, much of which will be described in Part II of this chapter. Much work was done on removing water from foods which had to be shipped, in order to save precious space. The introduction of spray-dried egg was one such innovation, but the solution of some of the bacteriological problems associated with this process did not occur until well after the war; many people still associate food poisoning and off-flavour with this product. During the war period many substitute foods were developed, and it became clear that a number of them contained food additives about which little was known in respect of their health hazards. Food legislation in Britain was fortunately not entirely unprepared for problems of this nature. In 1925 the Public Health (Preservatives in Food etc.) Regulations had prohibited, with certain exceptions, the addition of preservatives to food and required labelling declarations in the case of these exceptions. The Artificial Cream Act (1929) was introduced because it was found that this product was being made by emulsifying butter, skimmed milk powder, and water. The resulting product was sold at a lower price than cream, but had much the same chemical composition. The Food and Drugs Act 1938 incorporated—for the first time in one statute—food and drugs legislation with public health legislation relating to foodstuffs. Penalties were included for false or misleading labels and advertisements of food and drugs. The Emergency Powers of the Government during the war, despite the 1943 Defence (Sale of Food) Regulations, made it difficult for local authorities and public analysts in Britain to institute proceedings under these new laws, but the influence of American and Canadian food law was being felt. This had its accent not on prohibiting the use of certain substances in food but on giving in detail substances the use of which was permitted. In the consolidating Foods and Drugs Act of 1955, Ministers in Britain were empowered to make regulations which could do this. Through the guidance of the Food Standards Committee and the Food Additives and Contaminants Committee many regulations were formulated covering the use of most food additives. These are similar to, but not identical with the regulations in the U.S.A., Canada, and the Common Market (E.E.C.). The differences are mainly due to national tastes and customs and harmonization of British food law with that of the E.E.C. countries may take time, but the idea of having optional directives means that countries in the E.E.C. can, if they wish, still legislate in relation to their national preferences.

A further effect of the Second World War was to establish food science and food technology as university subjects in their own right. America saw the need first, and the department in the University of California at Davis, for example, gained a high reputation. In Britain, the National College of Food Technology was set up at Weybridge in the early 1950s and the first degree course in food science was taught at Glasgow University from 1958 to 1964, when it was transferred to Strathclyde University. This department, and that of Queen Elizabeth College, London, were the first in Britain to be named departments of food science and nutrition. Food science departments have also been established in other British universities and similar developments have occurred in Eire, as at Cork, where there is an active food industry.

The Second World War also focused attention on the importance of plant breeding (Ch. 13). In Britain the food scientist and technologist had long been aware of the differences in wheat properties required to give good biscuits, as compared with bread. The soft British wheats are suitable for the former and the harder more flint-like varieties—those, for example, of Canada, the U.S.A., the U.S.S.R., and the Argentine—have a protein of gluten more elastic and less extensible than the former and more suitable for breadmaking. Recent bread technology, as will be described later, has shown how softer wheats can be used also in breadmaking, making use of the mechanical development of dough. A work input during dough mixing of about 5 watt hours/lb, applied in under 5 minutes, is required. This process made Britain less dependent than formerly on the hard imported wheats, and more able to use the softer continental wheats, though this entailed a small reduction in the protein content of the final loaf. If the necessary electrical energy is available to drive the special machines, it is possible to make breads containing additionally proteins from non-cereal sources other than wheat, for example legumes such as soya flour. This makes it feasible to produce high-protein breads in areas of poor nutrition and as described in Part II of this chapter the use of *l*-cysteine hydrochloride made it possible to dispense with the special machines.

A major task of plant breeding institutes all over the world has been to try to produce cereals with a greater proportion of protein in them, to assist in overcoming the worldwide protein shortage. Thus in the U.S.A. in the late 1960s (but developed over many years) an improved maize, Opaque-2, has been produced, a hybrid with a better balance of essential amino acids, possessing more lysine and tryptophan, and with the protein content increased from 8–9 per cent to 10–12 per cent. This has had dramatic consequences in the treatment of kwashiorkor. In raw materials there can be two types of quality, food quality and technological quality. In cereals these are by no means always related to each other in terms of protein content.

Since the 1950s one of the most remarkable plant-breeding successes has been the development of Triticale, a cross of wheat and rye which contains about 10 per cent more lysine than wheat. This can grow successfully in arid areas, where wheat cannot grow well, and with yields as good as those of wheat under the most favourable climatic, soil, and fertilizer conditions (8000 kg/ha). The food technologist has shown that Triticale can convert into puffed products; it can be made into reasonable bread using high-energy dough mixing; it can make spaghetti, although darker in colour than that from durum wheat; it can be made into noodles, pancakes, chapatis, and Mexican tortillas; and it meets its avowed objective of being of maximum use in those countries where food shortage and nutritional shortcomings exist in the greatest measure.

Many social consequences arise from the partnership of food scientists with technologists and nutritionists. In the developing countries, criticism of their activities often arises from relatively simple causes, as was the case with Incaparina. This was a protein-rich baby food, developed from indigenous

foods in the Institute of Nutrition for Central America and Panama (INCAP).
Although accepted in Guatemala and a success in Colombia, where it was
commercially exploited, it was a failure in El Salvador because whereas in
Guatemala it was cooked like maize and drunk hot as a gruel, in El Salvador
the custom was to drink such products cool. In that case, it proved too thick
to drink and was a failure. In the developed countries, criticism is usually
about food sophistication. The development of snack foods with little
nutritional value, that is, foods of 'empty calories', has brought criticism, but
they may be useful to those compulsive eaters who also become obese.

The safety of food additives concerns many, although those most strongly
critical raise little demur at the presence of chemical substances in the form
of mycotoxins, derived as metabolites on mouldy foodstuffs. An example is
the potent poison, aflatoxin, which was isolated about 1960 from groundnuts
on which the mould *Aspergillus flavus* ex Link had grown. This gave a logical
explanation of a relationship, known since before the beginning of the present
century, between outbreaks of livestock poisoning and the feeding of mouldy
oil-cake from the tropics. This dichotomy of opinion arises from a false belief
that natural substances are safe, whereas chemical additives are not. Nevertheless, it is right that the work of food technologists is scrutinized. It is
right, too, that the public is interested in quality assurance. The latter is
something more than mere quality control over the raw materials used in,
and the consistency, purity, and freedom from health hazard of the finished
product. Quality assurance is the realization that textural properties—such as
bite, chewiness, aroma, and taste—are essential features of quality. Social
habits in various countries suggest that these attributes are not uniform
throughout the world population, but are highly individual. The food technologist of today must be aware of the psychology of food choice; so must the
nutritionist, because what you fancy does not necessarily do you good,
although a good and mixed diet without over-indulgence will.

The great challenge since the end of the Second World War, however, has
been more vital to us all than many of the problems so far discussed. It is
that of providing enough food for a world in which the population explosion
is the overriding factor (Vol. V, pp. 822–5). Mankind is facing a situation
unprecedented in history, adding close to 80 million people a year, equivalent to a new Europe each sixth year. Asia is adding a new Japan each second
year. It is Latin America, however, that is growing most rapidly. Brazil is
currently increasing with more people per year than the U.S.S.R., Mexico
with more than U.S.A. The 24 million of Colombia are adding per year

five times more people (800 000) than Britain, and so are Egypt's 37 million.

The energy crisis has exacerbated the problem of feeding this multitude. In terms of energy utilization, cereals emerge as very important food sources in terms of energy output to input ratios. That is, they utilize solar energy very efficiently in their growth and for this reason have energy output to input ratios greater than unity; in fact, grains generally have a value of 2 (2·3 for wheat and 1·8 for barley, showing that there can be intercereal differences). Bread, with a figure of 1·4,[1] is clearly a valuable food and still, in Britain, provides one-fifth of the daily protein requirement. Potatoes have a ratio of 1; sugar from beet 0·5; battery eggs 0·16; broiler poultry 0·11; meat about the same; and sea fish 0·073 (that is, nearly 15 kilocalories (about 60 kilojoules) of fossil fuel energy are used, nearly all of it from oil, for each kilocalorie eaten.) Thus we have entered an era of unexpected complexity—not unforseen but not provided for—which must inevitably lead to changing food habits, as we shall deduce from the content of Part II of this chapter.

BIBLIOGRAPHY

BARNELL, H. R. *Biology and the food industry*. Arnold, London (1973).

Chemistry at the Centenary Meeting of the British Association. Heffer, Cambridge (1932).

COPPOCK, J. B. M. The evolution of food science and technology in the UK. *Chemistry and Industry*, 455 (1973).

——. Food protein prospects. *Chemistry and Industry*, 292 (1970).

——. The green revolution. *Journal of the Royal Society of Health*, 270 (1974).

——. Triticale. *Nutrition and Food Science*, **39**, 15 (1975).

DAVIS, J. G. The evolution of food science and technology in the UK. *Proceedings of the Institute of Food Science and Technology*, 111 (1975).

DRUMMOND, J. C. and WILBRAHAM, A. *The Englishman's food*. Jonathan Cape, London (1957).

EGAN, H., HAWTHORN, J., and HULSE, J. Food in the developing countries. *Chemistry and Industry*, 58 (1973).

FILBY, F. A. *History of food adulteration and analysis*. Allen and Unwin, London (1934).

Food and nutrition research, H.M.S.O., London (1974).

FORBES, H. Rise of food technology 1500–1900. *Janus*, **47**, 101–27, 139–55 (1958).

HERSOM, A. C. and HULLAND, E. D. *Canned foods*. Churchill, London (1963).

KAY, H. D. A short history of the Food Group. *Journal of the Science of Food and Agriculture*, **23**, 127 (1972).

Manual of nutrition. H.M.S.O., London (1976).

McLACHLAN, T. *History of food processing*. Pergamon Press, Oxford (1975).

O'KEEFE, J. A. *Bell and O'Keefe's Sale of Food and Drugs* (14th edn.). Butterworth, London (1968).

PARKINSON, C. N. *The law and the profits*. Murray, London (1960).

---

[1] This figure does not include slicing, wrapping, and distribution.

PART II: FOOD PROCESSING AND DISTRIBUTION

The Second World War had dramatic effects on the scale and nature of food processing, which had been developing steadily throughout the century. Although much of this was related to the saving of shipping space, and therefore to the preservation and transportation of food in the dehydrated form, every area of food manufacture was affected and some of these developments will now be considered in detail. It is convenient to consider them under two main headings, namely those dealing with food preservation and those related to general food manufacture.

Before doing this, however, we must note another important factor that influenced the food manufacturer, and that is the changing pattern of the consumers' shopping habits (Fig. 56.2). Had the Second World War not intervened, the general change from the small grocer's shop to the multiple shop would have become significant earlier. In the event, the self-service supermarket, and later the hypermarket, was a post-war event in Europe, although in North America the trend had commenced earlier. The first self-service store opened in Memphis in 1912; by 1929 there were some 3000. To supply customers in this type of shop, where the constant picking up (and rejection) raised new problems of hygiene, the food manufacturer had to produce more and more of his products in unit packs capable of withstanding repeated handling. The wrapped loaf became the norm in such stores. Packaging became, therefore, a highly important part of food production, not only in the form of canned products but also by wrapping. Paper, often waxed, was the common material but after the Second World War polythene and other plastic materials were introduced; plastic bottles began to compete with glass and a whole set of new problems faced the food technologist. These ranged from devising the uniformly thick biscuit to fit a uniformly shaped pack, to satisfying himself that the plasticizers used in plastics manufacture were not leached out into the food or drink contained in them. The changing scale of operations involved problems of warehousing and distribution.

I. FOOD PRESERVATION

Methods of food preservation are essentially designed to prevent the deterioration by living micro-organisms (and enzymes) and the effect of

FIG. 56.2(a). A typical large food shop of the 1920s.

FIG. 56.2(b). A modern supermarket, in which very little food is directly handled.

oxidation. The methods fall into a few basic categories:

(i) Removal of 'active water' by salting, smoking, etc.; drying; or freezing.
(ii) Chemical methods, for example use of preservatives such as sulphur dioxide or antioxidants, and 'controlled environments' as in the storing of certain fruits in an artificial atmosphere.
(iii) Heat sterilization, as in canning.
(iv) Use of ionizing radiation (prohibited in Britain and some other countries).
(v) Cooling.
(vi) Selective action of an enzyme or micro-organisms on food, as in cheese-making.
(vii) Filtering.

Drying and dehydration. Dehydration is more complex than traditional drying and ideally involves the production of food capable of reconstitution substantially into its original form. The way in which water interacts with the various constituents of a food is important in three important respects. First, the nature of this interaction affects the readiness with which water is removed during dehydration. Secondly, the rate and completeness of reconstitution depends on the manner in which water recombines with the solid dehydrated mass. Thirdly, the influence of these interactions on the properties of the residual water in dehydrated foods; this in turn determines the efficiency of the process as a method of preservation. Failure to understand these factors led until recently to a degree of empiricism in the various processes developed.

As with other processes of food preservation, much progress has been made in providing new strains and varieties of plants of the necessary quality to withstand the process of dehydration. Having produced the right quality of vegetable, for example, the first criterion is to transport the product to the processing factory as quickly and as freshly as possible. Great care is then necessary in its preparation for drying. This includes cutting into dice or strips, followed by blanching or scalding; this consists in passing the material, particularly vegetables, through steam or hot water. This inactivates the enzymes on the surface, which would otherwise cause colour and flavour changes in processing and storage. The bacterial content is also reduced; this is important if delay occurs between reconstitution and consumption. Blanching or scalding must be done quickly to minimize deterioration of flavour and texture and the leaching out of essential nutrients.

Many kinds of hot-air driers have been developed over the past 50 years, but in all of them the material to be dried is placed on perforated trays, or belts, or sprayed into a tank. The trays are placed in cabinets or tunnels and hot air passed over or under them, the hottest air (*c.* 100 °C) being in contact with the wettest material and the cooler air in contact with the drier material.

Drum drying was used before and during the Second World War, particularly for milk. A film of the liquid is run over a heated roller, where it dries almost at once and is scraped off as the roller turns. There is some change in flavour in the milk, and loss of solubility. Variations of the process are used to produce potato flakes and breakfast cereals of the 'instant' type.

After the Second World War a much wider range of drying systems was introduced. These have been classified by S. D. Holdsworth as conduction heating; forced air convection; infrared radiation; and other forms of electromagnetic radiation.

In fluidized-bed drying the material is kept suspended and moving by a blast of hot air. This can be used, for example, for wheaten flours to dry them to consistent water contents; it provides a relatively efficient heat and mass transfer and a short drying time.

The spray-drying of eggs and milk was developed and much used during the Second World War. In this process the liquid material is sprayed into a large inverted cone, where droplets of the food meet hot air rising vertically from near the cone apex. The droplets dry rapidly and fall as a powder. One of the wartime problems was adequately to pasteurize the liquid egg, but despite the best endeavours from time to time food poisoning due to the bacterium *Salmonella* occurred. A second problem was the instability of the product; this was remedied by removal of the sugars from the egg white by treatment with the enzyme glucose oxidase.

Spray-dried skimmed milk proved difficult to reconstitute after drying, but instant milk was produced by the Instant Milk Company of America, which patented an agglomeration process in 1946. In this, the spray-dried particles were rewetted to 10 per cent moisture and agitated so that they adhered together to form larger granules. These, when finally dried again to 3–5 per cent moisture, reconstituted more rapidly and produced much more widely acceptable products. Many foods including coffee, milk, and flour are now agglomerated, yielding a free-flowing product. Spray-dried products now include such foods as coffee, tea, milk, fruit juices, and vegetable proteins. A typical post-war plant drying vegetable protein in the west of England is partly shown in Fig. 56.3. Many similar plants can be found all over

FIG. 56.3. A 'Niro' spray drier fitted with additional fluidized bed drying unit.

FIG. 56.4. A freeze-drying unit with tunnel section door open.

the world. Fig. 56.3 shows a composite plant in which the lower part of the drying chamber is connected to a fluidized bed. This exemplifies a further feature of modern food production, namely a combination of different drying systems to suit the needs of a particular product. This reflects the wide variety of foods marketed in the dehydrated form. Many kinds of packs are used for such foods, but in all of them the film or laminate requires to be waterproof and the product is commonly sealed in an atmosphere of nitrogen to reduce the chances of oxidative changes causing off-flavours.

It is appropriate at this point to mention the use of food additives. Spray-dried emulsions have become very useful for the production of a range of popular food products, such as topping mixes. These are composed of vegetable fat, protein, and carbohydrate together with surface-active agents, flavours, and perhaps a stabilizer. The components are initially emulsified and homogenized with water carrying the water-soluble ingredients, spray-dried, and then cooled. They have good shelf-life. When whipped with twice its weight of liquid milk a dried topping mix can be used to cover canned or fresh fruit salads; if whipped to a higher viscosity it can be used as a cake-filling or decoration.

Interest in labour-saving in the home (Ch. 47), and the greatly increased tendency towards eating out, led to a great increase in the consumption of dehydrated foods. Dehydrated soups have proved one of the most important growth-points of the dehydrated food market; they originated in America in the late 1940s. In addition to soup mixes, coffee, tea, and milk products, the other significant developments have been in the field of prepacked meals, dehydrated peas, and mashed potato powders. The last-named illustrates a specific demand linked with three technological advances, one of them involving the use of an emulsifier. Small amounts of glyceryl monostearate which links with free starch are added to the hot water. This, coupled with a three-stage cooking process entailing pre-cooking by water at 71–82°C, water cooling for 10 minutes, and then steam cooking for 30 minutes, produced the familiar instant mashed product now so popular.

Freeze drying (lyophilization) has been known since the 1930s and was developed in Sweden; it was first used for drying thermolabile pharmaceutical and biological materials such as penicillin and male spermatazoa. It uses the property ice has of subliming without liquefying—hence the disappearance of natural ice in sub-zero conditions. The first large-scale plant for freeze-drying fish and meat was established in the U.S.S.R. in 1954.

The simplest form of freeze-drier consists of a chamber connected to a vacuum and condensing system. The frozen material is placed on trays put on heated shelves in the cabinet. Heat is transferred to the material by conduction from the shelf to the tray, or by radiation from the shelf above. It is not a very efficient process, and is wasteful of energy. A high vacuum accelerates the drying process (which is therefore often referred to as accelerated freeze drying (AFD)), and if a pumping system of sufficient capacity is employed, capable of removing the large amounts of water vapour released at the peak period of sublimation, the efficiency is improved. It is also improved if various mechanical devices, such as ribbed trays, are used to increase the contact between the heated shelves and the material being dried.

Freeze-dried foods reconstitute exceptionally well and their original taste and aroma are very little impaired. They can be stored for a virtually unlimited time if the packaging is impermeable to water vapour and gases. Vacuum packing or storage in a dry inert atmosphere is therefore appropriate. It is claimed that compared with deep-frozen storage the extra energy costs counterbalance the high energy costs for transport and storage of frozen material (the refrigeration chain), the risks associated with electric power failure, and the costs of the necessary measures to avoid such risks. Fig. 56.4 shows a typical modern freeze-drying installation. Freeze-drying was developed particularly in connection with products that can command a high price, such as mushrooms, prawns, and, to a lesser extent, garden peas. The speed of reconstitution of vegetables is much greater than with the air-dried products. Attempts in Britain to use AFD for eggs proved unsuccessful; it proved unable to compete technologically with frozen whole eggs.

Another form of drying, which gives an open porous structure to the dried product, making it capable of rapid reconstitution, is puff-drying; this is a modern American technique, and there have been many U.S. patents since 1955. The vegetables are usually first hot-air dried to about 40–50 per cent moisture and then placed in a chamber in which the pressure is raised to 2–4 kg/cm^2. On releasing this pressure suddenly to atmospheric, explosion puffing takes place, after which a further short drying period is given.

This brief account of drying and dehydration would be incomplete without briefly mentioning another American process, foam-mat-drying (U.S. Department of Agriculture patent, 1960). In this method stable forms are produced by including such stabilizing agents as soya protein, egg albumen, glyceryl monostearate and other fatty acid esters, and sugar into liquid foods and by aeration or rapid mixing or whisking converting them into a foam. These foam mats are then dried conventionally on trays; dehydration is rapid and open porous structures again result. They reconstitute rapidly therefore, and this method has been used for dehydrated concentrated fruit juices, fruit purées, egg, whole milk, potato, and baby foods.

Many dehydration processes have benefited from a recent American development, reverse osmosis, which produces concentrates by de-watering liquid foods of all kinds including whole milk, skim milk, whey, cream, buttermilk, whole egg and its components, and even yogurt. It was first demonstrated in 1953, for the desalination of water. When a solvent is separated from a solution by a semipermeable membrane, the solvent passes through, diluting the solution. The osmotic pressure of the solution is the pressure that must be applied to it just to stop the passage of solvent. If very much higher pressures (of the order of 500 to 5000 lb/inch^2 (35–350 kg/cm^2)), are applied, solvent can be made to pass through the membrane from the solution, and so concentrate it by molecular filtration. For this reverse osmosis the semipermeable membrane must be very strong. To provide the necessary tensile strength, layers of glass fibre are wound on to a porous membrane of, for example, felt or paper, supported on a mandrel, spiralling alternatively to the right or left. This assembly is placed in a chamber and exposed to a vacuum in such a way that water will flow through the device when in operation, after which the strengthened membrane is treated to set resin contained in it to a solid state. The system, highly automated, has already done much to concentrate, and use in food production, the whey liquor from cheesemaking which can otherwise pose a severe effluent problem.

Pasteurization and sterilization. By the 1870s, reliable pressure retorts or autoclaves in which heating could be carried out by means of steam under pressure, or by superheated water prevented from boiling by applying an excess air pressure, were being used in canning (Vol. V, p. 39).

The art of canning consists in achieving the best time–temperature combination to give optimum product quality with an adequate margin of safety; the pathogenic and food-spoiling organisms originally present must be inactivated. Most attempts to improve the process have thus been related to improving heat transfer, followed by appropriate cooling. Cooling water must be bacteriologically clean, for there is always a risk that it can contaminate the contents of a can by seepage through minute pinholes. The Aberdeen typhoid poisoning disaster of 1964 was due to a failure of this kind; it originated in the Argentine in the processing of large cans of corned beef.

Cans are usually filled to leave a small amount of headspace. After filling the lids are firmly crimped on, and the cans then pass to the autoclave or cooker. Modern heat-processing equipment has two aims; first, to reduce handling, by the introduction of continuous cooker-coolers; secondly, to improve quality by high-temperature/short-time processes. The reel or spiral cooker, one of the earliest continuous devices for sterilizing cans, could rotate the cans and to some extent met these objectives. In this process the cans are propelled along a spiral track inside the shell of the cooker by flanges on the periphery of a slowly rotating reel. This causes an end-over-end agitation, mixing the contents and so improving heat penetration and reducing the process time.

Another established form of cooker-cooler is the hydrostat. In this the transfer valves used to introduce the containers from the pressure vessel are replaced by water columns sustained by the pressure in a steam chamber. The cans descend through the heating column, and then, after passing through a water seal, pass up a second column of water, after which they are cooled by air or water (Fig. 56.5). Most hydrostatic cooker-coolers impart little or no agitation to the contents of the can and are sometimes preferred for canned products that contain a jellied portion, although rough handling during cooling can render this advantage valueless.

Another post-war development is aseptic canning, one of the best known being the Dole process developed in America. To achieve the very rapid heat transfer rates required, particularly with more viscous products, it is essential to heat and cool the product continuously in heat exchangers specially designed for the purpose. The process operates best with products which have been previously homogenized. The product is then filled cold, and fillers working under aseptic conditions are used for the purpose. A typical Dole

FIG. 56.5. A model of a hydrostat; the size of the barometric legs is apparent in contrast to the height of the man at the control panel.

FIG. 56.6(a). An old vegetable cannery.

56.6(b). The Dole aseptic canning system; the can sterilizing unit is to the left, the filling and sealing unit on the right.

plant is shown in Fig. 56.6 where it is compared with an earlier cannery. Superheated steam is used for sterilizing cans and lids. Process time of 30 seconds at 140 °C are typical of this high-temperature/short-time process.

Flame sterilization was introduced in the 1960s. If cans of liquid are spun about their horizontal axes at 120 rev/min, heat transfer is so rapid that when gas flames at about 1400 °C are applied to the can surface this surface becomes little more than 1 °C higher than the can contents. A reciprocating shuttle bar rotates the cans first in one direction, then in reverse, as they are carried through the heat-transfer zone. Natural gas has made this an attractive process. Overall process times can be short, and products of good quality are obtained, but there are limitations to the can sizes and type of product that can be produced. The energy crisis led to some criticism of the efficiency of the process.

Big changes have taken place in the nature of cans. The two main types of internal corrosion associated with metal containers, particularly those made of tinplate, are electrochemical corrosion in an acid pack and sulphide staining in packs for sulphur-containing foods, such as meat, fish, certain vegetables, and some milk products. The best way of preventing this blackening is to apply an appropriate lacquer film.

The use of electrolytic tinplate has been accompanied by a gradual reduction in the weights of tin coatings. Increased reliance has therefore been placed on the use of lacquered plate to minimize corrosion effects. Acidic corrosion of lacquered tinplate is different from that of ordinary tinplate, for only very small areas of metal (where the lacquer does not penetrate) are in contact with the product. The area of iron exposed through damage during fabrication is relatively greater than that of exposed tin due to film imperfection. In these conditions iron is normally the anode, and corrosion is concentrated at these small areas. Sometimes perforation will occur, but more likely hydrogen evolution creates a swollen or 'blown' can. (Blown cans may also result from imperfect sterilization, when gas-producing micro-organisms are left alive.) Quality controllers in canning factories have to be continuously on the lookout for defects of this type, but fortunately they are not of frequent occurrence.

The aluminium can began to become established after the Second World War as the price fell. Lacquering of the can is nearly always essential. Such cans are very suitable for canned vegetables, since they avoid the risk of sulphur staining, and for canning low-acid fruits. The introduction of the ring-pull aluminium end opener proved a great success, particularly for beer and soft drinks, and for the gas packing of such easily oxidized products as peanuts.

Tin-free steel (TFS) has also come to be extensively used. The protective film of chromium or chromium–chromium oxide is about one-fifth the thickness of tinplating on the conventional tin can. Both sides of this plate are lacquered. It is free from the risk of sulphide staining, and the use of lacquered ends for food packs classed as strong de-tinners is significant. Rhubarb, for example, is packed in lacquered cans fabricated from hot-dipped tinplate bodies with TFS ends. Beer and other beverages have been successfully packed in tinplate bodies with TFS ends. Pure tin solder is used in cans for soft drinks and baby foods in order to avoid any risk of lead poisoning from lead-containing solder at the seams.

As in Appert's day, glass is still used as a container for sterilized foodstuffs. The closure is, however, of importance and it must be acceptable to the consumer. For long-life foodstuffs it may be of tinplate or aluminium with a rubber or plastic lining. Single- or multi-piece closures were developed, and could be of the pry-off; press–twist, roll-on, or lug type. The choice is governed by price, container size, the length of sterilization, the nature of the food, and how it is to be marketed. If the product is susceptible to oxidation, the question of oxygen leakage through the closure is paramount, because the product will discolour in the headspace, become rancid, and even be impaired nutritively owing to vitamin losses. The housewife, bottling in her traditional kilner jars, faced exactly the same hazards as the food processor.

Milk pasteurization has changed considerably in the last fifty years. Although from 1923 onwards in Britain some processing was carried out by in-bottle techniques, most of it was in bulk. The method known as the 'holder' process remained in general use until 1941; in this milk was heated to a temperature between $62.8\,^\circ$C and $65.6\,^\circ$C for at least 30 minutes and then quickly cooled to less than 10 $^\circ$C. This process has been replaced by the high-temperature short-time (HTST) method, defined in Britain as a heat-treatment at not less than $71.7\,^\circ$C for 15 seconds followed by immediate cooling to 10 $^\circ$C or less. This form of pasteurization is carried out in heat exchangers usually based on plate heat-transfer surfaces, although some are tubular. The heating medium is water, pressurized steam, or steam under reduced pressure. The process is continuous in operation and has more recently been modified to include an infrared heating stage for attaining the final pasteurization temperature, using quartz tubes surrounded by electrically heated elements.

The ultra-high-temperature (UHT) process for milk is based on work carried out by the National Institute for Research in Dairying at Reading and the British dairy industry. It uses temperatures of 135–150 °C with holding times of 2–6 seconds. Technologically there are two distinct systems: indirect methods of heating in tubular or plate-type heat exchangers, and direct methods using either injection of steam into milk or *vice versa*. These were developed also in Sweden in the 1960s. The second system is more efficient in terms of heat transfer, but a vacuum evaporation is necessary to remove the exact amount of steam condensed in the heating stage and restore the initial composition of the milk. For a long time this presented a legal complication, which prevented the use of the method. UHT milk can be aseptically filled into sterile containers and has an exceptionally long life.

Mention must be made of the increased awareness by distributors of liquid milk of the need for maintaining a low temperature at all stages during its transport and storage, both before and after processing. In many parts of the world, starting in the 1950s, there developed an increasing use of vehicles fitted with mechanical refrigeration, eutectic plates, and cryogenic gas cooling. In local delivery many vehicles, after the crated milk containers have been stacked, are maintained until required in insulated or refrigerated garages.

The chilling and freezing of foods. The use of ice for the purpose of chilling foods has long been known. From about 1820 until 1872 production of both natural ice, for example from Norway, and artificial ice, expanded rapidly. In 1880 clear ice, that is, ice containing no air bubbles, began to be produced and until the introduction of the modern refrigerator and freezers was extensively used in the transportation of perishable foods. Now much transport carries its own refrigeration, or uses solid carbon dioxide, a process first developed in 1925 by the Dry Ice Corporation of America. The aim in freezing is to lower the temperature enough to slow down both enzymic and chemical reactions which can take place in the food and to reduce or inhibit the development of micro-organisms, including bacteria and moulds. Such micro-organisms vary considerably in their behaviour towards cold. Thermophiles are usually most active between 30 °C and 50–60 °C. Mesophiles have a temperature range of about 10–45 °C, and probably multiply best at about 35 °C. Psychrophiles, however, can grow below freezing and have a temperature range of less than 0 °C to about 30 °C with an optimum about 25 °C. Thus some micro-organisms can grow at 0 °C and the limitations of the domestic refrigerator (introduced in the mid-1920s) for prolonged food storage, with an operating temperature of about 3 °C, is clearly apparent. Equally, the value of 'deeper freezing' to, say, −18 °C, is seen. In commerce, freeze storage is most often carried out at between −30 °C and −40 °C. Actual freezing of foods may require even lower temperatures, of −60 °C or less, but this should not be confused with freezer storage.

Freezing has disadvantages, however, and the nature of the foods themselves contributes to the problems. Most foods are complex in composition; on freezing, damage occurs to the food structure, and this is most apparent on thawing. Strawberries, unless freeze-dried, tend to lose their structure if wrongly frozen. Meat, poultry, and fish lose some of their textural properties and become prone to water loss, which in certain instances, particularly if accompanied by blood, can be unhygienic. Vegetables, too, lose much free liquid on thawing. Sometimes the increased water movement in the tissue leads to an increase in enzyme activity and an increased susceptibility to attack by micro-organisms, causing off-flavours and sometimes accelerated putrefaction. For this reason, it became usual, as in canning, to blanch vegetables in steam or hot water before freezing, particularly to inactivate the hydroperoxidase group of enzymes, and in green vegetables to inhibit destruction of chlorophyll.

For a long time there was a popular belief that food cooled to less than −2 °C became denatured. This was associated with the damage caused by ice-crystal formation, and it was many years before it was appreciated that slow freezing, through generating the largest ice crystals, was more likely to result in thaw damage. Quick freezing, however, causes very much less potential damage, the ice crystals being much smaller. It was not until 1929 that the full implications of rapid freezing were realized by Clarence Birdseye, who created the business which bears his name. Some foods, such as asparagus, peaches, peas, and fish, were found to require quick freezing; other foods require a less rapid treatment. Bread is an interesting example. If slowly cooled and then thawed, it is found to have staled, owing to the crystallization of starch. If, however, deep freezing is rapid, this phase is avoided and on thawing the bread is as soft as when baked. Baked goods lend themselves very much to this process, making it possible to smooth out production over the week, and yet meet peak demands for these products at weekends.

Freezing practices of this kind have been greatly helped by cooling in cold-air blast or tunnel freezers, and the growing availability of liquid nitrogen led to immersion freezing of great rapidity. Solid carbon dioxide is also a valuable coolant, as also is Freon 12 (dichlorodifluoromethane). Metal-plate surface freezers, and double metal-plate freezers, are also widely used, and in meat chilling the traditional form of mechanical refrigerator is still very much employed. Scrape-surface heat exchangers are used mainly for freezing foods which can flow, for example ice-cream. The choice of method requires a high degree of technological judgement; in particular, the overall heat transfer coefficient is a function of the thermal conductivity of the food, of the physical properties of any packaging material which may surround it, and of the external heat transfer coefficient, which depends on the type of equipment used. Most major groups of food require somewhat different technologies and nowhere is this better illustrated than with fish, poultry, and meat.

Freezing of whole fish and blocks leads to loss of weight and to 'freezer burn' of varying degrees of severity. Exposure of the tissue can lead to oxidative effects and severe dehydration to the fish becoming porous and of obviously poor quality. Variation in storage temperature can cause this last effect. A small increase in temperature from, say, -30 °C to -28 °C will prove enough to cause ice sublimation and therefore desiccation. Thus the cooling area was made large enough to minimize the mean temperature difference between the cooler and the product. Ice glazing of the product was found to act as a protection, because the ice will evaporate while the underlying tissue remains unaffected, and the onset of oxidative rancidity is delayed. A comparatively recent method has been to freeze the fish in polyethylene film or paper lined with polyethylene. Oxygen is thereby virtually eliminated all the spaces being filled up with water; the plastic film also prevents dehydration losses. Storage lives of fatty kinds of fish were particularly extended by this procedure, and there was also found to be a reduction in physical damage in handling.

Ice glazing was also introduced in attempts to reduce the effects of desiccation in the pack, but the greater dehydrating effect during distribution, in store, and in the home, was found to be caused by storing at too high a temperature, often greater than -6 °C. Even temperature, appropriately low, is essential if quality is to be maintained at all points in the food chain. The type of packing material is also of importance. Whereas a 6 oz pack of fish fillets in a polyethylene-lined wax board carton may lose only 0·1 per cent of its water in 3 months at -20 °C, and not show signs of deterioration until about 0·5 per cent moisture has been lost, an unwrapped block of peas would lose 16 per cent moisture in the same period.

In the freezing of meat and poultry it is desirable for rigor mortis to have set in before lowering the temperature without initially freezing. Adenosine triphosphate is the immediate energy source for muscle contraction, and in rigor mortis this substance decreases in quantity. A minimum retention is therefore necessary to prevent undue muscle contraction; too rapid freezing is the cause of 'cold-shortening'; that is, toughening. The ultimate source of energy is animal starch (glycogen); this becomes biochemically changed to lactic acid, which in turn determines the acidity of the flesh. This has a profound effect on the potential growth of micro-organisms and on the structure and water-holding properties of the meat, and additionally on the rate of cold-shortening.

Cold-shortened muscle is tough even after cooking. Pig carcasses can be cooled at somewhat higher rates without cold-shortening because the muscle is protected by fat. On the other hand, poultry should not be cooled too rapidly, since cold-shortening and toughening effects the breast muscle.

The food poisoning hazard with meat is thought generally to be contained if the storage temperature remains below 3 °C. Carcasses hung too close together after slaughter and dressing tend to retain body heat and increase the chances of raising the bacterial load and of spoilage. Meat at 0 °C keeps about four times as long as meat at 10 °C. At −1 °C meat has the maximum storage life without freezing. Food poisoning *Salmonella* bacteria grow well on meat, but 7 °C is the minimum temperature for their growth; hence the European Economic Community's requirement of transportation temperatures below 7 °C.

As has been mentioned for fish, refrigerated display cabinets in shops and supermarkets require good temperature control for maximum shelf life, the ideal being not more than 2 °C. Higher temperatures limit shelf life to two days.

Other preservation methods. Reference has been made above to the role of water in preservation. The availability of 'free' water for the growth of micro-organisms can be reduced by the use of sugar, as is traditionally done in jam-making; or by lowering the equilibrium relative humidity, as in fruit cakes of the Dundee type; or by the use of salt.

Dry-salting (Vol. I, Ch. 11) has been used for the preservation of meat and fish since ancient times and is still important. Well-cleaned fish, split, gutted and with the heads removed are placed in barrels in alternate layers of fish and salt. As water is extracted from the fish, brine is formed which finally penetrates the whole fish. After this penetration is complete the fish is packed in brine or dried.

Salting of meat is still traditional in Brazil, where sheets of meat are submerged in vats of saturated brine and then, after drainage, dry salted in much the same manner as described for fish. Most bacon is now prepared by injection methods using a sterile brine, the carcass portion being also enclosed in a bath of brine with a low bacterial count.

Mention of the salting of meat would be incomplete without commenting on two non-preservative functions, that of improving taste and of enhancing the solubilization and release of myosin, a most important proteinaceous globulin, from the muscle fibre.

Saltpetre (potassium nitrate) has been used for very many years for the preparation of 'cured' meats ('salt' beef, ham, tongue, etc.), and long before it was realized that it had a vital role in inhibiting the growth of *Clostridium botulinum*, which produces an exceedingly potent toxin. The original use was to preserve colour. Sodium nitrate and nitrite are also used as 'cures', although recently the formation of cancer-producing nitroso-compounds during the curing process and also in the stomach after eating have been regarded as possible hazards. This is an example where the concept of risk-benefit analysis is applied, and currently the danger from *Clostridium botulinum* is regarded as the greater risk.

Vinegar, another traditional preservative, is very much a product of national taste. In France and most European countries, the aroma and taste of wine vinegar is preferred; in North America cider vinegar; in Britain malt vinegar. Many technological improvements took place in the first half of this century. Barley yielding a high starch and low nitrogen content has been produced by the plant breeder. Malting has improved through better diastatic activity and the almost complete conversion of starch into sugars in the mash tun. Finally, improved fermentation converts most of these sugars to alcohols and better acetification by a continuously aerated submerged culture process yields a vinegar with an increased acetic acid content.

In Part I of this chapter reference was made to the trend in food legislation towards defining what substances can be added to food, and this includes the use of preservatives and antioxidants. Generally permitted preservatives include acid substances: sulphur dioxide, propionic acid, sorbic acid, benzoic acid; sodium nitrate and nitrite for the uses already described; methyl and propyl *para*-hydroxybenzoates; and antibiotics: tetracyclines and nisin.

Sulphur dioxide—and sodium sulphite, bisulphite, and metabisulphite—are widely used in beers, wines, ciders, pork and beef sausages, dried vegetables, peeled potatoes, fruit juices, soft drinks, pickles, and sauces. Some thought has been given to the potential loss of the B group vitamin, thiamine, in such foods as potatoes, for which sulphite is also effective in reducing browning. Benzoic acid, and its salts the benzoates, are also permitted in many products, often as alternatives to sulphur dioxide, and are used in fruit juices, tomato purée, pickles, and sauces. Both are also used in fruit pulps for jam-making; that is, in products liable to rapid spoilage if bacteria, moulds, or yeasts are allowed to grow on or in them. Many of these traditional products would not be available at all unless seasonal fruits and vegetables were preserved. Problems have arisen in the enlarged E.E.C. owing to the use of sulphur dioxide in wines in the wine-growing countries almost up to the maximum daily intake regarded as safe; that is, the acceptable daily intake (ADI). Preservatives are not normally permitted in milk and milk products. The surface of cheese under modern selling practices can become mouldy, and the use of sorbic acid has been permitted to reduce spoilage from this cause. In summer bread is susceptible to mould and 'rope' formation. Propionic acid and its salts are permitted to prevent this, with an upper limit of 3000 p.p.m.

The use of antibiotics in food to suppress bacterial growth is, of course, entirely a development since the Second World War. The permitted antibiotics, such as nisin, are either not used in medicine or their use is drastically controlled. This is to avoid the problem of the development of antibiotic-resistant strains of bacteria. In Britain, cheese, clotted cream, or any canned food can contain nisin, as may any food prepared from one or other of these substances. Tetracyclines can be used in ice for maintaining the freshness of fish but the residual amount must not exceed 5 p.p.m. In the U.S.A. it has become the practice for eviscerated poultry to be treated in tanks of ice-water containing 10–10 p.p.m. tetracycline for 2 hours, followed by storage at 3 °C. American law permits a residue of 7 p.p.m. in raw poultry; usually the cooked bird shows no residue.

Some substances having antioxidant effects are natural, such as vitamin C (ascorbic acid) and its salts. So also are the tocopherols, found in soya oil and wheat germ oil. Synthetic antioxidants, also developed mainly since the last war, are usually fat-soluble and are restricted in their use to prevent oxidation and off-flavour development in edible oils and fats, butter (for manufacturing purposes only), essential oils, vitamin oils and concentrates, and certain emulsifiers. Rancid oils and fats can constitute a health hazard leading, if consumed in quantity, to diarrhoea and severe malnutrition.

The number of permitted antioxidants is, in most countries, severely restricted, usually to the propyl, octyl, or dodecyl gallates, butylated hydroxyanisole (BHA), butylated hydroxytoluene (BHT), and ethoxyquinone for treating apples and pears at the very low limit of 3 p.p.m. Other permitted limits range from 80 p.p.m. for gallates in butter for manufacturing purposes, to 200 p.p.m. for BHA and BHT (or mixtures of them) in edible oils and fats, to 1000 p.p.m. for all these substances in essential oils. Carry-over into other foods is permitted; the antioxidants play an important role in inhibiting the rapid atmospheric oxidation of finely dispersed oil associated with fried products, such as potato crisps and other savoury snack foods. BHT is added to fish meals used in animal feeds, such as those from the Peruvian anchovy, which can ignite spontaneously if not treated.

This account of preservatives would be incomplete without some mention of irradiation pasteurization and sterilization, despite the fact that restrictive legislation in many countries, including Britain, largely prevents its use. This, too, is entirely a post-war development, arising from the atomic energy programme. Ionizing radiations from such sources as radioactive cobalt-60 or from machine-produced fast electrons can, in appropriate doses, kill moulds, bacteria, and insects and inhibit sprouting in potatoes and onions.

No temperature change occurs in this form of treatment; it is, indeed, a cold sterilization, but the higher dose levels are sometimes accompanied by off-flavour formation because the water in the food can be split into active free radicals which can combine with the organic matter of the food. In oils and fats, carbonyls can be produced and much toxicological work has been done to prove that the amounts formed are innocuous. Vitamin destruction is about the same as in normal cooking. It is claimed that there is a considerable reduction in rehydration and cooking times in dehydrated vegetables after irradiation and that there are no significant changes in overall nutritive value. The value of irradiation is not confined to the field of preservation. It includes such other effects as inducing delay in the ripening of the banana and the mango, of potential value in transportation; and botanical effects such as the inhibition of root hair growth in carrots, and the halting of development of button mushrooms.

II. GENERAL FOOD MANUFACTURE

Milling and baking. Throughout the twentieth century wheaten flour remained a very important source of energy to man in many countries, and even in Britain nearly a third is still derived from cereals. The wheat grain is rich in vitamins of the B group, and the embryo is rich in vitamin E and the essential fatty acids. The grain itself contains about 82 per cent of energy-giving carbohydrate (in terms of dry matter); 8–16 per cent of protein, according to its geographic source; and some 2–4 per cent fatty material or lipid. Apart from energy, people in Britain still derive about one-fifth of their daily protein requirements from flour products.

Wheat quality and protein quantity are closely, but not invariably, related in terms of milling and baking characteristics. Nutritionally, where lack of protein is a problem, the wheats containing the most protein are those of choice.

Wheats can broadly be classified as hard or soft. Both types are related to the heredity of particular wheats, and the plant breeders believe they know the genetic factors producing hard wheats (p. 1407). Hardness is a function of how the starchy endosperm, which comprises the greater part of the grain, breaks down during milling. Hard wheats give coarse, gritty flour which sifts well because it is free-flowing. Such wheats became established mainly in North America, Russia, the Argentine, and parts of Australia. They usually produce strong flours, with sufficient strength to withstand the exigencies of the bread-making process and produce a loaf of good volume, texture, and keeping properties. They are usually high in protein content.

In Europe, including Britain, the wheats are softer; they are not free-flowing and mill to a more fine and 'floury' flour. They usually possess a lower protein content than the hard wheats and the flour produced from them is also different, being less elastic and more extensible. They are not so good for breadmaking; the bread, like French bread, keeps less well and has a harsher crumb. On the other hand, soft wheats grown in Britain give a bread of good flavour and the flour produced from them is admirable for making cakes, and particularly biscuits.

The shape of the wheat grain, and in particular its crease, produces difficulties for the miller of wheaten flour. Technologically, there are two main objectives. First, to separate the endosperm from the branny outer layers and the germ, to give a flour of appropriate granularity, free from branny specks, of good colour and storage life; and relatively free from the enzyme α-amylase which gives a sticky bread crumb. This aim is due to the fact that the bulk of flour sold, certainly in the form of bread, is white and sliced. The second objective is to obtain the maximum extraction rate, this being the percentage of wheat converted into flour. White flour usually has an extraction rate of about 72 per cent, but small changes in extraction can be important economically. European and U.K. wheats are now used far more in bread grists than they were before 1962, when mechanical dough development was introduced. The U.K. bread flour grist can now contain well in excess of 50 per cent soft wheat, and the potential extraction of the new U.K. wheat varieties, for example, assumes greater importance. Recent varieties like Maris Widgeon and Bouquet can yield as much as 5 per cent more flour than Cappelle (grown widely in the 1960s) in comparable millings. Some varieties, bred for their high yields, and favoured therefore by farmers, have a high α-amylase activity and are therefore unsuitable for including in the bread grist. Among such we may mention Maris Huntsman and Maris Nimrod. Sometimes varieties of initial promise did not maintain it in later years, because unexpected interactions can take place in the grist.

These, then, are some of the complex factors that have influenced the development of the flour-mill in this century. The modern mill has been designed to use a form of grinding incorporating a combination of shearing, scraping, and crushing to exploit the differences in physical properties between the endosperm, the bran, and the germ and to overcome, by correct cracking or breaking and utilizing these actions, the problem caused by the crease.

In the milling process the wheat is first cleaned to remove impurities such as stones, other seeds, and ergot. The introduction of the combine harvester meant that cleaner wheats were delivered to the mill. In 1920 less than 5 per cent of American wheat was harvested in this way, but in 1938 this had risen to 50 per cent. The wheat is next conditioned to optimum moisture content, automatic equipment being available. The wheat is then ground using various kinds of steel rolls; break rolls, as the name implies, crack the grain between flutes or corrugations in the roll. Some starchy material from the endosperm is released, and is sieved off or, while still coarse enough, separated by air currents in a purifier. It then passes to a pair of reduction rolls, possessing a smooth surface, where it is further ground and then sifted. The stock from a number of pairs of break rolls goes in this manner to reduction rolls, while the material retained is fed through further pairs of break rolls. The break rolls also have a scraping action, so separating the bran from the endosperm,

FIG. 56.7. A modern mill room; the vibrating plansifters on the left, with purifiers and roller units on the right.

while the reduction rolls reduce the coarse semolina to flour. Sieving is performed through 'silks' of various mesh size; in modern milling nests of sieves are used called plansifters (Fig. 56.7). In both forms of rolls there is a speed differential between each pair, greater for the break rolls; this produces a shearing action and in the reduction system enhances the crushing action. Different kinds of flour can be made by varying the flow in the mill. The whole process is now carried out under pneumatic conditions. Cyclones collect the final 'dust'; the flour itself is then either stored in silos or, more usually, blown into bulk vehicles or tankers for transport to the user and stored in bins. Paper bags (containing 140 lb) replaced traditional hessian sacks when flour was to be transported in small quantities.

This century has seen three major changes in the milling process. First, the reduction of roll surface per unit capacity from about 120 inches per sack (280 lb) of flour to 30 inches or less, and an increase in starch damage influencing the water-holding capacity of flour and helping to satisfy the public demand for softer loaves. Second, the introduction of 'flake disruption' carried out in machines, originally designed to kill insects, called entoleters. This, with higher roll speeds, has created the conditions for short surface milling.

Fig. 56.8. The Alpine 'Mikroplex' classifier.

Rapid methods of determining the protein and α-amylase content of the wheat intakes have also improved gristing control and with the introduction of the computer tailor-made flour types became a practicality. Third, the separation of flour into fractions of differing starch and protein content by air-classification. The finest silk available for sieving in conventional milling has an aperture size of 61 μm, further separation of particles smaller than this is not possible. However, if flour is further ground in a pin mill or impact disc mill its granularity can be still further reduced giving particles ranging in size from a very few micro-metres to less than 61 μm. The very fine particles—as was first noticed in the cyclone dust-collectors in pneumatic mills —have a higher protein content than the larger particles. Separation of these very fine particles can be achieved by subjecting the flour to currents of air moving at differing speeds; for example, an air speed of 0·9 ft/min (0·27 m/min) lifts particles of 10 μm, but to lift a 30-μm particle an air speed of 7·6 ft/min (3·96 m/min) is necessary. Such a system has too small a capacity for commercial production, but higher air velocities can be used if gravitational force is increased. Air-classification uses the fundamental principle of subjecting particles to two opposing forces, namely centrifugal force, which is proportional to the cube of the particle diameter, and air drag, which is proportional to the square of the diameter. For any set of conditions there is a point of equilibrium above which the centrifugal force will be greater than the air drag, or *vice versa*. In a classifying chamber with a spiral air flow, coarse material therefore accumulates at the periphery and fine material is drawn off with the air from the central exit. One such classifier, a laboratory-sized one, is shown in Fig. 56.8. In this, the Mikroplex classifier, the air flow is controlled by adjustable vanes shown on the left; the rotating part, producing the centrifugal effect, is seen on the right. As an example of its action, a cut size of 22 μm can yield 70 per cent coarse flour of 9·1 per cent protein content and 30 per cent fine flour with a protein content of 10·5 per cent.

There are several other systems of classification, and they are put to various uses in different countries. In Britain coarse free-flowing flours have been produced for the self-raising flour market. In France, where much of the flour is weak, and similarly in the more westerly part of Australia, the process has been used to produce bread flours with better protein content while simultaneously producing weaker biscuit flours. In the U.S.A., where the wheats are mainly strong, the production of low-protein flours for cake-making has predominated.

Flour improvers. When flour is kept, it ages; that is to say, it improves naturally because of oxidative changes which enhance its colour and bread-making properties. When flour was imported into Britain from North America in the nineteenth century this ageing occurred during transport. When flour milling developed in Britain, in order to compete with imported flour artificial improvers were used. Nowadays, both in North America and Britain when storage is limited (and the risk of infestation reduced) and bulk transport extensively used, improvers are widely employed. In Europe, where breadmaking even now is not highly mechanized, their use has been much more restricted.

The use of improvers in flour has the further advantage that the inevitable natural variations in the quality of different wheats (and of the same wheat variety grown in varying environmental conditions) can be smoothed out, and the flour is of more uniform performance. Thus the miller, and sometimes the baker, uses improvers in the final milling stage, or at doughmaking. Regulations in Britain permit the use of ascorbic acid (vitamin C), azodicarbonamide, L-cysteine (a naturally occurring amino acid), potassium bromate; and the gaseous improvers chlorine dioxide (for bread flours), chlorine (for cake flours), and sulphur dioxide (for biscuit flours—or sodium metabisulphite if added to the dough). In bread-making and biscuit-making, they improve the handling of the doughs, a matter of great importance in mechanical bakeries.

In some countries, bread is still made by the traditional method of bulk dough fermentation that was current at the beginning of this century. Flour, yeast, salt, and water are mixed (sometimes with added fat, skimmed milk powder, and sugar) into a dough which is fermented for about two hours, 'knocked back', and fermented for a further hour in large bowls, using 560 lb of flour for every 30–32 gallons of water, according to the water absorption of the flour. After fermentation the dough is divided into pieces of suitable weight, given a short 'proof' or resting time to recover, and the pieces are then moulded (which also affects crumb structure). The pieces are then placed in tins in which they receive a longer second proof of about an hour and are then baked for approximately 30 minutes at about 230 °C. Many countries have very distinctive national tastes in bread. In France, 'tinned bread' is not common; although white, it is made into batons or sticks from a lean formula. In the U.S.A. tinned bread is widely known, made from a rich formula often containing 6–8 per cent (expressed on the flour weight) each of milk powder, fat, and sugar.

American bread lent itself to its continuous production using mechanical dough development (p. 1408) and the Do-maker and Amflow equipment is used extensively in the U.S.A. This form of dough development, first used by J. C. Baker in the U.S.A. in 1954, made it possible to do away with the 3-hour bulk fermentation stage, with all its attendant problems of space and difficult handling. In Britain, the Chorleywood Bread Process, now producing the bulk of British bread, was an adaptation of the American continuous process to batch conditions. Special mixers, in which the work input of 5 watt hours/lb is applied in 2–4 minutes, have been designed (Fig. 56.9). The process has the advantage of using the weaker flours that are of importance to the British economy, and the quantity of strong imported wheats has been drastically reduced. Its nutritional value is closely similar to that of bread prepared by the traditional methods but it has the advantage of (1) a time saving of 60 per cent; (2) a space-saving of 75 per cent in the dough room and a 75 per cent saving in the quantity of dough being produced at any one time; and (3) an increased yield owing to the retention of flour solids and water. For the smaller baker, 'activated dough development' using traditional equipment but using L-cysteine hydrochloride as an improver, enabled him to achieve much the same savings and technological advantages.

The batch system of doughmaking produces a continuous source of dough pieces, and in large bread bakeries the tinned loaves are baked continuously in gas- or oil-fired ovens, heated directly or indirectly; a typical modern oven

FIG. 56.9. A 'Tweedy' high-speed dough mixer, showing the mixing unit in the tipping position, and an elevator for dough tipping; automatic flour and water feeds are above the mixer.

FIG. 56.10. A typical bread-baking oven, illustrative of the hygiene of modern processing.

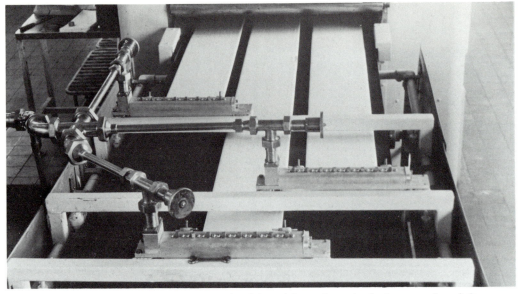

FIG. 56.11. Swiss-roll manufacture; the controls of the mixing unit are in the foreground, and three ribbons of sponge-cake batter are on the band taking them to the oven.

is shown in Fig. 56.10. Bread is also turned out of the tins automatically, followed by cooling to a temperature at which the loaf can be sliced without damage, and finally wrapped ready for distribution.

Biscuit-making, too, is carried out on the continuous-flow system, although in Britain the dough-mixing stage, except for biscuit rusk used as a cereal binder in sausage manufacture, still remains largely a batch process. After dough mixing, using either soft flours or flour doughs softened by sodium metabisulphite, the dough is sheeted and continuously fed through rollers until the desired thickness is obtained, after which the pieces are either stamped out or wire-cut. They then pass to a long continuous oven and are baked with varying degrees of top and bottom heat according to the type of biscuit being baked.

Certain types of cake manufacture have become highly mechanized in the course of this century. A typical modern plant is illustrated in Fig. 56.11 showing the mixing and continuous depositing by extrusion of a ribbon of cake batter which passes through the oven continuously; this can be automatically filled with jam, coated with chocolate, etc.

Oils and fats. Until the beginning of this century the baker had available to him only butter, lard, beef fat, and liquid vegetable oils. Once the hardening of oils by catalytic hydrogenation became available (the Sabatier–

Senderens reaction, 1899) coupled with advances in oil refining, many marine (especially whale) and vegetable oils became available for food manufacture. Blends with differing melting-points, a range of textures, and often with good creaming power, were produced. For the fish-fryer, fats were made which did not froth during frying and off-flavours caused by rancidity formation became better controlled; this was still further assisted by the use of anti-oxidants. Crystal size has been recognized as important in determining the properties of shortening, as the baker calls such fats; in general small crystals are favoured. For example, fats (triglycerides) can crystallize in various forms. The α-form is the smallest type of crystal, formed on rapid chilling. It changes, however, to the coarser β-form quite readily, but this is the least desirable in bakery shortenings. The instability of the hydrated α-form can be overcome by adding lactylated monoglyceride as emulsifier. This addition is of considerable value, for example in maintaning the volume of sponge-cake, which is dramatically reduced if reversion to the β-isomer occurs.

Margarine production has developed greatly since the original product of the 1880s. It entails refining the raw oils and fats to make them free of taste, odour, and colour. Oil began increasingly to be derived from such raw materials as rape, cotton seed, soya, palm kernel, and groundnuts. The use of whale oil diminished. The refined oil is hydrogenated in the presence of finely divided nickel to the degree of saturation (or hardening) desired, which materially influences the melting-point of the product. The melting-point can also be controlled by another chemical process, namely esterification. Several oils are then blended to produce the required melting-point, plasticity, and product consistency. Flavours, such as diacetyl which is part of the flavour of butter, are produced by adding fat-free or whole milk cultured with various bacteria. The product is then emulsified in a special machine known as a Votator. In this stage cooling is applied; crystallization occurs and is con-trolled to give various crystal sizes according on the use to which the mar-garine is to be put. The product, which has already had vitamins A and D added, is automatically packed and boxed. Some countries, though not Britain, still prohibit the use of colour so that the resemblance to butter is not too close.

Chocolate, sugar confectionery, and preserves. These industries are all craft-based. The change from batch processes to continuous ones was consequently prolonged and was made even more difficult because in the first two industries operatives were usually trained in the manufacture of a particular sweet.

This is well illustrated by the development of the milk chocolate crumb, introduced into Britain in the 1920s. The process entailed first pasteurizing and concentrating liquid milk; sugar was then added, followed by further concentration under vacuum to about 90 per cent solids. At this point of incipient sugar crystallization, cocoa liquor was introduced and the mass was then kneaded, further promoting crystallization. The paste was then dried under vacuum in large ovens fitted with shelves heated with steam or hot water. The process involved much handling and was labour-intensive. Belt and drum vacuum driers and a flow-tower drier are now used. These driers were specially designed, for research showed that much of the flavour was formed in the vacuum oven of the batch process. Without this design feature, crumbs weak in flavour were produced.

The raw material for chocolate is the cacao bean, and as with other foods, the agronomist has done much towards creating a consistent product. The criollo type, popular at the start of the century, was steadily replaced by the hardy high-yielding forastero variety. World production tripled in the first quarter of the century, rising from 150 000 tonnes in about 1900 to more than 480 000 tonnes in 1926. The bean, like cereals, requires cleaning; this is achieved in machines using a combination of vibration, sieving, and air lift. Roasting, originally accomplished in rotary roasters at about 140 °C, is now done in hot-air ovens with careful control of temperature. Winnowing, that is removing the shell, is done by crushing and effecting a separation of the 'nib' (containing a little over 50 per cent cacao butter) by sieving and air-lift or suction devices which lift the shell from the discharge point of each section of a bank of sieves. The grinding of nib to liquor is now done in pin mill pulverizers, or vertical ball mills. The chocolate paste is then passed through rolls in which the pressure is hydraulically controlled. The paste can be a mixture of pulverized sugar and cocoa liquor, or a mixture of partially pulverized nib and granulated sugar. 'Conching' is a process in which the chocolate liquor is subjected, in a tank, to the action of heavy rollers moving backwards and forwards. The purpose is further to liquefy the mass and reduce the particle size in the refined paste, and to remove water and unwanted volatile materials. The trend in later years has been to eliminate this noisy batch process by using one in which warm air is blown on to a thin film of ground chocolate, achieving the same aims as the conch. The smoothness and general texture of chocolate in the mouth is a combined result of these various stages in production.

Chocolates, and chocolate biscuits, are made by the process of 'enrobing', in which the confectionery centre or the biscuit is passed continuously through a curtain of chocolate, followed by cooling. Alternatively chocolates are made by making hollow shells by depositing liquid chocolate into metal moulds, inverting them to drain off excess liquid, and then depositing the filling into the shell followed by a liquid chocolate backing and cooling. Chocolate used in enrobing is first tempered. This consists of cooling liquid chocolate to about 30 °C, when it thickens visibly. This is followed by a reheating to 35 °C, when the 'seed' of cocoa-butter crystals throughout the mass is retained. Without this, the finished products do not have such a good colour and appearance, becoming 'bloomed' or whitish where the cocoa butter has separate and crystallized.

As with chocolate processing, most advances in the sugar confectionery industry have been in mechanization, although better raw materials and a wider range of them have also contributed. Specially designed fats have helped the sugar confectioners, like the baker and the chocolate-maker. In the realm of gelatinizing and whipping agents, gelatine, agar, pectins, and modified starches have all found their way into various products.

Boiled sweets are made by boiling a syrup of white sugar and glucose syrup until the solids reach 97 per cent or over. Modern vacuum cooking yields material of 99 per cent solid content which is, in essence, a very highly viscous non-crystalline glass. This remains plastic for a considerable time during cooling, allowing flavours and colours to be folded into it; the mass may then be pressed into shapes. Centre filling with fruit pastes or other soft confections or sherbet can also be done at this stage, which is carried out mechanically on a rotary cooling table.

Caramels and toffee consist of a high-boiling mixture of cane sugar, glucose sugar, milk, and fatty ingredients. The flavour derives from a non-enzymic browning, in this case produced by the reaction between milk protein and reducing sugars. This process is dependent on time and temperature, and continuous cooking processes were developed to take account of this. Basically they utilize a jacketed trough heated by high-pressure steam; a helical screw mixing device conveys the product through the hot trough. New materials of construction have helped considerably. For example, a machine has been made which deposits hot boiled caramel into flexible silicone rubber moulds, which became available after the Second World War. From these moulds they are ejected, after cooling, simply by passing through a pair of rolls.

For the manufacture of preserves, the horticulturist and the plant-breeding stations have done much to produce disease-resistant cultivars with high yields of fruit of good flavour, and of types which matched developing processing techniques. As processing methods have been given in some detail in relation to chocolate and sugar confectionery, quality control—of ever-growing importance in every aspect of food technology—will be used to illustrate various aspects in the development of the production of jam and preserves. In the late nineteenth century copper used to be a common contaminant in jam, because copper pans were used for the boiling process, their high thermal conductivity making for rapid heat transfer. Silver-plated copper pans are still used for this reason, but stainless steel has become more common, for both vacuum pans and specially designed open pans for rapid boiling.

U.K. law, and later E.E.C. law, has laid down standards for the fruit content of jams, although the quantities demanded are different, and somewhat lower in the E.E.C. countries. This can pose increased problems of microbiological spoilage if preservatives are not used, leaving sugar as the sole preservative. This is why European and American jams taste sweeter than U.K. ones. The jam manufacturer looks not only for fruit in first-class condition, but for specific varieties that will satisfy his manufacturing conditions. Thus in the 1950s problems arose in making jam from the strawberry variety 'Brenda'; these related to the penetration by the sugar of the berry, which stayed whole. The result was floating of the strawberries, with lowering of soluble solids at the surface. The variety 'Cambridge Favourite' had the opposite effect, breaking down all too readily. Although fruit production is seasonal, jam production is not, and deterioration of fruit in cold storage must be avoided. In some sulphited fruits, notably strawberries, the fruit has been known to break down completely because of certain fungi which can live in acid conditions. Acidity and pectin content and chemical constitution, aiding gel formation, are of great importance and so also is the rate of 'set'. Adjustment of acidity is important. It is normally in the range of pH 3·0–3·5. Small additions of fruit acids increase the rate of set; the addition of sodium bicarbonate in the boiling process lowers the acidity and lowers the setting rate. Set is also affected by the soluble solids in the jam and its temperature at the time of filling into the jar or can.

The introduction of machine filling caused new problems and the increased standards demanded by consumers highlights the need to avoid quality variations, especially from the 1960s. One problem was the tendency for air-bubbles to appear, and time was necessary for these to disperse. On the other hand, if too much time is allowed for setting, the fruit will not be evenly distributed.

When the machine-filled jar of hot jam has been sealed, it is then cooled, usually by sprays of cool water on a moving belt. The sprays are directed at the cap rather than the jar, but this can cause a problem if the headspace suffers a sharp drop in pressure; if the filling temperature is high this can cause boiling of the jam under reduced pressure, again causing bubbles to appear and disturbing the setting process. These and many other quality-control problems occur and if the jam is in a can and not a jar many of them cannot be observed, so that even more stringent controls are necessary.

Structured foods, snack foods, and novel proteins. The cheaper cuts of meat are a good and economic protein source, but are often too tough, fat, and gristly to be acceptable. Various processes have been developed, particularly since 1960, to use such meat after trimming, and also offal, by forming or restructuring them. One method of cold processing involves cutting wafer-thin slices of frozen meat and subjecting them to hydraulic pressure in a mould; incipient thawing occurs, enough for the pieces to adhere on releasing the pressure.

Another method of making a composite product is to cement meat pieces together with their natural protein by heating. This entails curing with a solution containing brine and sodium tripolyphosphate, pushing the small treated meat pieces into moulds, and heating. One of the most interesting American processes (Union Stock Yard, U.S. Patent 3 163 541, 1961) is to extrude a mixture of raw ground meat and methyl cellulose through dies to form filaments. These are then coated with collagen (exactly as nature does in the muscle fibre) producing parallel strands of meat substance. These can be made to adhere under pressure and then cut into steaks.

This principle of extrusion is used also in making many snack foods, and also in making one class of simulated meat products from soya protein. There are many kinds of equipment; Fig. 56.12 shows a Wenger extruder.

Soya concentrates and isolates are extensively used in various foods such as sausages, beefburgers, and meat loaves. Soya bean has been a major crop in China and Japan since time immemorial, but in the present century it has been established in the U.S.A. The American acreage was only half a million in 1917, but this had risen to more than eight million acres in 1939. Textured soya product has a protein content of about 52 per cent. A blander product with a higher protein content can be made by washing out soluble carbohydrates and salts with either dilute alcohol or acid to product a 70–73 per cent protein concentrate. Isolates with a protein content as high as 95 per cent can be made by extracting defatted soya flour with lime or sodium hydroxide. Most of the protein dissolves, the insoluble material is separated,

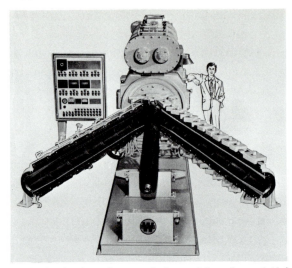

FIG. 56.12. A Wenger extruder, a typical extrusion cooking layout with the extruder assembly opened. This sectional illustration gives an idea of size, the type of steam-heated jackets used, and the design of the extruder. The product, which is forced through a die, can be shaped and then cut to size by a rotating knife.

and the isolate is precipitated by the addition of acid. After draining it can be washed and spray-dried. Such materials were used in making spun fibres, from which simulated meats were made. By the 1970s, however, this process was proved economically non-viable, probably because of its high technological content compared to extrusion processes. They can be made into a bacon-like material, sold as a snack food in the form of small chips. Beef, chicken, and ham products, sometimes heavily spiced with paprika, are also produced. Isolates can also be used in preparing structured meats.

Single-cell and other forms of protein production must also be mentioned, for research into the production of protein by yeasts, fungi, and bacteria has been proceeding apace since the Second World War. Much effort was unsuccessfully expended in Britain and Trinidad during the war to produce an acceptable yeast protein for human consumption based on *Candida* (*Torula*) *utilis*, using molasses as a basis for growth. Of apparently greater potential is the feeding of all classes of livestock using protein from yeasts which can be grown on certain simple petroleum and natural gas products, both hydrocarbons and methyl alcohol. However, these recent developments permit only a passing mention here. In any event, the main objective is animal feedingstuffs rather than food for direct human consumption.

Unicellular and multicellular algae have found limited use in foods in south-west Asia and in Africa. Of these, unicellular algae are the better protein sources. The *Chlorella* species have been studied, but more promising are the filamentous algae, such as *Spirulina maxima*, possessing a crude protein content of 62 per cent, but a rather low methionine–cystine content.

They have a colour problem and possess bitter tastes but material from Mexico has shown some promise in animal feeding and the U.S.S.R. and Czechoslovakia are reported already to be utilizing these products.

III. FOOD TECHNOLOGY AND THE CONSUMER

The expansion of the food industry in this century, and especially in the years immediately after the Second World War, created a problem which, although not technological in itself, is so directly related to its historical development that it cannot be ignored here. Throughout its history the food-processing industry has had to contend with a measure of prejudice that its products are, in some not very clearly defined way, not only not so 'healthy' as 'natural' foods, but may even be harmful. We are not concerned here with a mere matter of quality: obviously if meat, or fish, or vegetables are originally stale or otherwise of poor quality we cannot look to preserving processes to make good the defect. It would be absurd to suppose that the earlier brands of margarine were as palatable as butter. What is in question is a belief that processed food is intrinsically inferior to its natural counterpart.

The housewife knows that her life has been revolutionized: so-called 'convenience foods' have given her more leisure time; she and her family can eat out more; but doubts on wholesomeness have remained. She is concerned with the farmers' use of pesticides, insecticides, herbicides, hormones, and non-medical antibiotics as growth stimulants in animal and poultry feeding, and fears that the residues might contaminate her foods. Ever since artificial fertilizers became widely used in the 1920s many have believed them to be unsatisfactory substitutes for manure and compost. The housewife believes that intensive farming has created a loss of flavour in broiler chicken and veal and she does not accept the explanation that young animals cannot be so highly flavoured as the old and that the chemistry of their muscle proteins and fats is different. In Britain and France, the housewife prefers brown eggs to white, believing them to have superior flavour and nutritive value; her American counterpart, certainly in the northern states, believes a white egg is synonymous with cleanliness and prefers not to eat a brown one. Doubts, whether justified or not, are in the public mind and the food technologist cannot ignore them.

It is of minimal use to inform the public that the industrial revolution has created, in the western world, large conurbations of population which can be fed only by highly sophisticated farming and food-production methods; that many farming and horticultural products are seasonal, whereas food production has to be continuous; that production and distribution involve many forms of preservation, unless she is convinced that such food is as safe and wholesome as she believes her forebears ate. Post-war consumers have not experienced the poor hygiene current at the turn of the century. They do not remember, for example, that before milk pasteurization became general and dairy herds were largely freed from infection by the tubercle bacterium, the risk of tuberculosis was an ever-present worry, especially to mothers of young children.

What they hear now is that refined foods are the cause of many of the diseases of the West from which many primitive people are free. They are advised to reduce the amount of saturated fats in their meals and are told to utilize oils which are unsaturated, such as corn oil, as an alternative to lard and butter. White bread is frequently condemned, despite careful work done on German children just after the Second World War in which they were given, in groups, diets deriving 75 per cent of their energy from wholemeal flour or 75 per cent from white; both groups of children grew equally well. Conversely, it is known that wholemeal bread, as consumed in villages in Iran and Egypt, made from flour without yeast and baked immediately so that no phytic acid is lost, by no means represents an ideal diet. This high intake of phytate is believed to be the cause of zinc and iron deficiency in the villagers, and clearly shows how unwise it is to advocate wholemeal flour for the prevention and cure of all ills. It may prevent some but it can certainly aggravate others.

It is understandable that many turned to health foods, even though the reasons may be fallacious. In the U.K., sales of health foods increased in value from £11m. in 1965 to £18m. in 1970. In the U.S.A. at the same period sales were estimated as $200m. However, to keep the matter is perspective we must note that the American food industry had sales of $125 000m., so that the sale of health foods represented only about 0·16 per cent of the market. Nevertheless, consumption of health foods has increased because there are doubts regarding the safety of manufactured foods, whereas those grown naturally on compost-fertilized soil and free of additives are believed to be 'pure' and therefore health-giving. It is forgotten that some of the most powerful toxins known may appear in natural foods.

These are some of the complexities in the social acceptance of foods, and illustrate the emotive nature of the problem. Objective discussion is difficult to attain. Consumerism has exacerbated matters—understandably when, for instance, some food colours now banned have been showed to be carcinogens.

When legislation was introduced in the U.S.A. to the effect that no additive must be carcinogenic, it was not known that refined analytical techniques, capable of determining carcinogenic materials in parts per billion, rather than parts per million, would make the concept of zero tolerance unworkable. Nevertheless, a way must be found to reconcile opposing beliefs in view of the enormous problems caused by the world population explosion and the energy crisis.

The key could lie in increasing nutritional awareness in its broadest sense, and convincing the housewife that in cooking she can retain the heat-sensitive vitamins, such as thiamine (vitamin B_1) and ascorbic acid (vitamin C), no more nor less than the food processor can; that it is possible to have too much vitamins as well as too little, particularly with the oil-soluble vitamins such as A and D, which become positively harmful when taken to excess; and that to scrape off the mould on the outside of her foods is to risk potential poisoning from the residual mycotoxins which might be present as metabolites of mould and fungal growth. The food processor is better able to avoid these hazards because of the knowledge and experience gained by food scientists and technologists during this century.

BIBLIOGRAPHY

ADRIAN, W. *So wurde brot ans halm und glut.* Ceres Verlag, Bielefeld (1951).

BITTING, A. W. *Appertizing or the art of canning; its history and development.* Trade Pressroom, San Francisco (1937).

COPPOCK, J. B. M. Selling food technology, *Chemistry and Industry*, 358 (1974).

FENNEMA, O. R., POWRIE, W. D., and MARTH, E. H. *Low temperature preservation of foods and living matter.* Marcel Dekker, New York (1973).

FOOD STANDARDS COMMITTEE. *Report on novel protein foods.* H.M.S.O., London (1974).

Food Technology Reviews, Nos. 1–20. Noyes Data Corporation, New Jersey (1971–5).

FRANCIS, C. *A history of food and its preservation.* Princeton University Press (1937).

GOLDENBERG, N. and MATHESON, H. R. Off-flavours in foods, a summary of experience 1948–74. *Chemistry and Industry*, 551 (1975).

HOLDSWORTH, S. D. Dehydration of food products. *Journal of Food Technology*, 6, 371 (1971)

Improvement of food quality by irradiation. International Atomic Energy Agency, Vienna (1974).

INSTITUTE OF FOOD SCIENCE AND TECHNOLOGY OF THE U.K. Tenth Anniversary Mini Symposia (1974).

KAYDLEREAS, S. A. On the history of food preservation. *Scientific Monthly*, **71**, 422 (1950).

McCANCE, R. A. and WIDDOWSON, E. M. *Bread, white and brown: their place in thought and social history.* Pitman, London (1956).

PLANK, R. Die frischhaltung von lebensmitteln durch kälte. *Abhandlungen und Berichte des Deutschen Museums*, **12**, 139 (1940).

SPICER, A. (ed.) *Bread.* Applied Science (1975).

STURCK, J. and TEAGUE, W. D. *Flour for man's bread: a history of milling.* University of Minnesota Press, Minneapolis (1952).

57

TECHNOLOGY OF THE OCEAN DEPTHS

T. F. GASKELL

THE great voyages of discovery of the eighteenth century had demonstrated the interest to scientists of exploring new lands and finding new species of plants and animals. The application of scientific and mathematical expertise to problems of navigation showed that a mutual interest between the philosopher and the sailor was beneficial to both, and in Britain the association of the Royal Society and the Navy, so successful in the voyages of pioneers such as Captain James Cook in *Endeavour*, continued with a new target: the exploration of what lay beneath the sea surface. Practical consideration undoubtedly influenced active interest in finding out more about the ocean depths. Successful telegraph cables laid on the sea-bed in shallow water led to a desire to connect the continents by this new method of instant communication (Vol. V, p. 224). It was essential that some idea of the topography of the sea-floor should be obtained so that the factors concerning strains and wear and tear on cables, and the possibility of recovering them from deep water for repair, should be ascertained. Furthermore, it was important to find out what sort of hazard to the cables would be posed by the denizens of the deep. More recently, knowledge of the ocean bed and its underlying geological structures assumed immense technological importance as the search for natural gas and oil extended, from the 1920s, to off-shore fields (Ch. 16, p. 386).

The telegraph companies made many soundings using the traditional techniques of line and sinker. These and soundings taken by naval captains, who extended the standard 200-fathom sounding line in order to satisfy their scientific curiosity concerning the ocean floor, provided a U.S. Naval Officer, Matthew Fontaine Maury with information which he compiled in the form of charts of the oceans. His *Physical geography of the sea* (1853) was the first textbook of modern oceanography. The honour of first sounding oceanic depths of the order of a few thousand fathoms goes to Sir James Clark Ross, who in 1839–43 used a stout hemp line over a mile long. There was great difficulty in ascertaining when the sinker reached the bottom in places where the water was several miles deep, because the weight of rope supporting the sounding weight was so great that little difference in tension in the rope was apparent when the weight grounded. The technique in H.M.S. *Challenger*, which made a prolonged survey of the oceans of the world (1872–6), was to use a grass line which was almost buoyant. As the line paid out under the pull of the sounding weight, the time at which every 100 fathoms of rope unreeled was noted. This time increased with the depth of the weight, because of the added drag of the water on the rope. When the weight treached bottom, a marked increase of the time between 100-fathom intervals occurred.

The *Challenger* expedition marked the end of the older order of things and the beginning of oceanography as a precise science. A second advance, comparable to that begun by *Challenger*, was the institution in 1901 of the International Council for the Study of the Sea. Although the immediate object of this institution was the improvement of fisheries in the North Sea and the surrounding waters, a great deal of fact-collecting about the shape and composition of the sea-floor, and about the ocean currents and the transport of sea-bed material was initiated. Prince Albert I of Monaco founded the Oceanographic Institute in Paris (1906) and the Oceanographical Museum in Monaco, and made many pioneering experiments on the water circulation of the North Atlantic; he also devised many ingenious sample-takers for collecting both biological and geological samples from the sea-floor.

The study of the Gulf Stream by the U.S. Coast Survey was a lasting tribute to inspired seamanship and good instrumentation and experiment. Direct measurements of the current from ships at anchor in the fastest part of the Gulf Stream were made. These have been compared with subsequent calculations of water flow derived from measurements of the water density. It is estimated that this vast ocean current carries about 70 million tons of warm water northward every second from Florida to Newfoundland. It is possible to calculate ocean currents from a map of pressure distribution in a similar manner to that in which wind speed in the atmosphere is plotted from a grid of barometric pressure-readings. In the nineteenth century, water samples were collected and temperatures measured at a series of depths in order to calculate the density of water and hence the hydrostatic pressure. The concentration of salts in the water samples was measured in order to calculate the density; it had been discovered by analysing samples of sea-water from many parts of the world, collected by the *Challenger*, that the relative distribution of different minerals was universal, although total concentrations differed markedly in different places. This indicated that the salts in the sea, derived over thousands of million years from erosion of the continents, were thoroughly well mixed, and that differences in salinity were due to local concentration by evaporation, and to local dilution by mixture of fresh water from atmospheric precipitation or by melting ice.

Towards the end of the nineteenth century, the old *Challenger* hemp lines and heavy sinkers, with the hours of laborious watching and hauling needed to make a sounding and to collect a sample from the sea-bed, were being replaced by lines of fine steel piano-wire and weights of less than 70 lb. The sounding machine was fitted with a brake which was tensioned so that the wire drum would stop when the weight hit bottom, the depth being read directly from an indicator. Sounding was more rapid because of better winding gear, and the observations of temperature and salinity were made easier by improved mechanical equipment. The cable-laying companies had by then collected a considerable amount of information, which was added to that collected by British and U.S. Naval expeditions. An interesting discovery by cable-layers was that average profiles of the sea-bed can be obtained by observing the strain on the cable as it is being laid. Maps of the ocean basins were appearing with increasing frequency, and in 1899 the International Geographical Congress at Berlin organized a Commission to draw up a general map of the ocean basins, and to standardize the terminology of undersea features—such as trough, trench, ridge, plateau—which are familiar terms today. Albert I of Monaco undertook this task, and the Monaco ocean charts have been famous since 1904. The International Hydrographic Bureau (now the International Hydrographic Organization) was formed at Monaco in 1921 to keep the ocean charts up to date, and is supported by the main oceanographic nations of the world.

I. THE SHAPE OF THE FLOOR OF THE OCEAN

By far the greatest quantity of information about the deep sea-floor has been gathered by experiments conducted from ships at the surface. Because sea-water is opaque, most of the instruments needed to investigate the sea must use physical principles that are more complicated than the optical methods which, in general, are so satisfactory for studying the surface features of the land. To make matters worse, sea-water contains enough salt for it to be neither a really good conductor of electricity nor an effective insulator; in this respect also it is more difficult to work in than is the atmosphere. Salt water is corrosive, and the sea surface is seldom still, ensuring that experiments shall be conducted with the maximum of discomfort.

However, in spite of all these adverse features, oceanographers during the first half of this century managed to explore the shape of the sea-floor, and to discover a great deal about the rocks that lie beneath it. Partly because the ocean occupies more of the Earth's surface than does the land; partly because the oceans have turned out to be the active portion of the Earth in respect of the movement of plates of continental rock; and because, as with the Moon, there has been little erosion, so that the geological evidence is less disturbed than on land, it is oceanographic studies of geology that have led to the new theories and generalizations concerning the Earth's geological history. These, of course, have important practical implications for the exploitation of minerals.

The tools that are used to explore beneath the silent vastness of the sea-floor range from passive detectors of what the Earth emits—for example, its magnetic field—to probes utilizing sound pulses. To these must be added the drill, the ultimate probe developed by the oil industry. The first measurement to be made is that of the shape of the sea-floor. Although it is not possible to make surveys by aerial photography, as is common on land, the sea surface does provide a conveniently flat reference plane, so that it is necessary only to measure systematically the depth of water in order to draw a map of the topographical features of the sea-bed.

The modern echo-sounder, first introduced about 1925 and greatly developed during the Second World War, is an instrument which is precise to within a few feet even in the deepest parts of the ocean. With the great international effort that has been put into collecting soundings since the end of the last war, the main features of the ocean floor are now known, although the sea is so enormous that detailed maps are available only for small areas of particular interest.

The echo-sounder consists essentially of a source of noise which is fixed beneath the hull of the ship. Some early models used a metal hammer which struck a diaphragm in order to send out a pulse of sound; this spread out in the water and echoed back when it reached the solid sea-bed. Modern echo-sounders transmit a pulse of high-pitched sound by means of an electrically excited oscillator. At the instant that the pulse is sent out a zero mark is made by a pen on a moving paper chart. When the sound pulse arrives back at the receiver it is amplified and fed to the pen, which makes another mark on the chart. The paper moves at a constant speed, so that the distance between the two marks corresponds to the time taken for the sound pulse to travel from the transmitter to the bottom of the sea and back to the receiver. As the ship

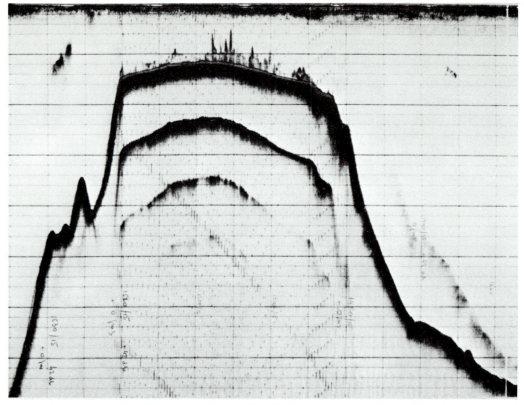

FIG. 57.1. An echo-sounding trace of the Gettysburg seamount in the Atlantic.

proceeds on its course, a picture of the sea-bed is drawn out (Fig. 57.1).

In shallow water, the echo-sounder draws a very accurate profile of the sea-bed, but in the great depths of the oceans a certain blurring of the picture is inevitable. The sound waves spread to a certain extent; high-pitched sound waves, so high as to be almost inaudible to the human ear, are used in modern equipment in order to minimize this effect. Even with the best apparatus, however, the sound waves fall on a patch of deep ocean-floor about a mile across, and echoes can be sent back to the ship from any part of this area of the sea-bed. The echo from immediately beneath the ship usually reaches the receiver first, because it has the shortest path to travel, but if the sea-bed is irregular in shape it is possible for echoes to be recorded that are sent back from elevations lying to one side of the ship's track. This is especially the case when steep slopes exist in the topography, and there is a tendency for such slopes and sharp features to be smoothed over in the record which is drawn by the echo-sounder. In many cases, also, a confused picture of crisscrossing echoes appears as echoes come back from different parts in close succession. While such observations are sufficient to give warning that rugged sea-bed conditions exist, they do not allow an exact estimate to be made of the real shape. In just the same way that it is impossible to see the clefts and fissures of a mountain viewed against the distant sky-line, so the fine detail of deep-sea features is hidden to the echo-sounder.

Some useful additional information about the shape and composition of the sea-bed can be obtained by pointing a narrow beam of sound pulses sideways, instead of vertically downwards as with the echo-sounder. An electro-magnetic pulse source is needed to give a narrow beam of sound, which traverses a swath of sea-bed as the ship moves forward. Hard rocks send a strong signal back to the ship, while soft mud provides a weak return. Obstacles such as wrecks or rocks show up as dark objects on the plotted display. The sideways sonar, as this device is called, has been used in the North Sea to follow the course of a pipeline to determine whether it is completely buried, or whether any dangerous scouring has occurred.

For the deep ocean the National Institute of Oceanography in Britain produced a giant sideways sonar ('Gloria'), which can obtain reflections in water depths of 3 miles or more with a beam that stretches 10 miles to the side of the ship operating the device. Gloria will probably make it possible to speed up the drawing of deep ocean topographical maps, as well as helping to discover new features because its width of cover as it traverses the ocean bottom is many times that of the echo-sounder.

The discovery in 1951 of the deepest part of the ocean, the Challenger Deep in the Marianas Trench (11°20'N., 142°30'E) by the 1950–2 *Challenger* expedition, was interesting in illustrating the different methods of measuring great depths and the ingenuity of oceanographers in devising new adaptations of old techniques in order to meet new problems. The echo-sounder in *Challenger* lost the echo at 4000 fathoms, mainly on account of fouling of the transmitter, since the ship was due for a refit. However, there are many other ways that a scientific ship can use to find the depth, and in this case it was particularly important to locate the axis of the trench in order to set out the seismic apparatus above the deepest part. Every few minutes the ship was stopped, and $1\frac{1}{2}$-lb explosive charges were fired, as in the normal reflection-shooting technique. The sound waves which echoed back from the sea-bed were picked up by a hydrophone and recorded on the photographic seismic apparatus. In many ways this gives a more accurate measurement of the travel time of the sound waves for their journey down to the bottom and back again, because the timing system of the recording camera is frequently checked against standard radio time signals, and because the arrival of the sound waves can be read at leisure from the photographic records. The method has, of course, the disadvantage of providing only occasional readings of the depth, rather than the continuous profile that is given by the echo-sounder.

A travel time of over $14\frac{1}{2}$ seconds, corresponding to a depth of almost 5900 fathoms was obtained. Since this was nearly a thousand feet in excess of the previously recorded greatest ocean depth in the Philippine deep trench, it was checked by the old method of lowering a sounding weight on a wire. A heavy iron weight (140 lb) was lowered over the stern of the vessel on thin steel piano wire. This was fed from a drum through a calibrated wheel, and the revolutions of the wheel were counted, so that the total length of wire that passed over the wheel could be calculated. This taut-wire apparatus, as it is called, is normally used for measuring horizontal distances at sea, by recording the length of wire paid out as the ship steams on a straight course. It is most suitable for measuring depth, provided the wire is kept vertical in the water as the weight is lowered to the sea-bed. It was to facilitate this that the wire was paid out over the stern, because the rounded stern of the ship could be kept headed to the slight breeze that was blowing, thus enabling excellent control on the wire to be maintained by giving small kicks astern on the engine.

An idea of the great depth of the ocean at this point can be obtained from the fact that it took an hour and a half for the iron weight to fall to the sea bottom, recording a depth of 5944 fathoms (2716 m).

On returning from New Zealand some months later with the echo-sounder in first-class condition, *Challenger* made a thorough survey of about 20 miles of the trench. It was found that a 20-mile by $\frac{1}{2}$-mile area deeper than 5900 fathoms existed. The echo was not strong enough to mark the recorder paper, but was easily audible in the headphones, and accurate determinations of depth were made by several observers. The echo faded a little at about 5600 to 5800 fathoms, when the slope was about one in three, but a strong echo was obtained from the bottom of the trench. This is to be expected, because the deepest part of the trench will tend to concentrate the reflected sound back to the ship while the slopes throw the sound away from it. The steepest slopes are of the order of 1 in 2 at least, while several slopes of 1 in 6 extend for 1–2 miles. On the other hand, flat stretches exist in some parts for a mile or two, so that the side of the trench must have ledges or steps in it. The average slope from 4000 fathoms to the bottom of the trench is about 1 in 7.

The approach to the trench from 3000 to 4000 fathoms is more gentle, about 1 in 18.

The deepest deep trench, then, is a giant valley about sixty miles across with occasional precipitous ledges, but with an overall mean slope that, on land, would be motorable. In 1957 the Russian oceanographic ship *Vityaz*, using a British-type echo-sounder, confirmed the great depth of the deep trench by obtaining a sounding which was, within the limits of experimental error, the same as that found by *Challenger*. Later (1960) the bathyscaphe *Trieste*, reached the bottom of this trench and determined the depth as 6000 fathoms, by measuring the pressure at the sea-bed.

Study of a bathymetric chart of the world's oceans shows that the continents are mostly entirely surrounded by a platform covered by shallow water. This is known as the continental shelf. Its width varies from almost zero, as along parts of the west coast of Africa, to a maximum of about 1500 km in the Gulf of Mexico off shore from the coasts of Louisiana and Texas. The average width is about 80 km and the surface dips gently seawards to a depth of about 130 m at the oceanic edge.

The shelf area in fact amounts to about 18 per cent of the total area of the land area of the earth, although it occupies only about $7\frac{1}{2}$ per cent of the marine area. Its significance, however, lies in the fact that it represents the seaward extension of the continents which were submerged following the melting of the ice after the last Ice Age. This means that the bedrock of the shelf actually forms a continuation of the geology of the adjoining land area.

The surface of the shelf may be smooth and consist of bedrock, but more often it is irregular, coated with recent sediment, and is cut by submarine valleys or submarine canyons which in places line up with major rivers on land such as the Congo River of West Africa or the Hudson River on the eastern seaboard of the U.S.A. These canyons have been cut by torrents of mud and sand-laden water which have travelled at high speed down the continental shelf and have then discharged their load when the water was checked on the sea-floor beyond the edge of the shelf. The sediments deposited in this way are known as turbidites.

Beyond the continental shelf the sea-floor consists of the continental slope (and/or rise) and the abyssal plain. Away from the edge of the continental shelf the sea-floor dips more strongly with a gradient of about 1 in 15 and falls steadily down the continental slope to the abyssal plain, where water depths average about 6000 m.

These deep trenches—such as the Pacific Marianas Trench and parts of the abyssal plain—contain deposits made up of clays and animal and plant remains that have accumulated very slowly and over long periods of time. Cores taken of these deposits show a record of deposition extending over tens of thousands of years.

The surface of the abyssal plain is interrupted by submarine ridges as well as by submarine volcanoes, some of which are active, as in the South Pacific, but others are long-since dead. The submarine ridges are of profound importance in understanding the origin of the continents and oceans. They have been recognized in broad outline for many years but their details have only recently been studied. It can now be seen that there is an almost continuous submarine ridge extending in mid-ocean for some 40 000 miles through the oceans of the world. The ridge is broken by fractures or faults and the crest itself is rifted by deep valleys. The best-known of these ridges is the Mid-Atlantic Ridge, which extends southwards from near Iceland, to form the North Atlantic Ridge, and then extends further south to form the South Atlantic Ridge midway between the continents of South America and Africa.

Below the veneer of sediment on the deep ocean floor is basaltic rock, which in turn overlies the deep mantle of the earth's crust. This contrasts with the continental areas which, together with the surrounding continental shelf are floored by granitic rocks, which in turn overlie the basaltic substratum.

The study of these submarine ridges and their relationship to the basaltic and granitic layers of the earth's crust led to a theory of sea-floor spreading which captured the imagination of geologists and geophysicists and revolutionized geological thinking in relation to the broad history of the continents and oceans. In 1911 A. Wegener propounded the theory that the continents originally formed a single land mass (Pangaea) which split into pieces which gradually drifted apart. The theory appealed to biologists, for it supported many established facts of evolution, but many geologists were sceptical, believing that the forces invoked by Wegener were inadequate.

In 1937, A. L. du Toit, in South Africa, postulated not one original land mass, but two: one north of the equator and one south. It was supposed that the continental masses, with their granitic basements, 'floated' apart on the basaltic floor carried by convection currents that were thought to exist because of physical changes of state in the upper part of the earth's crust. The deep oceans were regarded as old features of the earth's surface. Later evidence showed, however, that these are quite young geologically and what is happening is that the sea-bed is constantly changing; the oceans are growing outwards from the mid-ocean ridges and the continents are being pushed apart at the same time.

Detailed studies of the mid-ocean ridges by soundings, bottom sampling, and magnetic investigations have shown that the ridge is made up of basalts which have come from deeper in the earth's interior. On the crest of the ridge is a rift along which earthquakes are frequent; these are believed to be due to a cracking apart of the rift and an upwelling of liquid basalt which solidifies within the crack. Magnetic studies showed that this is a continuing process in which the ridge is cracking open, the sea-bed being forced apart by injection of basalt from below which forms the new ocean floor. So we have a process of continuous creation of the sea-bed in which the floor is spreading at a rate estimated at a few inches per year.

Continental drift is now accepted in principle, but not quite in the way envisaged by du Toit. Instead, we have a series of major plates incorporating continents and ocean floors and separated by the mid-ocean ridges along which the plates are moving apart. In places, the plates will therefore be 'colliding' and when this happens it looks as though one plate is 'sinking' below the other. Along the west coast of the U.S.A., for example, a plate forming the eastern part of the Pacific seems to be sinking below the north American continent. This line is marked by abnormal earthquake intensity, of which the San Francisco earthquake of 1902 is a notable example.

II. SEA-BED SEDIMENTS

The old sounding method of weight and line usually furnished samples of the sea-bed by means of a hollow plug in the sounding weight or by means of coring tubes. The recovery of a sample not only demonstrated the fact that the bottom had been reached, but could also show that life existed in the ocean deeps and provide evidence of movement of sand and mud along the slopes of the continents and ocean ridges to the abyssal plains. Further evidence concerning the sea-bed has been collected by underwater photographs. These have shown many plants, animals and the tracks of animals, and mineral deposits in the form of nodules. The specially designed underwater cameras (including television cameras) have been of great use in identifying sunken submarines and other vessels. Deep-sea vehicles, such as the bathyscaphe[1] (Fig. 57.2) have allowed the sea-floor to be observed by scientists *in*

---

[1] The bathyscaphe, designed by the Swiss physicist Auguste Piccard, consists of a flotation hull filled with petrol, to provide buoyancy, and a pressure-resistant cabin. Propellers provide a measure of mobility. The first descent was made in 1948.

Fig. 57.2. The F.N.R.S. **2** bathyscaphe built by Professor Auguste Piccard between 1946 and 1948.

situ. From the earliest days of sea-bed studies, dredges have been used to bring up rocks and mud from the sea-bed, and a great part of the many volumes produced by the *Challenger* expedition during 1872–6 are devoted to descriptions of plant and animal life brought to the surface by this means.

In order to penetrate below the surface of the sediments, long core tubes are driven into the sea-bed by various systems of falling weights, and cores of 20 m or so have been obtained from many parts of the world. Much deeper sampling of the ocean floor is now carried out by using techniques for drilling oil wells (Ch. 16). Oil has been found on the shallow water continental shelves since Lake Maracaibo in Venezuela proved (1924) to cover a large oil reservoir. Shallow-water (tens of metres) drilling was carried out by building structures from the sea-bed, but gradually, as oilfields were followed into water depths of a few hundred metres, it became economic to develop a technology of drilling from various types of floating craft.

In 1958 the Mohole Project was established in America by the National Science Foundation to investigate the possibility of adapting oil drilling vessels to work in the ocean at depths of 5000 m and to drill a hole through the Earth's crust in order to obtain a sample of the underlying mantle rock *in situ.* The mantle was considered to be much nearer to the surface under the oceans than beneath the continents, so that the difficulty of drilling at sea would be outweighed by the much shallower boring that would be required. The result of considerable design and field-work showed the project to be feasible, but adequate funds were not forthcoming to build and operate the special vessel required. However, the National Science Foundation was able to provide finance to support the Deep Sea Drilling Project, with a less ambitious objective. The basic goals were to learn more about the history and origin of the deep ocean basins and to gain increased understanding of the processes that have led to past geological changes. Incidentally, of course, it would provide a valuable opportunity to develop the technology of deep-sea drilling. These goals were achieved, and penetrations of several thousand feet into the sea-floor have provided direct evidence in support of modern theories of plate tectonics. As further experience is gained of ocean drilling, the mantle may one day be reached.

The drill ship used for the Deep Sea Drilling Project is the *Glomar Challenger*. This is a ship of 10 500 tons displacement, 400 ft in length, and of 65-ft beam. The 142-ft derrick is mounted centrally, and the drill is operated through a well 20ft by 22ft. The ship has twin screws, each driven by three-750 hp electric motors. In addition to this forward propulsion, which gives a maximum speed of 12·5 knots, four Schottel-Nederland tunnel thrusters, each providing 17000 lb thrust, are fitted fore and aft to keep the ship on station in deep water without the use of anchors. The perfection of this method of operating is largely due to the work carried out in connection with the Mohole Project before it was abandoned, and dynamic positioning, as it is called, has great potential in the oil industry within the next few years, both for floating rigs and for semi-submersibles. The laying-out of large anchors to keep drill ships firmly in position is expensive and time-consuming. The anchors drag in bad storms and sometimes strains make it necessary to cut the cables and let the craft drift. In severe storms even dynamic positioning would not be adequate to maintain station, but at least the craft could be kept head to wind. Dynamic positioning is a good example of a 'spin-off' from academic research to technology.

The drill string, of which up to 20000 ft may hang in water before the sea-bed is reached, is rotated by a turbo-drill. Sea-water is used as the circulating fluid, but drilling mud is available on board in case it is required for supporting the walls of the borehole. No rock chippings are returned to the surface, since the circulating fluid flows up the annular space of the borehole to the ocean at the sea-bed. Core samples are collected by core-barrels which are lowered and recovered by wire-line.

The cores are pumped out of the core-barrel on deck, and are encased in a clear plastic tube, which is subsequently cut into 5-ft lengths. These sections of core are submitted to a fairly comprehensive preliminary analysis on board. They are weighed, X-rayed, natural radiation is measured, and porosity and density are determined. The cores are then slit lengthwise, placed in specially designed plastic containers and photographed.

III. SEISMIC METHODS

As we have noted, sound waves through the water are used to find the depth of water by echo-sounder. In a similar way, sound waves through the Earth have been used to elucidate its geological structure. The primary division of the Earth into crustal rocks 10–30 km thick; 1500 km of mantle rock; and the rest liquid core, is known from the study of earthquake (seismic) waves. These are of very low frequency (fractions of a Hertz) compared with the 10–20 kHz used for echo-sounding.

It was observed that in some conditions an ordinary echo-sounder will show a hard rock basement below soft mud. This type of information is useful when planning the dredging of silted channels or the building of new jetties or breakwaters. Many special adaptations of the echo-sounder have been invented since the last war. In particular, various sources of sound have been developed.

The 'sparker' noise source is simply an electric discharge in the water, made originally by connecting a charged bank of condensers to an automobile sparking plug. Since the sparker there have been 'boomers', in which an electromagnetic pulse imparts sudden movement to a metal plate; the gas-gun, in which a gas explosion is generated; and the air-gun in which a pulse of air is let out into the water. The different characteristics of the various types depend on the power that they can develop, and on the frequency and length of the pulse of sound that is emitted.

In general, lower frequency gives greater penetration into the sea-bed, and a short signal gives more accurate resolution of different layers; higher power allows operation in deeper waters. Sparkers, gas-guns, etc. have proved of enormous value in the civil engineering work associated with off-shore drilling and pipe-laying. In deep ocean surveys, the air-gun has produced remarkable profiles showing the hard rock of the original sea-floor disappearing beneath flat ponds of soft sediment.

The seismic reflection technique for plotting the change in depth of underground rock strata is the premier tool in the oil geophysicist's equipment. Seismic reflection has for many years guided the drill to numerous successful oil and gas discoveries on land, and is much used for locating structures of potential commercial value in the continental-shelf zones of the world where the presence of up to a few hundred feet of water precludes normal geological methods of locating oilfields.

Reflection seismic experiments are really an elaboration of echo-sounding, using explosions as the source of sound pulses, and analysing the echoes by modern electronic and computer techniques. The method has been used to explore the deep oceans but our most interesting discoveries concerning marine geology have come from a variation that is more akin to earthquake-wave seismological studies.

In seismic 'refraction' experiments the source of sound waves is usually an explosion (Fig. 57.3), although vibrators, gas explosions, and dropping weights have been used to initiate the earthquake-type waves. Fig. 57.4 shows several different possible paths for sound waves sent out by the explosion at A. The 'direct' wave on the surface layer goes horizontally to the detector at B, and it is obvious that it will always arrive before the reflected wave ACB, because it always has a shorter distance to go. The 'refracted' wave travels along the path $ADEB$. Part of the path is down and up, AD and EB in the top layer, but the main part is the horizontal section DE in the underneath layer.

The wave travelling along AD is refracted at the boundary between the two layers, just as light is refracted or bent as it passes from air into a glass prism. The sound-wave is refracted again at E to travel upwards to the top layer and back to the detector at B, in a perfectly symmetrical manner. Now, although the path $ADEB$ is longer than either that of the direct wave AB or that of the reflected wave-path ACB, it is not necessarily longer in travel time. If the horizontal distance DE is great enough, the time saved in the fast layer will more than make up for the time spent in the slower top layer.

In order to make use of these refracted waves, several shots are fired at different distances and the travel times of the sound-pulses are plotted against the distance AB between shot and detector. At short distances it is the direct wave that is recorded, and this enables the speed of travel in the top layer to be determined. Beyond a certain distance the refracted waves reach the detector first, and from them the velocity of sound in the layer underneath is calculated.

The travel time for the refracted wave is made up of the constant intervals AD and EB, during which the sound waves go down to the fast layer and back again, and the horizontal section DE, where the travel time increases proportionately as DE is increased.

FIG. 57.3. A depth-charge exploding during seismic tests to determine the sub-structure of the sea-bed. Shock waves produced by such explosions are refracted and reflected in various ways by the materials they pass through before being picked up by detectors, which measure their time of travel (see Fig. 57.4).

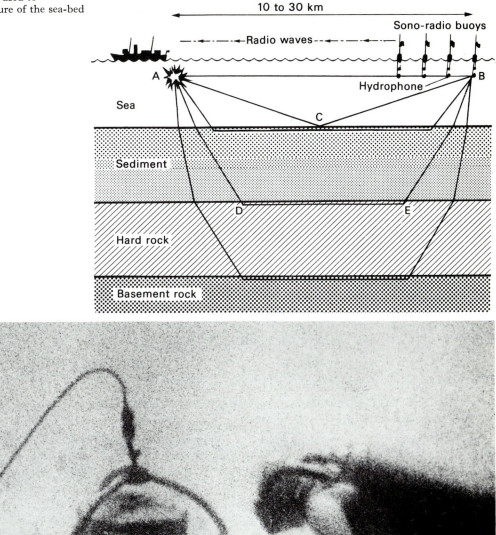

FIG. 57.4. The detectors used to determine the sub-structure of the sea-bed during seismic tests.

10 to 30 km

Sono-radio buoys

Radio waves

A

B

Hydrophone

Sea

C

Sediment

D

E

Hard rock

Basement rock

57.5. A gravity meter on the sea-bed off Abu Dhabi in the Persian/Arabian Gulf. Slight variations in gravity readings at earth's surface may indicate the approximate depths of heavy rock formations, and whether folding or faulting has occurred.

Seismic refraction experiments not only make it possible to calculate the depths of the various geological strata below the sea-bed, but also to some extent provide clues to the identity of the rock layers. This is because the experiments enable the velocity of sound waves in each layer to be determined. Although different types of rock may fall into the same velocity range, in general hard, tough rocks are characterized by high velocities, while softer sedimentary rocks have low seismic velocities.

IV. MAGNETIC MEASUREMENTS

Magnetic measurements at sea—first systematically plotted by Edmond Halley in 1701—were in early days associated with the use of the magnetic compass by mariners and the need to determine the angular difference at various parts of the Earth's surface between the true north and the direction in which a magnetic needle pointed. This difference changes slowly over the centuries, and is consequent on the magnetic poles being displaced from the axis of rotation of the Earth.

The Earth's magnetic field shows minor variations in magnitude on account of the different magnetic properties of rocks; it has long been an indicator, for example, of deposits of iron ore. Magnetic measurements may be made from aircraft—the saturable-core magnetometer was devised in the Second World War as an airborne detector of submarines—or by towing magnetometers behind a ship at a distance far enough for the instrument not to be affected by the magnetic properties of the ship. Small changes in the Earths magnetic field are detectable when the instrument passes over a local intrusion of volcanic rock—lava which has cooled and become strongly magnetized.

However, if the igneous intrusions are covered by several miles of sediment, the local effect on the magnetic field is smoothed out to a large extent. Oil companies use this fact to make preliminary surveys of sedimentary areas in order to confirm that a sufficient thickness of sediment exists to provide a source of oil. In the oceans the magnetic results have been instrumental in supporting the new theories of sea-floor spreading.

Magnetic observations in the Pacific Ocean off the coasts of Mexico and California have shown distinctive patterns of magnetic field variations, but these patterns along several east–west tracks show a large lateral misfit, suggesting sideways movements of the ocean floor of several hundred miles.

V. GRAVITY MEASUREMENTS

The Earth's gravitational attraction varies locally by a few parts in a million owing to variations in the density of buried rocks. For example, in the North

Sea, the presence of a thick blanket of halite (rock salt) which covers the gas reservoirs is revealed by abnormally low gravity readings, because salt is much less dense than normal sedimentary rock. It is difficult to measure the Earth's gravitational field at sea, because even slight movements of a ship give accelerations far greater than the minute changes caused by local geological effects.

The earliest reliable gravity records over the oceans were obtained by measuring the time of swing of pendulums in a submarine. A pioneer in this field was F. A. Vening Meinesz, who in the 1920s was enabled to use submarines of the Royal Netherlands Navy. By diving below the waves the water movements were minimized. Gravity meters can also be placed directly on the sea-bed (Fig. 57.5). Modern stable platforms, originally devised for naval gunnery, make it possible to measure gravity to 1 p.p.m. from surface ships and many of today's oceanographic vessels are equipped with gravity meters.

It is interesting to note that well before this gravity had been considered for oceanographic purposes other than that of learning about the geology of the ocean floor. In 1876 E. W. von Siemens invented an apparatus which was to be used at sea, and it was 'hoped that it would be possible for a captain to find the depth of water without a plumb-line'. The method was, in fact, impracticable, because the distribution of crustal rock between continents and oceans is such that the lack of attraction of the sea-water is compensated by the extra thickness of dense mantle rocks; in consequence, gravity values are not a reflection of water depth.

In the first decade of this century, gravity measurements were made by Hecker in the cabin of a liner by comparing the atmospheric pressure shown by the height of a mercury barometer with the value calculated from the boiling-point of water determined by a hypsometer. The height of mercury must be corrected for gravity, while the boiling-point is dependent only on the mass of air in the atmosphere above. While this experiment served to show the general agreement between gravity over the oceans and over the land, it also demonstrated gravity was of no immediate practical value for finding the depths of the oceans.

Gravity measurement could theoretically be used to calculate latitude, since the Earth is not a perfect sphere, and the Earth's surface is closer to its centre at the poles than at the equator. This might be useful for navigation of modern submarines which remain submerged for long periods and, therefore, out of contact with sun and star sights for many weeks. A good map of world-wide gravity anomalies caused by such features as deep trenches is, however, needed for accurate use.

VI. HEAT FLOW

Heat flows continually outwards through the Earth's surface because of the breakdown of radioactive elements in the crust. Since the active heat-producing elements are more abundant in the granitic crust beneath the continents than in the more basaltic crust below the oceans, it was expected that a smaller heat flow would be observed under the oceans. Heat flow is measured by dropping a temperature-measuring probe into the deep sea-bed. Such probes show readings similar to those on land, but with much larger variations. In particular, high heat flows over ocean ridges suggest the upward transport of hot material from below the crust, consequent on possible convection currents in the mantle.

VII. MINERALS IN THE SEA

Sea-water contains a total of 5×10^{16} tons of solids, representing all known elements. The dilution of most of the elements is great, and very few have been extracted economically. Common salt, fresh water, magnesium, and bromine are produced commercially from sea-water. In the future, other minerals, such as uranium, may be obtained from sea-water when the concentrated deposits on land have been used.

It is estimated that one-quarter of the world's oil lies beneath the sea-bed of the shallow continental shelf areas, and considerable off-shore oil production has already been established. It is questionable whether oil in commercial concentrations exists below the deep ocean floor, but some explorers hope that the continental slopes, at depths ranging from 0·5 to 4·5 km, may contain exploitable reserves. There is no doubt that oil production at these depths will be costly, but the technology that has been developed for the continental shelves could be adapted. The exploration techniques of seismic work and drilling have been used in deep water. There has been a continual interchange between oceanographers studying the ocean depths and oil explorers working in shallow water in respect of tools for carrying out their work. The earliest seismic experiments at sea were made by oceanographers on the eastern seaboard of the U.S.A. and in the western approaches to the English Channel, and their findings in respect of sediment thickness guided oil companies to productive off-shore areas. Acoustic devices designed to study the ocean bed have been adapted to shallow-water studies to assist the engineering of oil production structures, while the oil company drilling developments have made possible the important contributions to earth science provided by the

Deep Sea Drilling Project. The experience gained in deep ocean drilling will in turn provide the information necessary for deep-water oil production if it is ever needed.

Although the dilution of most elements, with the exception of sodium, chlorine, magnesium, and bromine, precludes their commercial extraction from sea-water, nature has provided some concentrating processes which may allow economic exploitation of the sea to provide two groups of useful metals. Manganese nodules, which are found in many parts of the deep ocean floor, could yield copper, cobalt, nickel, and manganese, and phosphorite nodules are a potential source of phosphorus. The muds and hot brines of the Red Sea contain iron, zinc, copper, lead, silver, and gold, all in much greater concentrations than is the normal for sea-water.

The deep-sea dredging carried out by the 1872 *Challenger* expedition showed that what are now known as manganese nodules were widely distributed throughout the three major oceans of the world. It is estimated that $1\cdot5 \times 10^{12}$ tons of these brown friable lumps, resembling potatoes, are scattered over the ocean floor. In some areas the density may be as high as 50000 tons per square kilometre. Manganese is, of course, an essential constituent of certain steels.

Manganese nodules may contain up to 2·5 per cent copper, 2·0 per cent nickel, 0·2 per cent cobalt, and 36 per cent manganese in some deposits; in others the cobalt content may be as high as 2·6 per cent with 57 per cent manganese. Since the values of the different constituent elements are different, some deposits are naturally more valuable than others.

The economic potential of mining manganese nodules is uncertain, in spite of ingenious systems of suction and bucket dredges that have been devised, because the more valuable metals—copper, nickel, and cobalt—are in low-grade ores compared with ores from land sources. However, the oceans contain all the manganese, iron, cobalt, nickel, and copper that mankind is ever likely to need. By the time the low-cost land sources are depleted, sufficient skill will no doubt be available to exploit the sea-bed reserves.

A second group of nodules has potential value. Oceanographic surveys have shown that phosphate rock is widely distributed on the sea-floor on continental shelves and slopes. The deposits are generally most abundant in areas of upwelling water, and it is possible that the deep ocean water, containing a relatively high concentration of phosphate from the sea-bed, deposits the mineral as a precipitate on meeting the warmer, more acid surface waters. The nodules contain the equivalent of about 20 to 30 per cent phosphorus pentoxide, P_2O_5, compared with a minimum of 31 per cent from land-based phosphate considered economic for fertilizer manufacture. The land resources of phosphate are still very large, and because of the high cost of working at sea it is unlikely that phosphate nodules will be mined in the near future.

Several oceanographic expeditions, in the course of making temperature and salinity measurements and taking bottom samples, located an interesting phenomenon on the floor of the Red Sea. The first observation was made in 1948 by the Swedish research vessel *Albatross*; subsequently other vessels discovered large pools of hot brine on the ocean floor. The brine pools are in water depths of about 2000 m, at about the median line of the Red Sea. The layers of brine are about 200 m thick, with a temperature of 56 °C and a salinity of 25 per cent, contrasted with 4 per cent for normal Red Sea water. They are probably associated with a line of activity and consequent high volcanic heat caused by the pulling apart of Arabia from Africa to form the Red Sea. Since there are many areas of the oceans where splitting similar to that in the Red Sea is taking place, there could be other pools of hot brine with the associated concentration of minerals.

Sediments below the brine pools were analysed for metal content and show: iron, 29 per cent; zinc, 3·4 per cent; copper, 1·3 per cent; lead, 0·9 per cent; silver, 54 p.p.m.; and gold 0·5 p.p.m. The upper 10 m of the sediments have been estimated to weigh 50 million tons, so that a considerable reserve of valuable metals, in concentrations which could be economically exploitable on land, has been identified on the floor of the Red Sea.

Even if these brines are not exploitable in the immediate future, their further study may be rewarding in showing how some concentration processes have operated in the geological past. A full understanding of natural processes may lead engineers to develop similar methods of upgrading conventional ore bodies.

BIBLIOGRAPHY

BULLARD, E. C. Minerals from the deep sea. *Endeavour*, **33**, 80 (1974).

DEACON, G. E. R. (ed.) *Oceans*. Hamlyn, London (1962).

ENCYCLOPAEDIA BRITANNICA. Vol. 19, p. 967 (1911).

GASKELL, T. F. *Under the deep oceans*. Eyre and Spottiswoode, London (1960).

——. *Physics of the Earth*. Thames and Hudson, London (1970).

——. *Using the ocean*. Queen Anne Press, London (1970).

HEEZEN, B. C. and HOLLISTER, C. D. *The face of the deep*. Oxford University Press, London (1971).

MAXWELL, A. E. (ed.) *The sea*. Vol. IV. Wiley, New York (1971).

SCHLEE, SUSAN. *Edge of an unfamiliar world*. E. P. Dutton, New York (1973).

STOMMEL, H. *The Gulf Stream*. University of California Press, Berkeley (1958).

58

TECHNOLOGY AND THE QUALITY OF LIFE

TREVOR I. WILLIAMS

I N the preface to these two volumes it was asserted that their purpose was not merely to display the principal events in the history of technology in the twentieth century, but to try to discern their significance. It is appropriate therefore that this extension of the *History* should conclude with some attempt to evaluate the contributions of technology to modern civilization. At the outset, it must be acknowledged that this is not a subject that lends itself to many unqualified conclusions. The facts, we may hope, have been adequately displayed in the various chapters but their evaluation is a very different matter. To begin with, it must be recognized that the topic is subjective, emotive, and illogical. For some, technology is essentially a destructive force: ruining the countryside and its wild life, poisoning our food and drinking water, spoiling the natural beauty of the environment, and generally destroying the traditional way of life. The stir created by Rachel Carson's *Silent spring* in 1962 was a clear indication of the depth of this feeling. At the other end of the scale are the, supposedly, more realistic thinkers who acknowledge these adverse consequences but regard them as a small price to pay for the undoubted benefits. Here there is room for legitimate differences of opinions between one country and another. In most of the Western countries, for example, whose economies are basically capital-intensive, technological developments that reduce the need for labour are very acceptable. In underdeveloped countries, on the other hand, where the basic need is to find some sort of work for teeming masses of unemployed, labour-saving devices are viewed very differently. Yet the people of such countries desperately need many of the products of modern technology: insecticides to eradicate mosquito-borne malaria; fertilizers and irrigation schemes to increase crop production; antibiotics and other drugs to combat infection; vitamins to supplement inadequate diets; and so on. Again, technology may be required to serve totally disparate ends. In Europe, countries anxious to increase their population have offered incentives in the form of family allowances, largely paid for by the greater national productivity engendered by improved technology. At the other end of the world, alarmingly over-populated countries offer the more sophisticated products of technology, such as transistor radios, as a spur to voluntary sterilization. In trying to reconcile these widely differing attitudes, perhaps the most that can be said is that almost nobody would like to see the clock put back altogether. Very few of the devotees of food that has never seen a chemical, or the opponents of atomic power stations, or those who demonstrate against new mining projects, would refuse a life-saving drug, or the use of the telephone to summon help, or a motor-driven ambulance to whisk them down the motorway to a fully equipped hospital. Nor would they see any illogicality in making use—so far as it suits them—of many of the other products of technology that have been discussed in these volumes.

The real difficulty is that everybody likes to be selective and this desire is strongest where it is most comfortably exercised. Thus, in the rich technologically advanced countries of the west, the food faddist can indulge himself very easily. But for hundreds of millions in the impoverished regions of Africa and Asia the anxiety over food is not whether it has been produced with the aid of chemicals, or grain has been ground between stone millstones or steel rollers, but whether there is any to be had at all. To this sweeping generalization we must make one important qualification: food will be refused, even *in extremis*, if it is of a kind that offends deeply held religious beliefs. Again, it is the rich countries that find this the least irksome. On the one hand, wealth confers a freedom of choice; if pork is to be avoided, or fish is commanded, there is no great problem in eating well all the same. Additionally, religious observance tends to become less strict as wealth and sophistication increase. In less advanced societies it is quite otherwise; religious laws, including many relating to diet, are strictly observed.

With this desire for selectivity, to enjoy the aspects of technology that appeal to us and reject those that do not, it is hard to quarrel. We cannot avoid asking, however, whether this is in fact generally attainable, and, if so, how far artificial constraints are desirable. If one lesson emerges clearly from this study, it is that technology advances on a broad front or not at all. Developments in one field point the way to new progress in others, often totally unrelated in their objectives. Thus the Manhattan atomic energy project, with all its tremendous consequences in war and peace, derived ultimately from purely academic research on the structure of matter. As late as 1933, Rutherford, who had contributed more than anybody to the basic science, dismissed as 'merest moonshine' the notion that atomic transmutation might be a source of power. It would not have been feasible without drawing deeply on the resources of every branch of engineering—mechanical, civil, electrical, electronic, chemical, and production—and of chemistry, metallurgy, hydraulic science, the technology of ceramics and glass, and others too numerous to mention. Again, the manufacture of synthetic ammonia, for fertilizers and explosives, was made possible only by the concomitant developments in the construction and use of high-pressure reaction vessels. High-pressure technology was to be one of the basic requirements for the manufacture of polythene. Progress on one front may bring to life another that had been quiet. The computer, for example, had limited possibilities as long as it was considered only in terms of a mechanical device. But the introduction of the thermionic valve, and later the transistor—both primarily developed for telecommunications—completely transformed the situation, with consequences we all know. Effectively, technology depends on evolution and cross-fertilization: it grows by feeding on itself. While the eye of genius may see how existing technologies can be combined to bring about a desired end, it is a very different matter to work the process in reverse: to define an acceptable end, and then create the technology necessary to achieve it. Space flight, for example, had been a dream for many centuries before it was ultimately achieved in our own time. But, with the benefit of hindsight, it is clear that, even with the promise of untold wealth and power as the reward for success, it could not have been achieved much before it was. Not until the middle of this century were all the technological ingredients available and— no less important—the political incentive there to provide the immense resources of men and money to make this remarkable advance possible.

If we may make another generalization, it is that the human race has shown itself extraordinarily resilient. If the beginning of a new technology is regarded not as the time of its inception but as the time when it begins to have a widespread social impact, the changes to which the oldest people now living have adapted themselves are quite extraordinary. They have seen a revolution in transport with the advent of the motorcar and the aeroplane. The oldest member of my own family clearly recalls seeing Blériot's first flight across the Seine and now almost daily sees *Concorde* flying overhead. Electricity has brought the boon of instant, brilliant light and power to remote homes beyond the range of the essentially urban gas supply industry. In communication, telephony and radio link the furthest corners of the world in a matter of minutes, compared with the days or weeks of earlier times. For leisure time, the technology of the cinema provided a whole new and exciting kind of entertainment for the masses. Later, the cinema industry, so immensely powerful and wealthy in the 1930s, was to find itself severely challenged by alternatives—radio, television, and the more sophisticated electronic versions of the gramophone—which could be enjoyed without leaving home and have changed the whole pattern of family and social life. These profound changes have been accepted with such aplomb that perhaps we are in danger of supposing that there is no limit to the accommodating powers of mankind. Whether there are limits to ability to adapt to further change, there is certainly some evidence of a growing reluctance to do so. In recent years much has been made of the so-called alternative technology, which in effect represents a compromise between the highly organized society of the west, utterly dependent on advanced technology, and the primitive community wholly dependent on its own resources. Its advocates do not eschew technology, but seek to avoid excessive dependence on it. For growing food they rely wholly on compost or natural manure; they generate electricity by windmills and store it in accumulators; they use solar panels to produce hot water; and so on. The weakness of this way of life is that it is not truly alternative: it depends on all kinds of devices and materials—batteries, ball-bearings, copper tubing, switches, electric light bulbs, and so on—which are really available only as a spin-off from the 'big' technology of the outside world. If that were to collapse, the alternative technology could not long survive: it is viable only under the umbrella of technology as a whole. Nevertheless, its very existence is a further reminder that the material benefits of modern technology certainly do not have a universal appeal. There is a growing number of people who have an expressed preference for a simple way of life, and we must not allow our judgement on this to be clouded by the fact that their ranks have been infiltrated by those with no enthusiasm for work of any kind. In a sense, there is nothing new in all this: communities of educated people deliberately living in isolation under primitive conditions are as old as civilization. Generally, speaking, however, they were religious orders, and great monasteries and convents still exist. The new communities seem—and often claim—to be united less by positive belief than by a revulsion against technology. Even so, we must be careful in forming an opinion: the revulsion may, in fact, not be so much against technology *per se* as against the complexity of modern civilization of which it forms an integral part. More than a century ago, Matthew Arnold spoke nostalgically of existence:

> Before this strange disease of modern life,
> With its sick hurry, its divided aims,
> Its heads o'ertax'd, its palsied hearts, was rife.

The material benefits of technology have done little to promote the universal brotherhood of man which has long been the goal of social reformers. Once, it was supposed that the main obstacle to this was poverty; that if once this were relieved, then the milieu would be created in which creative, cooperative endeavour would flourish. This, unhappily, has most certainly not proved to be so. In the industrialized nations, poverty in the sense in which it was understood only a century ago now scarcely exists, though social workers know all too well that there are no grounds for complacency. Yet the baser side of human nature shows itself as vigorously as at any time in history. Two world wars—the outcome of the second of them determined very largely by technological superiority—have been no more than violent eruptions of a constantly grumbling volcano. Governments based on tyranny and oppression still rule over a great part of the world's population. In our great cities, citadels of technological progress, violent crime is scarcely contained, and in many areas citizens cannot safely walk the streets after nightfall. The operation of international airlines is disrupted less by technical faults than by the necessity to enforce strict security precautions. Political ends are sought not by democratic methods but by the bullying of the powerful or the violence of minorities. Religious beliefs, which once maintained standards of behaviour, if only through fear of the hereafter, are on the wane—partly, at least, because they seem to many to be incompatible with the science upon which our new civilization is built.

All this is, of course, the tarnished side of a coin which has a much brighter one. For many, life today is not only more comfortable but lived with greater dignity and self-respect than would have been possible a few generations ago. Nevertheless, these dark and destructive forces are prevalent enough to demonstrate that science and technology have not provided the hoped-for means of salvation. Indeed, it is argued that by the very fact of creating wealth, and thus stressing the importance of material possessions, technology encourages the erosion of spiritual values. That there is some truth in this few would deny, but to quantify the argument is impossible. Indeed, perhaps the conflict between science and religion is more apparent than real. Science, after all, concerns itself with elucidating the mechanisms of the universe, and technology with turning this knowledge to useful ends. There is no particular reason why the mere possession of such knowledge should under-mine—or reinforce—religious faith, which is essentially personal and internal, and of the mind. Perhaps the fault lies as much with the organized religions of the world, which still tend to be insistent on the acceptance of dogma which has been disputed on the basis of fact. However, we must resist the tempta-tion to pursue such controversial views here, and acknowledge that the churches, like more worldly institutions, have their organizational problems. Let it simply be recorded that the rise of science and technology and the decline of religious belief are not necessarily an example of cause and effect.

To assert, contentiously, that science and technology have a different basis from that of religion is not, of course, to imply that they are independent factors in human life. This would, indeed, scarcely be likely, for both have been most powerful factors in shaping civilization as we know it. At times they have reinforced each other as, for example, in the many wars of religion in which military technology has been invoked to aid the faith; at others, they have found themselves in opposition. Both are concerned, in their different ways, with improving the quality of human life and it is ironic that this should be one area of conflict. Virtually all religions are concerned with the sanctity of human life. This concern extends literally from the cradle to the grave, and at both ends of the scale technology has had a powerful impact. Prenatal and infant mortality have been much reduced, and the expectation of life has been considerably extended. The principal factors contributing to this need not be considered in any detail here, as all are implicit in earlier chapters of this work. They include repression of infectious diseases, both by direct means, such as use of sulphonamides and antibiotics, and indirect ones, such as the control of insect vectors, like the mosquito, louse, and the tsetse fly, by new insecticides. They include also major public health measures such as the purification of drinking water and the disposal of sewage and garbage. The selective breeding of better plants and animals; the improve-ment of crop yields by use of artificial fertilizers and new methods of cultiva-tion; and better understanding of nutrition are among other major contributory factors. The overall consequence of technological progress in these areas has been not only a greatly increased world population, with the biggest increase in the least developed areas, but a changed pattern in the age of the popula-tion. The consequent practical problems are immense, but so too are the concomitant ethical ones. Are enforced policies of birth-control—implicit in which are the use of technical aids—ethically defensible? Should euthanasia be permitted—if at all—not only for those afflicted with painful and incurable diseases, but for those who suffer the general and depressing infirmities that are the normal accompaniment of the old age to which improved medical science has brought them? The dilemma was succintly stated by A. V. Hill in his Presidential address to the British Association for the Advancement of Science in 1952:

The conquest of disease has led to a vast increase in the world's population. The result may be starvation, unrest, and even the end of civilization. If ethical principles deny our right to do evil that good may happen, are we justified in doing good when the foreseeable consequence is evil? The forces of good and evil depend not on the scientist but on the moral judgement of the whole community.

For those blessed with a clear-cut religious belief in the absolute sanctity of life, even before birth, the answer is simple: life must be preserved regardless of the consequences. This must apply even if, statistically, the great majority of the new-born are foredoomed to lives of ill-health, starvation, and endless boredom and frustration. For those less clear-sighted—or less bigoted, according to the point of view—but no less intensely concerned with the welfare of their fellow men, the issue is far more complex. If technological factors alone were in question, there is no doubt whatsoever that ample food, clothing, shelter, and energy could be produced not only for the present world population but for a very much greater one. But the inescapable political, economic, and social problems of the modern world make it no less certain that anything resembling equitable distribution lies in the very far distant future. Régimes based on the most ardently egalitarian principles revert, when the dust of revolution has settled, to a hierarchical pattern in which material benefits are once again unevenly distributed, but according to new rules. Meanwhile, we must live in the world as it is and not as we would wish it to be. To assess the benefits of technology on the basis of reality is not unreasonable, for we have already noted that provision of the basic necessities of life—even on a quite generous scale—is by no means the sole ingredient necessary for human happiness. Let us, therefore, try to pull out the technological thread from the complex skein that makes up twentieth-century life and see what it reveals in terms of progress in the basic human needs enumerated above—food, clothing, shelter, and energy.

I. FOOD

The food industry falls into two parts: primary production of animal and vegetable products, and the processing of these for human consumption. In both these areas the first half of the twentieth century was a period of great activity. Productivity was increased in many ways, but particularly by the selective breeding of better and higher-yielding varieties of both plants and animals. Mechanization made enormous progress. At the beginning of our period draught animals were virtually the sole source of tractive power; at the end, except in primitive countries, the tractor and a wide variety of mechanical harvesting aids reigned almost supreme. The internal combustion engine, eventually used also for almost all ancillary transport, was the key to most of this, but the growth of the electrical industry provided an important alternative source of power; for example, in milking parlours. Irrigation schemes, and great land reclamation schemes like the Zuider Zee, opened up vast new areas for cultivation. It is true that huge areas also went out of production through soil erosion, mainly the consequence of mismanagement and ignorance, but towards the end of our period control measures were introduced. Additionally, of course, traditional methods of land clearance, and improved methods of transport lead to much new land being brought into productive use throughout the world. Chemistry made a powerful contribution. The Haber–Bosch process opened the way to intensive use of artificial nitrogenous fertilizers. Later, synthetic insecticides made it possible to control many of the most destructive pests, and to these were added selective weedkillers and new fungicides. The incidental consequences of some of these products were later to provoke a strong public reaction—to a considerable extent uninformed and often near-hysterical—but this was largely beyond the period with which we are here concerned. Unsatisfactory as some of the earliest products undoubtedly were, they served to demonstrate most forcefully the potential value of chemical agents and led the way to improved materials with less harmful side effects. We cannot ignore the fact, for example, that in 1971 three-quarters of the estimated 1800 million people living in the originally malarious areas of the world then lived in areas where the disease was virtually eradicated (*World Health Chronicle*, **25**, 498, 1971). Tens of millions of lives have been saved by mosquito eradication campaigns and tens of millions more people have been saved from lasting ill-health.

The preservation of food from time of plenty to time of need has always been a major problem, but it was aggravated in the twentieth century by the changing pattern of production. Huge new areas of production grew up remote—often by thousands of miles—from the areas of demand. Developments in food technology made this new pattern feasible. In particular, there were big improvements in canning, refrigeration, and drying processes. Food preparation shifted increasingly from the home or local bakery to factories supplying very large areas—sometimes, indeed, world markets. Food technology was not merely a matter of conservation: important public health principles were involved. Of particular importance was the control of tuberculosis by the pasteurization of milk. Harmful adulteration—often the result of ignorance as much as of lack of scruple—was brought under control. The development of the supermarket, with much food exposed to handling and consequent risk of infection, brought a revolution in packaging techniques and methods of sale.

On balance, the new technologies of food improved the lot of the housewife and her family, especially when greater attention was paid to the conservation of vitamins and other accessory food factors as the principles of nutrition became better understood. Food was safer, more dependable in its properties, and demanded less preparation. This last point was of increasing importance as domestic labour became increasingly scarce after the First World War. The possibility of transport over long distances not only introduced more variety but increased the duration of availability of normally seasonal products.

But not everybody would regard progress of this sort as being made without a penalty. For example, when exotic products are available all the year round, the pleasure associated with their brief seasonal availability is lost. Further, when year-round availability is the rule, deprivation is regarded as a hardship even though out-of-season prices may be several times the normal. In Britain, for example, rather tasteless imported tomatoes sell readily in mid-winter at more than five times the cost of the luscious home-produced summer fruit. Such prices are reflected in cost-of-living indexes and so increase the pressure for wage increases, with their attendant economic consequences. Convenience foods are aptly named and save much work in the kitchen, but few—on a free vote—would choose them in preference to the same dish well prepared by traditional methods. The captains of the food and catering industries are not commonly observed dining in establishments where the food comes from tins or polythene bags.

II. CLOTHING

For much of our present period, the provision of the basic materials for clothing was essentially a task of the agricultural industry, as it had been since the earliest days. Fibres for the textile industry were still almost entirely of animal or plant origin: wool, silk, cotton, and linen with rougher fibres like jute for coarser fabric. Leather remained the traditional material for footwear, and for many dress accessories such as gloves, belts, and the like. Man-made fibres made a slow start with rayon—only semi-synthetic as it derived from wood—in the 1920s, but the truly synthetic products, notably nylon and Terylene, did not make a really substantial impact until after the Second World War. Even at the very end of our present period chemical manufacturers did not foresee the speed with which the industry would grow. In the early 1950s they were still nervous of the giant natural textile industry and were protesting that their policy was not to supplant natural fibres but to complement them. Thus by mid-century man-made fibres had made little impact on the quality of life, except in the field of women's stockings—developed just before the war—where the popularity of nylon was enormous. Early fibres were unsatisfactory in respect of certain basic, if unquantifiable, qualities such as drape and handle; the lack of absorbency of the earliest nylon monofil shirts made them more of a penance than a pleasure. But the chemical industry—aided by its long connection with the textile trade—learned quickly, and far more satisfactory products were quickly developed, often combining natural and artificial fibres. So far as everyday life was concerned, their main merit lay, perhaps, in their labour-saving qualities. Drip-drying and permanent creasing obviated the need for ironing, qualities of great consequence as domestic labour became increasingly scarce and expensive. Moreover, the speed of drying was such that lightweight garments, such as stockings, shirts, and blouses, could be washed at night and be ready to wear again in the morning. Even men's suits in the new materials could be washed instead of being dry cleaned. All this was a great convenience; and also an economy, for fewer garments were necessary. Or, looked at in another way, the same budget could provide a more varied wardrobe.

Apart from having new materials at its disposal, the garment-making industry underwent a considerable transformation. Ready-made clothing had, of course, long been available but not generally for the better-quality products, such as men's suits and ladies' gowns. These were commonly made to measure by bespoke tailors and dressmakers, as they still are for the comparative few who can afford them, but during the first half of this century, and especially after the First World War, the ready-made clothing manufacturer made steady inroads into the territory of the individual garment maker. This was partly a matter of labour costs, but also a consequence of improved quality of material and finish and a more systematic statistical evaluation of the relevant dimensions of the human body. For the ordinary person, the overall effect was again that it became possible to afford a bigger and better wardrobe. Correspondingly, of course, the bespoke tailor and dressmaker found their business declining. As in so many other areas, the continuing tendency was to shift production from the small local establishment to the factory.

III. SHELTER

In the present context, we must consider the third of man's basic requirements, shelter, in rather broader terms than mere domestic dwellings. In fact, as has been shown in relevant earlier chapters, there were very considerable changes in building materials and methods in the first half of this century, but their direct effect on everyday life was not dramatic. The majority of people still dwelt in houses of conventional pattern or, increasingly, in blocks of flats of fairly standard design. There was little change, either, in basic furnishings. The impact on the quality of life lay much more in the amenities than in the basic unit. By the 1920s, gaslight—in its day a revolutionary improvement on candles and oil-lamps—had largely been replaced by electricity. Gas and electricity still competed, however, to provide clean and trouble-free heating as an alternative to the open fire. A hot water supply for washing and bathing became fairly general and great improvements were made in cookers, the heart of the kitchen. Indoor sanitation became the rule rather than the exception, though for an astonishingly long time local by-laws, in Britain at least, insisted on outside accommodation as well. A variety of appliances—vacuum cleaners, washing machines, refrigerators—combined to make housework easier. Certainly, the home comforts of the 1950s were far in advance of those at the beginning of the century.

But if his home was more comfortable, the householder might not be so fortunate in his surroundings. True, improvements in urban transport might allow him to live in the country and travel in to his work, but even then he might soon be engulfed in the horrors of almost uncontrolled ribbon development. In the industrial areas, however, many workers still lived in the bleak shadow of the factories. Town planning was in its infancy, but as the century progressed enlightened projects in the form of garden cities, and more closely controlled development of new sites, began to effect some improvement. The process was slow, however, and in many urban areas people might live in considerably greater comfort but in little improved environments. For the country dweller the way of life changed relatively little, though motor vehicles conferred a vastly increased mobility. This permitted not only more social life locally, but greater freedom to sample the pleasures of urban life, and perhaps to find employment there. To some extent, of course, the new mobility also promoted urbanization; it became increasingly feasible for the country worker to live in the town and go out daily to his place of employment.

Chief among the new pleasures of urban life in the years up to the Second World War was undoubtedly the cinema, which provided a wholly novel form of cheap and exciting entertainment for the masses; for the more discriminating, there were more serious productions made in an attempt to turn the cinema into a new art form. Simultaneously, entertainment was making its way into the home, first through the radio and later, at the end of our period, through television. To these must, of course, be added the gramophone, becoming the basis of an important section of the great new electronic industry. Unquestionably, the whole quality of life was transformed by the advent of these new forms of entertainment: and not merely entertainment, but a degree of popular instruction. How far they have been beneficial has become a matter of wide controversy. It is argued—but by no means universally accepted—that the constant exposure to sex and violence under the guise of entertainment is a root cause of some of the worst of our social ills. Others point to the benefit conferred by television in keeping families together at home and to its valuable role in supplementing education at both school and university level. Nor must we forget what a boon these new forms of domestic entertainment have proved to the aged, the lonely, and the sick. But much of the controversy is of fairly recent origin: up to 1950 most people simply regarded the cinema, radio, and television—then still in its infancy—as pleasant and harmless means of passing some of the additional leisure made available by a general shortening of the working week.

IV. TRANSPORT

Transport we have already briefly alluded to in the context of changing relationships between town and country. In a wider context, the advent of the motor-car had profound consequences, providing a measure of fast and comfortable individual mobility never previously possible. Again, however, we must remember that the social impact of the motor-car was not apparent until half-way through our period and was not overwhelming—especially in Europe—until after the Second World War. To many, this new-found freedom of travel seemed one of the greatest of all benefits conferred by technology on the quality of life. Sadly, many post-war planners thought otherwise and sought to restrict this freedom—which undeniably caused great practical problems—rather than adapt to it. In spite of its fairly obvious impracticability, they sought to drive travellers back to public transport. Latterly, high fares, curtailed services, inconvenience, and the erosion of city centres have begun to bring about a reversal of this policy.

During this period, the railways remained a more or less static factor so far as the travelling public was concerned. There were, of course, major technical developments: increasing use of electric or diesel power for traction, improved rolling stock, better and safer traffic control, and so on. But for the ordinary traveller the journey from, say, London to Edinburgh was not notably different in 1950 from what it had been in 1900. Much the same may be said of travel by sea: liners became larger, faster, and more comfortable but, again, a transatlantic voyage before the First World War was not very different, from the passengers' point of view, from one just after the Second.

It was in the air, of course, that the real revolution occurred, for this was for all practical purposes a form of transport peculiar to the twentieth century. The First World War saw a tremendous development of the aircraft industry in response to military needs and this paved the way to the beginning of serious commercial flying in the 1920s. Although a worldwide network of air routes was established in the 1930s, passengers were relatively few: aircraft were small and their range limited. The Second World War provided a further powerful stimulus to the development, not only of aircraft, but of navigational aids. It was only after this that flying became a recognized means of travel for the public at large, providing opportunities for completely new forms of holidays. In the sense of personal transport, therefore, flying can scarcely be said to have made a very direct impact on the quality of life until after 1950. There were, however, considerable indirect advantages long before this. In particular, airmail services transformed the speed of operation of intercontinental postal services. There had, of course, long been international telegraph, and later telephone, services but these were expensive and really suitable only for brief and important messages. When airmail services were extended, long personal letters could be sent to friends and relatives in the most distant parts of the world in as many days as it once took weeks or even months by sea.

To conclude this general survey of the ways in which progress in technology affected daily life we must consider two issues which have lately become the subject of deep public concern, though they were less so even at the end of the period with which we are here concerned. These topics are respectively the environment and energy.

V. THE ENVIRONMENT

It is of the nature of industry that it produces waste products, many of which are noxious and present serious disposal problems. There is nothing in this peculiar to the twentieth century. It must be remembered, however, that industry is not alone in this: collectively, private citizens make a formidable contribution. For example, before the days of smoke-control regulations, it was the domestic chimneys of London, and not its factories, that contributed most to the choking fogs for which the city, like many others, was notorious. Pollution of rivers and the seas near the coast can be attributed as much to inadequately treated sewage as to industrial effluent. A visit to any popular beauty spot provides ample evidence that the average citizen has no great conscience about how he disposes of his litter. Nevertheless, this can be no more than a mitigating plea for industry; it does produce unpleasant waste material and has not always been as responsible as it should be in its disposal. Some great rivers—of which the Rhine is perhaps the best known of far too many examples—are no more than open drains, devoid of all plant and animal life. Beaches are rendered unusable, and seabirds killed by the thousand, by oil-tankers discharging sludge from their tanks in defiance of international regulations. Wildlife is needlessly destroyed by careless use of chemicals. Electricity supply companies disfigure the countryside with striding lines of pylons. Tasteless building developments are an eyesore. But all this is really the dark side of a much brighter picture. Generally speaking industry takes its effluent problems very seriously. This is not necessarily so much a matter of virtue as of common sense. In the first place, much waste is potentially valuable and is worth treating before disposal. Secondly, starting—in Britain —from the Alkali Act of 1863, there is in most countries a very considerable body of enforceable legislation, infringement of which carries heavy penalties. Thirdly, industry is very much more sensitive to public opinion than it used to be.

Some measure of responsibility lies with the consumer, who is generally not prepared to meet the higher cost implicit in improved environmental measures. The electricity industry is a case in point: while underground transmission is feasible, its general adoption, on the basis of currently available technology, would force up the price to the consumer to a quite unacceptable level—unacceptable even to the environmentalists.

In the first half of this century a much more *laissez-faire* attitude prevailed, and it is no doubt because of this that the problem began to get out of hand

and thus is now receiving so much attention. At present, the pendulum has certainly swung too far—more nonsense is talked about the environment than most subjects of current concern—but at least the public has become aware of the issue and offenders have been put on the defensive.

VI. ENERGY

One basic requirement of industry, and of modern life generally, is energy; indeed, the consumption of energy per head of population is a recognized index of industrial activity. The first half of this century saw radical changes in the sources of the world's energy, and the overall requirement rose enormously to keep pace with the demands of industry and of domestic consumers. Among fossil fuels, world production of coal rose fairly steadily until about 1925 but then more or less levelled out: world production (excluding the U.S.S.R.) was around 1200m. tons in 1928 and about 1100m. tons in 1946. But the production of oil, the other major fossil fuel, rose prodigiously. From comparatively small beginnings, total world production up to the middle of the century was around 5000m. barrels (one barrel being 42 U.S. gallons). This was accounted for mainly by the growing demands of the internal combustion engine, including not only those required for road vehicles but for aircraft, ships, and railway locomotives. Natural gas, often associated with petroleum, must also be regarded as a fossil fuel. Used very substantially in America from the late nineteenth century its utilization in Europe was not undertaken on any large scale until after the Second World War.

The form of energy directly obtainable from fossil fuels is, of course, heat. For certain purposes, as in the open domestic fire, this can be used directly but usually it has to be converted—with some considerable loss—into more useful forms of energy. The internal combustion engine and the steam engine convert it into mechanical energy; the conventional power station into electrical energy. Much of the electrical energy is itself converted into mechanical energy in the motors that drive locomotives, factory machinery, domestic appliances, and so on. More electric energy is converted—very inefficiently until the advent of the fluorescent tube—into light energy. Water power, which had been the motive force of cumbersome machinery for centuries, found in the twentieth century a new and highly sophisticated application in hydroelectric schemes in those parts of the world—fewer than is commonly supposed—favourable to them. Finally, at the very end of our period a totally new source of energy, that locked up within the atom, began to be tapped.

Without adequate supplies of energy, industry cannot operate and it can, therefore, be argued that the whole quality of modern life, so far as it is affected by technology, is dependent on the energy industry in its various manifestations. At the same time, this is not something that impinges very directly on the consciousness of the individual. If he turns on an electric switch, it makes no difference whatever—provided the power is there—whether the electricity originated by mining coal, by harnessing a river, or by the splitting of atoms. Equally, the gas consumer obtains the same effect, and uses essentially the same appliances, whether his gas is generated by carbonization of coal, from petroleum, or by tapping vast underground reservoirs of natural gas. Most transatlantic passengers would have neither known nor cared whether their ship's engines were fired by coal or oil.

Up to the middle of the century there was, in fact, no particular reason why the ordinary citizen should think very much about such matters: energy was there as it was wanted, cheap and abundant. While it was self-evident that fossil fuels would eventually be exhausted, it was reassuring that new reserves were still being discovered at least as fast as existing ones were being exhausted. The rivers, presumably, would go on flowing and the sun would shine. Any real problem must surely lie generations ahead: let them worry. It is against this sort of background that we must judge the prodigal use of energy that characterized the early decades of this century, most particularly in the United States with its immense resources, but with other Western nations lagging behind not for any reason of prudence, but because they could not afford it. Of the two embarassing legacies that have been left to us by the technology of the first half of the twentieth century—the problems of the environment and of maintaining adequate energy supplies—it is the second that is the most pressing and will most tax the resources of the technologists —and the politicians—of the remaining years of this century and the years beyond.

A HISTORY OF TECHNOLOGY

CONTENTS

VOLUME I

FROM EARLY TIMES TO FALL OF ANCIENT EMPIRES

VOLUME IV

THE INDUSTRIAL REVOLUTION

c 1750 TO *c* 1850

CONTENTS

VOLUME V

THE LATE NINETEENTH CENTURY

c 1850 TO c 1900

PART I. PRIMARY PORDUCTION

PART II. PRIME MOVERS

I. Index of Personal Names

II. Index of Place Names

III. General Index of Subjects